G000123585

THE WILLING WORLD

In this time of unwillingness, the right kinds of global solutions are needed now more than ever. Climate change is here and intensifying. Anxieties over economic globalization grip many in the fear of change. While these fearful have turned inward into unwillingness, the world's willing are working harder than ever for international and other cooperative solutions. James Bacchus explains why most of the solutions we need must be found in local and regional partnerships of the willing that can be scaled up and linked up worldwide. This can be achieved only within new and enhanced enabling frameworks of global and other international rules that are upheld through the international rule of law. To succeed, these rules and frameworks must for the first time see and treat economy and environment as one. *The Willing World* explains how best we can build the right legal structure to attain our global goals – and summon and inspire the willingness needed to do it.

JAMES BACCHUS was a founding member and twice the chairman of the Appellate Body of the World Trade Organization – the chief judge on the highest court of international trade. He is Distinguished University Professor of Global Affairs and Director of the Center for Global Economic and Environmental Opportunity of the University of Central Florida. He is the author of *Trade and Freedom* (2004) and has written and spoken extensively on global governance in leading publications and on prominent platforms worldwide. For decades, he has been an advocate of freer trade and investment, and, starting with his service as a Member of the Congress of the United States before becoming a judge, he has long also been engaged in efforts to forestall climate change and further global sustainable development.

The Willing World

SHAPING AND SHARING A SUSTAINABLE GLOBAL PROSPERITY

JAMES BACCHUS

University of Central Florida

CAMBRIDGE
UNIVERSITY PRESS

CAMBRIDGE
UNIVERSITY PRESS

University Printing House, Cambridge CB2 8BS, United Kingdom

One Liberty Plaza, 20th Floor, New York, NY 10006, USA

477 Williamstown Road, Port Melbourne, VIC 3207, Australia

314–321, 3rd Floor, Plot 3, Splendor Forum, Jasola District Centre, New Delhi – 110025, India

79 Anson Road, #06–04/06, Singapore 079906

Cambridge University Press is part of the University of Cambridge.

It furthers the University's mission by disseminating knowledge in the pursuit of education, learning, and research at the highest international levels of excellence.

www.cambridge.org
Information on this title: www.cambridge.org/9781108428217
DOI: 10.1017/9781108552417

© James Bacchus 2018

This publication is in copyright. Subject to statutory exception and to the provisions of relevant collective licensing agreements, no reproduction of any part may take place without the written permission of Cambridge University Press.

First published 2018
Reprinted 2018

Printed and bound in Great Britain by Clays Ltd, Elcograf S.p.A.

A catalogue record for this publication is available from the British Library.

Library of Congress Cataloging-in-Publication Data
NAMES: Bacchus, James, 1949- author.
TITLE: The willing world : shaping and sharing a sustainable global prosperity / James Bacchus, University of Central Florida.
DESCRIPTION: Cambridge : Cambridge University Press, 2018. | Includes bibliographical references and index.
IDENTIFIERS: LCCN 2017059710 | ISBN 9781108428217 (hardback : alk. paper)
SUBJECTS: LCSH: Sustainable development. | Climate change mitigation. | Biodiversity. | Conservation of natural resources.
CLASSIFICATION: LCC HU79.E5 B327 2018 | DDC 304.2–dc23
LC record available at https://lccn.loc.gov/2017059710

ISBN 978-1-108-42821-7 Hardback

Cambridge University Press has no responsibility for the persistence or accuracy of URLs for external or third-party internet websites referred to in this publication and does not guarantee that any content on such websites is, or will remain, accurate or appropriate.

For Karen

For Karen

Contents

Preface

I am one of the willing.

All over the earth there are others who are also willing and trying to do their part and their best to find the right ways to help make life better for billions of people on our imperiled planet. The willing are fighting famine in Africa, furthering the flow of freshwater in the Andes, battling back against the rising seas on the small islands of the South Pacific, urging use of renewable energy in the cities of Europe and the United States, struggling against smog and air pollution in China, and sheltering endangered sea turtles on the beaches while preserving the coasts of my home state of Florida. And, in every part of the world, the willing are convening in meeting after meeting, conference after conference, year after year, to try to find and fashion the necessary legal architecture for the international institutions needed to achieve worldwide what they describe as "sustainable development."

Many of these gatherings of the willing center on the connections between the economy and the environment. In particular, my own work in many of these sessions has shown me firsthand the truth in the telling assertion by my insightful friend David G. Victor that, in considering and confronting these connections, the advocates of trade and the champions of the environment are on "two different planets."[1] Not only do the "two different planets" of trade and environment have two entirely different ways of looking at the world, they also have two different languages. Even on those rare occasions when the two do try to communicate, there is usually little mutual understanding.

Unlike most among the willing, I am from both of these "two different planets." Because I speak the languages of both "planets" (and because I know the meanings of the arcane acronyms of both), I have found myself, more than once, explaining and translating one to the other. I share the fundamental ambitions of each of these "two different planets," and the fact that I am someone from both of them has helped me to have a better understanding of both. This, I have found, has often helped me foster communication between the two. I hope it will help me in speaking to both about the inseparability of economy and environment in offering the suggestions in this book.

Concerted and collaborative action is much needed now by the willing aimed at discerning how, together, we can help forge an urgently needed consensus for the world. The consensus we seek must be made and manifested through much more international cooperation. This enhanced international cooperation must create effective frameworks of agreed rules for enabling global sustainable development. This book is one small contribution of mine toward that end. As will be seen in the pages that follow, I am a believer in learning by doing. Publicly and privately, I have had the good fortune in my life of serving others at every level of global governance, ranging from the innovative grassroots of the world up to the global pinnacles of public responsibility. The observations and recommendations in this book are a distillation of much I have learned – by doing – along the way about the economy, the environment, the connections between the two, and, most of all, the current necessity to unite the two in trying to build a consensus for sustainable development.

As will be seen, too, in what follows, I am also a firm believer in the value of beginning by identifying premises. While a judge on the Appellate Body of the World Trade Organization, my first question of the disputing countries appearing in an oral hearing was always, "What is the measure before us?" In other words: What is our subject? And, given our subject, what are our assumptions about it? What are our definitions? What are our philosophical foundations? If we know – and if we can agree – on the answers to these threshold questions, then we have a much better chance of building a consensus.

Moreover, as will be seen, I am a believer in experience. What have we already done on which we can build now in doing all we still hope to do? How did we get to where we are now? And what have those who have preceded us said they were doing and why? In other words, what were their premises? In my experience, rarely is anything so new in the world that we cannot benefit from a lot that has been said and done previously. Past experience can be instructive in understanding and dealing with a new challenge. This seems to me to be true even of so novel and unprecedented a global challenge as ours today in confronting and combating climate change as part of attaining sustainable development.

So I have divided all that follows into three parts. Part I begins with the premises of the willing – with what we hope to do. Part II continues with our experiences – with what we have done so far. Part III concludes with what, as I see it, we all must do together now. It concludes with my many specific suggestions, based on these premises and on these experiences, for the best approaches for building a global consensus for securing sustainable development. In other words, this book is about how all of us must learn by doing if we are to shape and share a sustainable global prosperity.

As will soon become clear, I believe as well that trade, investment, and other forms of economic globalization have been and can be enormously beneficial. But

I also believe that, like so much else we do in the world, how beneficial additional globalization turns out to be for all of us will depend on how we go about doing it. This said, however, if you are looking for a book that will focus solely and comprehensively on explaining and defending all the many reasons why trade- and investment-led economic globalization is good for the world, this is not that book. I have addressed that topic in my previous book, *Trade and Freedom*.[2]

Likewise, if you are looking for a book that will explain and elaborate in technical detail all the scientific reasons why climate change is real and why we frail and feckless human beings are causing it – if you are looking for a point-by-point scientific refutation of the denials of the reality of manmade climate change – this is also not that book. On the inescapable reality of manmade climate change, I urge you to read and consider the views of the overwhelming global consensus of climate scientists in the latest reports of the United Nations Intergovernmental Panel on Climate Change. All that follows in this book takes it as a given that those climate scientists are correct in concluding that our striving and struggling species is now facing significant and accelerating climate change of our own making.

But if you are looking instead for a book that acknowledges the reality of climate change and accepts the fact that we are causing it – and if you are looking also for a book that suggests to practical decisionmakers everywhere in the world some practical ways of confronting this fact that will help all of us in the world both survive and prosper through global sustainable development – if you are looking for a book that suggests how we should proceed from where we are now to where we hope to go economically and environmentally – then please read on.

What follows is akin to a "how-to" book for enhancing global economic and environmental governance. It is suggestive, not definitive. There are many sustainability issues I do not address and many desirable legal and other reforms I support but do not discuss. The specific suggestions in Part III are included because of my hope that highlighting them here will help the willing everywhere in the world in their continuing efforts to shape a sustainable global development in which we all can share. This is a book that offers not the magic wand of one technocratic "top-down" solution from the top of the world, but instead ardent support for an innovative "bottom-up" approach that can enable us to find the many partial solutions that can rise up and be scaled up from the grassroots of the world, and that can add up over time to the one global solution we all need.

This is a book about how to grow and govern the global economy in ways that will work economically and environmentally through sustainable development.

I am one of the willing, and what follows is what I see as our best way forward to the willing world.

Introduction

We live in an unwilling world. Preoccupied by day-to-day demands and by the ever-present threats of terrorism, oppression, and calamitous nuclear and other conflicts, most people in the world are either unaware of the broader urgent and existential challenges facing humanity or seem unwilling to face them squarely. The rising needs of a rapidly growing global population cast doubt on our hopes for a shared and lasting prosperity for all. The rapidly increasing global pressures on – and the intensifying competition for – our planet's limited natural resources renew our age-old fears of a war of all against all. The hastening onset of manmade climate change could soon threaten the survival of all. These and other intertwined global challenges demand interconnected global solutions.

Many people everywhere in the world are willing to find these solutions. In networked and worldwide webs of the willing, they are working as hard as they can in search of solutions. Every day, in a vast array of innovative local endeavors and in a vast variety of venues and ways, the willing worldwide strive to address urgent global concerns of all kinds by working together toward a goal they commonly call "sustainable development." Some focus their attentions on the unending avalanche of challenges threatening the global economy. They labor especially for the impoverished on our planet and for all those who have yet to share in the bounties of globalization. Others dwell on the threats to the global environment. They labor especially for the planet itself. And some of the willing devote their energies equally to both people and planet by connecting solutions for the economy and the environment. With their determined, driving idealism, all of the world's willing strive to serve humanity and to save the planet by shaping a bright future for everyone everywhere.

Yet, despite all this hard work, their professed goal of sustainable development remains an elusive and distant ideal – seemingly unreachable – and an unwilling world resists making many of the essential transitional changes needed to reach it. Despite all their well-intentioned labors, the willing in the world are increasingly finding they lack all the practical and realistic approaches needed for building the basic global architecture of a sustainable future. Worse, in every part of the world they lack the popular support indispensable for building it. Undaunted, the willing persist. There is ever the hopeful expectation of achieving, at last, the ultimate universal and comprehensive global solution for "sustainable development" at the next global summit – or perhaps the next.

Without doubt, there are successes worth reporting. But there are not nearly enough – not when compared to all the many more successes we urgently need. The impassioned pursuits of the willing worldwide have so far not come close to securing the sought-for success of global sustainable development. Moreover, their ardent labors have not yet inspired anything approaching the amount of global political will needed even to begin to make the hard choices that must be made to achieve it. The world as a whole remains unwilling to do all that must be done to advance the global economy and to enhance the global environment through international cooperation for sustainable development.

THE REACTION AGAINST GLOBALIZATION

In the wake of an unnerving global financial crisis, in the midst of an uneven recovery and lingering global economic uncertainty, and in the face of increasingly dire warnings from scientists of an approaching environmental catastrophe that few understand and many choose to deny, most governments in the world continue to try to come together and work toward common ends. Yet throughout the world many who would lead us are largely in retreat from cooperation and from a shared search for global solutions to our inescapably global economic and environmental concerns.

This retreat by so many of our national political leaders reflects the gravity of a much larger retreat in many places from engagement with the wider world. "Anti-globalization has gone global."[1] In the United States, in parts of Europe, and elsewhere, we have witnessed what has been widely described as a "populist" revolt against the international economic institutional arrangements established through long decades of determined international cooperation. Some say that the extent of the political reaction against globalization is such that "[t]he new age of deglobalization is on, and it is likely to last."[2]

In stark contrast to the ambitions of the willing are the apprehensions of the unwilling. In many countries, "populist earthquakes" have erupted in an overflow of anger and anxiety aimed at all things global.[3] As one baffled reporter for the *Washington Post* put it not long after the British vote to pull out of the European Union and the even more surprising outcome of the American presidential election in 2016, "[I]t seems that a nameless rage has seized global politics, and millions of people are voting to burn it all."[4]

Some of this rage is justified. Insufficient attention has been paid by many of the tribunes of globalization to the human costs of rapid and uprooting economic change. The economic insecurity of those paying those costs is real. So too is the growing economic inequality that adds to the pain of those costs. Sir Angus Deaton, a Nobel Prize-winning economist and a self-declared "optimistic defender" of globalization, points out that the world today is healthier and wealthier than it would otherwise have been without centuries of economic integration.[5] He adds, though, that this basic truth about globalization is obscured by the inequality resulting from what economists call "rent-seeking" – in his description, "a takeover of government by those who would use it to enrich themselves."[6]

This, Deaton says, "is the crux of the matter" behind the backlash against globalization. After decades of highlighting the human progress made possible by globalization, he worries now that there may be "an inextricable link between progress and inequality."[7] The Paris-based Organisation for Economic Co-operation and Development, an international organization of the world's wealthiest countries, points to "the stagnation of the well-being of many in the lower half of the income distribution in a number of OECD countries, in contrast to the situation at the top end of the income distribution."[8] Meanwhile, "In developing and emerging economies, while poverty levels have decreased significantly, income inequality levels have remained very high."[9] These are understatements.

In the United States, the pain of the human costs paid by those who have not benefited as they should from globalization is intensified not only by ever-widening economic inequality, but also by a deep-felt sense of injustice. Millions of people suffered in the United States, as many millions of other people did elsewhere, from the fallout of the global financial crisis of 2008. In the aftermath of that crisis, not one high-ranking executive of any of the major US financial firms that contributed to causing the crisis was held accountable. No one was fired. No one went to jail. Eventually some corporate fines were paid, but they added up to only a drop or two in Wall Street's money bucket.

Feeding this feeling of injustice in the United States is the fact that, when the American economy at last began to recover following the Great Recession, the financial "elites" and the "1 percent" in the uppermost income bracket were the ones who benefited the most, and not those in the middle class and down below who had suffered the most. In this context, a political reaction against know-it-all "elites" is not at all surprising.[10]

In 2017, one exemplar of the global "elite," the German finance minister, Wolfgang Schäuble, declared at yet another global gathering of the willing, "Nationalism and protectionism are never the right answer."[11] He is absolutely right. All the same, growing numbers of people in the world are unpersuaded, and more and more of the unpersuaded have been ascending to places of power with the surge of the reactive worldwide wave. The defenders of globalization are everywhere on the defensive, and the affirmative case for continued global economic integration can scarcely be heard above the protests.

The economic distress driving this reaction is mixed in many places with the cultural, ethnic, religious, and racial resentment of a resurgent and virulent nationalism. In the United States and elsewhere, we have witnessed the triumph of a so-called economic nationalism dictating an insulating protectionism. This is a triumph of economic myopia and mythic cultural nostalgia. It is in many respects equally "the triumph of those who preach strong action over rule of law, unilateralism instead of cooperation and the interests of the majority above the rights of ethnic and religious minorities."[12]

There is in this latest of the recurring historical outpourings of the poison of nationalism an aggressive hostility toward foreigners, immigrants, other races, other ethnic groups, other faiths, those of different sexes, sexual preferences, or lifestyles – toward all those who may think, look, act, believe, or live differently from how "we" do, whoever "we" may be in our different parts of the world. This widespread political revolt is not only an expression of a palpable fear of the economic changes wrought by globalization. It is also an expression of the timeless fear of the "other" that has, for millennia, kept our singular species from seeing that humanity is one and thus must act as one.

The worst of this popular reaction is manifested as an invitation to authoritarianism. In many countries – rich and poor alike – anger at supposedly arrogant "elites" and frustration with the slowness, the messiness, and the sheer lack of responsiveness of democratic institutions have created political openings for the ruthless who seek to exploit this anger and this frustration to secure a monopoly of personal power. Lost and alone, all too many are easy prey for those who promise them purpose and security in an authoritarian state. Demagogues reduce the complex to the deceivingly simple for the gullible and the uninformed, blame the foreign "other" for all that ails the nation, and proclaim that they alone embody the answer. The democratic habits of the disillusioned then bend until they yield to authoritarian impulses. The center does not hold. It folds. The rule of law succumbs to the rule of one "strong man." The call for more popular rule leads to precisely the opposite.

THE NEED FOR GLOBAL ECONOMIC SOLUTIONS

Amid this worldwide reaction against globalization, global economic solutions are needed more urgently now than ever. The world is not only interconnected; it is interdependent. One expert group of the willing – the global "thought leaders" who help set the annual global agenda of the World Economic Forum – has peered through all the political rhetoric and joined Deaton in seeing the top two global trends that are likely to have the biggest impact on the world as deepening income inequality and persistent jobless growth.[13] To these two global trends can be added, in much of the world, the closely related concerns of stagnant wages; vulnerable jobs; missing and mismatched job skills; racial, sexual, ethnic, religious, age, and other forms of job discrimination; and widespread structural unemployment. Periodic cyclical upswings in national economies and in the global economy may mask but do not mitigate – much less erase – these structural impediments to a widely shared prosperity. At the core of the economic reaction against globalization is this: More and better economic opportunities for good jobs and for secure livelihoods are needed by billions of people everywhere in the world. These opportunities will not be found unless we respond to our economic interdependence with more economic integration.

Additional economic integration through further economic globalization offers untold new opportunities for good jobs and secure livelihoods in a global transition to a sustainable economy. Yet, in the eyes of many wary people, globalization seems a threat, not an opportunity. In a globalized economy connected by ever-lengthening global supply chains, workers and businesses alike in wealthier countries fear competition from poorer countries. And, for their part, workers and businesses alike in poorer countries are in equal fear of competition from wealthier countries. There is a pervasive global fear of being swept away by the rising force of the allegedly "unfair" flow of foreign competition resulting from globalization.

Everywhere in the world, people fearful of change are clinging as best they can to what they have and know and think they can trust. Economically, the young are trying to get in, the old are trying to hold on, and the rest in between are just trying to get by without being passed by technologically or globally. All too many of all ages and all nationalities are lost between the past and the future and are lined up in the lines of the jobless and the hopeless. All of us everywhere are trying somehow to find some purchase and some piece of the future in a world that seems to be turning faster and faster, and that seems to be turning away from us. All of us are looking for something more and better, and the poorest among us are looking hardest of all.

Poverty still prevails in many parts of the world. The United Nations Development Programme (UNDP) speaks of poverty as "multidimensional." The willing of the world who work for the UNDP explain that measures of poverty are typically based on income or consumption, which can reveal much about deprivation but provide only a partial picture. As they point out, people can be deprived of many things besides income. "They may have poor health and nutrition, low education and skills, inadequate livelihoods and poor household conditions, and they may be socially excluded."[4] By their reckoning, 1.5 billion of the more than 7 billion people in the world live in "multidimensional poverty," and an additional 700 million are "vulnerable" to such poverty.[15] They add that three-fourths of the world's poor live in rural areas, "where agricultural workers suffer the highest incidence of poverty, caught in a cauldron of low productivity, seasonal unemployment and low wages."[16] Moreover, many of those who recently joined the middle class "could easily fall back into poverty with a sudden change in circumstances."[17]

We are not condemned to a world afflicted by immiseration. Our recent record of success in reducing global poverty gives us reason to believe we can do better still in reducing poverty, and particularly extreme poverty. Even with the setbacks of the global financial crisis of 2008, twenty-eight countries classified by the World Bank as "low income" made the jump to middle-income status between 2002 and 2015.[18]

The number of people in the world living in extreme poverty has diminished by about 1 billion since 1990.[19] Still, about 1.2 billion people in the world continue to live in extreme poverty on less than $1.25 per day.[20] This is about 15 percent of the world's population.[21]

The Pew Research Center underscores the concern expressed by the UNDP that recent global gains against poverty are precarious.[22] Many of those who have recently escaped the worst forms of poverty are "only a moderate step up the income ladder" and still on the edge of being poor.[23] In a world with few and often faulty safety nets, these new members of the global middle class could easily fall back down the ladder. Only about 16 percent of the people in the world live on incomes that put them safely above the official US poverty line of about $23,000 annually for a family of four.

Meanwhile, amid the vast wealth and opulence of the United States, the bottom 50 percent of Americans in income got just 3 percent of the gains from growth since 1980, and their income share diminished from more than 20 percent in 1980 to 13 percent in 2016.[24] A combination of stratification and stagnation helps explain the fear of many middle-class Americans that they, too, could descend the economic ladder into poverty. Confronted with the pressures of their own increasingly fragile economic existence, many Americans have little time left over to ponder the far more perilous position of so many others facing extreme poverty elsewhere. Instead, they strike back politically at the "elites" they believe have betrayed them.

The World Bank has adopted the goal of reducing the percentage of those in the world living in extreme poverty to less than 3 percent by 2030, and this goal was embraced by the United Nations in identifying a whole host of "Sustainable Development Goals" (SDGs) as part of its 2030 Agenda.[25] There is bold talk in abundance at the global "summits" about ending poverty. With the adoption of the Sustainable Development Goals by the United Nations, the whole world has now endorsed this goal. Eradicating global poverty will, however, be far from easy. Based on the latest projections by the World Bank of likely global growth by 2030, "growth is unlikely to be high enough across all developing countries to reduce poverty to the level sought by 2030. Developing countries would have to grow at an average of 4 percent each year – even higher than the growth rate of the 2000s and much higher than that of the 1980s and 1990s."[26]

By far the best way to jumpstart growth not only in the developing countries of the world, but in *all* the countries of the world, would be to eliminate many more of the tariff and non-tariff barriers to international trade and foreign direct investment. We have reduced global poverty as much as we have in the past generation in no small part because we have lowered the vast numbers of global barriers to trade and investment while embracing markets and market principles more widely in the world. But our global efforts to free trade and to free investment have faltered and fragmented as developing and developed countries alike have turned inward and largely away from the further economic integration that is intrinsic to most needed global economic solutions.

The willing of the world have long since lost count, to cite one glaring example, of just how many times at just how many summits in just how many places the world's governments have promised to conclude in some form and with some success long-deadlocked global trade negotiations under the auspices of the World Trade Organization. After years on life support, the latest round of talks seems at last to have expired. Trading countries are trying to regroup and to redirect their global negotiations. Making their task harder is talk, among the "economic nationalists" and other "anti-globalists," not merely of abandoning global trade talks, but also of abandoning the WTO itself. With the ascendency in the United States of a protectionist presidency, there is danger that this talk could turn into destructive action.

THE NEED FOR GLOBAL ENVIRONMENTAL SOLUTIONS

Global environmental solutions, too, are more urgently needed now than ever. For now comes climate change to complicate, all the more, our complex challenge economically with an unprecedented challenge environmentally. In 1896, a Swedish scientist, Svante Arrhenius, first predicted that increases in the levels of carbon dioxide in the atmosphere caused by the burning of fossil fuels could heat the surface temperature of the Earth.[27] For some time now, the overwhelming consensus of the world's climate scientists has been that he was right. The Earth is warming and the climate is changing as we release more and more carbon dioxide and other greenhouse gas emissions into the atmosphere.

Responding to this reality, in 1988 the World Meteorological Organization and the United Nations Environment Programme established a broadly representative international group of climate scientists called the Intergovernmental Panel on Climate Change (IPCC). The IPCC consists of about 800 climate scientists drawn from all over the world, including scientists from the National Aeronautics and Space Administration (NASA) and the National Oceanic and Atmospheric Administration (NOAA) in the United States. In reaching their conclusions and recommendations, these climate scientists draw on the results of the latest scientific research and on the ongoing reviews of their results by thousands of other scientists from across the globe.

The IPCC works under the auspices of the United Nations. It has been endorsed by the United National General Assembly and supports the work of the United Nations Framework Convention on Climate Change (UNFCCC), which is the UN treaty that forms the basis for global climate negotiations. The IPCC has been asked by the member states of the United Nations in their negotiating role as the "Conference of Parties" of the UNFCCC to assess and report periodically on the risks to the world of "anthropogenic" – human-induced – climate change and on the ways we might mitigate or adapt to it.

The IPCC has made five such assessments. The most recent assessment was finalized in 2014, when the consensus conclusion of these leading climate scientists was that the evidence of climate change is "virtually certain." Their consensus conclusion, too, was that we humans are causing it. They reported, "Human influence has been detected in warming of the atmosphere and the ocean, in changes in the global water cycle, in reductions in snow and ice, in global mean sea level rise, and in changes in some climate extremes ... It is *extremely likely* that human influence has been the dominant cause of the observed warming since the mid-20th century."[28]

The climate scientists have explained that by "extremely likely" they mean that they are "95 to 100 percent certain" that human activities – especially fossil fuel emissions – are the primary drivers of planetary warming.[29] Human emissions of carbon dioxide and other greenhouse gases began in earnest with the invention of the steam engine in the eighteenth century, have grown steadily since, and have rapidly accelerated in the past half-century. About half of all the CO_2 emissions resulting from human activity have occurred since 1970. As with the steam engines that began to fire the Industrial Revolution in the eighteenth century, these modern emissions are still largely due to our overwhelming reliance on fossil fuels.

The ever-increasing evidence of climate change that is caused by the ever-increasing concentration of carbon dioxide and other greenhouse gases in the Earth's atmosphere is all around us. The IPCC tells us in no uncertain terms that climate change is no longer coming; it has arrived. "Warming of the climate system," the scientists tell us, "is unequivocal, and since the 1950s, many of the observed changes are unprecedented over decades to millennia."[30] Our greenhouse gas emissions are causing the climate to change 170 times faster than natural forces.[31] Rising seas. Melting ice caps. Scorching heatwaves. Intensifying storms. Spreading floods. Prolonged droughts. Loss of natural habitats. All these and other reported damaging consequences of climate change are already threatening our food, water, health, safety, and security.

Every passing year adds to the urgency of addressing the unprecedented global challenge of climate change in a global way. Climate scientists have documented a relentless rise in overall global temperatures in the more than two centuries since the dawn of the industrial age. The ten warmest years in recorded history have all been since 1997. The hottest year on record was 2016;[32] 2017 was the second-hottest year on record – and the hottest year without the temporary warming effect of an El Niño event in the Pacific Ocean.[33]

Scientists insist this will only be the beginning of the heat from climate change if we do not find the right way to come together and act together now. The IPCC anticipates that, without additional efforts to slow emissions, temperatures will rise by between 3.7 degrees and 4.8 degrees Celsius by the end of this century – by 2100 – over what temperatures were in the pre-industrial year of 1750. (For my fellow Americans, that's between 6.6 degrees and 8.6 degrees Fahrenheit.)

Climate scientists have warned us for some time that setting a limit on the increase in global temperatures of no more than 2 degrees Celsius (3.6 degrees

Fahrenheit) above the pre-industrial levels is necessary to prevent the worst effects of climate change. Global temperatures have already risen since pre-industrial times by about 1 degree Celsius (about 1.8 degrees Fahrenheit).[34] Unfortunately, and for all the fanfare attending what we have, belatedly, agreed on globally, nothing on which we have so far agreed globally is expected to keep us from exceeding that "2C" limit.

In concluding a global climate agreement in Paris in 2015, the governments of the world pledged to do all that must be done to keep global temperatures from rising above that limit. The consensus of the UN science panel is that, to keep global warming below 2 degrees Celsius since 1750, global emissions of carbon dioxide and other greenhouse gases must be cut by between 40 percent and 70 percent below 2010 levels by 2050, and cut to "near zero or below" by 2100. These cuts would be much deeper than the insufficient pledges of emission cuts that have been made so far by the world's governments under the Paris Agreement. What is more, there may be no effective means of knowing or ensuring that even those insufficient promises will be kept.

An analysis by one thinktank, Climate Interactive, of the initial national climate pledges made under the Paris Agreement concluded that keeping those voluntary pledges would shift the world away from a course in which global emissions were expected to rise significantly to one in which emissions would remain the same by 2030. This shift would suffice to keep global warming "somewhat under control." It would not, however, be nearly enough to meet the 2C goal. Furthermore, 21 percent of the promised initial emissions cuts are expected to be made by the United States. If the United States does not keep its climate commitment, global emissions will keep rising through 2030.[35]

Such a course seems all too likely now that the United States – which was previously one of the strongest advocates for global climate action – has, under a new president, announced its intention to withdraw from the Paris climate agreement. Driven by a combination of climate denialism, economic nationalism, and sheer "know-nothing-ism," the new president of the United States announced in June 2017 the intention of the United States to back out of the agreement. The willing of the world held their collective breath in awaiting the global response to this perhaps worst of all the worldwide reactions against globalization. Would other countries rally and lift their own ambitions by taking additional climate action? Or would they follow the example of the United States and turn inward and away from global cooperation in addressing perhaps the ultimate global issue?

Carbon dioxide lingers in the air for an average of 100 years before breaking down. Even when emissions are cut, so long as they continue, CO_2 keeps accumulating in the atmosphere. The World Bank warns of what it describes as "the new climate normal" in the absence of much deeper cuts in global greenhouse gas emissions: "There is growing evidence, that even with very ambitious mitigation action, warming close to 1.5 [degrees] C above pre-industrial levels by mid-century is already locked-in to the Earth's atmospheric system and climate change impacts such as extreme heat events may now be unavoidable. If the planet continues warming to 4 [degrees] C, climatic conditions, heat and other weather extremes considered highly unusual or unprecedented today would become the new climate normal – a world of increased risks and instability. The consequences for development would be severe."[36]

In addition to all its other impacts, climate change is a leading driver of poverty. The rising seas harm the impoverished coastal areas of Southeast Asia and drown the poor island economies all over the world. The droughts cause crop failures that lead to more starvation in Africa. The natural disasters intensified by climate change devastate entire economies in the developing world.[37] The many and varied effects of climate change constrain growth in ways that will make it all the more difficult to achieve the World Bank's lofty goal of shrinking the percentage of extreme global poverty to only 3 percent by 2030. World Bank president Jim Yong Kim is entirely correct in speaking of "the intrinsic link between climate change and poverty."[38]

Adding to this challenge is the knowledge that climate change is only one of the many and interrelated environmental challenges so many in the world seem all too unwilling to face. Others abound. Air and water pollution. Water shortages. Ocean acidification. Deforestation. Desertification. The loss of fisheries stocks. The unprecedented loss of other plant and animal species. The depletion of all natural resources. The list goes on. And each and every one of these and numerous additional environmental challenges is complicated by the effects of climate change.

Moreover, each and every one of these challenges, while affecting all of us, affects the poorest among us the most. The poor know better than the rest of us the connections between the economy and the environment because the burden falls more heavily on the poor when those connections are ignored. Pope Francis rightly reminds us in his historic encyclical on climate change of "the intimate relationship between the poor and the fragility of the planet."[39] As he explains, "Both everyday experience and scientific research show that the gravest effects of all attacks on the environment are suffered by the poorest."[40]

THE NEED TO UNITE ECONOMY AND ENVIRONMENT FOR SUSTAINABLE DEVELOPMENT

The highest hopes of the willing are on display in a full flowering of all their optimism in the Sustainable Development Goals of the United Nations. Enormous effort has been invested by the willing all over the world in these SDGs as the shining centerpiece of the UN's 2030 Agenda. Literally hundreds of thousands of people from all points of view and from all over the world contributed to reaching global agreement on these supposedly shared goals. The list of economic, environmental, and social goals is long. The list of "targets" and means of implementation is longer. Going forward, the SDGs are meant to guide the UN's "global development agenda" toward full success in 2030. The global goals agreed by the nearly 200 member countries of the United Nations are designed to attain numerous noble and uplifting ends by blending a whole host of targeted means together in making an inclusive and uplifting sustainable development.

The distance we have to travel to accomplish these global goals is far. One study by some of the willing has concluded that no country in the world currently meets the needs of its people in a sustainable way.[41] As one commentator summarized the study's results, "The nations of the world either don't provide the basics of a good life or they do it at excessive cost in resources, or they fail at both."[42] The United States, for example, provides Americans with a relatively high quality of life when compared with other countries, but it "fails on every measure of sustainability in the study."[43] The study's threshold for carbon dioxide emissions per person per year was 1.6 metric tons. The United States emits 21.2 metric tons of carbon dioxide per person per year.[44]

From this imposing starting point, the questions inspired by these global ambitions are many. To be able to transform ours from an unwilling into the willing world, the willing among us must ask and answer: Are the Sustainable Development Goals of the United Nations the right goals for the world? If so, how can we, at a time when so many in the world seem to have turned away from global cooperation on global solutions, somehow help summon the necessary political will throughout the world to implement them? If we can help inspire the political will to try to implement these global goals, what are the best approaches for doing so? How can we best transform these hopeful words into global reality? Have we truly thought through how to unite economy and environment as one in achieving these global goals? Do we in fact know how to grow and how to govern the global economy in ways that will work economically *and* environmentally by shaping a sustainable development we all can share?

Do we even know and agree on what we mean when we say "sustainable development"?

On What We Hope to Do

1

On the Elusive Definition of Sustainable Development

The willing of the world are all pursuing the goal of "sustainable development." This, though, is a goal with a definition on which they do not all even begin to agree. In the most widely accepted definition, that of the United Nations Commission on Environment and Development in 1987: "Sustainable development is development that meets the needs of the present without compromising the ability of future generations to meet their own needs."[1] This definition is open to endless further defining. The definition we choose matters to all of us everywhere, for how we define "sustainable development" will do much to determine the extent to which all of us everywhere will be able to shape and share in a lasting global prosperity.

THE MEANING OF "DEVELOPMENT"

In pondering the definition of "sustainable development," it may be best to begin with the meaning of "development" itself. After all, we cannot determine whether "development" is "sustainable" if we do not first agree on the definition of "development." Plumbing the depths of the meaning of "development" is a task for us all, but the considerable extent of the difficulty of this task can perhaps best be illustrated by examining the evolving ways in which economists have defined it.

The traditional focus of classical "liberal" economics is on maximizing "the wealth of nations" by maximizing economic "growth." This focus on growth first emerged fully from the fertile mind of the Scottish moral philosopher Adam Smith – the world's first and arguably best economist – during the early days of the Industrial Revolution. Smith's view of how economies work has since enjoyed a long intellectual ascendency in a world where "the wealth of nations" has multiplied over and over again, in no small part due to his teachings. Following Smith, the enduring emphasis of classical economists has been on how much and on how fast all that is produced and consumed "grows" overall by increasing, over time, and thereby creating, over time, more "income." Thus, the prevailing focus of this conventional economics has long been on the creation and the evolution of more material wealth through an ever-increasing division of labor that "leads to productivity growth through specialization and the adaptation of skills to tasks."[2] Crucially, as Smith emphasized in *The Wealth of Nations* in 1776, the division of labor is limited only "by the extent of the market."[3]

The conventional economic understanding of "development" is that "development" is a matter that mostly involves "growth." Yet there has long been a broad understanding among mainstream economists that economic "development" includes much more than "growth." As one basic textbook explains, "The terms economic growth and economic development are sometimes used interchangeably, but a fundamental distinction lies between them. *Economic growth* refers to a rise in national or per capita income and product. If the production of goods and services in a country rises, by whatever means, one can speak of that rise as 'economic growth.' *Economic development* implies more."[4]

Most mainstream economists seem to agree that there must be something *more* to "growth" than merely a calculation of material growth,[5] and that economic "growth" is not an end in itself but is a means to the end of human "development."[6] Yet many economists remain deeply divided over the definitions of these basic terms. What is more, this academic debate says nothing at all about all the deep divisions about these definitions among all the rest of us who are not economists. Many of the willing of the world work diligently for "sustainable development" without examining their basic assumptions about what precisely it is they hope to sustain. So the question lingers: Given that "growth" is a means to the worthy end of "development," how should we define "development"?

In the first decades following the Second World War, "development" still "was generally seen in terms of increasing that newly invented measure, GNP,"[7] by increasing the sum total of all national production. Thus, foreign assistance was mostly funneled into technocratic assistance to stimulate "growth" in GDP. This approach often failed. There was little emphasis on increasing the individual rights of those in developing countries who were meant to benefit from "growth," or on how an emphasis on securing their rights could further "growth." According to development economist William Easterly, "The technocratic approach ignores . . . the real cause of poverty – the unchecked power of the state against poor people without rights."[8] The cause of poverty, he insists, is not "a shortage of expertise" but "a shortage of rights,"[9] and "free development" by "free individuals with political and economic rights" is the only way to end poverty in achieving "development."[10]

Over time, it became increasingly clear that frequently growth "was not bringing tangible benefits to the poor, and was often even leading to their further impoverishment."[11] Starting in the 1970s, this led some developmental theorists to extend their view beyond simply "growth" and to emphasize more broadly meeting "basic needs" as the proper gauge of "development." Their "basic needs" approach for the first time looked beyond the sheer statistics of production and also stressed education, health care, and other fundamental social criteria that contribute to meeting human potential.[12] This approach, too, proved limited. The notion of a "basic need" is one of those elastic concepts that can mean different things to different people. The British economist Wilfred Beckerman has explained, "People at different points in time, or at different income levels, or with different cultural or national backgrounds, will differ about the importance they attach to different 'needs.'"[13]

In addition, there is what psychologists describe as a "hierarchy" of needs. Even where a desire is in fact a "need," some "needs" are more important to some individual human beings than to others, especially when considered in their context.[14] Not least, the fullest extent of human "development" consists of much more than merely meeting the "basic needs" for food, clothing, shelter, and the like. As essential as it is to have a full stomach, clothes to wear, and a roof overhead, the human spirit strives for a whole lot more. Above all, it is our striving spirit that has brought us this far toward our "development."

THE PURSUIT OF "HUMAN DEVELOPMENT"

For these reasons, in defining the content of "development," today's economists tend to speak not in terms of "basic needs" but in broader terms of overall "human development." Every year since 1990, the United Nations has published a Human Development Report that relies on a carefully calibrated Human Development Index which ranks the countries of the world on three critical measures of "development": longevity, as measured by life expectancy at birth; knowledge, as measured by literacy and length of schooling; and living standard, as measured by per capita income.[15] The aim of this annual UN calculation is to tell us how much economic "growth" is truly contributing to fulfilling the end of actual human "development" in every country.

This emphasis on defining "development" as "human development" has been inspired in large part by the influential thinking of the Nobel Prize-winning economist Amartya Sen and by his central belief in – as the title of his most famous book expresses it – "development as freedom."[16] For Sen, "human freedom" is "the preeminent objective of development," and the "[e]xpansion of freedom" is rightly viewed "both as the primary end and as the primary means of development."[17] "Development," he contends, "consists of the removal of various types of unfreedoms that leave people with little choice and little opportunity of exercising their reasoned agency."[18] "Freedom," of course, is itself one of those elastic ideas with a meaning on which people can disagree. For Sen, human freedom is an individual act of choice made through the exercise of human reason, and, for him, "[d]evelopment can be seen … as a process of expanding the real freedoms that people enjoy" to make individual choices.[19] Furthermore, for him, the appropriate measure of whether we are expanding freedom is "the expansion of the 'capabilities' of persons to lead the kind of lives they value – and have reason to value."[20] He favors a "capabilities" approach to development that includes much more than merely a ritual accounting of the latest tally in the growth of GNP.

In linking economics to the notion of an ever-unfolding freedom, Sen follows in the footsteps of a pioneer in development economics, Peter Bauer, who argued that "the principal objective and criterion of economic development" is to extend "the range of choice" by expanding "the range of effective alternatives open to people."[21] In Sen's view of freedom itself, and in his stress on the centrality of freedom, he echoes the basic insight of the widely influential twentieth-century Austrian philosopher Karl Popper, who saw freedom as self-rule, as the autonomous act of choosing. For Popper, "every man is free, not because he is born free, but because he is born with the burden of responsibility for free decisions."[22] For him, the freest society is the one in which individuals are free to make the most possible choices – the most possible "personal decisions" – about how to live.[23]

Popper called the society in which the decisions of individuals are made for them by someone else "the closed society."[24] In contrast, he called "the society in which individuals are confronted with personal decisions ... the open society."[25] In the transition from a closed society to an open society in which personal decisions can and must be made, the received certainties of the past yield to uncertainties about today and about the future, the old world in which nothing is in doubt becomes a new world in which all is in doubt, and there is a "feeling of drift"[26] because "everything is in flux."[27] The open society is open-ended – because no one knows the destination of freedom. Popper's contrast between closed and open societies foreshadowed Sen's contrast between "unfreedom" and freedom, and provides a philosophical foundation for viewing the whole notion of human development.

Popper's fundamental premise of our need to choose between living in the freedom of open societies or in the "unfreedom" of closed societies says much to the willing about how we should frame our efforts to secure sustainable development. Our struggle in the world today is not a struggle *between* civilizations. It is a struggle *within* civilizations between those who wish to cling to the certainties of closed societies and those who are willing to confront the open-endedness of freedom. It is a struggle within civilizations between those who embrace freedom and those who fear it. In this struggle, the old ideological lines of left and right that prevailed for two and a half centuries no longer exist. The new lines of political division throughout the world are lines drawn between those who are willing to be open to new ways of living, working, thinking, and acting as part of the wider world, and those who are not. Nationally and internationally, our politics have not caught up to the reality of this new division. We still speak as we have long spoken in terms of the "left" and the "right." But a new and proper understanding of this new division is indispensable to doing all that must be done for sustainable development.

Globally, in this new geopolitical context, so-called postdevelopment theorists argue that development is nothing more than a disguised form of postcolonial

Western imperialism, an artificial construct intended to perpetuate what they see as the continued hegemony of the West by mirroring the West in the emergence of the rest of the world. These postdevelopment theorists are likewise equally "postmodern" in that they think of development as an artificial concept with no real existence outside the discussion of development. They feel the same way about the concept of poverty (which nevertheless seems real enough to hundreds of millions of impoverished people around the world).

Evidently less than persuaded by this line of argument, the members of the United Nations have declared that, whatever "development" may be, and whatever it may represent, we are all entitled to it. In 1986, in a United Nations Declaration on the Right to Development, the assembled nations of the world all agreed that "[t]he right to development is an inalienable human right by virtue of which every human person and all peoples are entitled to participate in, contribute to, and enjoy economic, social, cultural and political development, in which all human rights and fundamental freedoms can be fully realized."[28] This UN Declaration continues by saying that "[t]he human right to development also implies the full realization of the right of peoples to self-determination, which includes, subject to the relevant provisions of both International Covenants on Human Rights, the exercise of their inalienable right to full sovereignty over all their natural wealth and resources."[29]

If there is a "right to development," is there also a "right to *sustainable* development"? And, if so, what would that "right" be? For that matter, what is "sustainability"? And how (as I might have asked some weary legal advocate in a long oral hearing during my days judging WTO disputes in Geneva) is the definition of "development" altered by modifying it with the word "sustainable"? Most important by far, how does how we choose to define "sustainable development" change how the willing in the world should be seeking to shape and share a lasting global prosperity?

"SUSTAINABILITY" AND THE ENLIGHTENMENT PROJECT

For most of our history, the "dominion" of humanity over nature has been thought to be unlimited, and the natural resources of the Earth have been assumed to be inexhaustible. For many thousands of years, humanity exploited and sought to "subdue" nature in the belief that this was often the best way of surviving it. Civilization after now-forgotten civilization paid the price for refusing to heed the need to live consistently with and within nature, and yet the necessity of balancing economy with and within ecology remained a lesson unlearned.[30] The revolutionary philosophers who established the framework for our supposed "age of reason" largely shared the longstanding assumption that the Earth and all on it are ours to use as we see fit. Early in the seventeenth century, the French rationalist René Descartes described animals as mere automatons without any awareness of their own, and wrote that humans needed to become the "masters and possessors of nature."[31] At about that same time, the English champion of science – and of the practical application of science that in time came to be called "technology" – Francis Bacon likewise subscribed to the need for humanity to command nature. However, in an ominous foreshadowing of the future, he warned, "Nature, to be commanded, must be obeyed."[32]

The first intellectual antecedents of what might legitimately be called "sustainability" appeared later in the seventeenth century. The idea of sustainability literally came from the forests in reaction to the worldwide shrinking of woodlands occasioned by the multiplying presence of humanity. In France, Germany, Japan, England, and elsewhere around the world, protests began to be heard against the consequences of increasingly extensive deforestation. In some places, these protests resulted in better forestry practices that proved to be the first tangible accomplishments of an incipient environmentalism. Arguably the first summons to what would later be known as "sustainability" was a visionary tract written in 1664 by an English aristocrat named John Evelyn with the catchy title of "Sylva, or a Discourse of Forest-Trees and the Propagation of Timber in His Majesty's Dominions." Addressed to the attention of King Charles II, Evelyn's "Sylva" became the Restoration equivalent of a bestseller and inspired his fellow nobles to enlist their tenants in planting millions of seedlings in the English countryside.[33]

The term "sustainable" was coined by another European opponent of deforestation, the German Hans Carl von Carlowitz, in 1713. In the first book on forest management, Carlowitz contended that the "sustainable" use of forests could assure the supply of timber resources indefinitely.[34] Carlowitz not only invented the word "sustainable"; he was also perhaps the first to articulate the inescapable interrelationship between the economy and the environment.[35] Although Evelyn, Carlowitz, and others of like mind were writing about the immediate need for forestry management, they were writing equally about the relationship between economy and environment. These early advocates of sustainability maintained that we can continue to make use of natural resources for the benefit of humanity only if we replace those we use with others of equal or greater value while neither endangering nor destroying the natural systems that produce them. In other words, they insisted that only by "sustaining" natural resources can we continue to benefit from them. This belief in a human duty of replenishment was then, and it remains today, at the core of what many of the willing mean by the concept of sustainability.

These initial stirrings about sustainability occurred simultaneously with the first flickering of the Enlightenment that became visible in the eighteenth century and gradually spread throughout Europe and the United Kingdom and into the thirteen British overseas colonies that became the United States of America. The Enlightenment thinkers in England, Scotland, France, Germany, and elsewhere sought to liberate humanity from traditional oppressions of all kinds by applying reason to the world. Uniformly optimistic and profoundly cosmopolitan, they sought to emancipate and empower humanity by substituting science for superstition in the making of a "universal civilization"[36] in which every individual would be freed to flourish in freedom. They rejected the traditional static view of existence and eagerly embraced in its place the new idea of progress that is so much engrained in our modern world – the idea that tomorrow can be better than today if we only persist on our own and together in using human imagination to apply reason to all the unreason in our imperfect world.

Inspired by the Enlightenment, the idea of progress has become "the directing idea of humanity."[37] It is in between the lines of all we do in the modern world. The premodern belief that the world cannot be changed has been supplanted by the tacit modern assumption that everything can be changed. Indeed, the often-unspoken assumption in the modern world is that everything *will* change, that change cannot be stopped. In between the lines of all we do, too, is the Enlightenment belief that there are no limits to the possible scope of these changes. Progress is seen as a process without bounds and without end. At the core of the Enlightenment ethos is an outright refusal to accept any limits to human aspiration.

What has been called "the Enlightenment project"[38] has become in many ways an ongoing construction project for building the modern world. Scientific discovery. Political liberty. Religious toleration. Advances against disease, hunger, illiteracy, and child mortality. A longer life. A vastly improved standard of living since the eighteenth century. The antecedents of all this and much more can be found in the optimism of the Enlightenment. Without the historic lift of the Enlightenment, the vast majority of us everywhere would still be hungry and living in hovels while enduring the arbitrary rule of some potentate.[39] Likewise, a lot of the good we still hope to do in the world and for the world can be done only if we retain the confidence, the optimism, and the abiding belief in the possibility of human progress that characterized the exponents of the Enlightenment. As Stephen Eric Bronner has written, "The Enlightenment has always been – historically and politically – a force for securing liberty and fostering resistance against material oppression."[40]

And yet there are those who have professed to see a dark side to the Enlightenment, a hypocritical side that reveals as hollow its claim of seeking a brighter future for all of humanity. "Some post-modern and radical writers have adopted the cantankerous attitudes of the Frankfurt School to the Enlightenment, that it was a prelude to barbarism, controlling, manipulative, and dominating, to be dismissed, in the words of [the Marxist historian] Eric Hobsbawm … as 'anything from superficial and intellectually naive to a conspiracy of dead white men in periwigs to provide the intellectual foundation for Western Imperialism.'"[41] One aspect of the dark side they see is a subjugation of nature.[42] The contemporary British critic of globalization, John Gray, for one, argues that "the Westernizing impulse" the Enlightenment "embodies has transmitted to nearly all cultures the radical modernist project of subjugating nature by deploying technology to exploit the earth for human purposes."[43] Certainly no optimist, and no fan at all of what he views as a deeply destructive modern "humanism," Gray maintains that "[t]he project of subjecting the earth and its other life-forms to human will through technological domination is Western humanism in its final form."[44]

Economic historian Joel Mokyr tells us, "The belief in growth and improvement, and the specific notion that innovations and the growth of useful knowledge were the way to bring them about and thus a source of hope and excitement, were central to the entire Enlightenment movement."[45] In the wake of the Enlightenment, scientific advances led to a technological boom that transformed much of Europe from pastoral societies of villages into smokestack societies of factories. What became known as the Industrial Revolution caused sudden and sweeping economic, social, and political changes. These changes erased traditional ways of living and imposed enormous suffering. These changes also introduced us, culturally and psychologically, to the recurring nostalgia, so often so potent in politics, of "the world we have lost."[46] Not to be forgotten, though, is that these changes also enabled an ever-expanding portion of humanity to rise up for the first time from mere subsistence into an unprecedented prosperity.

The Enlightenment thinkers had been eager cheerleaders for these changes, for they foresaw, emerging from change, a new world of unprecedented abundance. It is too much to say that the Enlightenment caused the Industrial Revolution. Although the scientific spirit inspired by the Enlightenment led to some of the many inventions that revolutionized human industry, others might have occurred anyway. What can be said, and indeed has been said by Mokyr, is that "the Enlightenment was the reason why the Industrial Revolution was the beginning of modern economic growth and not another technological flash in the pan ... The Industrial Revolution marks the first time that technological advances and refinements were continued and sustained. The intellectual and ideological changes of the eighteenth century turned a few key inventions into a macroeconomic sea change."[47]

There is widespread acknowledgment that the Enlightenment Project "of applying knowledge and sympathy to enhance human flourishing"[48] consisted of both a political effort "that would create a better society" and a philosophical effort "that would replace religion with rational thought and an understanding of nature."[49] Less understood and less appreciated is the fact that, as Mokyr emphasizes, there was an equally important third part to the Enlightenment Project, "namely to make the economy produce more wealth and thus to increase what economists today call economic welfare."[50] In his judgment, "Of the three projects of the Enlightenment, the third has been by far the most successful even if on a global scale it is as yet incomplete."[51]

SMITH'S "SIMPLE SYSTEM" AND "SUSTAINABILITY"

Adam Smith, one of the most influential of all the Enlightenment thinkers, taught and wrote during the widely influential Scottish Enlightenment in the latter half of the eighteenth century. The eminent Yale historian Peter Gay, perhaps the leading authority on the Enlightenment, has gone so far as to describe Smith's *Wealth of Nations* as "the cardinal document of the Enlightenment," for "far beyond Scotland, in the German states and the American republic, economists wrote treatises and statesmen made policies in its name."[52] Both explicitly and implicitly, Smith's influence has endured to this day.

Smith's thought proceeded from the fundamental premise that all thinking about human endeavor must begin with an understanding of the uniformity and the immutability of human nature. Economically, in particular, he saw the human "propensity to truck, barter, and exchange one thing for another"[53] as a basic part of a human nature that is identical and unalterable in each and every one of us. Because of this human "propensity," he believed each of us "lives by exchanging," and so each of us "becomes in some measure a merchant," and our human society becomes a "commercial society."[54] Smith saw our "commercial society" as an expression of human nature resulting from a division of labor that maximizes individual human freedom and thereby magnifies the potential for human enlightenment.

This division of labor is therefore central to the Enlightenment Project. It results in the most efficient and thus the most productive allocation of economic resources. But this optimal division of labor does not emerge by design. It emerges and evolves over time from the combined consequences of the myriad individual actions each and every one of us takes in pursuing our natural propensity for exchange. In this way, the ever-evolving and open-ended development of our "commercial society" through the division of labor is led, in by far Smith's most famous phrase, by an "invisible hand." Each of us, he said, in pursuing our own interests, is led by an "invisible hand" to promote the broader interests of all of us.[55] This thought underlies much of today's liberal market capitalism.

The unintended end of Smith's "commercial society" is thus the mutual benefit of all. Smith saw what most would see as the merely mundane act of commerce as also a helpful and hopeful form of cooperation and communication with the potential to bring and bind humanity closer together. For him, "Economic life . . . is itself a sort of discussion."[56] From the commercial "discussion" of trade, he believed, could be derived much else of mutual benefit to humanity. To achieve these optimistic ends, Smith sought an economy based on private commercial decisions and not on arbitrary public dictates. He called for an end to the "mercantilism" that had led historically to government-ordained monopolies and to other restrictions that distorted the natural workings of the marketplace. He believed the division of labor would work best in a market economy based on private property, and not in a statist economy based primarily on government ownership or other state control of the means of production. He thought, too, that the "invisible hand"[57] of the marketplace would work best if freed from the visible hand of all unnecessary governmental regulations and restrictions.

Foremost among the systems of preference or restraint that Adam Smith saw as requiring elimination in 1776 were the many that had been imposed on international trade. He denounced then the results of "nations having been taught that their interest consisted of beggaring their neighbors. Each nation has been made to look with an invidious eye upon the prosperity of all the nations with which it trades, and to see their gain as its own loss."[58] Instead, he maintained that "the most advantageous method in which a landed nation can raise up artificers, manufacturers and merchants of its own, is to grant the most perfect freedom of trade to the artificers, manufacturers and merchants of all other nations."[59] Despite all the fears everywhere of the results of free trade, Smith insisted that "[e]very town and country, ... in proportion as they have opened their ports to all nations, instead of being ruined by this free trade ... have been enriched by it."[60] Arising from the freeing of trade, Smith envisaged a world of learning, invention, innovation, adaptation, and never-ending change in which the prosperity of all in the world would be multiplied again and again. He foresaw in such a world "the almost infinite growth of wealth."[61]

A crucial early refinement in Smith's "simple system of natural liberty" was the doctrine of *comparative advantage*. Smith had stressed the value of international trade where there is an "absolute advantage" in producing a good or service by producing it more efficiently than a potential trading partner. Four decades later, David Ricardo, one of Smith's British followers, took the next step intellectually. Ricardo saw that it is not necessary to have an "absolute advantage" in producing a good or service to profit from trade. His more subtle insight was that, to profit from trade, only a "comparative advantage" is necessary, and that, for both individuals and countries, a "comparative advantage" *always exists*.[62] In *The Principles of Political Economy and Taxation*, published in 1817, Ricardo demonstrated that individuals and countries alike can profit from trade even if they have *no* absolute advantage in producing *any* good or service. He showed that even those who are better or who are worse than everyone else at producing everything will be better off nevertheless if they concentrate on producing what they produce *relatively* the best when compared to their trading partners – and trade for the rest.

Ricardo's fundamental insight was that *all* of us can profit from international trade through an international division of labor in which *each* of us does what each of us does *relatively* the best when compared to others. This is true of all individuals. This is true of all countries. By each specializing in what we produce *relatively* – and thus *comparatively* – the best, when compared with our trading partners, we will each be our most productive, and we will each be able to afford to obtain through trade the most of all of the other things that we might need and desire and that we might otherwise have produced less efficiently. In contemporary terms, trade is not a "zero-sum" game. Trade is a "win–win" for all. Building on Smith's foresight, Ricardo envisaged a world in which all would pursue their comparative advantage in an ever-widening, ever-increasing, ever-subdividing division of labor.[63]

Smith's invention of his "simple system of natural liberty" is one of the greatest of all the accomplishments of the Enlightenment, and was, as Mokyr has observed, a driving force in the rise of the Industrial Revolution. Ricardo's later realization that comparative costs provide each and all of us with a "comparative advantage" when engaging in trade speeded up the Smithian drive for economic growth through commercial expansion of the division of labor then, and it still speeds that expansion now. Although the phrase "comparative advantage" appears nowhere in the treaty that established the World Trade Organization, underlying the WTO treaty and other international agreements of all kinds that further the freeing of international trade is the unstated belief that the gains from trade will be maximized worldwide if we each do what we can each do *relatively* the best when compared to others in the world marketplace.

Smith's views that contributed to this economic triumph were founded in part on his working assumption that there will always be a scarcity of natural and other resources. All the same, in all of his voluminous writings on political economy, Smith never dealt directly with the natural environment or with the impact of trade and commerce on the natural environment. He did not articulate his "simple system" in today's language of "ecology" (a term that was not invented until long after he died), and it has been contended in criticism of the Enlightenment that Smith "saw nature as no more than a storehouse of raw materials for man's ingenuity."[64] In contrast, his rough contemporary, the revolutionary sage from Geneva, Jean-Jacques Rousseau, had no love at all for commerce. A redeeming aspect of the erratic Rousseau was, however, his love of nature. In his "admiration of nature," Rousseau's "Arcadian philosophy" became an important "source of the sustainability movement."[65] As Canadian historian of sustainability Jeremy L. Caradonna has expressed it, Rousseau's "love of nature differed from that of mainstream Enlightenment philosophers, who saw nature as an abstraction or an inert object of study."[66] For Rousseau, "To be virtuous was to live in harmony with the natural world. Unlike John Locke, who thought that nature only had value if humans mixed their labor with it, Rousseau saw nature as intrinsically valuable."[67]

The intrinsic value of nature would become one of the recurring themes of many of those who reacted against the convulsive changes caused by the Industrial Revolution. Following Rousseau, this theme was at first taken up by the Romantic poets. In the long walks in the English countryside that summoned and gave cadence to his lyricism, William Wordsworth "learned to look on Nature," and felt "a sense sublime."[68] For Wordsworth, an engagement and oneness with nature offered transcendence from worldly travails. Soon enough, in the New World on the opposite shore of the Atlantic Ocean, Henry David Thoreau was taking his own long walks, and writing in his notebooks the eloquent origins of the modern environmental movement. Not nearly so well remembered as Wordsworth and Thoreau, and yet of considerable significance in the unfolding chronicle of sustainability, was George Perkins Marsh, who has been called "America's first environmentalist."[69]

A former Member of Congress from Vermont and a friend and ally of Abraham Lincoln, Marsh, after leaving the Congress, served for the last two decades of his life as the American minister in Italy. He despaired of the deforestation he saw in both the New World and the Old. In 1864, he published *Man and Nature*, in which he denounced in ringing rhetoric what he saw as our "reckless destruction" of the natural world.[70] "[M]an is everywhere a disturbing agent," he warned. "Wherever he plants his foot, the harmonies of nature are turned to discord."[71] Marsh "set the stage for the early conservation movement" by focusing on "the dangers of imprudence and the necessity of caution" whenever we "interfere with the spontaneous arrangements" of nature.[72]

There is nothing explicit in Adam Smith's famous treatise of 1776 on "the wealth of nations" that accounts for, or that clearly anticipates, these compelling thoughts about the utter necessity to a striving humanity of ensuring the sustainability of nature. The truth seems to be that it simply did not occur at that earlier time to most of those involved in the making of modern commerce that nature could be anything but bountiful, or that there could be constraints on how nature might be transformed for human purposes. Yet surely Smith would recoil at the environmental destruction that today puts "[d]ozens of Scotland's most famous historic sites ... at very high risk of being badly damaged by climate change," and surely he would want to do something to stop it.[73]

THE GLOBAL SEARCH FOR "SUSTAINABLE DEVELOPMENT"

For the most part, an endless wealth from nature was simply assumed as the Industrial Revolution multiplied and remultiplied human production. Throughout the nineteenth century and into and throughout much of the twentieth, the Industrial Revolution produced an abundance of unprecedented wealth from the seemingly endless cornucopia of the natural world. Little thought was given along the way to the environmental destruction that was often caused by ever-increasing industrial growth. The incipient idea of sustainability persisted, though, as a quiet undercurrent in reaction to industrialism, and it was often an implicit thread in the gradual unfolding of the competing strands of conservation and preservation that ultimately became the environmental movement. Environmental losses mounted, and eventually voices were raised and heard in asking about their costs. The thoughts of Marsh and others about the inescapable connection between "man and nature" influenced John Muir, Gifford Pinchot, Aldo Leopold, Rachel Carson, and the other environmental thinkers in the United States and elsewhere whose later writings and actions are far more familiar to us today. The idea of sustainability helped inspire and nurture the eventual emergence of a far-reaching environmental consciousness in the 1960s and 1970s.

Concerns about the environment first reached the United Nations in 1968 with the passage of UN Resolution 2398, which warned that "the relationship between man and the environment is undergoing profound changes in the wake of modern scientific and technological development."[74] The United Nations General Assembly agreed then that these changes presented "unprecedented opportunities," but also posed "grave dangers."[75] The UN delegates foresaw a "continuing and accelerating impairment of the quality of the human environment."[76] Resolution 2398 was approved at the urging of the Swedes, who were alarmed by the recent discovery of acid rain drifting their way from elsewhere in Europe. Acid rain became one of the first international environmental concerns to draw global attention.[77]

Global environmental concerns moved more prominently to the global stage in 1972 with the convening in Stockholm of the United Nations Conference on the Human Environment. The Stockholm gathering that year laid the international foundation for all the efforts of all the world's willing that followed. The famous "Stockholm Declaration" resulting from the conference stated that "[a] point has been reached in history when we must shape our actions throughout the world with a more prudent care for their environmental consequences. Through ignorance or indifference we can do massive and irreversible harm to the earthly environment on which our life and well-being depend."[78] Apart from the Stockholm Declaration itself, the most enduring achievement of the conference was the establishment of the United Nations Environment Programme (UNEP), which brought the United Nations for the first time fully into the business of environmental protection, and which has since become a reliable and relentless voice for achieving global "sustainable development." Stockholm also heralded the arrival of a new era of international negotiations resulting in a host of innovative international environmental agreements.

The concept of sustainability was not specifically on the agenda in Stockholm. That same year, though, it became the heated topic of worldwide discussion with the publication of a report entitled *The Limits to Growth* by a global group of technical experts called the Club of Rome.[79] Using newly invented computerized models of demographic, ecological, and other global trends, the report stated that, in the absence of change, "the limits to growth" on the planet could be reached within the next hundred years, and predicted, "The most probable result will be a rather sudden and uncontrollable decline in both population and industrial capacity."[80] The report of the Club of Rome became a best-selling global sensation in 1972. It was translated into thirty languages and sold 30 million copies.[81] Through the years, it has been much criticized for its methodology and for its apocalyptic tone in contemplating the prospect of a looming global ecological collapse. All the same, it imprinted once and for all in the global consciousness the notion that the Earth is finite and that we must live within the finite limits of the Earth. Expanding beyond the forests, "[t]he word *sustainable* appears for the first time in its broader, modern meaning" in *The Limits to Growth*.[82]

The phrase "sustainable development" was introduced eight years later, in 1980, by the governmental and non-governmental members from 114 countries of what was then called the International Union for the Conservation of Nature and Natural Resources (and later became the World Conservation Union) as the touchtone to their "World Conservation Strategy."[83] Among other reforms, they called for preserving genetic diversity in plant and animal species, protecting essential ecological processes, and using biological resources sustainably.[84] Their aim was to "help advance the achievement of *sustainable development* through the conservation of living resources."[85]

The term "sustainable development" was then embraced in full in 1987 by the United Nations Commission on Environment and Development and popularized in the Commission's pioneering report "Our Common Future," commonly called the Brundtland Report after Gro Harlem Brundtland, the commission's chairwoman and the former three-time prime minister of Norway. "Sustainable development" was also given its famous definition in the Brundtland Report. Significantly, the Brundtland Commission did not stop with offering its enduring if elusive definition as "development that meets the needs of the present without compromising the ability of future generations to meet their own needs." It then went on to explain that the definition of sustainable development "contains within it two key concepts: the concept of 'needs,' in particular the essential needs of the world's poor, to which overriding priority should be given; and the idea of limitations imposed by the state of technology and social organization on the environment's ability to meet present and future needs."[86] The two "key concepts" of economic needs and environmental limits are thus contained and entwined equally within the definition of "sustainable development" on which the nearly 200 countries that belong to the United Nations have long since agreed.

For several decades now, the goal of "sustainable development" as defined in the Brundtland Report in 1987 has been the rallying cry of the willing in all their work in an unwilling world. It has been heard in Rio and Bonn, in Bali and Geneva, in Lima and Paris, in Durban and Kyoto, in Cancun and Montreal, and in all the numerous other cities where global gatherings have convened to pursue this supposedly shared goal. It has been invoked endlessly at untold other earnest gatherings of the willing. This definition has taken and transformed the notion of sustainable development "from concept to movement."[87] Yet, despite all this, we still do not know what "sustainable development" means.

Must we first agree on the definition of "sustainable development" before we can begin to achieve it by transforming ours from an unwilling into the willing world?

On Defining Sustainable Development by Doing It

Although the Brundtland definition of sustainable development has become a rallying cry for the willing in the world, it is widely viewed as anything from vague to meaningless to dangerous. Some of the most ardent environmentalists see the linkage in this definition of what they consider the starkly contrasting concepts of "sustainability" and "development" as a betrayal of the environment and of future generations. Some of the most passionate champions of commerce see the binding of these two terms in this definition as an ominous hindrance to the magical workings of a free market. These usually opposing critics are united in thinking that the very notion of sustainable development is little more than a convenient political contrivance that glosses over numerous irreconcilable conflicts between economy and environment. They each fear the consequences.

The challenge is to eliminate this conflict by somehow reconciling the competing claims of economy and environment. The task in particular is how best to minimize needed trade-offs between these claims, and how best to guide the choices involved in these trade-offs where they must be made. When considered together, the "two key concepts" highlighted in this controversial definition – needs and limits – can unlock for us how to do so, and can thereby answer the question of whether we must first agree on a definition of sustainable development before it can be achieved.

THE DIVISION OF LABOR AND ECONOMIC NEEDS

The key concept of *needs* in the Brundtland definition is meant to remind us that, however we may choose to define our overall "needs," they must include the most pressing of the basic economic necessities of humanity. Emphasis is rightly given in the definition to the "overriding priority" of paying particular attention to the "essential needs of the world's poor." The key concept of *limitations* that follows in the definition reminds us of the environmental limits within which these economic "needs" must be met. Limitations are imposed by the state of technology and social organization on the environment's ability to meet "present and future needs." The punctuating words in the definition about meeting both "present and future needs" serve to underscore, once more, that "[s]ustainable development is development that meets the needs of the present without compromising the ability of future generations to meet their own needs."

It is this idea – the idea that our economic needs can only be met over time within our environmental limits, and only by balancing our needs within our limits – that remains the redeeming heart of the Brundtland definition. Only in a world without environmental limits could the pursuit of an economic future for a needy humanity ignore the environment. Only in a world without a striving humanity could the natural environment be unaffected by human economic demands. We do not live in either of those two worlds. Humanity strives within environmental constraints, and the economy and the environment are inevitably and inextricably intertwined. Understanding and acceptance of this inescapable fact are essential to defining and achieving "sustainable development." But how best can we strike, together, the right balance by meeting our needs within our limits? And how best can we balance, together, our needs within our limits in ways that will help us transform an unwilling into the willing world?

"Today, on average, people live more than twice as long and enjoy over eight times more goods and services than their forebears of the 1800s."[1] Much of this transformation of human life is the result of human exchange resulting from specialization in Adam Smith's ever-subdividing division of labor as part of the Enlightenment Project. Smith taught us that the division of labor is limited only by "the extent of the market."[2] Today, the extent of the market, and thus the extent also of the division of labor, is worldwide, resulting in the global reach of both international trade and international investment. As one of Smith's most outspoken modern apostles, the British writer Matt Ridley, has said, "The more people are drawn into the global division of labour, the more people can specialise and exchange, the wealthier we will all be."[3]

Not everyone agrees. The adversaries everywhere of international trade, international investment, and other border-breaching manifestations of a growing "globalization" recoil in reaction to what they see as the harmful effects of the global division of labor. The American agrarian essayist Wendell Berry speaks for many around the world who perceive specialization as dehumanization in arguing that "a person who can do only one thing can do virtually nothing for himself ... In living in the world by his own will and skill, the stupidest peasant or tribesman is more competent than the most intelligent worker or technician or intellectual in a society of specialists."[4] Berry and other critics of globalization on the left and on the right alike see the division of labor as a soulless device devoted exclusively to economic efficiency that severs each of us from all to which we once belonged, and leaves each of us fragmented and less than whole. They doubt the very possibility of progress as envisaged by the Enlightenment, and they doubt whether we can make a better future in a specialized and commercial society. Adam Smith anticipated this critique and acknowledged the deleterious effects of the division of labor into discrete and monotonous tasks on a factory assembly line. To counter these effects, he counseled that governments must take "some pains to prevent it" and advanced the then-revolutionary remedy that governments had an obligation to provide an education to workers and to "the children of the common people."[5]

Where the Enlightenment thinkers were optimists, many of the opponents of our modern market-driven and globalized world are pessimists. These outspoken opponents of our ever-expanding specialization worldwide through an ever sub-dividing division of labor seem to long nostalgically for a return to an imagined past, a mythical golden age of self-sufficient village and hunter–gatherer societies. We can sympathize with their sense that something more should be sought and derived from life than simply things and more things. But how, in the absence of some amount of material well-being, can life be more than merely a struggle to survive? Did the peasant have running water? Did the tribesman have a long life? Without specialization, the peasant and the tribesman alike are much more likely to live in poverty than are the specialists of the world.

Ridley, for one, has little patience with such criticisms, which are heard most often from those who were blessed to be born in some of the most prosperous parts of the world and need not, thanks to specialization, make the pens and the paper they employ in writing their critiques of globalization. "It is easier," he says, "to wax elegiac for the life of a peasant when you do not have to use a long-drop toilet."[6] The American libertarian thinker Virginia Postrel has no more patience than Ridley with such criticism of the supposedly dire effects of specialization. Like Smith, she sees the division of labor as emerging naturally from the irrepressible inclination to engage in commercial – and in countless other – human exchanges that is an unchanging and unchangeable part of human nature. "It is not human nature," she says, "to prefer poverty and hunger to the comforts of cold beer and four-wheel drive . . . The alternative to specialization is the great reactionary dream: a return to peasant life."[7]

Smith called the result of his "simple system" of human exchange through trade and investment a "commercial society." Nowadays we tend to call it liberal market capitalism. Much of the contemporary opposition to the continuing subdivisions of Smith's division of labor through ever-longer and ever-more-complex global value chains is really only a vocalization of a visceral suspicion of liberal market capital-ism. As Canadian financial journalist Peter Foster sums up the familiar stereotype, "For its more powerful ideological opponents, 'capitalism' is a satanic word, almost invariably attached to derogatory epithets such as brutal, vicious, casino, dog-eat-dog, cowboy, crony, no-holds-barred, unfettered, untrammeled, cold-hearted, hard-hearted, heartless, etc., etc."[8]

Human nature being what it is, there is often ample reason to be suspicious of the motives of some capitalists. All too much evidence of the legitimacy of such suspicion can be found in any consideration of the causes, for example, of the global financial crisis of 2008 and 2009. Crony capitalism, in which the powerful profit by influencing government to rig the economic rules in their favor, is not capitalism; it is a corruption of capitalism parading falsely by that name. It is often overlooked that Smith was the first to warn us about the enduring threat of such a greedy and excessive capitalism. "People of the same trade," he cautioned, "seldom meet together, even for merriment and diversion, but the conversation ends in a conspiracy against the public, or in some contrivance to raise prices."[9] Sounding like no one from Wall Street, Smith derided the rich as "a few lordly masters"[10] and denounced their "natural selfishness and rapacity" and the "immensity" of their "vain and insatiable desires" for "all the different baubles and trinkets which are employed in the economy of greatness."[11]

Yet the opponents of liberal market capitalism often forget the countless benefits of a market economy. They often forget that the cooperative human expression of the natural human "propensity" for exchange through capitalism has created our unprecedented material wealth, and that capitalism alone can create more. The undeniably bad behavior of some capitalists should not blind us to the constructive actions of others. Nor should it blind us to the undeniable benefits of capitalism as a whole. For all our legitimate reservations arising from the excesses of capitalism, and for all of the admitted failings of capitalism arising from myriad human frailties found in human nature, the fact remains: Capitalism works. Capitalism alone works, because capitalism alone among the economic arrangements so far devised by humanity is rooted in human nature. Unlike communism, unlike socialism, and unlike anarchism, capitalism does not require an alteration in human nature in order to work. Of all these "isms," capitalism alone reflects people as we really are. The British statesman and philosopher Edmund Burke may have been the first to underscore this point when he wrote to Smith not long after publication of *The Wealth of Nations* that "a theory like yours, founded in the nature of man, which is always the same, will last, when those that are founded on his opinions, which are always changing, will and must be forgotten."[12] Since then, we have had to rediscover this enduring truth generation after generation.

Other economic approaches usually begin by assuming that human nature can in some way be changed. It cannot be. Because capitalism begins with the premise of people as we really are, and not as we might wish we were and might ideally ought to be, capitalism has freed us from the bucolic confines of the past and led us into the modern world, and it gives us by far our best opportunity now to work together to shape an even brighter future for all humanity. It is our reliance on capitalism that has enabled billions of us in the world to stop using long-drop toilets. Capitalism has long been "the ultimate global antipoverty program."[13] In recent decades "a billion people have escaped poverty as their countries moved away from command and control, toward capitalism and freedom."[14] According to the American economist Edward P. Lazear, "[T]here is little doubt that the cause for the improvement has been a move toward markets and away from government-managed economies."[15]

The global evidence of declining poverty is irrefutable. In the most recent calculations, the World Bank tells us that the share of the world's population living in extreme poverty fell from 36 percent in 1990 to 15 percent in 2011.[16] The International Labour Organization reports that the number of workers in the world earning less than $1.25 per day fell from 811 million in 1991 to 375 million in 2013.[17] Based on current growth trends, the United Nations predicts that only about 5 percent of the people in the world will be mired in extreme poverty in 2030.[18] As the distinguished international trade economist Douglas A. Irwin has observed, "The credit goes to the spread of capitalism."[19] The scope of market capitalism has been enlarged by the lowering of many barriers to international trade and investment worldwide, and it has been enlarged, too, by the embrace (albeit ever so slowly) in important ways of many free market principles in India, China, and other emerging economies. The liberating economic transformations that first happened in Europe and then in the United States during the Industrial Revolution because of the Western embrace of market capitalism are now happening at long last in many other parts of the world.

Some critics of capitalism argue that the rise from poverty worldwide should not be credited to the countless decentralized trial-and-error transactions in the bottom-up and decidedly human exchange of the free market. Instead, they argue that the credit should be given to reliance, in China and elsewhere, on centralized government "planning" and on the other top-down statist solutions of an anti-democratic authoritarianism that, in its latest incarnation, is sometimes called, euphemistically, "state capitalism." They advise us to abandon liberal market capitalism in favor of having the state dominate, direct, and drive the course of the economy while restricting international trade and investment and otherwise controlling and constraining the natural workings of market forces. They lament the messy complexities of markets because markets reflect the messy complexities that come with being human. Often, too, they lament the similar messiness of democracy, and for the same reasons. They envy the apparent ease and the purported purity of authoritarian rule. They invite, often without realizing it, the rise of the "strong man" directing the strong state. But in the recent global rise up from poverty, the market solutions of market capitalism have made most of the difference. Market solutions have reduced poverty by creating more wealth for nations wherever market solutions have been permitted.

China began to move toward markets with the famous "opening" to the outside world by Deng Xiaoping in 1979. India began to move toward markets with major liberalizing reforms in the early 1990s. The movement toward markets by the two most populous countries in the world has been slow and often not sure. China now seems to be retreating from Deng's gradual embrace of freer markets into a planned and ultimately self-defeating mix of more restrictiveness on trade and investment, a strategic mercantilism, and an old-fashioned protectionism. India is struggling with the complexities of its transformation from a state-directed to a market economy in the largest democracy in the world. But the evidence of the positive effects of economic liberalization in both countries during the past several decades is clear. In China, where so much of world attention has focused on the supposed triumphs of state edicts, "the much more dynamic and productive private sector has been the driving force for change."[20] Similarly, in India, the most productive parts of the economy are those that no longer suffer from the crippling restraints of the previous statist "raj regime."[21]

American economist Alan S. Blinder has summed up the virtues of free markets in a single sentence that should be memorized by every single politician who professes to wish to serve the people, and also by every one of the willing in the world: "Throughout recorded history, there has never been a serious practical alternative to free competitive markets as a mechanism for delivering the right goods and services to the right people at the lowest possible cost."[22] This is true of the wealthiest countries of the world. Emphatically, this is equally true of the poorest countries in the world, and of the poorest people in those poorest countries, for they are the people who can benefit the most from continued economic growth.[23] Jasson Urbach, director of the Free Market Foundation in South Africa, concludes from this that, "[i]n simple terms, if you are poor, the best place to be is in economically free societies where government intervention is kept to a minimum. It is for this reason that we see millions of people trying to escape despotic nations that are controlled by overbearing states to seek refuge in the richest and most economically free nations on earth."[24] Confirmation of this conclusion could be obtained from anyone who arrived in Florida on a raft from Cuba.

And yet, for all our recent successes in reducing poverty worldwide, the fundamental economic "need" of escaping from poverty remains, and this "need" is rightly a key for our concern in the definition of sustainable development. Looking ahead hopefully to fulfilling the "post-2015 development agenda" of the United Nations, a "high-level" panel advising the UN offered this reminder to the world: "Every day, poverty condemns 1 out of 7 people on the planet to a struggle to survive. Many of those living in extreme poverty are ignored, excluded from opportunities, sometimes for generations." Today, they reminded us, "1.2 billion people suffer under the hardship of living on less than $1.25 per person per day."[25]

Not without reason did Prime Minister Indira Gandhi of India remind the United Nations Conference on the Environment in Stockholm in 1972 that "poverty is the worst pollution."[26] This has not changed. Decades later, in our unwilling world, there is reason aplenty to believe that "the real environmental crisis" is poverty.[27] Whatever our legitimate concerns may be about our climate and about our overall natural environment, these stark numbers tallying the reality of the continuing immiseration of billions of people simply cannot be ignored in any consideration of sustainable development.

ENVIRONMENTAL LIMITS AND THE "LIMITS TO GROWTH"

All this said about our *needs*, what, then, about our *limits*? How does the second of the two key concepts in the Brundtland definition of sustainable development link to the first? As a cure for the world's undeniable economic "needs," is the marvelous economic cornucopia of market capitalism as an endless means for furthering the continued advance of humanity in accordance with Adam Smith's "simple system of natural liberty"? Is there, as Ridley argues, "no inevitable end to this process"?[28] Or does the constant churning of capitalism have ultimate environmental limits?

The Brundtland Commission elaborated at some length on what it saw as the essential balance between needs and limits: "Growth has no set limits in terms of population or resource use beyond which lies ecological disaster. Different limits hold for the use of energy, materials, water, and land. Many of these will manifest themselves in the form of rising costs and diminishing returns, rather than in the form of any sudden loss of a resource base. The accumulation of knowledge and the development of technology can enhance the carrying capacity of the resource base. But ultimate limits there are, and sustainability requires that long before these are reached, the world must ensure equitable access to the constrained resource and reorient technological efforts to relieve the pressure."[29]

"Ultimate limits there are," said the Brundtland Commission, and these ultimate limits must be respected. But is this so? Given that there are clearly environmental limitations that constrain our actions in meeting human needs, are there also "ultimate" limits beyond which we cannot push in our pursuit of human prosperity? Are there natural boundaries beyond which we cannot go? The answer to this question is central to comprehending precisely how the two key concepts of sustainable development are interconnected. The outcome of the central query about the competing claims of our needs and our limits turns on whether we believe that there are "ultimate limits" to the capacity of our natural resources to support human life and to satisfy the seemingly never-ending array and accumulation of material human aspirations.

This is not a new debate, and this is far from a new question. The dividing lines in this prolonged debate were first drawn by a British country parson and political economist, Thomas Malthus, toward the end of the eighteenth century, and they have remained much the same ever since. Reacting to the utopian expectations of some of the more venturesome and visionary among the later Enlightenment thinkers,[30] Malthus tried to refute the optimistic assumptions of the Enlightenment about progress and the future. He published, anonymously, in 1798, a deeply disturbing pamphlet entitled "An Essay on the Principle of Population" that became a bestseller at the time.[31] This essay was the first rendering of the enduring divisions between economy and environment that are still with us now.

Malthus believed the optimists of the Enlightenment were mistaken in thinking that the increasing population supported by the increasing economic wealth derived from the application of Smith's "simple system" was beneficial. He had noticed that, although there were more and more people, there was, unfortunately, no more land. Stalks of grain were growing one by one in the English countryside while people were busy multiplying. Or, to put it as he did, the supply of food was growing *arithmetically* while the number of people was growing *exponentially*. Reasoning from this comparative calculation, the pessimistic parson predicted that the food supply would not be able to keep pace over time with the growth in population because of the finite productivity of the limited amount of land. The imbalance he described between our needs and our limits is today known as "the Malthusian trap."

Malthus was absolutely wrong, of course, in foreseeing that humanity would fall in the nineteenth century into the vise of the trap he saw between growing needs and non-growing resources. As Julian Morris has written in recounting what he refers to as "the persistence of population pessimism": "It is ironic that Malthus should have invented this 'principle' just at the moment when England was in the process of escaping the very trap he described. Various technological innovations had already resulted in increased agricultural productivity – and were beginning to result in new forms of industry. Since the late 1700s, a continuous stream of such innovations has resulted not only in dramatic increases in per capita output, but also in increases in life expectancy."[32]

In his own time, Malthus "was too quick to assume that population pressures would automatically reverse the gains of economic development."[33] But was Malthus a prophet for our time far ahead of his own time? For all the overwhelming evidence that Malthus was wrong in his conclusions in 1798, the debate has continued, throughout the more than two centuries since, about whether we are fated eventually to fall into the Malthusian trap. The unavoidable collision course that Malthus foresaw between our economic needs and our environmental limits is much the same course that many around the world see us taking today.

On one side of this debate are the pessimists, echoing Malthus. Counting more and more people, and anticipating the availability of fewer and fewer natural resources, they warn of the inescapable approach of disaster and doom unless fundamental changes are made in the way we live. On the other side are the optimists, echoing Adam Smith and all his followers. They still carry the torch of the Enlightenment, and see no necessity for any fundamental changes in how we continue to pursue the Enlightenment Project. In considering the link between our needs and our limits, they are confident that human ingenuity and the consequent transformations wrought by unforeseeable technological innovations will, as always in the past, enable us somehow to continue to escape the trap. Every discussion of sustainable development is a continuation of this ongoing debate.

In the eyes of the optimists, all our history teaches us that, through unforeseen technological innovations, we can escape from and transcend what seem now to be the straits of our confining limits. Furthermore, they believe the pessimists misunderstand the very nature of the concept of resources. The key, they say, is to do more with less through the relentless use of the human imagination in adding to the shared stock of human knowledge in shaping the world around us. The American economist Paul Romer explains, "The naïve intuition that people have about limits to growth is profoundly wrong. There is a scarcity of physical objects, but that's not the constraint on what we can do."[34] Rather, "the real constraint is not the number of objects but the ways of combining objects as ideas."[35] And the number of possible ways to combine ideas, as Virginia Postrel poetically puts it, "makes the number of atoms in the universe look close to zero by comparison."[36]

Thus, for the optimists, the emphasis when considering our limits should not be on the tangible – on physical objects – but on the intangible – on ideas. There is no limit to our ideas because there is no limit to our imagination. Implicit in this overarching optimism is the belief that "the relative abundance of a society's natural resources can change dramatically with technological advance."[37] Yesterday's grain of sand is today's silicon chip. Today's ocean wave may become tomorrow's power plant. We make new resources by imagining new ideas for making new technologies. In this view, resources are neither static nor limited. Rather, "[r]esources are simply those assets that can be used profitably for human benefit," and "what can be used productively changes with time, technology, and material demand" in the ongoing pursuit of human progress.[38]

The centuries-long and continuing debate about the connections between our economic needs and our environmental limits delineates the basic philosophical premises underlying our differences over these "two key concepts." Where each of us sees ourselves as standing in this debate is determinative in defining how each of us sees the appropriate approach to "sustainable development." Enters now into this debate the issue of *climate change*. Is the outcome of this ongoing debate altered by the arrival and acceleration of manmade climate change? Is progress still possible in this heat?[39] Or is Parson Malthus enjoying a posthumous revenge with humanity at long last in the snare of his trap?

"PLANETARY BOUNDARIES" AND SMITH'S "SIMPLE SYSTEM"

Some scientists affiliated with a research center in Stockholm shook up this debate in 2009 by maintaining that "new challenges require new thinking on global sustainability" and introducing into the debate the concept of "planetary boundaries."[40] They reported from their research that we are fast approaching nine planetary boundaries that regulate the stability and resiliency of the Earth, and they warned that these boundaries must not be passed. Keeping within these natural boundaries, these scientists assured us, should secure a "safe operating space for humanity." But, exceeding these boundaries, they cautioned us, will threaten not only the Earth's natural systems, but also our own survival.[41] In 2015, the same scientists updated their earlier report and announced that four of the nine boundaries had been crossed as a result of continuing increases in greenhouse gas emissions and other human actions.[42]

The nine planetary boundaries identified by the Stockholm scientists are: climate change; ocean acidification; ozone depletion; pollution caused by excessive flows of the nitrogen and phosphorus crucial to plant growth; the overuse of freshwater resources; deforestation and other changes in inland use; the loss of "biosphere integrity" through the loss of biodiversity; the buildup of chemical pollution; and the level of particulate pollutants in the "aerosol loading" of the atmosphere.[43] The four boundaries they now see us as having crossed are those for nitrogen and phosphorus cycles, land use, biosphere integrity – and climate change. Of these four, there are two – biosphere integrity and climate change – that these scientists see as "core boundaries."

The Stockholm scientists say, ominously, that significantly altering either of these two core boundaries through human actions has "the potential on its own to drive the Earth System into a new state should they be substantially and persistently transgressed."[44] Their fear is that we could reach a "tipping point" on the planet where "ecological systems shift radically and potentially irreversibly into a different state" that could cause widespread global economic and environmental destruction.[45] Moreover, some contend, this could happen because we push past any one of these boundaries, or, conceivably, it could happen through a combination of human actions even if we remain within all of them. Furthermore, it could happen not gradually, but all at once. No less than the *Economist* has intoned, "A sudden shift is plausible."[46]

Whether these tipping points even exist is a matter of some ongoing scientific debate. Another group of scientists, from the California-based Breakthrough Institute, in critiquing the Stockholm conclusions, maintains that the reality of "tipping points . . . remains unconfirmed."[47] Furthermore, they argue that the very concept of planetary boundaries should be "discarded" because it "does not capture the challenges involved in most of the environmental problems it lists."[48] Instead, they say the proper focus should be on how best to discern and to make the trade-offs that will be needed going forward between economy and environment.[49]

In believing the right trade-offs between economy and environment can be identified and made, these scientists offer one more optimistic echo of the Enlightenment. They argue that, "Human alteration of environments produces multiple effects, some advantageous to societies, such as enhanced production, and some detrimental, like environmental pollution with toxic chemicals, excess nutrients and carbon emissions from fossil fuels, and the loss of wildlife and their habitats."[50] According to these optimists and contemporary followers of Adam Smith, who appear supremely confident of our capabilities in confronting our impacts on the environment, "The key to better environmental outcomes is not in ending human alteration of environments but in anticipating and mitigating their negative consequences."[51] In reply, the Stockholm scientists say they "have never argued that there are planetary tipping points for all Planetary Boundary processes. Furthermore, there does not need to be a tipping point for these processes and systems in order for them to function as key regulators of the stability of the Earth system."[52]

Thus, the scientific debate continues. Whatever its outcome, and whether in fact there are actual tipping points or not, "the idea of planetary boundaries has taken root."[53] The view that there are boundaries to the environmental "carrying capacity" of the planet has become a familiar and a common currency in the peripatetic global conversation about the competing concerns of economy and environment. In much of the current global debate, the existence of planetary boundaries is simply assumed by those among the willing who believe in particular that climate change must be addressed. One of the most outspoken among the advocates for finding the right way to attain sustainable development that can satisfy our increasing economic needs while respecting our environmental limits is the American economist Jeffrey Sachs, who explains the significance of these supposed boundaries in this way: "When humanity trespasses on these planetary boundaries, meaning that human pressures on the environment become greater than the ability of the Earth's natural systems to absorb those human pressures, the result is a major change in the function of the Earth's ecosystems. These changes, in turn, threaten human wellbeing and even human survival when the shocks occur in places where populations are very poor and do not have the buffers of wealth and infrastructure to protect them."[54]

As the transcending expression of environmental limits, climate change does not change everything.[55] Climate change does not change the enduring value to humanity of Adam Smith's "simple system of natural liberty" as an indispensable catalyst for securing human freedom and prosperity by creating and shaping open societies. Within the context of our new environmental circumstances, we must continue to rely on Smith's "simple system." To survive in a world confronting the unprecedented challenge of climate change, we continue to need the unlimited innovation that only the individual and collaborative expression of freedom in the market economy of capitalism can provide. But, while it does not change everything, climate change does change a lot. It does change how we should see and use Smith's "simple system." Climate change alters how we must use the incomparable power of market forces worldwide to address the transformation of the climate while shaping and sharing a lasting global prosperity through sustainable development.

Our circumstances today are not those of the Enlightenment thinkers of the eighteenth century. The agricultural and industrial production that has created the prosperity of the modern world has also, in the twenty-first century, pushed the world to the brink of the ecological edge. If there are not absolute environmental limits, if there are not tipping points, there are clearly unprecedented environmental constraints on all we can do without grim consequence to the natural world of which our species is a part. At the very least, there are profound constraints imposed by the immediate and increasing need to confront and combat the threat of climate change.

However, contrary to what some so shrilly assure us, market capitalism need not worsen this growing global threat. Quite the opposite. The challenge before us is not one of "capitalism versus the climate."[56] The challenge before us is one instead of shaping and sharing a capitalism *for* the climate. To achieve sustainable development, we must have the bountiful benefits of the marketplace in a *sustainable* capitalism. To create a sustainable capitalism, we must make the most of Smith's "simple system of natural liberty" while using it in new ways. For Smith, the market was a manifestation of shared human imagination. He taught us that the magic on which we should always rely is the magic of the human imagination. All philosophical systems, he told us, are "mere inventions of the imagination."[57] This includes his own. His admonition to rely on our imagination should inform all of our thinking about how best to balance our economic needs with our environmental limits in achieving sustainable development through the creation of a sustainable capitalism. His "simple system of natural liberty" has helped us progress this far. If we take his advice and use our imagination, his system can continue to serve us now. It can be the key to our success in making the willing world.

MARKET PROGRESS TOWARD "SUSTAINABLE DEVELOPMENT"

One of the most eloquent champions of the Enlightenment, the Irish historian J. B. Bury, published a history of *The Idea of Progress* in 1920.[58] Progress, he wrote then, is the idea that "civilization has moved, is moving, and will move in a desirable direction" toward the "increasing happiness" of all humanity.[59] Somehow Bury was able to write his hopeful paean to progress even in the immediate aftermath of the unprecedented carnage of the First World War. He believed as much as anyone in the possibility that tomorrow can be better than today. In a prescient aside, though, he mentioned a single, striking qualification: "If there were good cause for believing that the earth would be uninhabitable in AD 2000 or 2100 the doctrine of Progress would lose its meaning and would automatically disappear."[60]

What is the Brundtland definition of sustainable development if not simply another way of stating what the followers of Adam Smith have long characterized as optimizing human welfare over time through the workings of his "simple system"? Yet, often missing from their view has been an express appreciation for the fact that the fulfillment of our economic needs is constrained by our environmental limits. Often the economy and the environment have been assumed to inhabit separate domains of human concern. This separation has led, subtly, to a resulting view that what happens in one domain does not affect the other. And this has led in turn to something other than sustainable development and other than a sustainable capitalism.

If it was possible to see the economy and the environment as separate at the turn of this century, it certainly is no longer possible now – not amid all the repeated warnings by the world's climate scientists about the urgency of addressing climate change, and not amid all the ever-intensifying natural evidence of this urgency. The economy cannot be seen as separate from the environment. The economy must be seen as *within* the environment. The economy must be seen as within and subject to the natural constraints of the Earth's ecosystems. To be able to meet our ever-increasing economic needs, we must internalize within our continuing reliance on Smith's system the inescapable fact that those needs can be met only within the confines of our environmental limits.

The search for global sustainable development is a continuation today of Smith's search for what he described as "universal opulence."[61] In this search, the temptation everywhere in the world is to try to devise some design for a system that can be imposed on the world from above. The temptation is to move away from reliance on the complexity and unpredictability of markets and toward the supposed simplicity and predictability of some overarching and singular statist solution. For many of the willing in the world, this temptation is all the greater given the urgency of confronting and combating climate change. Those so enticed ask themselves: Are we not in dire need now of "universal" and "comprehensive" solutions for addressing climate change? Would not such solutions best be assured by imposing them throughout the world as truly global solutions from the expert heights of grand global decisionmaking? Further, they ask, even if capitalism is not necessarily always evil, do not the inconvenient demands of markets for incentives, for profits, and for much else serve only to make the prospects for finding the global solutions we need all the more difficult?

If we were able to ask Adam Smith how we should transform today's unwilling world into the willing world, he would surely advise us to resist this temptation and continue to rely on markets. Smith's "simple system" is really the absence of a system. Like Karl Popper, he saw human freedom in the personal choices made through autonomous and individual human decisions, and not in collective efforts to dictate those decisions. Smith had no fondness for grand abstract systems that strive somehow to structure human experience beforehand instead of permitting human experience to flow and evolve naturally, and without predetermined end, from the creative confluence of free individual decisions. It is the unpredictability of the market that enables it to work. The "man of system," Smith told us, "is apt to be very wise in his own conceit, and is often so enamored with the supposed beauty of his own ideal plan of government, that he cannot suffer the smallest deviation from any part of it . . . [H]e seems to imagine that he can arrange the different pieces of a great society with as much ease as the hand arranges the different pieces upon a chess-board; he does not consider that the pieces upon the chess-board have no other principle of motion besides that which the hand impresses upon them; but that, in the great chess-board of human society, every single piece has a motion of its own, altogether different from that which the legislature might choose to impress upon it."[62]

We are not pawns to be manipulated from above. Abandoning the individual human interactions of market capitalism is not the way to win the human chess game of sustainable development. Turning away from markets would condemn billions of people to continued poverty and deny to billions more the hope for a brighter economic future. We will never meet our economic needs as part of sustainable development if we abandon the benefits of a market economy. We will meet those needs only by making the market economy work within the environment. Moreover, we will never be able to meet our economic needs if we do not imagine innovative solutions that acknowledge our environmental limits. But the imaginative innovative solutions we seek that blend economy and environment together into a brighter future for all of us cannot be found and imposed by government diktat. If human progress is still possible – if it is not a myth, if it is not a fantasy, if it is not an illusion left over from the fondest hopes of an earlier day – then human progress can continue to be made only through the trial and error of imaginative problem-solving.

Progress toward sustainable development cannot be achieved through one collective solution imposed from the top down by a central authority of some kind, no matter how benevolent or how well intentioned it may profess to be. Such progress can be achieved only through countless innovative and individual solutions that will ultimately add up to the one overall solution we need by evolving from the bottom up. And this improvisational evolution toward sustainable development will be possible only within the enabling framework of an economic approach that relies on the catalytic creativity of a market economy. Building on the insights of Smith and other earlier thinkers, the noted twentieth-century Austrian economist Friedrich Hayek spoke of a market-based commercial society as creating a "spontaneous order." A spontaneous order is one resulting from human actions but not from the specific intention or execution of any human design.[63] In the spontaneous order that is a free market, the coordination of the aims and purposes of countless individuals, acting in what they see as their own interests, is attained through the mechanism of prices. Changes in prices send signals "to 'automatically' produce that spontaneous co-ordination that *appears* to be the product of an omniscient mind."[64]

In other words, the spontaneous order is created by Adam Smith's "invisible hand." Coordination by an "invisible hand" is needed because, as Hayek explained, in a free market, there is not only a division of labor, there is also a "division of knowledge." Not only does the "man of system" bent on imposing some central plan lack all the knowledge he needs to move the pieces on the human chessboard. So does everyone else. All knowledge in a market economy is partial and fragmented. All knowledge is imperfect. All knowledge is divided. "What the market does is to bring all this decentralized knowledge together by co-ordinating the activities of the different agents, none of whom knows in detail every aspect of the whole of which they are a part."[65] A market economy works precisely because it is *not* imposed from above by some central authority; it works because it emerges and evolves from below through the repeated instances of mutual exchange that comprise human commerce. In this way, a market economy achieves through its spontaneous order "a more efficient allocation of societal resources than any design could achieve."[66] The market succeeds where other economic approaches do not because it is an improvisational exercise that prescribes no preordained conclusion. A market economy is a work of progress that is ever in progress. Implicit in a reliance on markets is the understanding that we cannot know, and so we cannot shape, the future in advance. The unexpected is always to be expected. The unforeseen will always, given time, be seen.

Smith's division of labor creates what Nobel Prize-winning economist Kenneth Arrow called "learning by doing."[67] There is, in a division of labor, an economic learning curve. As workers acquire experience in performing a task, they become more proficient and more efficient in doing it. They act both individually and collaboratively. They practice. They make minor improvements. They build on those improvements. Then they build some more. In this way, they become, over time, more productive. The more productive they are, the more they can and will produce, and the more "growth" there can be. Increased productivity is the engine of growth. The trial and error of learning by doing is ever open to new approaches and to new ways of problem-solving. It is in the very act of *doing it* that we learn what best to do as part of a division of labor.

The cumulative experience of "learning by doing" explains, along with much else, the source of innovation. Thus, it also explains how we create the innovations that become new technologies. From the first steam engine invented in the late eighteenth century, to the newest app on the latest smartphone in the twenty-first century, new technologies have been a powerful driver of productivity and growth. The most useful new technologies usually result from learning by doing. This same process must be used while we strive to harness market forces in a global division of labor devoted to achieving sustainable development. In all aspects of our search for sustainability, only by doing can we learn what best to do. Adam Smith, if he were still here, would doubtless tell us that "sustainable development" is one of those concepts, like "liberty" or "democracy," that cannot be defined beforehand but can be defined only through the act of doing. To shape and share in a sustainable global prosperity in a willing world, we must define sustainable development *by doing it*.

3

On the Indivisibility of Our Economic and Environmental Future

Whether we achieve "sustainable development" by doing it will depend on *how* we do it. How we do it will depend on how we see the relationship between economy and environment in shaping a shared future. The truth is: Our future economically cannot be separated from our future environmentally. If, in all we do together to try to make the willing from an unwilling world, we fail to appreciate and act on the basis of this inseparability, then we will fail both economically and environmentally, and there will be no sustainable development.

People everywhere in the world are wondering aloud whether we should continue with globalization. They fear the blurring and vaporizing forces of a hyperconnected world. Some see globalization as causing more economic disparity and deprivation, and leaving all too many people lost in dislocation in the transition between yesterday and tomorrow. Others see it as contributing to climate change and causing other environmental degradations, pushing ever closer up against the ecological boundaries of the Earth's ecosystems. Many believe we would all be better off overall if we retreated from a globalized world. The truth is, globalization remains a good idea – if we globalize in the right way. The right way requires us to see that economy and environment truly are one in seeking sustainable development.

Economy and environment have always been one. Since our primitive past in our prehistoric caves, humanity has been making an economy by shaping the environment in a struggle to survive and thrive. With our first tools, we carved enclaves from the wilderness. With our first fields, we were fed by the discovery of agriculture. With our first ships and our first caravans, we further magnified human production through the early embrace of what eventually became Adam Smith's division of labor. In all of human history leading up to the Enlightenment and to the Industrial Revolution, the truth of the indivisibility of economy and environment was largely left unspoken because it was simply assumed, and the bounty of nature seemed without end.

Now this has changed. This has changed because of the accelerating scale of the sheer human impact on the natural world. The extent of our impact is such that some scientists are now suggesting that nature no longer exists separate and apart from humanity, and that, from now on, the world in which we will live will be the world that, from our own fashioning, we make. They point in particular to climate change, which they see as a form of planetary engineering by humanity devoid of either human intention or conscious design. These scientists say that we have been living since the dawn of the Industrial Revolution in a new and unprecedented geological era, the age of the *Anthropocene* – the age of humans.

THE HUMAN AGE

The proposal to anoint ours the human age was made at the turn of the twenty-first century by the Nobel Prize-winning chemist Paul J. Crutzen and his collaborator, marine scientist Eugene F. Stoermer.[1] Crutzen explained, "For the past three centuries, the effects of humans on the global environment have escalated. Because of these anthropogenic emissions of carbon dioxide, global climate may depart significantly from natural behavior for many millennia to come ... The Anthropocene could be said to have started in the latter part of the eighteenth century, when analyses of air trapped in polar ice showed the beginning of growing global concentrations of carbon dioxide and methane. This date also happens to coincide with James Watt's design of the steam engine in 1784."[2]

Since then, in furtherance of the Enlightenment Project, humanity has conquered and commanded the Earth for our own purposes of production and consumption. We have cleared the forests from the land, taken the fish from the seas, and dammed the rivers and the lakes. We have carved up the landscape with our cities, our factories, and our highways, taking the habitats of other species and making them our own. We have recombined and exploited the basic chemical elements of nature. Above all, we have created an ever-increasing flow of carbon dioxide and other greenhouse gas emissions that now fill the air and warm the world. These accumulating emissions are a byproduct of the primary engine for the economic achievements so far of the Enlightenment Project.

Since the dawn of the Enlightenment, the rise of the freedom that enables us to make our own way in the world has been powered by fossil fuels. Yet, as historian Dipesh Chakrabarty observes, "In no discussion of freedom in the period since the Enlightenment was there ever any awareness of the geological agency that human beings were acquiring at the same time as and through processes closely linked to their acquisition of freedom."[3] Unaware until recently of our "geological agency," we have, unwittingly, led ourselves astray by making choices that have created circumstances where our freedom has arisen from, and has depended on, the unlimited use of fossil fuels. Since the eighteenth century, in the search for energy to power our ongoing pursuit of freedom, humanity has "switched from wood and other renewable fuels to large-scale use of fossil fuel – first coal and then oil and gas. The mansion of modern freedoms stands on an ever-expanding foundation of fossil-fuel use. Most of our freedoms so far have been energy-intensive."[4]

The central historical relationship between the accumulation of freedom and the burning of fossil fuels is almost always ignored in the debates among the willing about the nexus between economy and environment and, especially, between commerce and climate change. Given this relationship, all engaged in those debates must ask whether it is necessary for the pursuit of human freedom and the human domination of nature always to go hand in hand. We must ask whether humanity, despite all we have learned lately about the harmful effects of human impacts on the planet, must continue to "wield a geological force" that will dominate, degrade, and ultimately destroy our natural environment through the uncontrolled burning of fossil fuels.[5]

Chakrabarty says "No," and explains, "[H]uman beings have tumbled into being a geological agent through our own decisions. The Anthropocene, one might say, has been an unintended consequence of human choices."[6] Having "tumbled into" some wrong choices, however unwittingly, we can and must climb up now out of our ecological predicament by making the right ones. Freedom is indeed about choosing. With the benefit of today's sophisticated scientific hindsight, it is all too obvious now that we made some of the wrong choices along the way in pursuing freedom through the Enlightenment Project. But what we know now, thanks to the calculating of supercomputers in advanced laboratories and to the remote sensing of manmade satellites circling the Earth, could not have been foreseen in the eighteenth century by the inventors of the Industrial Revolution any more than it could have been anticipated then by Adam Smith. More than two centuries ago, they saw the opportunities offered by the use of fossil fuels. They could not foresee at the time the risks of our carbon dependency for nature and, hence, for us. Now, the novel idea of the Anthropocene as a new geological era offers us an opportunity for "a new way of seeing,"[7] and we must seize that opportunity in choosing all we see as ways to the willing world.

ECONOMY AND ENVIRONMENT AS ONE

Scientists continue to ponder whether ours should be labeled the Anthropocene age.[8] While they deliberate, we must internalize the essential insight that the economy and the environment are one and the same into all our efforts to achieve sustainable development by doing it. Informed by this insight, we would do well to begin by separating the facts from the fictions in the continuing debate about the complex interrelationships between "trade and environment" and "investment and environment." So much of what is usually said about these interrelationships in the debates of the willing bears little relation to reality. Perhaps above all else in meeting our economic needs within our environmental limits, these interrelationships between commerce and ecology must be seen in a new way, for increases in both international trade and international investment are indispensable ingredients of "sustainable development."

The nuance evinced by empirical evidence must matter most to our decision-making on the confluence of commerce and ecology. Factual nuance often reveals the "in between" where the answers are to be found. While still a student, the distinguished social critic Richard Sennett once exclaimed, in exasperation, to his teacher and mentor, the literary critic Lionel Trilling, "You have no position; you are always in between." Trilling replied, "Between is the only honest place to be."[9] As in so many other realms of public engagement, between is often the only honest place to be when reconciling the competing claims of economy and environment.

Environmentalists are inclined to assume that more international trade and more foreign direct investment must necessarily harm the environment. For their part, traders and investors are inclined to assume that more environmental protection must necessarily harm the economy. Based on the available empirical evidence, both of these rival assumptions are simplistic and wrong. They are based on caricatures that largely ignore the complexities involved. The more complicated truth is that whether economic and environmental actions will each be harmful to the other will always depend on how, with each, we go about doing it. "It all depends on the particular case."[10]

The truth is, too, that because the economy is contained within the environment, and because our economic advance in this new and hyperconnected world is now fast approaching our environmental limits, neither trade nor investment can be advanced any longer in any lasting way other than sustainably. Likewise, in a world burdened by the stark reality of continuing and ever-increasing human needs, climate change and other environmental challenges cannot be met and surmounted in ways that will not work economically. As the WTO Secretariat has put it, more prosaically, "The environment and the economy are two interdependent systems."[11]

The interdependence of economy and environment is becoming more and more obvious in our globalized world. Increasingly, *trade and investment* issues tend also to be environmental issues. One example is the global plague of fossil fuel subsidies. Increasingly, *environmental* issues tend also to be trade and investment issues. Take the competitive puzzle of environmental product standards. Which are better: Yours or mine? The issues confronting economy and environment today are, more than ever, one and the same. These issues cannot be addressed successfully economically without also addressing them environmentally – and vice versa. Whether economy and environment will be helped or hurt in addressing them will, again, always depend on how we do it.

Jagdish Bhagwati, the eminent trade economist, explains one divide between economy and environment: "Trade has been central to economic thinking since Adam Smith discovered the virtues of specialization and of the markets that naturally sustain it. Because markets do not normally exist for the pursuit of environmental protection, they must be specially created. Trade therefore suggests abstention from governmental intervention, whereas environmentalism suggests its necessity."[12] As with trade, so too with investment. Another divide results from the frequent absence of environmental considerations in market decisions relating to investment that often makes environmental damage a side effect of economic growth. Investment is often pursued without heed to environmental risks, and without any bottom-line consequence to the investors from environmental harms. With both trade and investment, while the allocation of economic resources is made possible through the legerdemain of Adam Smith's "invisible hand," the allocation of climate and other environmental risks is sometimes made instead by what environmental economist Michael Jacobs describes as the "invisible elbow."[13]

The commercial elbowing of our ecosystems causes environmental harm that economists commonly call an externality – a spillover effect from a market action by a producer or a consumer that is not included in the market price.[14] It is called an externality because it is "external" to the market, so the usual price signals from the market do not work as they should. An apprehension about the harmful effects of the "hidden" costs of "environmental pollution" not reflected in market prices was a particular concern voiced by the Brundtland Commission in 1987,[15] and the dilemma over environmental externalities remains at the core of much of the global debate among the willing. There are "positive externalities" of market actions on the environment that have a beneficial effect on others – such as those that often occur from market investments in basic research and development and in green infrastructure. These benefits "accrue to society but cannot be captured by producers."[16] There are also "negative externalities" of market actions that harm others – such as the increasing carbon dioxide and other greenhouse gas emissions caused by the production of a product when the price of those emissions is imposed on others and is not included in the market price. These costs are "borne by the population at large but not by individual producers."[17] As economists Gernot Wagner and Martin L. Weitzman have said, "Climate change is the mother of all negative externalities."[18]

Finding the best way of somehow accounting for, and thereby of minimizing, these and other harmful environmental results of economic production is a key to reconciling economy and environment through sustainable development. Left alone, markets cannot find the needed solutions because market forces do not automatically "internalize" environmental costs. The solutions are to be found only in the right kind and the right extent of enabling governmental actions that intervene to redress this "market failure" by internalizing environmental costs so they will be included in market prices.[19] The difficulty always is finding the right place between public and private delineating how much governmental intervention is needed. Should the state direct the market? In any particular context, is public ownership required, or is it sufficient in that context to smooth the rough edges of capitalism through governmental restraint? Can more be accomplished for the environment by restricting property rights or perhaps by expanding them? If governmental intervention is needed, should it take the form of taxes, regulations, standards, or laws ensuring and enabling competition? And at what governmental level should this intervention occur?

Furthermore, and significantly in any given instance, is the question of whether there can be an innovative and effective sharing of responsibility publicly and privately through a creative form of "multi-stakeholder" cooperation. Are there new ways of imagining and implementing the traditional relationship between public and private and between state and non-state that can enlighten and enable our efforts to attain sustainable development? This in particular is a question to be asked and answered by those among the willing who acknowledge that the right answers are to be found within the context of a global marketplace and "in between" the often irreconcilable extremes of the current debate.

A related difficulty resulting from the economic fact that markets do not ordinarily exist for the purpose of environmental protection is the continuing pervasive focus of so many of the willing on "the tragedy of the commons," a phrase made famous in an essay with that title published in the journal *Science* in 1968 by the biologist Garrett Hardin.[20] In considering the fate of the common inheritance of humanity, Hardin feared that where there is an absence of individual private ownership, common "resources, precisely because they are viewed as a common inheritance, are likely to be exploited to the point of depletion, with catastrophic results."[21] He saw it as inevitable that commonly held resources will always be depleted because individuals, when left free to choose, will always choose to maximize their own private advantage and externalize the costs to others. This logic might be applied, say, to the vast "global commons" of the open seas.

Considerably less common among the willing is an awareness of the subsequent research that shows that the "tragedy" that Hardin feared would necessarily be a foregone conclusion of private exploitation of the commons need not happen. The late Elinor Ostrom won the Nobel Prize in economics in 2009 for demonstrating how common resources such as fisheries, forests, water supplies, and grazing land can be, and have been, well managed by large and diverse groups of people, without the coercive involvement of a central government, and also without carving up the common resource into private property.[22] Ostrom saw great potential in "the evolution of institutions for collective action."[23] She "found, all over the world, an impressive number of cases in which communities run the commons in a sustainable way, getting the most out of them."[24] Preconditions to sustainability were, in Ostrom's view, clarity of the law, methods of collective and democratic decisionmaking, local and public mechanisms of conflict resolution, and no conflicts among the various layers of government. Thus, from the empirical evidence she found at the time, she identified a useful checklist for us now for creating new ways to choose triumph over "tragedy" in seeking to reconcile economy and environment through sustainable development.

TRADE-OFFS AND FALSE CHOICES

There are indeed some truly hard choices to be made between economic aspiration and environmental preservation. Many of these hard choices will involve the internalizing of environmental costs into economic prices. Rio Principle 4 proclaimed at the "Earth Summit" in 1992 contemplates such hard choices in saying "that the polluter should, in principle, bear the cost of pollution, with due regard to the public interest and without distorting international trade and investment."[25] Bhagwati says it should come as no surprise to anyone "that the objective of environmental protection should at times run afoul of the goal of seeking maximum gains from trade" and necessitates hard choices.[26] This, he adds, is why economists "invented the concept of trade-offs."[27] As others have acknowledged, the notion of a trade-off is "[a] concept that's ingrained in any economist's DNA."[28] A trade-off involving a utilitarian calculation of the anticipated costs and the anticipated benefits of a particular course of action is a familiar economic approach.

Whether they realize it or not, lawmakers everywhere are, like economists (and like the rest of us), usually practicing utilitarians. We all, almost always, weigh what we see as the costs and the benefits of a particular choice.[29] Seeing and making the right trade-offs between legitimate but conflicting concerns is the familiar stuff of everyday political decisionmaking. What has changed about the trade-offs between economy and environment is the balance of how we must see and make them in the light of our "new way of seeing" in the human age. The costs and the benefits in any such trade-off must be calculated according to the new arithmetic of sustainable development. The weight of the calculation now, and from now on, must be tipped to include an understanding that the economy and the environment are emphatically one and the same, and that our economic needs can therefore be met only within the unavoidable constraints of our environmental limits.

In the mystic spirit of Thoreau, Marsh, and the other patron saints of the environmental movement, environmentalists will rightly insist that the intrinsic value of some natural resources is beyond the mundane making of a mere utilitarian calculation. Their value is incalculable. This is true. Although some economists specialize to increasing effect in "environmental valuation," and some environmentalists also try to tote up the value in dollars of rare ecosystems,[30] the fact is that much of our shared natural inheritance is unique and irreplaceable, and so it does not lend itself easily, if at all, to the mere "cash nexus" of a price tag. As one example, the Everglades in Florida is irreplaceable economically as a source of freshwater for millions of people in Florida. It is also, for many other, non-quantifiable reasons, simply irreplaceable.

In weighing the calculations involved in trade-offs between economy and environment, too, due consideration must be given also to the costs and benefits to future generations. The Brundtland definition speaks of a sustainable development that "meets the needs of the present without compromising the ability of future generations to meet their own needs."[31] In like vein, Rio Principle 3 says there must be intergenerational equity. The "right to development" must be fulfilled by taking into account the developmental and environmental needs not only of present, but also of "future generations."[32] We have no right to exhaust their opportunity to live. We must be mindful of then as well as now. But how should we make this calculation?

When calculating the present value of future benefits as part of the trade-off between today and tomorrow, economists and environmentalists alike employ what they call a "discount rate."[33] As economists Wagner and Weitzman explain it, pithily, "Having \$1 today is worth more than having it ten years from now. How much more? That's discounting."[34] As with all other forms of finance, the *lower* the discount rate, the *higher* the cost in current dollars. Thus, where the costing of action on climate change is concerned, the choice of a *low* discount rate implies that future climate damages will be more costly in today's dollars and, thus, suggests the necessity for extensive and expensive climate action today.[35] In contrast, a *high* discount rate suggests precisely the opposite. As with interest rates, a difference of a percentage point or two in a climate discount rate can matter a lot. This is why the willing are often at odds with others and among themselves in disputing the seemingly esoteric matter of discount rates.

The thought that we are trustees for future generations is but a modern restatement of conservative icon Edmund Burke's timeless assertion in 1790 in his *Reflections on the Revolution in France* that human society is "a partnership not only between those who are living, but between those who are living, those who are dead, and those who are to be born."[36] Humanity, he contended, should never forget "what is due to their posterity,"[37] for, should we do so, "Men would become little better than the flies of a summer."[38] We would be here for a brief time, and then disappear without a trace. Not without reason has it been said that "Burke's notion of partnership across time accords well with sustainability."[39]

In contemplating and making needed trade-offs, there can sometimes be real conflicts between economy and environment. It is difficult to see, for example, how acid rain could have been curtailed and the Earth's ozone layer saved several decades ago without the Montreal Protocol on the Ozone Layer, the innovative international agreement that first froze and then reduced the production and use of chlorofluorocarbons (CFCs), "chemicals of great industrial utility and prodigious commercial profitability."[40] To curb acid rain, a hard choice had to be made in which important economic actors and essential environmental aims were clearly in conflict. We should not pretend that real conflicts do not sometimes exist.

Sometimes, though, there is no need for a trade-off between economy and environment. Sometimes the supposed choice between economy and environment is a false choice, and, where a false choice is made between the economy and the environment without due regard to both, that choice will invariably result in harming both by hindering a truly sustainable development. To cite only one

example, the choice that is sometimes posed in policymaking between the dissemination of new technologies and the preservation of the natural environment is often
just such a false choice. To be sure, the introduction of new technologies, especially
when done carelessly or in willful disregard of ecological consequences, can cause
environmental damage. Recalling the "silent spring" of Rachel Carson, an obvious
example is DDT.[41] Yet, if done in the right way, both international trade and foreign
direct investment can be effective means for spreading the benefits of new technologies and know-how in ways that will usually help and not harm the environment.
Once more, it all depends on our discernment of the "in between." It all depends on
how we do it.

International trade, foreign direct investment, and other aspects of globalization
have brought unprecedented prosperity to many parts of the world. Many environmentalists, though, in their balancing of the costs and the benefits, conclude that
the price of this global prosperity is too high. Alongside the historic economic
growth, they see "resource depletion, deforestation, species extinction, pollution,
and greenhouse gas emissions."[42] They lament that the hand of humanity on
the Earth is now heavier than ever. More than half of the planet's land surface,
for instance, has been changed by the hand of man.[43] Despite our considerable
economic gains from trade and investment, many environmentalists nonetheless
insist that the benefits of globalization "have clearly come at a considerable ecological price"[44] and that this price is just not worth it.

The economic and environmental plight of the poorest in the world is proof of
how, for them, as for us all, there can be no separating our economic and our
environmental future. Since the founding after the Second World War of what has
gradually become a fully global trading system, hundreds of millions of people
worldwide have been lifted out of poverty by the lowering of barriers to international
trade. Freer trade can be a liberating means of uplifting millions upon millions
more – especially the poorest among us.[45] Frank Garcia of Boston College speaks
of trade as a means to uplift the poor in terms of simple justice. He maintains,
"By allowing the principle of comparative advantage to operate, free trade moves
the trading system in the direction of operating to the benefit of the least advantaged,
by affording them the opportunity for welfare increases through specialization.
Moreover, in a contingent sense, since free trade can lead to welfare growth, it is
a precondition to a more just distribution of wealth and an improved standard of
living for the least advantaged, both of which fulfill one's moral duty to others."[46]

At the same time, some of the poorest people in some of the poorest countries in
the world are suffering the most from climate change, especially in sub-Saharan
Africa, the island nations, and the coastal areas of the least-developed countries.
Quite rightly, some increasing attention is being paid at last to the threats from the
rising tides along such wealthy urban centers as Miami Beach in Florida in the
United States. But much less attention is being paid to the fact that some impoverished island countries are being swallowed by the sea. The poorer countries have

done little to cause climate change, but they are often the most affected by it and have little means to confront it.

What is more, there is also the cumulative impact from continued "externalities" of what Rob Nixon has called, memorably, "slow violence" – the gradual shifting of many of the harmful environmental impacts of growth onto some of the most marginal and powerless communities of the world.[47] This is true within countries; it is also true between countries. With the acceleration of globalization, the fear is that a cleaner environment in rich countries will be purchased at the price of a dirtier environment in poor countries. A wealthy country may, for example, set high domestic standards for reduced carbon emissions but then turn around and, in substitution for clean domestic products, import cheaper like products made in a poorer country which has lower emissions standards. In effect, climate, pollution, and other environmental harms can simply be exported elsewhere by the wealthier countries.

Unquestionably, the rise of international trade as part of globalization has increased and intensified the pressures imposed by human endeavor on the natural environment. If there were no international trade, the human mark on the natural world would, unquestionably, be less. This, of course, is equally true of all of human commerce, international and otherwise. Indeed, it is true of all that our species does. If there were no tillage of the land, there would be no trespass of the meadow. If there were no trade between the villages, there would be no trail between the trees. If we restless humans, stirring and striving, did not have "the propensity to truck, barter, and exchange,"[48] then our primitive world would be a more pristine place. There would be no cities, no factories, no flights crowding the skies, and no fleets plying the seas. In venturing out in such a primitive, pastoral world from our hovels in our scattered villages to engage in our hunting and gathering, we would surely risk doing less harm to the environment.

In their intransigent opposition to economic globalization, this is the simpler world that some skeptics of international trade and investment seek (although they likely hope that their simpler world will be air-conditioned and well provisioned with app-filled smartphones and modern pharmaceuticals). It is easy to dismiss such reactionary romanticism. But some of the more thoughtful environmental skeptics of trade are more searching in their criticism. A more incisive critique of the impact of international trade and international investment on the environment is one that poses "a broader questioning of the logic of comparative advantage from an ecological point of view."[49] This broader question deserves an answer. In posing it, the British thinker Peter Newell observes, "While economic orthodoxy dictates that producing a product from components sourced from all over the world to capitalize on the lowest possible costs and comparative economic advantages of different countries makes perfect sense, the ecological costs can be very high."[50] He elaborates, "Critics suggest that the environmental impact associated with production across many sites is unacceptable. In conventional economic terms, it may be logical to transport components across hundreds of miles, using extensive packaging and utilizing vast amounts of pesticides and preservatives, in order to allow a product to endure large-scale transportation and enjoy a longer shelf-life. Ecologists insist, however, that the same product can often (though certainly not always) be produced locally at greater benefit to the community and with much lower associated social and environmental costs."[51]

THE ENVIRONMENTAL IMPACTS OF TRADE

We cannot begin to answer this broader question about the continuing logic and merit of reliance on comparative advantage in the light of the environmental results without first knowing the facts about the effects of international trade and international investment on the environment. Many in the world assume a clash between comparative advantage and ecology. Many assume that global value chains supplying goods and services must be chains of global environmental destruction. Setting aside the fantasies and the fears, what are the facts? How do trade and investment truly impact the environment?

By one estimate, as much as a quarter of global emissions is embedded in international trade.[52] International trade generates greenhouse gas emissions and causes other environmental effects in one of two ways. The first is through the international movement of traded goods, which has *direct* effects on the environment. The second is through the production of those traded goods, which has *indirect* environmental effects. The emergence in recent years of global value chains complicates this basic picture by increasing the transport of component parts along ever-lengthening lines of production that are further subdividing Adam Smith's division of labor.

As WTO and UNEP analysts have explained about the *direct* environmental effects of trade, "Merchandise trade can be transported by air, road, rail and water, or via pipelines in the case of oil. In most instances, international trade in merchandise will involve more than one mode of transport, since even goods that are carried by air or by water must often make an overland journey to the seaport or airport, and are generally transported by land on the final stretch of their journey to the ultimate consumer. At a global level, maritime transport accounts for the bulk of international trade transport by volume, and for a significant share by value," but, "[w]hile the greater part of international trade is transported by sea, the volume of goods shipped by air . . . has been growing rapidly."[53]

About one-fourth of the value of all world trade is between countries sharing a land border. Where trading countries do not share a land border, the vast majority of goods are moved by ocean or by air.[54] About 90 percent of the volume and somewhere between 60 percent and 70 percent of the value of international trade is transported by sea.[55] Container shipping transports 95 percent of all manufactured goods.[56] Aviation accounts for the transport of only about 10 percent of the volume of world trade, but some recent studies show aviation now reaching 40 percent of world trade in value.[57] Overall, one-third of worldwide trade-related emissions can be traced to international transport.[58] Global emissions from international marine bunker fuels – usually low-grade coal and heavy oil – have increased by more than two-thirds since 1990.[59] Between 2010 and 2050, carbon emissions from international freight transport are projected to increase fourfold outside the several dozen developed countries that are members of the OECD, and one and one-half times within the OECD.[60] Given these projections, it is not surprising that these direct effects of international trade on the environment are beginning to move closer to the center of the global debate.

Far more attention has been focused by the willing on the *indirect* effects of trade on the environment. In their utilitarian calculation of costs and benefits, mainstream economists have mostly concluded that international trade is, overall, beneficial for the environment. One reason they usually emphasize for this conclusion is that, in adding to economic growth, trade adds also to the tax revenues available for paying for more effective environmental protection. Bhagwati explains, "Growth enables governments to tax and to raise resources for a variety of objectives, including the abatement of pollution and the general protection of the environment. Without such revenues, little can be achieved, no matter how pure one's motives may be."[61]

In addition, there is the positive environmental payoff from the elongation of Smith's division of labor and from the application of Ricardo's concept of comparative advantage. By encouraging more specialization, freer trade increases productivity. This, in turn, enhances the ability to expand production while employing fewer resources, and thus improves the efficiency of the overall allocation and use of resources. Moreover, "by encouraging greater competition, trade drives efficiency gains all along a producer's supply chain, with the same potentially beneficial effect for the environment."[62] For this reason, Bhagwati has said, "Efficient policies, such as freer trade, should generally help the environment, not hurt it."[63]

There is empirical evidence that – over time – rising income in a country results in rising environmental protection. At first, in the early stages of development, as incomes start to increase, environmental degradation increases as well. But then, as incomes continue to rise, "[e]ventually environmental degradation peaks. It then begins a steep descent as economy and incomes continue to grow."[64] Economists call this the "Environmental Kuznets Curve." In what is known so far, this curve seems to hold for some specific types of air and water pollution, but there are "inconsistent results"[65] for others. One of those others is carbon dioxide emissions. It simply cannot be assumed that freeing trade will automatically lead over time to cuts in carbon emissions. Where the unprecedented challenge of climate change is concerned, there are grounds for seeking an unprecedented solution.

There is, too, a whole lot more to the complicated "trade and environment" equation than solely the level of a country's economic development. The WTO Secretariat has reported that, "Recent empirical estimates . . . suggest that countries' environmental performance depends not only on the level of economic development but also on several factors that are related to income, including political institutions, good governance and the diffusion of technological innovation."[66] There is also this: Before rising incomes start to give rise to an enhanced environmental consciousness supportive of protection and preservation, the environmental degradation that occurs during the early stages of development can do irreparable damage to the benefits we receive from ecosystems – "ecosystem services" – and to the irreplaceable splendor we see in so many of our natural resources. The loss today of food, freshwater, timber, fiber, and fuel from failing ecosystems cannot be easily recovered tomorrow. The loss today of a timeless natural treasure such as an irreplaceable coral reef or an ancient forest or a unique plant or animal species can never be offset. Here the usual calculations of costs and benefits cannot be made.

Among the supposed indirect effects of international trade and investment on the environment, one stands out in the minds of the unwilling. There is widespread fear in developed countries that freeing trade and foreign direct investment leads, inevitably, to fleeing jobs when producers – in search of sanctuary from environmental regulation – shift production from developed countries to dirty "pollution havens" in developing countries.[67] The generally unassailed assumption is that developed countries will lower their environmental standards to keep jobs, and that developing countries will lower their environmental standards to get jobs. Thus all the endless talk by the opponents of liberalizing trade and investment of a global "race to the bottom" of environmental protection.

But it turns out that, in fact, there is "very little evidence" of a "race to the bottom."[68] In particular, "there is actually little evidence that polluting industries relocate to jurisdictions with lower environmental standards in order to reduce compliance costs."[69] The empirical research thus far, as distilled in a study done for the World Bank, "has found little or no evidence that pollution intensive industry is systematically migrating to jurisdictions with weak environmental policy; hence maintaining a weak environmental policy regime appears to have little effect on a country's comparative advantage. Other factors such as labor productivity, capital abundance, and proximity to markets are much more important in determining firm location and output."[70] In describing the "race to the bottom" as a "non-existent threat," the American political scientist Daniel Drezner contends that, despite the generalized fears, "there is no indication that the reduction of controls on trade and capital flows has forced a generalized downgrading in labor or environmental conditions. If anything, the opposite has occurred."[71] Drezner notes that the countries that are the most open to trade and investment – the developed OECD countries – have the highest environmental standards, and that a number of developing countries have raised their environmental standards even as they have become more open to trade and investment.[72]

At the same time, it must be acknowledged that, in a world of complex global value chains, where fractions of fluctuating prices affect untold livelihoods, "downward pricing pressure has created economic incentives for violating environmental regulations and industry best practices, leading to the increased release of disease-causing pollutants and climate-change-related emissions. Cutting costs by engaging in negative social and environmental practices is a particularly acute trend in developing countries, which often lack the regulatory infrastructure to ensure compliance with the laws and/or have lower social and environmental standards in place as a result of the competitive pressures of [global value chains]."[73] As with the effects of trade on climate change, here, too, there is less than definitive evidence.

All this said, whether freeing trade in the pursuit of national comparative advantage will be a plus or a minus for the environment will depend, in any given case, on the combination of circumstances in which the trade occurs. The interplay of several economic factors can determine whether freer trade will have a beneficial effect or a harmful effect on the environment.[74] One factor is the way freer trade and the changes in relative prices resulting from trade affect the sizes of the various sectors comprising a country's economy.[75] Another factor is the increase in the scale of economic activity due to the freer trade.[76] Still another factor is the improvement in environmental conditions resulting from the advances in technological techniques caused by the freer trade.[77] Yet another is the type of goods that are traded.[78] And, as already seen, one more factor can be the level of income in the trading country.[79] To date, there seems to be no clear conclusion from the still-limited empirical evidence on how these various factors interrelate to alter the environmental outcomes from freer trade. It is clear, though, that the factual mix of these interrelated factors in any given instance of trade liberalization can do much to determine the bottom line of whether that instance of trade liberalization helps or harms the environment. As UNEP advises, "The impact of trade on a green economy transition depends in large part on how trade policies are designed and applied and whether an adequate national institutional infrastructure exists to manage the impact of trade liberalization."[80] Once more, it all depends on how we do it.

THE ENVIRONMENTAL IMPACTS OF INVESTMENT

How do the effects of foreign direct investment on the environment differ from those of international trade? In contrast with portfolio investments and with other forms of foreign investments such as contract rights, foreign direct investment (FDI) is generally defined as an investment establishing a long-term relationship that gives the investor a lasting interest and an effective voice in managing and controlling its investment in one country through an enterprise based in another country.[81] An investment by a foreign company in an overseas subsidiary or joint venture is FDI. A short-term purchase by an individual of stock is not.[82] In sum, "FDI should be distinguished from portfolio investment. FDI typically involves some form of effective control and active management of assets in host countries, while portfolio investment typically involves passive investments in host countries."[83]

FDI is a leading driver of global economic growth and the main means of delivering goods and services to foreign markets.[84] The Paris-based International Chamber of Commerce (ICC), which has national chapters in about 130 countries representing about 7 million businesses worldwide, has said, "The increasing level and expanding nature of international investment flows and associated transactions speak to the recognition by host governments – particularly in the developing markets – of the contribution international investment makes to their sustainable development. Businesses and governments in developing countries are keenly aware of the importance of investment as a driver of growth … [FDI] enables all firms to establish a presence in global markets, particularly the fast growing markets of emerging economies; and, increasingly, it enables emerging market firms to establish themselves in industrialized economies."[85]

One important way in which foreign direct investment furthers growth in developed and developing countries alike "is the spillover or indirect effect of technology transfer."[86] Another is the stimulation of infrastructure development. Still others, of course, are the creation of jobs and the addition of tax revenues to public coffers to help pay for public services. All this supports the contention of the United States Council for International Business that "[c]ountries that have pro-investment, pro-business policies and well-established rule-of-law systems attract more and higher-quality FDI – and their economies, workers, and citizens reap significant additional benefits."[87]

International trade and FDI are two sides of the same commercial coin, mutual drivers of global economic growth and of global economic integration. In a world in which multinational corporations have become "increasingly flexible in the location of their production or business activities and consequently in their market access,"[88] they "treat FDI and exporting as alternatives in their product sources and market access strategies,"[89] and they strive to combine them to maximize their gains. Mary Footer rightly compares the pull between trade and FDI to that of the "moth to the flame."[90] Many of the same factors of scale, composition, technology, and income that shape the effects of international trade on the environment also shape the environmental effect of foreign direct investment. Here too it all depends on how it is done.

As with trade, FDI can pose a special threat in some sectors in the use of exhaustible natural resources, such as mining and agriculture.[91] FDI can also be conducted in ways that undermine local environmental laws, regulations, and standards. There is the possibility as well of a constraining "chilling effect" on the local adoption of higher environmental standards, for fear of losing investment or confronting international legal challenges due to restrictions on investment.[92] The evidence suggests, however, that "FDI, particularly when originating from OECD countries, typically plays a positive role in the adoption of environmental standards."[93]

One attraction of foreign direct investment is the possibility that it will result in positive environmental spillovers through the introduction of higher standards or through the transfer of cleaner technologies and useful knowledge for improving environmental protection.[94] As the WTO Secretariat has elaborated, "It has been argued that multinational enterprises may impose particular environmental require-ments on their supply chain subsidiaries and external suppliers (for example, due to concerns about their reputation or economies of scale), inducing them to adopt environmentally friendly technologies."[95] Moreover, it has been found that, where there is FDI, "emission reductions are concentrated in those firms that face low implementation costs, have more understanding of procedures to meet standards and greater access to technology."[96]

Once more: How we choose to do it makes all the difference.

DOING TRADE AND INVESTMENT RIGHT

The answer to the broader question about the continuing logic of comparative advantage in a globalized world caught between the competing realities of growing economic needs and looming environmental limits is found in the nuances of these facts. The answer is not to turn away from trade and investment. The answer is to trade and invest in the right way. Done right, trade and investment can further our environmental goals. Done right, too, environmental protection can enhance trade and investment.

One important reason why ours is an unwilling world is that our global efforts on economy and on environment are structured to see the two as separate. The political will essential to address the convergence of our economic and environ-mental concerns is lacking everywhere in the world in no small part because these concerns are still seen as separate by so many of our decisionmakers. In policymaking worldwide – and especially in international negotiations – economy and environment remain separate silos of endeavor, each largely an alien mystery to the other.[97] For the most part, the environment is an afterthought in global economic negotiations, and the economy is an afterthought in global environmental negotiations. This goes a long way toward explaining why all too many of our

economic and environmental goals remain hopes and not achievements. The
political will essential to reach our economic and environmental goals can be
created only if those goals are seen and treated as mutually reinforcing aspects of
the single goal of sustainable development.

A convergence between our ongoing efforts on economy and environment is
imperative to help secure a just world that will not feel impelled, for example, to
make the false choice between confronting the persistence of global poverty or the
peril of global climate change. Caught as we are in the crosscurrents between
economy and environment, we must unite our economic and environmental efforts
to pursue a common course, treating the economy and the environment as one in
all we do. This can be done only if we make economy and environment one within
a global framework of agreed rules and uphold those rules through the international
rule of law.

4

On the Necessity of the International Rule of Law for Effective Global Economic and Environmental Governance

No one has done more to explain why we need the international rule of law than the ancient Greek historian Thucydides, more than 2,400 years ago. His "Melian Dialogue" brings alive even today an arbitrary exercise of power in the absence of the rule of law during the Peloponnesian War between Athens and Sparta. His brief account of one sad episode in that long war during that long-lost time is a lesson for all time about why the rule of law is necessary in the timeless struggle between might and right, and why, without it, might always makes right.

In 416 BC, after nearly two decades of intermittent conflict, the war was going badly for Athens. As so often happens in war, the early predictions of an easy Athenian victory had vanished amid the realities of the bloodshed.[1] With Pericles, the enlightened leader of democratic Athens, dead from the plague, the moderate and the temperate no longer held sway in the unruly popular assembly in Athens. An ancient form of populism prevailed. The Athenian empire consisted of a league of mainland and island city-states allied under Athenian leadership against the Spartans and their allies. Alone, the tiny island of Melos had refused to join the Athenian-led league, "which allowed them to enjoy the benefits of the Athenian Empire without bearing any of its burdens."[2]

Athens sent a military expedition to bring Melos forcibly into the Athenian empire. Badly outnumbered, and hoping for help from Sparta that never came, the Melians protested to the Athenian generals that the Athenians had "come to be judges in your own cause," and asked what would happen to them "if we prove to have right on our side and refuse to submit."[3] Bluntly, the Athenians replied, "[Y]ou know as well as we do that right, as the world goes, is only in question between equals in power, while the strong do what they can and the weak suffer what they must."[4]

In other words, might makes right.

Firmly believing they were in the right, and clinging to "hope, danger's comforter," the Melians refused to submit. The Athenians then besieged Melos for a number of months. As Thucydides tells the story, eventually the siege was "pressed vigorously," and "the Melians surrendered at discretion to the Athenians, who put to death all the grown men whom they took, and sold the women and children for slaves, and subsequently sent out five hundred colonists and settled the place themselves." The Athenians did what they could to the Melians simply because they could. In the dispute between Athens and Melos, might, in the end, did make right.[5]

Because of Thucydides, we still remember today, many centuries later, what would be "an otherwise forgotten act of oppression."[6] The laconic Greek historian refrained in his telling from any comment on the Athenian belief expressed in the Melian Dialogue that "superior power sanctions any conduct,"[7] and on the conduct of the Athenians on Melos. He "let the sentiments stand self-condemned,"[8] and let the actions speak for themselves. But his abhorrence of the Athenian actions is not in doubt. As one commentator summed up this famous passage, "In so far as philosophy is concerned the whole dialogue is an attack on the doctrine that might is right, that doctrine which Thucydides . . . abominated."[9]

The timeless lesson of the Melian Dialogue is that, in the unending human struggle between right and might, right can make might only if the strong and the weak are made, in the words of Thucydides, "equals in power." This equality is possible only through the rule of law. The rule of law equalizes the strong and the weak by establishing and upholding rules that make them equal under the law and before the law. The arbitrariness of power is thus replaced by the security and the predictability of impartial rules.

DEFINING THE RULE OF LAW

As with the need to define "sustainable development," there is need also to define the "rule of law." With the rule of power, it is power alone that matters. The law is uncertain and arbitrary. The law means only what those with power say that it means for any one person on any one issue at any one time. With the rule of law, power is subdued. The law is certain and not arbitrary. The law is written and the rules are known in advance. The rules are written to apply to all equally, and all – in practice – in reality – are equal under the law and before the law. No one – no one – is beneath the concern of the law, and no one – no one – is above the law. Anything less than this cannot rightly be called the rule of law.

Through all our long centuries of experience since the events on Melos, four basic elements have been identified as a "core definition of the rule of law."[10] First, the power of the state must not be exercised arbitrarily. There must be the "rule of law" and not the "rule of men." Second, the law must be applied to sovereign and to citizens alike, with an independent institution such as a judiciary "to apply the law to specific cases." Third, "the law must apply to all persons equally, offering equal protection without prejudice or discrimination. And lastly, for there to be the rule of law, the law must be of general application and consistent implementation; it must be capable of being obeyed." Words in a statute book or in a judicial ruling are not enough. The words must have reality. What matters is not only what the law *says* but, even more, what the law *does*. The rule of law is more than simply "law in words"; it is "law in action."[11]

There is a tendency in some places to equate "rule *by* law" with the "rule *of* law." But the two are not the same. "Rule *by* law" is a means for imposing the power of the state. Not surprisingly, it is favored by authoritarian rulers in authoritarian states. The "rule *of* law" is a means of ensuring individual freedom, including freedom from the arbitrary sway of the state. Where the law is subject to the whim of whoever happens at the time to be wielding power over the state, there may, as an expedient of autocratic rule, be "rule *by* law," but there is no "rule *of* law."

The truest test of whether there *is* the "rule *of* law" is whether there is an independent judiciary. As Anne-Marie Slaughter has explained, "The definition of an 'independent judiciary' is a judiciary that is not the handmaiden of State power, that answers to law rather than to the individuals who make it."[12] Those who advocate "rule *by* law" favor subordinating the judiciary to those who hold power in the executive branch of governance. In contrast, those who favor the "rule *of* law" understand that it can exist only if there is strict separation of the judicial powers from the executive and legislative powers of governance.

On this, as on so much else, Adam Smith got it right in *The Wealth of Nations*: "When the judicial is united to the executive power, it is scarce possible that justice should not frequently be sacrificed to, what is vulgarly called, politics. The persons entrusted with the great interests of the state may, even without any corrupt views, sometimes imagine it necessary to sacrifice to those interests the rights of a private man. But upon the impartial administration of justice depends the liberty of every individual, the sense which he has of his own security. In order to make every individual feel himself perfectly secure in the possession of every right which belongs to him, it is not only necessary that the judicial should be separated from the executive power, but that it should be rendered as much as possible independent of that power. The judge should not be liable to be removed from his office according to the caprice of that power."[13]

The Enlightenment thinkers were the first to see the need for an independent judiciary as being at the very core of the rule of law. The Englishman John Locke viewed the absence of an independent judiciary as an indication that a society remained uncivilized and in a "state of nature."[14] Baron de Montesquieu of France saw an independent judiciary as essential to his trumpeted separation of powers. "[T]here is no liberty," he said, "if the power of judging be not separated from the legislative and executive powers."[15] The American Founding Father Alexander Hamilton quoted him to this effect in one of his contributions to the Federalist Papers written in support of the ratification of the United States Constitution.[16]

The United Nations defines the rule of law in more detail but in much the same terms as "a principle of governance in which all persons, institutions and entities, public and private, including the State itself, are accountable to laws that are publicly promulgated, equally enforced and independently adjudicated, and which are consistent with international human rights and a principle of standards. It requires, as well, measures to ensure adherence to the principles of supremacy of law, equality before the law, accountability to the law, fairness in the application of the law, separation of powers, participating in decisionmaking, legal certainty, avoidance of arbitrariness and procedural and legal transparency."[17]

As with freedom, the rule of law is about the making of human choices. With the rule of law, we are each free to make our own personal choices about how best to live within the bounds of the law. Without the rule of law, those choices will be made for us by someone else – some bully, some bureaucrat, some autocrat, or some arrogant invading Athenian general. Thus, with the rule of law, freedom becomes possible, while, without the rule of law, we can never be free. Without the rule of law, we are all always the potential victims of the arbitrary rule of power, whether by the state itself or by someone with the power either to control the state or to escape the lawful constraints of the state. Without the rule of law, we are all Melians.

There is no lack of those in the world today who still believe, like the Athenians on Melos, that the strong, by right, should rule the weak. All of human history through all of the centuries since the Peloponnesian War can be seen as commentary on the events on Melos – as a struggle to curb and tame the worst in our nature by replacing the arbitrary exercise of power with the rule of law.[18] Today, as we consider how best to confront the historic challenge of meeting our economic needs while respecting our environmental limits in securing sustainable development, we have only two choices. We can choose the arbitrary rule of might in all its many manifestations, or we can choose the lawful rule of right through the rule of law. On this central issue, there is no nuance of the "in between." Anything less than the rule of law is only the rule of power as described long ago by Thucydides in his Melian Dialogue.

What occurred on Melos was Athens at its worst. Athens at its best in the classical era not only invented democracy but also did much to help invent the rule of law.[19] Not only in Athens, but in all of classical Greece, commercial competition among more than 1,000 city-states spawned a level of specialization, innovation, and cooperation that produced an unprecedented prosperity.[20] Greece became an "experimental laboratory" for establishing new institutions that supported this prosperity.[21] Within each city-state, the self-rule of self-governance created "rule egalitarianism."[22] Where there was equality under the law, there was a feeling of fairness and security that "drove economic growth, first by creating incentives for investment in the development of social and human capital, and next by lowering transaction costs."[23]

Where there was the rule of law, the citizens of the Greek city-states had a measure of freedom because they could make many of their own personal choices. This sense of individual empowerment contributed much to the economic and cultural flourishing in the "efflorescence" of classical Greece.[24] Nowhere in classical Greece was this truer than in Athens, where the economic benefits of the specialization and the innovation arising from individual initiative were "exemplified by the high-grade ceramics industry."[25] Today, we tend to think of the exquisite black-figure and red-figure Greek pottery in our museums solely as works of art. But Greek pottery was not primarily about art; it was mostly about art in the service of commerce.

The Greeks were followed by the Romans in developing the rule of law. After the fall of Rome, it was left to Rome's Greek heirs in the Eastern empire of Byzantium to codify Roman law in the Code of Justinian and bequeath it for eventual rediscovery later, after dark centuries of European discord, by Western Europe during the Middle Ages. In England, the rule of law emerged with the Magna Carta in 1215 and with the gradual development of the common law leading up to the English Civil War and to the Glorious Revolution in the seventeenth century. It may be too much to say, as Friedrich Hayek said, that "[i]ndividual liberty in modern times can hardly be traced back farther than England of the seventeenth century."[26] But extensive and expansive individual freedom emerged only with the emergence of the rule of law.

"[T]he end of law is not to abolish or restrain, but to preserve and enlarge freedom," wrote Locke, because "where there is no law, there is no freedom. For liberty is to be free from restraint and violence from others which cannot be, where there is no law."[27] Like Locke, Enlightenment thinkers in the eighteenth century insisted on the need for the rule of law as the assurance of individual freedom; they "maintained that the liberal rule of law incarnates the political exercise of reason."[28] Memorably, Alexander Hamilton, Thomas Jefferson, James Madison, Benjamin Franklin, and the other Enlightenment thinkers who embarked on the Enlightenment experiment that became the United States of America channeled Locke in crafting the Declaration of Independence and, later, the United States Constitution.

Despite all our progress through the centuries toward the rule of law, today we still see evidence everywhere of the rule of power and not of law in our unwilling world. Ours is a world where the willing talk a great deal about order and about rules, and where they talk a great deal, too, about the institutions that are intended to serve both. Yet, for all this talk, ours nevertheless remains in all too many respects a disordered world of lax and absent rules overseen by weak and weakened institutions. This gulf between talk and action lies at the heart of much of the world's unwillingness. Much of the growing disaffection with globalization and with governance everywhere in the world can be traced to the anxieties fed by the absence of the right rules upheld by the right strong and enabling international institutions.

Amid the noisy and seemingly never-ending global disorder resulting from the absence of so many of the international rules and of so many of the international institutions we need, and amid all our frustration at our endless difficulties in agreeing on those needed rules and needed institutions, and, then, in making them work, many of the willing in the world are, not surprisingly, tempted to retreat from frustrated labors for enlightened global governance through the rule of law. They are tempted, like Voltaire's Candide, to seek consolation in the tending of their own gardens. The frustrations seem without bound. But retreat is not an option. In our hyperconnected world, there can be no retreat from our confrontation with the myriad consequences of globalization. In this unavoidable confrontation, we must somehow transform the chaos into a just transition to the willing world.

In the exercise of our freedom, we must either shape the world by means and to ends of our own choosing, or we will surely be shaped by the world in ways we may not like. And, in shaping the world ourselves in accordance with our own choices, foremost among the means we use must be agreed rules that are upheld by effective institutions at all levels and in all the multiple realms and multiple levels of governance through the rule of law. Not only in the nexus of economy and environment, but also in numerous other ways, the disorder afflicting our unwilling world can be quelled only by an agreed framework of agreed rules supported by agreed institutions. Some of these rules may apply to some of us and to some of what we do. Others may apply to all of us and to all we do. All these rules will require the sustaining strength of supportive institutions.

SUPPORTIVE INSTITUTIONS AND THE RULE OF LAW

The distress in the world can best be eased, and the globalization of the world can best be turned away from popular apprehension and shaped ultimately toward practical global solutions, by strengthening our existing international institutions and creating the new ones we need. These international institutions must support and must promote a sustainable development in which all the world can share and prosper. They must be legitimate, accountable, effective, and fair. They must be consistent with and responsive to democratic governance. They must be flexible and able "to change when the environment changes."[29] They must make and uphold rules that are fair to all and that apply equally to all. They must give global reality to the rule of law.

Figuring out how best to bring people together to build the necessary legal architecture for these international institutions is the transcending task of the willing in defining sustainable development by doing it. The widespread inclination among many of the willing is to use the sharp saw of the state to construct from up above the needed architectural framework, and to let the chips fall where they may and along the way in the market down below. The shared task of constructing the legal architecture for sustainable development cannot, however, be fulfilled if we disdain the market and if we turn away from the bottom-up creativity of the market in our shared efforts to frame solutions. This task can be fulfilled only if we appreciate fully the utter indispensability of free markets and of free market solutions to finding the practical solutions we urgently need for sustainable development.

The rule of law is in no way inconsistent with free markets. Nor is it in any way in opposition to free markets. Far from it. Supportive rules upheld by supportive institutions are not just consistent with the concept of free markets; they are essential to free markets. The great German sociologist Max Weber, who devoted much of his life to explaining the rise of market capitalism, emphasized that the success of market capitalism requires the framework of a formal system of legal rules to provide the security and the predictability that are needed to facilitate market transactions.[30] Any Athenian potter would have said the same. So, too, would have Adam Smith.

Smith believed that, for the "invisible hand" to work best, it must be accompanied by "the visible hand of the state."[31] Moreover, he anticipated that the role of government would grow over time with the growth of an increasingly complex and expansive commercial society.[32] In fact, according to the eminent economic historian Jerry Z. Muller, "The need for institutions to direct the passions was the implicit premise behind Smith's work."[33] As he sees it, "For Smith, the state is the most important institution on which commercial society depends, because the authority and security provided by government are essential for the flourishing of 'liberty, reason, and the happiness of mankind.'"[34] And, today, despite our still decidedly Smithian preference for limited government, it turns out that large market economies in large states need a lot of the right kind of government.

How much weight should a single bolt be able to bear in a building? Should an airline pilot be licensed and certified? What is an acceptable risk in a side effect of a medicine? Who should pay for a road from farm to market or from city to port? How should we build and pay for the port? Who should be free to hold herself out to others for hire as a "lawyer" or a "doctor" or an "engineer"? Who should pay for health care and how? Who should pay for educating our children and for training and retraining our work force? How should we organize ourselves to explore outer space? What limits should there be on how banks use our money? Who, if anyone, should oversee and regulate the use by several billion people of the Internet? And so on.

The issue we face everywhere every day is not whether a commercial society requires governance in order to flourish. Without question, it does. The issue always and everywhere is just how much governance we require of the state, and just what kind. The issue always and everywhere is *where* we draw the line, *how* we draw the line, and – by no means least – *who* draws it. What we use to draw the line are rules. What we use to uphold the rules are institutions. The only way human institutions can further human freedom in upholding the rules is through the rule of law.

For Smith, "the supreme end of government was preserving the rules of justice" on which all else depended.[35] Like Locke, Smith understood that there can be no freedom without law, and without frameworks of rules and institutions that are upheld. He saw it as a "duty of the sovereign" to protect "as far as possible, every member of the society from the injustice or oppression of every other member of it."[36] A commercial society, in particular, simply cannot succeed where might makes right. At the most basic level, this means upholding such essential rights as property rights and contract rights. More broadly, it means much more. The rule of law is "indispensable ... if a market society [is] to be a civilized society."[37] Rules are "the bonds of life."[38] Rules in the form of laws "enable individuals to interact most productively in a material sense."[39] For individuals everywhere to be as productive as they can be in making their own choices while pursuing their own interests, there is need for regularity and for predictability. And there is need, above all, for certainty.

The twentieth-century champion of free markets, Friedrich Hayek, devoted whole chapters in a number of his many volumes to explaining the necessity for the rule of law as a supportive foundation for freedom. He saw certainty in law as the key. In *The Constitution of Liberty*, he wrote, "The importance which the certainty of the law has for the smooth and efficient running of a free society can hardly be exaggerated."[40] The basic differences between a market system and a legal system, he explained, make necessary some workable framework of legal governance to give the needed certainty to the law. The "invisible hand" of the market system benefits from the governing mechanism of prices that overcome the fragmentation of knowledge resulting from the division of labor. The "visible hand" of the state has no such automatic mechanism.

For this reason, Hayek, surely the foremost apostle of the spontaneous order of free markets in the twentieth century, readily acknowledged that "it is at least conceivable that the formation of a spontaneous order relies entirely on rules that were deliberately made ... and ... are entirely the result of deliberate design."[41] By following the right rules upheld by the right institutions, the deliberate design of the rule of law must be used to ensure the existence of an enabling economic atmosphere that will not only allow, but will also encourage the initiative, the improvisation, the innovation, and the sheer serendipity of human enterprise and human creativity that are all essential to the success of a commercial society. A dynamic commercial society with the capability and the capacity for evolving, improving, and (if you will) progressing will be graced by the rule of law through an established legal "framework within which people can create nested, competing frameworks of more specific rules."[42] The right legal framework will furthermore be one that allows ample elbow room for the trial and error of experimentation within the division of labor that enables us to learn by doing.

Importantly, too, to facilitate progress, the possibility must be provided within that legal framework for changing both the rules and the institutions. As economic historian Joel Mokyr has said of "the enlightened economy" of Britain during the Industrial Revolution, "A successful economy ... needs not only rules that determine how the economic game is played, it needs rules to change the rules if necessary in a way that is as costless as possible. In other words, it needs meta-institutions that change the institutions, and whose changes will be accepted even by those who stand to lose from these changes. Institutions did not change [during the

Industrial Revolution] just because it was efficient for them to do so. They changed because key people's ideas and beliefs that supported them changed."⁴³

With all this in mind, the deliberate design of the rule of law must likewise be used to establish the needed legal framework for shaping and sharing a lasting sustainable development as a continuation of the centuries-long Enlightenment Project. Just as the success of a private market economy depends on supportive institutions that uphold the rule of law, so too does the uniting of economy and environment for sustainable development. This is true domestically, and this is equally true globally. Nationally, internationally, at every level and in every kind of governance, we will never be able to bring economy and environment together as we must without enabling institutions that apply the glue of the rule of law.

In the end, if we achieve our shared goals of sustainable development, it will be because we will have succeeded in bringing like-minded people together – across all the artificial borders that divide us – into a vast and varied array of new human networks that lead to new innovations in producing, working, and living together. "Institution" is but another way of saying "network." An "institution" is simply a network of enabling expectations we weave together to construct and to sustain order. "Law" is the thread that weaves order out of disorder.

THE INTERNATIONAL RULE OF LAW AND "SUSTAINABLE DEVELOPMENT"

That institutions matter, and that the rule of law matters in ensuring the ongoing success of institutions, has become a common mantra in the contemporary discussion of the essential ingredients of economic development.⁴⁴ One study has gone so far as to conclude that the quality of a country's institutions "trumps" all else as a determinant in economic development.⁴⁵ The World Bank has found "strong correlations (and indeed strong causal relationships) between" such "indices" of the "institutional quality" of an economy as voice and accountability, political stability, government effectiveness, regulatory quality, control of corruption, and rule of law "and their measures of development."⁴⁶ In the "institutional" economics pioneered in the 1990s by economist Douglass North, "the institutional framework dictates the kinds of skills and knowledge perceived to have the maximum pay-off" in any economy.⁴⁷

The tendency among some of the willing is to indulge in reductionism in reciting the necessary conditions for sustainable development. The temptation is to look for that one all-explaining, all-embracing, all-purpose answer. Not surprisingly (and human nature being what it is), each of us is inclined to see that one answer in our own field of special interest, expertise, or employment. A cook will see the answer in the kitchen. A carpenter will see the answer in a toolbox. A lawyer is like anyone else; a lawyer is inclined to see the answer in the law.⁴⁸ In fact, there is no one answer to the mystery of making economies and societies grow and succeed. There are many answers to be found in many factors. Yet, clearly, one of the answers to that mystery is the necessity for an institutional framework that creates and respects the rule of law. Inclusive economic and political institutions enshrined in the rule of law are indispensable to sustainable development.

Officially, there is no dispute among the nations of the world that the rule of law is central to sustainable development.[49] One commission of the United Nations has estimated that 4 billion people in the world live outside the protection of the rule of law.[50] In 2012, the UN General Assembly declared, "The advancement of the rule of law at the national and international levels is essential for sustained and inclusive economic growth, sustainable development, the eradication of poverty and hunger and the full realization of human rights and fundamental freedoms, including the right to development, all of which in turn reinforce the rule of law."[51] That same year, these lofty words were echoed by the delegates assembled at the UN's Rio+20 Conference on Sustainable Development in an almost identical statement that, notably, made a specific reference to the need for the rule of law, both nationally and internationally, to ensure "environmental protection."[52]

Falling short of the rule of law has considerable economic consequences. Economists at the World Bank "have repeatedly found that the better the rule of law, the richer the nation."[53] They have devised a measure that they call the "300% dividend." They have concluded that, over the long term, "a country's income rises by roughly 300% if it improves its governance by one standard deviation. One standard deviation is roughly the gap between India's and Chile's rule-of-law scores, measured by the bank."[54] Given this "300% dividend," there is every reason for continuing to encourage respect for the rule of law *nationally* not only as essential to economic development, but also as essential, more broadly, to an overall sustainable development.

But what about *internationally?* We not only need the rule of law *within* countries. We need the rule of law equally – if not more – *between* countries. Indeed, the domestic rule of law and the international rule of law are connected. They are mutually dependent and mutually reinforcing. As Zhao Jun of Zhejiang University in China has written, "In the process of global governance, national and international rule of law are mutually interdependent and supportive and are interconnected in particular ways. They permeate and influence one another and show a clear state of interaction in practice."[55] In our globalized world, we cannot truly have one without the other.

How can we put an end at long last to the Melian dialogue between the powerful and the powerless by turning might into right *internationally?* Our search for the answer to this question must begin with the very idea of "international law." Before might can be transformed into right internationally, before there can be the reality of the international rule of law, there must first be an acceptance of the need for the international rule of law, and there must, too, be an acceptance of the need for international law itself. Before there can be any acceptance of these global needs, there must first be the belief that there can truly be such a thing as "international law."

Whether "international law" can even exist was debated for centuries before the British philosopher Jeremy Bentham coined the term in 1789 to describe what had previously been called "the law of nations."[56] A few decades later, in 1832, one of his acolytes, John Austin, identified what remains to this day the defining fulcrum for this continuing and contentious debate. As Austin saw it, "laws proper or properly so called are the commands" of a sovereign backed by threats or sanctions. There is no global sovereign. Thus, Austin reasoned, what we commonly call "international law" is not really law at all, and it should therefore be excluded from "the province of jurisprudence."[57]

In the nearly two centuries since, a long parade of legal philosophers has devoted entire careers to refuting the outright rejection by Austin of the very possibility of "international law." Perhaps most prominently, in 1961, the Oxford philosopher H. L. A. Hart, in *The Concept of Law*, argued that Austin's concept of law is entirely too narrow.[58] As described more broadly by Hart, a legal system consists of primary rules governing conduct, and of secondary rules governing how governments deal with the primary rules. He saw the most important secondary rule as a "rule of recognition" that allows people to recognize when a rule is valid. To be valid, the rule must be widely shared, and it must be widely followed in actual state practice.[59]

Employing this reasoning, Jens David Ohlin, one of the most insightful of the contemporary defenders of international law, has maintained that "it is clear that the commands of a sovereign are not an essential element of the concept of law. What matters is that there is some definite rule (or set of rules) that identifies what counts as law. Then there must be a shared attitude and practice with regard to that rule of recognition."[60] In other words, what matters in evaluating "international law," as with all other would-be "law," is whether there are agreed rules that are recognized as "law" by those to whom they are supposed to apply.

COMPLIANCE WITH INTERNATIONAL LAW

The two principal sources of international law are custom and convention.[61] Consistent with Hart's revision of Austin, the widely accepted legal test of whether rules are recognized as customary international law is whether there is "a general practice accepted as law."[62] The legal test for international custom is thus twofold. First, is there a "general practice" of states as a matter of custom? And, second, is compliance with this custom considered by states to be a legal obligation?[63] Conventions in the form of "lawmaking" treaties are, by definition, assumed to create legal obligations that are international law.[64]

Yet, as a practical matter, the test for conventions and for customs is really much the same. Regardless of whether they believe a legal obligation exists, what, in practice, do states actually *do*? Do states routinely obey the international rules that have been established by custom, by convention, or, increasingly, otherwise? Or do they obey the international rules on which they have agreed only when it seems to them convenient and expedient to do so? In the actual practical reality of making our unwilling into the willing world, this is the true test.

Article 102 of the United Nations Charter requires all UN member states to register all their treaties and agreements with the UN.[65] No treaty or agreement that has not been registered with the UN can be invoked in The Hague before the International Court of Justice.[66] About 4,000 treaties and related actions are filed annually in the UN registry and published as part of the UN treaty collection. The UN Treaty Series contains more than 50,000 treaties and a similar number of related actions in 142 languages on more than 1 million pages in more than 2,200 published volumes.[67]

If "international law" does not exist, then, clearly, there are many in the world who have not yet been told. The real question is not whether international law exists. That question can be left to the further musings of the legal philosophers. For all those who are so busily engaged in the practical day-to-day endeavors of making law, and of making law work, the real question, as Hart said, is instead whether the international rules that supposedly comprise international law are, in fact, recognized by those who are purportedly bound by them as having any real meaning in the real world. Rules have meaning only if they have force. Rules have force only if those who agree to be bound by the rules also deign to comply with them.

In a dictum quoted by champions of international law many times since, Louis Henkin said, in the 1960s, that "almost all nations observe almost all principles of international law and almost all of their obligations almost all of the time."[68] So they do. There is no lack of empirical evidence that international law affects the behavior of states.[69] But why? Why do states comply with international law? In the continuing absence of any global sovereign that can issue global commands backed by threats and sanctions, what is it that makes sovereign states recognize an obligation to uphold the international rule of law by complying with international rules?

A number of reasons have been advanced by advocates of international law to explain why states choose to comply with international law to the extent that they do.[70] One reason often suggested is simply because they have consented to do so.[71] Another reason is because they see an advantage in mutual cooperation with other states in solving some common problem or in managing some common task.[72] Still another suggested reason why states may comply with international law is because states see international law as being fair and legitimate where it has "come into being in accordance with the right process."[73]

Yet another reason why it has been maintained that sovereign states may choose to comply with international law is because they develop the habit of complying. Through an ongoing process of repeated interaction in "countless iterated transactions" in accordance with international law, states may develop patterns of behavior from which international norms emerge over time that are incorporated into their domestic legal structures.[74] In this view, it is not only the perceived fairness of the rules that matters most in compliance. It is also the actual repeated iterations of the process of implementing and upholding the rules over time with others with whom, importantly, one will have to continue to deal in making the rules work in the future.

As the leading advocate of this view, Harold Koh, has said of this possible explanation for compliance with international law, "It is through this repeated process of interaction and internalization that international law acquires its 'stickiness,' that nation-states acquire their identity, and that nations define promoting the rule of international law as part of their national self-interest."[75] Thus, a willingness to obey international law can evolve from the sustained process of being engaged with others on an ongoing basis in making international law work. An alternative way of expressing this perception of how international law can acquire "stickiness" might be that states learn to comply with international law by doing it.

Furthermore, it has been said that sometimes states may comply with international law mainly because they do not want to acquire a reputation for *not* complying with international law.[76] They may face peer pressure from other states to comply. They may fear the potential political and economic costs of not complying. Or they may fear other potential costs from the reputational damage due to a failure to comply.[77] Hence we see the compliance of these reputation-minded states with international law. Hence, too, we see the increasing inclination in international circles to rely, as a means of upholding international law, on the tactic of publicly "naming and shaming" those states that choose not to comply with international rules. Many international agreements rely mainly on "name and shame" as a means of enforcing the rules in those agreements.

Lastly, it has been suggested that a determining factor in whether a state may choose to comply with international law could well be whether that state is a "liberal" state graced with a representative form of government, guaranteed civil and political rights, a market economy based on private property rights, and a judicial system dedicated to the rule of law. In advancing this view, Anne-Marie Slaughter sees the domestic reliance on law of liberal democracies and "the distinctive quality of relations among liberal democracies" as leading them to greater acceptance of the need for international law and for the international rule of law.[78] This, in turn, as Koh has put it, makes them "more likely to 'do law' with one another, while relations between liberal and illiberal states will more likely transpire in a zone of politics" where, still, might makes right.[79] This may also incline democracies to try to "do law" with non-democracies in hopes that those non-democracies may grow more accustomed to and inclined toward the rule of law by doing it.

If this last suggestion is true, then the interrelationship between the rule of law and sustainable development becomes all the more significant in seeking the willing world. If "liberal" states are indeed more likely to support international law, then the ringing reminder by development economist William Easterly that "the real cause of poverty" in the world is "the unchecked power of the state against poor people without rights" assumes for the willing all the more meaning.[80] Not only does the "real development" that results from the existence and the expansion of individual rights depend on the domestic rule of law. The "real development" arising from increasing individual rights also helps create the international rule of law that is essential to sustainable development. The rule of law is not a sideshow to sustainable development; it is center stage.

What all these explanations for why sovereign states may choose to comply with international law have in common is that they all depend on how those states see their self-interest. Indeed, how states perceive their own interests is a common thread in the arguments both of those who are skeptical of international law and of those who defend it. How states perceive their interests is central to understanding how they pursue them. It is the key as well to determining whether states will pursue their interests by creating and complying with international law. This, in turn, will be crucial to determining whether we will succeed in achieving sustainable development by doing it.

"States do what they do," say the current skeptics of international law.[81] These skeptics think that the advocates of law are afflicted by an airy naïveté. They cast doubt on the whole enterprise of making international law as an unrealistic part of the Enlightenment Project. They place international law where the ancient Greek playwright Aristophanes put his caricature of the philosopher Socrates, hanging in a basket, floating in the clouds, far removed from the grounded reality of the actual motivations of states.[82] What states do, these skeptics insist, is pursue what they perceive to be in their own "rational self-interest."[83]

Thus, for example, in stressing "the limits of international law," legal scholars Jack L. Goldsmith and Eric A. Posner argue that "international law emerges from states acting rationally to maximize their interests, given their perception of the interests of other states and the distribution of power."[84] In their telling, "International law . . . is not a check on state self-interest; it is a product of state self-interest."[85] The skeptics of international law see themselves as realists. They say that states adhere to international law when it suits what they see as their self-interest at the time and ignore it when it does not. They would have us believe that international relations are exclusively about competition among nation-states in a dog-eat-dog, win-or-lose, up-or-down, "zero-sum" world. They see all international cooperation as purely transactional – as only about getting the best on the bottom line of an international bargain – as only about getting a return and an edge.

In echo of the Athenians long ago on Melos, these skeptics are saying, implicitly, that whether we like it or not, in our unwilling world, might still makes right. The correct question for them about the making and upholding of international law is: What do the mighty see at any given time as in their self-interest? Goldsmith and Posner specifically invoke the Melian Dialogue of Thucydides in support of their view. "This passage is striking," they say, "because the Athenians make no attempt to mask their imperialistic aims behind 'specious pretenses.' They simply assert that they have an interest in ruling the Melians and will achieve this end because they are more powerful."[86] In the eyes of the skeptics, many countries today, though usually much less candid, are nevertheless moved by the same motivations as the Athenians on Melos. Thus, it follows for them that international law is not law but only another form of politics. It is a selective expression of power.

Ohlin does *not* argue that states do *not* act out of "rational self-interest." Like Goldsmith and Posner, he believes that states strive to act rationally in service of their self-interest, but he contends that they "fail to understand rationality" by focusing on the supposed perception by a state of its self-interest "at each moment in time."[87] "This is incorrect," Ohlin says, "because it leads to paradoxical situations where doing what is best at each moment in time fails to maximize payoff when viewed from the perception of the agent's entire life."[88] In considering their actions, states can – and should – weigh the consequences in terms of both the payoff now and the payoff later. The perceived payoff from taking an action now may pale in comparison to the payoff later from *not* taking that action. In Ohlin's view, the "simplistic theory of rationality" voiced by the skeptics of the existence and the efficacy of international law "fails to take the longer view."[89] It is where states "take the longer view" of their own interests, Ohlin concludes, that international law becomes both real and effective, and the Enlightenment enterprise of international lawmaking thereby becomes worthwhile.

"THE PRINCIPLE OF INTEREST RIGHTLY UNDERSTOOD"

This is not a new thought. It has antecedents in both philosophy and theology dating back at least to the time of the ancient Athenian invasion of Melos. This is the enduring optimistic thought that the genuinely "rational" self-interest is in fact an "enlightened" self-interest that looks beyond the narrow concerns of the current moment and takes the broader and longer view. Perhaps most memorably, this timeless thought was described as "the principle of interest rightly understood" by the French political thinker Alexis de Tocqueville in the 1830s in his equally timeless book, *Democracy in America*.[90] What Tocqueville called "the principle of interest rightly understood" is a principle of rational self-interest that is not limited to the narrow demands of the near term. It is, instead, a way of seeing and seeking our self-interest that ranges both far afield and far ahead to take the broader and longer view. It is a way of seeing our self-interest in our *broader* as well as in our *narrower* needs, and in our needs *tomorrow* as well as our needs *today*.[91]

Tocqueville saw this enlightened way of viewing rational self-interest as the key to fulfilling the fullness of the promise of individual human freedom, which is of course the ultimate goal of sustainable development. He saw the optimistic new democracy in America as offering an example to all the world of the best way to keep this promise, and he saw "the principle of interest rightly understood" as the way Americans were trying to do so during the travels he recounted in the New World. Tocqueville saw this principle as finding "universal acceptance" in the America of the 1830s, and he saw the commitment of the American people to this principle in those early years of the youthful American democracy as "clear and sure."[92]

Tocqueville hoped that, over time, the American example of "the principle of interest rightly understood" would endure, and that it would be emulated as people in other countries likewise came to see that self-interest "rightly understood" is best served by helping others as well as ourselves, and by remembering and fulfilling the needs of tomorrow as well as those of today. As a tribune of the Enlightenment, he hoped that all this would be accomplished through the light of reason. He believed that an enlightened reason is especially needed in a democracy. "The natural tendency of the democratic soul," he thought, is "to get caught up in the moment."[93] It tends to "turn from day to day to chase some novel object of desire," and to try "to gratify without delay" the "smallest" of these desires.[94] Thus, in the absence of an enlightened leadership that posits and that pursues an enlightened self-interest, democracy tends toward the immediate personal gratifications of the here and now.

A singular focus on immediate gratification will not fashion a firm foundation for the future in making and upholding international law. Nor will it do so in any other necessary endeavor for sustainable development. Establishing long-term goals through the rational application of "the principle of interest rightly understood" is therefore government's "most important business."[95] Tocqueville said, "At all times it is important that those who govern nations act with a view to the future."[96] Because of the democratic tendency toward short-term thinking, he said, acting with a view to the future is "even more necessary" in a democracy.[97]

The skeptics of international law warn of the dangers of heeding a "cosmopolitan theory which argues that states have a duty in crafting international law to act on the basis of global welfare rather than state welfare."[98] But this is not the danger we face. There may be a theorist or two who voices such a variance of a "cosmopolitan" view. There is, however, not a single decisionmaker in any state in the world who would say that any state should set aside its "state welfare" and should act instead on the basis of an abstract "global welfare." Rather, the danger we face in the world is that, in seeing their "state welfare," decisionmakers will see only their narrower interests today, and not also their broader interests tomorrow, and that, as a result, they will not pursue "the principle of interest rightly understood." The danger is that they will look solely to the narrow concerns of the moment, and not also far afield and far ahead. Only if they embrace the enlightened principle of self-interest described by Tocqueville will they choose to make the international rules we need, and choose also to comply with them.

There are, to be sure, limits to international law and to what can be accomplished through international law. There are bounds to law. There are bounds, too, to how much we would and should be willing to be bound by law. But the existence of these limits should not blind us either to the need for international law or to the positive possibilities of international law. As it is, the need for international law is growing, not only in sustainable development, but also in numerous other areas of global concern, while most of the vast possibilities of international law remain, for now, unrealized.

One vital area of global concern where, until now, some of the possibilities of international law have been realized is international trade. All our trade gains are now much at risk, but the experience of the world so far in establishing and upholding the international rule of law in trade offers useful lessons for the willing in how to achieve sustainable development by doing it through a mutual reliance on enlightened self-interest. In trade, much progress has already been made toward making right into might, and toward proving that, through enlightened international cooperation, we can sail away, forever free, from the ancient oppression on Melos.

On What We Have Done So Far

PART II.

On What We Have Done So Far.

5

On the Nature of Competitiveness and the Need for World Trade Rules

For all who seek the willing world, by far the most important thing to understand about establishing the international rule of law in trade is that trade is about much more than merely commerce. Above all else, trade is about individual freedom and about the individual choices that are the essence of freedom. Being free is about being able to make as many personal choices as possible about how we each wish to live. The equation between trade and freedom is this: More trade equals more choices equals more opportunities for more freedom. More trade does not guarantee more freedom, but it does create more opportunities for the full attainment of freedom for us all. Without more trade, there are fewer opportunities for expanding freedom.[1]

WHY TRADE IS NECESSARY

Trade is necessary. Openness to the opportunities offered by more trade is a necessary means to the end of freedom. We cannot prosper in the enjoyment of the full measure of freedom by retreating from trade and from international cooperation on trade, and by rejecting and undermining the trading rules on which we have long agreed to help govern globalization.[2] No country has ever grown – and continued to grow over time – without opening economically to the wider world.[3] One common characteristic of all high-growth economies in the past half-century has been that "[t]hey fully exploited the global economy."[4] During their periods of fastest growth, the fastest-growing economies of recent years "all made the most of the global economy."[5] Their "sustained growth ... became feasible only because the world economy became more open and more tightly integrated."[6]

As first suggested long ago by Adam Smith, and as later spelled out by David Ricardo in his classic description of "comparative advantage," every individual can gain from trade, and thus, by extension, every country can gain from trade, by participating in an integrated global market.[7] Maximizing trade by maximizing the extent of economic integration through an integrated global market is in the mutual interest of all countries, and finding the most effective way of doing so is rightly the goal of those in all countries that choose to pursue the enlightened rational self-interest recommended by Alexis de Tocqueville. The longer and broader view of his "principle of interest rightly understood" reveals that the fulfillment of this goal can best be maximized for all of us by pursuing our comparative advantage – by doing what we each do *relatively* the best – while furthering an international division of labor. Paul Samuelson, the Nobel Prize-winning economist whose basic treatise on economics has taught many an undergraduate, maintained that "there is essentially only one argument for free trade or freer trade, but it is an exceedingly powerful one, namely: Free trade promotes a mutually profitable division of labor, greatly enhances the potential real national product of all nations, and makes possible higher standards of living all over the globe."[8]

Building on the insights of Smith and Ricardo, the British political theorist John Stuart Mill, in his *Principles of Political Economy* in 1848, identified three different kinds of "gains from trade." He saw direct economic gains from trade. He saw also indirect economic gains. In addition, he contended that "the economical benefits of commerce are surpassed in importance by those of its effects which are intellectual and moral"[9] in supporting peace and in speeding the peaceful spread of new ideas and useful knowledge. These three categories of trade gains continue to apply today in counting the benefits that can be derived from economic globalization.

First, trade leads to *direct* gains that arise from the specialization inherent in a division of labor. One of the leading advocates of free trade, Dartmouth College economist Douglas Irwin, sums up the basic textbook view: "By exporting some of its domestically produced goods in exchange for imports, a country engages in mutually advantageous trade that enables it to use its limited productive resources (such as land, labor, and capital) more efficiently and therefore achieve a higher real national income than it could in the absence of trade. A higher real income translates into an ability to afford more of all goods and services than would be possible without trade."[10] There is, moreover, "overwhelming evidence" that the direct gains from trading domestic exports for foreign imports include an improved economic performance provided "by increasing competition in the domestic market."[11] According to Irwin, who speaks for the vast majority of economists on this pivotal point, "This competition diminishes the market power of domestic firms and leads to a more efficient economic outcome."[12] Among the numerous manifestations of this improved performance are economies of scale, lower production costs, and bigger potential markets, at home and abroad.

Equally, there are direct gains from trade for consumers in the form of lower prices and broader choices, and often higher quality in a wider variety of marketed goods. Domestic consumers of course include not only individuals, but also domestic producers. Often overlooked in the political debate over trade is the fact that domestic producers gain directly from trade by securing, through imports, lower prices and broader choices in the inputs of what they produce. This in turn makes domestic producers more productive and, thus, more competitive, both domestically and internationally. Prosperity is a product of productivity, and almost any economist would say that the main reason to engage in trade is to be able to import goods and services so as to become more productive and, thus, more competitive, as part of an international division of labor.

But don't imports cost us jobs? To be sure, some do; but it is a mistake to assume that imports necessarily displace local jobs. On the contrary, imports often create and maintain jobs. In the United States, for example, half of all imports are intermediate goods that support American jobs through US production.[13] Anne Krueger, former chief economist for the World Bank, explains that many US jobs are directly connected to imports and depend on imports, and that still more US jobs are created and are supported by imports because using cheaper (and sometimes better) imports as inputs enables American manufacturers to compete more effectively with foreign firms in the United States and worldwide. Viewing the American economy as a whole, low-cost imports do not have the net effect of destroying American jobs. Businesses that become more competitive through trade by importing at lower costs can afford to expand at home and abroad, and, thus, to create more jobs. In sum, Krueger concludes, "Without imports, many jobs that exist today would disappear."[4] And even more American jobs would never be created. This jobs calculus from trade is true not only in the United States; it is true everywhere.

Second, trade leads also to *indirect* gains. Trade not only allocates resources more efficiently. It also makes those resources more productive by inspiring innovations and improving the process of production and overall economic performance. In so doing, trade contributes to the growth of *productivity* by increasing the ratio of what we produce as compared to what goes into producing it. Growth in productivity is the key to economic growth and much of sustainable development. As Nobel Prize-winning economist Paul Krugman famously said, "Productivity isn't everything; but in the long run it is almost everything. A country's ability to improve its standard of living over time depends almost entirely on its ability to raise its output per worker."[15] The higher our productivity, the higher our standard of living and the greater the extent of our overall national wealth and competitiveness.[16]

Third, as Mill said, in addition to the direct and indirect material gains from trade, trade also has *intellectual and moral* effects which are even more important than material gains. Over and above the opportunities for more freedom flowing from more trade as a result of the act of material exchange are the opportunities offered through the act of human exchange that is a necessary part of trade. Trade is a form of communication that communicates the idea of freedom itself. The ancient Persians despised the entrepreneurial Greeks for their "addiction to trade," and especially for "the free exchange of opinions that went with it."[17] What the Persians failed to comprehend – and what therefore contributed to their defeat by the upstart Greeks and to the rise of Athens – was that the Greek "addiction to trade" was one and the same as the Greek addiction to freedom. The Greek word for marketplace – *agora* – originally meant "place for assembly." The Greeks made no distinction between the two.[18] They equated free markets with free ideas.

So must we.

Karl Popper, who took the long view of history, declared that "the Greeks started for us that great revolution which, it seems, is still in its beginning – the transition from the closed to the open society."[19] He saw "the trade of Athens" as the catalyst for this revolutionary transition.[20] "Perhaps the most powerful cause of the break-down of the closed society" for the Athenians, said Popper, "was the development of sea communications and commerce."[21] As Popper saw it, this was because "trade, commercial initiative, appears to be one of the few forms in which individual initiative and independence can assert itself, even in a society in which tribalism still prevails."[22] In our still-tribal times, trade can also be a catalyst for transforming closed into open societies.

WHY TRADE IS NOT ENOUGH

But, while trade is necessary, trade is not enough. Trade alone is not nearly enough. The opportunities offered by more trade will not result in more freedom for all of us if more trade is not accompanied by domestic actions that better enable all of us to make the most of more trade. An increased openness to more and freer trade internationally must be matched domestically by actions that open the way for more people everywhere to share fully in the gains from trade. Without such domestic actions, the gains derived from more and freer trade will be fewer, and those gains will be enjoyed by fewer people. All too often, and in all too many places, this is precisely what has happened so far in this century.

Throughout the world, the domestic actions needed to ensure that everyone can make the most of the gains from trade are missing. In the United States, to take one example, too little has been done to help retrain, reemploy, and generally reen-gage workers caught short by the relentless and disruptive advance of technology and globalization. The anguish of the left out, the left over, and the left behind has done much to fuel the populist reaction in the United States against globalization. It has done much, too, to create a gullible and brittle political fodder for those who seek and perpetuate personal political power by fanning the flames of extremism with an incendiary demagoguery. This widespread domestic failure is what has most led to a misplaced opposition to freer trade from many in the United States who now fear rather than welcome the openness of trade, and who, in their fearfulness, invite unwittingly the further shrinking of their own economic future. Their assumption is that stopping trade will halt change and start anew the local engines of job creation. But stopping trade will not restart job creation. Freeing trade will.[23]

Openness to foreign trade, to foreign direct investment, and to all else offered by the wider world economy is indispensable to national growth. Open economies are enablers of growth. Closed economies will inevitably shrink, decline, and die. But, in addition to openness, there is the need in every country for a competitiveness that can be maximized only if there is openness.[24] As one group of the world's willing has said, "Openness alone does not lead to success. The competitiveness of economies in an integrated world [is determined by] how well they convert the potential created by access to global markets into opportunities for their ... people."[25]

The best path toward competitiveness will vary from country to country with differences in history, culture, geography, and other diverse local circumstances. This said, the basic ingredients of national and international competitiveness are everywhere much the same. These ingredients include free trade, free investment, and the reinforcement of the free and open markets that encourage trade and investment through supportive institutions, and, of course, through the rule of law. Also essential are financial stability and fiscal solvency. Moreover, the ingredients of competitiveness everywhere include maximizing the potential gains from trade and from other economic endeavor – and thus the potential for the enjoyment of individual human freedom – by finding and by combining the right mix of market and government actions.

The right line must be drawn everywhere between private and public – between markets and governments – while striving for inclusiveness by providing: creative lifelong education for both work and citizenship, starting with essential and cost-saving investments in early childhood development; practical, skills-based training and retraining and other forms of tested and proven wage and other transitional assistance; roads, transit systems, water systems, bridges, seaports, airports, spaceports, communications, green power grids, and all other kinds of needed infrastructure; a fair, limited, and broadly shared tax base; and a tax structure that does not result in an obscene extent of income inequality.

This right line of a mixed public/private economy must be drawn also while providing ease of labor mobility; accessible and affordable universal health care; abundant basic scientific research and development; an ample and reliable social safety net; a sufficient minimum wage; a supportive economic atmosphere for individual and cooperative initiative, incentive, and enterprise; effective protection and preservation of the environment; and all else necessary to enable each and every one of us to make the most of the opening of new economic opportunities through an open economy in an open society.

One essential ingredient of competitiveness everywhere must be an openness to change. The embrace of freedom demands a willingness to undergo "the ordeal of change" for the sake of a better future.[26] For any individual, any enterprise, or any country to be competitive in shaping such a future, there must be a firm and unwavering understanding that, as Nobel Prize-winning economist Michael Spence has put it, "Sustained growth and structural change go hand in hand."[27]

To be successful in generating economic growth, free markets must be free, if need be, to destroy the old so as to create the new. To be open to change, individuals must believe that they can survive change and ultimately prosper from the change from old to new.

Everywhere in the world, the older parts of economies will resist the counter-intuitive process of the "creative destruction" of market capitalism and also the equally counterintuitive logic of comparative advantage.[28] Those who obtain power and profit from the way things are will seek to forestall the way things could be. The older and less competitive parts of economies will resist yielding to the new, and will seek always and everywhere to survive by securing the subsidizing support of local governments. Entrenched interests that are no longer competitive will do all they can to try to preserve their entrenchment while denying to themselves the incentivizing benefits of competition, and while denying to others the new opportunities that should be theirs to share in the gains from more trade and more investment. Those engaged in the economy as a whole will pay the opportunity costs of this protection of the old at the expense of the new through higher costs, higher taxes, and lost innovation.

Part of being competitive is being willing to compete. The spur of competition – both foreign and domestic – is necessary to the ongoing process of structural change. Growth involves a structural transformation that "is the result of competitive pressure."[29] Without the incentives from the pressures of competition, there will be less growth. Thus, "Governments committed to growth must ... liberalize product markets, allowing new, more productive firms to enter and obsolete firms to exit. They must also create room to maneuver in the labor market, so that new industries can quickly create jobs and workers can move freely to fill them."[30] Trying to protect and preserve jobs in uncompetitive parts of the economy by insulating them from competition, Spence tells us, "is the functional equivalent of throwing sand in the gears of an otherwise well-oiled machine. It will negatively impact productivity and incomes – and, eventually, growth."[31]

As this image illustrates, comparative advantage "shifts continuously over time, in parallel with investment, human capital acquisition, and, ultimately, with prices and wages."[32] National competitiveness is everywhere and always about comparative advantage. To remain competitive, a nation must be willing to shift with it.[33] Although more jobs will be created, some jobs will inevitably be lost along the way in these shifts because of the competition that comes from commercial open-ness, both foreign and domestic. As Spence asserts, "The main job of government is to facilitate structural change by investing in human capital, protecting people in the transitions through income support and access to basic services, and then to let the market forces and investment incentives work."[34] Putting this another way, we must protect people, not jobs.

Trade creates many more jobs than it destroys, but trade does destroy some jobs. New technologies also destroy jobs – many more jobs, in fact, than trade.

International trade is often blamed for causing what in reality are transitional consequences of fashioning the new from the old through the innovations of new technologies.[35] Robert Lawrence of Harvard University and Lawrence Edwards of the University of Cape Town in South Africa have observed that, in the United States, "trade has been assigned a villainous role that far exceeds its actual impact on America's economic difficulties. To be sure, some imports have caused harm, as trade-related job losses hurt specific communities and prove to be costly for displaced workers. However, trade accounts for only a small part of America's economic problems, and many myths surround its role in causing them."[36]

One of these myths is that international trade is the main culprit in the decline in the number of manufacturing jobs in the United States. It is almost universally held all along the widening spectrum of American politics that US manufacturing job losses in the past few decades have been primarily due to the ways in which trade rules and trade deals have permitted "unfair" trade competition with imports and have spurred the "offshoring" of untold numbers of the jobs of American workers. But the main cause of these manufacturing job losses is not trade; it is the increasing growth in labor productivity due mostly to advances in technology. As Douglas Irwin has emphasized in defending freer trade, "[a]lthough imports have put some people out of work, trade is far from the most important factor behind the loss of manufacturing jobs. The main culprit is *technology*. Automation and other new techniques have enabled vast productivity and efficiency improvements, but they have also made many blue-collar jobs obsolete."[37]

Irwin and others point to one economic study concluding that productivity growth due to automation and other technological improvements has accounted for more than 85 percent of US manufacturing job losses while just 13 percent of those job losses can be attributed to trade.[38] They underline the fact that manufacturing employment has been declining for more than half a century in the United States – since long before the surge in world trade and the birth of the WTO as an accelerator of still more trade in the 1990s. They highlight as well the fact that these manufacturing job losses are not limited to the United States; they are global. They are part of a worldwide growth in manufacturing labor productivity and a worldwide "shift in demand away from goods toward services."[39]

What is happening in the United States to manufacturing employment now is similar to what happened to agricultural employment a century ago. Jobs on farms shifted then to jobs in factories as Americans left the countryside for new opportunities in the burgeoning cities. A new transition is occurring now as factory jobs have shifted to jobs in health care, finance, real estate, information and communications technology, and numerous other services. The hardship in this latest transition lies in part in that, in contrast to most other industrialized economies, the United States has a frail and frayed safety net for displaced workers, and in part in that many displaced workers have no notion of what to do next. They are left on their own with nowhere to go and with no answer to the question: What comes next?

Some Americans blame this quandary on increased US trade with China. US imports from China have surged since China became a member of the WTO in 2001. Research by David Autor and two other economists from MIT and the University of Zurich led them to estimate in 2012 that import competition with China caused job losses for nearly 1 million US manufacturing workers in the first years of this century.[40] This research has been widely cited by those who would abandon free trade. It has also been criticized. Krugman has questioned the Autor approach of starting "with an empirical analysis, using cross-section data, of the impact of the China shock on employment, wages, and so on at the regional level" to generalize about "the aggregate effects of the China shock" on the whole US economy.[41] Similarly, Scott Sumner has noted, "Trade with China undoubtedly cost jobs in specific industries. However, there is no evidence that it has any impact on the overall number of jobs in the [United States]."[42]

One newer economic study concluded that "the risk of layoff and unemployment to workers in trade-exposed sectors is comparable – or even lower – than the risk to workers in non-traded sectors and that these risks have not increased during the period of more intense competition with Chinese imports."[43] Similarly, another newer study found that trade with China reduced costs and allowed US companies to expand "their total manufacturing employment in industries in which the [United States] has a comparative advantage relative to China, even as specific" parts of the same company got smaller.[44] Noting these two studies, the editorial writers of the *Wall Street Journal* commented, "Somewhere David Ricardo is smiling."[45]

Every single layoff causes personal pain to the laid-off worker and that worker's family. Lost jobs can lead to lost lives. All that can be done to help those who have lost their jobs must be done. Much too little has been done to help jobless Americans in the past generation. Yet, in the United States, in an economy of nearly 150 million jobs, about 75,000 workers are laid off or fired *every day.*[46] That adds up to more than 27 million firings and job losses *annually* – as compared to the nearly 1 million manufacturing jobs that Autor and his colleagues calculate have been lost altogether in US manufacturing to Chinese trade in the years since the turn of the century. Even if they are correct, their work explains only a very small part of the job losses resulting from the job churn in the United States' market-based economy. Of course, too, and as they concede, their calculation ignores the jobs gained.

Economists at the Peterson Institute for International Economics have concluded that the personal costs suffered by displaced workers are "much smaller than gains from expanded trade" and that "*permanent* gains from liberalization and technology advances far outweigh *temporary* adjustment costs."[47] To help displaced workers, they recommend, not a resort to trade protection, but rather "sharply improved adjustment programs ... to compensate those who [have] lost from deeper integration and from newer technology." They stress, "Adjustment costs should not be used as a reason to say 'no' to liberalization or new technology. Free trade, like technological advances, will continue to raise incomes and the standard of living," but adjustment assistance is imperative.[48]

Like the Luddites in Britain in the early nineteenth century, who destroyed the mechanical looms that had replaced them in the workforce, we can resolve to halt the automation that is replacing workers with robots.[49] But we are likely to have as much success in the end in stopping innovation as the Luddites did. In a world ever in search of the greater wealth derived from greater productivity in the marketplace, automation, like the mechanical loom, is here to stay. The real solution to securing jobs with a future is to figure out how to create more and better jobs while transitioning toward more robots and other forms of automation. In contrast to the mistaken perception of the extent of the job losses from trade, without the right transitional policies, the prospective job losses from automation could be substantial. Two prominent economists, Daron Acemoglu of MIT and Pascual Restrepo of Boston University, have calculated that each new robot added to the workforce means the loss of between 3 and 5.6 jobs in the local commuting area and that, for each new robot added per 1,000 workers, wages in the surrounding area will fall between one-fourth and one-half of 1 percent.[50] In response to these alarming numbers, all we have are educated guesses about how Americans (and other humans) might be educated and trained for jobs with a future – such as making robots; engaging with robots; working with robots; and marketing, licensing, and repairing robots.[51]

In contemplating the future of work, we should focus on new technologies and on the automation that is resulting from them, not on trade. There is nothing even remotely resembling a public strategy in the United States for how best to blend human intelligence with artificial intelligence to prevent humans from becoming redundant in a more fully automated economy. Always in the past, new technologies have created new and unforeseen jobs that have been better and better-paying than the jobs they have replaced. This time, will the new technologies leave displaced workers behind, bereft of their familiar manual looms, and left with no way to support themselves and their families? Like others in the world, we Americans simply do not know. In part, we do not know because, as always, we cannot foresee the future. In part, too, we do not know because we are busy, instead, debating the pros and cons of continuing with international trade.[52]

For the vast majority of economists everywhere, saying that we should free trade so that each of us can capitalize on our comparative advantage by doing what we each can do *relatively* the best in the market is a long-settled statement of the obvious. But this statement is by no means obvious to all. There is timeless truth in the frustrated comment by the British historian and politician Thomas Macaulay in 1824 that, "Free trade, one of the greatest blessings which a government can confer on a people, is in almost every country unpopular."[53] Some in every country of the world always prefer to "protect" local producers in incumbent industries from the "threat" of "foreign" competition by raising tariffs and regulatory and other non-tariff barriers to more international trade and investment. Self-styled economic nationalists tend to wrap their indignant rhetoric against trade and investment in the righteousness of their local flag. In the Congress of the United States, their call has long been to "Buy American." Nowadays, this is accompanied by a call to put "America First." But the call of protectionism is everywhere the same in the world, varying only with the flag that is waved. For all the fervent flag-waving, protectionism everywhere is a futile effort to preserve the past at the price of the future, a self-seeking alliance of the privileged few against the billions of people everywhere who stand to benefit from sharing in the many gains from trade.

Whether it takes the form of a tariff at the border, an import quota, a discriminatory standard, a needlessly costly regulation, an overt or covert market-distorting subsidy, a domestic-content requirement, a "jaw-boned" jettisoning of some foreign trade or foreign investment opportunity, or some other form of trade-distorting government intervention that creates an unfair advantage for local producers in the marketplace, protectionism is a tax on all we buy, all we do, and all we hope to do. What is more, because tariffs and other forms of protectionism are usually applied across the board and without regard to personal income, protectionism is a regressive tax, falling most heavily on the poorest among us. In addition, protectionism is a tax that comes with a price tag in the form of what the economists call an "opportunity cost." Sacrificing the future to try to prop up the past keeps us from being, and from becoming, as productive and as competitive as we would otherwise be. In protectionism's vain effort to preserve jobs and firms that can survive and struggle to compete only if they have the crutch of government largesse, we cede to others and to other countries the opportunity to create jobs and firms that can be competitive. In this way, perhaps more than all others, protectionism keeps us from realizing fully the gains that ought to come to all of us from more trade.

RULES TO MAXIMIZE THE GAINS FROM TRADE

Sustainable global development requires the gains that can be made from trade. The global sustainable development sought by the willing can be achieved only by a combination of openness and competitiveness that maximizes the gains from trade while making the most efficient allocation and ecological use of our natural resources. The gains from trade can be maximized globally only within the enabling context of an international framework of rules. Within this framework, there must be rules that facilitate the flow of trade, and those trade rules must be followed and enforced globally. In realization of this, many of the governments of the world have long labored to build and strengthen a global framework of rules for the international rule of law in trade. They have agreed on global trade rules. They have tried over time to improve those rules to meet the ever-changing challenges of an ever-changing global economy. And they have agreed to uphold and enforce those rules together through their cooperative efforts as members of the World Trade Organization, which is a modern vanguard in the continuing Enlightenment Project.

The flow of trade in world markets is smoothed by the certainty that comes from having rules for world trade. Traders need to know that mutual obligations will be met. International traders especially need to know that mutual obligations will be met in and by other countries. Why ship a product to the far side of the world if you are not sure you will be paid? And why take the risk of such a faraway transaction if you fear your product will face trade discrimination? The WTO treaty refers to the sense of certainty sought by traders as "security and predictability."[54] Security and predictability in trade have long been sought through rules. Throughout history, the gradual spread of trade has coincided with the development of rule-making and rule-enforcing institutions.[55] In supporting the spread of trade, these institutions have supported the spread of freedom. As Easterly has said, "[F]ree institutions create free values, and vice versa, for a virtuous feedback loop."[56] The WTO is an international institution that seeks through international cooperation to maximize the gains from trade and thus maximize the opportunities for freedom by establishing and upholding international trade rules.

Since its modest origins with the conclusion by twenty-three countries of a General Agreement on Tariffs and Trade (the GATT) in the hopeful wake of the Second World War, the international institution that has evolved into the WTO has labored to lower barriers to trade by establishing the international rule of law in what has gradually grown into a world trading system. The "main function" of the WTO "is to ensure that trade flows as smoothly, predictably and freely as possible."[57] The members of the WTO currently consist of 164 countries and other customs territories that, altogether, account for about 98 percent of all world commerce. (Twenty more countries have applied for membership.)[58] The rule-based world trading system under the auspices of the WTO is an international expression of a rational decision by these countries to follow Tocqueville's advice by taking together the broader and the longer view through international cooperation. From its beginnings as the GATT, and throughout its long expansion and evolution into the WTO, the international rule-making and rule-enforcing institution known as the World Trade Organization has worked because all its members have seen the need for the WTO to work as being in their own self-interest "rightly understood." The WTO will work and will progress in the future only if this enlightened view endures and prevails.

The economic conference of the victorious Allies at Bretton Woods in New Hampshire toward the end of the Second World War was the beginning of what is now the WTO-based multilateral trading system. Both the World Bank – to promote global development – and the International Monetary Fund (IMF) – to stabilize global monetary policies – were born at Bretton Woods.[59] Born there also was the idea of an "International Trade Organization" intended to promote the liberalization of world trade and investment. The so-called ITO was supposed to prevent a renewal in the postwar world of the short-sighted and self-defeating "beggar-thy-neighbor" trade restrictions that had contributed to the outbreak of the war by causing the global collapse of trade during the Great Depression. Trade protectionism did not cause the Great Depression, but it deepened and widened it. By far the most notorious of those harmful protectionist measures were the Smoot–Hawley tariffs enacted by the United States in 1930 which raised US tariffs on more than 20,000 goods to record levels and prompted other countries to raise their tariffs in response, causing a downward spiral in world trade.[60]

Unfortunately, the idea of an "ITO" as a "third leg" of the Bretton Woods system to facilitate the freer flow of trade and investment was not approved by the United States Senate. It fell victim to the American isolationism that soon returned following the war. Fortunately, an initial international agreement on the most basic rules of trade had been negotiated as a prelude to the "ITO" in Havana, Cuba, in 1947 – the General Agreement on Tariffs and Trade. Because of the urgent need for some ground rules for trade to help guide postwar economic recovery, the GATT rules entered into force on a provisional basis. Provisional soon became, in effect, permanent when it became apparent that, as those at Bretton Woods had antici-pated, the postwar world not only needed rules to help facilitate the increased flow of world trade; the world also needed some kind of a supportive institution to uphold and enforce those rules. So the provisional piece of paper called "the GATT" also became a permanent place called "the GATT" in Geneva, Switzerland. From this *de facto* trade institution in a villa on the shores of the lake of Geneva, generations of trade negotiators labored through the years that followed to create a "rule-based" world trading system.

According to Spence, who echoes many others, "The GATT was the beginning of the creation of what we now call the global economy ... Together with cost-reducing technological advances in travel, transportation, and communication, the GATT was an essential catalyst to a second economic revolution, a much more inclusive one in which hundreds of millions of people started to experience the benefits, if also the turbulence, of growth. It is this revolution ... that is shaping the way we live."[61] Thanks to this economic revolution, during the second half of the twentieth century, "the world performed better ... than at any time in the past. World GDP increased six-fold from 1950 to 1998 with an average growth rate of 3.9 percent a year compared to 1.6 percent a year from 1820 to 1950, and 0.3 percent from 1500 to 1820."[62] Even with the turmoil of the global financial crisis beginning in 2008, and with the widespread backlash against globalization since that crisis, the growth triggered by this economic revolution continues in the twenty-first century.

During the nearly half a century that followed 1947, the twenty-three countries that were the original Contracting Parties to the GATT multiplied, and the limited scope of the trade coverage of the GATT broadened to include most of world commerce touched by trade. Over time, the international footnote that began as the GATT grew toward maturity in what ultimately became the WTO through a series of extended and increasingly complicated "rounds" of multilateral trade negotiations involving an ever-increasing number of countries that, round by round, lowered many of the global barriers to trade on a multilateral basis. There were eight such rounds during the nearly five decades between the agreement on the GATT and the establishment of the WTO. The eighth round was the Uruguay Round, which concluded in 1994 with the Marrakesh Agreement establishing the World Trade Organization – the WTO treaty. Much – but not yet all – of what was originally envisaged in the charter of the "ITO" is found today in the text of the WTO treaty, which changed the letters on the door of the world headquarters of the world trading system in Geneva from "GATT" to "WTO."

THE SUCCESSES OF THE WTO

Contrary to popular misunderstanding in many places, the World Trade Organization is not a free trade organization, and the WTO treaty is not a free trade agreement. The WTO treaty does not require free trade. Although the abundant benefits of freeing trade are assumed in numerous provisions throughout the treaty, the phrase "free trade" nowhere appears in it. The WTO treaty is instead an agreement that establishes the WTO as an enabling framework for facilitating trade negotiations, trade oversight, and trade dispute settlement. It is a rulebook that can be used by the members of the WTO to the extent they choose to maximize their gains from trade by the lowering of barriers to trade.[63]

Today's level of global prosperity can be traced to a great extent to the existence and persistence of this supportive legal framework for more openness internationally to trade. Since the establishment of the GATT/WTO trading system, the share of world GDP from trade has grown dramatically, and the volume of world trade has grown exponentially. As summarized by the WTO and the World Bank, "Tariffs have fallen steadily since the end of the Second World War, along with progressive liberalization of capital controls, and greater connectivity through new technology in transportation and communications," resulting in an ever-expanding circle of prosperity.[64] "This accelerating circle of development was possible only because the world economy grew more open and integrated. At each stage, expanding trade was a powerful driver of economic development – opening up new markets, improving access to raw materials, promoting international specialization and stimulating technological diffusion and innovation – which in turn drove further trade expansion."[65] The value of world exports of goods has multiplied more than fourfold since 1980.[66] Trade in commercial services has grown even faster over the same period.[67]

Through all the years since the agreement on the GATT in 1947, an increasingly global framework of trade rules has helped create an unprecedented extent of global prosperity. The European countries left devastated in the wake of the Second World War have recovered and grown. Developing countries in Asia, Africa, and Latin America have advanced as well. China and India especially have lifted hundreds of millions of people from the depths of poverty. The integration of the global economy has benefited every country that has chosen to connect to it. Not least among those who have enjoyed a higher standard of living because of the benefits of the world trading system and of an open society have been the people of the United States of America. Economists Gary Hufbauer and Zhiyao (Lucy) Liu of the Peterson Institute have concluded that "past integration through policy liberalization and technology advances generated annual and recurring income gains of roughly $2.1 trillion in 2016 for the United States. This translates to an increase of $7,014 in GDP per capita and $18,131 in GDP per household. Estimated future gains that the United States might realize from fresh policy liberalization are $540 billion [annually], implying that US GDP per capita could increase by $1,670, and US GDP per household could rise by $4,400 by 2025."[68] These are averages. Going forward, with the right domestic policies to accompany an openness to freer international trade, all Americans could share as they should in the gains from trade.

Trade is a favor we do for ourselves, and not for others. Almost any economist would affirm that it would make perfect sense for any one country to eliminate its barriers to trade even if others did not. To paraphrase a familiar aphorism from the pithy nineteenth-century French free trader Frederic Bastiat: Why should we throw rocks into our harbors simply because others choose to throw rocks into theirs?[69] But it is never easy for any politician anywhere in the world to explain to the skeptical voters back home why "we" should lower our barriers to trade even if "they" do not. The WTO-based trading system has long acknowledged this universal political reality. Economics aside, from the beginning, the approach of first the GATT and now the WTO in lowering trade barriers has been to exchange trade *"concessions"* mutually as a matter of *"reciprocity."*

Central to the historic success of the world trading system in securing mutual trade concessions through mutual trade reciprocity has been the long-standing reliance by the members of the WTO on an overarching principle that international trade negotiators describe routinely and sometimes almost reverently as *"multilateralism"* – acting globally. Multilateralism applies to all kinds of international cooperation. In trade, the enduring goal of multilateralism is to act *globally* so as to reduce the barriers to trade *globally*.

This has long been accomplished within the WTO-based world trading system through the working of one of the fundamental trade rules – the rule requiring *"most-favored-nation"* treatment. Dating back nearly a thousand years to innovations by the Baltic traders of the Hanseatic league, and embedded in the commercial DNA of the modern trading system at Bretton Woods and at the later conference in Havana that proposed the ITO and concluded the GATT, the WTO requirement of *"most-favored-nation"* treatment – or, commonly, MFN treatment – is widely misstated and is even more widely misunderstood. Most-favored-nation treatment is mistakenly thought by many to mean that in lowering a tariff or another barrier to international trade, one country will give to the products of another country treatment *more favorable* than it gives to those of all other countries. Actually, this basic rule of trade means precisely the opposite. Most-favored-nation treatment means giving to the products of every other country the same trade treatment that you give to the products of the *most favored* of all countries. The MFN treatment rule forbids discrimination between and among the like traded products of other WTO members.

This fundamental trade principle is enshrined as a general obligation of all WTO members in the very first article of the GATT in the WTO treaty.[70] Thus, whenever a concession on trade in a product is made by one WTO member to another WTO member, that same concession must also be made to trade in the like products of every other WTO member. In this way, the reciprocity of trade concessions is multilateralized. In this way, too, the lowering of barriers to world trade has been globalized again and again, and the gains from trade have been maximized again and again, in the successive rounds of multilateral trade negotiations now conducted under the auspices of the WTO. Through the operation of the requirement of most-favored-nation treatment, a multilateral agreement has vastly more potential to lower trade barriers and, thus, to lift trade and, thereby, the potential for prosperity, than any one or series of bilateral or regional agreements between just two or a few countries.

Often, and increasingly, a pair or other small group of countries will take advantage of a general exception to the MFN obligation in the GATT and conclude a free trade agreement between or among themselves involving mutual trade concessions applying only to those countries participating in the free trade agreement.[71] A mutual trade concession made as part of such a free trade agreement between only two or only a few countries can be beneficial to those who make it. But the same concession made by those same two or few countries within the context of global WTO negotiations will automatically be globalized because of the MFN obligation, which requires that concession to be granted automatically to every member of the WTO. In this way, every country in the WTO can benefit from the concession, and not just two or a few. By reducing barriers to trade everywhere, the operation of the MFN rule increases the volume of trade everywhere, and thus increases the potential for prosperity.

In addition, there is another very practical advantage of global negotiations that involve many countries over negotiations that involve only two or a few countries. Because they involve many countries, global negotiations multiply the numbers and the kinds of goods, services, and issues involved in the negotiations. So they multiply, too, the opportunities for trade-offs in making mutual trade concessions. Thus, there are many more chances for making a trade deal multilaterally in global negotiations than there are bilaterally in negotiations that are less than global. (For sports fans, think of the additional trading opportunities offered by trades of player contracts among three or more teams, and not just two.) These are the reasons why the biggest possible payoff in the gains from trade resulting from additional trade liberalization comes from the multilateralism of global negotiations. These, too, are the reasons why multilateral global negotiations maximize for all countries the opportunities for more freedom offered by more trade.

The incentive to join the WTO and to agree to be bound by WTO rules is considerable because the trade benefits of WTO membership are considerable. The WTO's most-favored-nation obligation does not apply to countries that are not WTO members. Members of the WTO are therefore free to discriminate with impunity against the trade of countries that are not WTO members. Moreover, in their trade with non-WTO members, WTO members are not limited to the low tariffs and the obligations of non-discrimination agreed in the WTO. They can impose tariffs without limit and discriminatory regulations of whatever kind they choose. Should the United States (to cite one hypothetical example) decide to withdraw from the WTO, every one of the 163 other members of the WTO would be free under international law to discriminate against US goods and services in the absence of any other trade commitment to the United States outside the WTO.

Of equal importance to the MFN rule in maximizing the gains for all from world trade is another fundamental WTO rule of non-discrimination – the rule requiring *"national treatment"* of imported products. Protectionism frequently assumes the form of discriminatory taxes or internal regulations that deny imported products an equal competitive opportunity in the local marketplace. The market access that is supposed to be provided by tariff cuts is often denied by such "non-tariff" barriers to trade. The national treatment obligation counters this practice by forbidding WTO members from discriminating by means of taxes or internal regulations in favor of the products of local producers over like imported products once they have entered the domestic market.[72]

Although these two basic WTO principles of non-discrimination – most-favored-nation treatment and national treatment – are crucial to the success of the world trading system, these two rules are far from being the only WTO rules. The vast scope of the rulebook that is the WTO treaty now covers almost everything that is traded in the world and almost everything that is done by governments in the world that affects trade. Trade of all kinds affected by taxes and regulations. Trade in manufactured goods. Trade in agricultural products. Trade in services. The trade-related aspects of intellectual property rights. Trade-related investment actions. The standards and technical regulations affecting thousands upon thousands of traded products. Governmental actions dealing with human, animal, and plant health and safety. Various governmental actions taken as trade remedies to address unfair trade practices. Such arcane but significant trade issues as import licensing procedures, preshipment inspection, and "rules of origin" for traded products. The WTO treaty covers all this and more, and all this and more, in world commerce, can give rise to international disputes.

Perhaps the greatest of all the many accomplishments of the WTO is the mundane fact that almost all world trade is conducted almost all the time by almost all the members of the WTO in compliance with almost all the tens of thousands of pages of WTO rules. WTO rules are binding treaty obligations with which WTO members are supposed to comply as a matter of international law to ease the flow of trade. The fact that WTO members do comply with WTO rules is due in no small part to the existence of the WTO dispute settlement system. Whenever there is a dispute about the meaning of a WTO rule, WTO members can ask WTO jurists to help them resolve the dispute. Any WTO member can be summoned to the bar of global justice in WTO dispute settlement whenever another WTO member complains that it is not complying with WTO rules. WTO members almost always agree to comply with the rules when they are judged not to have done so – because the price of refusing to comply is the loss then and in the future of some of the lucrative trade benefits of belonging to the WTO and adhering to the WTO treaty.[73]

THE WTO AND THE EVOLUTION OF INTERNATIONAL COOPERATION

The multivolume treatise written by the German jurist and Cambridge University scholar Lassa Oppenheim and first published in 1905, is now, more than a century and many editions later, still considered the standard authority on international law. Oppenheim foresaw that international commerce would, over time, prove to be a leading driver in the development of international law. In the first edition of his treatise, he predicted that "the more important that international economic interests grow, the more International Law will grow."[74] The gradual growth of the WTO confirms his prediction.

There remains no lack of skepticism in the world about whether the largest stakes for the world will ever be resolved through a reliance on "international law." The expectation persists among the skeptics that, no matter what those who have power in the world may say along the way, they will always end up insisting – implicitly if not explicitly – that might makes right. Such skeptics believe a professed commitment by the powerful to multilateralism, no matter how nobly stated, will always conceal a willingness to resort in the end, if need be, to the unilateral *Realpolitik* of the Athenian generals on Melos. With this skepticism in mind, one recent view is that "international law is most likely to affect outcomes when there are many repeated interactions and each of those interactions involves relatively small stakes."[75]

The stakes involved in the work of the WTO on trade in goods and services are, of course, far from small. Billions of dollars in trade – annually – are frequently at stake in WTO disputes. WTO rules apply to trillions of dollars in annual global commerce. The commercial exchange in everything from apples and bananas to semiconductors, supercomputers, and steel falls within the extensive scope of the WTO treaty. Yet, from all their "many repeated interactions" through the years in dealing with the often-mundane matters of trade, the members of the WTO have developed certain habits of cooperation. Their many successes give credence to the view that international law is most likely to affect outcomes where, compared to the existential issues of war and peace, the stakes are small and where there are repeated interactions. The routine working of the WTO demonstrates every day that international law truly can work in, as WTO jurists have put it, "a real world where people live and work and die."[76] But does the success so far of the WTO in developing these practical and prosaic habits of international cooperation also tell us something more that extends beyond trade?

The overriding challenge in making and in upholding international law is one of inspiring and institutionalizing cooperation. Where countries see the need to act internationally, they will have the will to act internationally. But where there is the will to act internationally, there must also be the willingness to do what it takes to cooperate. Because trade is only another name for a division of labor, trade is also a form of cooperation. Adam Smith saw trade as being as much about cooperation as it is about competition. In transforming an unwilling into the willing world, so must we. The questions arising from our continuing cooperation on trade through the international institutional framework of the WTO are these. First, can our habits of multilateral cooperation on trade developed in the latter half of the past century continue to evolve sufficiently to meet the evolving complexities of trade in this century? And, second, can our experience of cooperation in trade offer useful lessons for us in cooperating also in establishing the international rule of law in other areas of global concern where there are other and even larger stakes?

In his provocative thoughts on the process of "the evolution of cooperation," Robert Axelrod tries to derive a formula for facilitating the emergence of cooperation in "a world of egoists without central authority ... where each individual has an incentive to be selfish."[77] The world he posits is a world "of individuals who pursue their own self-interest without the aid of a central authority to force them to cooperate with each other."[78] This world sounds a lot like the contentious commercial world of the sovereign states joined in membership in the WTO. In quest of a formula for cooperation, Axelrod relies on a thought experiment familiar from game theory (and familiar also from the personal experience of any international trade negotiator): the Prisoner's Dilemma. As he describes it, "In the Prisoner's Dilemma game, there are two players. Each has two choices, namely cooperate or defect. Each must make the choice without knowing what the other will do. No matter what the other does, defection yields a higher payoff than cooperation. The dilemma is that if both defect, both do worse than if both had cooperated."[79] Given such a dilemma, how can cooperation develop? Axelrod concludes that, "What makes it possible for cooperation to emerge is the fact that the players might meet again. This possibility means that the choices made today not only determine the outcome of this move, but can also influence the later choices of the players. The future can therefore cast a shadow back upon the present to affect the current strategic situation."[80] Two of the ways he suggests for promoting cooperation among the players are to "enlarge the shadow of the future" and to "change the payoffs" for cooperation.[81]

Axelrod specifically cites "the mutual advantages of free trade" as one example of the Prisoner's Dilemma.[82] In international trade, the "players" in this dilemma meet, again and again, every day in every part of the world. They meet every day not only in Geneva in the councils of the WTO but in the many ways that general adherence to WTO rules eases the flow of trade all over the world. If the trade "players" in the game of trade see the future "as sufficiently important relative to the present," then they can, within the enabling framework of the WTO, "enlarge the shadow of the future" through "more durable" and "more frequent" interactions.[83] If, further, they increase the gains from trade that can result from their cooperation, then they can "change the payoffs" for cooperation by making "defection less attractive." Asked for his reaction to this contemporary exercise in game theory, Alexis de Tocqueville would no doubt reply that all this adds up simply to saying that the trade "players" can solve the Prisoner's Dilemma if they take the longer and the broader view of his "principle of interest rightly understood." This is precisely what trading countries have done in establishing and adhering to their habit of cooperation in the open and rule-based system of the WTO.[84] The practical challenge ahead lies in sustaining and extending such an enlightened expression of mutual international self-interest to maintain and strengthen the trading system while achieving global sustainable development.

6

On Our International Economic Efforts on Trade and Investment

During the global financial crisis in 2008 and 2009, the WTO helped prevent the Great Recession from becoming another Great Depression. The members of the WTO reaped the benefits of their habits of cooperation when the very existence of a global legal framework of binding and enforceable rules for trade kept the worst from happening to international trade. There was no repeat of the punitive tariffs of the 1930s. There was no turning inward in the tit-for-tat "trade wars" that prolonged and deepened the Great Depression. By and large, WTO members continued to comply with their WTO obligations. During the crisis, "the system worked" with the WTO, as it generally did with the other Bretton Woods institutions.[1] The system worked because agreed rules were in place, because countries had acquired the habit of complying with those rules, and because they faced real commercial consequences if they did not.

THE RETREAT FROM GLOBAL TRADE SOLUTIONS

Even so, there was much increased protectionism during the global financial crisis, and there has been even more since then as part of the worldwide backlash against international cooperation and globalization. By one reckoning, more than 70 percent of all the trade actions taken in the world since 2008 "have curbed trade, rather than spurring it."[2] What may be most interesting about this new protectionism is the extent to which it has been applied in ways that acknowledge the boundaries of WTO rules and are not inconsistent with WTO rules. Violations of WTO rules continue to occur, of course. At the same time, a great many new barriers to trade have been raised in ways permitted by loopholes in WTO rules and occurring in areas of trade not yet addressed by WTO rules. Likewise, a great many restrictions on foreign direct investment have been imposed in areas that are not covered by WTO rules on trade-related investment measures. These are all instances of "legal protectionism" – of protectionism that has not yet been rendered illegal by agreement on new WTO rules.[3]

The postcrisis global backlash now threatens in places to become a full-blown turn into economic nationalism and economic isolationism. Certainly for Americans, but also for the rest of the world, the saddest aspect of this backlash is that it has been led lately by the United States of America. Under newly elected leadership in 2017, a new administration bent on turning away from "globalism" has pulled the United States back from its longstanding global obligations and global undertakings, including in international trade, and has pushed ahead with an aggressive and impulsive "economic nationalism" that has estranged longtime American friends and allies and, in trade and elsewhere in global affairs, has left the United States standing increasingly on its own on the world stage. "America first" has become "America Alone."[4] As a result, continued commitment by the United States to international cooperation through the WTO – which the United States helped create and has long supported – and through numerous other international institutions and cooperative endeavors can no longer be assumed.

The unilateralism of acting alone in imposing trade restrictions against perceived unfair trade practices – even if it is outside the agreed rules – seems increasingly to be favored by the United States. The current United States Trade Representative has denounced what he derides as "an unthinking, simplistic and slavish dedication to the mantra of 'WTO consistency,'" and has hailed "the potential benefits of derogation" from the WTO rules.[5] The new president of the United States has acted outside the WTO dispute settlement system and has promised to ignore any WTO rulings he thinks threaten US sovereignty.[6] Instead of showing a willingness above all else to seek cooperative global approaches to global challenges, the United States is turning from multilateralism toward unilateralism while embracing the might-makes-right mentality of the Melian Dialogue. Many of the willing are rightly concerned that the new United States view that its WTO obligations are optional will lead to more unilateral US trade actions and to more reactive trade actions by other countries that will unravel international economic integration and the WTO-based world trading system.[7]

One of the most ominous aspects of the overall retreat from globalization is this retreat by the United States and also by other WTO members from global solutions in trade. Desiring not only to remain open to trade in the face of an intensifying political pull backwards toward global protectionism, but also to maximize their gains from trade through more openness, the members of the WTO have been trying for a very long time to agree on more and better global rules for trade. So far, for the most part, they have failed. Since the establishment of the WTO in 1995, the members of the WTO have, despite years of off-and-on negotiations, largely been unable to forge a consensus on almost all the new global rules for trade they have all agreed are needed in some agreed form. In addition, they have largely found it impossible even to agree on needed revisions and improvements to the global rules we already have. In this collective failure, they have facilitated the unwilling world, and their continued failure only adds to the world's unwillingness.

The ninth round of multilateral trade negotiations by the WTO-based world trading system – the Doha Development Round – was launched in 2001 not long after the September 11 terrorist attack on the Twin Towers of the World Trade Center in New York. The goal of this anointed "development" round of global trade negotiations was to help spark more development worldwide by continuing to lower barriers to trade worldwide. The potential stakes certainly justify the effort. Economists have estimated that sealing a global trade deal would add $11 trillion to the world economy and pull 160 million people out of poverty by 2030.[8] Yet, despite the lure of these potential gains, the Doha Development Round degenerated into the longest international trade negotiation in the history of the world. Year after year, the members of the WTO failed to conclude the Doha round, freezing the further development of the world trading system. The manufacturing, agriculture, services, and other significant market access and other trade issues long on the Doha round agenda remain unresolved. A much-needed rollback of the new trade protectionism applied during the global financial crisis remains unattempted. What is more, a lengthening list of new trade issues has emerged and evolved since 2001. These new issues are not on the Doha round negotiating agenda, and thus they remain largely unaddressed multilaterally by the WTO.

A successful conclusion of the Doha round was prevented in part by certain of the habits of cooperation on which the members of the WTO have long relied, and on which they chose to rely once more in the Doha negotiations. WTO rules do not require that trade negotiations be conducted on an all-or-nothing basis, but this has long been the preferred approach. Thus, the Doha trade round was pursued as what is called a *"single undertaking."* In a single undertaking, WTO members cannot pick and choose which new trade concessions they wish to make. To get the benefit of any of the new trade concessions, WTO members must each agree to make and to be bound by them all. Agreement is reached by what the WTO treaty calls a *"consensus."*[9] Nothing is agreed on anything until all WTO members have agreed on everything.[10] As a practical and political matter, this means that any one of the 164 members of the WTO can singlehandedly block a global trade deal, and can do so for any reason. Seeking a consensus in a single undertaking worked well in the past when many fewer countries with many fewer differing trade interests were part of the rule-based trading system. But this practice did not serve the WTO well during the Doha round.[11] Now there are too many countries, too many issues, and too many obstacles to achieving a consensus.

There have been some breakthroughs on the commercial margins along the way. For example, frustrated by their years of impasse, the members of the WTO did at last secure some results by severing the issue of "trade facilitation" from the Doha agenda. "For manufactured goods and other merchandise, logistics costs today pose a greater barrier than tariffs. Such costs include corrupt and inefficient customs bureaucracies, inadequate ports and airports, and poor intermodal connections between ships, airports, railroads, and highways. Better trade facilitation is essential to reduce these assorted costs."[12] With this in mind, in 2013, in Bali, Indonesia, the members of the WTO concluded by consensus a global agreement to streamline customs procedures, reduce red tape, increase transparency, and generally ease crossborder trade.[13] Once the WTO Trade Facilitation Agreement (TFA) is fully implemented, it could add more than $1 trillion in world export gains annually by moving goods more quickly and more cheaply, and by otherwise smoothing the way worldwide toward more trade.[14] The WTO itself has predicted that the TFA will lead to annual export gains of between US $750 billion and US $1 trillion[15] and to a decrease in global trade costs of 14.3 percent once it is fully implemented, country by country.[16] Developing countries have the most to gain.[17] Welcome as they are, though, the anticipated gains from the Trade Facilitation Agreement will be small when compared to the potential gains that could result from the successful conclusion by the WTO of a comprehensive global trade agreement.

THE SEARCH FOR NEW TRADE APPROACHES

In 2015, the members of the WTO met with high hopes in Nairobi, Kenya, to celebrate the organization's twentieth anniversary. The disappointments there were many. Although there had been high hopes of finding some way there to progress on their long-stalled negotiations, the members of the WTO could not even summon a consensus there to agree on their usual ritual reaffirmation of their unfailing support for marching on with the Doha round. Rather, they more or less agreed to disagree on the central issue of how to proceed with their continuing global negotiations. The headline the following day in the *Financial Times* read, "The Doha Round Finally Dies a Merciful Death."[18]

Not the least of these disappointments were two missed opportunities to demonstrate that the WTO could contribute positively to sustainable development – by eliminating the duties on "green" environmental goods and services, and also by establishing needed disciplines on the subsidies that are contributing to depleting the world's overfished fisheries. Yet, despite these disappointments, there was a modicum of progress in Nairobi. Although a global farm deal remained as elusive as ever, some limited progress was made at long last toward combating global agricultural protectionism with some new disciplines on the agricultural export subsidies that have for decades distorted world trade. Agreement was also reached to update the existing WTO Information Technology Agreement (ITA), which freed more trade by eliminating duties on a great many more information and communications technology products.[19]

The WTO treaty does not mandate only fully global trade deals; it also permits smaller trade deals.[20] Frustrated by their inability to move forward multilaterally, and eager to meet changing economic demands for enabling rules, various subsets of

WTO members sometimes have not waited for a consensus on a global deal before going ahead. Instead, like-minded countries have made progress through smaller trade deals in the form of "plurilateral" agreements among some – but not all – WTO members. *Ad hoc* alliances of willing WTO members seeking more ambitious "WTO-plus" obligations have negotiated and concluded these plurilateral agreements within the legal framework of the WTO treaty.

One example of this alternative form of reaching a WTO agreement is the Information Technology Agreement, the 1996 agreement concluded shortly after the establishment of the WTO which was updated and modernized in Nairobi in 2015. A significantly expanded ITA agreed by fifty-three WTO members has brought this plurilateral WTO agreement into the twenty-first century by eliminating tariffs on MRI machines, GPS devices, CT scanners, video game consoles, advanced medical products, and numerous other information technology products that did not exist back in the 1990s when the agreement was initially concluded.[21] The 201 products it now covers account for 10 percent of all international trade, and the substantial trade gains from this expanded deal are estimated at US $1.3 trillion annually.[22]

The approach taken to freeing trade in information and communications technology should be emulated by the WTO in future negotiations on numerous other issues. Yet WTO negotiations since the Nairobi conference have mostly remained at a standstill while WTO members have debated whether in fact the Doha round is truly over. The timeless traditional issues relating to agriculture and to "non-agricultural market access" for manufactured goods, intertwined and intractable, remain mired in impasse. The increasingly important issues of trade in services have migrated to some extent to parallel negotiations on the sidelines of the WTO in Geneva on a proposed "Trade in Services Agreement." The twenty-three WTO members engaged in these sideline talks have left unclear whether their notion of a "TISA" would, in the end, be concluded as an agreement within the legal framework of the WTO. These services talks were frozen at the end of 2016 because of uncertainty about continuing US support for the negotiations in the wake of the outcome of the US presidential election. The TISA negotiations remained frozen thereafter as the new American administration expressed indifference to a deal that could benefit much of the 75 percent of the American economy that is services. Negotiations on services must be revived, ideally within the WTO.

Meanwhile, pressures have been intensifying for the negotiation of more and better WTO rules on, in addition to services trade, such "new" commercial issues as digital trade, intellectual property, production overcapacity, competition (antitrust) policy, export restrictions, food supply, food safety, technical standards, labor rights and standards, investment facilitation, and services facilitation. Pressures, too, have been building to address some of the trade-related issues of sustainable development, such as fisheries subsidies. A number of these issues are now being discussed to varying extents within the WTO for the first time in efforts to place some of them on the WTO negotiating agenda. Yet, constrained by the necessity that is still seen by most WTO members of first forging a consensus among *all* WTO members before enacting *any* new trade rules, the WTO as a whole seems largely unable to respond to these growing global demands arising from global economic change.

The continued dysfunction of the WTO as a forum for modern international trade negotiations was again displayed at the WTO ministerial conference in Buenos Aires, Argentina, in 2017.[23] There was no multilateral trade outcome at all. The members of the WTO could not even agree on the usual conference-concluding declaration. The one hoped-for multilateral outcome – an agreement limiting fisheries subsidies and illegal fishing – failed once more. "The sad reality," lamented European trade minister Cecilia Malmstrom, "is that we did not even agree to stop subsidizing illegal fishing."[24] Headlines afterward proclaimed, "The WTO May Have Reached Its Breaking Point," and "It's the End of the WTO as We Know It ..."[25] Probably more accurate was the verdict of the *Economist*: "The WTO remains stuck in its rut."[26] Despite the absence of any multilateral trade achievement in Buenos Aires, world trade continued in the aftermath to flow largely in accordance with WTO rules, WTO dispute settlement continued, and WTO negotiators vowed to press on. Moreover, despite the failure at the conference to produce any multilateral outcome, there were some encouraging signs of systemic evolution on several sectoral and other fronts as subsets of like-minded countries pledged to proceed with plurilateral negotiations on such "new issues" as digital trade, investment facilitation, disciplines for fossil fuel subsidies, trade opportunities for "micro, small, and medium-sized enterprises," gender equity in trade, and more.[27] Yet, even so, the ongoing global stalemate on global trade solutions evidenced anew in Buenos Aires only reinforces the inclination of many WTO members to look elsewhere for the solutions they need, and it does nothing to counter the forces against trade and against globalization.

Because of their prolonged frustration with the snail's pace of the multilateral WTO negotiations, many WTO members – including most of the largest economies and trading countries – have gradually shifted the principal focus of their trade-negotiating attentions away from the WTO. They have concluded a proliferating array of free trade agreements (FTAs) and other preferential trade arrangements outside the WTO that now number in the hundreds worldwide. The majority of these new arrangements are bilateral agreements between just two countries. Others, more and more, are regional. Potentially the most significant of all these non-WTO initiatives have – until their setbacks following the most recent US election – been thought to be two extensive regional "mega-deals" among two separate subsets of WTO members bordering the Atlantic Ocean – the Trans-Atlantic Trade and Investment Partnership (TTIP) – and the Pacific Ocean – the Trans-Pacific Partnership (TPP).

Although the proposed TTIP and TPP trade deals have suffered setbacks due to the headlong post-election retreat of the United States from freer trade, both of these mega-deals may yet have a major impact on shaping world trade. This seems to be happening with the TPP. The eleven other countries along the Pacific Rim that negotiated the TPP vowed to move ahead without the United States following the US withdrawal. They achieved success in Santiago, Chile, in March 2018, where a reconfigured TPP – rechristened by the TPP-11 as the "Comprehensive and Progressive Agreement for Trans-Pacific Partnership" – was concluded without the United States.[28] Even without the United States, the new TPP-11 agreement accounts for about one-sixth of all world trade.

The Trans-Pacific Partnership in particular is a good example of how mega-deals could be useful proving grounds for twenty-first century WTO-plus commitments that could be tried regionally and then scaled up incrementally to become fully global trade and investment obligations. As concluded before its later rejection by the United States, the TPP includes WTO-plus obligations on a number of "new" trade and investment issues that extend beyond the existing obligations in the WTO treaty or in other preferential trade arrangements – such as intellectual property, government purchases, digital trade, competition with state-owned enterprises, regulatory coherence and convergence, and labor and environmental protections.[29] With the withdrawal of the United States, a number of these innovative TPP provisions have been suspended by the TPP-11 until the United States may decide to return. Thus, having withdrawn from the TPP, the United States has been left with the task of trying to renegotiate what it had already successfully negotiated in the TPP in bilateral and other negotiations with the TPP-11, which has not so far produced much in the way of results.

Bilateral FTAs and regional mega-deals such as the TTIP and the TPP can be helpful generally in lowering the barriers to trade by serving as laboratories for introducing new issues and for exploring through trial and error new approaches in freeing and facilitating trade. They are also easier to conclude than global deals because they do not require a consensus of all the WTO members. These departures from multilateralism, however, are not fully global agreements. Moreover, when these agreements are concluded outside the WTO, they are not part of the legal framework of the WTO-based world trading system, which creates the potential for conflict between these arrangements and WTO rules and obligations. Although free trade agreements and regional mega-deals on trade lower some of the barriers to trade among some countries, they are by definition discriminatory in favoring trade between and among those countries over trade with others. A decision to give a preference in trade to one country over others is equally a decision to discriminate against those others – often small developing countries. Furthermore, such deals may not create trade. They may only divert existing trade to different markets – often away from developing countries. The continued global proliferation of these other, "second-best" agreements outside the WTO has the potential to undermine the basic WTO principle of non-discrimination enshrined in the WTO obligation of most-favored-nation treatment.[30] Instead of a world of freer trade for all, the outpouring of FTAs and would-be mega-deals could result in a Balkanized world of ever-more-complex and ever-more-nuanced international trade discrimination.

The hope of the willing is that somehow, in some still unforeseen way, the cumulative conclusion of all these many preferential trade agreements *outside* the WTO will in time lead trading countries back to a "multilateralizing" *inside* the legal framework of the WTO of all that has been concluded outside it. The benefits of freer trade limited solely to some countries by these non-WTO trade deals would then somehow be extended to all the countries that are members of the WTO. But nothing has been done so far to make this happen, and no plan for making it happen is in place or even under discussion. Jagdish Bhagwati is far from alone in fearing that the continued proliferation of "free trade" arrangements outside the framework of the WTO will put "termites in the trading system" by distorting and diverting trade instead of truly freeing and maximizing it.[31]

THE NEED FOR NEW RULES FOR TRADE

Trade has long been a driver of global growth. For decades, the expansion of global trade significantly exceeded the expansion of overall global growth. Global trade grew considerably faster than global production and income, increasing 27-fold between 1950 and 2008 – three times more than the growth in global GDP.[32] The momentum from the growth of world trade has spurred more growth while also forging international economic integration by binding the world's economies ever closer together. In recent years, however, the growth of trade has fallen behind overall global growth.[33] Economists do not agree on why this has been happening. Some contend that the reasons are mostly "structural." They say exceptional historical forces in the form of declining trade barriers, shrinking transport costs, and newly dynamic emerging economies combined to spur trade at extraordinary levels in the years leading up to the crisis, and that these unique forces have now been absorbed into a "new normal" of slower global trade growth.[34] In contrast, others say the reasons for "the great trade slowdown" are primarily "cyclical,"[35] and that the sluggishness in trade growth is due not to the structural changes in the global economy, but to the weakness in global demand.[36] While this debate continues, trade is still growing, but not by as much as before, and it is "back to crisis levels."[37] Facing this slowing growth in world trade, traders everywhere continue to believe that by far the best way to jumpstart global trade would be by concluding international trade agreements that lead to global trade solutions.[38]

Solutions are much needed for communications and connectivity, which are being transformed in endless and intertwining ways in the globalized economy of the twenty-first century. Global trade rules must, in response, be transformed to make certain that the rules framework for trade keeps up with these trends and these technological developments, and that the WTO-based trading system does not become increasingly irrelevant to the new commercial realities of international trade. The continuing evolution of the trading system must mirror the continuing evolution of the churning, constantly changing, hyperconnected, and highly inter-dependent global economy. This is so on numerous economic fronts, but this is especially so with services trade and with digital trade.

Global rules on services trade have not been changed since 1997 – when less than 2 percent of the people in the world had access to an exotic innovation called the "Internet."[39] Both global and plurilateral efforts alike to modernize the services rules have so far failed. The OECD tells us that services account for about 75 percent of GDP, 80 percent of employment, and two-thirds of the inflows of foreign direct investment in the United States and other OECD countries.[40] Moreover, services account for 40 percent of the GDP and 70 percent of the employment in major emerging economies.[41] Furthermore, "[A]ccounting for the value added by services in the production of goods shows that ... services as intermediate inputs [into the production of final products] represents over 30% of the total value added in manufactured goods."[42]

Barriers to trade in both embodied and embedded services amount to the equivalent of an invisible tariff on global services suppliers.[43] WTO services rules currently address some of these barriers, but far from all. Significantly, in contrast to the rules on trade in goods, the national treatment rule forbidding discrimination in favor of local producers and suppliers over foreign producers and suppliers does not apply automatically to trade in services. It applies only if a country has made a specific trade concession in its schedule of concessions annexed to the WTO treaty. All WTO members have made such concessions so far for some – but not nearly for all – traded services. In many sectors of services trade, WTO members remain free to discriminate in favor of domestic suppliers over foreign suppliers of like traded services. The WTO should begin by reconsidering the efficacy of this approach for liberalizing services trade. WTO members should no longer be free to discrimin-ate in services trade unless they *"opt in"* to an obligation of non-discrimination in a particular services sector. Instead, they should be obligated *not* to discriminate in a services sector unless they have successfully negotiated an *"opt out."* Indeed, this very approach has been taken in the negotiations on the stymied Trade in Services Agreement.[44]

The rise in digital trade parallels the rise in services trade. While, overall, the growth in world trade has slowed in recent years, trade in digital goods and services has multiplied 45-fold in the past decade.[45] In demonstration of the death of distance, the algorithms of digital trade are everywhere a potent accelerant for globalization and have changed the conduct of commerce profoundly. Business-to-business digital commerce is estimated to account for 90 percent of all global electronic commerce.[46] Today's digital revolution in commerce has lowered trans-action costs, lifted productivity, and contributed in countless ways to a more efficient and, thus, a more sustainable growth. Digital trade and services trade overlap. About half of all traded services are now enabled by information and communications technologies.[47] So, too, with digital trade and goods trade. In the brief span of about one decade, crossborder electronic commerce has increased to more than 10 percent of all world trade in goods.[48] One trillion connected objects and devices on the planet were generating data by 2015, and machine-generated data is projected to contribute to fifty times as much Internet traffic in 2020 as in 2010.[49] These fast-multiplying crossborder data flows have accounted for between 15 and 20 percent in GDP growth in many countries, including developing countries.[50]

Faced with the arrival of the digital age, some countries have responded with digital protectionism – where governments impose data localization and other restrictive requirements on companies and on crossborder data flows, not because of any legitimate concerns about preserving privacy or safeguarding national security, but simply to limit foreign competition (and, in some instances, to limit also the free flow of speech and ideas). To curb the growth-preventing trade distortions caused by this new kind of protectionism, there is need for new trade rules and commitments to ensure that online information can be accessed and that there will be a free flow of data across borders. To some extent, the existing WTO rules are sufficiently capacious to accommodate digital trade. In some respects, digital trade issues are not unlike other, traditional trade issues. But most WTO rules are hopelessly out of date for dealing with the novel concerns of digital trade. WTO rules are analog, not digital. A redrawing of many of the lines in the trade rules to adjust and align to the new commercial realities of digital trade is much needed and long overdue.[51]

Perhaps the most far-sighted of the willing working on the legal issues relating to digital trade, Joshua Meltzer of the Brookings Institution, has suggested that much can be accomplished by the WTO for digital trade by: making permanent the current WTO moratorium on customs duties on electronic transmissions, expanding rules on trade facilitation to support digital trade, updating guidelines in the services rules on anti-competitive behavior to include more sectors of digital services trade, incorporating the legal obligations of Internet treaties by reference into the WTO intellectual property rules, and encouraging much more regulatory cooperation in agreeing on balanced and mutually supportive rules that do not discriminate in digital trade without sound reason.[52] At the most basic level, too, WTO members must decide whether different kinds of digitally enabled trade should be characterized as trade in goods – for which non-discriminatory national treatment is automatic – or trade in services – for which it is not.[53]

Much of this could be done as part of a plurilateral digital trade agreement among those WTO members willing to boost their economies by agreeing on new WTO rules to stimulate even more the surge in digital trade. Other WTO members could then enlist over time in this digital agreement as they realized that complying with its commitments would benefit their economies. An encouraging sign was the announcement by about seventy WTO members at the WTO ministerial conference in Buenos Aires that they would begin "exploratory work together toward future WTO negotiations on trade-related aspects of electronic commerce."[54]

Meltzer says it all in saying that, today, "Data flows underpin how the global economy works."[55] It follows that WTO rules for world trade will not work unless they underpin data flows. In the twenty-first century, a world trading system that does not address digital trade is not truly a world trading system. Negotiating a plurilateral agreement on digital trade within the WTO is one way the WTO can move fully into the twenty-first century. On digital trade, on services trade, and on some other new "twenty-first century" trade issues, we can begin with a smaller deal among some WTO members and then build up over time to a fully global deal among all WTO members.

THE NEED FOR NEW RULES FOR INVESTMENT

Despite all the global growth in foreign direct investment in the past several decades, frustrations with trade rules are matched today by frustrations with investment rules. For the past decade, national governments have been adopting investment measures at a rate of about one hundred annually.[56] There is ambivalence in many of these national investment measures, with "simultaneous moves to liberalise and promote investment and to regulate and restrict it."[57] One of the most dedicated of the willing, James Zhan of the United Nations Conference on Trade and Development (UNCTAD) in Geneva, has calculated that, although most investment measures taken in recent years have tended toward "investment liberalization and promotion, the overall share of regulatory or restrictive measures has been on the rise (from an average of 5–10 percent in the early 2000s to an average of 25–30 percent in the past few years),"[58] which has "increased the risk of investment protectionism."[59] Amid this global ambivalence, the international framework of rules for enabling and balancing foreign direct investment has been tested and found, in many respects, wanting, not least as it relates to sustainable development.

As the flip side of trade, FDI is the opposite but equally significant side of the coin of global growth. Although there is a tendency to think of trade and investment separately, our "existing economic reality," the WTO informs us, "is characterized by increasing international factor mobility, mainly in the form of FDI flows that finance investment . . . Multinational firms, with their headquarters in one country, establish operations under their operation and managerial control in another country. Given that two-thirds of world exports are governed by these multinational firms, deciding where to invest is simultaneously deciding from where to trade."[60] Trade and foreign direct investment are therefore intertwined and are often mutually reinforcing. Intermediate goods that are components of production account for 60 percent of all global commerce, and about 30 percent of total world trade is conducted across national borders between the affiliates of the same multinational corporation.[61] More trade leads to more FDI by creating more markets amenable to foreign direct investment. In turn, more FDI leads to more trade by shaping supply chains, spreading technology, shifting relationships between importers and exporters, strengthening financial relationships, and more.[62] One particular area where trade and investment are intertwined is in trade in services when they are embedded in product supply chains.[63]

In principle, the concepts of a division of labor and of comparative advantage apply to foreign direct investment the same as to trade,[64] for both "are concerned with the efficient allocation of resources. Adam Smith's 'invisible hand' and David Ricardo's comparative advantage are not only theories of international trade – the international mobility of goods (and services) – but also theories of investment, because they may be equally understood as explanations of investor responsiveness to market returns from manufacturing activities (e.g., the decision to invest in production of cloth or wine)."[65] Like traders, investors will maximize their gains if they do what they do relatively the best where they can do it most efficiently and most productively. Therefore, in principle, the world is just as much in need of global rules to free foreign direct investment as it is of global rules to free trade. Yet, apart from a few rules in the WTO treaty on trade-related investment measures,[66] global rules to help us maximize the gains from investment largely do not yet exist.

So far, we have accomplished much less toward establishing a global framework for freer investment than we have toward creating one for freer trade. Although we have an abundance of international rules on foreign direct investment, most of these investment rules are in a vast profusion of bilateral investment agreements. Some, too, are in chapters in some of the newer free trade agreements. There are also, of course, customary rules of international law on investment. But, to date, we have few globally negotiated and globally agreed investment rules, and we have no global equivalent in international investment of the WTO dispute settlement system. There is no WTO for investment.

As a part of international law, international investment law has long been an uneasy mix of custom and convention. In both practice and treaty, there has long been a conflict between the expectations of foreign investors and the desires of host states. In a world where private property rights are not universally acknowledged and respected, foreign investors seek the assurance of protections for their property against mistreatment and uncompensated expropriation by host states, while host states in turn often seek as much regulatory and other control as they can over invested property while still attracting foreign direct investment. As with other international rule-writing, there is a line that must be drawn between these competing interests.

Through the centuries, protections for private investments developed as customary international law in "rules for the protection of aliens on foreign territory as part of the law of State responsibility."[67] A premise of the early "friendship, commerce and navigation" treaties was that foreigners residing in a host country "carried their own law with them wherever they went" and were "entitled to better treatment" than local citizens. As David Collins has explained the evolution of this legal concept, "Over time this superior treatment came to be defined by reference to an *international minimum standard of protection* with which all aliens should be treated, which survives today as a check on the arbitrariness of a state's exercise of its power over individuals."[68]

In the modern world, a number of common provisions have been included in almost all international investment agreements to assure the protection of foreign direct investment. One of these common provisions has been an investment equivalent to the trade obligation of most-favored-nation treatment. Contemporary international investment agreements almost always contain MFN clauses that assure participation in foreign direct investment opportunities on a non-discriminatory basis with other foreign investors.[69] The assurance of national treatment is likewise common in today's international investment agreements. However, non-discriminatory national treatment only assures treatment no less favorable for foreign investors than that granted to local investors, which is often not enough to guarantee sufficient protection for foreign direct investments. States do not always protect the private property rights and other basic investment rights of their own citizens. For foreign direct investments, national treatment therefore does not always rise to an assurance of the standards generally accepted by most nations. Consequently, just as international traders have supplemented the national treatment obligation in trade with many additional obligations,[70] international investors have spent nearly a century trying to establish in international investment rules – in addition to the basic rule of non-discrimination – an international minimum standard of protection for the property rights of foreign investors.[71]

The classic example of this continuing conflict between many developed and developing countries is the confrontation between the United States and Mexico in 1938 following Mexican expropriations of agrarian lands and oilfields owned by Americans in Mexico. Mexico took the position that it had treated American citizens the same as it had its own citizens by providing national treatment.[72] In reply, United States Secretary of State Cordell Hull asserted what he saw as the "international minimum standard" required for investment protection by customary international law. He said, memorably, that "no government is entitled to expropriate private property, for whatever purpose, without provision for *prompt, adequate, and effective payment* therefrom."[73] This "Hull Formula" demanding "prompt, adequate, and effective" compensation for governmental expropriation as a matter of customary international law has remained at the center of all efforts to write rules for the protection of foreign direct investment ever since.[74]

Founded on their territorial sovereignty, and on their consequent right to control property and other resources within their own territory, host states have the right under international law to expropriate alien property. As Collins relates, international investment agreements generally acknowledge this right by reiterating that "the taking of property by a state within its territory is fundamentally lawful."[75] For the most part, the treaty law on expropriated investments centers on "only the conditions and consequences of an expropriation."[76] Where the legality of the expropriation is concerned, customary international law and most international investment agreements require that, to be legal, a taking of private property must serve a public purpose, not be arbitrary and discriminatory, follow principles of due process, and be accompanied (as Hull insisted) by prompt, adequate, and effective compensation.[77] One of many matters giving rise to modern investment disputes is whether there has in fact been an expropriation. Rarely nowadays does a host state simply seize title to a foreign direct investment. Frequently what is in dispute today is whether there has been an "indirect expropriation" – an action by the state interfering "with an asset that, while damaging, falls short of resulting in an actual transfer of title."[78] Increasingly, such disputes arise from local laws and regulations, including those relating to the environment and to other aspects of sustainable development.

Yet another common obligation in international investment agreements that provides protection for investors is that of "fair and equitable treatment," which "in its essence guarantees fairness in dealings with the host state government and in so doing controls the manner in which laws and regulations are applied to foreign firms."[79] This obligation has proven in practice to be "an alternative means of providing investment protection where there are no clear grounds for [claiming] expropriation."[80] "Fair and equitable treatment" is an elusive concept, as evidenced by a long string of arbitral jurisprudence inviting a broad scope and a wide range of interpretation. Generally, such treatment seems to require due process, but it has also been seen and adjudged to require more. Additionally, a still-unanswered legal question is whether the treaty obligation of "fair and equitable treatment" can be equated with the customary obligation of an "international minimum standard" of investor protection, or whether it has an autonomous existence that confers additional rights on foreign investors and their investments over and above customary international law.[81]

The rise in investment protectionism has paralleled that in trade protectionism. As with trade, part of the impetus is the backlash against globalization. Investment restrictions often exist for the same reasons as trade restrictions, mainly due to a misguided desire to protect politically connected local producers from foreign competition. Moreover, with their memories of the many excesses of colonialism, developing countries have sometimes viewed foreign direct investment as a new form of foreign exploitation. What foreign investors today see as a simple request for the protection of their property and contract rights is still seen by many people in developing countries as a foreign drive for domination. Thus, the extent of the worldwide flow of investment is affected by an endless array of market-distorting governmental actions as developed and developing countries alike have discouraged investment "through regulations pertaining to local sourcing, minimum export requirements, restrictions on exports, trade-balancing requirements that restrict the value or volume of imports to the value or volume of exports, technology transfer requirements, and so on."[82] One area where this new protectionism is most likely to be found is in industries engaged in the extraction and other exploitation of natural resources – where environmental concerns are imperative and often paramount.

Some of these investment restrictions fall within the scope of WTO rules, which impose some limits on trade-related investment measures. But these WTO rules are limited in scope. There is a national treatment obligation but not a most-favored-nation obligation.[83] There is a non-exhaustive "illustrative list" of the kinds of trade-related investment measures that are inconsistent with national treatment, such as domestic-content requirements and limits on import purchases.[84] But this list applies only to trade in goods, not to trade in services.[85] Separate WTO rules on services apply to investment by including within the definition of "trade in services" the "commercial presence" of a "service supplier" of one WTO member in the territory of another.[86] Apart from these limited obligations, though, most WTO rules do not apply to most investment restrictions.

All efforts so far to establish global investment rules have failed. In 1947, "embryonic rules on foreign investment protection" were included in the Havana Charter that would have established an ITO.[87] In the 1990s, the OECD launched a controversial effort to craft a "Multilateral Agreement on Investment" that would have established global investment rules in a global investment framework. The proposed MAI was swept away by a storm of opposition from developing countries and NGOs that were excluded from the OECD process. The inclusion of broader investment obligations in WTO rules was part of the original negotiating mandate for the Doha round in 2001, but investment was removed from the Doha agenda in 2003 after a clash between developed and developing countries.[88]

In the absence of either a WTO for investment or broader coverage of investment in the WTO treaty, rules for international investment have emerged and evolved over time through the gradual development of customary international law. In recent decades, international investment rules have resulted mostly from the negotiation of myriad bilateral investment treaties and other forms of international investment and free trade agreements. FTAs have increasingly included provisions requiring investment protection. According to UNCTAD, by the end of 2016, there were 3,324 bilateral investment treaties (BITs) and other international agreements with investment provisions worldwide.[89]

This multitude of agreements is intended to promote investment, and foreign direct investment has increased as the number of these agreements has increased. Cause and effect have not been clearly established. As Simon Lester has observed, "[D]espite arguments that investment obligations help 'promote' foreign investment, the evidence on this point is mixed. Examinations of the impact of such rules on investment flows are inconclusive."[90] Even so, it is difficult to see how the rising number of restrictive investment measures prompted by mounting investment protectionism can be constrained without international rules, and it is all the more difficult to see how a shift in foreign direct investment toward sustainability can be enabled without incentivizing rules. We cannot rely on market forces alone to promote sustainable investment while the rules that govern investment impose no price on unsustainable investment impacts.

These thousands of international investment agreements contain many similar provisions, but they also "differ significantly in their content."[91] More and more, there are practical problems for governments and businesses alike in trying to deal globally with some of the differences in the obligations in these thousands of different treaties. The solution to these problems will not necessarily be found in negotiating still more bilateral investment treaties and other partial investment agreements. As UNCTAD has explained, "With thousands of treaties, many ongoing negotiations and multiple dispute-settlement mechanisms, today's [international investment] regime ... offers protection to only two-thirds of existing global FDI and covers only one-fifth of possible bilateral investment relationships. To provide full coverage a further 14,100 bilateral treaties would be required."[92] Clearly, just as in trade, a new global approach is needed in investment.

THE RISE AND ROLE OF GLOBAL VALUE CHAINS

The need for multilateralism in trade and investment alike has risen along with the rapid rise of the supply and production links commonly known as "global value chains" – results of the decentralization of the process of production from one place to many places driven by the death of distance. The extent of the economic impact of globalization is seen most clearly in these far-flung connectors of global commerce. Noted trade economist Richard Baldwin goes so far as to say, "[T]he 'global value chain revolution' redrew the boundaries of knowledge. The contours of industrial competitiveness are now increasingly defined by the outlines of international production networks rather than by the boundaries of nations."[93] The OECD tells us that "most trade today is in intermediate inputs – over 50% of goods trade and about 70% of services trade" – much of it through global value chains.[94] All told, about 70 percent of world trade in goods and services is related to global value chains.[95]

Global value chains are the latest commercial manifestations of the enduring logic of David Ricardo's explanation of comparative advantage as the pivot of Adam Smith's "simple system of natural liberty." Because they extend in length to embrace the entire world, global value chains create more opportunities for more trade, and thus they also create more opportunities for more personal choices in the exercise of more freedom. Global value chains also increase the need for more and better global rules to further the freeing of trade and investment. Toward this end, in some respects a reexamination of the basic premises of the existing rules will be required.

Almost all international trade disputes involve controversies between products that are perceived to be "from" one country and in competition with products "from" another country. But, increasingly, traded products are not "from" anywhere; they are "from" everywhere. Both trade in goods and trade in services are, increasingly, trade in tasks as part of an ever-dividing and ever-subdividing international division of labor. As the OECD has explained, "The whole process of producing goods, from raw materials to finished products, is increasingly carried out wherever the necessary skills and materials are available at competitive cost and quality."[96] This ubiquitous "fragmentation of global production ... has resulted from technological innovations in communication and transportation, which have lowered coordination costs, allowing countries to specialize in production of specific tasks or components, rather than entire final products."[97]

The best way for many countries to grow by creating more trade and more investment – the best way for countries to create more opportunities for more of their people to increase their income and enjoy more freedom – is to connect to these global value chains, and to use them as platforms for increasing productivity and thus competitiveness. The WTO and the World Bank have emphasized the role of global value chains in describing the role of trade in helping to reduce poverty. "The emergence of global value chains," these institutions tell us, "has been an important driver of developing country participation in the global economy. Countries no longer need to develop competitiveness in whole industries to be able to trade."[98] Individuals and micro, small, and medium-sized enterprises in developing countries in particular can begin to engage in trade simply by connecting to global value chains.[99]

There is "evidence that a slower pace of expansion of global supply chains is an important determinant of the trade slowdown" in world commerce. This slower pace of supply chain expansion keeps trade and investment from contributing as much as they could to global growth from a "finer international division of labor."[100] As the domestic markets and the domestic capabilities of emerging economies have grown, and as automation has offset some of the international differentials in labor costs, some previously international production lines have been pulled back behind national borders. All the same, the OECD continues to assert that, "Looking ahead, there is still considerable scope to enhance the international division of labor by drawing in regions that have been at the margin of global supply chains, such as South Asia, Africa."[101] We can capitalize on these "untapped opportunities" for maximizing the gains from trade and investment through linking to global value chains only if we are open to more trade and more investment, and only by creating and adding competitive value to the global trade in tasks.[102]

Solutions that are global are needed to maximize the gains from the additional trade and investment – and from the additional opportunities offered by both – that global value chains create. As Mahlstrom has put it, "[M]ultilateral trade deals are the best response to a world of global value chains. Trade rules that apply [to all the many] WTO countries are much easier to use than a web of subtly different bilateral agreements."[103] Economists advising the World Economic Forum have estimated that reducing supply chain barriers to trade worldwide could increase GDP by nearly 5 percent and trade by 15 percent.[104] This, they say, "could increase GDP up to six times more than removing tariffs," which are already much lower every-where in the world because of the past successes of the WTO.[105] Still more gains can be made by global reductions in the barriers to investment.

Notably for sustainable development, these economists explain that reducing the non-tariff barriers to trade in global value chains would produce these positive economic effects by eliminating "resource waste."[106] Thus, it appears that the best path to freer trade and freer investment in a world of global value chains can be a sustainable path that gives priority to the protection, preservation, and most efficient use of our natural resources. At the same time, UNCTAD warns us of the environ-mental threats posed by global value chains, pointing out that "downward pricing pressure has created economic incentives for violating environmental regulations and industry best practices, leading to the increased release of disease-causing pollutants and climate-change-related emissions."[107] Once more, it all depends on how we do it. Defining sustainable development by doing it demands our constant attention to the indivisibility of these connections through global value chains, just as it does to every other way in which the economy and the environment are connected through trade and investment. Yet, despite all the increasing focus of the world on sustainable development, the question of sustainability is still rarely raised in the many multilateral and other efforts to free trade and to free investment. In most of these efforts worldwide, the economy and the environment still remain, for the most part, "two different planets."[108]

Complicating this task of the willing is the fact that our progress so far in establishing and upholding the international rule of law for the global economy has vastly exceeded our progress in establishing and upholding the international rule of law for the global environment. The shortfalls so far in our international endeavors to forge more and better multilateral solutions in trade and investment are many. The shortfalls in our international efforts for multilateral environmental solutions are many more. This mismatch has left us with international rules frame-works that have sometimes seemed to value economy more than environment, and that have not done nearly enough to erase the lines between them and to turn the two into one. To make the willing world, these lines between economy and environment must be erased, and a convergence of economic and environmental concerns must be established, in all our international rules frameworks.

7

On Our Climate and Other International
Environmental Efforts

There is as much need for the international rule of law environmentally as economically. Many would maintain – not without reason – that there is more. Yet, to date,
we have done much less to establish it. The willing of the world are busy working
with high hopes of extending and improving how we govern the global environment
by negotiating and implementing the new global and other rules we need on a
whole host of urgent international environmental issues. Not least among these
urgent issues is the pervasive and unprecedented global issue of manmade climate
change.

   During the chill of the last ice age, the carbon dioxide level in the Earth's
atmosphere was about 180 parts per million. Now it is more than twice as much,
having reached – as a price of carbon-fueled human progress – more than 400 parts
per million. These continuing and lingering accumulations of carbon dioxide and
other greenhouse gases in the atmosphere have pushed average global temperatures
up by about 0.85 degrees Celsius (about 1.5 degrees Fahrenheit) since the first
emissions of the Industrial Revolution around 1750. Climate scientists say an
increase of 2 degrees Celsius (3.6 degrees Fahrenheit) is the tipping point beyond
which lie severe climate consequences. Heat waves. Shifting rain patterns. Extreme
weather events. Ever-worsening floods, droughts, and storms. And ever-rising seas.
Keeping the rise in global temperatures to less than "2C", the scientists say, will
mean reducing global carbon dioxide and other greenhouse gas emissions to zero by
the end of the twenty-first century. Their best estimate is that, to stay below a
temperature rise of 2C, we must keep our carbon "spending" within a total historical
global "carbon budget" of about 1 trillion tons of carbon emissions. We have already
consumed about two-thirds of this "carbon budget."[1]

   Clearly, global rules are needed to counter the inherently global issue of climate
change and to confront other intensifying environmental concerns. But most of
the rules we need remain unwritten, unenforced, or otherwise unrealized in our
unwilling world. Paramount as our environmental concerns must be, we have

constructed a legal edifice adding up to considerably less than the international rule of law for the environment. Many of the willing are working to remedy this by trying to paint international law green. Given the imposing scale of our global environmental challenges, the greening of international law has begun none too soon.[2] It took a long time to begin introducing environmental concerns into international law, and there is still much to do. The paint job is only partly finished. The eloquent American entomologist Edward O. Wilson writes, "Civilization is at last turning green, albeit only pale green."[3] So, too, is international law.

OUR THREATENED ECOSYSTEMS

Slowing our progress toward constructing the supportive framework of international environmental rules we need is the growing multiplicity and complexity of the threats to the planet's ecosystems. The extent of all that remains to be done in the ongoing development of international environmental law grows every day as the list lengthens of all our diverse and interconnected environmental concerns. Moreover, not even on this list, for many people, are all the intricate and indivisible connections of those environmental concerns with trade, investment, and the other dimensions of the global economy.

Soon after the new millennium, the United Nations asked about 1,300 of the willing from 95 countries – leading experts on all aspects of global ecology – to assess "the consequences of ecosystem change for human well-being," and to establish the scientific basis for actions needed to deal with those consequences.[4] The findings of their unprecedented, four-year-long audit of the entirety of the global environment revealed the alarming extent of the impact of the arrival of the Anthropocene – the human age – on the continuing capacity of the full range of the Earth's ecosystems to provide benefits to humanity. The bottom line of the Millennium Ecosystem Assessment in 2005 was this: Human actions are putting such a strain on our natural environment that the ability of the planet's ecosystems to serve and to sustain future generations can no longer be taken for granted. The situation is not hopeless. Many of the losses can still be reversed. But the changes required in what we do and in how we do it relating to the Earth's ecosystems are substantial, and, in 2005, the willing who conducted the global assessment did not see those changes underway.

These expert ecological auditors reported that, in the second half of the twentieth century, humans had "changed ecosystems more rapidly and extensively than in any comparable period of time in human history, largely to meet rapidly growing demands for food, fresh water, timber, fiber, and fuel. This has resulted in a substantial and largely irreversible loss in the diversity of life on Earth."[5] They acknowledged that "[t]he changes that have been made to ecosystems have contributed to substantial net gains in human well-being and economic development," but they stressed that "these gains have been achieved at growing costs in the form of the degradation" of the ability of many ecosystems to serve human needs.[6] This alarm arose from the scary specifics of some of their findings. Approximately 60 percent of the ecosystem services – the services that ecosystems provide for humanity – that were examined "are being degraded or used unsustainably, including fresh water, capture fisheries, air and waste purification, and the regulation of regional and local climate, natural hazards, and pests."[7] Although difficult to measure, "[t]he full costs of the loss and degradation of these ecosystem services ... are substantial and growing," and "[t]he degradation of ecosystem services could grow significantly during the first half of this century" and poses a "barrier" to achieving sustainable global development.[8]

Significantly, already in 2005 there was "established but incomplete evidence" that changes in the Earth's ecosystems were increasing the likelihood of nonlinear changes in ecosystems that would have important impacts on human well-being. The phrase "nonlinear changes" is one of those terms scientists tend to use that disguise and minimize the stark extent of what they are trying to say. Changes in ecosystems usually occur gradually. What scientists call nonlinear changes are "accelerating, abrupt, and potentially irreversible" changes.[9] With the occurrence of a nonlinear change in an ecosystem, "once a threshold is crossed, the system changes to a very different state."[10] Examples mentioned by those scientists in 2005 of such possible nonlinear changes were "disease emergence, abrupt alterations in water quality, the creation of 'dead zones' in coastal waters, the collapse of fisheries, and shifts in regional climates."[11] Since then, there have been more worrisome signs all over the world of the threat of these and other such nonlinear changes.

Equally alarming were the direct effects the ecologists found of these environmental degradations on the extent of human deprivation. They underscored that the harmful effects of degradations in the capacities of ecosystems to serve human well-being are increasing, and that these harmful effects "are being borne disproportionately by the poor, are contributing to growing inequities and disparities across groups of people, and are sometimes the principal factor causing poverty and social conflict."[12] For example, although increased food production "has helped to lift many people out of poverty or hunger," resulting changes to ecosystems "have harmed other individuals and communities, and their plight has been largely overlooked."[13]

There was no question whatsoever in the minds of these ecological experts from nearly 100 countries that the economy and the environment are one. To address the dangerous degradation of the world's ecosystems, they suggested, in part, market-based solutions. In particular, they highlighted a number of trade and investment issues that are also environmental issues, such as the market and other distortions caused by agricultural production subsidies, the depletions of fishing stocks worsened by fisheries subsidies, and the harm to global biodiversity exacerbated by the growing geographical span and intensity of development.[14] In these and other areas, the Millennium Ecosystem Assessment concluded, "Economic and financial interventions provide powerful instruments to regulate the use of ecosystem goods and services."[15] But "[m]arket mechanisms can only work," the ecologists advised, "if supporting institutions are in place, and thus there is need to build institutional capacity to enable more widespread use of these mechanisms."[16] They added, "The adoption of economic instruments usually requires a legal framework."[17]

Among the changes recommended by the Millennium Ecosystem Assessment were changes in the frameworks of "institutional and environmental governance" to "create the enabling conditions for effective management of ecosystems."[18] More and better cooperation and coordination were needed, they said, in many existing institutions. Some new institutions were also needed. Existing national and international institutions, the ecologists said, were not designed to deal with today's global environmental challenges.[19] In other words, the considered conclusion of these leading ecologists from all over the world was: We need rules. To halt the horrific march of environmental degradation and preserve the fragile ecology of the planet, we need international rules, and we need supportive institutions to uphold them. We need rules in the form of international environmental law, and – to give that law meaning, to give it real effect – we need the international rule of the law for the environment.

To help us confront the ever-increasing and ever-intensifying imprint of humanity on the balance of the Earth's ecosystems, we have international environmental law in abundance. By one count, there are now at least 1,190 multilateral environmental agreements, 1,500 bilateral environmental agreements, and 250 other international environmental agreements.[20] More are in the works. What we do not have is an enabling global framework that links this ongoing proliferation of environmental rules together coherently in seeking sustainable development by establishing and upholding the international rule of law for the environment. We do not have a WTO for the environment.

THE GREENING OF INTERNATIONAL LAW

Like the international rules we have devised for trade and investment, our international environmental rules frameworks have advanced together with the advance of our growing awareness that such rules are needed to meet our needs here and now and also to meet our needs more broadly and over the long term. Awareness of the need for international economic rules developed, however, long before the emergence of any comparable awareness of the necessity for international rules to sustain the ecosystems of the global environment. Consciousness always precedes law. Before there can be law, there must first be the perception of the need for law and, ideally, of the need to be bound by it.

Concern for the condition and for the fate of the international environment is a relatively new subject for international law as part of what is commonly called "the Westphalian system."[21] Classical international law is generally considered to have begun with the conclusion by rising nation-states of the Treaty of Westphalia, which ended the bloody Thirty Years' War of religious strife between Catholics and Protestants in Europe, in 1648. Since then, the subject matter of international law has largely been the relations between and among sovereign and (in theory) equal states in a world in which the only "actors" are states. Thus, the public international law of the Westphalian system is about solving problems between and among sovereign states.

Daniel Bodansky is right in pointing out that, among states, "[o]nly in recent years ... have pollution and depletion of natural resources been *perceived* as problems. The growth of international environmental law is sometimes portrayed as a single cause-and-effect relationship between the growing scale of environmental problems and the political-legal response. But whether a particular phenomenon is considered a 'problem' depends, in part" on the human perceptions and values prevailing at any given time.[22] As he illustrates, wolves disappeared from Britain in the 1500s, but the disappearance of the wolves there five centuries ago "did not occasion much interest, let alone concern."[23] In contrast, fast forward to today when scientists forecast that habitat loss and extreme droughts caused by climate change will result in the local extinction of six species of common butterflies by 2050 in the same Britain where the wolves once roamed. Headlines across the world warn, "Climate Change Could Harm British Butterflies."[24] A peril that was, for far too long, largely overlooked – the threatened loss of endangered species and the common need to preserve the biological diversity of the planet – is now increasingly and widely *perceived* as a problem to be solved.

The general absence for so long of a perception of worsening environmental degradation as a problem in need of our solving – the general lack of an environmental consciousness – explains why for so long rules to protect and preserve the environment comprised so little of international law. The gradual rise of consciousness of our enveloping environment explains why literally thousands of international environmental agreements have been concluded in recent decades, and why many more such agreements are sought in so many negotiations underway today. The absence today of an even higher level of global environmental consciousness explains the heights of the hurdles we face in fashioning the new international environmental rules and institutions necessary for sustainable development. A world that does not see the need to act is, and will remain, an unwilling world.

But believing there is a problem in need of solving is only the prerequisite to action. It is only the first step. Actually solving that problem is the next and necessary step. We may care about the disappearance of the butterflies today where we did not care about the demise of the wolves 500 years ago, but will we do what we need to do to stop it? To lead to the right results, consciousness must be matched by the right amount and the right kind of commitment. Even where we already see the need to act – as we do with the British butterflies – we must also be able to summon the will that is needed to act as we should. A world that sees the need to act, but nevertheless refuses to act as it must by taking the broader and longer view of Tocqueville's "principle of interest rightly understood," will likewise remain an unwilling world.

Not surprisingly, the first signs of an environmental consciousness in international law appeared in the nineteenth century at about the same time as some of the first expressions of a general environmental concern.[25] National conservation efforts began, and gradually became international, once it became clear that not all the problems of conservation could be solved solely within national boundaries. As the eminent British barrister and scholar Philippe Sands has described it, international environmental law has developed along with the development of "a growing awareness that the exploitation of natural resources could not proceed unchecked, that industrialization and technological developments brought with them pollution and associated problems, and that international measures were needed."[26] Rachel Carson's *Silent Spring* in 1962 signaled the discovery of environmental limits and inspired a mass environmental movement characterized by an outpouring of environmental energies in the decades that followed. The scope of international environmental law widened to include international protections against pollution of the air, the seas, the wetlands, freshwater, and more.

For the most part, though, these international environmental agreements have dealt with economic issues only piecemeal and only incidentally, just as the simultaneous growth of international trade and investment rules has unfolded largely without reference to environmental concerns. There has been no real awareness that international economic law and international environmental law should not be treated separately. The two have remained on their "two different planets." Now, all our cumulative environmental concerns have converged in the worldwide call for sustainable development. Sustainable solutions can be secured only by making more international environmental rules, establishing more international environmental frameworks, and upholding those rules through those frameworks. To find sustainable solutions, international law must get much greener – and the shade of green we select must blend economy and environment into one.

THE ROLE OF SCIENCE

Science has played a critical role in the evolution of environmental consciousness and, therefore, in the greening of international law. "Most of the major developments in international environmental law have had their origin in science."[27] Equally, and necessarily, science must play a critical role in the problem-solving of constructing international environmental rules and rules frameworks. The continuing unfolding of new and useful knowledge through science can give us "early warning" of an environmental problem, help us identify the nature of the problem, and help us determine how best to deal with it.[28]

The ongoing evolution of our scientific understanding of ecosystems is an example of the provisional nature of science at any given time. Other kinds of international law deal solely with human interactions with other humans, which are decidedly unpredictable. International environmental law deals mostly with human interactions with nature, and is dependent on science, which is supposed to be predictable. As we have experienced in the debate over climate change, one of the challenges in dealing with science as a tool in the making of international environmental rules and regimes – and one of the challenges in summoning the political will to do so – is being able (and willing) to rely on science while also acknowledging and accepting the limits of scientific predictability.

Karl Popper is best known as a philosopher of science. The empirical scientific spirit of ongoing observation is one of his requisites for an "open society."[29] He equated the open society with a "scientific" society, because he believed we can live in freedom only if we learn to live and thrive amid the uncertainty that comes with freedom, even as science lives and thrives amid uncertainty.[30] Popper derived his equation of science with freedom from the foundational premise of his fundamental explanation of science: Science always stops short of certainty. Science is "the ultimate, systematic search for truth," employing hypothesis, prediction, testing, and observation to draw conclusions and to establish facts.[31] But science is never certain. Science is science only if it can be tested – and possibly refuted – by further observation.[32] Any belief that cannot be tested by observation is not science; it is faith. Faith may well turn out to be justified, but it is not science. Thus, despite the common use of the phrase – even to the point of including it in some international conventions – there is no such thing as "scientific certainty." In the making of international environmental law – and in the wider making through the international rule of law of the willing world – the absence of certainty in science has profound implications. For sustainable development, "[t]his means that we have an ongoing fundamental question concerning the reliability of what we think we know and do not know about environmental processes."[33]

What is more, unlike much else in the world, science is one and the same everywhere. It is universal. The Enlightenment Project of making and upholding international law aspires to such universality. The state-centered Westphalian system of international law was not, however, constructed in the seventeenth century with science or the Earth's ecosystems in mind. It extolls the sovereign right of a state to control its own territory – including the natural resources in it.[34] Principle 2 of the Rio Declaration from the Earth Summit of the United Nations in Rio de Janeiro in 1992 affirms that states "have the sovereign right to exploit their own resources pursuant to their own environmental and developmental policies."[35] There is a potential contradiction in the exercise of this sovereign territorial right. States have the right to do as they choose in their own territory, but implied in the existence of this sovereign right is the right of states not to have their territory harmed by the exercise by other states of *their* sovereign territorial rights. This potential contradiction is addressed in Principle 2, which goes on to say that states likewise have the responsibility, in the exercise of their sovereignty, "to ensure that activities within their jurisdiction or control do not cause damage to the environment of other States or of areas beyond the limits of national jurisdiction."[36]

In addition to not harming their neighbors, states must not harm the global commons – the vast expanses of the upper atmosphere, the high seas, the common lands, and the other common resources of the world that lie beyond territorial boundaries. These common resources provide humanity with "public goods" – with "the kind of goods that one individual may consume but cannot exclude access to by others."[37] The concept of territorial sovereignty does not fit easily into a planetary biosphere comprising many ecosystems in which our environmental problems increasingly transcend all our artificial borders, and tend to spill over from legal place to legal place. In greening international law, our universal international insistence on the legal letter of sovereign independence bumps up time and again against the increasingly inescapable reality of our ecological interdependence.

A growing global environmental consciousness has inspired a growing recognition of global environmental concerns, slowly shading international law toward green. Some of this shading has occurred with the slow accrual of international customary law as state practices in protection of the environment have approached universality over time, and have also been acknowledged over time by states as international legal obligations.[38] But most international environmental law today is treaty-based in a multiplying array of international environmental agreements.

The number of multilateral environmental agreements doubled in the twenty years following the Stockholm conference in 1972.[39] A growing environmental consciousness was woven into the obligations of international agreements to regulate the dumping of hazardous wastes at sea,[40] to preserve world cultural and natural heritage sites,[41] to restrict trade in threatened and endangered species of plants and animals,[42] and to protect vital and vanishing wetlands.[43] Foreshadowing and laying the foundation for contemporary campaigns on the climate was a United Nations agreement in 1979 to combat the then-growing phenomenon of acid rain, which showed no respect for national borders.[44] Negotiations on the ocean began under the auspices of the United Nations in 1958. Eventually, these negotiations succeeded, in 1982, in concluding the United Nations Convention on the Law of the Sea – commonly known as UNCLOS.[45] Later in the 1980s, when scientists discovered a widening hole in the ozone layer threatening the very survival of the planet's biosphere, the nations of the world found a way to come together to conclude the Montreal Protocol on Substances that Deplete the Ozone Layer in 1987,[46] which in some ways is a model for addressing climate change. In this gradual greening of international law, the continuing accumulation of scientific understanding has played a central role.

THE EARTH SUMMIT AND THE RIO PRINCIPLES

The world in which we live is still Thomas Hobbes' perilous world in which "there is no common power."[47] And it was Hobbes, of course, who told us that, "Where there is no common Power, there is no Law."[48] The Westphalian system of international governance has been a prolonged experiment in international cooperation conducted over nearly four centuries in an effort to prove Hobbes wrong on this fundamental point. Because there is no single, overarching global sovereign, international law as a whole is necessarily fragmented and possesses no overall coherence as part of one overall global legal framework. As a consequence, it is divided among numerous separate and distinct international legal regimes. Within this fragmentation of international law, international environmental law is fragmented all the more. Although much has been done lately to green international law, much less has been done to paint all the green the same shade, or to paint it all on one common canvas. This greening of international law has been done *ad hoc* and issue by issue. It has sometimes been done within the legal framework of the United Nations, and sometimes not. Even when this painting by rule-making has been done well, it has not been done in any coherent way as part of an overall global environmental regime.

Furthering this environmental legal fragmentation have been the economic suspicions dividing the global "haves" from the global "have-nots" in what has long been described as the "North–South" divide, and is now usually characterized as the divide between "developed" and "developing" countries. Distrust of "developed" countries in "developing" countries has long persisted, and frequently not without reason. The fury and the frustration of the global "South" with what they saw as their continued economic exploitation by the "North" after the end of centuries of colonization and imperialism were memorably manifested in their call during the 1970s and the 1980s for a "New International Economic Order." Reacting to the all-too-frequent rapaciousness of capitalism as a part of the previous imperialism, and responding also to the trendiness at the time of the reassuring nostrums of various forms of socialism, the "NIEO" was light on practicality and heavy on cookie-cutter statist solutions. Ultimately, it proved considerably more useful as a potion for protest than as a prescription for sustainable (or any other kind of) development.

But the notion that there are injustices in the economic imbalances between the "North" and the "South," and that these injustices must in some way be acknowledged and redressed in international rule-making, has had lasting influence in the context of the evolution of international environmental law. Specifically, it is seen in the lingering conviction in much of the developing world that developed and developing countries should be expected to bear different levels of environmental and trade obligations. It is clearly seen also in the continuing global influence of "Our Common Future," the seminal report of the World Commission on Environment and Development – the Brundtland Commission – in 1987 that gave us the definition of sustainable development to which so many of the willing of the world subscribe.

In 1992, twenty years after the Stockholm conference, representatives of more than 180 countries – including 100 heads of state – gathered in Rio de Janeiro, Brazil, for what was called, grandly, the Earth Summit. The assembled UN members agreed there on the Rio Declaration on Environment and Development, which set out twenty-seven non-binding environmental principles. They also agreed on a non-binding but foundational declaration of what came to be called the Forest Principles, which had added credence because it was crafted in a country that is home to the imperiled Amazon rainforests.[49] At a time when severe droughts and spreading deserts were especially afflicting Africa, the Rio conference adopted a proposal to begin negotiations on a convention on desertification.[50] Amid intensifying concerns about threats to global biological resources, the Convention on Biological Diversity – the Biodiversity Convention – was opened for signature.[51] So too was the international agreement that was to become the main focus of the willing for the next quarter of a century – the United Nations Framework Convention on Climate Change, the UNFCCC.[52] Lastly, the countries convened in Rio created the UN Commission on Sustainable Development, with a mandate to meet every five years to monitor the world's progress toward achieving the Earth Summit's goals.

There were some lasting successes in the first years that followed the Earth Summit: the convention on desertification, in 1994.[53] A UNCLOS convention to conserve and manage declining fish stocks in the seas, in 1995.[54] A protocol on biosafety to the Biodiversity Convention, in 2000.[55] A treaty protecting plant genetic resources, in 2001.[56] An agreement regulating persistent organic pollutants, in 2001.[57] An agreement protecting tropical timber, in 2006.[58] Further, a large part of what the willing have sought since the Rio summit has been recognition of the twenty-seven non-binding principles in the Rio Declaration of 1992 as basic principles of international environmental law. One means has been to include important aspects of many of the Rio principles in the continuing proliferation of international environmental agreements of all kinds. Another has been to weave those principles into an endless array of other international directives, standards, and guidelines that have been produced by an endless variety of international undertakings. In these and other ways, those trying hard to fulfill the goals of the Earth Summit for sustainable development have endeavored to add more green to international law.

Prominent among the Rio principles that have gradually given an increasingly green tint to international law are: Principle 2, which posits a balance between preserving national sovereignty and ensuring no environmental harm; Principle 16, the "polluter-pays" principle, which encourages internalizing the externalities of environmental harm by stating that the polluter should bear the costs of pollution; and Principle 17, which establishes the duty of states to conduct an environmental impact assessment before taking any national action that risks causing serious transboundary harm.

Perhaps the most famous of the Rio principles, and one with profound implications, is Principle 15, the "precautionary principle," which provides sweepingly that "[w]here there are threats of serious or irreversible damage, lack of full scientific certainty shall not be used as a reason for postponing cost-effective measures to prevent environmental degradation." (The use of the undefined phrase "scientific certainty" in Principle 15 would, no doubt, have confounded and dismayed Karl Popper. Not surprisingly, the proper framing of the need for precaution has inspired and continues to inspire no end of global controversy.) Despite Principle 15, there is no global consensus on how much or what kind of precaution is needed, or when it is needed.

Because the Rio Declaration was a declaration on both environment and development, it did not ignore trade. Echoing in part the wording of the general exceptions in the GATT to global trade rules,[59] Principle 12 stated: "States shall cooperate to promote a supportive and open international economic system that would lead to economic growth and sustainable development in all countries, to better address the problems of environmental degradation. Trade policy measures for environmental purposes should not constitute a means of unjustifiable or arbitrary discrimination or a disguised restriction on international trade. Unilateral actions to deal with environmental challenges outside the jurisdiction of the importing country should be avoided. Environmental measures addressing transboundary or global environmental problems should, as far as possible, be based on an international consensus."[60]

Affecting all the Rio principles is the Brundtland Commission's earlier and enduring statement of the principle of sustainable development as a blending of economy and environment with both today and tomorrow in mind at all stages of development. The central principle of sustainable development is reflected in a number of ways in a number of the Rio principles. It is the theme threading throughout the Rio Declaration, as it was with the whole Earth Summit. To cite one example, Principle 4 envisages the intertwining of economic development with environmental protection by stating: "In order to achieve sustainable development, environmental protection shall constitute an integral part of the development process and cannot be considered in isolation from it." Here is an injunction in 1992 to see economy and environment as one.

In a victory for the willing, the principle of sustainable development is today said, more and more, to be a part of international law. Notably, there has been a growing recognition of this legal status in international jurisprudence. In a separate opinion in a case between Hungary and Slovakia in 1997, the Vice-President of the International Court of Justice in The Hague, Judge Christopher Weeramantry, of Sri Lanka, set the current tone when he said, "The principle of sustainable development is . . . a part of modern international law by reason not only of its inescapable logical necessity, but also by reason of its wide and general acceptance by the global community."[61]

The hope of those trying to green international law has been that the "logical necessity" of the sustainability principles in the various global environmental declarations will lead over time to many of them acquiring the force of law.[62] Most of these green principles, however, remain for now "twilight norms" lingering in the dim political terrain between the dawning international awareness of the need for common environmental action and the daunting task of mustering the political will to take it.[63] The trend in recent years has been to place environmental affirmations "in non-binding political instruments such as declarations, resolutions, and programs of action," and to signal "that compliance is expected with the norms that these texts contain. Commentators refer to these instruments as 'soft law' and debate whether the practice of adopting them constitutes evidence of new modes of international law making."[64] The non-traditional approaches of the willing in relying on such "soft law" in trying to green international law are one manifestation of an era in which the world has shifted in many ways in its international endeavors from the traditional Westphalian emphasis on the coexistence of states to a stress on the cooperation of states, and on the cooperation of states with a variety of non-states.[65]

Since the Earth Summit, the ongoing work of the willing to establish the international rule of law for the environment, more and more, "has concerned longer-term, irreversible, global threats, such as depletion of the stratospheric ozone layer, loss of biological diversity, and greenhouse warming."[66] Increasingly, this effort has focused on the environmental damages of all kinds that all states are causing to the global commons.[67] As Judge Weeramantry eloquently summarized our predicament when giving the concept of "sustainable development" his own personal imprimatur as a part of international law: "We have entered an era ... in which international law subserves not only the interests of individual States, but looks beyond them and their parochial concerns to the greater interests of humanity and planetary welfare ... International environmental law will need to proceed beyond weighing ... rights and obligations ... within a closed compartment of individual State self-interest, unrelated to the global concerns of humanity as a whole."[68] In the international rules we are making we must address the common concerns of all the world.

THE UNITED NATIONS CLIMATE REGIME

The search for common solutions to global environmental concerns has inspired the establishment of a number of international environmental frameworks. Foremost among these frameworks is the elaborate United Nations Framework Convention on Climate Change. In the First Recital on the first page of the UNFCCC, the members of the United Nations acknowledge "that change in the Earth's climate and its adverse effects are a common concern of mankind."[69]

The achievement of the world's climate goals as set out at the Earth Summit in the UNFCCC is an indispensable part of confronting the comprehensive global challenge of securing sustainable development. To be sure, there is much more to greening international law and to providing for the overall protection and preservation of global ecosystems than dealing with the causes and the consequences of manmade climate change. But everything about the environment is affected in some way by climate change. If we do not soon find a global solution for confronting climate change, we will not be able to shape and share a sustainable global development. In calling for international cooperation to confront climate change, the UNFCCC is the quintessential expression of how the willing have so far strived to turn our unwilling into the willing world.

Although scientists had known since the 1890s that pumping greenhouse gases into the atmosphere could cause global warming, it was not until the middle of the 1980s that the ever-increasing accumulation of those gases began to draw widespread global attention. In 1988, in response to the increasingly dire warnings of scientists about signs of climate change, the United Nations first declared climate change "a common concern of mankind."[70] That same year, UNEP and the World Meteorological Organization together established the IPCC to conduct ongoing studies of the Earth's altering atmosphere. In 1990, the IPCC produced its first assessment report. Against this backdrop, through the years, an entire generation of the willing has invested enormous energies in fighting climate change through the UN climate framework that was one of the achievements of the 1992 Earth Summit.[71]

The UN climate convention is designed as a basic legal "framework" on which comprehensiveness in confronting and forestalling climate change can be built, block by legal building block, over time. The UN climate regime aspires to a global climate solution, but the UN framework convention leaves the details of what that solution should be to a later legal filling-in of the blanks. Global success in filling in those blanks has been slow in coming. A first multilateral effort to fill in the blanks of a global solution for climate change was the conclusion of the Kyoto Protocol to the convention in 1997.[72] Unfortunately, the basic structure of the protocol, coupled with the changing over time of the political equation of climate change, kept it from becoming comprehensive and thus rendered it increasingly irrelevant. The Kyoto Protocol was "very logical and Cartesian."[73] It took the form of a "top-down" treaty imposing specific targets for carbon emission cuts. But, because the vast majority of carbon emissions historically had been made by the industrialized countries, and not by their former colonies and other poorer countries, the protocol imposed targets for cuts in emissions only on the developed countries of the "North," and not on the developing countries of the "South." Rapidly emerging economies such as China, India, South Korea, South Africa, and others were given no targets, and were thus left free to increase their emissions at will.

Believing the United States should not be bound to mandatory emissions cuts when many other countries – including a growing number of new commercial competitors – were not, the United States Senate refused to ratify the Kyoto

Protocol. By the time the protocol eventually entered into effect without the United States, in 2005, the global geopolitical landscape that had shaped it had changed considerably, and it no longer reflected altered political realities. China and a number of the other "emerging" economies had by then truly emerged, and their growing share of global GDP not only gave them greater clout in the global economy, but also caused the developed economies to call on them to assume greater global responsibilities – including a commitment to cuts in carbon emissions. China surpassed the United States as the world's leading source of carbon emissions in 2006. Most of the growth in global emissions is now coming from developing countries.

There was much that was useful in the Kyoto Protocol. It provided for the development of an international emissions trading system, which inspired the European emissions trading system and a number of other innovative carbon-cutting efforts elsewhere. It also created what was called a "Clean Development Mechanism," which enabled industrialized countries to get credit in such trading schemes for emission reduction projects in developing countries.[74] Moreover, the Kyoto Protocol allowed for the possibility of getting credits for certain forest and agricultural activities that remove carbon dioxide from the atmosphere. (In climate speak, these are known as "sink activities.") All the same, the search for a global climate solution continued. Many countries – including many in the developing world that were not required by the protocol to cut their own carbon emissions – clung to Kyoto. But eventually, as it became clear that the Kyoto Protocol would never become the needed global solution, the Conference of Parties to the UNFCCC – familiarly known as the "COP" – reluctantly decided to seek another. New global negotiations were launched in 2007 aimed at reaching an "agreed outcome" on a global climate solution at the COP in Copenhagen, Denmark, in 2009.[75]

COPENHAGEN AND THE ROCKY ROAD TO PARIS

Regrettably, no one had agreed on even the basics of what an "agreed outcome" would be. The Copenhagen conference turned out to be a grim global anticlimax. Tens of thousands of the willing descended on the Danish capital for a week of dramatic non-stop negotiations during the darkest days of a cold December. In the end, there was simply no way of overcoming in Copenhagen the wide and deeply entrenched differences among most of the negotiating countries involved in the negotiations, and of agreeing on targeted cuts in carbon emissions.

In a last-ditch effort to salvage something from the conference shambles outside the actual deliberations of the COP, the leaders of the United States and China, along with a few other larger countries, agreed on a brief statement that came to be known as the "Copenhagen Accord."[76] The Copenhagen Accord salvaged something from the disappointing outcome of the conference, and was noteworthy in a number of important respects. First, the accord cut through the thousands of pages of periodic scientific assessments by the IPCC to endorse "the scientific view that the increase in global temperature should be held below 2 degree Celsius" (3.6 degrees Fahrenheit). Second, it called for "deep cuts in carbon emissions . . . so as to hold the increase in global temperatures below 2 degrees Celsius." These two statements together established a legal hook for the 2C goal that has since become a universal rallying cry of the willing worldwide.

Moreover, and most of all, for the first time, all the world's developed countries *and the biggest developing countries* agreed to limit their greenhouse gas emissions. Although the differing proposed emissions cuts set out in the annexes to the accord fell short of what would be needed to achieve a "2-degree world," they were much more than had been made before. And the mere fact that developed and developing countries alike agreed to commitments marked a fundamental shift from the North–South divide of the Kyoto Protocol. The rich countries also promised in Copenhagen to provide needed money to help poor countries harmed by climate change. The accord called for the creation of a Green Climate Fund to help support mitigation, adaptation, and technological cooperation. Developed countries promised developing countries $100 billion *annually* by 2020 – of which a "signifi- cant portion" was to be channeled through the new fund. The Green Climate Fund was established in South Korea in 2013 to help channel these monies for dealing with climate change from the developed to the developing world.

The main provisions of the Copenhagen Accord– including the 2C temperature goal – were built into the UN climate process in 2010 in Cancun.[77] Then, in 2011, in Durban, the COP launched yet another new try at concluding a new and comprehensive climate agreement.[78] With scientists pleading ever more urgently for climate action, the fervent hope of the willing was that the global solution the world had long sought for climate change would at last be found in Paris in December 2015.

On the long and rocky road of the UN climate regime from Rio in 1992 to Paris in 2015 were a number of recurring themes that posed recurring obstacles to a global solution. Not least, from the beginning, the UN climate process was heavily burdened by the tacit assumption of many of those engaged in the process that *there is one and only one global solution for climate change*, and that *this one solution must be imposed from the top down through one universal and comprehensive global agreement among all the governments of the world*. Proceeding from this assumption, the professed goal of vast numbers of the willing enlisted worldwide in combating climate change was, for many years, to deliver that single global solution once and for all in the form of a "universal and comprehensive climate treaty." Yet more than two decades of global conferences on climate change demonstrated that insistence on a single ideal solution – and nothing less – is a guarantee of no solution at all.

Another obstacle has been the process of decisionmaking. The effort to negotiate a global climate treaty was prolonged by the same need to reach a "consensus" that confounded the WTO in its vain travails to succeed in negotiating the Doha Development Round. The UNFCCC encourages consensus; it does not require it. It quite clearly permits voting, with each member of the COP having one vote.[79] But the COP has been unable to agree on procedures for voting, and thus, by default, a "consensus" is necessary for all decisionmaking. Consequently, as with the WTO, any one country has an effective veto over any global climate agreement. Furthermore, if the COP could ever get around to agreeing on how to vote, every state would be equal to every other state in voting. But is every state equal to every other in sharing the responsibility for addressing climate change? From the outset, the UNFCC has said "No." The UNFCCC speaks of "common but differentiated responsibilities and respective capabilities," and adds, "[a]ccordingly, the developed country Parties should take the lead in combating climate change and the adverse effects thereof."[80]

Other obstacles also frustrate global climate action. Most pervasive is the persistent deep division in the COP between the developed countries – the minority – and the developing countries – the majority – over whether the leading *historic* carbon emitters or the leading *current* carbon emitters should bear the greater burden of emissions cuts. In addition, there have been divisions among the developed countries between those that have favored binding quantitative limits on carbon emissions – such as many of the European countries – and those that have not – such as, for the most part, the United States. There have been divisions, too, among the developing countries. The island nations facing rising seas and, therefore, at most immediate climate risk, seek quick and decisive climate action. In contrast, many of the most populous and poverty-stricken of the developing countries seem more concerned about ensuring continued economic development than about taking ambitious climate action.[81] The sides along these climate dividing lines still do not yet see economy and environment as one.

Not least, there are also divisions *within* each country, developed and developing alike. Climate change may be global, but, true to the truism, all politics remains persistently local. The United States has been perhaps the noisiest about its own internal political divisions over how – and whether – to deal with climate change. There is a stubborn and short-sighted denial by many Americans of the reality of manmade climate change, and therefore of the need to do anything about it. This denial is fostered and financed by the deceit of vested fossil fuel interests that have a huge stake in perpetuating the carbon economy and oppose decarbonization. The ascendency of this denial to the upper reaches of the US government since the 2016 presidential election now sets the United States apart from every other country in the world in opposing climate action.

Running through all these divisions over how to confront climate change are the two separate threads of economic and environmental concern. Most of the willing from all over the world who have worked for so long and in so many ways for a global climate treaty have largely been motivated by the urgency of what they see as an imminent environmental crisis. So they have tended to see such a treaty mainly as the ultimate environmental agreement. Despite all the mounting evidence to the contrary, all too many of those committed to confronting climate change continue to see economics as only incidental to the environmental task of driving the world toward combating climate change. They tend to overlook the vital political fact that the economic aspirations affected by climate change make it also very much an economic issue. No matter the environmental urgency, and no matter the promises made in any climate agreement, unless and until climate change is addressed also as an economic issue with a multitude of economic manifestations, there will be no suitably ambitious climate solution.

Driving the popular resistance everywhere to taking national action to address climate change in the United States and elsewhere is the belief that taking such action is a "job-killing" threat to continued economic development. In reality, climate change itself is the threat to continued economic development. It is in *not* taking action on climate change that we threaten to undermine economic development. The prevailing perception of climate action as a "job-killer" must be changed. It can be changed only by changing how we see the relationship between the economy and the environment. The only effective and enduring response to the threat posed by climate change is a convergence of economy and environment that seeks economic development that is supportive of the climate, and that is therefore truly capable of achieving a sustainable prosperity for all.

THE PARIS CLIMATE AGREEMENT

At 7:26 p.m. Paris time, on Saturday evening, December 12, 2015, in the suburb of Le Bourget just north of the City of Light, delegates from 195 countries, weary and bleary-eyed after thirteen days of intense round-the-clock negotiations, and surrounded by extensive security following a lethal terrorist attack, joined in a consensus of the United Nations Conference of Parties in support of a new Paris climate agreement. For the first time, nearly every country in the world, rich and poor alike, committed to take action of some kind against the global threat of climate change by lowering emissions of carbon dioxide and other greenhouse gases. The more than 36,300 of the willing who had traveled from all over the world to participate as delegates in COP-21 joined in celebration of what they hoped would mark a historic and world-changing global "turn from fossil fuels."[82] The previous night, the Eiffel Tower had been illuminated with Ban Ki-Moon's ringing rallying cry – "No Plan B."[83] The COP had responded by achieving, at long last, a consensus. But on what precisely had 195 countries agreed as Plan A, how did they intend to implement their plan, and would their new global plan actually achieve the global goals for fighting climate change that were first agreed in the UNFCCC in 1992 – nearly a quarter of a century before the celebration in Paris?

Strictly speaking, Plan A consists of two linked international understandings, both reached at the same time in Paris. One is the twelve-page Paris Agreement, which adds some new bricks to the legal framework for the intended climate actions of the member countries of the COP, starting in 2020.[84] The other is an accompanying nineteen-page Decision, which describes what needs to be done by 2020 to "give effect" to those intended actions.[85] The Paris Agreement is legally binding; the accompanying Decision is not. The first of the 140 "decisions" made by the COP in the document accompanying the new climate agreement was to adopt the new agreement "under the United Nations Framework Convention on Climate Change."[86] So the Paris Agreement is, legally, an elaboration of the preexisting and thus previously ratified UNFCCC, which remains in force. It is a part of the still-evolving architecture of the UN climate framework. Chosen at the urging of the United States, this legal approach had the appealing political benefit of sparing the US administration at the time a pitched battle over ratification of a new treaty with a reluctant United States Senate.

Standing out above all else in the Paris Agreement is the extraordinary level of professed global ambition for climate action. The 195 countries reiterate in the agreement their 2C goal of "holding the increase in the global average temperature to well below 2 C above pre-industrial levels." In an expression of greater ambition, however, they also venture considerably beyond that familiar goal of climate campaigners by promising as an additional and aspirational goal "to pursue efforts to limit the temperature increase to 1.5 C above pre-industrial levels, recognizing that this would significantly reduce the risks and impacts of climate change."[87] To achieve these ambitions, the parties to the agreement "aim to reach global peaking of greenhouse gas emissions as soon as possible" and "to undertake rapid reductions thereafter . . . to achieve a balance between anthropogenic emissions by sources and removals by sinks of greenhouse gases in the second half of this century, on the basis of equity, and in the context of sustainable development and efforts to eradicate poverty."[88] Cutting through this typically convoluted COP wording, this talk of "balance" has the effect of legally committing these 195 countries to a common goal of carbon neutrality – to overall global carbon emissions of *net zero* – by the second half of this century.

The dozen pages of the Paris Agreement, which are largely procedural, bind every country and make clear that something of some sort is expected of every country in tackling climate change.[89] In this, the Paris climate agreement differs from the Kyoto Protocol. But, in expecting some climate action from each country, the Paris climate negotiators left it to each country to choose its own emissions-cutting and other climate-related targets and to pick its own preferred ways and means of meeting them. What is more, nothing whatsoever in the Paris Agreement mandates the meeting of these voluntary national targets, which have been described since the conclusion of the agreement as "Nationally Determined Contributions" – NDCs. The Paris Agreement does not impose a legal obligation on any country to do anything to cut carbon and other greenhouse gas emissions. Furthermore, there is nothing in the climate agreement that imposes any penalties on a country that does not meet its voluntarily announced climate targets.

Why should any country in the world bother to comply with a global climate agreement that is voluntary and non-binding and without penalties for non-compliance? Because, after a quarter of a century of trying, of failing and repeatedly failing, a consensus of almost every country in the world has at last put into place a global framework for addressing climate change that makes more ambitious cuts in carbon and other greenhouse gas emissions by every country possible. And because, without this global climate framework, global cuts in greenhouse gas emissions will surely fall far short of forestalling the worst damages of climate change. As David Victor explains the necessity of this global climate framework, "Paris is about the long game – laying a foundation for deeper cooperation as countries learn more about what they are willing and able to do."[90]

The shift from the "top down" to the "bottom up" in the global approach to international emissions-cutting is a central innovation of the Paris Agreement. Departing again from the Kyoto Protocol – and from all other previous attempts to reach a global climate agreement – no across-the-board cuts in carbon emissions are imposed on any country by the Paris climate accord. The COP abandoned in Paris its long-held top-down approach of cutting emissions across the board, and embraced instead the voluntary bottom-up approach of the Nationally Determined Contributions. Individual countries have pledged in their NDCs to begin by 2020 to cut their own carbon emissions by certain amounts of their own choosing either by 2025 or by 2030. The preparation, communication, and maintenance of these entirely voluntary national climate pledges are mandated by the new climate agreement.[91] The national climate pledges are nowhere incorporated in the Paris Agreement but have simply been recorded by each country in a form entirely of its own devising in a "public registry" of the UN climate framework.[92]

As to the precise content of these national pledges, the climate negotiators were able to agree only that, in communicating them, countries "shall provide the information necessary for clarity, transparency and understanding" in accordance with COP decisions.[93] Little more is specifically required. Furthermore, there are neither common definitions nor common metrics to employ in evaluating the implementation of the national climate pledges. Because the negotiating countries could reach no agreement on common standards for what should be included in these national pledges, or on what format they should assume, the pledges have little in common. They have assorted lengths and sundry forms. The measures, baselines, targets, terminology, and professed goals in the various national pledges are all vastly different. India, in its own climate pledge, movingly quotes the wisdom of Gandhi.

Unfortunately, the sum total of these voluntary national climate pledges does not add up to anything approaching the ambitious – but essential – level of global emissions cuts set out so boldly in the Paris Agreement. There is a considerable shortfall in the national pledges. Official UN estimates suggest that – even if all the pledges are kept – there would still be a rise of 2.7 degrees to 3.5 degrees Celsius (4.9 degrees to 6.3 degrees Fahrenheit) above pre-industrial levels. To be sure, this would be better than the temperature rise of between 3.3 degrees to 4.7 degrees Celsius (5.9 degrees to more than 8.4 degrees Fahrenheit) predicted by an MIT study if no climate actions were taken.[94] But this amount of global warming would be significantly above the goal of 2C set to avoid the worst ravages of climate change.[95] And it would be more than twice the ambitious goal for curbing climate change in the Paris Agreement of only 1.5 degrees Celsius.[96]

In reiteration of the UNFCCC, the new climate agreement reaffirms that developed countries "should continue taking the lead" in cutting carbon emissions.[97] In contrast to the Kyoto Protocol, however, the new agreement provides that – in accordance with their "respective capabilities" and "in the light of different national circumstances"[98] – developing countries "should continue enhancing their mitigation efforts, and are encouraged to move over time towards economy-wide emission reduction or limitation targets in the light of different national circumstances."[99] In plain words, the developing countries, like the developed countries, are all expected to pitch in to fight climate change as best they can, and to contribute more over time as they continue to grow.[100] As their circumstances change, as countries emerge and grow, as they grow richer, and as they contribute more to the accrual of global carbon emissions, they will be expected by other countries to do more to reduce them.

Even keeping global emissions relatively flat until 2030 will depend on the cooperation and participation of all countries. This is especially so of the largest emitters – such as China, the European Union, India, and the United States, which together are responsible for most of the world's greenhouse gas emissions. The United States now trails China as the world's leading emitter, but the United States has emitted more carbon historically than any other country, and the United States still leads the world by far in per capita carbon emissions. Twenty-one percent of the anticipated emissions cuts under the initial NDCs depend on the United States keeping its national pledge. "If the United States does not meet its commitment, global emissions will keep growing."[101] The United States thus remains central to combating climate change, and the continuing obligation of the United States to help provide global leadership on climate change must be made clear to all Americans.

The Paris Agreement is supposed to be "a progression over time."[102] A crucial part of Plan A for confronting climate change is to narrow the wide gap between the modest initial climate commitments by individual countries and their professed collective climate ambitions through a detailed follow-up "pledge-and-review" process that is described in the agreement. Anticipated is the facilitation through this process of a "ratcheting-up" over time of the initial ambitions of these voluntary national climate change pledges – with a stress on the sooner, the better.[103]

The success – or not – of this process will be the crucial factor in determining the ultimate success – or not – of the Paris Agreement.[104] Toward this end, countries have been encouraged to move ahead before 2020 with implementation of the necessary domestic measures to keep their initial climate pledges. National pledges may be adjusted by a country "at any time ... with a view to enhancing its level of ambition."[105]

Starting in 2018, the COP will meet every five years to take stock of global emissions cuts to date, compare them to what is needed to keep below 2C in global warming, and then determine how to "ratchet up" their climate ambitions.[106] The first such "global stocktake" has been set for 2018 so as to occur in concert with a scientific update of the climate situation by the IPCC. The next global stocktake will be in 2023.[107] By 2020, countries will be expected to submit new, updated climate pledges. This second set of pledges will be reviewed in 2023 to assess the extent to which they help meet the 2C goal. Unless decided otherwise, the COP will continue with these global stocktakes every five years after 2023, with countries repeatedly urging other countries to improve their voluntary national pledges. Implicit in the Paris Agreement is the expectation that it will work in no small part through continuous international peer pressure. The hope is that ongoing mutual peer pressure will contribute to an accelerating ratcheting-up of national climate actions, and that, through this unfolding global process, emissions-cutting will accelerate rapidly and will close the current gap between national climate pledges and international climate ambitions.

Along the way, mutual reporting of progress in keeping the national climate pledges is intended to reinforce and to enhance this expected ratcheting-up of national climate ambitions through the working of the new "transparency" rules in the Paris Agreement.[108] In negotiation after negotiation, the United States and other developed countries have long sought a common approach to "monitoring, reporting, and verification" (MRV) on climate matters for all countries. In particular, these developed countries and some others have maintained that professed national targets for climate action are meaningless without transparent MRV requirements. Before Paris, developed countries already reported their carbon emissions annually, and they also reported their progress toward emissions targets every two years. Up until Paris, developing countries had no such obligations. Overcoming the longstanding resistance of China and some other developing countries, the Paris Agreement has now changed this by establishing an "enhanced transparency framework" under which *every country* must "regularly" report its emissions and report its progress toward implementing its national climate pledge.[109]

The Paris Agreement establishes a new goal for "adaptation" – the offsetting measures that countries can take to prevent climate damage, such as by building defenses against flooding.[110] More stress on adaptation had been sought by poorer and more vulnerable countries, which are at much greater imminent risk of climate harm and cost. Previously, there was apprehension that a focus on adaptation might undermine efforts on mitigation. This concern remains but has now diminished. For many in the world, what once seemed the long term has become the now and the near term amid the results of melting glaciers, rising seas, intensified storms, and altered landscapes. In addition, the Paris Agreement acknowledges the importance of dealing with "loss and damage associated with the adverse effects of climate change" – such as storms and rising sea levels.[111] This was a hard-won negotiating victory for the same poorer and more vulnerable countries, which would like to be compensated by the developed countries for their climate losses and damages. It is, however, made clear in the accompanying Paris Decision that this part of the agreement "does not involve or provide a basis for any liability or compensation."[112] The international legal consequences of transboundary climate harm will thus be left to be litigated outside the UN climate regime.

Under the agreement, the technology efforts of the climate framework are to be vastly enhanced to help scale up the new innovations for climate mitigation and adaptation needed by developed and developing countries alike.[113] The shared aim is "fully realizing technology development and transfer in order to improve resilience to climate change and to reduce greenhouse gas emissions."[114] Toward this end, a "technology framework" has been established under the "technology mechanism" previously set up under the UNFCCC.[115] A particular purpose of this technology framework is to facilitate "collaborative approaches to research and development, and . . . access to technology" for developing countries, "in particular for early stages of the technology cycle."[116] Also, there is a whole series of provisions in the Paris Agreement intended to help countries confront the corrosive ravages of climate change. These provisions are supposed to facilitate "capacity-building" in developing countries – with priority for those with the least current capacity – for the construction of low-carbon, climate-resilient economies.[117] This will require money. The otherwise-varying national pledges of the developing countries are identical to the extent that they are all conditioned to at least some extent on the availability of the financing they claim they need to keep their national climate pledges.

Unquestionably, the developing countries need financial help to be able to succeed in the fight against climate change. This needed help will cost billions upon untold billions of dollars – annually. Where will we find all the money needed to pay for all this climate action? The answer emerging from the climate negotiations depends in no small part on the balance that is struck between the respective rights and obligations of developed and developing countries in dealing with climate change. How much of an obligation do the richer, developed countries that were the main original sources of climate-altering carbon emissions have to pay to help the poorer, developing countries confront the altered climate? And how much of a "right to development" do the poorer countries have to rely on carbon to catch up in their growth to the richer countries now that we know what the consequences are of such emissions – and now that the richer countries are no longer the major sources of emissions? People in the poorer countries think the rich in the world have no right to tell them they should not tap the cheap and abundant fossil fuels they see as the best currently available source of energy to lift them out of poverty.

The Paris Agreement does not provide an answer; but it does, in its legal bricklaying, begin to put into place a process that could lead to an answer. Despite the pleas of developing countries, there is no specific reference in the legally binding Paris Agreement to the amount of $100 billion annually that was promised by developed countries in Copenhagen as assistance to developing countries in confronting climate change.[118] That specific amount is mentioned only in the non-binding Paris Decision, where the sum of $100 billion annually is described as a "floor" for climate financing set through 2025.[119] Sometime before 2025, the Decision states, the parties to the Paris Agreement "shall set a new collective quantified goal."[120] The agreement provides that developed countries "should continue to take the lead in mobilizing climate finance."[121] It also says that "Other Parties are encouraged to provide such support voluntarily."[122] (For "Other Parties," read, in the minds of the climate negotiators: China.) What is more, the funds to be mobilized for climate finance are to come "from a wide variety of sources, instruments and channels, *noting the significant role of public funds.*"[123] This last phrase betrays a continuing bias in climate thinking – especially among the developing countries – toward traditional sources of funding in the form of direct governmental foreign aid. There is no specific mention of "business" or of "the private sector" in the provisions on climate finance in the Paris Agreement.

Nor, for that matter, is there any mention in the Paris Agreement of the "market." Despite the repeated urgings of the numerous business leaders and other allied advocates of private-sector solutions on the "observer" sidelines of the Paris negotiations, the COP could not, in the end, summon the needed consensus to include the word "market" in the climate agreement. As one analysis drily put it, "There was … a certain ideological opposition by some countries to the inclusion of any provisions that referred to markets, or could be seen as facilitating markets."[124] Instead, the Paris Agreement speaks only, and more vaguely, of "voluntary cooperation" in implementing the national climate pledges, and of "engaging on a voluntary basis in cooperative approaches that involve the use of internationally transferred mitigation outcomes."[125]

Even if these phrases are intended as surreptitious references to carbon trading, the apparent price of even these indirect allusions to the market and to market solutions to climate change was the inclusion also in the agreement of elusive language extolling the significance of "integrated, holistic and balanced non-market approaches" – whatever those may be – to implementing national climate pledges.[126] In implementing the agreement, one task is to pin down what else these "non-market approaches" are intended to be. So far, the nature, direction, and implications of these approaches are considerably less than clear.

There is likewise no specific mention of "carbon pricing" in the Paris Agreement. Although some countries sought to include the concept of putting a price on carbon in the climate agreement, there was considerably less than a consensus for such a bold act. Draft language on carbon pricing was dropped from the final text of the agreement, and instead a single orphan sentence was shoehorned into the tail-end passages of the non-binding Decision stating that the COP "recognizes the important role of providing incentives for emission reduction activities, including tools such as domestic policies and carbon pricing."[127] Whether this recognition would acquire any practical reality was left to the post-Paris proceedings.

There are other omissions from the Paris Agreement. Although aviation emissions and shipping emissions are growing rapidly as contributors to overall global carbon emissions, all references to both were deleted from the final text. Although efforts to reduce emissions from deforestation are covered, and although the threat to "food production" is mentioned once, short shrift is given overall to agriculture, which significantly affects and is much affected by climate change.[128] In addition, although the oceans soak up almost all the heat that accumulates in the atmosphere because of human activity, and are central to confronting climate change, the oceans are mentioned only once – in the preamble to the agreement – as being included in the planet's ecosystems, and are not specifically mentioned anywhere else.[129]

The word "trade," too, does not appear anywhere in the Paris Agreement; nor does the phrase "foreign direct investment." Trade and foreign direct investment both seem simply to have been left out of Plan A. There is much in the agreement that could affect trade or could be affected by trade. Indeed, about 45 percent of the national climate pledges include a direct reference to trade or to trade measures.[130] Trade-related elements in the NDCs that can present opportunities but can also pose conflicts between trade and climate governance include "reducing trade barriers, regulating trade on climate grounds, regulating timber trade, standards and labelling, border carbon adjustments, renewable energy, fossil fuel subsidy reform, international market mechanisms, technology transfer, response measures, and co-benefits" such as cleaner energy, improved health, and additional revenues for financing the achievement of education and other Sustainable Development Goals.[131] Yet there is nothing in the Paris Agreement that tells us how the trade and the climate regimes are to coexist – much less how they are to work together toward addressing climate change or achieving the other global goals of sustainable development. Much the same can be said of the treatment in the climate agreement of foreign direct investment. There is much in the agreement about money and much about climate finance; but there is no specific mention of the catalytic role of FDI.

There are some potentially significant legal implications in how the Paris Agreement deals with national measures that may be taken to respond to climate change. The preamble to the binding Paris Agreement does recognize that countries "may be affected not only by climate change, but also by the impacts of the measures taken in response to it."[132] In like vein, the non-binding Paris Decision states that due consideration must be given to "the social and economic impact of response measures."[133] Of more legal import, the binding agreement states, "Parties shall take into consideration in the implementation of this Agreement the concerns of Parties with economies most affected by the impacts of response measures, particularly developing country Parties."[34] Presumably, this admonition includes the impacts on international trade and on foreign direct investment. But there is no definition in the Paris Agreement of response measures, and there is no guidance on which national responses are appropriate as genuine climate measures and which are not.

Although trade is not mentioned in the Paris Agreement, the agreement was concluded "under" the UNFCCC. Thus, legally, respect must be given in actions in furtherance of the Paris Agreement, and in any disputes arising from those actions, to UNFCCC Article 3.5, which provides: "The Parties should cooperate to promote a supportive and open international economic system that would lead to sustainable economic growth and development in all Parties, particularly developing country Parties, thus enabling them better to address the problems of climate change. Measures taken to combat climate change, including unilateral ones, should not constitute a means of arbitrary or unjustifiable discrimination or a disguised restriction on international trade."[35] This last phrase is, of course, identical to that in the GATT setting out the conditions that must be met in justifying an exception to what would otherwise be a WTO trade obligation.

There is no climate enforcement system in the Paris Agreement. There was never even a real effort by the COP to contrive and include one. To be sure, the agreement does say that the provisions of the UNFCCC on the settlement of disputes shall likewise apply to the new agreement.[36] What the agreement does not say, though, is that the UNFCCC provisions on dispute settlement have never been used.[37] Since it was formed in 1992, the COP has never even been able to agree on procedures for conducting dispute settlement under the UNFCCC. This is one of the most significant shortcomings of the UN climate framework.

What will pass for dispute settlement under the pledge-and-review approach of the Paris Agreement will be a new and novel "mechanism to facilitate implementation of and precise compliance with" the provisions of the agreement.[38] It is emphasized, however, in the Paris Agreement that the transparent "expert-based" and "facilitative" implementation and committee contemplated by the agreement will be "non-adversarial and non-punitive."[39] Furthermore, it will have no enforcement powers. As with many multilateral environmental agreements, some of which have shown some success with this approach, the hope is that the peer pressure of "name and shame" will prove to be enough to promote compliance with the Paris Agreement.

After the initial euphoria in Paris, the early assessments of the Paris Agreement were mixed. Some disappointed climate scientists lamented that, because of the wide gap between the stated goals and the promised cuts, and because there was no clear way of enforcing the fulfillment of those promises, the agreement offered "false hope."[40] James Hansen, the NASA scientist who first drew US attention to climate change in the late 1980s, said, "It's a fraud really, a fake."[41] He and others fear the world will now mistakenly conclude that the problem of climate change has been solved, and move on to other, self-indulgent endeavors. For his part, Bjorn Lomborg, the provocative Danish developmental gadfly who styles himself "the skeptical environmentalist,"[142] said the agreement would achieve too little at too much cost because it was burdened by an abundance of misplaced priorities.[143] He and others compared the naïve idealism they saw in the aftermath of the Paris Agreement to the ill-fated Kellogg–Briand Pact – which outlawed war in 1928.[144]

Yet, many of the weary willing were elated in Paris by the success of their exhaustive efforts to conclude a universal climate agreement after more than two decades of trying.[145] They saw the new agreement as sending a strong signal of global commitments to a low-carbon future for the world.[146] Did the new climate accord in fact send such a signal? Post-Paris, this seemed to be the crucial question. Meanwhile, the willing assembled anew in the far-flung corners of the world to go about the tedious but urgent business of implementing the Paris Agreement – and of figuring out how the new climate agreement would fit into the wider work of accomplishing the world's newly agreed goals for sustainable development.

8

On Our Global Goals for Sustainable Development

Easier than defining sustainable development is to reduce it to a set of goals. In this way, the pursuit of sustainable development becomes a process, first of setting goals and then of striving to implement them. There are skeptics of such goal-setting who see it as a way of simply assembling a wish list of all that any of us might possibly desire. There are also defenders of such goal-setting who see it as a way of focusing collective actions toward specific shared ends. Some see setting goals as "the evolution from a primarily rules-based to a more goals-based system" of global governance.[1] Others see is as a prelude to more international rule-making. One of the exponents of goal-setting is the United Nations, which has been listing and pursuing development goals since shortly after the turn of the century, and is now busily pursuing its most ambitious goals yet.

SETTING GOALS FOR SUSTAINABLE DEVELOPMENT

The willing of the world have long sought to integrate what are commonly called the "three pillars" or the "three dimensions" of sustainable development – economic development, environmental sustainability, and social inclusion – into global goals on which all the countries of the world have agreed. In September 2015, they converged in the many thousands from all over the world in New York for the 70th General Assembly of the United Nations and for the announcement and celebration of their success in this prolonged undertaking with their agreement on global goals for the willing world. There – 43 years after the Stockholm convention first gave global voice to the concern for sustainability, 28 years after the Brundtland Commission gave initial global definition to "sustainable development," and 23 years after the Earth Summit in Rio de Janeiro gave global hope to all those who sought to give that elusive definition real meaning in the real world – 154 heads of state and other High Representatives of 193 countries adopted by consensus a declaration of their common goals entitled "Transforming Our World: The 2030 Agenda for Sustainable Development."[2]

"Transforming Our World" is "a call for action" in twenty-nine pages for a grand global experiment "to change our world" between 2015 and 2030.[3] It is "a broad and universal policy agenda" that can be seen as the ultimate expression of the Enlightenment Project.[4] Seventeen "Sustainable Development Goals" have been established as bold watchwords for all who seek the willing world. Listed along with these global goals are 169 "associated targets," including many that are seen as "means of implementation" to advance these goals in concrete ways.[5] The 17 goals and the 169 targets are described in this sweeping centerpiece of the "post-2015 development agenda" of the United Nations as "integrated and indivisible, global in nature and universally applicable."[6] They are "a to-do list for people and planet."[7] These 17 SDGs (in the inevitable acronymic parlance of the willing) together with their accompanying 169 targets set out "a supremely ambitious and transformational vision" of "a world free of poverty, hunger, disease, and want, where all life can thrive."[8]

Goal 1 of the seventeen is nothing less than to "End poverty in all its forms everywhere." This primary global goal is an absolute goal without even the quibble of a qualification. Those who signed the UN declaration for "Transforming Our World" have made this their first goal because "[w]e recognise that eradicating poverty in all its forms and dimensions, including extreme poverty, is the greatest global challenge and an indispensable requirement for sustainable development."[9] This first goal is imposing enough – but it is only the beginning. The remaining sixteen of the seventeen Sustainable Development Goals are all equally and "spectacularly ambitious," adding up to a long list of the loftiest long-held dreams of people everywhere.[10] Through several years of unprecedented outreach by the United Nations, literally millions of people in every part of the world participated in shaping this ultimate checklist for the willing. Since these grand global goals were officially blessed by the United Nations and "received with rapture" in New York in 2015, billions more people have been told about them again and again in an unprecedented UN outreach campaign of implementation.[11]

What are we to make of these global goals for sustainable development? Are they merely a chimera consisting of wishful words? Or are they truly goals around which the willing can rally to transform our unwilling into the willing world? Can these visionary goals be implemented? How can we implement them? How can we pay for implementing them? How can we monitor and measure our progress so we will know if and when they are in fact implemented? In search of the answers to these and other questions about the SDGs, we must recall first the MDGs – the Millennium Development Goals that preceded them.

THE MILLENNIUM DEVELOPMENT GOALS

Following the fanfare of the 1992 Earth Summit in Rio de Janeiro, the high hopes of the willing were dashed by the beginnings of the backlash against globalization. The Asian financial crisis of 1997 renewed the reservations of those in the developing world about the globalizing economy. The "Battle in Seattle" of anti-global protests at the WTO ministerial conference in 1999 symbolized the similar suspicions of many in the developed world. Trust in the United Nations and in other international institutions began to decline in every part of the world, diminishing hopes for increased international cooperation. Worldwide, there was little geopolitical elbow room at the turn of the century for pushing forward on all the global promises made in Rio.

Seizing on the fortuitous numerical fact that a new millennium was about to begin, the United Nations decided in 2000 to try to jumpstart global action for sustainable development with the identification of eight ambitious goals for development which soon came to be known as the Millennium Development Goals. Few in number and straightforward in expression, they were: (Goal 1) eradicate extreme poverty and hunger; (Goal 2) achieve universal primary education; (Goal 3) promote gender equality and empower women; (Goal 4) reduce child mortality; (Goal 5) improve maternal health; (Goal 6) combat HIV/AIDS, malaria, and other diseases; (Goal 7) ensure environmental sustainability; and (Goal 8) develop a global partnership for development. To achieve these eight goals, the MDGs included a limited number of mostly specific targets for each goal. Ultimately, there were twenty-two of these targets.[12]

The Millennium Development Goals theoretically applied to all countries, but actually the eight goals and twenty-two targets were focused mainly on developing countries, and mainly on the presence and the persistence of different aspects of extreme poverty in developing countries. In their specificity, the MDGs offered the world a gauge for calculating progress toward reducing global poverty.[13] In the fifteen years that followed, they provided the world with – as one of the ablest of the willing, John D. MacArthur, has put it – an "overarching vision" that "unified, galvanized, and expanded efforts to help the world's poorest people."[14]

At a United Nations conference on development finance in Monterrey, Mexico, in 2002, the developed countries agreed that – in exchange for a commitment to certain basic reforms by developing countries in poverty, health, and education – the "developed countries that have not done so" would "make concrete efforts toward the target of 0.7 percent of gross national income (GNI) as official development assistance to developing countries."[15] This aid target "implied more than tripling total global support" in aid for foreign development.[16] The Monterrey commitment was later reaffirmed by developed countries in 2008 – even amid the onset of a global financial crisis.[17] This ambitious aid target grabbed all the headlines in Monterrey. More foreshadowing of the future, though, was the bare beginning there of a broadening of the discussion of development finance – one that would in time come to include much more than merely direct governmental foreign aid.

Significantly, other sources of development finance besides direct governmental foreign aid were also considered at the Monterrey conference, such as international trade, foreign direct investment, and domestic savings and taxation. For development advocates long accustomed to viewing development as overwhelmingly a governmental endeavor, including the commerce of the private sector in the development discussion was a decided departure. Underscoring this departure was the mention in Monterrey of the central role of the market. For all the focus on governmental assistance, there was an inkling there of the potentially pivotal role that must be played by the private sector in sustainable development. Over time, it has become increasingly clear to many – although still far from all – that the market and the private sector are utterly indispensable means to attaining the global ends of sustainable development.

Looking back later, most of the willing seemed to see the role of the MDGs as largely that of a catalyst – as a practical and useful tool for inspiring more – and more varied – collective action.[18] But many also came to see the MDGs as too few and "too narrow" because they left out much that is essential to sustainable development.[19] In particular, Goal 7 of the MDGs – to "ensure environmental sustainability" – seemed to some to be an afterthought.[20] Moreover, the few targets listed for the goal of ensuring environmental sustainability seemed insufficient. As one example: The overall emphasis on reducing global poverty was most certainly right, but the goal of poverty reduction was not truly tied in the MDGs to the centrality of sustainability. Of most concern, there was no integration in the MDGs of economy, environment, and social inclusion. The "three dimensions" of sustainable development were left unlinked in their three separate silos of global endeavor.

At the end of 2015, the United Nations declared victory in its final assessment of the MDGs.[21] Highlighted in particular by the UN was the progress made toward the achievement of the targets of Goal 1 – eradicating extreme poverty and hunger. The final UN assessment noted that, "Globally, the number of people living in extreme poverty [had] declined by more than half, falling from 1.9 billion in 1990 to 836 million in 2015."[22] Similarly, on the global goal on hunger, the UN reported that the proportion of undernourished people in the developing regions of the world had fallen by almost half – from about 23 percent to about 13 percent over roughly the same period of time.[23] Significant progress was likewise claimed by the United Nations on the other goals. For example, the UN estimated that 7.6 million deaths had been prevented from HIV/AIDS, and that 6.2 million deaths had been averted from malaria – primarily of children under five in sub-Saharan Africa.[24]

All in all, MacArthur may be right in speaking of "roughly 15 million success stories, measured in lives saved" due to the MDGs.[25] Even so, and despite the UN's victory declaration, the MDGs had a "mixed report card."[26] Only five of the rich countries had kept the promise of foreign financial assistance they all made at the Monterrey conference in 2002.[27] Extreme poverty had indeed been reduced by half by yearend 2015, but it is unclear whether the MDGs caused this to happen. Most of the progress in reducing poverty during that time occurred in China – where there is scant evidence that any particular attention was paid during that time to the global clarion call of the MDGs. Ever eager (and rightly so) to remind their readers of the essential role of the market in making a more prosperous world, the leader writers for the *Economist* firmly concluded, "Most of the credit ... must go to capitalism and free trade, for they enable economies to grow – and it was growth, principally, that has eased destitution."[28]

And yet the businesses that drive economic development were not at the table where most of the most important decisions about the MDGs were made. Businesses and other advocates of market-based solutions were seated in the backs of the conference rooms and shunted to the sidelines of the unfolding succession of UN goal-setting summits. From there, they protested – to scant avail – that in the global pursuit of the Millennium Development Goals, all too much emphasis was being accorded to familiar pleas for old-fashioned top-down international governmental largesse, and all too little to free markets and the central catalyzing and growth-driving role of the initiative and the entrepreneurialism of free private enterprise.

THE SUSTAINABLE DEVELOPMENT GOALS

The din of the drumbeat of the willing in favor of crafting a set of new and updated global goals reached a crescendo amid the rain, the mud, and the noisy, endless traffic jams that graced the United Nations Conference on Sustainable Development held in Rio de Janeiro in June 2012, twenty years after the famous 1992 Rio Earth Summit – a conference that, in the inevitable shorthand, is widely known as Rio+20. The rain-soaked delegates to Rio+20 applauded the usefulness of goal-setting as illustrated by what they saw as the growing success of the Millennium Development Goals.[29] They called for the negotiation next of "Sustainable Development Goals" for the world that would "address and coordinate in a balanced way all three dimensions of sustainable development and their linkages" – economic, environmental, and social – and that would be integrated into the United Nations development agenda beyond 2015.[30] Toward this end, the United Nations then began an elaborate three-year global process that led ultimately to the global adoption of the Sustainable Development Goals.

In "Transforming Our World," the members of the United Nations state up front that their aim is to "build upon the achievements of the Millennium Development Goals and seek to address their unfinished business."[31] But the SDGs reach far beyond that. In establishing for the world "universal goals and targets" that "are integrated and indivisible and balance the three dimensions of sustainable development," those agreeing to the goals "pledge that no one will be left behind," and they pledge further that they "will endeavour to reach the furthest behind first."[32] Following this ringing declaration is a recitation of the 17 Sustainable Development Goals, accompanied by a list of the 169 targets that have been identified as means for fulfilling them. Remembering all these goals is no easy task.

Reportedly (and understandably), Ban Ki-Moon resorted to relying "on a laminated cheat sheet that he [kept] in his coat pocket,"[33] one that likely said:

- Goal 1: End poverty in all its forms everywhere.
- Goal 2: End hunger, achieve food security and improved nutrition and promote sustainable agriculture.
- Goal 3: Ensure healthy lives and promote well-being for all at all ages.
- Goal 4: Ensure inclusive and equitable quality education and promote lifelong learning opportunities for all.
- Goal 5: Achieve gender equality and empower all women and girls.
- Goal 6: Ensure availability and sustainable management of water and sanitation for all.
- Goal 7: Ensure access to affordable, reliable, sustainable and modern energy for all.
- Goal 8: Promote sustained, inclusive and sustainable economic growth, full and productive employment and decent work for all.
- Goal 9: Build resilient infrastructure, promote inclusive and sustainable industrialization and foster innovation.
- Goal 10: Reduce inequality within and among countries.
- Goal 11: Make cities and human settlements inclusive, safe, resilient and sustainable.
- Goal 12: Ensure sustainable consumption and production patterns.
- Goal 13: Take urgent action to combat climate change and its impacts.[34]
- Goal 14: Conserve and sustainably use the oceans, seas and marine resources for sustainable development.
- Goal 15: Protect, restore and promote sustainable use of terrestrial eco-systems, sustainably manage forests, combat desertification, and halt and reverse land degradation and halt biodiversity loss.
- Goal 16: Promote peaceful and inclusive societies for sustainable development, provide access to justice for all and build effective, accountable and inclusive institutions at all levels.
- Goal 17: Strengthen the means of implementation and revitalize the global partnership for sustainable development.

What stands out above all in the Sustainable Development Goals is the focus on fighting poverty. But, in contrast to the MDGs, the goal of the SDGs is not merely to eradicate extreme poverty; it is to *eliminate* all poverty. Goal 1 is purely and simply to "End poverty in all its forms everywhere." The targets linked to this goal are equally ambitious. Among them, first: "By 2030, eradicate extreme poverty for all people everywhere, currently measured as people living on less than $1.25 a day."[35] Next: "By 2030, reduce at least by half the proportion of men, women, and children of all ages living in poverty in all its dimensions according to national definitions."[36] In explaining why ending poverty is their primary goal, the shapers of the Sustainable

Development Goals say, forthrightly, in "Transforming Our World": "Billions of our citizens continue to live in poverty and are denied a life of dignity. There are rising inequalities within and among countries. There are enormous disparities of opportunity, wealth and power . . . We are committed to ending poverty in all its forms and dimensions, including by eradicating extreme poverty by 2030. All people must enjoy a basic standard of living, including through social protection systems."[37]

But an end to poverty is to be sought in a certain way. In contrast to the MDGs, the SDGs place the fight against global poverty within the wider context of the global struggle for sustainable development. The SDGs are not aimed primarily at poorer countries, but rather "involve the entire world, developed and developing countries alike."[38] These globally agreed goals are professed to be "integrated and indivisible," are said to "balance the three dimensions of sustainable development,"[39] and are intended to give global reality by 2030 to the Brundtland Commission's landmark definition in 1987 of "sustainable development."

Not surprisingly, the critics worldwide were quick to line up to lampoon these lofty new global goals. The sheer number of the goals and targets in the SDGs – many more than in the MDGs – drew by far the most immediate attention. There were, it was widely said, entirely too many of them.[40] How, it was widely wondered, would anyone ever be able to remember all seventeen of the global goals? Not everyone else in the world could carry along in a coat pocket a handy laminated cheat sheet listing all the seventeen goals. And wouldn't an extra pocket or two (or three) be needed to carry along also a list of all the 169 targets? What is more, even if some way were found to remember all the seventeen goals, how would any priorities be established among them?

To be sure, ending poverty is generally acknowledged as the primary goal. In theory, too, all the goals are interrelated and supposedly equal in priority. Yet, as the *Financial Times* intoned, "If everything is a priority, nothing is a priority."[41] Not to be outdone, and seemingly even less impressed, the *Economist* archly observed, "Moses brought ten commandments down from Mount Sinai. If only the UN's proposed list of Sustainable Development Goals (SDGs) were as concise."[42] Even more than the number of goals, the critics were concerned about the much more lengthy number of targets, with Bjorn Lomborg speaking for many others in saying, "Having 169 priorities is like having none at all."[43]

On the right, George Russell of the self-proclaimed "fair and balanced" Fox News in the United States grumbled that, "A better description of the SDGs than a 'transformative vision' might be a sprawling and shapeless bid to establish a truly global and socialist agenda, not to mention a blank check required for trillions of dollars annually in development spending to achieve – if achievable."[44] At the same time, on the left, the American historian Glen David Kuecker said that, "Like lipstick on a pig, the SDGs are a continuation of the thinking within the [MDGs'] approach to global poverty offering nothing more than a cosmetic makeover . . . putting lipstick on the pig of colonialism. The [MDGs'] brand of lipstick attempted to lift people out of poverty by promoting economic growth, while refusing to acknowledge that this capitalist cure was the cause of the ill it created in the first place. The [SDGs] retain the growth paradigm, while tinting the lipstick's color with 'sustainability.'"[45]

Thus, with the SDGs, as so often, the extremes of competing ideological views of the world offer only rhetoric, not answers. They proceed from their contrasting conceptions of the world. They do not proceed from facts or result from reasoned analysis. They leave no room for finding common ground. One of the two extremes claims that the SDGs seek to abolish global capitalism; the other claims that the SDGs seek further to enshrine it. Perhaps the truth of what the SDGs are – and, more important, of what they can become through the collaborative labors of millions of the willing in the world between now and 2030 – is to be found somewhere in the "in between" of doing it.

The combined effect of an assembled army of the willing is evidenced in the text of the SDGs. There was "intense political lobbying by every group that wants their issue represented on the international agenda."[46] In the skeptical eyes of some, "[t]he result is a long and entirely unattainable wish-list of development targets that utterly fails to prioritize those areas on which international coordination and goal setting is both desirable and feasible."[47] The International Council for Science and the International Social Science Council – active supporters of global goal-setting and also of the Sustainable Development Goals – have reported that fewer than one-third of the SDGs are "well developed," and that more than one-half "should be more specific."[48] Now, in the evolving process of implementing the global goals, reductionism reigns. Each of the global interest groups that invested so much effort during the run-up to the New York summit in securing a foothold for their favorite interest in the form of a passage, or at least a passing reference, in the SDGs has been equally assiduous since the summit in explaining why their particular interest is the one that transcends all the rest.

Thus, it has been asserted – with equal fervor and with equal conviction – that the single key to the success of the Sustainable Development Goals is agriculture,[49] education,[50] environmental protection,[51] forest protection,[52] water management,[53] curbing youth unemployment,[54] ensuring gender equality,[55] reducing extreme inequality,[56] weaning ourselves off fossil fuels,[57] and establishing peace and just-ice.[58] It has been said also that the key to attaining global sustainable development is adopting new eating habits that move us toward a mostly plant-based diet in which we choose kale over steak by eating less red meat, "which consumes 11 times more water and results in five times more climate-warming emissions than chicken or pork."[59]

Reducing all the world's agreed goals into the one goal that seems to stand out as the most important of all can hardly be avoided in an endeavor fueled by the combined passions of so many of the willing in the world who have devoted so much of their lives to so many singular – and singularly essential – causes. And, of course, almost every one of these assertions is in its own way absolutely and undeniably correct. Yet, this conceded, the main message of sustainable develop-ment is that, in the end, all these essential and seemingly separate global causes are in fact *connected*. In the final analysis, too, there is something to be said for managing somehow to express in writing the complex connections of all the vast and varied wants of the world in a mere seventeen goals on which nearly 200 countries have agreed.

The United Nations has established a "High-Level Political Forum on Sustainable Development" to monitor and mobilize continuing support for the accomplishment of these global goals as a central part of the UN 2030 Agenda. This forum is meeting annually and, every four years, convenes as a meeting of heads of state. It is also "voluntary and country-led" and features "reviews at regional and global levels" of national progress toward sustainable development.[60] Forty-three countries presented "voluntary national reports" at the forum's annual meeting in 2017. One group of the willing, however, described the session as "lackluster and wanting in the urgency and leadership that the 2030 Agenda and the state of the world today seem to demand."[61] The United States, under new leadership after the US presidential elections, "suggested that its support of the entire Agenda may be in question."[62] And a grand total of 90 minutes was devoted to the topic of global partnerships.[63]

How do we get from here to fulfillment of the SDGs by the UN's agreed deadline of 2030? In one of the many celebratory speeches at the New York summit that approved the SDGs in 2015, Prime Minister Erna Solberg of Norway summed up this global challenge by invoking "the famous philosopher Elvis Presley," who urged, "[a] little less conversation, a little more action please."[64]

MEASURING AND FINANCING THE SDGS

Action began in earnest on any number of SDG fronts soon after the New York summit. Take one example among many worldwide: Goal 3 – "Ensure healthy lives and promote well-being for all at all ages" – which is accompanied by thirteen targets, including Target 3.3 – "By 2030, end the epidemics of AIDS, tuberculosis, malaria and neglected tropical diseases and combat hepatitis, water-borne diseases and other communicable diseases."[65] Toward this end, less than one week after the summit, the World Health Organization announced stepped-up efforts to get HIV antiretroviral medications out for early treatment and prevention of AIDS.[66] Simul-taneously, billionaire philanthropist Bill Gates announced that the Bill and Melinda Gates Foundation would focus on the eradication of malaria.[67] Actions, however, must be measured by some agreed means to determine whether they in fact fulfill goals, and many have wondered whether progress toward fulfilling the vast hopes given voice in the SDGS can truly be measured. Just three weeks after the summit, newly minted Nobel economics laureate Angus Deaton, certainly a supporter of a shared global development, said of the SDGs, "I'm not a big fan. There's no way to measure them."[68]

Those who advised the UN on making the SDGs identified the crucial need for a "data revolution for sustainable development," explaining that there is a worldwide need to strengthen the extent and the quality of data and of statistics "for accountability and decision-making purposes," and especially to make certain that the SDGs "reach the neediest, and find out whether they are receiving essential services."[69] Equally, there is need for "new technology, crowd sourcing, and improved connectivity" that offer new opportunities for enhancing data, particularly in the least-developed countries.[70] The SDGs and their targets are to be reviewed systematically using a set of more than 300 global – and largely quantitative – "indicators." These indicators are needed because "[q]uality, accessible, timely and reliable disaggregated data will be needed to help with the measurement of progress and to ensure that no one is left behind."[71] Data is often incomplete. Or it is inaccurate. Or it is out of date. Or it is driven by donor priorities or corporate interests or bureaucratic biases. Or even deception. What is more, all too often, available data omits those on the margins of society.

Consider, for instance, Goal 5 – "Achieve gender equality and empower all women and girls." (And note that, whereas the goal of the MDGs was to "promote" gender equity, the far more ambitious goal of the SDGs is to "achieve" it.) Women and girls account for half of the world's population and represent half of its economic and other potential. Yet gender discrimination is evident everywhere in the world. At the same time, the metrics we need to measure such abuses as child marriage, female genital mutilation, human trafficking, and other forms of violence against women are sorely lacking. Only 13 percent of countries dedicate a budget to gender statistics. Only 15 percent of countries have legislation that mandates specialized gender-based surveys. Only 41 percent of countries regularly produce data on violence against women.[72] The same absence of data hinders the measurement of progress on many of the other Sustainable Development Goals.

Given that the overarching goal of the SDGs is literally to "[e]nd poverty in all its forms everywhere," it may be that the moving target of measuring the global level of poverty is the best illustration of the elusiveness of data. What, after all, is "poverty," and how should we measure it? On these questions, there is an ongoing evolution in metrics that will have much to do with determining whether we will, in the end, measure this primary goal of the SDGs as having been achieved by 2030. Not long after the New York summit, the World Bank raised the international poverty line from $1.25 per day to $1.90 per day, taking into account its calculations of the "purchasing power parity" of different levels of income in different countries.[73] As a result, the bank's economists were able to report that global poverty had fallen below 10 percent for the first time.[74] Reacting to this announcement, one economist compared the official data to the early European maps of the unknown interior of Africa, saying that such conclusions about the level of poverty "are still basically built on tall tales of mythical creatures."[75] To diminish such doubts, the willing are proceeding with what they hope will be a "data revolution" resulting from the pursuit of the SDGs. The monitoring of the SDGs requires significant additional investments in data collection of all kinds and at all levels.[76] Although the World Bank says it is an overstatement, one of the experts advising the Copenhagen Consensus Center has estimated a cost of $250 billion just to monitor and measure the SDGs.[77]

Assuming we can figure out how to measure progress toward achieving the SDGs, where will the money come from to pay for achieving them? And how much money will be needed to achieve them? The United Nations estimates the needed funding at $37 billion annually to achieve universal health care, $42 billion annually to achieve universal primary education and to expand access to lower secondary education, and $62 billion annually to eradicate extreme poverty.[78] The UN tells us, too, that $5 trillion to $7 trillion will be needed annually worldwide to meet investment requirements in infrastructure, and that in order to fulfill the goals and targets relating to climate change, several trillion dollars more per year must be spent on "additional requirements" for "sustainable development."[79] International financial institutions have pegged the total global price tag for the SDGs during the fifteen years from 2015 to 2030 at $172.5 trillion. The sticker shock of this huge number is eased somewhat by the fact that the vast majority of this needed funding will come from the ordinary course of national budgets. Even so, estimates are that about $3 trillion – annually – in what the willing call "new money" must somehow be found to fulfill the SDGs. To put the tidy sum of this global funding gap in some perspective, the advocacy group One – founded by the Irish rock star Bono – has pointed out that $1 trillion is enough to buy every person on the planet – each and every one of the more than 7 billion of us – a Starbucks latte every day for a month.[80]

There is, in "Transforming Our World," a dutiful reiteration of the original goal of the Monterrey conference in 2002 that developed countries will devote 0.7 percent of their gross national income to overseas development assistance.[81] This goal is no closer to being achieved now than it was in 2002. The OECD average in 2014 was about 0.39 percent.[82] The total of governmental spending earmarked for foreign aid by developed countries worldwide that year was $135 billion – substantially less than private foreign direct investment of $680 billion and foreign remittances of $430 billion.[83] For this reason, the World Bank and other international financial institutions have coined the phrase "Billions to Trillions" to suggest the steep ascent of the funding slope facing the world in pursuing the global goals, which requires an entirely new way of approaching development.[84]

Slowly, ever so slowly, it has begun to dawn on some – but still far from all – of those in search of global sustainable development that the money to pay for much of it must come from somewhere other than the public treasuries. This is evident in the declaration of the United Nations' Third International Conference on Financing for Development in Addis Ababa in July 2015 – the Addis Ababa Action Agenda – which was, soon afterwards, made legally a part of the SDGs as a part of "Transforming Our World."[85] The familiar recitations about foreign aid are still there; despite all, it remains the hope of the poorer countries that the richer countries will eventually ante up through further "international development cooperation."[86] But also a target of a proposed "global framework for financing development post-2015" is "domestic and international private business and finance."[87] In words that did not often appear in the global developmental declarations of the previous decades, the Addis Ababa declaration goes so far as to say, "Private business activity, investment, and innovation are major drivers of productivity, inclusive economic growth, and job creation."[88]

This belated acknowledgment by the UN of the role of the private sector as a driver of growth prompted at least one group of NGOs to criticize the declaration for a "misplaced optimism towards private finance."[89] Civil society organizations lamented that, in terms of traditional governmental foreign aid, the Addis Ababa conference "had brought no new money to the table."[90] They could not see what any economist could have told them: All money is fungible. All money is equally available to be spent, if we choose, in pursuit of sustainable development. As an example, the private sector will, unavoidably, play a major, inevitable, and indispensable role in one of the "systemic" innovations established in the Addis Ababa Action Agenda and later folded into the Sustainable Development Goals – the so-called Technology Facilitation Mechanism,[91] and also in the new technology framework established by the Paris Agreement to confront climate change, which is meant to include the private sector.[92] The development and diffusion of the new green technologies that are drivers of sustainable development cannot be accomplished without the active engagement of the principal source of the innovations leading to new technologies – the private sector.

TRADE, INVESTMENT, AND THE SDGS

Trade was addressed – but not particularly emphasized – in the MDGs.[93] In contrast, trade appears in many places in the Sustainable Development Goals. Trade-related targets are found throughout the pages of "Transforming Our World." As with the MDGs, two of the SDG targets are to promote the multilateral trading system and to increase "significantly" the exports of developing countries.[94] Added now in the SDG targets are specific references to concluding the Doha Development Round and to succeeding in the current initiative to provide "duty-free and quota-free" access for least-developed countries to the markets of the developed world.[95] Scattered elsewhere among the 169 targets of the SDGs are other references to trade and to trade-related concerns.

One target is to increase "Aid for Trade" to help provide developing countries – "in particular least developed countries" – with the technical capabilities to engage in trade.[96] Another target – and an all-consuming but ever-elusive goal of the global trading system for decades – is to "[c]orrect and prevent trade restrictions and distortions in world agricultural markets, including through the parallel elimination of all forms of agricultural export subsidies and all export measures with equivalent effect, in accordance with the mandate of the Doha Development Round."[97] Yet another target contemplates access in developing countries "to affordable essential medicines and vaccines, in accordance with the Doha Declaration on the TRIPS Agreement and Public Health" of the WTO, which affirms the right of developing countries to use the flexibilities of WTO intellectual property rules "to protect public health, and, in particular, provide access to medicines for all."[98] Still another SDG target contains a reminder that – in pursuit of Goal 10, to "[r]educe inequality within and among countries" – countries should "[i]mplement the principle of special and differential treatment for developing countries, in particular least developed countries, in accordance with World Trade Organization agreements."[99]

Standing out also among the many trade-related targets are two at the intersection of trade and sustainable development that are likely to draw much attention in the years leading to 2030. One of these two targets is to "prohibit certain forms of fisheries subsidies" that contribute to overcapacity and overfishing; "eliminate" others that contribute to illegal, unreported, and unregulated fishing ("IUU" fishing); and refrain from introducing new such subsidies.[100] These abuses and distortions affecting the livelihoods and the food supply of billions of people worldwide are already on the Doha Development Agenda of the WTO and the subject of ongoing negotiations. The other target is to "[r]ationalize inefficient fossil-fuel subsidies."[101] This profoundly significant global issue is not – yet – a negotiating topic in the WTO.

Without the slightest qualification, "Transforming Our World" identifies trade as a means of implementation for the Sustainable Development Goals, declaring that "[i]nternational trade is an engine for inclusive economic growth and poverty reduction, and contributes to the promotion of sustainable development."[102] The Addis Ababa Action Agenda – which has, again, been made a part of the SDGs – goes even further in listing trade as one of the seven "action areas" of financing for development: "Meaningful trade liberalization encourages long-term investment in productive capacities. With appropriate supportive policies, infrastructure and an educated work force, trade can also help promote productive employment and decent work, women's empowerment, and food security, as well as a reduction in inequality and contribute to achieving the SDGs."[103]

For these reasons, the members of the United Nations pledged in Addis Ababa that "[w]e will endeavor to significantly increase world trade in a manner consistent with the SDGs," and, in a telling statement with potentially profound and funda-mental implications for global trade policy and for many of the same countries in their guise as the members of the WTO, "[w]e will integrate sustainable develop-ment into trade policy at all levels."[104] Tellingly, UN members have included in their declaration of the SDGs the following assertion echoing the UN climate frame-work convention: "States are strongly urged to refrain from promulgating and applying any *unilateral* economic, financial or trade measures not in accordance with inter-national law and the Charter of the United Nations that impede the full achievement of economic and social development, particularly in developing countries."[105]

All this is entirely too much for some of those who oppose trade and yet profess to support sustainable development. One joint "civil society" response to the conclusion of the Addis Ababa conference lamented that it included "no critical assessment of trade regimes: Instead of safeguarding policy space, the Addis Agenda fails to critically assess international trade policy in order to provide alternative paths."[106] At least one anti-globalist group has insisted that an unraveling of the entire trade regime away from the basic principles of free trade is needed to fulfill the SDGs.[107] The truth is precisely the opposite. Largely overlooked in all the discussion of the Sustainable Development Goals has been the fact that, of the SDG targets offering the biggest likely returns for every dollar spent, by far the biggest bang for the buck is to be found in lowering barriers to trade, "which achieves far more per dollar spent than any other option."[108] Economists commissioned by the Copenhagen Consensus Center to do a cost–benefit analysis of the SDGs calculated that completing the unfinished Doha Development Agenda of the WTO would return $2,000 to the world as a whole for every dollar spent – and would return to developing countries $3,400 for every dollar spent.[109] They added that merely freeing trade on a regional basis among some of the Asia-Pacific countries – such as contemplated through the Trans-Pacific Partnership – would return $1,200 to the world for every dollar spent – and would return to developing countries $1,900 for every dollar spent.[110]

The Copenhagen analysts have suggested that additional gains could result from freeing trade in services, which "account for increasing shares of total value-added in production and trade as well as of employment in virtually all economies."[111] They have argued also that additional gains can be derived from focusing on reducing the costs of trading, because this would allow governments to work with all involved to lower all the barriers to trade, including non-tariff trade barriers, trade infrastructure, and other domestic trade hurdles.[112] In addition, they say, there is much to be gained by improving the global connections to global value chains – especially in developing countries. Small and medium-sized enterprises all over the world link to the wider world economy by climbing onto the global value chains of larger companies. Special attention must be paid, the Copenhagen economists advise, to the WTO Aid for Trade initiative and other efforts to tackle the "supply-side capacity constraints" that developing countries frequently face in trying to link to and profit from these chains of global production.[113]

World Bank models suggest that a global free trade agreement "could add $5 trillion to the world's GDP by 2020, $3 trillion of which would go to developing countries. And, by the close of this century, such a deal could increase global GDP by more than $100 trillion, with most of the gains accruing outside developed nations."[114] Moreover, as the flip side of trade, foreign direct investment cannot be ignored in the furtherance of the SDGs. If freeing trade is the best means of implementing the SDGs, then freeing investment must be among the best. Economies advance everywhere when they are open to more foreign investment. The challenge is to free investment in a sustainable way. Scrutiny of the vast majority of the processes relating to the SDG targets shows that all of them "will, one way or other ... increase demands for quantitatively more investment that is also qualitatively more sustainable."[115]

Toward this end, an UNCTAD Action Plan for investment in sustainable development focuses on mobilizing and maximizing private investment in sectors related to the SDGs while minimizing the environmental risks of investment.[116] All this must be done, say the UNCTAD analysts, within an "investment policy framework" for sustainable development.[117] Creating the need for sustainable investment, UNCTAD says, is an "investment gap for developing countries" of "about $2.5 trillion per year, mainly for basic infrastructure, food security, climate change adaptation, health, and education."[118] A major role for the private sector through trade and investment in closing this sizeable "investment gap" is indispensable, for the investment needs of the world simply "outstrip the ability to finance investments through public expenditures, even in developed countries."[119]

THE PIVOT OF PARTNERSHIPS

Partnerships are the pivot of the Sustainable Development Goals. The last of the global goals – Goal 17 – is to "[s]trengthen the means of implementation and revitalize the global partnership for sustainable development." This one goal is central to all the others. Finance, technology, trade, and capacity-building in developing countries are all seen as essential means for achieving this goal. So too is the "data revolution." So also – and significantly – are "multi-stakeholder partnerships," for which there are two listed SDG targets.

One of these two SDG targets is to "[e]nhance the global partnership for sustainable development, complemented by multi-stakeholder partnerships that mobilize and share knowledge, expertise, technology and financial resources, to support the achievement of the sustainable development goals in all countries, in particular developing countries."[120] The other of these targets is to "[e]ncourage and promote effective public, public–private and civil society partnerships, building on the experience and resourcing strategies of partnerships."[121] Wordy and windy as these two particular targets for global partnerships may be, they may also turn out to be the key to unlocking the ultimate achievement of the Sustainable Development Goals. One especially clever group of the willing has drawn a Venn diagram consisting of a number of overlapping circles to illustrate the interrelationships among the seventeen "integrated" SDGs. At the center of the diagram – and part of each of the overlapping circles – is a shaded area captioned "Global Partnerships."[122]

The eighth of the Millennium Development Goals – much less precise than most of the others – was to "develop a global partnership for development." This was an amorphous goal, entirely without definition. Even so, this MDG goal inspired such successful global initiatives as the Global Fund to Fight AIDS, Tuberculosis and Malaria and the Gavi Alliance on vaccines. Inspired by these and other successes in furtherance of the MDGs, those assembled for the Rio+20 conference in 2012 established a registry in the United Nations for voluntary initiatives throughout the world that promote sustainable development, and launched an effort to track these "action networks" and to inspire more.[123] By the time the Sustainable Development Goals were adopted three years later, about 1,800 such initiatives had been registered. They ranged all across the sweep of global concern, from health to education to transportation.[124] The vast variety of voluntary action manifested in these multi-stakeholder partnerships is shown merely by listing only a few random examples: the Sustainable Energy for All Initiative, the Action Network on Sustainable Transport, the Partnership for Small Island Developing States, the Higher Education Sustainability Initiative, and Every Woman Every Child. There was little of shared concern to the willing of the world that was not already on the UN registry list in the final run-up to the adoption of the SDGs in New York in 2015. That list continues to lengthen now.

If partnerships are the pivot of the Sustainable Development Goals, then the private sector will, necessarily, often be the pivot of many of the most vital of those partnerships. Where once the role of the private sector was an afterthought in the thinking of most of the willing about how they might attain their global goals, now many of them are rightly and increasingly seeing business as central to their hopes for "transforming our world." Tucked into the back pages of their bold declaration of the SDGs is a spare paragraph acknowledging that "[p]rivate business activity, investment and innovation are major drivers of productivity, inclusive economic growth and job creation," and calling "on all businesses to apply their creativity and innovation to solving sustainable development challenges."[125]

Some who are mindful of the catalytic role of the private sector in making the most of market opportunities maintain that "the only UN sustainable development goal needed is economic freedom."[126] They have a point – to a point. Economic freedom is indispensable to the attainment of the global goals. But economic freedom works best through a competitive market capitalism in an enabling environment blessed by the rule of law and by the right mix of market freedom and common-sense regulation. To achieve the Sustainable Development Goals, this right mix must be found in blending economy and environment into one in the willing world. If, in the end, the SDGs are to be more than merely words, then businesses worldwide must be much in the midst of giving those words reality in defining sustainable development by doing it.

Furthermore, if partnerships of all kinds are to prove effective in catalyzing the global accomplishment of the SDGs through markets and other means, then many of our goals must be transformed into enabling rules and rules frameworks at multiple levels of governance. As Oran Young, a leading thinker on global governance, has said, "Goals in the absence of rules are apt to degenerate into vague aspirations that everyone embraces conceptually but that no one knows how to fulfill in practice."[127] Goals are not universal substitutes for rules. To be achieved, goals must often be forerunners to rules.

9

On the Unfolding of International Economic and Environmental Law in Our Unwilling World

Globalization compels improvisation in the quest for the international rule of law. While the willing of the world continue their quest for consensus on new and universal economic and environmental arrangements, the world continues to turn, and economic and environmental concerns continue to collide. These collisions reveal the inadequacies of current rules and give rise to international and other transnational disputes that require the drawing in each instance of the right line between the competing claims of the economy and the environment.

A difficult challenge confronts those entrusted with cooperating in drawing the right lines when agreeing on international rules and when rendering judgments in resolving disputes about what those rules mean. This challenge is made all the more difficult in a world where so many of the international rules we need are still missing because we have not yet been able to summon the political will to agree on them. Where relevant rules already exist in the form of international agreements, the challenge is to uphold those rules, and to delineate the right lines in upholding them by interpreting and applying them in the right way. Where no relevant rules exist, the temptation is to try to fit a dispute into the scope of the existing rules – not always a ready fit. Where relevant rules exist in both international economic and environmental agreements, the challenge is to shape coherence by drawing a line that rightly resolves the seeming contradictions between them while giving the intended meanings to both of them. Meeting this challenge in this ongoing improvisation demands a scrupulous respect for the international rule of law.

The framers of the Sustainable Development Goals are mindful that the willing world is a world blessed by the rule of law. On the rule of law, as on so much else, there are bold words in the SDGs. Goal 16 is nothing less than a call to "[p]romote peaceful and inclusive societies for sustainable development, provide access to justice for all and build effective, accountable and inclusive institutions at all levels."[1] Among the dozen equally ambitious targets listed for measuring the fulfillment of Goal 16 is

Target 16.3 – to "[p]romote the rule of law at the national and international levels and ensure equal access to justice for all."

It took quite a struggle to get Goal 16 on the list. On the eve of the New York summit where the SDGs were adopted in 2015, the ambassador of the United States to the United Nations at the time, Samantha Power, recalled the difficulty of this diplomatic struggle: "Today the data linking peace, justice, and good governance with sustainable development is overwhelming ... And yet, in spite of this overwhelming evidence, when the world came together to lay out a roadmap for sustainable development for the next 15 years, there was adamant resistance to including a goal on advancing peace and good governance. Not only from autocratic governments – though of course they fought against it – but also, counterintuitively, from some democratic countries with vibrant civil societies, whose recent history is testament to the growing opportunities and the growing prosperity that come with increasing stability and accountability."[2]

To date, the worldwide engagement of the willing on behalf of the rule of law has centered on the daunting task of establishing and upholding the rule of law *within* countries, and not so much *between* them. The importance of ensuring the rule of law *within* countries can hardly be overstated. Equally important, though, is ensuring the rule of law *between* countries. As Target 16.3 states, the rule of law is essential "at the national and international levels" to "ensure equal access to justice for all." To meet this target, the rule of law must be established and upheld nationally *and internationally*, and success at both levels must be pursued simultaneously. Making the achievement of such success all the more difficult – both nationally and internationally – is the complicating fact that the need for the rule of law at one level is linked to the need at the other.

Adam Smith understood the twofold need for the rule of law *between* countries as well as *within* countries, lamenting that: "The love of our nation often disposes us to view, with the most malignant jealousy and envy, the prosperity and aggrandizement of any other neighbouring nation. Independent and neighbouring nations, *having no common superior to decide their disputes*, all live in a continual dread and suspicion of one another. Each sovereign, expecting little justice from his neighbours, is disposed to treat them with as little as he expects from them. The regard for the law of nations, or for those rules which independent states profess or pretend to think themselves bound to observe in their dealings with one another, is often very little more than mere pretense and profession. From the smallest interest, upon the slightest provocation, we see those rules every day either evaded or directly violated without shame or remorse."[3]

Smith's observation in the eighteenth century applies equally to the thinking of many countries in the twenty-first century. In our unwilling world, "having no common superior to decide their disputes," and expecting little justice from their neighbors, what then are sovereign states to do? What is there to stop the most powerful of states from simply imposing their sovereign will on other, less powerful states, like the ancient Athenians did on Melos? To have any real meaning, rules must be followed. Sometimes international rules are followed simply because they ought to be. This is as it should be. Yet this thin reed of national compliance with international law is nothing on which we can rely too much in a world in which human nature has not changed. More often, international rules will be followed only if there is a price to be paid for not following them. International rules must, therefore, be enforced through the international rule of law.

Economically, the world is much farther along toward the international rule of law on trade than on investment. Environmentally, approaches toward upholding general international environmental rules are much more advanced than those relating specifically to climate change. Economically and environmentally, the silos of separate concern that prevail and persist in other ways likewise prevail and persist legally. Moreover, all in all, what progress we have managed to make so far in our unwilling world toward establishing and upholding the international rule of law on the economy and on the environment has accomplished all too little toward heeding the imperative of sustainability by seeing the economy and the environment as one.

THE JEWEL IN THE CROWN

According to one insightful legal scholar, Cesare Romano, "the law and procedure of international dispute settlement [have] long been the Cinderella of international law, neglected both by international legal scholarship and [by] diplomats."[4] Yet, inspired first by the need to establish international ways of preventing a Third World War, and sped lately by the need to find ways of furthering globalization and also of dealing with the fallout from globalization, there has been an explosion of international law – and equally a proliferation of what purports to be international law – since the end of the Second World War. And much of the legal pioneering on the pristine cutting edge of international law has been done through international dispute settlement.

While the willing have labored and so far largely fallen short in fashioning the global architectural framework of rules the world requires for sustainable development, what there is of an international legal structure to spur and to support sustainable development has been shaped in no small part *ad hoc* through the accumulation in various international legal settings of a proliferation of international dispute rulings. These legal rulings highlight many of the most pressing of the new issues of sustainable development, rendering judgment on some of those issues that can no longer be ignored and hinting in their holdings at the way forward. Nowhere is this prevailing practical reality more evident than in the rulings now routinely emerging from the peaceful resolution of international trade disputes in WTO dispute settlement.

It is in the dispute settlement mechanism of the WTO where we have seen most of all the recent unfolding of the international rule of law. More than 500 international trade disputes resulted in formal legal complaints in WTO dispute settlement during the first two decades of the WTO.[5] This total is several times the number of disputes heard by the United Nations International Court of Justice in The Hague during the entirety of its century-long history. A great many more than this rapidly growing number of WTO trade disputes were resolved during that same time without formal legal action by means of the consultations between disputing countries that are required by WTO rules before a formal legal complaint can be filed. This demonstrated and historic success of the WTO dispute settlement system is the reason why the former director-general of the WTO, Pascal Lamy, in sentiments similar to those voiced also by many others worldwide, has said, "[t]he dispute settlement system is widely considered to be the jewel in the crown of the WTO."[6]

One source of dispute settlement can be traced to what the Scottish philosopher David Hume, a friend of Adam Smith, called "the jealousy of trade."[7] The two Enlightenment thinkers saw international trade as what modern game theory would describe as a "win–win" exchange from which all engaged can benefit. In contrast, others, now as then, see trade as a "zero-sum" game in which there must always be a "winner" and a "loser." The supposed "zero-sum" calculus of trade is a core belief of many of the protectionists and mercantilists who hope to halt globalization and have galvanized the retreat from it. They think another country's gain must be our own loss because surely it is impossible for our trading partners to prosper other than at our expense. In the eyes of some, any commercial competition coming from "them" over there and not from "us" right here must, by definition, be unfair; and any trade or other economic success by another country equates to economic failure for us.

Of course, too, in addition to the persistence of "the jealousy of trade," there will always be perfectly legitimate trade grievances. There will always be commercial disputes in need of resolution between trading countries, just as there will always be commercial disputes in need of resolution between competitors in the same business, and between local buyers and sellers in any small town. The numbers of such international trade disputes grow as the volume of international trade grows. The peaceful resolution of such inevitable disputes should be seen as routine in any commercial marketplace, and the WTO dispute settlement rules are clear in saying that actions in dispute settlement "should not be intended or considered as contentious acts."[8]

Having agreed beforehand on rules for trade tends to prevent many of the disagreements that would otherwise cause trade disputes. Having rules that can be enforced tends to enhance compliance and thus to minimize the need for actual enforcement. Sometimes, though, the countries engaged in trade cannot agree on what the rules mean. And sometimes, of course, countries clearly violate the rules and must be held accountable for their violations before the bar of international legal justice. Their trading partners will need and seek a legal remedy. Hence, there is need for a rule-based system of dispute settlement in which the international rule of law can be upheld because dispute settlement rulings can be enforced.

Apart from the centuries-long evolution of the English common law, the decades-long development of first the GATT and now the WTO dispute settlement system is perhaps the best of all the examples of practical and incremental legal improvisation in search of and in service to the rule of law. Like the common law, the WTO dispute settlement system is based and built on the accumulation of practical experience. As an international institution, it has been built up from the bottom up. What began not long after the Second World War as merely informal "working parties" of trade diplomats, assembled whenever needed to offer non-binding views on the recommended outcome of trade disputes, has evolved in the course of seven decades into a formal and fully binding system of international dispute resolution through legal rulings by panels of impartial jurists picked by the members of the WTO. What began as trade diplomacy has become trade law.

Central to the success of this "jewel in the crown" of the WTO have been two aspects of its dispute settlement system that make it unique among all the international tribunals in the world and in all the history of the world. First, all WTO members have agreed to "have recourse" exclusively to WTO dispute settlement in all their disputes over matters falling within the scope of the treaty.[9] WTO dispute settlement is mandatory for all WTO treaty-related disputes.[10] In other words, the dispute settlement system has what lawyers call "compulsory jurisdiction." This mandatory "jurisdiction" is extensive. The 164 countries and other customs territories that belong to the WTO account for almost all global trade.[11] Virtually every action taken by WTO members that affects trade – either internally or at the border – falls within the scope of the WTO treaty and is therefore subject to WTO dispute settlement.

But why, it might be asked, should any sovereign country belonging to the WTO feel in any way compelled to "have recourse" to the WTO dispute settlement system instead of resorting to the "self-help" of unilateral trade retaliation or, worse, some other less-than-peaceful reaction to a trade dispute? What encourages compliance? The answer to this question is the second way in which WTO dispute settlement is unique. In all the world, and in all the history of the world, the WTO dispute settlement system is alone among international legal tribunals in having real enforcement powers.

The WTO has neither the legal authority nor the actual power to make any member of the WTO do anything at all. A sovereign country that is a member of the WTO is free to choose not to go to the WTO to resolve an international trade dispute. It can instead choose to take unilateral trade action. Legally, too, it can act unilaterally on matters not covered by the WTO treaty. Likewise, a country that is judged in WTO dispute settlement to have acted inconsistently with its WTO treaty obligations can, in an exercise of its sovereignty, choose simply to ignore an adverse

WTO ruling. This, thus far, has rarely happened in the WTO. The members of the WTO are constrained from refraining from WTO dispute settlement and are constrained from ignoring adverse rulings in WTO dispute settlement for the simple reason that there is an economic price to pay if they do.

The price can be high in many international trade disputes. Countries that choose to act unilaterally rather than go to the WTO to resolve a trade dispute, or that choose not to comply with a legal verdict that goes against them in WTO dispute settlement, face the "last resort" of the imposition by other members of the WTO of economic sanctions in the form of the loss of previously granted trade concessions in other areas of trade. These economic sanctions – what the WTO treaty calls a "suspension of concessions" – can in some disputes add up to billions of dollars of lost trade – *annually*.[12] This potential price for non-compliance is a powerful incentive for countries to comply, however grudgingly, with WTO rulings that go against them. The enforcement power of the WTO dispute settlement system is the power of economic suasion.

At the apex of the WTO dispute settlement system is the WTO Appellate Body – a standing global body of seven jurists who are of "recognized authority, with demonstrated expertise in law, international trade and the subject matter" of the WTO treaty, "unaffiliated with any government," "broadly representative of membership in the WTO," and appointed by consensus of the members of the WTO. These seven global jurists hear appeals on the legal rulings by the *ad hoc* panels of three jurists chosen by the disputing countries to judge each particular dispute.[13] Anti-globalists everywhere denounce the Members of the Appellate Body as "faceless foreign judges."[14] But, within the informal councils of the WTO, only rarely are the seven Members of the Appellate Body called "judges." They do not wear wigs. They do not wear robes. The innocuously named Appellate Body does not indulge in the familiar trappings of most other legal tribunals, international and otherwise. Few outside the councils and corridors of the WTO even know their names. Although they sign their names to their opinions, the media habit is merely to report that a decision has been made by "the WTO." Almost never are the Appellate Body Members mentioned by name.

The absence of the usual accoutrement of adjudication in WTO dispute settlement is in part due to the low-key nature and informal tradition of WTO proceedings; it is also due in part to the unique legal structure of WTO dispute settlement. Under the GATT, panel decisions were not legally binding. Under the WTO, they are. For this reason, the WTO Appellate Body was created to provide a desired security and predictability for the "multilateral trading system" by ensuring the legal consistency of WTO rulings.[15] Strictly speaking, the legal structures of the WTO dispute settlement system are "quasi-judicial." Technically, the rulings of the Members of the Appellate Body in appeals from the judgments of WTO panels are only recommendations to the members of the WTO in their collective role as the WTO Dispute Settlement Body. But, in perhaps the most significant of all the innovations implemented with the transformation of the GATT into the WTO, the rulings and recommendations of WTO panels and the WTO Appellate Body are adopted automatically by the members of the WTO unless *all* the members of the WTO agree by consensus that they should *not* be.[16] As a practical matter, this "reverse-consensus rule" means that, in any trade dispute, for the rulings and recommendations of WTO jurists *not* to be adopted, the WTO member that won that dispute would have to agree with every other WTO member to set aside its own winning verdict. Not surprisingly, this has yet to happen in any dispute since the establishment of the WTO dispute settlement system in 1995. This will probably never happen. Technically, though, the mere possibility that it *could* happen keeps the WTO dispute settlement system from being fully "judicial."

Fully "judicial" or not, the Appellate Body has the full clout of a court. Moreover, it is widely considered as tantamount to a court, and, increasingly, it is seen as an influential one in construing and upholding international trade law and other public international law. The Appellate Body has been described by the *New York Times* as "essentially the supreme court of international trade."[17] Philippe Sands has gone so far as to pronounce the Appellate Body "arguably the most powerful court in the world."[18] Wigs and robes aside, the unique coupling internationally of mandatory jurisdiction with real enforcement powers gives considerable legal weight to all that the Appellate Body says and does in WTO dispute settlement, and makes it a global tribunal that cannot be easily ignored.

Perhaps contributing the most to the global stature of the Appellate Body is its consistent demonstration of independence from any and all outside political pressures. WTO rules state that jurists on the Appellate Body "shall be unaffiliated with any government."[19] This requirement has been read to mean that they shall be *independent* of any government – including their own. Appellate Body Members – who serve the whole trading system – routinely sit in judgment of their own countries. In contrast to other international tribunals – including the International Court of Justice – it is commonplace for Members of the Appellate Body to rule against the legal pleadings of their own countries when they conclude there has been a violation of the WTO treaty. The judicial independence consistently demonstrated by the Appellate Body has had the effect of reinforcing and adding still more to the credibility of WTO judgments. Although the political pressures on the Members of the Appellate Body, individually and collectively, have intensified in recent years, their legal rulings are proof that they have ignored these pressures and continued to render independent judgments.

The persuasiveness of the legal conclusions of the Appellate Body can be – and often is – disputed. The extent and the appropriate reach of their legal rulings can be – and sometimes are – disputed. That their conclusions in WTO appeals are exclusively *legal* conclusions has never been disputed with any justification. More than two decades of judgments strongly suggest that it is law alone that motivates the WTO Appellate Body. In a world in which true judicial independence is all too rare, whatever their legal merits, there has never been even an inkling that any legal ruling by the Appellate Body has been in any way influenced by non-legal, political considerations. Like all the other jurists for the WTO, the Members of the Appellate Body have been bound from the beginning by strict WTO rules of conduct that bar any conflicts of interest.[20] Within the WTO itself, and within the ranks of all those outside the WTO who have any actual familiarity with its proceedings, the scrupulous independence of the WTO Appellate Body is now widely assumed. The Appellate Body has for some time now rightly been seen as "impartial and unflinching."[21]

Adding further to the legal force of Appellate Body rulings has been the practice of the Appellate Body – rare among international tribunals – in ruling always by consensus. There is no bar in the rules to dissents by Members of the Appellate Body. In fact, WTO dispute settlement rules clearly permit individual expression in a separate opinion by a Member of the Appellate Body in a WTO appeal – so long as it is "anonymous."[22] On a few occasions in recent years, a Member of the Appellate Body has dissented anonymously to the ruling on a particular legal issue raised in an appeal. But throughout the first two decades and more of WTO dispute settlement, no Member of the Appellate Body has ever dissented to the ultimate outcome in any appeal. As in the formative years of the Supreme Court of the United States after John Marshall became the Chief Justice and the US Court first enunciated the principle of judicial review, the Members of the Appellate Body have sustained during the first decades of the WTO a consistent public consensus. The Appellate Body has chosen to speak to the members of the WTO – and to the wider world – in the strength and solidarity of a single voice. The singularity of the consistent single voice of the Appellate Body has added strength to its verdicts and has also had the positive effect of magnifying and maximizing the global impact and influence of WTO rulings.

Especially striking in their strength and their positive effect have been those rulings that have addressed the complicated relationship between "trade and environment." Having no international tribunal on the environment akin to that on trade, and having no sufficient political will to resolve their ever-increasing numbers of "trade and environment" disputes by means of further global rule-making, the members of the WTO have instead left the growing number of their disputes over environmental actions that affect trade to be resolved in WTO dispute settlement. The WTO rulings in those disputes say much about the need for international rules that treat economy and environment as one.

"TRADE AND ENVIRONMENT" DISPUTES

The nexus between "trade and environment" is only one of the numerous "trade and" linkages that increasingly occupy those debating international trade. Another is "trade and labor." Still another is "trade and human rights." Almost every aspirational aspect of global sustainable development bumps up against the buy–sell of trade for the simple reason that the economy and the environment – and all that are affected by both – are in fact one. The leading authority on the nexus between "trade and environment," Steve Charnovitz of George Washington University, reminds us that this particular "trade and" issue is far from new, and that "[i]nternational policies on trade and on environment have always intersected."[23] As he notes, the very first multilateral environmental agreement – the Convention for the Protection of Birds Useful to Agriculture in 1902 – used an import ban as an environmental tool,[24] and the very first multilateral trade agreement to pursue freer trade – the Convention for the Abolition of Import and Export Prohibitions and Restrictions in 1927 – included an exception for trade restrictions to protect public health and to protect animals and plants against diseases and against "extinction."[25]

These connections exist, Charnovitz explains, because "[e]nvironmental problems will always be a challenge on a planet where governmental units do not exactly match ecosystems. Another way of saying this is that so long as the policies in one country can impose externalities on others, and so long as prices in the market are not fully reflective of environmental costs, there will be a need for international governance to manage the transborder conflicts that will inevitably ensue … Because all major ecological problems affect the world economy – for example, climate change, biodiversity, forestry, fisheries, and pollution – linkages between the world trading system and environmental policies are inevitable."[26]

What *is* new is not the relationship between trade and environment; what *is* new is the extent to which globalization and the increasing overall impact of human endeavor on groaning global ecosystems have combined to confront the willing and the unwilling alike all the world over with a whole host of hard choices on the relationship between trade and environment. Yet many of the most pressing and most difficult of the "trade and environment" issues are not even on the WTO agenda. The tendency of the trading countries that belong to the WTO has been to defer confronting the hard issues of "trade and environment" while dumping them into the legal laps of the jurists in WTO dispute settlement.

Why does the WTO itself not intervene by bringing legal actions against countries whose trade actions harm the environment? This very question betrays a misunderstanding of the nature of the WTO. There is no "WTO" that can intervene. Because the WTO is only an alter ego for the WTO members acting collectively, there is no "WTO" that can initiate any legal action in dispute settlement. To trigger WTO dispute settlement, one of the WTO members engaged in a trade dispute must decide to initiate dispute settlement proceedings. If it chooses to do so, it cannot be stopped.[27] If it chooses not to do so, it cannot be compelled. Pulling this legal trigger is the exclusive prerogative of the members of the WTO, which alone can be legal "parties" to WTO disputes. Private parties have no "standing" – no legal status – to invoke or to participate in the exclusively state-to-state and government-to-government proceedings in WTO dispute settlement.[28] There is no legal action in the absence of one of the 164 members of the WTO filing a formal legal complaint.

What is more, every WTO dispute is really two disputes. It is a dispute specifically about certain traded goods and services involving certain countries. It is also a dispute generally about certain legal principles applying not only to trade in those, but also in many other goods and services, and applying to all countries. Thus, for example, the long-running "bananas" dispute inherited from the GATT and litigated at length in the WTO in the 1990s among several dozen countries on several continents was not only about the terms of billions of dollars annually in the global trade in bananas but was also the first WTO case to clarify some of the most basic of the WTO obligations on trade in services.[29]

Legally, every WTO dispute is distinct. Strictly speaking, there is no *stare decisis* – no rule of precedent – in the exclusively state-to-state subject matter of public international law.[30] Thus, every public international dispute is an entirely new dispute, even if it involves the same legal principles, including disputes in WTO dispute settlement. Yet, as a practical day-to-day commercial matter, the security and predictability of the multilateral trading system that are the overarching goals of WTO dispute settlement are not possible without a consistent view of trade obligations that does not vary from dispute to dispute.[31] Basic trade obligations must mean the same thing every day for every trading country if world trade is to flow smoothly. For this reason, Appellate Body rulings are generally treated by WTO members and by the Appellate Body itself as if they were legal precedents. In this way, in effect, the legal "clarifications" of WTO obligations made by WTO jurists in each case become principles that apply in every case.[32]

This approach to the steady accumulation of WTO jurisprudence can be seen in the range of WTO disputes that have touched so far on the issue of the relationship between "trade and environment" as well as, increasingly, other dimensions of sustainable development. The topics of these WTO disputes have been many and vastly varied: environmental standards for reformulated gasoline;[33] a ban on growth hormones in beef in the name of food safety;[34] a requirement for the use of devices to protect endangered sea turtles when fishing for shrimp;[35] a ban on imports of retreaded tires;[36] a restriction on the use and import of asbestos;[37] standards for biotechnology products;[38] feed-in tariff incentives for renewable energy;[39] governmental subsidies for solar energy panels;[40] the treatment of seals;[41] and the encirclement of dolphins when fishing for tuna.[42]

Starting with its first appeal, in the *US – Gasoline* dispute, in 1996, the Appellate Body showed – to the surprise of some both inside and outside the WTO – that it would not view trade law in isolation from other international law, nor view trade issues in isolation from other issues of global concern. Some supporters of the GATT trading system had long seen the GATT and GATT rulings as a body of law separate and apart from the rest of international law, but, when musing in that initial appeal on the meaning of one GATT obligation, the Appellate Body observed in passing that it reflected "a measure of recognition that the General Agreement is not to be read in clinical isolation from public international law."[43] This single statement in that first WTO appellate report has been said to mark "a genuine turning point in the relationship between international law and international trade law," which many in the commercial legal silo of the original GATT suddenly discovered had a great deal to do with other international law.[44] As Philippe Sands has said, "For old-style GATT aficionados, the Appellate Body's decision was revolutionary. It signaled a seismic shift."[45]

Clearly shown as well by the Appellate Body in its first appeal was that – contrary to the apprehensions of many in the world – trade would not automatically trump the environment in WTO dispute settlement. True, the United States measure there – which established standards for the fuel additives in gasoline to improve air quality – was found by the WTO jurists to be inconsistent with the WTO obligations of the United States. But largely overlooked at the time was the fact that the United States was found by the Appellate Body not to be entitled to the benefit of an environmental defense in that dispute only because it had acted in an arbitrary and unjustifiably discriminatory way by imposing higher environmental standards on imported than on like domestic gasoline products. In *US – Gasoline* and in a string of subsequent disputes, the Appellate Body has consistently confirmed the basic right of WTO members under the WTO treaty to protect the environment and, in so doing, has, for all but the most biased of observers, put paid to the notion that there is no room for environmental protection within the WTO-based global trading system. Rather, the truth, as was acknowledged by the Appellate Body at the outset in *US – Gasoline*, is that under the terms of the WTO treaty, "WTO Members have a large measure of autonomy to determine their own policies on the environment (including the relationship with trade), their environmental objectives and the environmental legislation they enact and implement."[46]

But this autonomy is not without limits to which WTO members have agreed by signing and ratifying the WTO treaty. Significantly, the Appellate Body stressed from the start in *US – Gasoline*, and has emphasized again and again in judgments since, that under WTO rules the exercise of this sovereign right to protect the environment "is circumscribed only by the need to respect the requirements" of the GATT and the other agreements of the WTO treaty.[47] Often pivotal are provisions in the WTO agreements that require "even-handedness" in applying environmental measures that affect international trade.[48] At the founding of the GATT following the Second World War, environmental exceptions were written into the multilateral trading system. Those exceptions remain unchanged in the WTO treaty. Actions "relating to the conservation of exhaustible natural resources" and "necessary to protect human, animal, or plant life or health," for example, are clearly permitted under WTO rules.[49] Such potentially lawful actions will, however, violate WTO rules if they are "applied in a manner which would constitute a means of arbitrary or unjustifiable discrimination between countries where the same conditions prevail, or a disguised restriction on international trade."[50] Whether any particular purported environmental measure will fall within the scope of these environmental exceptions to what would otherwise be binding WTO obligations will be determined "case by case" on the basis of the facts as they are found in each case.

Where environmental measures taken by WTO members have been faulted in WTO dispute settlement, it has usually been on the basis not of *what* was done, but rather of *how* it was done. As in *US – Gasoline*, for example, higher environmental standards cannot be imposed on foreign products without imposing them on like domestic products. Or, as in *EC – Hormones*, a food safety measure affecting imports cannot be maintained without being based on the scientific risk assessment required by WTO rules. Or, as in *US – Shrimp*, efforts to negotiate a multilateral environmental arrangement affecting like traded products cannot be made with some countries in one region but not with other countries in another region. Or, as in *Canada – Feed-in Tariffs*, incentives for renewable energy cannot discriminate in favor of the "domestic content" of local providers. Or, as in *EC – Seals*, a measure regulating products derived from seal hunting that is motivated by "public morals" cannot discriminate arbitrarily between and among seal hunts and seal hunters.

The most significant of all these WTO rulings may be the ruling by the Appellate Body in the appeal in *US – Shrimp* – the "shrimp–turtle" dispute – in 1998, "a decision that has been widely seen as evidencing the greening of GATT/WTO jurisprudence."[51] In *US – Shrimp*, the Appellate Body ultimately upheld a *unilateral* United States measure aimed at protecting endangered sea turtles by banning imports of shrimp that were not caught while employing an environmentally friendly turtle-excluder device. The WTO jurists expressed a clear preference in *US – Shrimp* – under WTO law as under all public international law – for multilateral over unilateral actions. Yet in words that echoed throughout the WTO trading system when the *US – Shrimp* ruling was announced – but were little noticed at that time by those outside the trading system – the Appellate Body observed, "[i]t appears to us … that conditioning access to a Member's domestic market on whether exporting Members comply with, or adopt, a policy or policies *unilaterally* prescribed by the importing Member may, to some degree, be a common aspect of measures falling within the scope of one or another" of the exceptions in the WTO treaty.[52]

With these few words, the Appellate Body quietly opened the door in the WTO to the potential legality of *unilateral* trade measures intended to influence the *local* environmental actions of other countries *in their own territories*. For the most part, the legal question in the WTO since this far-reaching WTO ruling has no longer been *what* but *how*. If an environmental measure, unilateral or otherwise, is in fact an environmental measure that fits within the shelter of one of the environmental exceptions, how has it been applied? Is, for instance, the application of the measure "even-handed" or not? The answer to this and other related questions will usually determine the legal outcome of the WTO dispute.

Recall that the fundamental trade rules of non-discrimination – national treatment and most-favored-nation treatment – are rules that forbid discrimination between "like" traded products.[53] Historically, whether traded products are like has been determined on the basis of their physical characteristics, end uses, tariff classification, and consumers' tastes and habits.[54] Historically, how products are produced has not been relevant to determining whether products are like and, therefore, because they are like, should not be subjected to trade discrimination. So it was equally noteworthy in *US – Shrimp* that the unilateral measure ultimately upheld there was a measure that turned in its discrimination not on a comparison of the products themselves, but rather on a comparison of *how those products were produced*. The ruling in *US – Shrimp* did not alter WTO law as it relates to a determination of the "likeness" of traded products for deciding whether there has been a WTO violation. The legal question of the meaning of likeness was not raised by the parties in that appeal and thus was not before the WTO judges. And yet the Appellate Body ruling in the shrimp–turtle case was unprecedented in upholding a WTO defense excusing a WTO violation for an environmental measure that discriminated on the basis of the process and production method of the relevant traded product (in the trade jargon, the "PPM"). Furthermore, it did so for a PPM that did not affect the physical characteristics of the end product (a "non-product-related PPM").

Shrimp are shrimp. They are exactly the same whether they are caught while using a turtle-excluder device or not. The use of a turtle-excluder device does not change the physical characteristics of the shrimp. It does, however, change how the shrimp as products are produced. Thus, with this added dimension, the legal door opened by the Appellate Body in the shrimp–turtle case to the permissibility of unilateral environmental measures affecting trade was, potentially, opened wide indeed. How wide can this door be opened under the current rules in the context of future trade disputes? The Appellate Body left this question unanswered in *US – Shrimp*. Sea turtles swim. They swim far, and they swim wide, and they swim for thousands of miles. So a sea turtle swimming in one territorial jurisdiction today could well be swimming in another, an ocean away, tomorrow. For this reason, it was not necessary in the shrimp–turtle dispute for the Appellate Body to decide whether there is an *implied jurisdictional limit* to the permissible reach of a lawful unilateral environmental measure that restricts trade. The WTO jurists reserved for a future dispute "the question of whether there is an implied jurisdiction limitation" to the environmental exceptions in the WTO treaty "and, if so, the nature or extent of that limitation."[55]

That was in 1998. The Appellate Body has not been called upon since to be more definitive on this key legal statement. So we can only surmise at the full extent of its potential implications. To pick just one among a whole host of environmentally related possibilities: We do not know whether a trade restriction imposed by one country on imported products from another country because that other country does not do enough in the eyes of the importing country to combat climate change by controlling carbon emissions when making those products would be upheld in WTO dispute settlement.[56] If this perhaps most central and crucial of all the many "trade and environment" questions is not answered by global rules resulting from global negotiations, it may be answered instead by the Appellate Body in future WTO dispute settlement.

What, then, of all the many other lineaments of the nexus of trade and environment? The ongoing accumulation of WTO jurisprudence occurs, necessarily, case by case. The lines of legal judgment are drawn one by one. A challenge in judging any one case is, always, not to prejudge others. Legally as otherwise, the shape of the future can never be foreseen. Some line-drawing is simply unavoidable in clarifying legal obligations when resolving international trade disputes, but it is always best not to draw too long or too sharp a line, and no line can be drawn that either adds to or diminishes the mutual obligations agreed in the WTO treaty.[57] Because WTO jurists, in following their instructions from WTO members in the WTO treaty, tend to take (quite rightly) a cautious approach in their inevitable line-drawing, there are many more questions about the relationship between trade and environment that remain unanswered than have been answered so far in WTO dispute settlement.

Above all, and potentially affecting all, unanswered still in the case-by-case approach of WTO jurisprudence is the extent to which, in future disputes, the Members of the Appellate Body will – as they did decisively in *US – Shrimp* – find a real legal significance in "the explicit recognition by WTO Members of the objective of sustainable development in the preamble of the WTO Agreement."[58] Going forward, the full appreciation by the Appellate Body of this clearly expressed objective of the members of the WTO when they concluded the WTO treaty could have far-reaching consequences in the future clarification of WTO rules in WTO disputes. These consequences will be all the more far-reaching if most of the drawing of the needed legal lines on trade and environment is left in an unwilling world to WTO dispute settlement. However wise and however far-sighted the WTO judges may be, it would be far better if these lines were drawn in the rule-making process of negotiation rather than in the rule-clarifying process of dispute settlement. The judges themselves would be the first to say so.

"INVESTMENT AND ENVIRONMENT" DISPUTES

The numbers and varieties of international economic arrangements have multiplied many times over since the turn of the twenty-first century while frustrated negotiators have struggled with scant success to conclude new global agreements. In the absence of a more successful multilateralism, the first two decades of the century have largely been characterized by efforts by two – or by a few – countries at a time to agree to lower their mutual barriers to international trade and investment. These hundreds of trade agreements and thousands of investment agreements deal in many different ways with both trade and investment. Many among these ever-evolving economic arrangements also include specific provisions on dispute settlement. Where they have been used, these new dispute settlement systems, have – as with the WTO dispute settlement system – revealed the considerable overlap between international economic and environmental law unfolding in an unwilling world. In particular, this overlap has been seen in these non-WTO dispute settlement proceedings when considering the knotty issue of the nexus of "investment and environment."

At their best, bilateral, regional, and other preferential economic arrangements can be useful demonstrations of the trial and error of testing new ideas and new approaches in both trade and investment. Since its creation in 1993, one of the most prominent of these preferential proving grounds for new ways of approaching the relationship between economy and environment has been the trade and investment arrangement among the United States, Canada, and Mexico called the North American Free Trade Agreement (NAFTA). From the outset, NAFTA has served as a regional laboratory for new experiments in trying to reconcile economic and environmental concerns through regional integration, with mixed results.[59]

One problem with NAFTA in the eyes of many environmentalists is its controversial chapter on investment, which includes sweeping investor protections. Chapter Eleven of NAFTA provides for the "fair and equitable treatment and full protection and security" of foreign direct investments from a variety of measures, including those actions that fail to meet a "minimum standard of treatment," fail to provide the better of national or most-favored-nation treatment by federal governments, and are "tantamount to" nationalization or expropriation.[60] In significant contrast to the exclusively state-to-state proceedings in trade dispute settlement in the WTO, NAFTA Chapter Eleven gives legal "standing" to private parties in investment disputes. Under Chapter Eleven, private investors can challenge actions of the three NAFTA parties that affect their foreign direct investments in a process called "investor–state dispute settlement" (ISDS). This ISDS process did not originate with NAFTA; it can be found in literally thousands of bilateral investment treaties worldwide.[61]

Some of the decisions in NAFTA investor–state dispute settlement have been highly controversial. ISDS decisions are not made by a standing body of previously selected jurists such as the seven-member WTO Appellate Body. These NAFTA decisions are made instead by *ad hoc* panels of three arbitrators specifically selected and convened by the parties to a particular dispute for the purpose of judging it in "confidential" proceedings that are – like other, purely private arbitral proceedings – closed to public scrutiny. These ISDS arbitrators are private jurists unaffiliated with any governments who can make "awards" – decisions – that judge governmental actions to be illegal under the international law in NAFTA. There is no appeal from their awards because there is no equivalent of the WTO Appellate Body in international investment. Thus, there is no appellate safety valve to help guarantee that the rulings of these *ad hoc* tribunals of arbitrators will be coherent, consistent, or correct.

The "investment and environment" cases in ISDS under NAFTA have – like the growing number of "trade and environment" disputes in the WTO – ranged far and wide, and, over time, they have grown in number. NAFTA "investment and environment" disputes have dealt with such sensitive issues as gasoline additive restrictions, bulk water export bans, bars on pesticides containing persistent organic pollutants, bans on the deep sea disposal of nuclear wastes, regulations on waste disposal facilities, subsidies for wind energy, natural gas pipeline approvals, and natural gas "fracking" restrictions. Because of the understandable sensitivities about these issues, ISDS has become extraordinarily controversial in the United States – even though the United States government has never lost an ISDS case. ISDS has likewise become equally controversial in Europe and elsewhere where it has been employed under other international agreements. Central to the outcome of many of these disputes over the nexus of investment and environment have been questions of whether national environmental regulations and other national restrictions have fallen short of "fair and equitable treatment" of – or have resulted in indirect expropriations of – foreign direct investments. The definitions embraced by arbitrators of both "fair and equitable treatment" and "indirect" expropriation have been elusive and, in some cases, expansive, reaching into "issues of environmental protection, human rights, and labor standards."[62] The verdicts in the increasing number of environmentally related Chapter Eleven disputes under NAFTA have reached a variety of results. Yet, in one way or another, they all pose the same question: Precisely how much regulatory space should be preserved for sovereign states when their regulations affect foreign direct investment?

All countries – and especially all developing countries – need the additional capital that foreign direct investment can provide. To say the least, FDI is needed to confront the multifold and multifaceted challenges of facing and adjusting to climate change in the developing world. As Annette Magnusson, the secretary general of the Stockholm Chamber of Commerce, has said, "To tackle the risk of climate change, we need investment in new technology and infrastructure. This is fundamental ... But another element also needed is stability in policy, and predictability ... [T]he legal framework needs to be predictable."[63] Clearly, this predictable legal framework must include appropriate protections for foreign direct investment. FDI can, however, present real risks of many kinds to all countries in their efforts to achieve sustainable development. Ideally, international investment agreements can, "[b]y promoting environmentally sustainable investments ... help overcome unsustainable resource exploitation and industrial practices involving foreign investors ... [and] can help ensure that unsustainable practices are replaced by environmentally sustainable ones, and new industries or activities are equally beneficial to the natural, social and economic environments in which they take place."[64] Whether NAFTA does this has been put in doubt in the minds of many by a string of Chapter Eleven rulings.[65]

To cite two recent examples of awards that have raised legitimate concerns, in 2015, a NAFTA investment tribunal found for due process and other procedural reasons in *Bilcon v. Canada* that Canada had breached its NAFTA investment obligation when a projected quarry expansion in Nova Scotia was rejected for environmental reasons.[66] A dissenting arbitrator, the eminent Canadian jurist and scholar Donald McRae, described the majority decision of the other two arbitrators as "not only an intrusion into the way an environmental review process is to be conducted, but also an intrusion into the environmental public policy of the state."[67] Then, in 2016, another NAFTA investment tribunal, in *Windstream Energy LLC v. Canada*, concluded that the province of Ontario's moratorium on offshore wind power projects had breached the "fair and equitable treatment" obligation in NAFTA.[68] Canada argued that the moratorium "fell within the legitimate policy-making power of the Government of Ontario to regulate in the public interest."[69]

As with the overall opposition in some quarters to NAFTA itself, much of the opposition to ISDS under Chapter Eleven distorts the facts, peddles misinformation, and in general is vastly overblown. But some who voice reservations are more thoughtful. In the view of Cambridge University law lecturer Kate Miles, "Recent framing of host state environmental regulation as an investment treaty violation is a particularly insidious manifestation of the traditional relationship between foreign investors and the environment ... The lack of weight that is given to the public welfare role of government by arbitral tribunals in investor–state disputes is troubling ... The concern is that even where states enact regulation in good faith, they can leave themselves open to investor claims of a violation of the stable legal and business framework component of the legitimate expectations requirement of fair and equitable treatment. It is difficult to overestimate the potential repercussions of this development in interpretation."[70]

This concern extends beyond investment arbitrations in NAFTA dispute settlement to include the growing number of "investment and environment" rulings and awards worldwide in similar arbitrations under a whole array of bilateral investment treaties, and also of free trade agreements that, like NAFTA, contain investment obligations. One among many such results is the outcome of a dispute that arose under the bilateral investment treaty between Argentina and the United States after contaminated water supplies led to undrinkable water in an Argentine province. Argentina fined an American-owned company, Azurix, for failure to comply with its obligations under a concession agreement to operate the provincial water facilities. In reply, Azurix brought an action under the investment treaty between the two countries alleging a breach by Argentina of its obligation of fair and equitable treatment of foreign investment. Azurix won and was awarded compensation in excess of $165 million.[71]

Another outcome that causes justifiable environmental concern is the award by a tribunal of the International Centre for Settlement of Investment Disputes in a dispute between Costa Rica and an American-owned company called Santa Elena over the amount of compensation due the company because of the expropriation by the Costa Rican government of coastal lands and rainforests rich with biodiversity for the purpose of establishing a nature preserve. The arbitrators there held that, in calculating the amount of compensation, the application of the traditional international rules protecting foreign direct investment was not changed by the environmental objectives of the expropriation, or by the fact that it was done in fulfillment of international environmental obligations.[72] The implications of the *Santa Elena* ruling in a world faced with the need for profound changes in land use to confront climate change, preserve ecosystems, and advance sustainable development are obvious.

Miles and others are not only worried about potentially harmful environmental outcomes from investor–state dispute settlement. They are equally worried about the "chilling effect" of the mere prospect of ISDS. Their apprehension is that the omnipresent threat of ISDS could cause governments to refrain from enacting and implementing necessary health, safety, environmental, and other social protections. Researchers debate whether this is truly happening.[73] There may be no good way to test this governmental apprehension. Governments do whatever they do – or do not. But, worldwide, many environmentalists are asking: Will we be prevented by the threat of ISDS from doing all that must be done domestically to protect the environment and otherwise to promote sustainable development? In Europe, for example, in the aftermath of the global financial crisis, there has been a retreat by a number of revenue-short countries from previously granted programs providing for feed-in tariffs, subsidies, and other incentives for investments in the production and supply of renewable energy. Foreign investors affected by this policy retreat have brought ISDS cases against Spain, Italy, Germany, and other European countries contending that these policy changes violate the international obligation of fair and equitable treatment, which generally prohibits actions that defeat an investor's legitimate expectations for its investment or create an unstable atmosphere for investments.[74]

Unquestionably, FDI still faces discrimination and expropriation, direct and indirect, of many kinds from host countries in many parts of the world. Foreign investors are asking whether latitude for more local discretion in regulating investments will lead to open season for investment discrimination and "creeping" expropriation through the accretion of regulatory requirements that empty foreign direct investments of all their rightly anticipated value. At the same time, states that are hosts to investments are asking whether they are forever frozen from responding to ever-changing economic and environmental circumstances by the legal constraints of these investment rules. They wonder: Where should we draw the lines? How broad, for example, is the definition of an "investment" to which these legal obligations apply? What in fact are the basic "minimum" standards that are required in protecting FDI? What kinds of regulatory and other governmental actions can result in an "indirect" expropriation? And to what extent – if at all – is a legal obligation relating to an investment affected if the governmental action that results in an expropriation of that investment has an environmental or sustainability purpose?

To date, there is no investment equivalent of the WTO shrimp–turtle decision to help us begin to find the answers to these questions for foreign direct investment. Arbitrators in investment disputes have barely begun to come to grips with the necessity of viewing the meaning and the import of international legal obligations within the context of sustainable development. In no small part this is because, for the most part, the substance of most existing investment rules simply does not take the environment or other aspects of sustainable development into account. Nor is there any global counterpart in investment to the WTO Appellate Body in trade. There is no avenue for appealing arbitral awards that might lead toward ensuring the security and predictability needed every bit as much in international investment as in international trade. For this reason, rulings such as those in the *Santa Elena* dispute are left to stand – and to stand out – in stoking the fears of all those who see investment as necessarily harmful to the environment, and, more, as an obstacle to sustainable development. So we are left – as Philippe Sands has aptly put it – "searching for balance" between "investment and environment" in our unwilling world.[75] As he has rightly added, such balancing is an essential part of what sustainable development is all about.

ENVIRONMENTAL AND CLIMATE DISPUTES

Alongside the unfolding of the evolution of international trade and investment law, the progressive development of overall international environmental law continues as well, and the broad enterprise of making and upholding international law edges closer and closer to the ultimately unavoidable topic of climate change. Here it confronts what most characterizes the evolving international framework of rules relating to the environment – and potentially also to climate change – which is fragmentation. The fragmented "institutionalized structure" that exists for implementing and upholding a mounting multitude of international environmental rules is not only "highly decentralized"; it is also seen by some as "chaotic."[76]

The number of international environmental disputes has increased with the increasing environmental consequences of globalization, and recourse by states to international litigation has increased with it. "Environmental matters are now routinely litigated in a growing array of international courts and tribunals,"[77] which are rightly described by Australian scholar Tim Stephens as a "patchwork of jurisdictions."[78] Standing international tribunals and *ad hoc* international panels of arbitration totaling – by one count – more than 80 worldwide have issued a legal cornucopia of nearly 13,000 decisions, opinions, and rulings since 1990.[79] Likewise patchwork is the law they apply. In addition to customary international law, this proliferation of possible paths to environmental dispute resolution presents the task of discerning the legal meaning of a proliferating number of international environmental rules that can be found in – at last count – more than 1,100 multilateral environmental agreements, more than 1,500 bilateral environmental agreements, and more than 250 other international environmental agreements.[80] International jurists must ask: How does this multitude of agreements fit together, and how do the obligations in these agreements fit into the broader picture of international law, including trade and investment law?

Added to the imposing task of stitching together all this international environmental jurisprudence coherently and consistently is the increasing need for this assorted patchwork of jurisdictions to determine the international legal import of the prolific phenomenon of environmental "soft law" – of the multiplying mix of environmental guidelines and other purported standards emerging from a whole plethora of specialized and compartmentalized international institutions and endeavors.[81] Thus, international jurists must also ask: Which among this mix of lofty international expressions of international expectations and international aspirations rise to the level of something that can be called "law" and that can therefore be said to be a binding obligation of sovereign countries? When does "soft law" become "hard law"?

The fragmentation of jurisdictions offering answers to these and to other questions about international environmental law threatens to fragment the law itself. In contrast to international trade law in the WTO, and in common with international investment law, there is no mandatory court of final appeal in international environmental law to ensure security and predictability in knowing what the law means. Nor is there any international environmental tribunal with any real and effective authority to enforce its judgments. In stark contrast to that of the WTO, the dispute settlement mechanisms in multilateral environmental agreements – where they exist – generally lack the legal teeth of full and effective enforcement powers. Some multilateral environmental agreements (MEAs) employ trade sanctions in ways that do not undermine WTO obligations – such as restrictions on trade in endangered species, and restrictions on trade in substances that deplete the Earth's irreplaceable protective ozone layer. Most MEAs, though, rely instead on a combination of monitoring, reporting, verification, and other forms of mutual cooperation and hortatory oversight that all add up merely to voluntary compliance. Non-adversarial dispute resolution in such environmental settings works more often than might be expected, but it does not work all the time.[82] And it is less likely to work well when environmental claims are pitted against powerful economic interests.

The fragmentation of international environmental law also raises the possibility of "forum shopping" in search of a favorable judgment. The specter of such forum shopping arose in 2000 when, in a purported effort to protect depleted swordfish stocks (and not just to protect the market share of the Chilean fishing industry), Chile banned Spanish vessels fishing for swordfish in the high seas adjacent to the Chilean coast from landing at Chilean ports. The European Union – on behalf of Spain – began dispute settlement proceedings in the WTO. In reply, Chile began parallel proceedings in ITLOS – the International Tribunal of the Law of the Sea Convention. Ultimately, the disputing parties resolved their dispute without need of a legal judgment, and both legal proceedings were suspended indefinitely. Left unresolved was the answer to the question: Which forum had legal jurisdiction – the legal authority to make the judgment – in that "trade and environment" dispute?[83]

The fragmentation of international environmental law raises, too, the possibility of legal conflicts. This includes not only the possibility of conflicts with other kinds of international law, such as with international trade law and international investment law, but also – and maybe even more worrisome – the possibility of internal conflicts *within* international environmental law. To avoid such conflicts, and otherwise to fashion order from the "chaotic" world of international environmental law, Timo Koivurova has echoed a suggestion supported by many among the willing worldwide: "When institutional changes for international environmental law and policy are debated, the idea of an organization comparable with the World Trade Organization (WTO) is often proposed: a 'world environmental organization' (WEO). If an organization were created along the lines of the WTO, all the global environmental protection treaties could be integrated under its governance. This would certainly enhance the scope for synergies between the treaties that currently operate on overlapping tasks. If a WEO had an automatic dispute settlement system comparable to the WTO, states could take each other to WEO dispute settlement panels, gradually creating the foundation for a unified regulation of international environmental law."[84]

Conceivably, a World Environment Court with an automatic dispute settlement system might not be limited to state-to-state dispute settlement in the venerable Westphalian tradition. It might also be open to parties in addition to states. As it stands, there is no international judicial forum open to individuals seeking to hold either states or private parties accountable when they cause environmental harm. Judge Christopher Weeramantry of the International Court of Justice, in a separate opinion in an International Court of Justice (ICJ) case, suggested that international law should develop beyond simply state-by-state resolution to begin to hear matters of "global concern for humanity as a whole."[85] He would presumably open the doors of global judgment to "non-state political actors."

At first glance, the International Court of Justice, the principal judicial organ of the United Nations, appears to be best placed to fulfill such a specialized environmental role.[86] The ICJ is, after all, the only international tribunal with both general subject-matter jurisdiction and a global reach. In fact, the ICJ has already tried and failed to make itself the equivalent of a World Environment Court. In 1993, responding in the aftermath of the Earth Summit to what they perceived as the need to further the inclusion of environmental consideration in overall public international law, the judges of the world court established in The Hague what was meant to be a permanent environmental chamber devoted exclusively to environmental cases. In 2006, the same judges, in effect, quietly disbanded it. The new Chamber for Environmental Matters had no cases.[87]

One obstacle facing the late environmental chamber of the ICJ was that the ICJ, unlike the WTO, has neither mandatory jurisdiction nor enforcement powers. Another obstacle was a question of definition. There is no separate category of what can be defined as solely "environmental" cases. As with the WTO and other disputes involving "trade and environment" and "trade and investment," all disputes over the "environment" are also always disputes, too, about something else.[88] Any dispute involving the environment – or involving any aspect of sustainable development – is "likely to be a part of more complex disputes involving questions of trade, production, investment, rights of the individual, policy of international organisations and other matters that are inseparable from the general body of international law."[89]

Despite its setback on establishing an environmental chamber, the ICJ has contributed usefully to constructing the emerging framework of international environmental law, notably as it relates to building environmental law into the framing of customary international law.[90] The Hague Court has begun to nail together the basic architecture of the principles of customary international law in a way that takes the environment into account.[91] In a 1997 dispute between Hungary and Slovakia over a dam project, the Hague Court gave sustainable development explicit recognition for the first time, but did not spell out its legal status. The Court said that the concept of "sustainable development" expresses "the need to reconcile environmental protection and economic development."[92] It spoke of sustainable development, however, only as a "concept." The ICJ did not develop any further analysis of the "concept"; much less did it declare sustainable development to be a principle of customary international law. For his part in that case, though, Judge Weeramantry did say more. In a separate opinion, he stated that the principle of sustainable development is "a part of modern international law by reason not only of its inescapable logical necessity, but also by reason of its wide and general acceptance by the global community." He concluded, "I consider [sustainable development] to be more than a mere concept, but as a principle with normative value ... [T]he law necessarily contains within itself the principle of reconciliation. That principle is the principle of sustainable development."[93]

Now comes the unprecedented human challenge of climate change. The need to limit and to adapt to climate change is the fulcrum around which we must fashion a legal structure for facilitating a convergence of economy and environment through sustainable development. Now, too, a further fragmentation of international environmental law seems likely to occur because of the decision by UN climate negotiators not to include a mandatory and comprehensive system of dispute settlement in the Paris Agreement. National actions on climate change will lead without doubt to international disputes about those actions. Moreover, national *inactions* on climate change will lead to a proliferation of legal disputes as well, both domestic and international.

Already, a global search is underway for legal alternatives offering legal remedies for addressing climate change. Lawyers (being lawyers) are displaying considerable creativity in concocting new causes of action to drive carbon emissions cuts in the absence of a political willingness by policymakers to address the need for more and better rules to confront climate change. In the absence of rules, these climate lawyers pursue rulings. With these rulings, they hope to inspire new rules and, thus, new carbon-cutting actions. In the Netherlands, for example, in 2015, in the first climate liability suit brought under human rights and tort law, a Dutch court ordered the Dutch government to take additional action to cut greenhouse gas emissions.[94] The following year, in the United States, a group of twenty-one children and young adults between the ages of eight and nineteen pursued a suit against the federal government on US constitutional grounds for not doing more to cut emissions.[95] In 2017, a nine-year-old girl filed a lawsuit against the Indian government over its alleged failure to act against climate change.[96] A total of 884 climate cases had been filed worldwide by March 2017 – with the largest number of cases in the United States.[97]

Because of the absence of a mandatory climate dispute settlement system, there is, in particular, the looming possibility of a fragmenting and politically explosive collision between the international legal systems of trade and climate change. The decision by UN climate negotiators *not* to include a mandatory climate dispute settlement system in the Paris Agreement is *not* a decision not to engage in dispute settlement where there are international climate disputes that affect trade. Rather, for the 164 countries that are parties to both the Paris Agreement and the WTO treaty, it is, in effect, a decision *de facto* to leave the settlement of trade-related climate disputes to the judges of the WTO.[98] A governmental measure that is ostensibly taken in response to climate change and that affects trade – whether it is truly a climate response measure or not – falls within the scope of the WTO treaty. It is therefore subject to WTO dispute settlement. Nothing whatsoever in the Paris Agreement in any way alters this mandatory WTO jurisdiction. Indeed, the provision in the underlying UN climate framework convention that warns against a resort to measures affecting trade seems, at least implicitly, to cede such a collision to WTO jurisdiction.[99]

Furthermore, the absence in the Paris Agreement of any agreed definition by climate negotiators of what constitutes a climate response measure amounts, in effect, to a decision *de facto* by the 164 parties to the climate agreement that are also members of the WTO to leave the determination of what is and what is not a climate response measure to WTO judges on a case-by-case basis in WTO dispute settlement. When a WTO member enacts and applies a measure that affects trade, and then defends it as a climate response measure, the judgment of whether it is in fact a climate response measure which should be excused from what would otherwise be trade obligations will be made not by the COP in the climate framework, but by the WTO and most likely ultimately by the WTO Appellate Body in WTO dispute settlement. Entrusting WTO judges with resolving such disputes is not necessarily the wrong result. WTO judges have shown time and again that they will not give short shrift to the environment. They are unlikely to do so in any consideration involving climate change. Yet this is not a jurisdictional result that should have happened inadvertently. As it is, this jurisdictional outcome seems never to have been contemplated by climate negotiators in their prolonged deliberations on the Paris Agreement. Nor does it seem to have been discussed by their counterparts engaged in negotiating WTO trade agreements in Geneva.

At some point soon after the 2020 effective date of the Paris Agreement, or perhaps even at some time before that date if countries heed the call for early action in fulfilling their climate pledges, a WTO member will ask WTO judges to resolve a dispute over the effects on its trade of another WTO member's alleged climate response measure. That other member will reply that its measure has been enacted and applied in keeping with its climate pledge as part of the Paris climate agreement. WTO dispute settlement will then proceed to an unforeseeable outcome that will be largely determined by the specifics of the challenged measure and the facts that are proven about it. What will be the harm caused to both the climate system and the trade system by the global political firestorm that will surely result while the world waits several years for the eventual final verdict by trade judges on the meaning of climate treaty obligations? How much more unwillingness will be heaped on our unwilling world while we debate anew, in the heated glare of global controversy, the age-old question of "who should judge?"? And what will be the consequences of the eventual decision of the Appellate Body, whether it rules in favor or against the contested measure? This looming collision between the trade and the climate regimes is only one of many likely consequences of the world's continuing failure to confront the need for erasing the lines between economy and environment in new rules that will be upheld through the international rule of law.

PART III

On What We Must Do Now

On the Need for New Approaches to Global Economic and Environmental Goals and Governance

The willing of the world face increasing numbers of the unwilling. Darkening the sunny optimism in the global goals of the willing for freeing trade and investment, battling climate change, preserving the environment, and shaping and sharing a sustainable global prosperity is a gloomy pessimism that begets and nurtures a growing unwillingness worldwide. Everywhere, in differing ways but with strikingly similar motivations, people are turning inward and away from the wider world in a grim, growing backlash against globalization and against the economic, demographic, and cultural changes that accompany it. Everywhere, the unwilling of the world are less than welcoming to the grand global designs of the willing.

THE UNWILLING

On the evidence of recent experience, outright opposition to globalization would seem to make no sense. According to the McKinsey Global Institute, "Today, 35 percent of goods cross borders, up from 20 percent in 1990. More than a third of all financial investments in the world are international transactions, and a fifth of Internet traffic is cross-border."[1] Nothing is certain, including globalization. There will continue to be stumbles, hesitations, and populist, nationalist, nativist, and other political reactions aplenty along the way toward a more integrated world. Nevertheless, short of a Third World War, or of some global financial or ecological collapse, some considerable extent of a continuing and ever-more-connecting economic globalization seems here to stay.

There would, on these inescapable facts, seem to be every reason for humanity to work together to find better ways to do more to maximize the size of the overall global economic pie and share it more fairly through further economic integration. Given all we have learned, and given all we are still learning, about the profound human impact on the Earth's ecosystems, there would seem also to be every reason to do so in new ways that work both environmentally and economically. The question should not be: Should we globalize? The question should instead be: *How* should we globalize? It should be: How, through the right approaches to continued globalization, can we grow and govern the world in ways that will work both economically and environmentally for sustainable development?

Yet, for the most part, these questions are not being asked; much less are they being answered by the vast majority of those who must answer them in our unwilling world. Instead, there is an increasing reaction everywhere in the world against the global aspects of spurring economic growth, against the perceived environmental consequences of connecting further economic growth to the global economy, and against the continued calls by the willing for more effective global governance. There is an increasing concern everywhere that the ever-rising flow of trade, investment, and other forms of commerce across borders is neither serving nor uplifting the economic well-being of people or the environmental well-being of the planet.

All in all, the world as a whole has never before seen such prosperity. In China, India, and elsewhere, hundreds of millions of people have emerged from millennia of poverty by connecting to the global economy and embracing globalization. Economist Xavier Sala-i-Martin calculates that global poverty rates have fallen 80 percent and global welfare has soared between 128 percent and 145 percent in less than fifty years because of globalization.[2] In contrast to the widely prevailing popular perception, the fact is, global poverty in the current age of globalization is falling, not rising. Moreover, global inequality is also falling, not rising. The *global* income inequality *between and among countries* – although still huge – has been falling, particularly since 2000.[3] What is more, while vast disparities remain, the gaps between global "have" and "have-not" countries have been narrowing.[4] Whether this economic "convergence" among countries will continue depends to a considerable extent on whether the "emerging" economies can continue to emerge, and also on whether other poorer countries can enlist in the "convergence."[5]

During that same time, though, inequality has been rising *within* most countries, and therefore the already-yawning gap between the rich and the poor within most countries has widened as well. The wealthiest 5 percent of the people in the world have gotten 44 percent of the absolute income gains from globalization. The wealthiest 1 percent of the world's people have received 20 percent of those global income gains[6] (12 percent of Americans are in that global 1 percent).[7] By far the greatest gains have gone to the 1,426 billionaires in the world – who now control altogether about 2 percent of all the wealth on the planet. That is "twice as much wealth as exists in all of Africa."[8] This growing gap between the rich and the poor *within* countries has been most prevalent within those countries worldwide with the *highest* incomes. Mostly, in these wealthier countries the income gains from more globalization have been concentrated at the very top of the economic ladder, and the standard of living of most workers in the middle class has not risen at all. Workers and families in the middle classes of these high-income countries of the world – including those in the United States – have, for many years, seen little or no gains in their real incomes. In the United States, "Income inequality has been rising since the early 1980s, and the median household income is now lower than it was in 1999."[9]

The rise in the popular support for trade protectionism in the United States and in these other higher-income countries is in part one consequence of this phenomenon. In the United States and elsewhere, after simmering for years, the cumulative frustrations from this income stagnation, and from this furthering widening of the income gap, have led at last to a broad political reaction against globalization and all that comes with it in the form of an angry surge in populism, nativism, and economic nationalism. And, in the United States and elsewhere, this reaction has now reached the pinnacles of political power, replete with disinformation and demagoguery. In the forefront of this worldwide political reaction are the beleaguered in these countries who have paid a human toll for change, and who see themselves as the "losers" from their national embrace of the encroaching global economy. In their search for a culprit, they have seized on trade specifically and on globalization generally as by far the easiest targets for blame. In their anxiety and their uncertainty, in their frustration and their anger, they have become easy prey for those politicians who point the accusing finger of blame most of all at the foreign and at the foreigner.

In the developed world, new proposals by the willing may attract the attention, the scrutiny, and even the support of the "elites." But such new proposals are usually ignored or dismissed by those who are persuaded they have been abandoned by the "elites" to the merciless grindings of globalization. Worse, these proposals are scorned as more patronizing "pie in the sky" baked by the intrusive and abusive few who are seen as at fault for the plight of the many who are not perched on the top of the economic ladder. Nor is it at all surprising that, even in those many emerging economies and developing countries where international trade, foreign direct investment, and other aspects of a growing globalization have been catalysts for reducing poverty, there is likewise fervent opposition. In the developing world, the same globalizing forces that have reduced poverty have upended traditional arrangements, undermined traditional certainties, and threatened the entrenched interests that have profited and persisted in many developing countries by forbidding economic and other individual freedoms, and by keeping long-closed societies from opening to the wider world.

Thus, there is an intensifying political resistance almost everywhere in the world to proceeding further with global integration. The reality is that, despite the successes of the willing in concluding a global climate agreement and in agreeing on global goals for sustainable development, there is, in the wary aftermath of the global financial crisis, in the midst of erratic and uncertain global economic growth, and in the maw of a highly unpredictable global politics fueled more and more by extremism and irrationalism, a paucity of global political sentiment for implementing these two vital global agreements, for negotiating new international agreements, and for otherwise cooperating in the construction of new international arrangements.

All this together helps make for an unwilling world. Consider, for a moment, the United States and its slow and uncertain reaction to climate change. Opinion polls have shown that, on climate change, American "voters are best described as worried but unwilling."[10] A clear majority of Americans sees climate change as real, but they do not see climate change as even the most pressing of their environmental concerns; much less are they willing to pay substantial sums for climate action.[11] Still less is climate change – all-affecting as it may be – the only issue that so many anxious people there and elsewhere in the world seem unwilling to address. The willing of the world can come together and contrive all the well-intentioned and ambitious "Sustainable Development Goals" we may wish at grand United Nations summits. The UN can engage in unprecedented "outreach" in the run-up to those summits in a commendable endeavor to involve as many people as possible in shaping and supporting their outcome. But how many among the billions of people on this planet truly are willing to face change to fulfill the UN goals for "transforming our world"?

THE FEAR OF CHANGE

One reason for our unwilling world is the fear of change. In the early 1950s, when we did not yet have any real awareness of what ever-increasing emissions of carbon dioxide and other greenhouse gases were gradually doing to poison the Earth's atmosphere and thus imperil our civilization and our planet, the American philosopher, longshoreman, and autodidact Eric Hoffer described what he called "the ordeal of change."[12] "It is my opinion," he wrote, "that no one really likes the new. We are afraid of it."[13] To illustrate, Hoffer recalled his own early days as an itinerant farm laborer in California during the depths of the Great Depression: "Back in 1936 I spent a good part of the year picking peas. I started out early in January in the Imperial Valley and drifted northward, picking peas as they ripened, until I picked the last peas of the season, in June, around Tracy. Then I shifted all the way to Lake County, where for the first time I was going to pick string beans. And I still remember how hesitant I was that first morning as I was about to address myself to the string bean vines. Would I be able to pick string beans? Even the change from peas to string beans had in it elements of fear."[14]

Hoffer went on to explain, "In the case of drastic change the uneasiness is of course deeper and more lasting. We can never be fully prepared for that which is wholly new. We have to adjust ourselves, and every radical adjustment is a crisis in self-esteem: we undergo a test, we have to prove ourselves. It needs inordinate self-confidence to face drastic change without inner trembling."[15] It is one thing to contemplate the looming prospect of "drastic change" from the tenured cloisters of academe or from the cozy sanctuary of some governmental posting. It is quite another to confront it "without inner trembling" beneath the hot sun in a strange field of string beans.

The baffled billions of the world stand now in a field of string beans, and they are told now by the willing that they must start picking. "Drastic change" is needed, they are informed, because we face – all of us in the world – a daunting and unprecedented challenge. We face a global challenge that is "wholly new." So, all of us must change. All of us must, the willing say, take up together the task of "transforming our world." All of us must, they advise, seek together a global "sustainable development." And we must all, they insist, do it now. But those billions of people wonder: Have we truly picked our last peas? If there are no more peas to pick, can we change now from picking peas to picking string beans? If we can somehow summon the confidence to seize the opportunity to make this change, what will it cost us? What will fade and vanish in lost money and lost time, lost culture and lost community, lost life and a lost, and forever forsaken, future? And what if, with the last peas gone, there are no string beans to pick?

For many millions of people in the world, what for so long seemed a certainty about their lives and their livelihoods has now been rendered, wrenchingly, into a searing uncertainty. Amid a "liquid modernity,"[16] everything that once was solid is melting into air.[17] Left without their ancient anchors, these bewildered people are not prepared for this uncertainty. They are locked in the grip of an "inner trembling." They lack the "inordinate self-confidence" they need to face the future. So they fear not only change; they fear the future. And many of them strive – fervently, but futilely – to stop the future from happening.

In the United States, we once believed in progress. Because of our belief in progress, we Americans helped invent the modern world. Lately, though, too many of us who are Americans have resembled the ancient Romans, who, "lacking any perception of the dogma of progress – for it had not yet been invented – regarded novelty with distrust and aversion."[18] Yes, we may greet with eager delight every new version of the smartphone, and we may fill all our plenitude of personal devices with every new app. But is this truly the same thing as still believing in progress and still believing optimistically in the Enlightenment Project? When we can manage to peel our eyes away from the screens of our devices, many of us wonder how we in the United States – and all the rest of humanity everywhere else – will be able to summon the confidence we all must have to share and to manifest a firm belief in progress, face and seize the future, and change our unwilling into the willing world.

A SUFFICIENT CLIMATE AND SUSTAINABILITY SIGNAL?

In a televised address from the White House at the conclusion of the Paris climate accord, Barack Obama, then the president of the United States, said, "[t]his agreement sends a powerful signal that the world is fully committed to a low-carbon future."[19] Despite these confident words, it remains unclear in the aftermath whether the Paris Agreement does in fact send a sufficient signal to the market that the governments of the world fully intend to move their national economies away from fossil fuels and toward renewable fuels in a low-carbon future. Only if it does send such a strong signal will the Paris Agreement succeed. And only if the Paris Agreement succeeds can we hope to succeed also in accomplishing our much broader Sustainable Development Goals.

There are staggering gaps between the money we have and the money we must pay to fulfill the high hopes of the willing as expressed in these international agreements. The International Energy Agency reports that an additional $13.5 trillion in funding for investment in efficiency measures and in low-carbon technologies is needed to implement the Paris climate agreement by 2030.[20] All this money must be spent as part of an overall transition to a new kind of economy – an economy in which economic growth and environmental protection can be mutually reinforcing – a green economy of the future in which economy and environment are one and the same, and so coexist.

As it is, the world is awash with fossil fuels – with oil, coal, and natural gas. Cheap and seemingly ever-more-abundant fossil fuels continue to dominate the global energy marketplace. Energy production and use account for two-thirds of the world's greenhouse gas emissions. All told, the combined stock value of the oil, coal, and natural gas companies of the world is about $5 trillion. In comparison, stocks related to renewable energy are valued at only about $300 million.[21] The size and the disparity of these numbers suggest the need for a powerful signal to inspire a shift from fossil fuels to cleaner energy.

Nuclear power should be part of the energy transition, but its future remains uncertain because of concerns over costs, safety, and the disposal of nuclear waste. Hydropower is an important part of the energy equation in some parts of the world, such as South America. Solar energy and wind energy are rising rapidly as energy sources. The costs of solar power, wind power, and other forms of renewable energy have dropped dramatically in recent years. For the most part, though, these options for renewable energy are still unable to compete with fossil fuels on price. So worldwide we keep producing more than 32 billion tons of "anthropogenic" – manmade – carbon emissions every year.[22] The dangerous atmospheric concentration of greenhouse gases continues to increase steadily, and the long lifetime of these accumulating gases in the atmosphere makes it harder every year for us to act against climate change. If the climate scientists are correct, this is decidedly unsustainable development.

In a market economy, prices are signals the market sends to help chart the course of the market. In most parts of the world – including the United States of America – there is no price on carbon. The costs of using carbon – the climate and other environmental costs of cumulative carbon emissions – remain economic "external-ities." They are costs paid by society as a whole and not by the producers of these emissions; so they are not reflected in the prices of products produced by using carbon. Where there is no price on carbon, where the costs of using carbon are not "internalized" and thereby included in the market price, the market assumes that the use of carbon has no such costs. Carbon remains cheap, and thus the fossil fuels that emit carbon continue to dominate the market.

The world's 100 highest-emitting businesses account for about one-fourth of all global carbon and other greenhouse gas emissions.[23] But businesses drew little attention in Paris. They were largely kept on the sidelines as "observers," not participants. And yet quite a few businesses were there. More than anything, the multinational corporations and other companies, trade associations, and business alliances that showed up for the climate summit were there because they sought one result most of all from the Paris pact: a market signal in the form of a price on carbon.[24] They did not get one. What they got instead was only a passing mention of "carbon pricing" in a throwaway line in the non-binding Decision accompanying the binding agreement. What they got was a global climate agreement in which the word "market" does not appear.[25]

In the wake of Paris, businesses in search of a price signal on the continued use of carbon were left to find some consolation in the euphemistic mention in the climate agreement of what are described in Article 6 of the agreement as "cooperative approaches that involve the use of internationally transferred mitigation out-comes."[26] The resort by the climate negotiators to this phrase was a backhanded way to refer to carbon markets. Even this roundabout phrase was opposed by those countries in the COP that are allergic to "markets." The emphasis of the govern-mental negotiations in Paris was on governments. The focus in the aftermath of the Paris negotiations on implementing the Paris Agreement has likewise been on governments. Largely overlooked in all but the obligatory UN and COP rhetoric has been the ultimately unavoidable fact that the role of business and of the entire private sector in addressing climate change is both central and crucial. The ultimate test of the success of the Paris Agreement will be whether it sends a loud and clear signal to the world's private businesses and financial investors to shift their money from fossil fuels to clean renewable sources of energy.

Happily, to some extent, this shift to renewables may already be happening. "For all the lingering political uncertainty ... the economics of clean energy appear to be improving so rapidly that a radical acceleration of the clean transition can become possible, if governments push it along with new policies."[27] The majority of the capital being spent worldwide on building new power plants is being spent on renewables – twice as much as on fossil-fueled power plants.[28] More broadly, there is some limited evidence that in some places economic growth is decoupling from carbon emissions.[29] According to the International Energy Agency, global energy-related carbon dioxide emissions have stayed flat even as the global economy has grown, "signaling a decoupling of emissions from economic activity."[30] These encouraging signs about renewable energy investments must, however, be seen in the light of the stubborn fact that, even with all the recent growth, solar, wind, hydro, nuclear, and other sources of renewable energy still represent only about 12 percent of overall global energy.[31]

Up to $24 trillion in non-bank financial assets around the world could be vulnerable to climate change.[32] Concerted action against climate change makes sense for these investors and for their investments. Numerous studies have shown that private investment could exceed what governments can spend on climate change and, if used efficiently, could help combat climate change while reaping corporate profits.[33] Yet, despite their growing awareness of the climate threats to their portfolios, most investors have been slow to act on climate change. Of the top 500 investors in the world – pension funds, insurers, sovereign wealth funds, foundations, and endowments that manage a total of $38 trillion in assets – almost half are reportedly still doing nothing to address climate change through their investments.[34]

Most investors do not yet seem to have gotten the strong signal they need to accelerate the shift to renewable energy for a "green economy." While they wait for a sufficient market signal, they continue to proceed with "business as usual" in their energy and other sustainability-related investments. They do so despite the fact that climate scientists, ecologists, energy analysts, and mainstream economists are all insisting that "business as usual" will not prove to be nearly enough to prevent investment losses from climate change. As it is, one global energy fund manager has said, "[t]he vast majority of investors don't think climate change is an issue they should take into account."[35]

The strong signal investors and others await will not come *directly* from the Paris Agreement. If it does come, it will come *indirectly* from the actions taken by individual countries domestically to comply with the voluntary climate pledges they have made in connection with the Paris Agreement.[36] It will come from an early and a widespread compliance by national governments with – and especially from a significant ratcheting-up over time of – their climate pledges. It will mainly come not from the necessary international follow-up to the Paris deal – but from the hurly-burly of the domestic politics of national governments. If investors and markets see from their actions in response to the global climate accord that countries are indeed serious about keeping and even increasing their commitments to cut carbon emissions, then there will be an accelerated energy shift.

But if the signal to shift away from a carbon economy comes *loud and clear*, it will be because climate and sustainability actions are not confined to national governments. In the hard follow-up work of treaty implementation that must send the strong signal of a societal shift, the most important of the decisions relating to the Paris climate agreement and, equally, the most important of the broader Sustainable Development Goals may well prove to be some that have, so far, received little attention. These decisions and these goals reach beyond governments to encourage a whole host of climate and sustainability actions taken by "non-state political actors" *outside governments*.

The decisions accompanying the Paris Agreement reach beyond Westphalian states to include the "efforts of all non-Party stakeholders to address and respond to climate change, including those of civil society, the private sector, financial institutions, cities and other subnational authorities."[37] These groups other than national governments are "invited ... to scale up their efforts and support actions to reduce emissions and/or to build resilience and decrease vulnerability to the adverse effects of climate change,"[38] and the Parties to the COP are encouraged to "work closely" with them "to catalyze efforts to strengthen mitigation and adaptation action."[39] These decisions are in furtherance of the last – and the most significant – of the seventeen Sustainable Development Goals, which asserts the imperative for a "global partnership." Goal 17 of the SDGs is to "strengthen the means of implementation and revitalize the global partnership for sustainable development" that was first proposed around the turn of the century.[40]

Broad-based partnerships in action networks across different sectors and value chains, and at varying local, national, and regional levels[41] are supposed to become "the glue for implementation" of the Sustainable Development Goals.[42] Endeavors to "enhance" the "global partnership," it is explained in the SDGs, should be "complemented by multi-stakeholder partnerships that mobilize and share knowledge, expertise, technology and financial resources, to support the achievement of the sustainable development goals in all countries, particularly developing countries."[43] Among the listed target areas of Goal 17 are finance, technology, capacity-building, data monitoring and accountability, and trade.[44] None of the targets in these areas can be reached without these partnerships.

These words extolling the value of partnerships to sustainability will not be enough to send a sufficient signal that how we grow and how we govern the world must now be changed. New and energizing economic and environmental approaches are needed to send the right signals to the marketplace to help ensure the success of our fight against climate change, and to secure the success, too, of our overall struggle for global sustainable development. Continued and intensified international efforts by the willing are, of course, essential to reaching these global goals. The right kinds and the right amounts of national governmental actions continue to be required. A shared sustainable development must continue to be sought too in national capitals. We need new international and national approaches alike. Through the continued international cooperation of governments consistent with Tocqueville's "principle of interest rightly understood," we must build – brick by brick – a global architecture for enabling climate and sustainability actions of all kinds.

But, in addition to all this, we must look to more than merely governments if we hope to make the willing world. In much of all that is being accomplished cooperatively by crosscutting partnerships at the global grassroots, governments are engaged with a variety of others from outside governments. Yet, in much of all that is happening there is no governmental involvement at all. Sometimes there is a need for governmental engagement and participation. Sometimes there is not. The "global partnership" envisaged by the SDGs is not only a partnership of governments. It is a partnership of people. All our essential and ever-evolving national and international actions for climate and sustainability advances must be supplemented and complemented by the combined efforts of all kinds by business, civil society, educators, scientists, and volunteer activists rising up from the innovative grassroots of the world, so fertile everywhere with ideas, with enterprise, and with innovation.

"TOP DOWN" OR "BOTTOM UP"?

To help fulfill nearly 200 national climate pledges, to forge beyond the initial pledges to make additional emissions cuts, to weave economy and environment together for sustainable development, and to do all we must do in trade, investment, and other areas of commerce to support these ends, we must see and seize the potential of new approaches that are not limited solely to governmental action. We must also inspire and rely on the vast and varied abundance of innovative bottom-up approaches all over the world that can first be shown to work locally and can then be scaled up over time to serve more of the world and, in some cases, all of the world.

New approaches toward sustainable prosperity must emerge from the practical experience and the practical results of the learning by doing of *ad hoc* coalitions and action networks of solution-finders everywhere on the planet. They must rise up from the bottom up all over the world by telling us the living story of defining sustainable development by doing it. These new bottom-up approaches can help send the right signal of a real shift to a shared prosperity in a new green economy. They can help free us from the fear of change. They can help give us the renewed confidence that will come from believing that we can not only confront change. We can also prosper from it. Working together in new ways, we can learn how to pick many new kinds of string beans.

But, to be successful, not just some but *all* of these multi-stakeholder partnerships must embrace and must engage with not only the local and regional governments, not only the NGOs and other parts of civil society, but also with the investors, the businesses, and all those in the private sector that have largely been left on the sidelines of our global summits and in the background at our grand global pronouncements. To send a signal loud and clear of the necessity and of the certainty of a global shift to a green economy, the word "market" must no longer be avoided by the willing. It must be heard loud and clear. What is more, the creative forces of the market must be heeded far and near as we define sustainable development by doing it.

Two of the most committed of the willing, Peter Orebach of Norway and Martin Chanock of South Africa, have written much that is insightful on the relationship between international law and global sustainability. Yet they say, "Sustainable development is a top-down, internationally developed norm of social justice."[45]

No. It is not. It must not be. In its origins, it may be true to say of sustainable development that it was conceived as top-down. The foundational Brundtland Report in 1987 was certainly not the end product of a planet-full of consensus-building town meetings. The United Nations has done somewhat better since then in reaching out for the multitude of views in a diverse and divided world. Still, it is fair to say that the impetus for sustainable development still flows down from the top of the world and not up from the bottom where more than 7 billion people live. If this inclination toward the top-down persists in the work of the willing, there will be no sustainable development. To succeed, sustainable development cannot be top-down. It must be bottom-up. We will never find the solutions we seek for sustainable development if we begin by believing that we have already found them.

Noted environmental blogger Andrew Reskin points out that the Paris Agreement has departed from past "visions of some magical top-down accord."[46] So it has – to the extent that it relates to *governments*. Unlike the Kyoto Protocol, and unlike the long-held expectations of the "universal and comprehensive" treaty that a global climate agreement was long anticipated to be, the climate deal ultimately concluded in Paris at the end of 2015 is not centered on targets and timetables. Furthermore, it does not impose any across-the-board obligations on any of the governments of the world to cut their emissions of harmful greenhouse gases. Instead, national governments choose their own targets for cutting their emissions, and they choose their own timetables. They have made and announced these sovereign choices as their Nationally Determined Contributions – as their purely *voluntary* national pledges.

This reliance on voluntary national pledges in the climate agreement did not happen because the climate negotiators no longer desired to impose "top-down" obligations on governments. It happened because the negotiators did not have the makings of a consensus to impose them. It was out of sheer political necessity that the climate negotiators abandoned in Paris their "magical" vision of a top-down solution on global climate change. Most of the climate negotiators and advocates held fast to their ideal of the top-down for as long as they could. Had they been able to muster a consensus for it, the climate negotiators would surely have concluded in Paris yet another fully top-down agreement that would have imposed a slew of new international legal mandates on nearly 200 countries. In the aftermath, many among the willing continue to hold fast to a belief in the top-down "magic." For all the attendant rhetoric to the contrary, the "2030 agenda" of the United Nations that sets out the seventeen Sustainable Development Goals is still centered on governments. Yes, there is a grudging and obligatory nod in these products of the contemporary international diplomacy of sustainable development to some role for "actors" other than states. But, for the most part, the central focus still remains on states, and the knees of the negotiators still jerk first toward state-centered solutions.

The American philosopher Dale Jamieson has plumbed the psychology of the persistent "magical" belief that climate change can be solved by a global deal: "What these people have in common is *a state-centric view* of how the climate change problem can be solved ... Many activists and world leaders share the view that climate change is at heart a problem of justice *between states*."[47] With this in mind, we should not be deceived by the inclusion of language in the Paris Agreement and in the accompanying Paris decisions – or by the inclusion of similar language in the Sustainable Development Goals – that seems to anticipate the full and active participation of a variety of "actors" other than states in the fulfillment of those international agreements. That innovative language aside, the two agreements are nevertheless fully conventional international arrangements in the simple fact that they are *international*. To the extent that they are binding, they bind only states. To the extent that they impose obligations, they impose them only on states.

The timeless temptation of those who would see the world shaped in a new way is to devise some grand design for the world, and then require that all human actions fit within that design. The bold dreams of the most idealistic among us, and the restive minds of the most ambitious among us, turn most easily to the abstract thinking and the soothing symmetry of the top-down. If there is one big problem that must be solved, then surely there must also be one big solution to that problem. Cannot all of that one question be reduced to one same answer for all people, for all places, and for all purposes? This temptation to submit to the lure of imposing one grand design on all the vast variety of human endeavor has been called by American journalist Bret Stephens "the tyranny of a big idea."[48]

The enduring appeal of the abstraction of the big idea for constructing and for applying a grand design top-down to solve some societal problem appears in the guise of the obsessed painter in the famous short story by the nineteenth-century French author Honoré de Balzac entitled "The Unknown Masterpiece." In his story, a talented painter tries time and again to paint a glorious picture that he sees in his head. He touches and retouches his waiting canvas over and over again. In the end, the painter puts on the canvas only a shapeless collage of colors – which seems nevertheless to his biased eyes to be a perfect replica of the masterpiece in his mind. To his son-in-law, the image of Balzac's painter was the image that lingered in his mind of Karl Marx.[49]

One need not be Marx – or Mao or Robespierre – or Pol Pot or Hitler – to see a perfect masterpiece of human design that exists only in one's own mind. The timeless lure of the grand design does not appeal only to the tyrannical and the malevolent. It appeals equally – indeed most frequently – to some among us with the best and with the noblest of intentions. In their haste to do their best and their noblest, they extol from the heights what they see as the certain solution, and they seek to rain that sole solution down from the verdant heights onto the dry and thirsty plains of the needy masses below. But seeing it in the abstraction of our mind's eye is not the same as realizing it. Mere assertion must not be equated with action, much less with accomplishment. Simply saying it does not make it so – not even if it is said well.

There is also the unavoidable fact that, in conceiving a grand design in our head, we each design differently. Each of us sees a different painting. Another painter's conception of the ideal masterpiece will never be identical to our own. The tempting concept of imposing from above some grand design does not allow for the sheer diversity of humanity in inspiration and in aspiration, in culture and in circumstance. One person's soothing landscape may be another's bleak and barren plain. One person's utopia may be another's nightmare. The shapeless collage of colors that is the grand design can sometimes become a destructive force in the hands of its designers. If we let it, the train carrying Lenin will arrive in the Finland Station.

One of the most unfortunate results of a weakness to the appeal of the grand design is that it can lead to undue reliance on the long arm of the state. The utopian visions of all those who would somehow see the all-too-human messiness of our imperfect society transformed into a perfect masterpiece can lead not only to an inclination toward imposing some grand design. Those visions can lead also to a grand design that is imposed and controlled by the state. The state, these designers reason, can be singular. The state can be malleable. The long arm of the state can be as far-reaching as we may wish it to be. Besides, they ask, what else but the top-down of the state could fulfill our hopes for the grand design? What else but the state could be the engine of human progress?

Alas, in yielding to the allure of the grand design, some of the willing, as imaginative as they may otherwise be, seem somehow unable to see beyond the state. They seem incapable of imagining the usefulness – or even the legitimacy – of the vast and varied gallery of individual human endeavor that does not originate with and proceed from the state. They may see – and they may strive to serve through their "top-down" designs – the abstraction called "the people." But they may not see or absorb the lived experience of individual human beings trying to find some measure of freedom, fulfillment, and dignity in an unwilling world. While those who succumb to the lure of the grand design are busy trying to paint the perfection of Balzac's unknown masterpiece, they often miss the other bright colors of the human palette.

THE TRUE BOTTOM-UP

To learn how to shape and share in the bounty of the willing world, to define sustainable development by doing it, we must begin not at the end, but at the beginning. We will never find the innovative solutions we must find for fighting climate change and for forging sustainable development by beginning at the end, top-down. We will discover the solutions we need only by beginning at the beginning, with the true bottom-up.

The worldwide climate and sustainability solutions of the true bottom-up will never be identified and implemented by contriving and by then imprinting on a reluctant world some grand global design that presumes to tell us all the answers before we even know all the questions. The solutions will not be found by trying somehow to shape the rough contours of reality to fit the pristine purity of some predetermined abstraction. The climate and sustainability solutions of the true bottom-up will be revealed only by engaging in and by learning from the hard-won practical and cumulative experience of cooperative and creative human actions of all kinds down at the imaginative and innovative grassroots of the world. If we make the mistake of beginning at the end and not at the beginning, if we try to impose some grand global design, then we will end up like Balzac's painter. We will paint something much less than a masterpiece.

The assumption behind the grand design is that humanity can be moved by the conscious and concerted direction of designers toward predetermined ends. History teaches us that this is not so. Since our ancestors decided to abandon hunting and gathering and take up agriculture ten thousand years ago, most of all that we have achieved of any benefit to an aspiring humanity has been achieved through the workings of a "spontaneous order" – through spontaneous results that have emerged unforeseen and uncontrolled from the accumulation and the combination of countless improvisational human actions that cannot be foreseen and that cannot be directly controlled by any one person or by any one group of people according to some previous plan or design.[50] As the twentieth-century political economist Friedrich Hayek rightly reminded us, "The mind can never foresee its own advance ... Human reason can neither predict nor deliberately shape its own future. Its advances consist in finding out where it has been wrong."[51] Thus, the path of human advance cannot be reduced to writing upfront in some neat and tidy plan, no matter how noble the motivation or felicitous the pen of the planner. The bright future we must seek together in transforming our unwilling into the willing world cannot be designed beforehand. It must be lived together day by day.

The future cannot be designed because the future cannot be foreseen. The future must be shaped along the way by seizing the unforeseen opportunities that arise from the lived experience of freedom and from the sheer serendipity of the creative unfolding of individual and cooperative human endeavor. The future must emerge from the day-to-day dynamism of a decentralized and a self-organized spontaneous order that no one of us can foresee and that no one of us can ever direct on our own. A spontaneous order does not lend itself to direction because no one person – no one group – no matter how highly motivated or how supposedly "expert" – can ever possess sufficient knowledge to know *how* or to know *where* to direct it. The notion of a spontaneous order in human economy, and in human society as a whole, dates back to the Enlightenment and to the Enlightenment's departure from the assumption of a received, ascribed, and usually hierarchical order in all the arrangements of the world. In enduring words made famous by Hayek two centuries later, Adam Ferguson, an exemplar of the Scottish Enlightenment and a contemporary and friend of Adam Smith, declared, in 1767, that, "[e]very step and every movement of the multitude, even in what are termed enlightened ages, are made with equal blindness to the future, and nations stumble upon establishments, which are indeed the result of human action, but not the execution of any human design."[52]

In this century, Cesar Hidalgo, of the MIT Media Lab, has said much the same thing, in more contemporary terms, while channeling Ferguson's initial insight in his own attempt to explain "why information grows" from the stumbling along of myriad cooperative human actions.[53] In Hidalgo's more modern telling, "Knowledge and knowhow are embodied in humans and networks of humans that have a finite capacity to embody knowledge and knowhow. The finiteness of humans and of the networks we form limits our ability to accumulate and transmit knowledge and knowhow, leading to spatial accumulations of knowledge and knowhow that result in global inequality. So the need for knowledge and knowhow to be embodied in humans and networks of humans can help explain the unevenness of the world."[54]

A spontaneous order is essential because of its superiority in transmitting information and in thereby making information grow. Commercially, by far the most direct and telling means of transmitting information is through a price signal. In slowing and adapting to climate change, and in otherwise shaping sustainable development, a part of the "spontaneous order" must include the transmission in the form of a price signal to the marketplace of a shift away from carbon emissions and toward the climate-friendly sustainability of a green economy. This is the signal – loud and clear – that has been sought by the market from the Paris Agreement and from the Sustainable Development Goals. Trade is a crucial part of this. Those of our human networks that we call "trade" have an important role to serve in the transmission of this signal and in the transition to a green economy. Because trade is a division of labor, trade inspires specialization. Because trade inspires specialization, trade inspires innovation. The more we trade, the more we specialize, and the more we innovate. The more we trade internationally, the more we innovate globally, in part through the discovery and the development of new technologies. There is, therefore, a straight arrow connecting the flow of trade and the flourishing of the innovations needed to achieve sustainable development.[55]

AN ENABLING FRAMEWORK OF RULES

But rules are required. There are limits to the spontaneous order of the marketplace. A crucial task of government is to discern how much of "the unevenness of the world" should be evened out by rules through governmental intervention. At the same time, government must support the market, and a crucial part of supporting the market is ensuring the existence of an enabling framework in which market forces can work as they should. Market forces work as they should only in the context of an enabling framework consisting of the right rules. In the absence of the right rules, the market cannot succeed. Order soon descends into disorder. The market becomes chaos.

Because the market is necessarily a spontaneous order, the actual market itself cannot be designed deliberately. The market must emerge over time from the spontaneity of repeated human interaction. Yet certain of the rules needed to facilitate and to further the right workings of the market can and must be designed. Hayek himself, in insisting on the indispensability of an agreed framework of enabling rules for the market, not only conceded but even went so far as to stress that a successful spontaneous order can in fact exist that "rests on rules that are the result of deliberate design."[56] It is hard to imagine a successful market that does not rely on rules that are at least to some extent designed deliberately.

Agreeing on the right rules through the right kind of rule-making is therefore an essential part of defining sustainable development by doing it. Making and upholding the right framework of rules for supporting and enhancing market forces for sustainable global prosperity must be the overarching aim of the willing in seeking the willing world. Which are the right rules? As is so often true of so much else, the right rules are usually found somewhere in the "in between." "Between is the only honest place to be," the liberal thinker Lionel Trilling told us, and the effort to draw a line in the right place and in the right way "in between" is almost always the essence of the right kind of rule-making.[57] This is true of almost all rule-making. This is certainly true of almost all commercial rule-making in the endless stirring of a mixed economy that seeks the best from the market while seeking also to blunt the sharpest elbows of market forces. Almost everywhere, and almost always, a line must be drawn somewhere "in between."

The eminent nineteenth-century British historian and Whig politician Thomas Babington Macaulay may have summed up better than anyone else has done since the timeless challenge facing lawmakers and other rule-makers when discerning where and how to draw the right line "in between." In his speech to the House of Commons in 1846 in support of the then-novel idea of limiting the working day to ten hours, Macaulay lamented, "I hardly know which is the greater pest to society, a paternal government, which intrudes itself into every part of human life, and which thinks that it can do everything for everybody better than anybody can do anything for himself; or a careless, lounging government, which suffers grievances, such as it could at once remove, to grow and multiply, and which to all complaint and remonstrance has only one answer: 'We must let things alone; we must let them take their course; we must let things find their level.' There is no more important problem in politics than to find the just mean between these two most persistent extremes to draw correctly the line which divides those cases in which it is the duty of the state to interfere from those cases in which it is the duty of the state to abstain from interference."[58]

The "just mean" somewhere "in between" is, almost always, the right line for a rule-maker to draw. The drawing of the right commercial line only rarely involves an absolute. Human slavery is absolutely wrong; therefore, human slavery and the products of human slavery should be banned absolutely. Cancer kills; therefore, the sale of products that cause cancer should be controlled. Trade in elephant ivory threatens elephants with extinction; therefore, such trade should be outlawed and punished severely. There are more instances of such absolutes. But almost all commercial rule-making does not involve absolutes. It involves the assessing of degrees of difference. It involves the weighing and the balancing of costs and benefits. It involves the drawing of a line in an exercise of judgment.

Moreover, in discerning the right role for government, in determining just the right kind and just the right extent of government intervention as a part of right rule-making, the choice is rarely one between the utter absence of government or the total domination of government in the marketplace. The straw men of these two extreme choices are familiar foils from our divisive political debates, but, as Macaulay suggested, the choice is rarely between a total hands-off *laissez faire* by the government on the one hand or a total governmental intervention, direction, and control on the other. The choice is almost always somewhere "in between" the two extremes. We must, therefore, determine what should instruct and inform us in our ongoing efforts to draw the right lines in the right rules that will provide the necessary enabling framework for the marketplace. We must, especially, know what we should keep in mind when trying to write the right rules to enable the market to address climate change and also to shape a sustainable global prosperity in which we all will share. Rules are the glue that holds the market together, but we need rules that enable us, not rules that confine us. What should guide us as rule-makers in discerning the right place "in between"?

Above all, we should be guided in our rule-making by *humanity*. Right rule-making must be done in an atmosphere of freedom amid a free flow of ideas. It must be done with an appreciation of the necessity of the free flow of ideas to the continuing evolution of an enabling framework to support sustainable development. The right rules "in between" will leave room for the emergence of new ideas and for the testing of those new ideas in the marketplace through what the American economist and historian Deirdre McCloskey describes as "trade-tested better-ment."[59] The ideas that must animate us most in our search for the right rules for the right enabling framework for sustainable development are those ideas that have done the most in the past few centuries to advance humanity. Those ideas are the endlessly useful ideas inspired by a belief in the vast potential of human freedom. They are the still and forever revolutionary ideas of human liberty, human rights, and human dignity. They are the life-affirming and world-changing ideas of liberty and rights and dignity, not just for some of us, but for all of us.

McCloskey sees these ideas as having made our modern world. She maintains, "The original and sustaining causes of the modern world ... were ethical and not material. They were the widening adoption of two mere ideas, the new and liberal economic idea of liberty for ordinary people and the new and democratic social idea of dignity for them."[60] She sees "the one scientifically proven, social discovery" during the emergence of the modern world as the fact "that ordinary men and women do not need to be directed from above, and when honored and left alone can become immensely creative."[61] In her view, these revolutionary ideas of a sense of dignity and of rights for all have done the most to spur economic growth.[62] We must never overlook these ideas in our endeavors to find and draw the right lines "in between." Right rule-making should respect the individual capacity of "ordinary men and women" to give reality to human freedom by making their own choices. It should respect their ability to find their own future. In this way, it will not restrain but will reinforce the human creativity of the true bottom-up.

In addition to humanity, we should be guided in our rule-making by *humility*. We must share one and all in an understanding of the inevitability of our own fallibility. There will be no human perfection. There will be no one universal solution to the challenges we must face. The solutions we find will need to be inclusive and pluralistic. They will need also to be pragmatic, fit to purpose in keeping with the reality of what we actually discover to be true, and not fit only to some preconceived notion of what we may assume at the outset to be true. And these solutions will be imperfect at best – just as we are imperfect – and in need therefore of constant and continuing improvement.

The best of our willing intentions must be informed by the *facts* of how the world really is, instead of our fancies of how we simply wish it would be. Right rule-making demands rational thinking and reasoned judgment based on findings of fact. The reliance on rational thinking and reasoned judgment may not always have an immediate popular appeal. The facts are not always what a majority of the people who are affected by the rule-making may think the facts to be at the time when the rule is made. One of the lessons of the Enlightenment that is sometimes forgotten by those who hope to make ours a better world is that reason alone is not enough. The logic of reason must face the facts of reality. Thus, in bringing reasoned judgment to our rational rule-making, we must face the facts. We cannot rely entirely on our abstractions *a priori* – our preliminary judgments about the effects of a proposed rule before the experience of seeing what happens when we apply it. Our rules must be framed to be able to yield in practice to the reality of what does happen after they are applied. There must be flexibility in our rule-making that allows for a reconsideration based on what we later learn of the facts, and on what we later learn of the ever-changing reality around us.

Cultural differences, to cite one example, can often be stubbornly persistent and therefore resistant to rule-making. Culture cannot be ignored. "Culture matters."[63] We ask ourselves: We have always done it this way; why should we now do it differently? The best of our rule-making intentions may sometimes have to yield to the reality of cultural and other circumstances. Surely it is laudable to try to solve the global problem of household pollution by providing cook-stoves to poor women in poor countries. But what if we learn that those women won't use the stoves, or that the stoves won't work, or that the stoves we provide can pollute as much as the open fires they are supposed to replace?[64]

The right line "in between" must leave room for the rich diversity of all the cultures that comprise human civilization. While seeking harmony and some right measure of harmonization from globalization, the shaping of sustainable development should not impose a bland and sterile sameness on the world. While acting together as one, humanity can still be many. Humanity can and must be expressed in countless varieties consistently with the values of human freedom and human dignity. Indeed, it will be in some of these varied cultural expressions of our common humanity that we will find some of the new ideas we need for scaling up to sustainable development. The SDGs rightly speak of appreciating "culture's contribution to sustainable development."[65]

Part of the humility of facing the facts is that we must be guided in all our rule-making by human *experience*. The right rule-making for an enabling framework for sustainable development must be based not on theory, not on the masterpiece in our mind, but on experience. Yes, some of the right rules will, unavoidably, result from deliberate design. But most should not. Most of the right rules should emerge from the actual experience of life, and emerge especially from the practical experience of learning by doing. Most of the right rules that should be scaled up to serve more of us, and perhaps all of us, will be based on the proven experience of some of us as part of the diverse, flexible, empowering, and emphatically practical human interaction of the true bottom-up.

In contrast to the approach frequently taken by some other international institutions, a reliance primarily on experience has, for the most part, long been the approach generally taken to rule-making by the rule-based world trading system that has evolved over more than half a century into the World Trade Organization. The embracing rule-driven architecture of the global trading system – the enabling framework of thousands upon thousands of pages of WTO rules and of WTO rulings clarifying the meanings of those rules – has been built by WTO members over time and largely on the basis of their shared and cumulative experience in increasing trade by lowering the barriers to trade. In this respect, the WTO trading system is bottom-up and not top-down.

Another of our guides in drawing the right lines for the right rules must be *science*. Experience results in no small part from experimentation. Many of the right rules and the right solutions for sustainable development will rise up from the bottom-up experiments in learning by doing that are conducted by the creative and crosscutting voluntary networks of the willing throughout the world. Many of these experiments will be scientific experiments. Many others will be based on science. The rules we derive and scale up from these experiments will be the right rules only if they result from the application of scientific methods. The "useful intellectual tools" of science include the finding of facts through testing by observation, and the reliance on established facts in the hypothesis of the best approaches to conclusions suitable for rule-making.[66] These scientific tools have served humanity well in "the painstaking, evidence-based, self-correcting, centuries-long effort by scientists to elucidate how the universe works."[67] They must serve us now – and from now on – in all our rule-making for sustainability. The methods of science are the epitome of the true bottom-up. These tools for producing knowledge do not reason top-down by "deduction" – prior to any experience and premised on preconceived conclusions in which life is an abstraction. Instead, they reason bottom up by "induction" – based on observations that test hypotheses in the trial and error of actual experience, where life is lived.

"Bottom-up" rules derived from the scientific method are also rules that proceed from the assumption that the future is uncertain. Scientific knowledge is everywhere and always tentative and subject to what Popper labeled "falsification" – to future refutation by further testing by observation. Science is therefore open-ended, "a form of progressive knowledge in which established truths may always be disputed and in which an ultimate truth is never attained."[68] Science, like freedom, is thus a triumph of open-ended experience from below over the dictate of predetermined prescription from above. Science is a product of the exercise of the freedom of thought that is at the heart of human freedom. This relationship between science and freedom is why Karl Popper saw the free society, the open society, as, necessarily, a "scientific society."

Thus, humanity and humility alike suggest that the right rules will be scientific rules in which the right lines are drawn somewhere short of an absolute certainty. Accordingly, an enabling framework of rules for sustainable development must be seen not as permanent, but, rather, as provisional. It must be seen as a construct for use now, but subject to change later in the light of the learning of new facts. In the same way that the scientific method expresses – in science historian David Wootton's phrase – "the principle that intellectual systems are merely temporary constructions which may need later to be revised and improved," so too must this principle be expressed in the framework of rules established to enable markets and other human networks.[69] Because the future is uncertain, and because it will always be uncertain, we need flexible rules that look to the long term and that can be adapted to fit new facts over time.[70]

In particular, considerable humility is warranted in right rule-making for sustainability because rule-making for sustainability involves *nature*. Part of the signal we must send to the market through our rule-making must be that the impact of the market on nature can no longer be ignored. That impact must always be taken into account. The fate of nature is also our own fate. Nature is necessary to us. Nature has value to us because of what we can do with nature, and because of what more our ever-unfolding scientific understanding of nature can one day help us to do. Nature also has value in and of itself. Human understanding of the intrinsic value of nature is a part of "humility in the Anthropocene."[71] In the age of humans, we humans must tread carefully on the rest of Creation. As one environmentalist, Emma Marris, has rightly expressed it, in words that could as easily have been written by Henry David Thoreau, "Humility before the awesome complexity, great evolutionary age, and sheer beauty of wild nature is the key virtue. [We must] value the rest of nature in and of itself, and this requires that we accept that we are not the center of the universe or the determiner of value. It requires humility."[72]

Inevitably, our rule-making will affect the future of nature. Humility should insist that we hesitate before we proceed with rules that will affect nature. There is much about nature and about our effects on nature that we simply do not yet know. For this reason, in the eyes of some scientists, in the task of "shaping the future" through rule-making and other decisionmaking, our current environmental "problems are simply too complex and contingent for scientists to make definitive predictions. In the presence of such deep uncertainty, the machinery of prediction and decision making seizes up."[73] These scientists have concluded that the best approach in rule-making that strikes the right balance between economy and environment is to draw the line somewhere "in between" the extremes of any absolute certainties about either one or the other. The best approach in making rules that affect nature, they advise us, is to "frame strategies that work well over a very wide range of plausible futures."[74] In all our rule-making for sustainability, we must employ, going forward, "adaptive strategies" within an "alternative framework focused on flexibility – finding, testing, and implementing policies that work well no matter what happens."[75]

The best approach is to acknowledge uncertainty. The right lines will be drawn in the right rules with the uncertainty of the future of nature much in mind. As every rule-maker must always remember, every rule is really two rules – one for today and one for the unforeseeable tomorrow. As every jurist must always ponder, every case inspiring a ruling is really two cases – the one case today and all the future cases that cannot be foreseen but could be affected by today's ruling. These general admonitions for writing rules and for clarifying rules assume an added urgency because of our uncertainty about what today is doing to the tomorrow of nature. We have reached the point as a species where all our efforts to establish and to uphold an enabling framework of rules for the market must take fully into account all that the impact of our myriad market decisions is doing to the Earth's other species and to all the rest of nature. In the drawing of lines, in the writing of rules, in the weaving together of a rules framework to serve both the economy and the environment, we are due for a healthy dose of what the naturalist Edward O. Wilson calls "ecological realism."[76] There must be realism about all we are doing to nature, and there must be realism about our inescapable relationship with nature.

In exploring "the ordeal of change," Eric Hoffer observed that human freedom has long been seen in no small part as a process of enabling humanity "to break away from, and rise above, nature."[77] Humanity cannot be freed from nature. Humanity is a part of nature. The only way we can be free is *within* nature. The only way we can sustain ourselves and can sustain human civilization is by sustaining also the global ecosystems of which we are an inseparable part. As Wilson explains about one vital aspect of sustainability, "Biodiversity as a whole forms a shield protecting each of the species that together compose it, ourselves included . . . [D]uring the Anthropocene,

Earth's shield of biodiversity is being shattered and the pieces are being thrown away."[78] Such existential considerations cannot be reduced solely to a utilitarian cost–benefit calculation. The making of the rules we choose to use to help shape our future must be infused also by an understanding of the inseparability of humanity and nature.

Thus, a new awareness of the inescapable interconnectedness of humanity with nature must be evidenced in the incentives included in our rule-making for the necessary transition to a new green economy. The most important of those incentives is the sending of the needed price signal announcing the arrival of that green economy. Other needed incentives will be found as we ask and answer together the question common to all rule-making for sustainability: Where is the "just mean" of the right rules somewhere "in between"?

THE MAKINGS OF WILLINGNESS

The makings of willingness are there to be found in the voluntary cooperative networks comprised of all those who are busily engaged all over the world in the collaborative actions of the true bottom-up. The raw material for the making of the willing world is there to be shaped and scaled up through an incremental and improvisational approach to further rule-making that can frame and fashion over time the right global architecture for sustainable development. A great many of the answers we urgently need to our questions about how to shape and share a sustainable global prosperity will not be found in the "top-down" tutelage of states or in the "state-centric" abstractions of collaborations consisting solely of states. Those answers will be discovered only through the experience of the innovative networks of groups of volunteers in communities of all kinds all over the world who are defining sustainable development by doing it.

These action networks are coalitions of the willing. They have usually come together and combined together for the sole purpose of achieving a common goal they believe can be achieved only if they do combine together. These willing coalitions range across and cut across all the conventional lines of interest, expertise, and nationality. Often they link business, civil society, and local or regional governments together in pursuit of a common task through a "global partnership," a "global network," a "global alliance," a "public–private partnership," or some other form of shared endeavor. Usually these networks of volunteer workers learn by doing in the same ways as commercial workers in the division of labor in the marketplace. This world-full of many and vastly diverse coalitions "can often achieve, through collaboration, what governments working alone cannot, especially for those in developing countries."[79]

Worldwide, these ambitious networks of grassroots volunteers are largely self-started and self-directed, often local, and often not involving governments at all. These action networks involve governments whenever and wherever they think they need to do so. They do not, however, simply wait on governmental actions; nor do they necessarily depend on governmental actions to attain their goals. If need be, these voluntary networks of "non-state political actors" find ways to forge ahead without governments toward new forms of rule-making and new forms of governance. Every day, willing volunteers throughout the world find together the new ways we need for defining sustainable development by doing it. However and wherever these new ways may happen to emerge in the world, what some of the willing learn in an initiative in one part of the world can help demonstrate how, together, we can define sustainable development by doing it elsewhere and perhaps even everywhere in the world. Thus, global rule-making need not always be or always begin at the global level. Successful experimental local rules for one place can become a part of the basis for the local rules for other places, and some of these local rules can be scaled up over time to become global rules for all places.

Examples of these bottom-up networks and initiatives abound: the Consumer Goods Forum, dedicated to sustainability in the supply of consumer goods; the Green Touch program, enhancing the energy efficiency of Internet networks; the Global Fund to Fight AIDS, Tuberculosis and Malaria; the Gavi Alliance for vaccines and immunization; the 2030 Water Resources Group, helping manage the nexus of water, food, land, and energy; the African Cocoa Initiative, helping improve sustainability in cocoa farming; the Lights for All initiative, helping reduce poverty by eliminating energy exclusion; the C40 Cities Climate Leadership Group, greening cities across the borders of the world; the Coral Triangle Initiative on Coral Reefs, Fisheries, and Food, a partnership of a number of countries helping to halt coastal and marine degradation in the South Pacific; and thousands more.

The Friends of Rio+20 – a broad cross-section of the willing assembled by the World Economic Forum – urged in 2012 that these voluntary networks and initiatives be the focus of the ongoing work of addressing climate change and promoting sustainable development because "[t]here is now substantial evidence that clearly defined coalitions of willing and able actors from across government, business, science and civil society can mobilize their combined skills, innovation and resources to make clear progress at scale against specific sustainable development goals."[80] By the time of the adoption of the Sustainable Development Goals in September 2015, the voluntary commitments of nearly 2,000 "multi-stakeholder partnerships" had been listed on an interactive online platform of the UN's Sustainable Development in Action website.[81] By that time, too, about a dozen voluntary governmental commitments and more than two dozen voluntary commitments by non-governmental groups had been listed on the online registry established for the Addis Ababa Action Agenda of the third United Nations Conference on Financing for Development.[82]

After the Paris Agreement, there is also now the United Nations Conference of Parties' Non-State Actor Zone for Climate Action (in the inevitable and unfortunate UN acronym, NAZCA). Promoted especially by Peru, which preceded France in presiding over the climate COP, this "zone" is an online site for the listing and the totaling of bottom-up commitments of all kinds to take climate action.[83] It is also a forum for idea-shopping and idea-swapping on climate action – a meeting place for the willing of the world. In the first months following the success in Paris, nearly 12,000 commitments were uploaded onto the site. These included more than 70 cooperative initiatives involving more than 10,000 participants from 180 countries. For example, 73 companies, investors, and regions committed to end forest loss entirely by 2030. More than 800 companies and regions promised to use a carbon price, and 57 companies and investors committed to go 100 percent renewable.[84] Of course, some skepticism is justified. Some of these ballyhooed but non-binding pledges may be merely "greenwash" – the promise of climate action without any real intention of the reality of it. Some, too, may be simply attempts at smoothing public relations through the pretense of supporting climate action. Still others are no doubt well intended and sincere enough, but are without any assurance of fulfillment. There is, for now, no effective way of monitoring progress toward the fulfillment of all these promises. Much less is there any real way of enforcing them.

All this said, this climate registry does offer a useful setting for the exchange of learning by doing. Furthermore, it foreshadows the rudiments of a framework on which a future can be built that will – as contemplated by the seventeenth and last of the UN Sustainable Development Goals – include a central and crucial role in the seeking of sustainable development for such government-plus and non-governmental "Global Partnerships." As it is, the appeal of the top-down and of the state-centric persists in the prevailing attitudes of many in our international institutions. Despite all the words to the contrary in the SDGs and in the decisions of the Paris Agreement, the view of all too many international bureaucrats continues to be that the global partnership envisaged by these international agreements is a partnership consisting solely of governments.

Left on the outside and looking in at many of the ongoing deliberations of the willing is the private sector. Bill and Melinda Gates, when they choose to show up for a global gathering on climate or sustainability, will always have a seat at the head table. They will be heard at the press conference later. For the most part, though, business representatives at such summits are reminiscent of the rivals of the radical Jacobins during the French Revolution, the more moderate (and doomed) Girondins. They speak, when they are permitted to speak, from the far corners of the assembly hall, urging that we fix what is wrong with the market while keeping what is right. They speak, but they are rarely heard. Yet business must be at the center of the global partnership and at the center of a great many of our climate and sustainability solutions because markets must be at the center of those solutions. In business, "the quest for sustainability already is starting to transform the competitive landscape, which will force companies to change the way they think about products, technologies, processes, and business models. The key to progress . . . is innovation."[85] Innovative solutions for businesses are much of the answer for sustainable development. Solutions that do not work for the world's businesses in the world's markets will not be solutions.[86] In drawing the right lines of the right rules for sustainable development, we must be ever mindful of where those lines will fall in the global marketplace.

Thus, far from excluding business, we should be seeking new ways to include business in more of our deliberations. In particular, we should be exploring new ways to bind businesses and other political actors besides governments *legally* to the letter of their proclaimed climate and other sustainability commitments. Since the establishment of the current international system in the Treaty of Westphalia in 1648, what we call "public international law" has been seen solely as law between and among states. States are legal parties to such law. Businesses and other "non-state political actors" are not. Conceptually, in the further making of the international rule of law, it may be time to put the confining strictures of the seventeenth century behind us, and push past Westphalia.

In the run-up to the Paris climate summit, some of the more ambitious among the willing suggested something largely new and post-Westphalian in the structuring of public international law. They proposed that, in addition to the negotiating national governments, a "broader set of climate leaders," including "cities, states and provinces, regions, civil society and businesses within the international climate process," should be invited to sign and thereby to become legal parties to the Paris Agreement.[87] In the event, in Paris, this did not happen. But why should we not experiment with making this happen as part of our pursuit of the right enabling framework for a shared and sustainable global prosperity?

Recall in this context Alexis de Tocqueville and the extensive and expansive scope of the idea of individual "self-interest" in his fundamental "principle of interest rightly understood."[88] Worried about what he anticipated would be the atomized and increasingly self-centered isolation of individuals in an egalitarian state, Tocqueville looked for a remedy to counter this isolation during his travels in the 1830s in an egalitarian America. He found it in something he saw flourishing then in American civil life outside American government – "the immense assemblage of associations" being formed throughout the new country by the American people during those early days of democracy.[89] Tocqueville marveled that "Americans of all ages, all conditions, and all dispositions, constantly form associations" in their civil life.[90] He reported, "If it be proposed to advance some truth, or to foster some feeling by the encouragement of a great example, they form a society . . . [They] have in our time carried to the highest perfection the art of pursuing in common the object of their common desires, and have applied this new science to the greatest number of purposes."[91] He saw this inclination to form "associations" as a welcome contrast to what had passed for democratic government during the darkest days of revolutionary France. "[W]hat political power," he asked, "could ever carry on the vast multitude of lesser undertakings which the American citizens perform every day, with the assistance of the principle of association?"[92] We can certainly share his view that private associations can be better at circulating new ideas than governments.[93] In search of sustainable development, new ideas are surely needed.

Perhaps most important, Tocqueville viewed the active participation of individuals in public-spirited and right-minded associations of all kinds as helping foster the "habits of the heart" that led to a flourishing of virtue and enlightened citizenship. He believed, "Feelings are reciprocated, the heart is enlarged, and the human mind is developed by no other means than by the reciprocal influence of men upon each other."[94] He concluded, "[T]his can only be accomplished by associations."[95] Thus, he perceived the widespread American participation in associations as generating a widespread adherence to a broad-minded and far-sighted view of self-interest "rightly understood."[96] Not only in America, but worldwide, the same might be said equally today of the eager and rapidly proliferating participation of business, science, civil society, educators, and so many others in all the voluntary alliances and networks of the willing aimed at achieving sustainable development. The participation of the willing in this global multitude of bottom-up initiatives leads each and all of these volunteers to take the broad view and to look to the long term. As it did for the Americans in the new American democracy of Tocqueville's time, it leads the willing now toward the virtue and the enlightened citizenship of seeing their self-interest as it is "rightly understood."

These are the origins of the makings of willingness. Seeing our self-interest as "rightly understood" leads straight from here toward a sustainable global prosperity. This clear line of sight leads also to this optimistic thought: In scaling up for sustainable development, we can rise up together through the true development of human community. Tocqueville might tell us: This alone is reason enough to put the bountiful bottom-up partnerships of the willing at the pivot of our search for climate and sustainability solutions – for this is the way to the willing world.

11

On Reimagining the Relationship Between Economy and Environment in International Economic Law to Support Sustainable Development

There is no lack of imaginings of how we should get from here to the shining there of sustainable development. In their visions of a shared and sustainable prosperity, the willing of the world have been prolific. Visions abound. These visions all reimagine the world. Yet each of these visions reimagines the world differently. In seeing as their goal the sharing by everyone of a prosperous and a sustainable world, the willing all agree. In supporting the United Nations Sustainable Development Goals, they have all agreed on all they hope to achieve in such a world. On exactly what that world should look like, and on precisely how we should arrange to get from here to there, the willing have, in their varied visions, voiced less agreement.

NO LACK OF IMAGININGS

Among the suggested scenarios set out in the abundance of well-intended imaginings for "transforming our world," there are proposed "pathways," proffered "principles," "ten-point plans," and other pointed plans numbering more and numbering fewer. In these sundry scenarios, there are differing mixes of the top-down and the bottom-up. In these differing mixes, there are differing degrees of submission to the ever-present allure of the grand design, ranging along the long reach from the appealing abstraction of the presupposed to the practical self-directed action of the "spontaneous order." Some of these visions, more than others, leave room at the top for the catalyzing creativity of the true bottom-up.[1] For the most part, the wish lists of the willing have been made with the pervasiveness of climate change foremost in mind, and also with an awareness of the looming presence of all the other pressing demands of the broader dimensions of sustainability. Each and all, these scenarios insist on the imperative of some type of a decisive transition beginning here and now to what most call a "green economy." In so insisting, each and all invite the same question: Just what kind of an enabling framework will be needed to shape and share global prosperity in a sustainable world?

In its simplest expression, a green economy is one which is "low carbon, resource efficient and socially inclusive."[2] Like sustainable development as a whole, a green economy must be defined by doing it. It cannot be predesigned. It cannot be imposed from above. It must rise up from the learning by doing down below through the liberation of human imagination. The new economy we seek for the willing world can emerge only from the catalyzing effects of the free flow and the free exchange of imagination in accumulating and in accelerating creative human collaboration toward the discovery of new knowledge and, thus, toward the innovation of new technologies and other new approaches to living and prospering together within sustainable ecosystems.

Recall the primacy placed by the economist and historian Deirdre McCloskey on the broadening diffusion over time of the idea of freedom as the fundamental generator of the "great enrichment" of the world during the past few centuries of economic progress.[3] She traces it all to the liberation of ordinary people to pursue their own dreams of economic betterment. As she sees it, "The answer, in a word, is 'liberty.' Liberated people, it turns out, are ingenious. Slaves, serfs, subordinated women, people frozen in a hierarchy of lords or bureaucrats, are not . . . You might call it: life, liberty and the pursuit of happiness."[4]

Catchy phrase, that.[5] As McCloskey acknowledges, Adam Smith said much the same thing in 1776 when he explained that the success of his "simple system of liberty" turned on "allowing every man to pursue his own interest his own way, upon the liberal plan of equality, liberty and justice."[6] In this respect, a green economy is not unlike any other economy. A green economy will arise and succeed only within an enabling framework that is founded on human freedom. The challenge is found in fashioning that framework, and of then filling in that framework with the right rules drawing the right lines and building the right institutions in support of the essential transition to sustainable development.

There is ever-increasing urgency in making this transition. Economically, we remain far short of our goals for a shared global prosperity. Environmentally, scientists are telling us that we are now degrading the world's natural resources faster than the planet can recover.[7] Our very perception of nature has been altered by the extent of our imprint on it. Through the glow of artificial light, we have cloaked the planet in a luminous fog of "light pollution"; so much so that, even on the clearest night, one-third of the people in the world can no longer see the Milky Way.[8]

We humans have been busy imposing our imprint on the Earth for millennia. The pace quickened with the Industrial Revolution and has accelerated since; and now, nothing "pristine" remains.[9] Now scientists warn us that, without immediate cooperative action to enhance global sustainability, it will be impossible to maintain current global levels of prosperity, much less to increase prosperity and to extend it to include the poorer people of the world.[10] In seeking sustainable global development, the right lines and the right rules forming the basis for the right institutions of the enabling framework must soon be found.

THE EMANCIPATION OF IMAGINATION FOR INNOVATION

An enabling framework for sustainable development must be founded on the primacy of human freedom. Above all, this framework must value and must defend the freedom of thought, which is the very essence of freedom and the necessary foundation for all human creativity and human endeavor. Freedom of thought is the first freedom because it is the freedom that makes all other freedoms possible.[11] The certain assurance of the freedom of thought is the emancipation of imagination. The freeing of imagination from the constraints that confine it is the indispensable catalyst for innovation. The right lines in the right rules of the enabling framework we need for shaping a green economy for sustainable development must help ensure the free thought and the free exchange of ideas that feed individual creativity and foster constructive collaboration. The lines and the rules in the framework, *to be right*, must lead straight from imagination to innovation.

The willing in the world on the Global Commission on the Economy and Climate, led by former Mexican president Felipe Calderon, have stressed the critical role of innovation in their imagining of a "new climate economy." In their view, "Innovation and technological progress are by far the most important drivers of long-term growth in productivity and output. It is also becoming clear that innovation is likely to be the most important long-term driver to mitigate climate change, in particular by fostering new technologies that can supply energy that is not only clean but also cheap and abundant. The latter condition is critical if the world is to satisfy rapidly growing energy demand in developing countries while also abating GHG [greenhouse gas] emissions and climate change."[12]

In an enabling framework of freedom, ideas can spread and multiply rapidly. Most goods are "rival" because the use of them by one person precludes the use of them by anyone else. But ideas are "non-rival" because the use of an idea by one person "does not preclude anyone else from using the same idea for their purposes."[13] The multiplier effect of ideas as "non-rival" goods illustrates in the most fundamental way why the search for new ideas and the spread of new ideas must be at the center of our efforts to construct an enabling framework for a green economy that will further a sustainable global development. Central to these efforts must be science. Although science is increasingly assailed by the unwilling who equate science with mere opinion, science is essential to making new discoveries that can then be transformed into the new technologies needed for the success of a new, green economy – because the methods of science emancipate the imagination.

The climate crisis is, as the environmental writer Dan Turello has expressed it, "at its core, a crisis of imagination."[14] If every one of the nearly 200 countries that have made voluntary national pledges as part of the Paris Agreement do all they have promised to do to confront climate change, they will still fall far short of doing all that the scientists tell us must be done. The gap must be filled by the freeing and the flourishing of our imagination.[15] From now on, climate change and other environmental considerations must be embedded in all we imagine economically. The natural nexus of food, water, land, forests, and energy must be seen clearly. Likewise, all the interrelated dimensions of the living as well as the physical environment, biodiversity, other species, and burdened ecosystems must be part of our new way of seeing. These broad ecological concerns must all be part of how we think our way to and through the new ideas that can become new technologies and can create new products for a new, green economy.

Edward O. Wilson is one naturalist who is optimistic that market forces can be enlisted through innovation for the sake of sustaining nature. In an impassioned plea for new ways of thinking, he points to the alarming rate of species loss – now "a multiple of close to one thousand" of what it was before human ascendency in the world, and still "accelerating."[16] Yet Wilson predicts confidently that innovative uses of technology in the free market "will yield more and better results with less per capita material and energy, and will reduce the size of the ecological footprint."[17]

Perhaps the most optimistic of those who are confident of the potential of innovation and technology to provide new climate and other environmental solutions are the eighteen academics and activists who issued what they styled as "An Ecomodernist Manifesto" in 2015.[18] These Ecomodernists trumpet the potential of technological innovation as a tool for confronting climate change and other environmental challenges while expressing "the conviction that knowledge and technology, applied with wisdom, might allow for a good, or even great, Anthropocene"[19] which "demands that humans use their growing social, economic, and technological powers to make life better for people, stabilize the climate, and protect the world."[20] They insist that "modern technologies, by using natural ecosystem flows and services more efficiently, offer a real chance of reducing the totality of human impacts on the biosphere. To embrace these technologies is to find paths to a good Anthropocene."[21]

Such confidence in the positive potential of creating new technologies has long been characteristic of the Enlightenment thinking echoed by the Ecomodernists. Modern science and modern technology are contemporary manifestations of the Enlightenment, products of the human ingenuity unleashed by human freedom. The enduring Enlightenment assumption is that the challenges presented by climate change and sustainable development are no different from the many other challenges confronted by humanity in the past. They are challenges that can be overcome by coupling human imagination with human ingenuity.

Yet some who are a part of humanity are not at all certain of the truth of this assumption of the benefits of technology. For some environmentalists and for many anti-globalists, "The technological solutions offered up by Western science are not a potential savior ... The technological transfers of globalization are in fact often a deceptive solution, the heroin of market liberals and institutionalists, temporarily allowing societies to deflect a problem into the future or into another ecosystem."[22] These skeptics of technological solutions argue that, "Ingenuity and technology can certainly help to mitigate particular problems. Yet technology cannot solve the ecological consequences of globalization. Solutions can begin to occur only once the human species accepts that it is now beyond its carrying capacity."[23]

Point taken. New technologies alone will not save us from the worst impacts of climate change and unsustainable development. We must see the natural world and our place in it in an entirely new way. Yet examples are endless of how new technologies help us to protect and to preserve the environment. NASA and other space agencies of the world have called for a new generation of global satellites that would be precise enough to be able to pinpoint from orbit the greenhouse gas emissions from individual nations – and could thus help monitor compliance with national climate pledges under the Paris Agreement.[24] An increasing number of environmental NGOs are already relying on satellite imagery to monitor oil spills, mining damage, illegal fishing, and other environmental degradations.[25]

Both the past evidence of material human progress and the pressing present imperative for much more such progress suggest that the rapid spread of new technologies derived from innovations inspired by the free exchange of new ideas must be central to our efforts to confront climate change, and must be central also to our entire pursuit of sustainable global development. Certainly the centrality of innovation and technology to these efforts is taken as a given by the members of the United Nations in their shared vision for the implementation of the Sustainable Development Goals.

In the task of "transforming our world" by achieving those goals, the question posed by the SDGs is not *whether* to seek new innovations leading to new technologies but rather *how* best to secure them. Here is where innovative and catalyzing bottom-up partnerships enter into the global sustainability picture. The members of the United Nations have expressed in the SDGs a common desire to enhance all kinds of "regional and international cooperation on and access to science, technology and innovation and enhance knowledge sharing on mutually agreed terms, including through improved coordination among existing mechanisms, in particular at the United Nations level, and through a global technology facilitation mechanism."[26] In this important respect, the global search for sustainable development is very much a modern extension of the Enlightenment Project, and there is compelling cause to hasten ahead with this part of the project.

The OECD and the International Energy Agency report that, of the twenty-six technologies they follow that determine the rate of global greenhouse gas emissions, only three – electric vehicles, energy storage, and the combination of solar photovoltaics and onshore wind – are on track to meet the 2C goal on climate change.[27] In pursuit of innovation to further the low-carbon transition, we need more spending on basic research and development, including especially much more funding for energy-related research. We must also have more targeted tax incentives and other innovative incentives to inspire new entrants into the shift to a green economy. Governmental purchases total about 13 percent of the GDP in OECD countries, and this percentage is much higher in some developing countries. Public procurement must likewise be used in climate-friendly ways as a "driver of innovation."[28]

At the same time, it is equally clear from the numerous environmental dimensions of the Sustainable Development Goals that the potentially harmful impact of some new innovations and of some new technologies must be ever in mind. New fertilizers can help feed the world; if made or used unwisely, they can also poison the water we drink and the air we breathe. Innovative sea walls may contain the rising sea; they may also keep sea turtles from reaching their nesting places on the beaches behind the walls.[29] Just as, in constructing an enabling framework for a sustainable global development, we must hesitate before proceeding with rules that will affect nature, so too must we hesitate before developing and deploying new technologies that will do so.

Some of the willing have long contended that, instead of investing all our energies in trying to cut carbon and other greenhouse gas emissions, we should be trying to manipulate the environment to halt rising temperatures.[30] Conceivably, this could be done either by removing carbon dioxide from the atmosphere or by employing some kind of solar radiation management to cool the planet. Here a sky-full of caution is required. The purported panacea of non-existent and still unproven "geoengineering" technologies can be an excuse for not cutting greenhouse gas emissions. Also, some scientists warn that removing carbon dioxide from the atmosphere is "no silver bullet" for fighting climate change.[31] Scientific studies are still underway. Much is yet to be determined. We must never underestimate the potential for discovery, and we must do all we can to help make it happen. But, at least for now, for example, the European Academies' Science Advisory Council, which advises European policymakers, has reported that such technologies as carbon capture and storage, afforestation and reforestation, land management to increase and fix carbon in soils, and ocean fertilization have "limited potential to remove carbon from the atmosphere" and not at the scale that some have forecast of several gigatons each year after 2050. These scientists say "our main focus and best hope for avoiding the worst effects of climate change still needs to be reducing our own emissions."[32] Furthermore, geoengineering presents some fundamental legal questions that must be answered before using any such new technologies. We may discover how to alter the Earth's atmosphere. But, before we do, we need to ask whether any one country has the right to do so. If, as some have suggested, an effort were made to mimic the eruption in 1991 of the Mt. Pinatubo volcano in the Philippines, which cooled global temperatures by about 0.4 degrees C in the following year, "by shooting sulphur dioxide into the stratosphere to create a giant sunshade," which country or countries in the world would have the right to pull the trigger?[33] The Philippines? Only the Philippines? Only all of the world's countries working together? Or no country at all? These are not only unanswered legal questions; these are also largely unasked legal questions. Should we undertake geoengineering, global rules and global governance will be necessary.

Our technological progress must be matched by other human progress, including progress in legal rule-making. Our past experiences with DDT, asbestos, chlorofluorocarbons, and more should all remind us of the significant potential environmental "dangers of well-intentioned innovations that misfired."[34] In the press of the ever-accelerating pace of technological change, we should pause to consider that, like the proposed devices for geoengineering, new and innovative technologies of other kinds may well have unexpected consequences that cause unforeseen environmental harm. As just one example: The new technology of gene editing may bless us with whole species of mosquitoes that no longer carry malaria; yet it may also inflict us with ... the unforeseen.[35] Genomics is advancing at an accelerating rate unmatched by our understanding of how to use it wisely.

In addition, the tendency toward "path dependency" can perpetuate technological "misfires." Too often, "current choices determine future options."[36] The interstate highway system in the United States was a good idea in the 1950s. For decades, interstate highways have been drivers of US economic development. But our highways have also trapped most Americans in the inertia of the carbon-fueled technology of the internal combustion engine. So we tend to choose variations on more of the same instead of real change in our means of transport. It might well be asked – as the *Economist*, certainly no adversary of the market – has asked, rhetorically, "If the internal combustion engine had, from the start, carried its full environmental costs, would the car have ever become so central to the western economies?"[37] As economists for the World Bank have explained the behavioral pull of path dependency, "economic actors generally prefer to do what they are already set up for and are good at, so they tend to innovate and invest in technologies that are already mature and have a large market share, thereby locking in carbon-based technologies and sectors."[38] An enabling framework for a green economy must push against this natural pull.

The necessity to hesitate before introducing new technologies that may affect nature is reinforced by the fact that sometimes the natural effects of those technologies are not foreseen.[39] Sometimes, "things bite back."[40] Often, though, whether a new innovation leading to a new technology has a harmful effect is a matter of human choice, of human decisionmaking through human rule-making. Often it is a matter of assessing and controlling the factor of risk, and of choosing the most appropriate level of risk avoidance. Whether a new technology is harmful or not may depend on how we use it. Is the nuclear energy used in a nuclear power plant or in a nuclear bomb? Should we tell the indigenous peoples of Panama they should stop using drones to monitor the success of their efforts to replenish their endangered tropical rainforests?[41]

Humility in our rule-making should be evidenced in part by more humility in our making of innovations and of new technologies. Innovation – yes. Technology – yes. Optimism – yes, always yes. But the audacity of human ingenuity must be accompanied by a constant awareness of the enduring reality of human limitations.

In framing, together, how we hope to shape and share a sustainable development, we must demonstrate an abiding understanding especially of the sometimes-unintended ecological and other consequences of our technological innovations. In his heedless hubris, Icarus flew too high and too close to the sun. Like his, our wings too can melt; like him, we too can fall.

"CRYSTALS OF IMAGINATION"

Trade, the OECD informs us, is "an important driver of economic growth through the diffusion of technologies and know-how."[42] Trade helps inspire innovation, and, thus, trade helps spur the development and deployment of new technologies in the "mutual reinforcement" of a "two-way process."[43] In this process, while more trade provides more of the "necessary inputs" for innovation, in turn, that innovation sparks more trade, which then, again, stimulates more innovation.[44] Matt Ridley sums up this multiplier effect of trade on innovation succinctly in saying, "Trade makes innovation a cumulative phenomenon."[45]

Foreign direct investment – the flip side of trade – produces similar results in innovative productivity growth. The capital and the competition provided by increased FDI have the same positive effects as increased trade. Foreign direct investment can introduce and disseminate new innovations and new technologies. Furthermore, foreign direct investment can seed still more innovations and still more new technologies by widening the imaginative circle of those who share in making them. In particular, the international technology transfers so much needed by the people living in developing countries depend to a great extent on attracting foreign direct investment. The challenge lies in turning FDI more toward sustainable investments. The UN's Addis Ababa Action Agenda affirms, for instance, that significant investment in sustainable infrastructure – such as low-carbon electricity and power generation – can play a signal role in the energy transition to sustainable development.[46] Goal 9 of the Sustainable Development Goals, it will be recalled, is to "[b]uild resilient infrastructure, promote inclusive and sustainable industrialization and foster innovation."[47]

Together, investment and trade are inspiring innovative results especially among developing countries along the global value chains that increasingly characterize global production in the world economy. By fragmenting production, global value chains become conduits for change. Because they eliminate the need to acquire competency in all aspects of the production line of a particular good or the delivery line of a particular service, and because they promote local specialization in a part or parts of overall production and delivery, global value chains offer countries seeking economic development more of "the potential for technological transfer and knowledge spillovers to the local economy."[48]

In trade and investment alike, a sore subject especially for many in developing countries that are much in need of new technologies is the concept of the ownership of an idea – the legal notion of "intellectual property." An exclusive entitlement to the use of an idea for a certain period of time – a patent, trademark, copyright, trade secret, or the like – is an "intellectual property right." These "IP rights" are generally recognized as exceptions to free trade in the rules of the WTO and in other enabling international rules frameworks. They are likewise protected in many international investment agreements. To encourage new ideas, and to make the most of new ideas for all of us, an enabling framework for confronting climate change and for promoting overall sustainable development must include the recognition, and also the enforcement, of intellectual property rights. Although new ideas are non-rival goods, we are, as individuals, much more likely to conceive more good new ideas if we are free – at least for a limited time – to profit exclusively from them. How much time is a matter of legal line-drawing somewhere "in between."

Moreover, most economic studies conclude that market tools are the most effective tools for "incentivizing the diffusion of new technologies."[49] Property rights – including intellectual property rights – are the most primary of market tools. Property rights provide and strengthen the incentive for originating new ideas. The legal protection of property rights in innovative technologies has been an enabling force for economic growth since the dawn of the Industrial Revolution. Yet, at the same time, to be able to make the most of new ideas, we must be able to spread new ideas widely and quickly. The need for extending and speeding the spread of innovation is underscored by the urgency of countering climate change. So there must be a balance. In the pursuit of a climate-friendly sustainable development, the right enabling rules for intellectual property rights must draw the right lines between innovation and dissemination.

All in all, trade is just as much about the exchange of ideas as it is about the exchange of goods and services – maybe more. At the most basic level, trade is an exchange of imagination. The goods and services traded in the world are – in Cesar Hidalgo's elegant phrase – "crystals of imagination."[50] The rules of the world trading system are an enabling framework for the sharing of imagination through the free flow of ideas as incorporated into traded goods and manifested in traded services. Furthermore, all of history attests that traded products rarely travel alone; new ideas often travel with them. Often, these new ideas in transit are the leavening ideas of personal as well as commercial liberation. Free trade is thus an enabler of the very idea of freedom. Because freer trade and freer investment alike advance and accelerate the global flow of new ideas, they are rightly seen as agents of freedom.

PUTTING A PRICE ON CARBON

The absence of a price on carbon inhibits imagination and is, therefore, a disincentive to imagination. The OECD tells us that energy taxes in the major developed economies are too low to fight climate change.[51] If the developed countries do not confront the consequences of refusing to price carbon, it is hard to see many of the developing countries doing so. "Putting a price on greenhouse gas emissions is perhaps the most important policy" in shaping a new green economy[52] because it can help ease and enable the needed shift to a low-carbon economy by unleashing human imagination through the power of incentive in the marketplace.[53] Incentive is empowered and imagination unleashed because placing "an explicit price on carbon ... can send important signals across the economy, helping to guide consumption choices and investments towards low-carbon activities and away from carbon-intensive ones."[54]

Some say that carbon pricing is not needed, that "[h]uman ingenuity and prosperity are the best insurance against climate change."[55] Certainly both are important parts of the climate equation. But human ingenuity is misdirected and prosperity is limited where no price is placed on the climate and other environmental harms caused by carbon emissions.[56] The existence of a "market failure" in the form of such a negative "externality" that is not reflected in the price of a product results in an inefficient allocation of limited natural resources that justifies – indeed necessitates – a qualification on the general virtue of a generous measure of market freedom. Nicholas Stern, the eloquent climate economist and activist, maintains that emissions of greenhouse gases "may be the largest market failure the world has ever seen,"[57] while others agree that "[c]limate change ... is the biggest of all global externalities."[58] Analysts for the International Monetary Fund tell us that, in the absence of a carbon price, this externality amounts to an "implicit subsidy from the failure to charge for environmental costs."[59] Including the hidden costs of products to the climate in their market price sends the needed economic signal to remedy this market failure. Internalizing these costs compels energy producers and energy consumers alike to decide whether to cut their emissions – or pay the price for not cutting them. Putting a price on carbon will accelerate the energy transition by spurring innovation.[60]

Where there is no price on carbon, emitters are free to continue to pour more carbon into the air at will – without paying the costs of the societal and environmental harms that result. But where there is a price on carbon, emitters have an incentive to reduce their carbon emissions, and to do so at the lowest possible cost. Where there is a carbon price, energy and other producers must innovate. They have an incentive to invest in the development and the deployment of cleaner and, therefore, more cost-efficient technologies. The introduction of a carbon price into the mix of economic decisionmaking helps shift the flow of private finance to green innovations and thereby spur and speed the green transition to a decarbonized world. Also, carbon pricing helps generate additional public revenues needed to pay for the necessary transition to a green economy, whether through more government spending targeted toward green growth, through tax cuts for consumers and producers that can also stimulate green growth, or through a combination of both. Furthermore, and far from the least, "by aligning economic growth and emissions reductions, carbon-pricing policies can ultimately promote cross-border cooperation and more ambitious climate action."[61]

Basically, there are two ways to put a price on carbon. One way is through the market. The other way is through regulation or some other form of governmental intervention. Market-based measures provide incentives. Regulatory measures impose requirements. Market-based measures are more flexible. Regulatory measures may mandate the installing of a particular technology or the meeting of a specific performance standard. By relying on incentives and disincentives, market-based measures leave the ultimate decision to the private producer or consumer. By relying on governmentally imposed mandates and other requirements, regulatory measures are more akin to state-directed "command and control" by public decisionmakers.

Of course, separate and apart from carbon pricing, sometimes a regulation or some other governmental requirement can be more effective than a market solution. Consider the crimes committed against elephants, their tusks taken, and their lives lost, for the sake in part of some fanciful notions in the darker corners of the marketplace about the powers of the shorn tusks. The United States has banned commercial trade in African elephant ivory, and international efforts to stop elephant poaching and trade are intensifying.[62] With such an utterly unspeakable crime, the solution is simply to eliminate the market.[63]

In the fight against carbon emissions, however, market-based measures can cost less than regulatory measures, and they can be more environmentally effective. The costs of regulatory approaches "substantially exceed the cost" of market approaches.[64] Regulatory tools are less efficient because they allow less "abatement flexibility" and are, by their nature, selective.[65] Because they are broader, price-based tools are more efficient. They spread the costs of change evenly throughout the whole economy.[66] Market approaches can also be more environmentally effective than regulatory approaches. They are open-ended in allowing for experimentation. They do not improve the one-size-fits-all of many supposed command-and-control solutions. They enlist the profit motive in altering human behavior. "Harnessing market forces allows for reductions to come more efficiently, and [bring] about innovations necessary to achieve sustainable economic and environmental conditions."[67]

The simplest and most straightforward market-based approach is a carbon tax that sets a price on each unit of pollution, which is usually a price per ton of carbon emitted.[68] Thus, the pollution from carbon emissions is no longer an externality excluded from the price of a product. In paying the carbon tax, the taxpayer incurs an additional cost based on the amount of the carbon pollution produced. This additional cost is incorporated into the price of the product. This in turn gives the taxpayer a financial incentive to reduce carbon pollution by changing to new energy sources, adopting new technologies, or otherwise altering production methods. In this way, a carbon tax "provides a continuous incentive for innovation."[69]

Another market-based approach is "cap-and-trade." With this approach, instead of putting a price in the form of a tax on each unit of carbon pollution, a determination is made about how much total carbon emission will be allowed – the cap. Emitters then buy and sell their rights to produce carbon emissions – the trade. These rights take the form of tradable certificates that permit certain amounts of carbon emissions based on individual emitter needs – "allowances." Because the number of these emission allowances is limited, the resulting scarcity creates a demand for them and thus a market for them.[70] Under a cap-and-trade scheme, individual emitters cannot produce carbon emissions beyond those permitted in their allowances. Furthermore, the fact that they can profit by trading their allowances gives them an incentive to reduce what would otherwise be their carbon emissions in their own production. Although reality has not always lived up to this theory, there have been some notable successes with cap-and-trade approaches. Arguably the most successful of all the multilateral environmental agreements is the Montreal Protocol on the Ozone Layer, which features a cap-and-trade scheme.

Although both a carbon tax and a cap-and-trade program are market-based approaches to setting a carbon price, and although economists say their effects can be mostly the same, the two approaches to pricing carbon differ in some important respects. Carbon taxes impose a uniform price on carbon pollution – but permit the amount of pollution to fluctuate. In contrast, cap-and-trade schemes impose a cap on the amount of pollution – but permit the carbon price to vary. In addition, with carbon taxes, the polluter pays, consistent with the spirit of Rio Principle 16.[71] In comparison, with cap-and-trade schemes – uncomfortably for many environmentalists – polluters are permitted to buy and sell the right to pollute.

The alternative to a market-based approach to pricing carbon is a regulatory approach. Such regulation can assume many guises. One regulatory approach is a sectoral approach – such as, in the United States, the Corporate Average Fuel Economy (CAFE) standards used for regulating the fuel economy of motor vehicles. Another was to have been the Clean Power Plan for power plants proposed by President Barack Obama as a means of fulfilling the national pledge made by the United States under the Paris climate agreement – a proposal later withdrawn by his successor. If the MIT study is to be believed, such a regulatory approach, as compared to a market-based approach, could have accomplished less environmentally while costing more economically. (Even so, it would have been better than the only alternative at the time – no action at all from a recalcitrant Congress.)

Many economists would contend that by far the most effective and the most efficient of all conceivable carbon taxes would be a *global* carbon tax – one that would be the same all over the world,[72] would prevent competitive distortions among various jurisdictions, and would provide clarity for investors. Yet discussion of any such global tax was not even remotely on the agenda of a global climate summit that, in the end, could not even summon the will to include the word "market" in the Paris Agreement. All the same, there is increasing worldwide momentum for pricing carbon, and this momentum seems to have been enhanced by the conclusion of the Paris Agreement.

To date, more than fifty national and subnational jurisdictions – countries, regions, states, provinces, and cities that represent more than 1 billion people altogether – have created and have combined in different forms of carbon markets by implementing policies that have put a price on carbon. The number of carbon-pricing initiatives, implemented or scheduled, doubled in the five years from 2012 to 2017.[73] Nearly 40 percent of global GDP is produced in jurisdictions with carbon emissions trading systems.[74]

China, now the world's largest emitter of greenhouse gases, launched a number of "pilot" regional emissions trading arrangements leading up to the Paris summit and, in December 2017, launched a national carbon trading system, focused initially on the power sector.[75] China's national carbon market will be the largest carbon-pricing initiative in the world, surpassing the size of the European Emissions Trading System.[76] China's full national engagement in carbon pricing would double to more than 2 billion the number of people worldwide living in jurisdictions with some form of carbon pricing.[77] Nor is China alone in moving toward carbon pricing.

Established in 2005, the European Emissions Trading System (ETS) is the world's oldest and largest, including thirty-one countries, the twenty-eight member states of the European Union plus Iceland, Norway, and Liechtenstein. It limits emissions from more than 11,000 heavy energy-using installations and airlines operating between the thirty-one countries while covering about 45 percent of the EU's greenhouse gas emissions.[78] The European ETS has been plagued by a low carbon price due to an oversupply of carbon permits that has weakened its carbon price signal, resulting in a decline in prices by almost 70 percent since 2008. In February 2018, the European Parliament adopted a much-debated reform of the ETS intended to reduce the glut of permits and strengthen the EU's carbon price signal. The aim is to help attain the EU's pledge under the Paris Agreement to cut greenhouse gas emissions by at least 40 percent compared to 1990 levels by 2030.[79] In addition, post-Paris, South Korea, Japan, Chile, Colombia, Quebec, Ontario, Alberta, and California and the New England states of the United States have all also been fine-tuning and linking their carbon-pricing systems.[80] Eight new carbon-pricing initiatives were implemented in 2016 alone.[81]

The appeal of such approaches has been enhanced by the accumulating evidence that carbon pricing need not prove costly to businesses and consumers. Economic studies show that – if not offset – the burden of a carbon tax will fall most heavily on those with lower incomes.[82] But the economic costs of the green transition can be offset by the revenues produced by putting a price on carbon. While acknowledging the likelihood of higher conventional energy prices and other transitional costs, the staff of the IMF has emphasized that revenues from carbon pricing "could be used for lowering taxes on labor and capital that distort economic incentives, producing a counteracting economic benefit to the costs of higher energy prices."[83] A carbon tax can be structured in a way that is "revenue-neutral," resulting in no overall increase in government revenues. Moreover, businesses and consumers alike can be reimbursed through other tax changes for their transitional costs in ways that will smooth the green transition.

Even where there has not yet been any governmental action on carbon pricing, many businesses have, in the expectation that such action will eventually happen, been engaging in "shadow" carbon pricing.[84] More than 100 of the Fortune Global 500 businesses worldwide with a combined annual revenue of about $7 trillion – including both energy producers and energy consumers – have disclosed that they use an internal carbon price in shaping decisions on their operations and investments.[85] All told, CDP – formerly the Carbon Disclosure Project – reports that more than 1,200 companies are currently using an internal price on carbon or plan to do so within two years.[86] The actions of these 100 businesses are "a simple but powerful example of the importance of valuing carbon emissions and incentivizing reductions."[87] In many respects, and in many places, businesses are ahead of governments in acknowledging the necessity for carbon pricing. But the fact that these businesses have not been joined by thousands more worldwide is evidence of the need for the signal of carbon pricing.

Worldwide, the current level of greenhouse gas emissions covered by carbon-pricing mechanisms is about 12 percent. Soon after the conclusion of the Paris Agreement, the World Bank and the International Monetary Fund convened a High-Level Carbon Pricing Panel that includes the presidents of a number of countries and the heads of several leading international institutions (as well as, from the United States, California governor Jerry Brown). In April 2016, the panel announced the goals of doubling the amount of greenhouse gas emissions covered by carbon-pricing mechanisms from the current level to 25 percent of global emissions by 2030, and of doubling it again to 50 percent within the following decade. Technical experts have advised that these goals can be achieved "if existing and planned carbon pricing programs are augmented by additional actions."[88]

One needed additional action is the "linkage" of carbon markets. More than ninety of the countries that are the members of the Conference of Parties to the United Nations Framework Convention on Climate Change have expressed an interest in using carbon markets to meet the targets for carbon emissions cuts in their voluntary national climate pledges made pursuant to the Paris Agreement. Many of those countries have conditioned their climate pledges in one way or another on having access through linkage to a regional or other international carbon market, relying on the open door in Article 6 of the Paris Agreement to enable the linking of carbon markets in "internationally transferred mitigation outcomes."[89] Our trade rules must not only permit such outcomes. They must help achieve them.

BEYOND PRICING CARBON, A "JUST TRANSITION"

The signal needed – strong and sufficient – from the Paris Agreement of a world-wide shift to a low-carbon economy will be amplified if the new climate agreement proves to be a global catalyst for the continued embrace of carbon pricing and carbon markets. An enabling framework for confronting climate change and for achieving sustainable development begins with carbon pricing. It does not end there. Putting a price on carbon is essential, but carbon pricing will work only if it is accompanied by additional actions supportive of a shift to a green economy. Beyond the pricing of carbon, there must be broader actions that empower the true bottom-up of a successful green transition. These actions must be enabled by the drawing of the right lines in the right rule-making in the right economic mix of government and market.

In this mix, there must be a complete realignment of our current policies to support the sustainability shift. In their various imaginings, the willing seem to agree that the policies supportive of the necessary transition must include, among others: increasing the support for basic research and development of new, green technologies; scaling up and broadening the scope of innovation in key low-carbon and climate-resilient technologies; shrinking the capital costs for low-carbon infrastructure investment and other forms of climate finance; speeding the shift away from coal-fired power generation; decarbonizing the production of electricity; stopping deforestation and restoring forests as natural carbon sinks; strengthening incentives for sustainable land use and agriculture; streamlining cities to make them more compact and more connected through green urbanization; realigning tax policies to support a green transition; and improving efficiency and reducing waste throughout the economy.[90]

Lengthening this to-do list for the transition to sustainable development even more is much that must also be done that is not even on this list – because it cannot yet be foreseen. In tackling this to-do list, top-down support for preconceived solutions continues to color too much of the thinking of some of the willing. Needed instead is the bottom-up thinking that is practical and incremental and posits no preconceived solutions. Bottom-up thinking is what works; it is the Enlightenment in action. Therefore, central to the ultimate success of a policy framework supportive of carbon pricing will be the endless array of voluntary cooperative networks of the willing everywhere that are busy working diligently on climate and sustainability solutions down at the grassroots of the world. From the cumulative successes of these creative expressions of the true bottom-up can emerge the scaling up of a mounting momentum for the broad scope of the many more successes needed to make the transition to a green economy. Above all, the crucial role of these modern emissaries of the Enlightenment as creative catalysts for change is precisely why these voluntary cooperative networks make the "global partnership for sustainable development" of Goal 17 the very pivot of the UN Sustainable Development Goals.

But none of this – not the carbon pricing and not the other policies intended to provide a supportive framework for carbon pricing and for the transition to a green economy – will have any real chance of working unless, as a central part of our transitional policies, we strive also to confront and to overcome the fear of change. In Hoffer's example from his own experience working in the fields of California, people everywhere in the world must have confidence that they can change from picking peas to picking string beans; and they must have confidence, too, that there will be string beans to pick. We must help individual people find their way through the green transition. There will be a green transition only if it is a "just transition,"[91] for only if the shift to a low-carbon economy is seen as just in the eyes of all the many millions of people throughout the world who fear they will be harmed by that shift will there be enough popular support to enable it to succeed. The widespread fear of change must be overcome with the help of domestic policies that distribute the benefits and the burdens of change fairly; that help create new and well-paid employment for those who are dislocated by change; and that help affected businesses become more competitive in a green economy because of change.[92]

The ever-willing and ever-optimistic "thought leaders" for the World Economic Forum advise us that, among our greatest "global risks" today is that, "The fabric that binds citizens to the state and to each other is fraying,"[93] and that there is therefore compelling necessity for "overhauling the social contract."[94] Anyone who doubts such a fraying of societal ties or the necessity for restoring them need only look to the saddened streets of Barcelona or Brussels, Charlottesville or Las Vegas, where terrorists have preyed. The centrifugal forces of the modern world pull families and communities apart. These forces are aided and abetted by the emptiness of unemployment and by the absence for so many people of any sense of having a future or being able to shape a future. The resulting anxieties lead the rootless to try to reclaim and to reassert their roots by clinging to their perceived identity and to the memory of a lost and often-mythical past. This separates them from all the "others" who seem to threaten them merely by being unlike them. It also causes the uprooted to lash out at those "others" with words, with votes, and, alas, sometimes with violence. Above all else, the enabling framework for sustainable development must include policies that help mend the torn fabric of the social contract worldwide by promoting equity and security and by affirming the ties of our shared humanity and the transcendent human values all of us everywhere ought to share.

Toward this end, as one important part of this framework, the further freeing of trade and investment internationally as much-needed catalysts for the coming shift toward a sustainable economy must be accompanied and complemented domestically by a political liberalization that can help make the shift possible. The fact is, international trade and foreign direct investment are simply not the job-stealing culprits that many allege they are. Overwhelmingly, in recent years, the displacement of workers in the constant churning of the globalizing economy has been caused not by more openness to trade and investment, but by more productivity resulting from automation and other efficiencies in production due to the introduction of new technologies.[95] In the United States, while the total of production jobs fell by about 5 million between 1987 and 2017, manufacturing output, due largely to productivity increases from automation, rose by more than 86 percent.[96] Jobs have been lost not to foreigners, but to machines.

Not for the first time, it is technology, and not trade, that truly fuels the fear of change. Since the early days of the Industrial Revolution in Great Britain, when the Luddites, in fear of change, and in fear of losing their jobs, dismantled the newfangled technology of textile looms, there have been fears of job losses because of technological change. Up until now, these fears have always eased with the passage of time as new technologies have created new jobs, often in entirely new and unforeseen occupations and industries. Ask any smartphone app designer about the technological unforeseen. Now, once again, these fears have returned, and they have been intensifying with the accelerating pace of technological change. Economists and technologists are divided in their thinking, but, in the view of many today, "new technology does seem more fundamentally disruptive than technologies of the past."[97] All the supposed experts on the future of work foresee more and more of our current jobs vanishing. Some of them foresee ever fewer new jobs on the horizon. Those pessimists who predict an ever-shrinking number of new jobs do so mainly because they foresee human labor being increasingly supplanted by computers with sensors and mobility – by robots.[98]

Ten thousand years ago, human labor was transformed when we shifted from foraging to farming. Two hundred and fifty years ago, human labor was transformed again when we began the shift from farming to manufacturing. Now human labor is on the verge of transformation yet again, and now many of us rightly ask: When we all have self-driving cars, what will become of all the transport workers? And, when the robots have learned how to learn on their own, what, pray tell, will become of all the many other service workers? What will be the job-creating app for that?

An inquiry into the job markets in just twelve countries by the International Trade Union Confederation in 2012 suggested that investing 2 percent of GDP in the green economy could create a total of up to 48 million jobs in five years in those countries. The United States was first on their list in new green job creation.[99] If these projections are accurate, what would be the wider job-generating results of making the shift to a green economy in not merely a dozen countries, but in all the nearly 200 countries in the world? Economists for the World Bank have emphasized that green environmental policies will lead to substantial job creation only if other inefficiencies – including those of labor markets – are tackled. In other words, "green growth policies are no substitute for good growth policies."[100]

Those fearing job losses from facing climate change tend to overlook the job losses if we do not face climate change now. In 2015, a study by financial institution Citi concluded that unchecked climate change could cost up to $72 trillion in global GDP by the middle of the century. The Citi study also found that, by building a low-carbon economy, the world would save $2 trillion in energy infrastructure and ongoing fuel costs.[101] Fears of job losses also cause us not to focus on the potential economic gains from addressing climate change. In 2017, the International Energy Agency and the International Renewable Energy Agency reported that the cumulative gain from the green energy transition in global GDP from now to 2050 will amount to $19 trillion.[102] They explained, "Increased economic growth is driven by the investment stimulus and by enhanced pro-growth policies, in particular the use of carbon pricing and recycling of proceeds to lower income taxes."[103] As for job losses, they predicted, "The energy sector (including energy efficiency) will create around six million additional jobs in 2050. Job losses in [the] fossil fuel industry would be fully offset by new jobs in renewables, with more jobs being created in energy efficiency activities. The overall GDP improvement will induce further job creation in other economic sectors."[104] Also in 2017, the OECD reported that treating economy and environment as one by combining national and international agendas on growth and on climate would lift global output by 2.8 percent by 2050. According to the OECD, if we factor into the calculation the economic benefits of avoiding such impacts of climate change as coastal flooding and storm damage, the increased global GDP from the green transition would be 5 percent.[105] From this new green growth can come new green jobs – if the green transition is well implemented.[106]

Even Edmund Burke, the quintessential conservative, conceded, "We must all obey the great law of change."[107] All too true. But what should be the terms of our obedience? The ever-churning creative destruction of the marketplace results in job losses as well as in job gains. If we seek a world of useful work for us all on the far side of the green transition, then the freer trade we need and the new technologies we employ to help make the green transition must be accompanied by generous and effective transitional assistance to the workers who lose their jobs because of it. And this adjustment aid should be only a small part of all that is done to smooth the pending labor shift. We would be short-sighted if we focused exclusively on the job losses caused by trade when it is the productivity gains from new technologies that are driving most of the changes in the job markets. Whatever may have caused the loss of a job, displaced workers must never be left without a helping hand.

An enabling framework will be one that enables each and all of us to make the essential transition to a green economy. Trade, technology, and general adjustment assistance must only be the beginning in making that transition. Lifelong education. Apprenticeship. Skills-based training and retraining. Affordable child care. Universal health insurance. Wage insurance. Other transitional compensation. Labor reforms that ensure improved worker protections. Strengthened social security. A stronger overall social safety net. Expanded earned income tax credits. Relocation assistance. Targeted community and regional assistance. The right new green infrastructure. All these supportive planks, and more, should be part of the framework of a just transition.

Commercial openness at the border must also be accompanied by policies behind the border that ensure fairness.[108] It is true that no nation has ever become successful and remained successful over time without opening and remaining open to the wider world. It is equally true that no nation can ever make the most of openness without domestic policies that help ensure that the gains derived from openness are widely and fairly shared. In the absence of policies for ensuring fairness, people will remain unwilling. They will turn away in anger and in frustration from the wider world. Then there will be even less chance than exists now for the creative and cooperative international actions that should be happening everywhere now in parallel and in concert with the domestic pursuit of new policies for competitiveness and fairness.

In the United States, the bottom half of Americans have gotten just 3 percent of the growth since 1980.[109] The top 1 percent of American households now own 40 percent of the country's wealth and more wealth than the bottom 90 percent combined.[110] Worldwide, between 1980 and 2016, the wealthiest 1 percent of humanity got 27 percent of the world's income while the bottom 50 percent got only 12 percent.[111] In 2017, 82 percent of the new global wealth went to the wealthiest 1 percent of the people in the world (including the wealthiest 12 percent of Americans) while the bottom 50 percent received no increase at all.[112] Billionaires worldwide saw their wealth increase by $762 billion in 2017.[113] (And this was before the tax cuts passed by the United States Congress near yearend.) In addition to the sheer greed and utter disregard for the well-being of the majority of the people in the world that this extreme extent of inequality represents, it also has significant negative economic consequences. The OECD estimates that economic inequality diminished economic growth in OECD countries by 5 percent between 2000 and 2015. The OECD countries are the wealthiest countries in the world. What of all the rest? "Nowhere has the distribution of the pie become more equitable."[114]

Goal 10 of the Sustainable Development Goals is to "[r]educe inequality within and among countries."[115] Today, just eight people in the world have, combined, the same amount of total wealth as half the people on the planet – 3.6 billion people.[116] Is this sustainable development? Is this fair? Fairness, of course, lies always in the eye of the beholder. The right line is never drawn on fairness that will please everyone. Freedom demands equality of opportunity, not equality of results. An extreme egalitarianism has never worked and never will work. It is founded on a faith in the possibility of a fundamental change in basic human nature. Down that road await the gulag and the guillotine. Yet the current extent of economic inequality in the United States and in all too many other countries can only be seen as obscene. It is no part of any just transition. It poses an increasing risk to the survival of the mutual societal trust that sustains democratic institutions. It feeds the resentment that gives rise to the retreat from democratic institutions toward a tinderbox tribalism and an enticing authoritarianism. If too high, taxes on wealth and on the wealthy can reduce incentives for production. But some measure of income redistribution through taxation is surely required by almost any moral or rational concept of justice.[117]

The first recourse of many today is to distributive justice, and understandably so. In a world widely afflicted with vast and widening economic inequalities, the inclination is to focus primarily on the justness of redistribution rather than on the necessity for growth. But prioritizing less inequality over more growth will result in less growth and more inequality. In the United States, in the name of fairness – and also competitiveness – please do raise minimum wages, enact more progressive taxation, address the gender pay gap, and fill in the gaps in the social safety net. Please do fight – endlessly – for equal rights and against all kinds of discrimination. But please do not focus solely on redistribution. Focus instead on growth. Focus on making the economic pie larger instead of squabbling over how to divide up the pieces of what an exclusive focus on redistribution will make a smaller pie. Focus on sustainable growth by refocusing the direction of the entire economy. Make growth green. And make the most of green growth by remaining open to the wider world.

One of the "progressive" thinkers on the American left, Robert Atkinson, has it right: "[C]ontemporary progressivism must come to terms with globalization ... Rather than fighting economic innovation, progressives need to embrace innovation policies that help workers navigate the tricky waters of the new knowledge economy. We should continue to fight for a more equitable distribution of wealth and a stronger social safety net in order to help workers manage the creative destruction that a vibrant, postindustrial, and 21st century economy must strive for. But progressive opposition (and indifference) to innovation is profoundly misguided. Attempting to constrain innovation and productivity growth in order to avoid short-term economic disruptions is self-defeating."[18]

Opposition to change is often well intended, but such opposition is often also counterproductive. Often, where it fails, the effects of failure are compounded. Often, where it succeeds, it only shrinks what should have been the larger size of the economic pie, leaving less of a future for us all. We must, indeed, overcome our fears and "obey the great law of change." Yet we will never overcome our fear of change by yielding to fear and fleeing from change. Fortunately, justification for optimism can be found in this: We need neither fear nor flee. With the right transitional policies in place, and with the right kind and the right amount of resources in hand to help make those policies work, we can face and overcome the fear of change. The unwilling can become the willing, and can join in the making of the willing world.

REIMAGINING INTERNATIONAL TRADE LAW

Unquestionably, openness to trade, coupled with a much more pervasive and persuasive explanation to the public of why such openness is indispensable to their future, must be one of the central transitional policies for overcoming the fear of change and for securing sustainable development for all through our imagined shift to a new green economy. Openness to trade as a critical component of the commercial dimension of an "open society" is a necessary tool for the true bottom-up of the green transition. Being open to trade offers more options for the creative learning by doing in the competitive and the collaborative down below of the marketplace. It offers more opportunities for defining sustainable development by doing it.

There must, however, be considerably more to the trade focus of the green transitional framework than ensuring openness to trade. Concerns about climate change and other aspects of sustainable development must be integrated into all our trade policy.[119] Crucially, this includes the trade rules we write to help fulfill our trade policy. In particular, trade rules must not only be compatible with combating climate change. Trade rules must also be affirmative and active agents for combating climate change. To make this happen, the inescapable reality that the economy and the environment *are one* must be internalized by imagining them *as one* in all our endeavors to draw the right lines in the right trade rules. This new imagining must be reflected in a transformation of all our trade rule-making. As part of the necessary realignment of all our economic and environmental policymaking, of the just transition to a green economy, and of the existential struggle to confront climate change and secure sustainable development, there must be a *reimagining* of international trade law.

This legal reimagining must begin with how we treat carbon. Trade rules do not prevent carbon pricing, but they also do not facilitate it. The integration of the global struggle against climate change into global trade rules must mean – at the very least – that, from now on, we will treat carbon differently. What is more, because carbon emissions present a *unique* threat to humanity and to the entire world, it follows that carbon must be treated not only differently, but also *uniquely*. Unique ways must be found to craft and to construe trade rules so as to advance the flow of trade while also imposing a price on trade when it is fueled by carbon.

Worldwide, there is resistance to ambitious national actions that put a price on carbon because of fears of the possible impacts of such actions on local firms and local workers due to the changed terms of competition. There are disincentives and disadvantages to one country acting on its own by putting a price on carbon. If one country decides unilaterally to limit its own emissions of greenhouse gases while other countries do not, that one country bears all the costs of such actions, but most of the benefits accrue to those other countries. This gives those other countries an incentive not to take climate action. They have an incentive to be "free-riders."[120] Hence, the ideal of climate action has always been cooperative global action toward a singular global solution – the approach long taken by climate negotiators before Paris, and largely to no avail. Now, in the aftermath of Paris, in implementing the Paris Agreement, countries confront back home the political reality of the practical necessity they acknowledged and embraced in the global climate compromise reached in Paris. The members of the climate COP have committed to a voluntary "second-best solution" that is politically expedient but that is considerably less than the ideal. Each country has pledged to act on its own, and to act largely on its own terms. As each country tries now to keep its Paris climate promise, people everywhere back home are asking: What if we act and others do not?

Everywhere in the world, domestic economic interests are voicing concerns that local carbon pricing "will increase energy costs and leave an economy, sector, or firm at a relative disadvantage" in the marketplace.[121] Domestic producers and workers fear a loss of their competitiveness in domestic and foreign markets if they pay carbon taxes or otherwise face carbon emission restrictions that their foreign competitors do not. This fear is especially widespread in those basic energy-intensive and trade-exposed industries – such as steel, glass, cement, aluminum, paper, pulp, chemicals, and others – that depend extensively on carbon emissions in making their products. Throughout the world – and prevalent especially in the industrialized economies of the United States and of the European Union – is the apprehension that, here at home, addressing climate change by putting a price on carbon will raise energy costs for certain sectors in ways that will do grievous harm to the local economy.

Thus, it is everywhere believed that, as a result of our local climate actions, our foreign competitors will have an unfair advantage when competing with us in our own markets and in the wider global marketplace. It is anticipated that domestic producers – especially those producing carbon-intensive and globally traded goods and services – will flee "offshore." The expectation is that, in search of lower costs, domestic producers will ship our jobs from here over to some foreign there – over to some other country where carbon is not taxed and where carbon emission rules are less restrictive or perhaps do not exist. The assumption, further, is that domestic consumers will risk the loss of our jobs here by flocking to buy imported products that are cheaper than competing domestic products because carbon is not taxed and emissions rules are more lax in the countries where these imported products are produced. This manifestation of the fear of change is the fear of "carbon leakage," and this fear inhibits climate action everywhere.[122]

Economists disagree about the reality and the likely extent of carbon leakage. Despite the fears, the OECD tells us that, generally, "more stringent environmental policies ... have had no negative effect on overall productivity growth."[123] Development economists for the World Bank say, "Evidence from developed countries suggests that there are no discernible impacts on productivity and jobs from intro- ducing cost-increasing environmental regulations or pricing schemes."[124] Similarly, advocates of a "new climate economy" assure us, "There is substantial evidence suggesting that the direct competitiveness impacts are small for a country which is an early mover in legislating climate policy."[125] Even in such carbon-intensive industries as metals, cement, paper, and chemicals, "most studies fail to find evidence that" climate actions "have had a significant effect on business competitiveness."[126]

Seen purely as economics, these documented doubts about the likely economic damage from carbon leakage may well be warranted. But practically, as politics, this evidence does not matter. The prevailing perception in politics is that a singular embrace of carbon pricing while other countries remain free to refrain from any such comparable pricing will lead to the loss of local jobs from the loss of international competitiveness. When added to all the mistaken popular misperceptions about the supposed job losses caused by trade, the weight of the prospect of still more job losses due to carbon pricing or other ambitious climate actions can more than suffice to sink any local climate progress politically.

Alongside these economic fears are the equally prevalent and more warranted fears of carbon leakage harbored by environmentalists, who worry that national actions to price carbon will – in the absence of comparable actions by other countries – only export carbon pollution from richer countries to poorer countries through a form of what some call "eco-imperialism." They anticipate that "green" domestic products will simply be replaced in local markets by "dirty" foreign products with no real cuts in total global carbon emissions. What is accomplished if local climate action does not result in global climate progress?

Spurred by these economic and environmental fears, as countries begin to comply with their national climate pledges under the Paris climate agreement, many of them will undoubtedly enact climate response measures that restrict trade and will therefore fall within the legal scope of the WTO treaty. Carbon taxes, cap-and-trade programs, emission allowances for importers, performance standards, technology standards, technical regulations, and border and other measures of all kinds intended to prevent the specter of carbon leakage are all likely to restrict trade in various ways. When highly charged WTO trade disputes then arise over the legitimacy of these many and differing restrictive measures under international law, and when WTO jurists try to sort out which of them are lawful and which are not, a host of uncertainties will be revealed about the meaning and the import of some of the current rules of trade.

As it now stands, there is no way of preventing an approaching legal collision between the international rules that govern the WTO-based world trading system and the national and international means that are being constructed and implemented to confront climate change. Furthermore, as it now stands, in the likely continued absence of a functioning climate dispute settlement system, the coming legal collision between trade and climate change will occur in the WTO. In the continuing aftermath of Paris, sooner or later, a trade-restrictive national measure will be applied. The country applying that measure will maintain that it is a climate response measure taken in fulfillment of its national climate pledge made pursuant to the Paris Agreement. The country suffering the trade restriction will claim that it is not. If both those countries are members of the WTO, then the WTO will have jurisdiction over the resulting dispute. And, in the end, the WTO Appellate Body will decide whether the disputed measure is legal or not under WTO law. In the meantime, the worldwide political fallout from this head-on collision between trade and climate rules and regimes will be disastrous for both.[127]

The alternative is to reimagine WTO trade rules now to reflect the reality of the urgency of combating climate change. First of all, and above all, this needed reimagining of international trade law must make ample legal room under the

WTO rules for carbon pricing. Trade law must facilitate and reinforce carbon pricing. If trade rules are not reimagined to accommodate carbon pricing and other climate ambitions, then those ambitions will not succeed. Without the right trade rules (and without the right trade rulings), carbon pricing in particular will not succeed. It will be buried beneath a global avalanche of alleged trade law violations, both specious and legitimate. Because putting a price on carbon is indispensable to confronting climate change, trade rules must be reshaped by the members of the WTO so as to sharpen the sending of the essential price signal from carbon pricing. Moreover, this sharpening of the carbon price signal through the reconfiguring of trade rules must have the intended green effect, no matter the form in which WTO members may choose to fulfill their national climate pledges. Trade rules must provide affirmative support for all kinds of ambitious climate measures.

BORDER TAX ADJUSTMENTS AND A CLIMATE WAIVER

The price signal of a green transition will be sharpest in the form of a carbon tax. For this reason, trade rules – at the very least – must not be obstacles to the success of carbon taxes. Nor should the existence of trade rules be an excuse for refusing to impose carbon taxes. Fortunately, legal hindrances under the trade rules to climate action in the form of carbon taxes need not happen. Generally, the trade rules require that tax measures be applied consistently with obligations of non-discrimination and with concessions made and then listed in each WTO member's "schedule of concessions." Since the birth of the global trading system in 1947, however, the trade rules in the GATT – which is now part of the WTO treaty – have specifically permitted what are called in international trade law "border tax adjustments." Under the GATT rules, *a border tax adjustment equivalent to an internal tax is permitted as a charge on imported products, and is permitted also as a remission on exported products.*[128]

Simple enough? Hardly. Only indirect taxes on products – such as sales taxes – may be adjusted at the border. Direct taxes on producers – such as income taxes – may not be. To date, there is no WTO case law clarifying whether a carbon tax is a direct tax on a producer or an indirect tax on a product. So there is no certainty as to whether a carbon tax is a permitted border tax adjustment under the WTO rules. Nor is there any climate-relevant WTO case law that tells us whether a tax on inputs – such as fossil fuels – that are not physically incorporated into a final product is a tax that can be adjusted at the border under WTO law. These uncertainties in international trade law are disincentives to the enactment by any WTO member of a carbon tax.

So far, the closest the world trading system has come to clarifying any aspect of these legal uncertainties was the report of a working party of the GATT – in 1970.[129] Although it has sometimes been cited by panels and the Appellate Body, this sole GATT report some half a century ago is not binding on WTO judges. Also, it left numerous questions about border tax adjustments unanswered. Furthermore, and significantly, it occurred before the emergence of climate change as a global concern. In 1970, the pioneering Stockholm Conference on the Human Environment of 1972 was then still on the global horizon, the pivotal Brundtland Report of 1987 proclaiming "Our Common Future" was years away, and climate scientists had not yet begun to amplify worldwide their worsening warnings about the dire effects of manmade climate change.

Since that early date, legions of WTO legal scholars have suggested no end of intended clarifications of the legal meaning of a "border tax adjustment."[130] No doubt, as some of the most thoughtful of the WTO scholars have surmised along the way, it could be possible to craft a carbon tax in a way that could thread the needle of WTO legality in applying offsetting border tax adjustments consistently with the current WTO rules.[131] Conceivably, too, even if a specific carbon tax did not meet the GATT definition of a border tax adjustment, it might nevertheless be excused and upheld by WTO judges under one of the environmental exceptions in the GATT. But such a judicial outcome cannot be assumed, and the possibility that a carbon tax might somehow survive WTO legal scrutiny one way or another does nothing to eliminate this lingering uncertainty at the core of the carbon-pricing debate. Nor will needle-threading WTO legal scholars with an eye to WTO compliance be doing the drafting of the national climate response measures. Politicians will be doing it amid the heat of domestic political give-and-take. Experience suggests that, amid that heat, political decisionmakers may not be altogether mindful of their WTO treaty obligations in trying to assuage fearful local interests and muster the votes to pass the legislation.

Certainly, in the near term, the easier course politically would be to await an eventual ruling by the WTO Appellate Body in the outcome of some future international trade dispute over a climate-related trade measure. The members of the WTO could wait (as politicians often do) and "let the courts decide." But WTO dispute settlement takes time. The outcome of the ultimate judicial decision in an initial challenge to a trade-related climate measure would not be known for several years. Furthermore, that outcome would be framed by the unique specifics of the challenged measure and the proven facts of that initial "trade and climate" dispute. Even if that judgment is thought to be right in drawing the legal line between trade and climate change, it will be only a partial judgment, and the line that is drawn will be incomplete. The fullness of WTO jurisprudence emerges only incrementally on a case-by-case basis.[132]

Moreover, such a course would only add to the current extent of commercial and climate uncertainty during the lengthy duration of such a WTO dispute. One consequence could be a "chilling effect" on needed climate actions. The discretion reserved for WTO members in WTO rules for enacting and applying domestic measures is of little use to them if they are hesitant to act because of legal uncertainty. So long as policymakers are concerned that a climate measure they are considering might breach WTO rules and pose the possibility of trade sanctions – and they will know this for certain only once the measure has been litigated in WTO dispute settlement – they may refrain from enacting and applying it. Greater clarity provided now by WTO members about the extent of actual domestic discretion for climate policymaking could enhance national climate actions and add to national climate ambitions.[133]

Furthermore, the first prolonged litigation in the WTO to resolve such a fundamental "trade and climate" dispute in WTO dispute settlement would undoubtedly impose a high political cost on the global stature and legitimacy of both the trade and the climate regimes. During the long wait for a final legal ruling, the WTO trade regime would be diminished by seeming to impede progress in addressing climate change, and the UN climate regime would be hindered by having trade rules threaten to frustrate effective carbon pricing. Whatever the outcome of the first "trade and climate" dispute in the WTO, both the trade and the climate institutions will be damaged and diminished as they continue thereafter to strive to weigh and balance competing trade and climate goals. Far better, the members of the WTO should summon the collective political will to go ahead now, first of all, and before such a dispute arises, and eliminate the uncertainties about the application of current WTO rules to national climate measures.

The members of the WTO should begin by deciding that a carbon tax or any other similar tax based on the amount of carbon emitted in making a product is an indirect tax on a product that is therefore eligible for border tax adjustment.[134] This requires no change in the current WTO rule; it requires only a clarification of the meaning of the rule. This clarification can be accomplished through the adoption by the WTO members of a formal legal interpretation of the WTO obligation on border tax adjustments.[135] The WTO Ministerial Conference and the WTO General Council have the "exclusive authority" to adopt legal interpretations of WTO obligations either by consensus or, if there is no consensus, by vote of a three-fourths majority of the WTO membership.[136] This authority has never been used and, thus, has not yet been tested. Given the magnitude of the unique challenge of climate change, this authority must be used and tested now. Any such formal legal interpretation by the members of the WTO would be legally binding on WTO jurists in WTO dispute settlement.

The basic legal clarification that a carbon tax is eligible for border tax adjustment is the first task in the reimagining of international trade law. But this initial task is far from the only task facing the WTO in conceiving and in constructing a more enabling legal framework for addressing climate change. Although a carbon tax is the ideal way of putting a price on carbon, there are many other ways in which sovereign countries will choose to price carbon. These other ways will include cap-and-trade programs, emission allowances for importers, clean-energy performance and technology standards, targeted sectoral and broad-based technical regulations, and a whole assortment of border carbon adjustment measures that affect trade and thus fall within the scope of the WTO treaty and thus the jurisdiction of the WTO dispute settlement system. In addition to clarifying that border tax adjustments are permitted for carbon taxes, the members of the WTO must also reimagine trade rules to permit other ways of pricing carbon through national climate measures.

In particular, in would-be fulfillment of national climate pledges under the Paris climate agreement, a vast variety of trade-restrictive border measures will be implemented by many of the 164 WTO members for what they will all solemnly profess to be purely climate reasons. Some of these national measures will truly be climate measures. Others will, in reality, be only pretexts for protectionism. They will be disguised protections for domestic interests wary of competition and fearful of change. Further complicating matters, some of these national measures will contain elements of climate action *and* trade protection. The practicalities of politics being everywhere what they are, some of these national measures will, without doubt, provide a dose of palliative trade protection as a presumably necessary political antidote to the domestic fears of carbon competition and leakage. Nationally, trade protection in the guise of a border measure or some other trade restriction will be seen as an unavoidable part of the political price for carbon pricing or other imperative climate action.

"Carbon taxes." "Carbon tariffs." "Carbon credits." "Carbon offsets." "Carbon allowances." "Carbon bans." "Border carbon adjustments." The esoteric nomenclature of carbon pricing as it affects trade runs on and on. The creative options are many, and they have many names. In trade rules, there must be sufficient room for pricing carbon to help enable the variety and the creativity of the true bottom-up. Equally, there must be sufficient respect for allowing comparative advantage to maximize the gains from trade. But which among the miscellany of likely national climate response measures should be seen as consistent with WTO legal obligations? And which should not be? Answers to these questions are much needed now to prevent a legal collision between trade and climate change.

Recall that the fundamental WTO rules requiring most-favored-nation treatment and national treatment forbid discrimination between and among *"like"* traded products. At the most basic level, these two central obligations of non-discrimination in the WTO-based world trading system can work in the day-to-day commercial flow of international trade "only if we have some way of identifying which particular traded products are to be compared when determining whether these obligations are being respected."[37] It is for this reason that trade rules have long required that the comparison must be between "like products." The concept of "likeness" is thus crucial to supporting the very cornerstone of the global trading system, which is non-discrimination.

The WTO concept of "likeness" is endlessly elusive. In this elusiveness, "likeness" in the WTO is not altogether unlike the basic scientific concept of classification, which requires an ordered discernment when comparing one thing with another. Science historian Jacob Bronowski once described the "ability to order things into likes and unlikes" as "the foundation of human thought."[138] He declared, "Habit makes us think the likeness obvious; it seems to us obvious that all apples are somehow alike."[139] He stressed, however, that not all "likeness" is obvious. It required, for instance, an Isaac Newton "to see the likeness which no one else had seen, between the fall of the apple and the swing of the moon in its orbit round the earth."[140] No doubt WTO jurists would concur that the concept of commercial "likeness" is often anything but obvious – even as it relates to apples.[141]

The concept of a "like product" is nowhere defined in the GATT or in any other part of the WTO treaty. This concept has therefore had to be clarified through the years on a case-by-case basis in WTO dispute settlement. Making the clarifying of this key treaty term even more difficult has been the fact that the meaning of "like product" is clearly meant by the members of the WTO to vary from place to place in the trade agreements comprising the WTO treaty.[142] To illustrate this varying meaning, the Appellate Body has gone so far as to compare "likeness" to an "accordion" that "stretches and squeezes in different places as different provisions of the WTO Agreement are applied."[143] Therefore, not surprisingly, what is, and what is not, a "like product" has been the subject of endless debate and dispute, case by case, in the WTO-based trading system. Recall that, after some seven decades of struggle with clarifying this central concept of WTO law, the general view in WTO case law is that the "likeness" of traded products will be determined on the basis of their physical characteristics, their end uses, their tariff classification, and con-sumers' tastes and habits.[144] In this view, a determination of "likeness" should be made solely on the basis of these four criteria. It therefore follows that this determin-ation should *not* be made on the basis of how products are made or on the basis of what goes into making them.

The implications of this traditional view of the meaning of "like products" could have profound potential climate consequences. Supported by the weight of much WTO jurisprudence, if two competing products from Country A and Country B have the same physical characteristics, end uses, and tariff classifications, and if consumers' tastes and habits for them are all the same, then they will be seen as "like" *irrespective of how much carbon is emitted in making either one of them*. In this view, "likeness" has nothing to do with a "process or production method," whether it is "product-related" (having an impact on the physical quality of the product) or "non-product-related" (not showing any trace in the product).

In a series of appeals since its founding in 1995, the WTO Appellate Body has generally reinforced this long-prevailing view. Yet Appellate Body rulings have occasionally seemed to imply that, in a discrete factual context when evaluating the competitive relationship between traded products in some future trade dispute, they might see "likeness" somewhat differently. In particular, the Appellate Body ruled in the EC – Asbestos dispute in 2001 that the fact that a legal determination of "likeness" depends in part on consumers' tastes and habits implies that whether two products are "like" or not could depend in some instances on whether they are *seen* as "like" by the consumers in some particular market.[145] More recently, in the *Canada – Feed-in Tariffs Program* dispute in 2013, the Appellate Body observed in passing that, "[w]hat constitutes a competitive relationship between products may require consideration of inputs and processes of production used to produce the product."[146]

What, then, if the consumers in Country A see two competing domestic and imported products as not being "like" because the domestic products from Country A are "green" products and the imported products from Country B are "dirty" products produced in ways causing extensive carbon emissions? Are those two products "like products" that therefore cannot be subjected to trade discrimination? Or are they not "like" because they are not in a competitive relationship because of the fact that they are not seen as "like" by consumers? How wide has the legal door been opened by the Appellate Body to a different view of "likeness"? Can a consideration of how products are made be appropriate in determining whether there is a WTO *violation* in need of a defense, or is such a consideration appropriate only in determining whether there is a *defense* to a WTO violation?

First written in the 1940s, the basic WTO trade rule setting out "general exceptions" as defenses to what would otherwise be WTO obligations is long overdue for an update. One helpful reimagination would be to add new exceptions for actions taken by WTO members in compliance with an agreed list of multilateral environmental agreements. This list could include the Paris climate agreement. This rule has, however, proven – so far – to be sufficiently capacious to accommodate much of the modern world.[147] There is room in the "general-exceptions" rule for much in the world that should rightly trump trade – if applied in the right way. This capaciousness has been revealed through the years in the rulings of the Appellate Body. By taking into account how a traded product is made only in determining whether there is a *defense* to a trade law violation, instead of in determining whether there is a *violation* in the first place, the Appellate Body has – so far – been able to give due regard to legitimate environmental and other non-trade concerns without delving too deeply into the definition of a "like product." In this way, the WTO jurists have been able to avoid shaking the very foundations of the WTO trading system.

Starting with the *US – Shrimp* dispute in 1998, the WTO Appellate Body has dealt with disputes involving environmental PPMs largely while clarifying the environmental exceptions set out as potential defenses to what would otherwise be trade violations. Where justified by the facts of a particular dispute, this interpretive approach has made it possible for the WTO jurists to fashion fine legal distinctions in support of environmentally motivated trade restrictions on a case-by-case basis – without having to make any sweeping systemic statements that could lead to a more constrictive view of the "accordion" of "like products." The Appellate Body has, however, been able to take this approach in *US – Shrimp* and in subsequent disputes only because the legal issue of whether the products involved in those disputes are in fact "like products" has not been raised by the disputing countries in those WTO appeals. Should the legal issue of whether PPMs can be considered when making a "like product" determination be raised in a future appeal, the WTO jurists will not be able to dodge the issue. The WTO rules do not allow the Appellate Body to decline to hear an appeal, and the rules state that the Appellate Body "shall address" every legal issue raised in an appeal.[148] Thus, the Appellate Body will have no legal discretion *not* to address the issue. In the meantime, as with the meaning of a border tax adjustment, the legal meaning of the term "like products" as it applies to climate-related and other PPMs remains a source of uncertainty that constrains trade and threatens to inhibit needed climate action.

The widespread worry of trade advocates is over what Jagdish Bhagwati, the noted trade economist, calls the "slippery slope." He explains that "the fear" in the WTO trading system is "that an open-ended grant of exception on values-related PPMs could lead to a slippery slope and to a flood of exclusions that could not be challenged as countries passed unilateral legislation and executive orders that asserted moral objection to a practice they did not like and denied others market access."[149] If, when determining whether there has been a WTO violation, a distinction on the "likeness" of products can be made on the basis of the amount of carbon that is used or emitted in making them, then what other distinctions on what other bases can be made relating to a vast world of varying PPMs? Where will it stop? Where will we draw the line?

This is a legitimate worry. If taken too far, such distinctions could render meaningless the basic rules of non-discrimination at the heart of the WTO-based world trading system. There is no end of worthy causes, all much deserving. Human rights. Labor rights. Rights relating to health, to safety, to security. And many, many more. A flood of objections, "moral" and otherwise, could conceivably arise in the WTO against equal market access for any number of foreign traded products for any number of reasons. Down Bhagwati's slippery slope could flow a long list of non-commercial values imposed by some countries on other countries – usually by rich countries on poor countries – through the legal making of such distinctions between traded products.

This is also not a new worry. This apprehension of a slippery slope down from the longstanding view of "likeness" has been a consistent concern since the start of the trading system. Back in 1952, soon after the dawn of the GATT, Belgium sought to discriminate against trade from Denmark and Norway because those two other countries did not have family allowance programs that Belgium deemed comparable to its own. A GATT working party ruled then against legalizing and legitimizing under the trade rules such an intrusive degree of trade discrimination into sovereign domestic discretion, which could have extended far beyond queries about PPMs to question the basic domestic social policies underlying foreign production.[150]

The view that the legal line must be drawn somewhere short of an endless, open-ended series of such discriminatory distinctions in traded products has remained the consensus view of trade advocates ever since that early GATT report, first in the GATT and now in the WTO. And trade advocates wonder: If now, when we are confronted by the challenge of quelling climate change, we redefine the long-standing definition of "like products" to permit international trade discrimination on the legal basis that two competing traded products are not "like" where the processes and the production methods of one involve carbon emissions and those of the other do not, then where will it end? How far will we permit one country to go in second-guessing the sovereign domestic policymaking of another country by impos-ing trade restrictions on the basis that competing products are not "like"?

Thus, in the reimagining of trade rules to confront climate change, the need is urgent for a carefully crafted, carefully limited, and carefully confined construction of trade rules that permits trade discrimination on the basis of the carbon used or emitted in making a traded product – but does not have the effect of inspiring an unending flood of demands for an array of much more sweeping trade discrimin-ations that would risk the integrity and the future of the world trading system. This crafting of the right balance between trade and climate change cannot be done by redefining "like products," which would surely send the trading system down Bhagwati's slippery slope, or by trying to add a climate defense to the list of the general exceptions in the WTO rules, a tactic that would require a basic change in the WTO treaty and would doubtless sink from the weight of competing demands for other additions to the list.

The right balance can, however, be struck through the adoption by the members of the WTO of a single discrete and self-contained *climate waiver* to respond to the unique challenge of climate change with a unique solution as part of the needed reimagining of WTO trade rules. A WTO climate waiver should declare that all national measures that impose trade restrictions based on the amount of carbon used or emitted in making a product, and all other climate response measures that apply trade restrictions and are in compliance with international climate obligations and are taken to fulfill them, are legal under WTO law. If done right, such a WTO climate waiver could combine the most benefit for the climate with the least risk to trade.

Central to the success of a WTO climate waiver would be measurement, calibra-tion, and definition. An agreed international standard would need to be established for calculating the amount of product-related carbon emissions.[151] Ideally, the establishment of the right carbon metrics would be accomplished in concert by the trade and climate regimes. Climate negotiators are trying to establish such a standard as part of the climate "rulebook" under the Paris Agreement. Also, some calibration could be needed to afford different treatment to different products and sectors facing different challenges in shifting to low-carbon production. Moreover, a definition would be needed of what constitutes a climate response measure. Ideally, this key term will be defined by the climate regime, which has made little progress so far post-Paris in settling on such an agreed definition. Otherwise, the meaning of a climate response measure will have to be defined on a case-by-case basis by WTO jurists in WTO dispute settlement.[152]

Although not currently on the WTO agenda, or even seriously being considered by the members of the WTO, a WTO climate waiver is nevertheless available as an avenue for trade reimagining.[153] Exceptions and waivers to the basic rules of trade non-discrimination and to other trade rules are far from unprecedented in the WTO. WTO members have previously granted about two dozen waivers. The two best-known are a 2003 waiver granting least-developed countries the right to compulsory licensing of essential medicines for treating HIV, malaria, and other life-threatening diseases, and a 2006 waiver allowing some WTO members to take domestic measures under the Kimberley Process established in 2003 to prevent "conflict diamonds" financing African bloodshed from entering the mainstream global market for rough diamonds.[154]

Under the WTO treaty, WTO members may decide to waive what would otherwise be WTO treaty obligations "in exceptional circumstances"[155] by proceeding as follows: One or more members of the WTO must first be persuaded that framing a WTO climate waiver will be much better for the world trading system than waiting for the approaching legal collision between trade and climate change that might topple it. Next, the separate silos of the trade and climate regimes must be brought together to discuss and to define the nexus between the two. Then the topic of the relationship of trade and climate change must be placed formally on the WTO agenda. The "exceptional circumstances" justifying a climate waiver must then be set out clearly by interested WTO members in requesting WTO action. A working party of WTO members must then be established. The specific terms of the waiver must be identified by the working party in a proposed waiver submitted to all WTO members. Then, lastly, the waiver must be approved – either by consensus of the members of the WTO or, failing that, by a three-fourths vote.[156]

What other circumstances could possibly be more exceptional than those arising from climate change? Certainly the countless challenges facing our unwilling world cannot all be reduced to the one challenge of confronting climate change. In this, as in all else, reductionism must be resisted. Climate change is, after all, only one dire consequence of the ongoing human ravaging of the Earth's ecosystems. And yet, in the whole world over, what will be untouched by climate change? Each and every other worthy cause for worldwide concern has been affected in some way by climate change – or soon will be. In touching all else, in encompassing all else, in encapsulating all else, the global circumstance of climate change is not only "exceptional"; it is uniquely so.

The *uniqueness* of the challenge we face in fighting climate change fully justifies the adoption of a climate waiver by the members of the WTO that treats carbon differently from how we treat all else affecting trade. Ultimately, trade entangled with the unique climate harms caused by carbon emissions cannot be sustainable trade. Certainly the right line of the right climate waiver will be anything but easy to draw. But the fact that a line is hard to draw is not a reason for not drawing it. And the fact that there is no will politically at this time even to try to draw the line between trade and climate change does not mean that the unwilling cannot become the willing.

To varying extents, these are common challenges in all rule-making. The special challenge with a WTO climate waiver will not only be summoning the will to draw the line and then drawing the right line. It will also be sticking to that right line after it is drawn. The hardest part of this legal reimagining will be to make certain that the unique challenge of forestalling climate change is indeed met uniquely both in conception and in application. A WTO climate waiver must be upheld, and it must be upheld in a way that keeps it from becoming what trade advocates fear it might become – the legal basis for a slide down the slippery slope toward an abyss of unlimited and unjustified trade discrimination.

The broader necessary task for the members of the WTO will be to introduce and then to uphold a WTO climate waiver as just one part of a more extensive reimagining of trade law to help us not only counter climate change, but also shape and share an overall sustainable development. Like all other human actions, the human action of commerce through trade must be conducted within the bounds of nature. The rules we make to govern international trade must be guided from now on by this realization.

12

On a New Approach for Sustainable Energy in International Trade Law

The realization that we must live and work within the bounds of nature – the realization that the economy and the environment are one – is already reflected in the words of the treaty that established the World Trade Organization. The first paragraph in the preamble on the first page of the Marrakesh Agreement of 1994 proclaims that "trade and economic endeavor" should be conducted while "allowing the *optimal use* of the world's resources in accordance with *the objective of sustainable development,* seeking both to protect and preserve the environment and to enhance the means for doing so."[1] Compare these words to those in the preamble to the General Agreement on Tariffs and Trade of 1947, which speaks instead of "developing the *full use* of the resources of the world" and makes no mention of what has since become known as sustainable development.[2]

SUSTAINABLE DEVELOPMENT AND THE WTO

The WTO Appellate Body sees this differing wording in the preamble to the WTO agreement and the preamble to the original GATT as a textual distinction that makes a significant difference in how the content of WTO obligations must be viewed in the WTO-based trading system. In 1998, in the ruling in the appeal in the US – Shrimp dispute, the WTO judges expressed the view that the negotiators of the WTO treaty "evidently believed . . . that the objective of the 'full use of the resources of the world' set forth in the preamble of the GATT 1947 was no longer appropriate to the world trading system of the 1990's. As a result, the negotiators decided to qualify the original objectives of the GATT 1947" with new and different language that "demonstrates a recognition by WTO negotiators that optimal use of the world's resources should be made in accordance with the objective of sustainable development."[3]

The preamble to the Marrakesh Agreement establishing the WTO does not create any additional WTO obligations. The preamble is, however, context within the agreement evidencing its object and purpose, and, thus, it is highly relevant to the mandatory task of interpreting the current obligations in the agreement in accordance with "the ordinary meaning to be given to the terms of the treaty in their context and in the light of their object and purpose."[4] Furthermore, the "context" for the purposes of interpreting a treaty includes "[a]ny relevant rules of international law applicable in the relations between the parties."[5] It has been argued, with some merit, that sustainable development has now attained the status of a principle of international law that should be seen as relevant context in construing the content of those WTO obligations that relate to sustainability.[6]

Equal and parallel endeavors in reimagination are required to revise and revitalize current WTO rules through negotiation in order to realize the original imagining of the World Trade Organization as a catalyst for sustainable development. The WTO is meant to be not solely a forum and a framework for lowering barriers to trade, but, more, an agent for advancing trade while also achieving sustainable development. "The objective of sustainable development" was plainly invoked by the members of the WTO in their "Decision on Trade and Environment" annexed to the WTO treaty at the conclusion of the Uruguay Round in 1994. WTO members agreed that "there should not be, nor need be, any policy contradiction between upholding and safeguarding an open, non-discriminatory and equitable multilateral trading system on the one hand, and acting for the protection of the environment, and the promotion of sustainable development on the other."[7]

The WTO Committee on Trade and Environment – comprised of all WTO members – was instructed in that initial decision "to identify the relationship between trade measures and environmental measures, in order to promote sustainable development." The new committee was told also "to make appropriate recommendations on whether any modifications of the provisions of the multilateral trading system are required, compatible with the open, equitable and non-discriminatory nature of the system."[8] More than two decades later, the world still awaits those recommendations. The WTO Committee on Trade and Environment should be a source of much imaginative rule-making. Yet, despite the clarity of its original instructions, and despite long years of deliberation, this critical WTO committee has not made a single recommendation that has resulted in a single legally binding decision by the members of the WTO.[9] Thus far, the making of legal rulings clarifying the relationship between economy and environment in the world trading system has been left entirely to WTO judges in WTO dispute settlement.

Trade negotiators have hoped that such decisions would be part of a successful outcome of the Doha Development Round. Among all else that has been thwarted because of those failed negotiations are a number of announced trade-related environmental goals – including "the identification of any need to clarify relevant WTO rules" as part of "enhancing the mutual supportiveness of trade and environment."[10] In addition to listing this goal as well as other environmental goals, the Doha Declaration that launched the round in 2001 reiterates the continuing allegiance of the members of the WTO to "the objective of having sustainable development."[11] Elsewhere, the nearly 200 UN members that have endorsed the Addis Ababa Action Agenda of the United Nations, in furtherance of the SDGs[12] – almost all of them also members of the WTO – have pledged as part of it to "endeavor to significantly increase world trade in a manner consistent with the sustainable development goals." In addition, importantly, they have promised to "integrate sustainable development into trade policy at all levels."[13]

So far, the members of the WTO have not done much more than merely recite now and again a ritual reaffirmation of this stated objective. To help fashion the enabling framework of new economic approaches so urgently needed to transform our unwilling into the willing world, they must weave the objective of sustainable development into international trade law in ways it never has been before. Just as we must internalize the environmental costs of carbon emissions into the prices of our products in the marketplace, so too must we internalize the overarching goal of sustainable development into the enabling rules of all our international institutions – including the WTO.

In the eyes of the Appellate Body, as seen through the lens of the *US – Shrimp* dispute, the intent of the negotiators of the WTO treaty to further the flow of trade while also furthering sustainable development "must add colour, texture and shading" to the interpretation of WTO rules.[14] This is true of existing WTO rules. This must be equally true of any new WTO rules we negotiate. The same economic *and environmental* objective must "add colour, texture and shading" to the making and the remaking of WTO rules through the reimagining of international trade law. In many places throughout the WTO treaty, and in many places throughout the WTO trading system, the color that must be added is green. A broader and greener perspective in trade must begin with the stated objective of sustainable development.[15] Fulfilling the objective of sustainable development must begin with confronting climate change. And confronting climate change as a central and indispensable part of achieving sustainable development must begin – but only begin – with reimagining trade law to help put a price on carbon.

CARBON MARKETS AND CLIMATE CLUBS

Clarifying that carbon taxes are eligible for border tax adjustments under WTO law will help boost carbon pricing. So will adopting a waiver from WTO obligations for trade restrictions that are based on the amount of carbon used or emitted in making a product, and for other climate response measures taken in compliance with international climate obligations in order to fulfill them. But still more can be done by the members of the WTO to help accelerate climate actions and help generate more ambitious climate actions. A climate waiver should also support carbon pricing by permitting the international linking of carbon markets and the successful operation of "climate clubs" of willing countries that wish to join together to do more to fight climate change by cutting carbon emissions beyond the extent of their current commitments. Ultimately, these climate clubs could themselves be linked to create a single global carbon market.

Article 6 of the Paris Agreement extolls "voluntary cooperation" by the United Nations Conference of Parties in implementing their voluntary national climate pledges. Furthermore, and importantly, Article 6 urges "voluntary cooperation" in the pursuit of "higher ambition" through additional national "mitigation and adaptation" actions to counter climate change and "promote sustainable development and environmental integrity."[16] Significantly, in Article 6, the fulfillment of the highest aims of the agreement is seen by the negotiators as occurring "on a voluntary basis in cooperative approaches that involve the use of internationally transferred mitigation outcomes."[17] This treaty provision can be read as an invitation to the true bottom-up to enter through this back door left open in the global climate agreement. What is more, Article 6 establishes for use by countries "on a voluntary basis" a new "mechanism to contribute to the mitigation of greenhouse gas emissions and support sustainable development."[18] If the open back door to increased global carbon trading in the climate agreement is opened wide enough, this mechanism "could offer a universal carbon allowance or credit for those countries that choose to use it" and, thus, could offer "the prospect of carbon pricing in many economies."[19]

These aims can be achieved only by the means climate negotiators could not bring themselves to mention by name in the Paris climate agreement – the market. After Paris, climate-minded business leaders and other advocates of market solutions to climate change quickly seized on the tongue-twisting treaty circumlocution of "internationally transferred mitigation outcomes." They have made it central to their shared struggle to maintain and – they hope – to increase the growing global momentum toward putting a price on carbon. With the current carbon markets struggling – despite this momentum – to establish and to maintain their carbon prices,[20] with many countries having conditioned their voluntary Paris climate pledges on having ready access to a regional or other international carbon market, and with the global hopes expressed in the Paris Agreement for "higher ambition" for combating climate change hinging more and more on ensuring the success of the growing number of carbon markets in connecting across national borders, a central concern has become determining how best carbon markets can be made more successful by being "linked."

In climate parlance, the word "linkage" refers to the formal recognition by one carbon market – whether regional, national, subnational, or sectoral – of carbon emissions reductions undertaken in another carbon market for purposes of compliance with local emissions reduction obligations. In effect, linkage binds different carbon markets together into a single common market. Carbon markets in one place are increasingly reaching out to carbon markets in other places to establish market linkage. Many of these links are transnational, and some of the most creative of these transnational links are between state and provincial rather than national governments – such as the one between California and Quebec. The potential variations of these transnational links multiply with the worldwide multiplication of individual carbon markets. So do the potential advantages in cutting carbon emissions. Linking carbon markets creates more opportunities for more emitters to cut their carbon emissions, making emissions cuts more cost-effective and, thus, more extensive. "[T]he broader the base for a given carbon price, the more efficiently it operates and the lower the overall cost of managing emissions to the economies within which it is operating."[21] The transfer of emissions trading allowances and credits between linked carbon markets can also stimulate climate-related investment by directing "large scale financing towards mitigation activities."[22] These advantages, in turn, have the market consequence of encouraging still more emissions reductions.

The key to securing these advantages from linkage is facilitating the trading of carbon emissions allowances between carbon markets. The linking of carbon markets enables more successful carbon pricing, which is the crux of countering climate change, by encouraging the global shift to a green economy. One of the leading climate economists, Robert N. Stavins of Harvard University, has explained this connection by noting that market linking "facilitates cost-effectiveness, that is, the achievement of the lowest-cost emissions reductions across the set of linked systems, minimizing both the costs for individual jurisdictions as well as the overall cost of meeting a collective cap."[23] The "higher ambition" of the Paris Agreement is quantified by the goals of the High-Level Carbon Pricing Panel of the World Bank and the International Monetary Fund: to double the current level of only about 12 percent of global greenhouse gas emissions covered by carbon-pricing mechanisms to 25 percent by 2030, and then to double it again to 50 percent within the following decade.[24] Although technical experts have advised that these goals can be achieved "if existing and planned carbon-pricing programs are augmented by additional actions," it is difficult to foresee how these goals can be accomplished if those additional actions do not include the linking of carbon markets.[25]

The momentum for carbon pricing may also speed up with the formation of voluntary and *ad hoc* "climate clubs" of like-minded emitters willing to work together to do more to cut carbon emissions now than can currently be agreed in a fully global consensus.[26] A climate club could begin with an alliance of the willing who wish to adopt a common set of rules cutting across legal jurisdictions in order to go ahead now to make deeper emissions cuts in exchange for mutual commercial, technological, and other concessions. A climate club centered on carbon pricing could help overcome the lack of funding and the lack of a market that are the main challenges to renewable energy innovation in such key sectors as gas, oil, mining, and electricity.[27] This alliance of the willing could then build from there incrementally to include more emitters as more emitters witnessed the success of the climate club and wished to enlist in it to secure its benefits while lifting their own climate ambitions.[28] Beginning at the global "bottom," beginning at far less than a fully global level, such a club could be a spur to useful energy and governance experimentation; it could "encourage innovation and practical experiences that might best be described as learning-by-doing."[29] What is learned in the learning by doing of that climate club about how best to battle climate change could then be scaled up over time and applied first regionally and, eventually, globally. A climate club could become the epitome of the true bottom-up by growing over time toward more fully global approaches, just as the GATT grew over time into the WTO.[30]

A climate club of two or more COP members desiring to coordinate the measures they take to address climate change appears to be permitted within the United Nations Framework Convention on Climate Change.[31] Such a club could be legally located, however, either inside or outside the United Nations climate framework. Membership in a climate club formed outside the UN framework need not be limited solely to national governments; it could, in addition, include subnational regions, states, provinces, and cities, and even businesses, NGOs, and other non-state actors. Because it would be a "club" and not an "international agreement," a climate club could include, and could bind, parties other than governments; it could, legally, be post-Westphalian.

Whether located inside or outside the UN framework, a climate club could in fact be structured as a "club of carbon markets" which could set an emissions cap, issue and accept carbon emissions units, require compliance, and penalize non-compliance. Club members could receive a range of benefits from belonging to the club – including financial and green technological assistance, lower overall pollution abatement costs, potentially greater price stability, and greater market liquidity. Conceivably, these benefits could also include WTO-plus trade benefits over and above those currently provided by the WTO treaty.[32] Because a club of any kind can succeed only if the benefits of belonging to it are reserved exclusively for its members, those not in the climate club would be denied the benefits.

There could also be trade penalties. One leading advocate of a climate club, the noted climate economist William D. Nordhaus, sees the biggest obstacle to the success of international climate agreements as the prospect of free-riding – which "occurs when a party receives the benefits of a public good without contributing to the costs."[33] To prevent free-riding enjoyment of the benefits of being in a climate club consisting of countries by those countries that are not members of the club, he says there must be penalties for those countries that refuse to pay the costs of joining the club. He emphasizes, "Economic modeling indicates that the most promising penalty is uniform percentage tariffs on the imports of nonparticipants in the club region."[34] Whether in the form of higher tariffs, or in some other form, the availability of restrictions on trade is generally seen as essential to the success of climate clubs in advancing global carbon pricing.[35]

Neither the linking of carbon markets nor the bottom-up creativity of climate clubs will be successful without a further reimagining of the international trade rules by the members of the WTO as part of a WTO climate waiver. The reason is this: In their nexus with trade, all these emerging and possible climate arrangements aimed at furthering carbon pricing would more than likely be inconsistent with the rules of the WTO in their current imagining. Economic journalist Eduardo Porter has summed up the challenge posed by current WTO rules in pursuing carbon pricing in these new ways: "A system like that proposed by Professor Nordhaus would require some agreement to amend the rules of the World Trade Organization, to prevent countries hit by the tariff from retaliating with tariffs of their own. Those countries most dependent on fossil fuels may not quickly come on board."[36] This may be an understatement. How then must the trade rules be reimagined in the content of a WTO climate waiver to help facilitate and further the linking of carbon markets and the success of climate clubs?

First, there is the threshold issue of the legal status of the emissions units of carbon markets. As a matter of international trade law, what are they? In the content of the WTO climate waiver, WTO members must make it clear that emissions units are neither goods nor services under the WTO treaty, and, thus, the mere act of trading emissions units internationally is not subject to the varied array of non-discrimination and other WTO obligations that would apply if those units were goods or services.[37] If emissions units were deemed by the WTO to be either goods or services, then all sorts of high legal hurdles would be hoisted by the global trading system against carbon market links and against climate clubs.

Next, the WTO climate waiver must be expansive enough to embrace the linking of carbon markets and the working of all kinds of climate clubs. It should include a waiver of what would otherwise be the illegality under WTO law of the international trade discrimination resulting from any trade benefits provided by a climate club solely to club members and not to other members of the WTO, or resulting from any trade penalties imposed by the club on any WTO members in the pursuit of carbon pricing. All trade sanctions by carbon markets, by linked carbon markets, or by clubs of carbon markets that are based on the amount of carbon emissions resulting from a traded good or service should fall within the scope of the WTO climate waiver.

One option would be for the members of the WTO to establish up front the prerequisites for the kinds of carbon markets and climate clubs, and for the kinds of actions by those markets and by those clubs, that would be eligible for the climate waiver. For example, it could be required that, to be eligible for the climate waiver, a market or club would have to be open to any outsiders that may wish to become insiders by accepting the obligations and by bearing the costs of that market or that club. It could be affirmed, too, that, so long as the market or club is open to new members willing to pay its costs and to be bound by its rules, then the offering by that market or club of WTO-plus trade benefits exclusively to its members – and not to the other members of the WTO remaining outside that market or club – would not be in violation of WTO rules.

Another option would be for carbon markets and climate clubs simply to become part of the WTO. The agreements establishing them could become plurilateral WTO agreements that would be open to all WTO members but would bind only those WTO members that chose to be a part of them. This approach would have the advantage of streamlining and of simplifying legally some of what will surely be the multiplying legal complexities of structuring the likely increasing number of carbon markets and climate clubs. Moreover, this approach would offer to the markets and the clubs – if they chose – the advantages of access to use of the WTO dispute settlement system. Most of all, it would help in the transcending task of uniting economy and environment into one through the continued development of international law.

In addition, conditions could be included in the climate waiver to help limit the risks to the trading system while facilitating carbon pricing. Robert Howse, for example, has suggested that a climate-related WTO waiver could: spell out the specific suitable objectives for eligible carbon markets and climate clubs in furthering climate mitigation, halting environmental harm, and supporting the clean energy transition; contain language identical to that used for qualifying general exceptions to trade obligations, including that policies pursued under the waiver must not be applied in a manner that would constitute arbitrary or unjustifiable discrimination; and be conditioned on the markets and the clubs giving notice to the WTO of the policies that would be imposed, coupled with "a detailed plan about removal of discriminatory aspects within a defined time-frame."[38]

Ordinarily, long tradition in trade rule-making would urge a surge toward the ramparts by trade advocates to battle against the breadth of such a waiver of the basic obligations against trade discrimination. But now we all face the unique challenge of climate change, a challenge unlike any we have faced before. In reimagining international trade law to help us combine to confront this challenge, we must remember the timeless wisdom of Thomas Macaulay's "just mean" of the "in between." The progress of science is revealing to us now an ever-accumulating avalanche of alarming facts about all we are doing to harm nature – and thus to harm ourselves – through carbon emissions and through myriad other environmental degradations. Trade policymaking can no longer be largely oblivious to this. As with all our rule-making, our trade rule-making must acknowledge and accommodate the consequences of these scientific facts. Without positive action by the WTO, trade rules threaten the pricing of carbon that is the essential primary response to these scientific facts.

The imperative of carbon pricing will not work without a climate waiver from trade obligations. A climate waiver will not work unless it is sufficient in scope to support the success of all aspects of carbon pricing. If carbon pricing does not work, then the Paris climate agreement will not succeed. All our elaborate global efforts to combat climate change and to accomplish sustainable development will fail. The "just mean" of the "in between" must be a line drawn in the reimagining of trade rules that preserves the integrity of the rule-based world trading system while also helping the world prevent a cataclysmic climate failure.

THE MERITS OF SUBSIDIES

Macaulay, as both historian and lawmaker, had the right mix of historical perspective and practical experience required to know that, in right rule-making, the timeless task, the endlessly daunting and difficult task, is, again, "to draw correctly the line which divides those cases in which it is the duty of the state to interfere from those cases in which it is the duty of the state to abstain from interference."[39] In this respect, the challenge is no different now, for us, than it was for him in the British House of Commons in the 1840s. The question is still the same: Where is the right line of state interference?

Driven as we are by the urgent demands of science and by the relentless accumulation of fact upon scientific fact revealing the ever-accelerating impact of our carbon emissions on all of nature, we must ask ourselves, in all our rule-making, where that right line may be in fashioning a sturdy and supportive framework of rules in which the spontaneous order of human cooperation and creative human interaction can flourish in a swift transition to the low-carbon world of the green economy. Sending the right and, what is more, the sufficient price signal of the immediate necessity for this shift is central to inspiring and to easing the green transition. With the right support from the right reimagining of international trade rules in the right enabling framework, useful tools of transmission in the form of carbon taxes, carbon markets, carbon market "links," and climate clubs can all help to send this essential signal to the marketplace. Still more can be done to help send the sufficient price signal by reimagining the right course of the right line of state interference in the international trade rules relating to the grant of governmental *subsidies*.

In the willing world, the introduction of carbon taxes for carbon pricing would internalize the full environmental costs of burning fossil fuels into market prices, and the market would then react as markets do through a more efficient allocation of limited economic resources. In our unwilling world, the intense political opposition everywhere to imposing new "taxes" of any kind – certainly including carbon taxes – will continue to frustrate the use of carbon taxes and other purely market-based tools for fighting climate change. This is why David Victor has said that carbon taxes are the best way to control greenhouse gas emissions "but the worst way to mobilize political support."[40]

Although carbon taxes and other market-based solutions are surely much to be preferred, political reality suggests that these tools may not be available widely enough or soon enough to quell climate change. Moreover, these market-based tools may also not add up to enough on their own to raise the reach of global achievement to the heights of the higher ambitions of our Paris climate goals. For these reasons, many of the willing believe that some additional form of governmental interference aimed at shaping the choices and the outcomes in the global energy marketplace is needed to reinforce and to supplement market-based actions by providing added incentives for the investments and the innovations that are urgently needed to help spur the green transition. Thus it is that they tend to turn to the practical political expedient of governmental subsidies.

In particular, many of the willing support governmental subsidies because they see a pressing need for additional governmental initiatives to help speed and spread the green transition by giving consumers, companies, and whole industries additional incentives to develop and deploy clean energy.[41] Given the considerable gap still existing between the market prices for "modern" renewable energy and much cheaper fossil fuels, they all see governmental subsidies for the use of renewable energy as necessary to accelerate this shift. A risk is that the plea for "green subsidies" could become simply the latest example of the self-defeating fallacy of the top-down state-directed solution. But – if green subsidies are framed rightly – and if they are applied rightly – such subsidies can instead become a productive part of the enabling framework of rules furthering a faster green transition. To ensure that such interference by the state in the makeup of the energy marketplace will be productive, that it will be enabling and not self-defeating, our reimagining of international trade rules must locate Macaulay's right line of the "just mean" that is "in between" for renewable energy subsidies.

In international trade law, these are far from being new questions. In the reimagining of international trade law to counter climate change and to advance sustainable development, these may, however, be questions with some new answers. On the one hand, the very thought of a government granting subsidies to favored producers is anathema to the notion of non-discrimination that is the core of the trading system. On the other hand, the grant by a government of some kinds of energy subsidies may well be useful to speeding the green transition against the ticking clock of climate change. In the reimagining of international trade law, there must be a reimagining of some of the current trade rules as they relate to state subsidies generally and to energy subsidies specifically. Some energy subsidies may be impediments to the green transition; however, other, green energy subsidies may turn out to be indispensable ingredients to making that transition a success. In our reimagining of the trade rules on subsidies, the right line must be drawn in the right place and in the right way between the two.

Subsidies can be "good" when they correct for market failures. Subsidies can be "bad" when they distort what should otherwise be market successes. The debate over how to tell the "good" subsidies from the "bad" goes back at least to Adam Smith and the eighteenth century.[42] Smith believed that most governmental subsidies of favored market activities are "bad" because they cause harmful distortions to the unfettered exchange of the free marketplace at the core of his "simple system of natural liberty." Instead of "subsidies," Smith spoke of what he called "bounties," meaning the same thing. "The effect of bounties," he insisted, "like that of all the other expedients of the mercantile system, can only be to force the trade of a country into a channel much less advantageous than that in which it would naturally run of its own accord."[43]

For the most part, the advocates of trade have long sided with Adam Smith in asserting that most subsidies are "bad." Thus, they have long favored trade rules that impose disciplines on the use of subsidies because of the vast range of economic inefficiencies and economic distortions that subsidies can create. In echo of Smith, trade advocates explain, "Subsidies can potentially or actually distort trade, competition and investment decisions. Some subsidies have encouraged behaviours that have proven to be highly destructive of the environment (e.g. leading to over-fishing of ocean-going fish stocks, or leading to increasing emissions of greenhouse gases). Subsidies can also lead to massive waste, inefficient use of scarce resources and, possibly, even subsidy wars in certain industries or specific situations, while the benefits of the subsidies are captured by the few at the expense of the many. The use of subsidies can increase the development gap between rich nations (those that can afford to subsidize) and poor nations (those that cannot)."[44]

Throughout the world, local producers go to local politicians with their hands out seeking an unfair advantage in the market. The governmental subsidies they are given lower the costs for local producers and, thus, allow them to sell their products for lower prices. This artificial price difference reduces the access to local markets for competing foreign producers, and it gives local producers an unfair advantage in exporting their products to the home markets of those foreign producers as well as to other, "third" markets. Through this governmental intervention, subsidies can distort trade by distorting what would otherwise be the free functioning of competitive forces in the domestic and global marketplace.[45]

But others in this debate have long maintained that subsidies can sometimes be "good." While agreeing that governmental subsidies may distort the market, and may therefore result in an inefficient allocation of limited resources, these defenders of governmental subsidies contend that there are times when subsidies can "correct or compensate for market imperfections or externalities that would otherwise exist, and thus enhance efficient-resource allocation."[46] Today, they see ours as one of those times, and they see state subsidies for wind energy, solar energy, and other forms of renewable energy as offsetting the still-considerable price advantages of competing fossil fuels, with their harmful climate consequences, in the marketplace.[47]

Among the trade rules in the WTO treaty are disciplines on the governmental subsidies affecting trade that aspire to draw the right line between "good" and "bad" subsidies. Elaborate subsidies rules that took nearly half a century to negotiate apply to financial contributions by governments that confer a benefit on recipients in the marketplace. (Significantly, these rules apply to governmental *actions* and not to governmental *inactions* which could also be seen as subsidies – such as a failure to protect the environment or a failure to cut greenhouse gas emissions.) These WTO rules impose strict restrictions on the use of certain kinds of these defined subsidies, and also on the use of the "countervailing measures" in the form of "countervailing duties" that are permitted by the WTO treaty as neutralizing offsets against foreign subsidies.[48]

These WTO subsidies rules are generally true to the spirit of Adam Smith. They provide that governmental support may not be conditioned on exporting or on using domestic instead of imported goods as inputs in production. They provide also that such support may not be targeted to specific domestic industries in ways that have adverse effects in the marketplace. As part of the continuing legal chore of discerning the "good" subsidies from the "bad," exhaustive labors have been expended in WTO dispute settlement in an effort to clarify these WTO rules in ways that draw the right lines between the subsidies that are permitted and the subsidies that are not.

ENERGY SUBSIDIES

Against this backdrop of international trade law is arrayed, in this age of climate change, a vast and a varied range of energy subsidies. In our reimagining of international trade law to help forestall climate change, and to help also to advance overall sustainable development, two of the most important questions are: Which of these energy subsidies are "bad" – because they distort trade without facilitating and furthering (or because, worse, they frustrate) the green transition? And which of these energy subsidies can be "good" – because, although they distort trade, they also support the green transition?

In the warming world, production and consumption subsidies for fossil fuels perpetuate our dependency on the fossil fuels that are causing climate change. Fossil fuel subsidies "discourage investments in clean energy and energy efficiency, tilting the balance in favor of fossil fuels and making it difficult for renewable energy and energy-efficient equipment to compete."[49] Perhaps worst, fossil fuel subsidies "lock societies into carbon-intensive pathways for decades to come at the expense of cleaner alternatives."[50] Fossil fuel subsidies are likewise "locked in" to the inertia of domestic politics all over the world. Consumption subsidies for fossil fuels are popular almost everywhere, and in many places consume between 15 and 20 percent of GDP.[51]

Subsidies for fossil fuel use are frequently defended as a means to help the poor – especially those in poorer countries – by providing them with cheaper fuel through such means as inexpensive gasoline or fuel vouchers or heating energy grants. But such subsidies, however popular, are in fact "highly inequitable"; one study of how fossil fuel subsidies actually work in developing countries reveals that the wealthiest 20 percent of the people get 43 percent of the benefits.[52] The truth is, fossil fuel consumption subsidies do not favor the poor. Instead, they "tend to favor well-off urban middle classes, who can afford large cars and multiple electrical appliances at the expense of taxpayers or the poor who would benefit more from targeted pro-poor public spending."[53] We should help the poor in ways that do not encourage them to use fossil fuels.

Fossil fuel subsidies are pernicious in every respect. The International Monetary Fund has reported that energy subsidies "aggravate budget deficits, crowd out public spending on health and education, discourage private investment in energy, encourage excessive energy consumption, artificially promote capital-intensive industries, accelerate the depletion of natural resources and exacerbate climate change."[54] As journalist David Wessel of the *Wall Street Journal* has noted, tongue in cheek, "Other than that, there is nothing wrong with them."[55]

Not only do these pernicious subsidies not support the green transition; if they are not soon curbed and disciplined, they may well stop that transition. The signal of carbon pricing may well be silenced if we continue to subsidize fossil fuels. Yet many of the same countries that came together in bold consensus to trumpet the conclusion of the Paris climate agreement are also, at the same time, continuing back home to provide enormous subsidies to encourage the increased production and consumption of fossil fuels. The International Energy Agency reports that the total of consumer price subsidies and other forms of support for fossil fuels is "in the vicinity of" $500 billion to $800 billion a year.[56] When the cost of damage from pollution and climate change is factored into the tally, the International Monetary Fund has estimated that the sum total of governmental subsidies for fossil fuels rises to the staggering amount of $5.3 trillion a year – or $10 million a minute. With no price on carbon, polluters are not paying the costs imposed on governments by the burning of coal, oil, and gas.[57]

Beginning in Pittsburgh in 2009, the G20 leaders of the world's major industrial economies have promised repeatedly to cut fossil fuel subsidies – with little or no follow-through.[58] Now the United Nations has adopted Goal 12 of the Sustainable Development Goals: to "[e]nsure sustainable consumption and production patterns."[59] A target of this global goal is to "rationalize inefficient fossil-fuel subsidies."[60] (Line-drawing is much needed to determine what an "efficient" fossil fuel subsidy might be.) To achieve this target of this goal, to take real action against fossil fuel subsidies worldwide, we must take international action that can be enforced by the international rule of law. In the WTO, such action can best be taken as part of a WTO climate waiver by reimagining the international trade rules on subsidies to help discipline the subsidizing of fossil fuel production and consumption.

In the midst of the malaise of general disappointment at the WTO Ministerial Conference in Buenos Aires in December 2017, one potentially promising breakthrough was the endorsement by twelve WTO members of a ministerial statement on reforming fossil fuels.[61] (The United States was not among these dozen WTO members.) These countries urged putting disciplines on fossil fuel subsidies on the WTO negotiating agenda. In confronting this task, WTO members could use current WTO rules to challenge fossil fuel production subsidies where they have adverse effects, including where those adverse effects "include harm to the human and natural environment, without regard to whether there is harm to competitors."[62] So far, there have been no WTO cases challenging fossil fuel production subsidies. The alternative is negotiation, ideally leading to a multilateral solution.

As part of this solution, WTO members should either add fossil fuel subsidies to the list of subsidies that are prohibited under WTO law – and thus are automatically illegal – or (more easily done), as with agricultural subsidies, establish categories of different kinds of fossil fuel subsidies and caps for their permissible amounts that can be used as a negotiating base for reducing and eventually eliminating them over time.[63] Allowances should be made during this transition to keep from harming the poor. Once eliminated, fossil fuel subsidies could then be prohibited. As a start, all WTO members should disclose the details of all their fossil fuel subsidies to the WTO – something they have been slow to do – and risk facing WTO dispute settlement if there are adverse effects because they do not.[64] If there is resistance by some countries to *changing* the rules to discipline fossil fuel subsidies, then willing countries can – to begin – aim instead to *waive* the rules to discipline fossil fuel subsidies in the content of a climate waiver.

In contrast to subsidies for fossil fuels are subsidies for wind, solar, geothermal, and other "modern" renewable energies. The world added a record amount of renewable energy in 2016.[65] Headlines proclaim: The "balance of power tilts from fossil fuels to renewable energy."[66] Looking past the headlines, though, we are reminded that, "[w]hile renewable energy has been growing fast, it is coming from a very low base."[67] Despite the rapid growth of renewable energy, fossil fuels continue to provide 85.5 percent of our energy supply. This is less than the 94 percent of global energy demand met by fossil fuels a half century ago, but "[e]ven at the current, more rapid rate of change, they could still be supplying the majority of the world's energy needs for decades to come."[68]

Costs for renewable energy have indeed fallen fast as renewable energy sources "have emerged . . . as large-scale, and increasingly economically viable, alternatives to fossil fuels."[69] Costs of wind power dropped 71 percent and costs of solar power fell 83 percent between 2008 and 2017.[70] So far, however, costs of renewables have not fallen fast enough. Amid the striking success of the technological shale revolution, in most markets, a wide gap between the prices of fossil fuels and the prices of renewables remains. So those favoring the green transition have resorted to seeking subsidies to help narrow this gap.

Although state support for fossil fuels continues to exceed the sum of the subsidies for renewable energy worldwide "by a considerable margin," subsidies for renewable energy have increased in recent years.[71] Renewable energy subsidies totaled $121 billion in 2013, and they are predicted to rise to $230 billion in 2030.[72] These green subsidies run the gamut from grants to tax breaks to feed-in tariffs that guarantee better prices for using what would otherwise be more expensive renewable energy. Because WTO rules do not currently take into account any purposive policy justification for a subsidy, the fact that these subsidies are meant to correct for a market failure does not provide a legal excuse for them internationally.[73] As a result, international legal disputes over the trade effects of renewable energy subsidies have multiplied in the WTO. Worldwide, the proliferation of "tit-for-tat" WTO trade disputes over renewable energy subsidies has reinforced the view that the WTO opposes state measures to protect the environment and to fight climate change.

If fossil fuel subsidies are "bad," can renewable energy subsidies be "good"? The two can be distinguished by their effects. Fossil fuel subsidies are *market-distorting*. They push the market toward fossil fuels by underpinning fossil fuel production. Renewable energy subsidies are *market-correcting*. They eliminate the market failure caused by the omission of climate and other environmental costs from the prices of fossil fuels and of products made by using fossil fuels.[74] Market failures justify governmental interventions. So, yes, it makes sense to describe fossil fuel subsidies as "bad" and renewable energy subsidies as "good."

How, then, must we make legal room for renewable energy subsidies in WTO rules? Answering this question requires revisiting an age-old trade debate that continues to engage trade thinkers and trade negotiators to this day – the debate over the protection of "infant industries." The logic underlying the case for green subsidies relates to the assumed need to intervene in the market to establish a beneficial new industry in circumstances that would otherwise hinder and perhaps even prevent it.[75] This logic is not unlike the logic long used by many countries to justify market interventions to support new – "infant" – industries where it has been thought that those new industries would otherwise be unable to secure a commercial foothold sufficient to compete with more established foreign producers.

It has long been maintained by some that protection of infant industries should be an accepted exception to free trade. The infant-industry argument for trade protection "can be traced at least as far back as the Elizabethan period" in England.[76] Adam Smith firmly opposed policies of "preference or restraint" to insulate infant industries from competition.[77] John Stuart Mill gave the protection of infant industries a "qualified endorsement" – and then spent the rest of his life further limiting his limited support after being criticized for it.[78] WTO rules reflect the ambivalence of WTO members on the issue by permitting temporary deviations from trade rules to protect infant industries by countries with economies "which can only support low standards of living" and are "in the early stages of development."[79]

The difficulty with the argument that the protection of infant industries should be an exception to free trade has always been threefold. First of all, *which* infant industries should government choose to protect? Here is the impertinent and presumptuous peril of governmental bureaucrats intervening to pick market "winners" and "losers." How can they foresee the future? Second, *how* should infant industries be protected? There is an additional impertinence and presumption in assuming that politicians and bureaucrats can know the most effective ways to help nascent industries grow. And, third, *how long* should the protection last? One of Mill's unwavering qualifications about supporting infant industries was that any state support for infant industries should be "strictly limited in point of time," and that it should be phased out on "a gradually decreasing scale" over time.[80] But just how long should that limited time be? The common experience of many countries has been that many of the infant industries they favor with subsidies refuse to grow up. Rarely do they petition the government to end their subsidy.

For a brief time, too, following the creation of the WTO, there were WTO rules that permitted distinctions among subsidies on the basis of their professed purpose by carving out limited exceptions from the subsidies rules for assistance to research, to disadvantaged regions, and "to promote adaptation of existing facilities to new environmental requirements."[81] The last of these three exceptions seems especially relevant during this time of "new environmental requirements" imposed by the transitional challenges of climate change and of sustainable development. There was, in addition, at the outset, an exception for one-time-only subsidies "given merely to provide time for the development of long-term solutions and to avoid acute social problems."[82] This, too, seems highly relevant today. Unfortunately, these exceptions have long since lapsed and are no longer a part of WTO law. Ironically, the effort by the members of the WTO to negotiate an extension – and perhaps an expansion – of these developmental and environmental exceptions failed when the negotiations were curtailed because of the environmental protests against the WTO at its ministerial conference in Seattle in 1999.

As part of the reimagining of trade law to fulfill the original intent of the WTO – that of promoting sustainable development – the climate waiver adopted by the members of the WTO should include a restoration and a reimagining of these lapsed exceptions to the subsidies rules. Drawing from both the long experience of the trading system with the pros and cons of infant industries, and also from the brief experience of the system with the lapsed exceptions, these reimagined exceptions for green subsidies should be limited in time, limited in scope, and limited as well in the latitude they allow for trade discrimination. They should be structured in ways that will do the most for the green transition while doing the least to risk the basic integrity of the world trading system.

For example, domestic-content requirements that condition the grant of subsidies on the use of domestic over imported inputs in final production are already generally illegal under WTO law. Domestic-content requirements should be prohibited by the climate waiver.[83] Discriminatory sourcing requirements are tempting as devices to secure domestic support. But they distort trade while denying domestic producers and consumers alike the benefits of the competition, the lower prices, and the broader choices of the more effective energy and environmental alternatives offered by being open to foreign trade and to foreign direct investment.[84] Swiss trade scholar Thomas Cottier has observed that, "From the point of view of decarbonisation, a local content requirement does not make sense as it increases costs for hardware and installations. Imported and competitive products are likely to contribute to more rapid deployment of the technology."[85] The truth is, Robert Howse has added, "domestic content requirements and other discriminatory measures actually undermine environmental objectives, by shifting production to higher-cost jurisdictions, and therefore making clean energy, or clean energy technologies, more expensive than they need to be."[86]

In addition, the emissions permits and allowances that are often doled out for free to favored local producers as a political concession to secure their support for the enactment of cap-and-trade emissions trading schemes should be acknowledged as subsidies, and it should be affirmed that they are subject to WTO subsidies disciplines. What one participant in a market must pay for, but another gets for free, is a subsidy for the one that gets it for free. By distorting market competition, the free passes on emissions handed out as a part of carbon trading schemes have a discriminatory and therefore a protectionist effect in world trade.[87] This leaven of trade protectionism is supposedly justified because these allowances are politically expedient in passing climate legislation and also serve a climate purpose. In fact, they serve only to distort international trade while often accomplishing little or nothing for the climate.[88] In the 2018 reforms of the European Emissions Trading System, the share of emission permits granted for free will remain 43 percent.[89] This is an invitation to WTO litigation.

Under the current WTO rules on subsidies, the "serious prejudice" to the interests of another WTO member that is caused by a subsidy, and is one example of the "adverse effects" that are needed for a subsidy to be illegal under WTO law, must be economic in nature. It must be an economic consequence in the marketplace. The subsidy must discipline or impede imports into the market of the subsidizing country or exports into a third market, or have the effect of a significant price undercutting, price suppression, or lost sales in the same market.[90] Currently, the impact of a subsidy on the environment is not a consideration in determining whether it is illegal under WTO law. A WTO climate waiver should add environmental harm to the adverse effects that can make a subsidy illegal. Furthermore, climate protection should be recognized in the reimagining of international trade law as a lawful defense that can justify a subsidy. As part of a WTO climate waiver, the environmental and other general exceptions to most WTO rules relating to trade in goods and to trade in services should likewise be applied to subsidies for goods and for services.[91] After all, if the environmental exceptions in the trade rules can apply to some national measures that distort and restrict trade, then why not allow those exceptions for other national measures with similar trade effects – such as subsidies? The reimagining of international trade law in a WTO climate waiver should allow exceptions for green subsidies while ensuring that, as with all other claims to the shelter of those exceptions, such state measures "are not applied in a manner which would constitute a means of arbitrary or unjustifiable discrimination ... or a disguised restriction" on goods or services trade.[92]

Michael Trebilcock and James Wilson, two of the willing in Canada, point toward the "just mean" of the right line "in between" in structuring a WTO climate waiver to include green subsidies by suggesting that such subsidies should be lawful only if they are "winner-neutral."[93] They reason "that if our ultimate goal is to abate emissions as rapidly and cost-effectively as possible while laying the groundwork for a green energy future, as well as to advance ancillary goals that will help to sustain this progress, such as saving resources and creating green jobs, then providing technology-specific subsidies for renewable energy power generations ('picking winners') runs a considerable risk of failure, because some currently available clean-energy technologies are not green in every jurisdiction, and because public investment in sub-optimal technologies may have the effect of 'locking in' these technologies because of interest group politics and other features of path dependence."[94]

Trebilcock and Wilson identify, instead, another and better approach to providing green subsidies. Instead of subsidies that target particular *technologies*, they advocate green subsidies that target particular *outcomes*. They recommend "a 'winner neutral' approach that prioritizes public investments from which many different market actors can benefit as they compete to discover and to develop 'winning' (i.e. environmentally friendly and economically viable) energy technologies."[95] The goal, after all, is not to develop renewable energy "for its own sake" but instead to reduce emissions of greenhouse gases.[96] Therefore, subsidies should be provided to those in the market that achieve desired outcomes as measured by actual emissions cuts.[97] In particular, they urge "winner-neutral" investments in new energy infrastructure – such as new "smart" electricity grids – and early-stage investments in the basic research and development – the basic R&D – that is often indispensable to innovation, in clean energy as in much else.[98] They rightly say, "The importance of public funding for basic research, on one hand, and pilot projects, on the other, cannot be overstated."[99] Much of basic R&D is usually beyond the limited resources of would-be innovators and beyond the interest of potential investors, who are usually inclined to shy away from such an expense and from such an extent of risk. What is more, in its very nature, basic R&D is winner-neutral.

Apart from furthering carbon pricing, an emphasis on basic R&D is what may be most needed to facilitate the green transition. As both the Paris climate agreement and the Sustainable Development Goals acknowledge, global investments in basic research and development of new green technologies must increase significantly to meet the Paris climate goals and to achieve the SDGs.[100] As for energy technologies, the climate scientists on the UN Intergovernmental Panel on Climate Change have cited estimates for the required increase in energy-related R&D that range up to $78 billion – annually – through 2029. Currently, only about $50 billion annually is spent on energy-related R&D worldwide, with about $35 billion of that coming from the private sector.[101]

This recommended approach focusing on basic R&D ought to be especially appealing to decisionmakers in a country such as the United States, where scientists and others warn of the threat of declining innovation. The percentage of federal spending going to basic R&D in the United States is less than half of what it was a half-century ago, down from about 10 percent to less than 5 percent. Among Americans, there is, quite rightly, "widespread concern over a growing US innovation deficit, attributable in part to declining public investment in research," which is, now more than ever, "tightly coupled to national economic competitiveness."[102] Basic R&D on new energy technologies must be a critical part of US competitiveness strategy.

A line legalizing "winner-neutral" approaches would be the right line "in between" when reimagining trade law to allow certain green subsidies. Drawing the line there would correct for the market's failure to price the climate harm caused by carbon emissions while also minimizing the distortions in trade resulting from the subsidies. Where subsidies are "winner-neutral," the winners should win in the market because of the proof in the market of their own worth, and a state subsidy provided through R&D could thus be seen as deserved.

A SUSTAINABLE ENERGY TRADE AGREEMENT

"A safe and sustainable energy pathway is crucial to sustainable development," declared the Brundtland Commission back in 1987. "We have not yet found it."[103] Now, some decades later, we still have not found it. Energy is the "oxygen" of the global economy.[104] Despite this, there is no overarching framework for global energy governance. Rafael Leal-Arcas and Andre Filis have lamented, "'[G]lobal energy governance' today is a theoretical concept that does not exist in actuality ... [T]he currently fragmented and multi-layered global energy governance is not conducive to energy security that is truly global ... [and] fails to address global energy security needs."[105] In energy trade, literally hundreds of transnational organizations deal with international governance.[106] This concatenation of organizations does not begin to address in any comprehensive way the urgently needed transition from a high-carbon to a low-carbon and eventually a no-carbon economy.

Ricardo Melendez-Ortiz and others among the willing have pointed out that, "Currently, there are no energy-specific rules or commitments in the WTO, nor any structured discussion in the organization on issues relating to renewable energy."[107] "Internationally, there is more trade in oil than in anything else."[108] Historically, however, countries participating in the now WTO-based world trading system have been mostly concerned with reducing import restrictions; and, in a world where energy sources are spread unevenly among nearly 200 countries, few countries have restricted energy imports. This remains so today. Yet today there is need for global governance that helps enable the shift in energy production and use toward sustainable energy sources. One of the answers to the absence of global energy governance can be provided by ultimately transforming the reimagined trade law in a WTO climate waiver disciplining fossil fuel subsidies and permitting "winner-neutral" green subsidies into parts of a broader, comprehensive WTO sectoral agreement conceived as a sustainable energy trade agreement. Such a sectoral agreement could begin as part of a climate waiver or as a plurilateral agreement including those WTO members willing initially to agree to it. Over time, it could evolve into a multilateral agreement including all WTO members.

In furtherance of Goal 13 of the SDGs, the Paris Agreement aspires to "foster climate resilience and low greenhouse gas emission development."[109] Goal 7 aims to "[e]nsure access to affordable, reliable, sustainable and modern energy for all."[110] One target of Goal 7 is to, "[b]y 2030, increase substantially the share of renewable energy in the global energy mix."[111] The conclusion of a sustainable energy trade agreement by the WTO could do much to help achieve these global goals.[112]

Although much of the ongoing global debate over the green transition has centered on the wealthier, developed countries, the growing demand for sustainable energy is surging most of all in the developing world. World energy use has increased by more than 50 percent since 1990, and the demand for energy in developing countries "will continue to increase as these countries industrialise and as hundreds of millions more people move out of poverty. Many of these people will be gaining access to electricity for the first time."[113] Estimates are that nearly 600 million people in Africa – about 70 percent of the population of the continent – still do not have access to electricity.[114] Worldwide, 1.4 billion people still have no access to electricity.[115]

Amartya Sen, who sees "development as freedom," is concerned that, in our singular focus on cutting carbon emissions, we have been "ignoring the benefits from greater energy use on which the lives of billions of deprived people in the world depend."[116] He worries that there may well be "insufficient recognition" among the willing of the world that sufficient energy is "essential for conquering poverty." Sen reminds us that, "In thinking about expanding human freedom today and sustaining it into the future, we have to take fuller note of the need for greater energy use for a larger number of deprived people in the world."[117] If we tell poorer countries to stop using fossil fuels, we must provide them with an alternative. Access to energy is essential to human development.

Given the growing global demand for energy, especially by many who have for so long been left out of growing global prosperity, the global challenge is not one of using less energy; rather, it is one of using different kinds of energy in different ways. The renewable energies, the new energy technologies, and the new energy efficiencies resulting from the green transition can enable us to cut greenhouse gas emissions while also providing enough light and power for all of humanity. Toward this end, what, in addition to disciplines on fossil fuel subsidies and a permission slip for "winner-neutral" green subsidies, are some of the reimaginings of international trade law that might be included in a sustainable energy trade agreement?[118]

One is the long-sought WTO agreement to eliminate tariff and non-tariff barriers to trade in clean energy and energy-efficient technologies – the proposed Environmental Goods Agreement. As one of the willing, Sonja Hawkins, has said, "In a sector where finished products consist of many components that cross borders numerous times – a typical wind turbine, for example, contains up to 8,000 components – even small tariff cuts would reduce costs, making the technologies more affordable and competitive in the global market, particularly if combined with a phasing out of fossil fuel subsidies. This would not only help mitigate climate change, but also enhance energy access and security, generate jobs in associated sectors, help build domestic low carbon industries, and spur innovation through competition in an open global market. Another valuable role trade can play is to drive the diffusion of products with lower levels of embodied carbon, thus enabling a global shift from high to lower carbon products."[119] The subset of WTO members producing 90 percent of the world's environmental goods that are striving to eliminate duties on nearly $1 trillion in trade in those goods annually and share the benefits worldwide fell short of concluding a deal at the WTO ministerial conference in Buenos Aires. They continued afterward to strive toward eliminating duties on several hundred products ranging from clean energy to energy efficiency, and from air pollution control to environmental monitoring.

Next for the members of the WTO should be freeing the extensive trade in environmental services. A first task is identifying these green services. A next task is determining how best to deal with the fact that green goods and green services are often integrated. Because services are increasingly embedded in traded goods, their delivery is increasingly intertwined, and so their trade treatment should often be integrated. As examples of this integration: Freeing trade in green goods will boost services trade through international shipments of the makings of wind power plants, and freeing trade in green services will lift the obstacles to providing the international services that are often needed to maintain those plants.[120] Melendez-Ortiz, an ardent advocate for both trade and sustainable development, has, as he often does, stated the bottom line: "Trade in services plays a critical role in the deployment of clean energy and comprises a major input into clean energy projects."[121]

Rules for standards and technical regulations relating to climate-friendly and environment-friendly products should likewise be included in a WTO sustainable energy trade agreement. More so than tariffs, non-tariff trade barriers are major impediments to sustainable energy trade. These trade barriers can take the form of discriminatory standards and technical regulations. Sufficient latitude should of course be allowed for addressing legitimate domestic regulatory concerns locally. Some right amount of local regulatory discretion is certainly always needed, in energy trade as in all else, to address legitimate domestic regulatory concerns. But, in discerning and drawing the right lines of that discretion in energy use, it should be kept uppermost in mind that "[d]iscriminatory regulatory measures may not only inhibit the supply, transmission, and distribution of renewable energy, but also the foreign suppliers who are intent on investing in and providing these services."[122]

Here the right line in the right rule for many new green technologies might turn out to be the global line of harmonization.[123] Where standards and technical regulations are many, where such rules are diverse and are fragmented, they can lead to "fragmented global markets." This fragmentation of the global market can "potentially act as a brake on innovation efforts in low-emissions technologies. In addition, divergent standards or policies may raise transaction costs, restrict the benefits of economies of scale and raise the costs of compliance to industry and of policy-making to national authorities."[124] Ideally, it may be best in some instances to have one right universal and uniform standard or regulation. For example, one obvious type of standard "with potential to promote a green economy" is a standard for energy efficiency in the use of a product. As it is, different countries have different standards. This translates into higher costs for exporters and less dissemination of new energy efficiency standards and new green technologies. As Aaron Cosbey has pointed out, the global harmonization of such standards would be a solid step toward lowering the barriers to entry into needed new technologies.[125]

In the absence of one agreed standard, it may suffice instead to move toward regulatory convergence by agreeing on the mutual recognition by different countries of certain differing standards and regulations if they achieve much the same results. The WTO rules rightly permit countries to set their own standards and regulations and, if they choose, to have even higher standards than any globally agreed standards.[126] But the same rules also limit the use of standards and regulations to impose trade restrictions and other unnecessary obstacles to international trade.[127] Moreover, those rules also envisage "harmonizing technical regulations on as wide a basis as possible."[128] In a world in which trade negotiators have succeeded through their long labors during the past half-century in negotiating away the high tariffs on most manufactured goods, international trade disputes are increasingly about non-tariff barriers to trade, and international trade negotiations are nowadays aimed increasingly at freeing trade by eliminating arbitrary regulatory discriminations. This goal can often best be achieved through the establishment of more international regulatory consistency and coherence. The flow of trade always thrives where there is a common gauge.

Furthermore, to fulfill their national climate change pledges, countries will need large amounts of clean energy to be able to connect to networks, including for the purpose of crossborder trade in clean energy. To be able to shift away from fossil fuels, many countries will need to import clean electricity. In addition, long-term investments in clean energy infrastructure will be needed. Necessary too will be measures to guarantee the availability of fixed infrastructure and to ensure timely access to transportation pipelines, networks, and distribution systems.[129] For all these reasons, a sustainable energy trade agreement should also include provisions encouraging the harmonization of clean energy standards and technical regulations, and assuring the timely transit of clean energy.

Then there is the ever-contentious issue of technology transfer and development, which should be addressed in a climate waiver and also included in a sustainable energy trade agreement. Well-developed systems to protect patents and other intellectual property rights stimulate innovation and technological diffusion. They are an important means of commercializing new technologies, especially for small and medium-sized enterprises, most notably in developing countries. But diffusion never seems to happen fast enough, and diffusion is urgent in this age of accelerating climate change. Thus, the hard truth for many of the willing remains that "[g]reen technologies, no matter how advanced, are essentially useless until they are actually deployed and used."[130] Getting new green technologies to developing countries, and then scaling them sufficiently for widespread use, will be a key to enabling and ensuring the success of both the Paris climate agreement and the Sustainable Development Goals. Generally, technology is transferred across borders by means of licensing, trade, or foreign direct investment. Aspects of each of these conduits for technological advance must be part of the reimagining of international rules to blend economy and environment.[131]

As they see it, the developing countries made significant concessions in other trade sectors when agreeing in the Uruguay Round to a new WTO agreement that requires all WTO members to respect and also to enforce patents, copyrights, trademarks, trade secrets, and other intellectual property rights.[132] In that agreement, they were assured that they would get much in return from the developed countries through a rising flow of technology transfer, including the know-how for the new green tools they need now to do more locally to fight climate change and to fashion sustainable development. Two of the main objectives of the WTO intellectual property rights agreement – the so-called TRIPS Agreement – are the promotion of technological innovation and the transfer and dissemination of technology.[133] Pointedly, the rich developed countries are required by the agreement to provide incentives to "enterprises and institutions in their territories" to promote and encourage technology transfer to the poor least-developed countries "in order to enable them to create a sound and viable technological base."[134] So far, nothing concrete has been done by the developed countries to fulfill these now-longstanding WTO obligations (thus presenting the interesting legal question of whether the poor countries could challenge the rich countries in WTO dispute settlement for not fulfilling them). Similarly, the developed countries have given only "cursory followup" to like entreaties long enshrined in the UN climate framework for speeding tech transfer to developing countries.[135]

The conclusion of the Paris Agreement presents the perfect opportunity for the belated fulfillment of these trade and climate obligations to developing countries. Products made in the developing and emerging world often have the highest carbon content and would thus be burdened most by climate-related trade restrictions. Therefore, those who live in the developing countries of the world – the poor, not the rich – would bear the brunt first and most of a reimagining of trade law that legalized international trade discrimination based on the carbon used or emitted in making a product. For this reason, fairness demands a balancing of the burden of compliance by the developing countries with reimagined trade rules with the certainty that those countries will get something more than an empty promise in return as part of a climate waiver and a sustainable energy trade agreement. In exchange for agreeing to these reimaginings of WTO rules, the developing countries should get a ticket to the green transition. The billions of people who live in the developing world should get ready access to the new green technologies they urgently need to transform their economies and their environments into one in shaping and in sharing their own growth and prosperity. They should get to turn the lights on.

Innovations happen in the market if property rights in those innovations are protected by the market. The incentive provided by the protection of the exclusivity of intellectual property rights for an agreed period of time is essential to green innovation, as it is to all innovation. A whole host of disincentives confronts the holders of patents and other intellectual property rights in commercializing their climate-friendly technologies in the developing world – trade barriers, investment barriers, regulatory and harmonization barriers, the lingering lack in so many places of the rule of law, and more. Through all these disincentives runs the thread of the tension between innovation and access, which impacts the tenor of the debate over the location of the right line "in between" the two. That right line will be somewhere between, on the one hand, providing the incentive to create intellectual property and providing also, for a limited time, an exclusive legal right to intellectual property, and, on the other hand, disseminating as soon as possible and as much as possible the use of that intellectual property as an urgent universal necessity. The "just mean" of that right line somewhere "in between" the competing claims of innovation and of access should be found and drawn into a climate waiver and a sustainable energy trade agreement.

A WTO sustainable energy trade agreement could create new exceptions, change existing obligations, and add new obligations for those WTO members that choose to be bound by it. In a useful expression of the true bottom-up, in such an agreement, WTO members might zero in on making special transitional arrangements for specific industrial sectors such as glass, steel, cement, paper, and aluminum that are emissions-intensive and export-sensitive – and therefore are especially anxious about the possible consequences of new climate arrangements. These industries might, for example, establish, within the legal framework of the WTO, either as a sectoral agreement or as part of a sustainable energy trade agreement, their own agreed compilation of "best practices" on emissions and sustainability, and perhaps even their own industry standards, which could, if desired, be enforceable in WTO dispute settlement. Such an arrangement could be constructed similarly to the innovative "Reference Paper" on basic telecommunications services in which most WTO members have committed to regulatory principles that largely reflect "best practices" in telecoms regulation.[136] These industries could also set up cap-and-trade systems or other carbon markets or climate clubs, which might then, in turn, be linked with others.

In fashioning a sustainable energy trade agreement, we might also be so bold as to assault that global bastion of flag-waving protectionism that in many places comprises a considerable amount of the local economy – government purchases. The WTO Government Procurement Agreement (GPA), although ambitious, still, after more than two decades, binds only a few dozen WTO members.[137] The Government Procurement Agreement must become a fully multilateral agreement. A sustainable energy trade agreement would help hasten this globalizing of the GPA, help counter climate change, help secure a much broader market for sustainable energy, and help maximize the potential for green growth, by encouraging the non-discriminatory purchase by governments of green goods and services. It should bar discrimination against foreign green goods or foreign suppliers of green services by any party to the agreement. While the shift to green energy and to a green economy proceeds throughout the world from the bottom up, governments everywhere must each also do their part to provide the right enabling framework to speed that shift.

13

On How International Investment Law Can Be
Reimagined for Sustainable Development

With the transformation of the world in utterly unprecedented ways, a sustainable energy trade agreement is only one of the reimaginings needed to make our trade and investment rules relevant to the altered world economy and ensure that those rules are supportive of sustainable development. In calling for the application of our imagination to these and other twenty-first century tasks, Klaus Schwab, the thoughtful founder and executive chairman of the annual World Economic Forum in Davos, Switzerland, refers to our time of "abrupt and radical change" as the "Fourth Industrial Revolution." In his view, the First Industrial Revolution, of mechanical production, spanned about 1760 to 1840; the Second Revolution, of mass production, started in the late nineteenth century and continued into the early twentieth century; the Third Revolution, of computer and digital production, began in the 1960s and continued throughout the 1990s; and the Fourth Revolution envelops us now.[1] The green transition is occurring within this latest technological revolution in how we work and live together on this planet.

THE FOURTH INDUSTRIAL REVOLUTION

This new Fourth Industrial Revolution, Schwab explains, "builds on the digital revolution. It is characterized by a much more ubiquitous and mobile internet, by smaller and more powerful sensors that have become cheaper, and by artificial intelligence and machine learning."[2] The digital hardware, software, and networks that were developed in the late twentieth century now "are becoming more sophisticated and integrated and are ... at an inflection point where the effect of these digital technologies will manifest with 'full force' through automation and the making of 'unprecedented things.'"[3]

In trade and in investment, digital technologies are being employed and rapidly integrated all along the complex and attenuated global value chains that increasingly characterize our fragmented international production.[4] In the workings of these extended chains of supply and production, the trade in tasks flowing back and forth across national borders – sometimes crisscrossing borders dozens of times in the making of just one product – gives striking new meaning to Adam Smith's division of labor through specialization in providing ever smaller pieces of a much larger overall production.[5] Ours is still a Smithian world, but it is a world spinning on digital steroids. We have long since surpassed the productive potential of the pin factory Smith used as an illustration of the magical multiplying effect of a division of labor.[6] With the digitizing of global value chains, we can multiply all the world's modern pins of production many times over.

Traditionally, fundamental international trade rules of non-discrimination have been based on where a good is "from." Trade discrimination has been between one product "from" one country and a like traded product "from" another country. Today, though, the traditional trade questions about where goods or services are "from," with the answers to these questions turning on the legal twists of elaborate and esoteric "rules of origin," bear less and less relation to actual commercial reality. Today, more and more, traded goods and services are truly "from" everywhere, because different pieces of them are produced in different places everywhere. The foundational basis for some of the most fundamental WTO trade rules has been turned inside out and upside down by the global revolution in trade in tasks. Addressing the legal implication of this denationalization of global production must be part of the reimagining of international trade law.

Further contorting this legal knot is the fact that it is increasingly difficult to trace and to attribute to one country or another the services shared through global value chains. Services can be "embodied" through delivery within a product or "embedded" through delivery alongside a product. Knowledge-intensive business services are now the fastest-growing component of world trade, usually as part of global value chains for manufactured, agricultural, and natural resources products, including those that relate to climate change.[7] Some of these services help deploy new technologies to cut greenhouse gas emissions; others help with the mitigation of emissions in general.[8]

Schwab assures us that the Fourth Industrial Revolution "offers significant opportunities for the world to achieve huge gains in resource use and efficiency."[9] New technologies and other new innovations could be used to help restore and regenerate our natural environment, and could be employed to produce much more for us while imposing much less on our planet. A potential model of a useful approach toward providing the enabling framework to help make this happen is the new WTO Trade Facilitation Agreement that entered into force in 2017. The TFA is designed to streamline the process of engaging in trade and shrink the costs of linking many more micro, small and medium-sized enterprises to global value chains.[10] This is the first WTO agreement that proceeds from an awareness that what happens to traded products at the port is connected to what happens to them before they get to the port and after they leave it. It couples commitments made by small countries with assurances of the financing they will need to fulfill those commitments. Moreover, by cutting much of the red tape in customs and border procedures, this new WTO agreement will enhance efficiency – and thus sustainability.

Money is required to realize the imaginings of the Fourth Industrial Revolution through continued innovations. Money is especially required to achieve the sustainability that must be sought through those innovations. Sustainability requires not only openness to trade but also finance in the form of investment, including foreign direct investment. The imperative of sustainability demands the facilitation of all kinds of investment. Needed in particular worldwide – and especially in developing countries – is foreign direct investment. Needed also is a shift in FDI toward sustainability.

FDI can serve sustainability in any number of ways. It can, for example, enable the facilitation of the global digital economy, one of the best sources today of growth and development. According to UNCTAD, "A comprehensive digital development strategy should cover investment in digital infrastructure, in digital firms, and in digital adoption by firms across all industries."[11] One of the numerous and far-reaching challenges of the Fourth Industrial Revolution is to facilitate all kinds of *sustainable* investment globally amid the speed and the swirl of all Schwab describes. To do so with FDI, our enabling frameworks of international investment rules must be reimagined to speed the necessary shift to sustainable investment as a vital part of the green transition.

THE IMPERATIVE OF SUSTAINABLE INVESTMENT

One group of the willing, the Green Growth Action Alliance, informs us that "greening investment at scale is a precondition for sustainable growth" in "the water, agriculture, telecoms, power, transport, buildings, industrial and forestry sectors."[12] They warn us that "business-as-usual investment will not lead to a stable future unless it achieves environmental and sustainability goals. Beyond the known infrastructure investment barriers and constraints, the challenge will be to enable an unprecedented shift in long-term investment from conventional to green alternatives."[13] This "unprecedented shift" must result from an unprecedented flow of finance. Estimates are that about $89 trillion in infrastructure investment alone is needed by 2030 "to achieve global growth expectations."[14] About 60 percent of this required investment is needed in emerging and developing countries.[15] This sum is more than $7 trillion per year. Current annual global investment is about $1.7 trillion. As another example, the United Nations estimates the overall need for funding for climate adaptation at between $140 billion and $300 billion annually by 2030, which may prove to be an understatement due to the rising numbers of extreme weather events and other natural disasters.[16]

For now, the front lines in the gathering fight to adapt to climate change are in some of the more isolated and impoverished corners of the world. Having done the least to cause climate change, many small island states, for instance, have been among the first to suffer from some of the worst of the effects. They are much in need, for the sake of their very survival, of immediate funds to pay for climate adaptation – or else they may sink forever into the sea. With promises of forthcoming funds from the larger, wealthier countries for climate finance still mostly only promises, some of these small islands have resorted to the originality of their own resources. In their desperation to secure the money they so much need to adapt to climate change, they have turned to selling – passports. Picturesque as a postcard, but highly vulnerable, the Caribbean island of Dominica, for one, has been sending its emissaries abroad to peddle the small island's usefully far-ranging passports as an "investment option."[17]

This global "frequent flyer card" is not at all what the willing of the world have in mind when they speak grandly of climate finance. The OECD estimates that the financial needs for fulfilling the Sustainable Development Goals *in the developing countries alone* will total between $3.3 trillion and $4.5 trillion *per year.*[18] In their search for these "trillions, not billions," most developing countries continue to look for all that missing money first of all, and most of all, to the generosity of the governments of the rich countries, which have promised to donate $100 billion annually to assist developing countries with climate change. This promised money has been slow to appear and may also to some extent be "double-counted" along with other previous aid commitments. On top of that, the rich countries have not yet come close to keeping their promise made in 2002 at the first global development summit, in Monterrey, to increase the annual percentage of their "overseas development assistance" – their foreign aid – to 0.7 percent of their GNP.

In our unwilling world, it is unlikely they will keep this promise. Indeed, some of them are rolling back their level of foreign aid. But even doubling the recent annual global amount of about $132 billion in overseas development assistance would not move the money needle all that much closer to the target that must be met to pay for the green transition.[19] Unquestionably, the promise made of "0.7 percent" in aid should be kept. In particular, the additional money could help leverage the donation of other needed assistance from other sources. It could not, however, come close to closing the gaping money gap for climate finance.[20] The inescapable fact – all too little acknowledged by many of the willing – is that the vast majority of the missing money for climate finance for developing and developed countries alike must come not from governments, but from *the private sector.*

The truth is, in this unwilling world, with the besieged and befuddled governments of the richer countries constrained as they are by the lingering effects of the global financial crisis, the continuing constrictions of their domestic austerity programs, and the heel-digging resistance of their disgruntled voters to the "giveaway" of their hard-earned money as aid to "foreigners," some of whom are also increasingly competitors, the vast sums needed globally for climate finance must come *almost entirely* from the private sector.[21] For all the global emphasis on governmental assistance, 75 percent of all climate finance currently comes from private sources.[22]

The contribution of trillions of dollars by businesses and investors for climate finance and for other aspects of sustainable development is complex, and it cannot be planned. Indeed, "[t]he private financing component" of the Paris Agreement and of the Sustainable Development Goals of the United Nations agenda for 2030 "is complex precisely because it cannot be planned."[23] These complexities can produce positive results for addressing climate change and other dimensions of sustainable development only if businesses are actively enlisted, fully engaged, and warmly welcomed at the global table where the rules will be written to provide an enabling framework for market-led growth supportive of climate action and other sustainable development.

Given all this, it might have been assumed that, in the first gatherings of the willing following the approval of the SDGs in New York and the approval of the climate agreement in Paris, most of the discourse would have been about how best to engage businesses more fully in the implementation of both the SDGs and the Paris Agreement. There is certainly rhetoric aplenty in the SDGs and in the Paris Agreement that seems to invite extensive business engagement, including especially through global partnerships. Yet, the emphasis of some at these gatherings was not on how best to *engage* businesses but rather on how to *ban* businesses – even as mere "observers" – from taking any part in further global deliberations on climate change and sustainable development. Painting with a broad brush, a handful of countries and some allied NGOs charged that all observing businesses were merely defenders of fossil fuel interests or simply shills for phony greenwash and, therefore, have conflicts of interest that should preclude them from taking part in climate and sustainability policymaking. Without evidence, these business observers were accused of wanting to write the rules. In fact, as mere observers, most of them were not even allowed into the rooms where the actual writing of the rules was to take place.

There is certainly no shortage of historical examples of rapacious businesses despoiling the environment, both individually and in combination. Sadly, this list still lengthens every day. The poorest people in the world are often the ones victimized by corporate avariciousness and caught in the middle between growth and preservation. For example, in the little Andean town of La Oroya in the interior of Peru, wedged between barren mountains more than 12,000 feet above sea level, the townspeople have long depended for their livelihoods on a mineral smelter that has spewed industrial pollution causing many local illnesses. Now, in considering the use of new environmental standards, they must choose – between their livelihoods and their very lives.[24] In this little Peruvian town, as in so many other places on our imperiled planet, the right line "in between" must be drawn for domestic and foreign investment alike. But the line we draw must not be based on stereotypes. It must be based on facts.

As in Peru, so too in every other part of the world. Yes, there are some greedy capitalists. They are right down your street, they are way up on Wall Street, and they are way over on the far side of the world. And they will stop at nothing to squeeze a profit, including climate and other environmental harm. Adam Smith warned us about them, and about the need to constrain them with the rule of law. Recall his caution that "[p]eople of the same trade seldom meet together, even for merriment and diversion, but the conversation ends in a conspiracy against the public, or in some contrivance to raise prices."[25] But the facts separate and apart from the stereotypes show that foreign direct investment by most multinational companies in developing countries results in higher environmental, labor, and other standards.[26] And the facts show that companies of all kinds and of all sizes and from all parts of the world have proven their willingness in recent years to rise to the challenge of the green transition.

This is certainly not all greenwash. Typecasting so many willing businesses and business leaders as devious villains gives short shrift to decades of genuine and dedicated work against climate change and for sustainable development by countless numbers of the willing in the private sector.[27] Such stereotyping is symptomatic of the top-down mentality that continues to afflict all too much of the thinking about global governance and rule-making, much to the consternation of all who favor the true bottom-up. What is more, it is counterproductive. Many of those casting doubt on the green motivations of the private sector are also those who are seeking several trillions of new dollars in investments from private business to help accomplish the Paris climate goals and the SDGs.

In addition to securing trillions of dollars in investments from the private sector, the other, equally significant goal of climate finance is to *redirect* those trillions of dollars away from carbon-intensive projects and toward clean alternatives that will further the green transition. The achievement of both of these goals for climate and sustainability finance requires genuine regard for those with the skills and the experience to make markets work. It also requires the willingness to let markets work. Shunning business leaders who share your goals, and who want to work with you to achieve your goals, is surely not the best way to achieve them. Necessarily, businesses must be central to ensuring that, from now on, every investment will be made with the impact on the climate and on the overall environment much in mind.

This redirection of investment can be achieved only within an enabling framework of international investment rules that "internalizes" the costs to climate and the overall environment from investment. As in international trade law, in international investment law the economy and the environment must be reimagined as one to help facilitate the shift to global financing of the green transition. Within this facilitating framework, private investment must be aligned with public investment, and the two must be made mutually reinforcing. There must be a better understanding of the domestic laws and conditions that work best in attracting foreign direct investment. Equally, there must be a better understanding that the foreign direct investment most attractive for the green transition is investment that does not injure, but rather supports and sustains the climate and the overall environment. On the one hand, foreign direct investment can supply the financial, technological, and other resources essential for climate mitigation and adaptation and other environmental protection. On the other, FDI can also destroy biodiversity, pollute water resources, introduce hazardous waste and dangerous chemicals, and wreak all other sorts of environmental damages.[28] This is well known, for example, to the towns-people of La Oroyo in Peru.

Developing countries will not be able to attract the trillions of dollars they need in FDI to fund the green transition unless they provide an enabling framework of rules locally that contains much that has long been highlighted globally as essential to prospective foreign investors: respect for contract rights. Respect for property rights – including patents, trademarks, copyrights, trade secrets, and other intellectual property rights. Protections against direct or indirect expropriation without due process and full, effective, and prompt compensation. Effective rules and actions against corruption and against bribery. Transparent rules that are not "rigged" for locals but that treat foreigners equally and fairly. No governmental discrimination where there is commercial competition between foreign competitors from different countries or between foreign and local competitors. And, above all, access to justice rendered by independent courts that uphold and enforce the rule of law.[29] All of this is certainly needed; however, attention must equally be paid in local frameworks to identifying and supporting the kinds of foreign direct investments needed to facilitate and further the necessary shift to a low-carbon and ultimately a no-carbon economy.

Needed is not just investment. Needed is *sustainable* investment, which has been defined in the deliberations of the willing as "commercially viable investment that makes a maximum contribution to the economic, social and environmental development of host countries and takes place in the framework of fair governance mechanisms."[30] Note that, as Karl P. Sauvant and Howard Mann have observed, "This is a definition that goes beyond 'do no harm' and calls for efforts on the part of foreign affiliates to make an active contribution to sustainable development. In other words: sustainable FDI for sustainable development."[31]

THE INCOHERENCE OF INTERNATIONAL INVESTMENT LAW

As it is, the vast majority of international investment agreements say very little about sustainable development. They are almost always entirely about investor rights and protections. This was the original goal of such agreements, and this remains by far the main goal. The G20 group of leading economies quite rightly asserts, "Investment policies should establish open, non-discriminatory, transparent and predictable conditions for investment," and those policies "should provide legal certainty and strong protections to investors and investments, tangible and intangible."[32]

The challenge when reimagining international investment rules is to attain these aims in balanced ways that have positive overall impacts for sustainable development. Investment policies must "serve two potentially conflicting purposes."[33] They must create the right conditions in the right enabling framework to attract foreign direct investment to where it is needed, and they must do so while ensuring "that any negative social or environmental effects are minimized."[34] Striking the right balance that will resolve these "potentially conflicting purposes" requires leaving appropriate room for host countries to regulate. This necessitates "the mainstreaming of sustainable development issues" by embedding them in international investment rules and agreements.[35]

In only a small minority of international investment treaties is sustainable development an explicit goal. To some extent, this has been changing. References to the objectives of sustainable development have been included in a number of recent and proposed international agreements affecting investor rights. As with the WTO treaty, these references are mostly in the preambles to these agreements. Also, as with the WTO treaty, these references can help treaty interpreters discern the intended balance between investment protection and regulatory space by serving as legal context in construing the meaning of specific investment obligations. References to achieving the objectives of sustainable development should be in the preamble of *all* international investment agreements because achieving these objectives must be the overarching goal of all foreign direct investment. Additional objectives that should be cited because they would further sustainable development include "the protection of public welfare and human rights, including the protection of public health, labour standards, safety, and the environment."[36] To be consistent, however, with the objectives of sustainable development, the reimagining of investment rules must extend beyond the limited contextual bounds of the preambles to international investment agreements and deeper into the treaty texts.[37]

Reimagining investment rules to favor sustainable investment is complicated by the incoherence of the current international framework for dealing with foreign direct investment. As Howard Mann laments, because of variations in the wording of investment agreements and variations in the reasoning of arbitral awards, "for almost every investor right ... there are two or three strands of jurisprudence mostly irreconcilable without legalistic gymnastics."[38] "[T]he system needs certainty," he insists. Yet, for investors and governments alike, there is no certainty.[39] In the intricate web of thousands of differing agreements are "gaps, overlaps, and inconsistencies" that make it difficult to reimagine existing investment rules for sustainable development.[40] Making this harder still is the tendency of some arbitrators to give priority to investment law over environmental and other types of public international law – as if there were some ladder of international law in which investment law occupies a higher rung while environmental law and sustainability law cling somewhere down below.[41]

Which investments and investors should be protected by international investment agreements? Broad definitions are needed of an "investment" and an "investor" to ensure that genuine foreign direct investments made in accordance with applicable local laws will fall within the scope of the protections afforded by international investment agreements. These definitions should be broad enough to include those investors exercising indirect control over FDI, and to include those investments that are intangible as well as tangible.[42] These legal definitions should not, though, be so broad as to encompass, and thus to accord legal rights to, businesses and individuals with only remote or illusory relationships to the host state.

Some investment arbitration tribunals have maintained that, to meet the legal definition of an "investment," an economic action must make an economic contribution to the host state.[43] The gauge of whether a contribution is made by a foreign direct investment must be sustainable development. Not only should an economic action be required to make a positive *economic* contribution – properly identified and measured – to the state hosting the investment in order to fit within the definition of an "investment." To fall within that definition, that action should, in addition, make a positive contribution to the *sustainable development* of that host state. Furthermore, investor protections should be available under international investment agreements *only* to those economic actions that promote sustainable development. Mann expresses this well in saying that there must be "a shift in focus from looking at the *quantity* of an investment as the *only* issue, to the *quality* of that investment as the *key* issue."[44]

Generally, international investment agreements impose obligations on states but not on investors. Because such agreements are between states, and because investors are not parties to those agreements, imposing obligations on investors under those agreements can be questioned. However, as Kate Miles contends, "It is not unreasonable to assume that where investors have been granted rights under an international agreement between states ... they can also be burdened with responsibilities under that same agreement."[45] This is in keeping with a reimagining of international law overall to include "non-state political actors," a category that includes foreign direct investors. As part of this reimagining, investor rights should be accompanied by investor obligations to act sustainably.

Acting sustainably includes acting with all who are affected by an investment in mind. Frank Garcia, who urges us to see trade through the prism of justice, says the same about how we must see investment. He asserts, "The international investment regime ... is not solely about private actor rights – it is also about state responsibilities to the larger society. [International investment agreements] are part of a governance system meant to ensure justice and the rule of law for everyone in the allocation of investment capital."[46] Needed, he contends, "are efforts to make investment law more *just* by ensuring it embodies essential civil and political values, such as procedural fairness, equality before the law, the rule of law, and the right to political voice for all affected parties."[47]

Because international investment agreements have until now almost entirely "focused on the protection of capital and the return of capital," one result has been that "[n]o such protection has been extended to labor, indigenous people, migrants, or consumers, all of whom have linkages with investment."[48] In reimagining investment law, states host to investment must have the legal latitude to make certain that these and other groups of people are protected against any environmental or other social harm that may be caused or threatened by foreign direct investment. In addition, these groups must be legally empowered to assert their own rights under international investment law.

It is noteworthy that, in a number of places, the guidelines for international investment written by the largest international business organization, the International Chamber of Commerce, contemplate sustainable investment. The ICC guidelines say that an investor "should seek to create shared value by developing business opportunities that contribute to the economic, social, and environmental progress of the host country" and "should support sustainable economic growth by considering the financial, environmental, and social impacts of its investment in the host country at the outset of planning and during operations."[49] In particular, the ICC guidelines say that an investor "should assess environmental impacts, in the host country and elsewhere, before starting a new activity or project and before decommissioning a facility or leaving a site," and should "cooperate with the government of the host country in examining the impact of its operations on the environment, based on accepted norms, and take steps to minimize damage as far as it is economically and technically practical in the local situation."[50] Plus, the investor should, "where possible and practicable, give preference in local operations to environmentally-sound technologies and operational practices, and extend [the] same standards to local partners."[51] Ideally, these should be preconditions to all foreign direct investments.

Yet another obligation of investors should be "corporate social responsibility" (CSR). A "best efforts" clause on CSR in an international investment agreement would be a helpful start, leaving it to the arbitrators to decide, in the case of a dispute, whether "best efforts" were in fact made by an investor. A better approach would be to link specific international standards, such as the OECD Guidelines for Multinational Enterprises or the ten principles of the United Nations Global Compact on sustainability and social responsibility (signed by nearly 15,000 international businesses in 170 countries), to investments made under an international investment agreement. Investors could then be held to these specific standards through enforcement of that agreement.[52] Ideally, a post-Westphalian multilateral convention on corporate responsibility could be negotiated with both states and businesses as legal parties that could be legally binding in international investment agreements as well as in other international agreements.[53]

One sustainability concern relating to investment liberalization is that freer foreign direct investment must be accompanied by a national regulatory framework that enables sustainable investment and that insists that FDI be done sustainably. Otherwise, not only will there be a *perceived* loss of local control. There will be a *real* loss of local control, with unknown consequences for the climate, other ecosystems, and other elements of sustainability. This is a particular problem for developing countries, which have less mature and less comprehensive institutions of local governance, and thus often have less capacity to regulate. Investment liberalization should everywhere be accompanied by capacity-building for effective local regulation.

One of the best ways in which a state can ensure that investment will be sustainable is by the line-drawing of regulating.[54] A balance is needed in international investment rules between investment protection and the "right to regulate." The right line establishing the right balance in international investment agreements can be drawn in part by affirming the host state's right to regulate. If the reimagined purpose of such agreements is to promote sustainable development, then it is necessary as part of the reimagining to give host states "the right to regulate in the interest of legitimate public policy objectives," and also to affirm that right in those agreements.[55] Sovereign states must be free to act as sovereign states within the bounds of their international commitments.

The "common understanding" is that a state "fully retains its regulatory powers" once it has entered into an international investment agreement.[56] Nevertheless, "[t]he impact of the uncertainty" over the precise meaning of investment obligations "adds to the risk of regulatory chill" that can inhibit the enactment of the requisite local framework for enabling sustainable development.[57] Views differ on whether there is such a "chilling effect."[58] But, amid this legal uncertainty, how are host states to sort out which climate, environment, and other sustainability regulations are permitted by investment rules, and which are not, even with the benefit of an affirmation of the right to regulate? Legislation may be difficult to enact if it is seen as simply inviting prolonged and expensive international litigation. Yet new science and new circumstances may demand new legislation. A leading authority on the relationship between investment and environment, Jorge Vinuales, says that the possibility of a "chilling effect" is especially pertinent to "environmental regulation, which, by its very nature, is constantly evolving, either through new norms or measures or simply through the evolving interpretation of existing measures."[59]

Among the needed reimaginings of rules relating to foreign direct investment that would help to thaw this "chilling effect" are: a requirement that environmental standards not be lowered to entice foreign direct investment;[60] a carve-out, akin to that on trade in the WTO treaty, of general exceptions for certain environmental and other sustainability measures if they are not applied in ways that constitute arbitrary or unjustifiable discrimination or a disguised protection of competing domestic investors;[61] the incorporation by reference of an agreed list of multilateral environmental agreements that are thereby made enforceable under the investment agreement; and a commitment going forward to ongoing cooperation on sustainability that includes investors as well as other members of civil society.

Reservation of the right to regulate FDI to ensure sustainability must also be aligned with the promotion of FDI. Toward this end, the G20 advises that investment promotion by host states "should . . . be . . . matched by facilitation efforts that promote transparency and are conducive for investors to establish, conduct and expand their businesses."[62] The business advisers to the G20 spell out what is meant by investment facilitation in saying that, from their perspective, "we mean efforts to remove barriers to FDI, whether they are policies, administrative obstacles, logistical barriers, or efforts that include technical support to improve investment capacity. These efforts have broad benefits: they help investors as well as recipient markets and complement countries' unilateral efforts to encourage FDI flows."[63]

Standing out in these recommendations is the fact that these business leaders go on to say, "Investment facilitation is thus also crucial to the achievement of the SDGs."[64] They know that investment facilitation must be fit for sustainable development. With the need in mind for trillions of investment dollars to address climate change and otherwise further sustainable development, some in the business community and others among the willing have joined in advocating a sustainable investment facilitation agreement that "would focus on practical ways and means – the 'nuts and bolts' – of encouraging the flow of sustainable FDI to developing countries and, in particular, the least developed countries."[65] Such an agreement would help convey technical and other useful knowledge to help make possible the fulfillment of the Sustainable Development Goals. Karl Sauvant and Khalil Hamdani have observed that, to fulfill the mandate of the SDGs, such an international investment facilitation agreement would also need to help inspire more FDI for purposes that historically have gotten little of it, such as infrastructure, health, and education.[66]

At the WTO Ministerial Conference in Buenos Aires in December 2017, a large group of WTO members comprising both developed and developing countries endorsed a joint statement agreeing to start "structural discussions with the aim of developing a multilateral framework on investment facilitation."[67] Two months later, Brazil submitted a draft proposal to jumpstart the promised negotiations. The Brazilian proposal includes voluntary principles and standards of corporate social responsibility for investors to meet in other countries.[68] This is a good start toward using an investment facilitation agreement to help inspire and support sustainable investment. Ideally, such an agreement should be a multilateral agreement negotiated by the members of the WTO inside the WTO. Once concluded, this multilateral agreement could function within the WTO system as an investment counterpart to the multilateral WTO Trade Facilitation Agreement. In this way, the two innovative facilitation agreements could be linked and made mutually reinforcing under the WTO treaty. If a multilateral investment facilitation agreement cannot be concluded by all WTO members, then those WTO members willing to do so should conclude a plurilateral agreement within the WTO that could, over time, become fully multilateral.

Solid guarantees of rights of most-favored-nation treatment, national treatment, and full payment for expropriation are all fundamental and essential to investor protection. These protections should be included in all international investment agreements. This said, the meanings of these obligations have proven elusive as different arbitral tribunals under different investment agreements have reached different conclusions. These divergent conclusions have fed uncertainty and frustrated efforts to encourage FDI. In the reimagining of investment law, the content of these basic investor protections must be interpreted consistently and within the broader context of the urgency of advancing sustainability.

The definition of an "indirect" expropriation has proven particularly elusive. Foreign investors should be protected against "indirect" expropriations that interfere with and that sometimes even prevent the use of their property while stopping short of taking title to it. Nowadays, governments rarely send in armed troops to confiscate title to foreign property through a direct expropriation. The usual legal question today is whether there has, instead, been an indirect expropriation through some other governmental action or combination of actions. But, while there must be investor protections against indirect expropriations, the concept of an indirect expropriation should not be so expansive as to include necessary regulations to protect climate, health, or environment, or otherwise regulate the use of property in the public interest.[69]

In investment law, the same is true of the meaning of most-favored-nation treatment, which, as UNCTAD recounts, "has been subject to diverging and unanticipated interpretations by tribunals."[70] Foreign investors from one country should benefit from a most-favored-nation obligation that assures they will be treated by the host state no less favorably than it treats investors from other countries. In considering, however, in individual cases whether the reach of such MFN obligations in investment agreements should be as far as to "import" obligations from investment agreements between the host state and third countries, and also in considering in individual cases the exceptions to the MFN obligations that are sometimes included in investment agreements, account must be taken of any and all resulting implications for sustainable development.[71]

The meaning of national treatment, too, has been hard to pin down in international investment law. A national treatment obligation is essential to ensure equality of competitive conditions for foreign and domestic investors. Because it prevents discrimination against foreign investors and their investments, the guarantee of national treatment, as David Collins of City University London has explained, helps to "encourage a healthy economy overall because it emphasizes quality and price of goods and services rather than regulatory favoritism."[72] Yet, as he adds, although national treatment "eliminates discrimination against foreign investors on the basis of nationality or ownership of an investment and in theory should promote FDI, National Treatment can also significantly interfere with a nation's capacity of self-government on a wide range of issues."[73] Among those issues can be those relating to environmental protection and other expressions of sustainability.

Sustainability issues relating to the non-discrimination obligation of national treatment are likely to arise, first, when asking who is entitled to national treatment. In newer agreements, the national treatment obligation often applies to investors and their investments that are "preestablishment" (*before* the investment is made in the host state) as well as to investments that are "postestablishment" (*after* the investment is made in the host state). Where there is only postestablishment protection in an agreement, a host state is free to discriminate against the foreign direct investment before it is made. Depending on the quality of the investment, and on the discernment of the domestic regulatory framework, this discrimination may be good or bad in any given case for sustainability. On balance, it seems likely that sustainable development will be advanced if protections against discrimination are afforded both pre- and postestablishment, which will provide certainty of protection to more rather than fewer potentially positive and sustainable investments. Countries should not deny themselves sustainable investments for the sake of discriminating in favor of local interests that may or may not act sustainably.

National treatment also generally applies only where foreign investors and domestic investors are "in like circumstances." In some ways, this "likeness" requirement in investment law is comparable to the "likeness" requirement in trade law.[74] But it differs in one important respect as to sustainability. As Vinuales has explained, "trade is primarily about the transboundary movement of goods and services and only secondarily about production," while "investment is mainly about production and only secondarily about transboundary movements of goods and services."[75] Thus, issues relating to the environmental consequences of process and production methods – PPMs – and to other sustainability impacts of production are more likely to arise in "likeness" determinations in investment than in trade. In the reimagining of investment rules, this contrast gives support to the argument made by some of the willing that a determination of whether there are "like circumstances" in investment should not be based solely on commercial considerations. It should also be based on the environmental and social impacts of an investment. Further, the contrast between trade and investment on their opposite sides of the commercial coin strengthens the case for emulating trade agreements by including environmental exceptions in international investment agreements.

As reflected in the concerns of Cordell Hull in the 1930s, the conviction of foreign direct investors has long been that something more than merely national treatment is required to protect investor rights where host states may not provide protections to their own private investors. Hence we have had the evolution of the notion of a minimum international standard of treatment for FDI in customary international law. The contemporary manifestation in treaty law of this perceived need is the obligation of "fair and equitable treatment" that is enshrined in many international investment agreements. The availability of this additional investment obligation guarantees that, even if there is no expropriation and no discrimination, investors and their investments are protected against governmental treatment that is arbitrary, abusive, or unfair. The relationship between the customary minimum international standard of treatment and the treaty-based standard of "fair and equitable treatment" has been much debated and much litigated but remains unclear.[76] Lacking clarity, too, is the meaning of "fair and equitable treatment." What is "fair"? What is "equitable"? Unavoidably, these are subjective determinations that depend on the judgments of *ad hoc* arbitrators who serve as the treaty interpreters in investment disputes under the several thousands of international investment agreements. For investment, there is no common court of appeal such as the WTO Appellate Body in trade to ensure consistency in the world-full of these *ad hoc* arbitral rulings.

The obligation to provide "fair and equitable treatment" is "the most frequently invoked standard in investment disputes."[77] The wide range of the arbitral rulings about the content of this "inherently unclear" obligation has led, as UNCTAD has reported, to "a great deal of uncertainty."[78] Especially uncertain is where the scales of judgment should be balanced by drawing the right lines between the environmental, social, and other dimensions of sustainability governance by host states and the protection of the "legitimate expectations" of foreign investors for their direct investments in those states.[79] In the absence of any clarity about where the right lines should be drawn to strike the right balance, there is the risk that an unqualified guarantee of "fair and equitable treatment" will inhibit host states in changing local laws, regulations, and policies as needed to fulfill their climate commitments under the Paris Agreement and to meet the targets of the Sustainable Development Goals. To eliminate this risk, it must be clarified that the "fair and equitable treatment" obligation does not require host states to forgo regulatory and other public measures adopted in good faith to fulfill climate and other sustainability objectives.

One legal option is the inclusion in international investment agreements of a closed list of specific criteria – such as due process – that are agreed to be contained in the "fair and equitable treatment" obligation. Although closed, such a list could be made subject to review and revision over time as climate actions, sustainability actions, and other imperatives of international investment governance continue to evolve. Where the line of balance will be drawn on this and on other international investment obligations will depend on how much room and on what kind of room is reserved in the evolving rules framework for foreign direct investment for imposing discretionary domestic regulation.

REIMAGINING INTERNATIONAL INVESTMENT LAW

An opportunity for constructive international cooperation in the needed reimagining of international investment law may have been presented by the endorsement by the heads of state of the G20 countries at their summit in Hangzhou, China, in September 2016 of the "G20 Guiding Principles for Global Investment Policy-Making."[80] As James Zhan of UNCTAD points out, this endorsement marked "the first time in decades of international investment policymaking that consensus [was] reached among such a varied group of countries (the G20 membership includes developed, developing, and transition economies). Moreover, collectively the G20 represents more than three-fourths of global foreign direct investment."[81]

The shared hope of the willing is that the constructive international cooperation that resulted in these G20 guidelines will be "a stepping stone for multilateral rules on investment" as the core of a fully global investment framework.[82]

There are nine G20 Guiding Principles. In their brevity, all nine can be printed and read easily on just one page. These "non-binding" FDI principles highlight as one objective "fostering an open, transparent and conducive global policy environment for investment."[83] The fulfillment of this objective is envisaged in part through efforts by host governments to "avoid protectionism"; to "establish open, non-discriminatory, transparent and predictable conditions for investment"; to "provide legal certainty and strong protection to investors and investments," including access to "fair, open and transparent" and also enforceable dispute settlement; and to ensure "an institutional framework based on the rule of law."[84]

What is especially striking about the G20 Guiding Principles – and what appears to the willing to point the way ahead – is the emphasis placed by the G20 on achieving sustainable development through foreign direct investment. Not once, not twice, but three times in the short length of the statement of these principles, the goal of sustainable development is cited by the G20. First, a stated "objective" of the investment principles is that of "promoting inclusive alternative growth and sustainable development."[85] Second, national and international policies on investment are to be "consistent with the objectives of sustainable development and growth."[86] And, third, the G20 Guiding Principles, considered together as a "coherent whole," are supposed to take "into account national, and broader, sustainable development objective and priorities."[87]

Although these principles do not say so explicitly, they seem to imply that the 17 goals and the 169 related targets of the United Nations Sustainable Development Goals (which had been adopted less than a year earlier) should be considered the basis of the universal criteria that are needed to identify sustainable investment. Yet these goals and these targets are only the bare beams of the framework. They await further construction. In filling in the empty spaces in this framework, we must figure out how to recognize sustainable investment when we see it, what specific criteria to employ as commonly agreed "indicators" of sustainable investment, and how to measure the progress of foreign direct investment toward sustainability. The work by the willing in settling on globally accepted economic, environmental, and social indicators for judging whether there is progress toward sustainable investment is one part of the broader task of identifying progress on each of those "three pillars" of sustainable development. Equally important is the parallel task of identifying the best "metrics" for measuring such progress – a prerequisite to progress in which many of the willing are much engaged, both on climate change and on sustainability generally.

In agreeing internationally on common criteria for assessing our advance toward sustainable investment, it must be remembered that the true bottom-up is always to be preferred over the siren's lure of the top-down. It must be understood by decisionmakers everywhere that sustainable investment – like all of sustainable development – must be defined *by doing it*. Sustainable investment must be defined not by the seductive abstractions of the top-down, but by the hard-won practical experience of the bottom-up of *learning by doing* by alliances, networks, public–private partnerships, and assorted other *ad hoc* coalitions of the willing of all kinds all over the world. All we have learned by doing, and all we have yet to learn by doing, in our myriad pursuits of the Sustainable Development Goals down at the innovative and catalytic grassroots of the world, must be a central source of inspiration for identifying and measuring the common characteristics of sustainable investment.

With this in mind, as Karl Sauvant and Howard Mann have urged, national governments should routinely subject potential foreign direct investments – before they are made – to local scrutiny of their likely help or harm to sustainable development. Already, they remind us, "[i]n many instances, especially for larger-scale and natural resources projects ... governments may have set out criteria regarding the sectors in which investments may be made, and for the approval of these investments."[88] Why not also require similar national tests to make certain that foreign direct investment will be sustainable?

What precisely is tested will be critical. A mere cost–benefit calculation is not enough for ensuring sustainable investment. An assessment of whether any proposed FDI will be sustainable must be founded more inclusively on an understanding that the economy and the environment are one and the same; that the human economy is contained within, constrained by, and fueled and facilitated by the natural environment; and that some environmental harms to natural resources, other species, and fragile ecosystems are so harmful that they are irreparable, and therefore result in unacceptable long-term damage to the environment and the economy alike.

As Sauvant and Mann report, there are any number of international standards, voluntary guidelines, and other assorted "checklists" from which we can select as "sources and examples" in assembling "an indicative list of sustainability characteristics."[89] One obvious place for doing this is the follow-up by the United Nations to the Sustainable Development Goals.[90] Such a list could be agreed in a joint public–private undertaking in that or in any number of other institutional settings, and then, over time and with experience, be scaled up for worldwide use in assessing whether individual instances of foreign direct investment are sustainable and therefore consistent with reimagined rules in a reimagined international investment framework. Some of these standards can remain voluntary. Others can be made binding – perhaps by inclusion or by reference in reimagined bilateral or other international investment agreements.

Building on the G20 Guiding Principles, considerably more international cooperation is needed to help give international investment obligations a meaning that draws the right lines to balance investor rights with host state rights to help achieve the Sustainable Development Goals through sustainable investment. In our reimagining, we must overcome the legal inconsistencies and incoherence that currently frustrate the fostering of foreign direct investment and, thus, slow the advance toward sustainable development. One of the stated objectives of the G20 Guiding Principles is "promoting coherence in national and international policymaking," and doing so in ways "consistent with the aims of sustainable development and inclusive growth."[91]

In giving life through further international cooperation to the "coherent whole" of these G20 Guiding Principles in international investment rules and rulings, the stated objectives of international investment agreements, the identity of an "investor," the scope of a foreign direct "investment," the extent and the nature of investor obligations, the affirmation of the right to regulate, the exclusions and the exceptions made for environmental and other public policy measures, the provisions for investment promotion and facilitation, the guarantees against uncompensated expropriation, the exact meanings of the non-discrimination obligations of most-favored-nation treatment and of national treatment, and the meaning of "fair and equitable treatment" must all be harmonized, and they must all give appropriate recognition to, and must all be consistent with, shaping and sharing a lasting global prosperity through sustainable development.[92]

Equally important in promoting sustainable development is eliminating legitimate investor concerns in ways that will stimulate and facilitate the increased flow of foreign direct investment to all those places where it is much needed. A sampling of these increasingly common investor concerns includes: the need to secure market-opening preestablishment as well as postestablishment state obligations to investors; forced localization requirements that coerce foreign companies into investing in, buying from, exporting from, or otherwise "localizing" in, a host state as a condition of their investment; the related phenomenon of data and server localization requirements that raise concerns about investor security, increase costs, and distort digital trade; sweeping definitions of "national security" in host state investment screenings that can block legitimate foreign investment for purely protectionist purposes; and domestic measures that restrict foreign direct investment to protect the market share and the competitive advantage of favored and often heavily subsidized state-owned enterprises.[93]

The G20 stopped short of discussing the substance of the existing investment obligations in the world's several thousand investment agreements. It is on the substance of these obligations that the endeavors of the willing should be centered going forward. Once we have agreed on how to define the indicators that are the universal characteristics of sustainable investment and of overall sustainable development, and once we have agreed also on the common metrics for measuring our progress toward those goals, we must next turn our cooperation to giving actual content to the meanings of those markers for sustainability through the writing, the rewriting, and, not least, the interpretation of international investment obligations. As the G20 Guiding Principles express, private finance in the form of more foreign direct investment must be promoted and facilitated in ways that will create sustainable development, not undermine it. This task can be accomplished only if international investment rules are reimagined to give priority to sustainable development and to establish a proper balance between investor rights and state obligations.

14

On Policy Space and Post-Paris Climate Action

The willing call it "policy space." The concept of a sovereign space reserved for domestic policymaking, a space beyond the reach of international economic rules and rulings, is at the heart of much of the national and international debate and decisionmaking about how best to further sustainable development. Locally, the details differ, but everywhere the same questions are asked: Must we – as the price for securing the benefits of foreign direct investment and the gains from trade – surrender so much of our sovereign discretion to the international rules of international institutions that we cannot choose for ourselves, here where we live, how we wish to provide our food, protect our health, treat our workers, ensure our safety, preserve our environment, promote our economic growth, and otherwise arrange our public services and pursue our national life? Must we submit to the global sway of distant but intrusive "foreigners" concealed by the trappings of supposedly impartial international institutions? Must we acquiesce to the edicts of "faceless foreign judges"?[1]

POLICY SPACE

There are competing and contrasting voices among the advocates of more policy space. The vast majority of the willing are entirely sincere in extolling the right to make differing economic choices locally and the right to regulate locally as the right remedies to what they see as the slow loss of local popular control due to the creeping and increasingly constraining encroachment of international rules and rulings. They aim to ease the jarring impact of the societal disruptions of market-based globalization by reasserting a maximum of local control of economic destiny and – in some laudable instances – ensuring a just transition to a green global economy.

But some of the most vocal defenders of policy space should not be numbered among the willing. Worldwide, online, on the streets, and on the darker traces of the political campaign trails, some of the tribunes for policy space are simply seizing on the anger and the anxieties resulting from the fear of change for other, often hidden purposes. They are sowers and reapers of discord. They are demagogues and opportunists. Their opposition to the supposed transgressions of trade and investment is often really only a ploy for seizing and holding political power, devoid of any sincere political agenda.

For still others, their opposition is a visceral ideological opposition to market-based capitalism itself. They see capitalism – even liberal democratic capitalism – as requiring, and even delighting in, more environmental degradation, more human exploitation, and, not least, ever more social and economic inequality. Many of them still remain in the discredited Marxist past, whether they acknowledge it or not. Many of them still dream the deathless utopian dream of something else, of something entirely and profoundly different in how we shape our world so as to shape ourselves and perfect our nature.

Against all the evidence of history, against all the memories of bodies heaped by the millions in slaughtered sacrifice to utopian dreams, many still cling to the vain belief that we can best shape the future of human civilization in ways that assume the perfectibility of human nature and, thus, of human society. This is why they recoil reflexively against a mixed economy based on market-based capitalism, an imperfect economy which assumes an imperfect and imperfectible human nature, an economy which works best, and which works most justly, when it is structured by democratic governance in ways that appeal not to the worst, but to the best in human nature. These among the advocates of policy space have no faith that justice can even exist while there remains a market-based capitalism.

In this corrosive atmosphere, we are, all too often, left with only dueling stereotypes. Even some of those who do not wish to abolish capitalism fear that what they see as the global hydra of multinational corporate trade and investment could eliminate all their seemingly waning control over the course of their own lives in their own countries. For their part, the advocates of trade and investment fear that the populist call for more policy space will lead to a contagious surge of global protectionism that will shrink global economic growth and perhaps even plunge the world into a prolonged global depression. All too often in this rhetorical duel, neither side seems to appreciate or even acknowledge the nuance of the "in between."

One of the sincere – and one of the most articulate – among the many advocates for more policy space is Dani Rodrik, a professor of international political economy at Harvard who says he is not an anti-globalist. He claims, instead, to be trying to identify the nuanced "in between" that will save globalization from what he perceives as the overreach of the globalists. Rodrik says, "We must redress the balance between national autonomy and economic globalization. Simply put, we have pushed economic globalization too far – toward an impractical version that we might call 'hyperglobalization.'"[2] In his view, one of the events signaling "the transition to hyperglobalization" was the establishment of the WTO.[3] As a remedy, he argues for a "more moderate form of globalization" that will surrender less of national sovereignty to international rule-making while somehow slowing the speed at which globalization seems to some to be overwhelming the role of local decisionmaking.[4] Rodrik recommends "placing some sand in the cogs of globalization."[5]

This debate goes back at least to the back and forth between Adam Smith and the British mercantilists in the eighteenth century about the degree to which political judgment should be substituted for that of the market. The problems with what appears to be Rodrik's preferred approach to finding the right lines "in between" through more local policy space for economic development are many, but several stand out – both old and new. The oldest and the most familiar of these problems is found in the sad and lingering history of the failed struggles of the poorer countries during the middle decades of the twentieth century to liberate themselves from what they perceived as a state of unending underdevelopment and ongoing economic subservience to the developed world by "placing some sand in the cogs of globalization" to insulate their local economies against competition from foreign trade and investment.

The "dependency theory" of Raul Prebisch, Hans Singer, and other theorists of the time held that, to be able to grow, diversify, and develop their economies over time, the poorer countries "needed to embark on a separate or autonomous development path and reduce their dependence on trade with developed economies, including by embarking on programmes of infant industry protection and replacing imports with domestically produced goods."[6] Embracing this theory, many of the developing countries sought, in the first few decades following the Second World War, to create a "New International Economic Order."[7] A number of them still, tacitly, seek such an "order" now. This proclaimed new order was doomed because it turned inward and away from the rest of the world and because, in blaming all local economic ills on foreign interests, it gave poorer countries an easy excuse for not facing up to the need to fix structural economic problems that were homegrown. This "new" order was doomed, too, because it was a top-down statist approach to economic growth that distrusted and undermined the marketplace. For the most part, it comprised state-imposed and state-directed policies that were anything but new, and that relied primarily on the old mercantilist panaceas of import substitution, high tariffs, and other familiar forms of state direction and protectionism.

The supporters of this failed new order forgot the first and foremost requirement of national competitiveness – being an open society open to the wider world, a society that, by being open, liberates human imagination and enables the full flourishing of human imagination to discover and develop the technological and other needed innovations that help make a brighter future. Thus, not surprisingly, by the 1980s, dependency theory "had failed."[8] Under its sway, "a significant number of [less developed countries] had become heavily burdened by huge debts, their governments were running unmanageable budget deficits, and their economies suffered from high inflation rates that discouraged productive economic activities and foreign investment."[9]

A reprise of the siren song of this supposed new international economic order would result in the same failure today. Yet Rodrik parrots the tired tropes of this failed "dependency theory" in contending that, "Developing countries ... need to enshrine the notion of 'policy space' in the World Trade Organization. The goal would be to ensure that developing countries can employ the kind of trade and industrial policies needed to restructure and diversify their economies and set the stage for economic growth. All countries that have successfully globalized have used such policies, many of which (e.g., subsidies, domestic-content rules, reverse engineering of patented products) are currently not allowed under WTO rules."[10]

Setting aside for the moment the facts that domestic-content rules, though popular politically, often do nothing to advance sustainability,[11] that, currently, WTO rules *do* allow ample policy space for many subsidies, and that the "reverse engineering of patents" is nothing other than a euphemism for theft, Rodrik appears to be calling, in the main, for state-determined and state-directed approaches to attaining global sustainable development, and not for the market-based solutions that are generally much more effective. His is an enticing call for the top-down instead of the bottom-up.

Without question, Rodrik is right that "in the absence of a more concerted governmental response, too much globalization" can "deepen societal cleavages, exacerbate distributional problems, and undermine domestic social bargains."[12] The evidence is all around us. The grievances of the disaffected and the dislocated are real. But turning inward and away from the rest of the world will not lead to a just transition. If a return to protectionism in the pose of an "industrial policy" akin to that of the failed New International Economic Order is what Rodrik and other champions of policy space have in mind when they plead for "greater space" for more local latitude in decisionmaking by developing countries under international economic rules, then the result will be economic diminution and economic decline as those countries deny to their people the gains from trade, the benefits from investment, and the bottom-up innovations of an imaginative marketplace.

As one group of the willing has put it, when properly framed, a "modern industrial policy emphasizes *the promotion rather than restriction* of trade and investment."[13] Through more economic openness, more local producers can benefit from cheaper imported inputs into their local production than may otherwise be available, and local enterprises can link up to the global value chains that now characterize so much of global commerce. In these ways, they can become more competitive, locally and internationally. Empirical studies conclude, too, from the evidence of recent experience, that developed and developing countries alike will not shape and share a lasting prosperity by pursuing domestic policies that single out and favor specific industries with infant-industry or other special treatment. Rather, every country will become most competitive by pursuing domestic policies that will vary from place to place but will always include "improvements in infrastructure, education and training, enterprise development, entrepreneurship, innovation, finance and social policies" that will "create the potential for spillover effects" allowing the early successes of new ideas "to take root and spread locally."[14]

This kind of "modern industrial policy" is one that "requires a systems approach,"[15] one that demands a "a recognition that successful industrial development is a process involving the ongoing upgrading particularly of skills, infrastructure and economic institutions."[16] This process of ongoing upgrading will not work where countries hide behind trade and investment barriers that deny domestic workers and companies the benefits of competition, and the benefits of broader and better sources of inputs and of expertise in their production. Nor can a shared and a sustainable national prosperity ever be attained through a crony capitalism that discriminates in favor of vested local special interests in their economic rent-seeking – in the use of their wealth and their position to influence local politics for their selfish gain.

What is entirely new in the global debate over policy space is not the long-held desire for more elbow room under international rules for many *developing* countries; it is the mounting demand for more policy space that is heard in the streets and that is heard, too, and more and more, in the legislative assemblies of many *developed* countries. This demand in the wealthier countries is driven not by a desire for trade and investment protection as such, but, rather, by a long and seemingly ever-lengthening list of non-trade and non-investment concerns that can all be summed up as a subset in the developed world of the fear of change.

The intensifying fear of many in Europe, in the United States, and in other parts of the wealthier, developed world is that international trade and investment rules and institutions, in service to selfish and shortsighted multinational corporate interests, will overrule numerous local laws and local regulations that serve other vital, non-commercial societal values and establish higher standards than those that apply in the rest of the world. This, it is widely feared, will lead – if trade and investment are allowed to trump all else – to tainted "Frankenfoods," other toxic products, diminished labor protections, shrinking public services, and a long list of harmful risks to public health, public safety, the environment, and much more.

Those out campaigning against new regional and global trade and investment agreements fear that international economic rules and rulings will undermine local efforts to guard against these risks by overturning existing laws and by having a "chilling effect" on the enactment of needed new laws. They characterize and castigate the making and the upholding of international trade and investment rules as a "neoliberal" enterprise aimed at instilling a strict *laissez faire* – a rigid policy of hands-off that privatizes public services, rips holes in the social safety net, and shuns any and all local governmental laws or regulations that might impede the utterly unrestricted flow of global commerce.

POLICY SPACE UNDER WTO RULES

This is not so. This charge is one of the politically convenient but imaginary inventions of the unwilling world, one more example of how the public perception of international trade rules and the actual reality of those rules are far apart. WTO rules are anything but global edicts for *laissez faire*. WTO rules create a framework for freeing trade but in no way mandate free trade where WTO members have not agreed to it. WTO members have, in addition, imposed many limits on free trade in trade rules. WTO rules allow considerably more local policy space than many trade critics realize or – in some cases – will admit.

The basic WTO rules on trade in goods generally intrude on the reserve of the sovereign right to regulate only if local laws or regulations discriminate between and among like internationally traded products, either in favor of domestic over foreign products or in favor of some foreign products over others.[17] Much the same is true in the reservation of policy space under the WTO rules on trade in services. The services rules, to cite just one instance, allow ample room for domestic regulation of financial services for "prudential reasons . . . to ensure the integrity and the stability of the financial system."[18]

Likewise, although intellectual property rights must, rightly, be protected under WTO rules, considerable latitude is allowed to WTO members to provide such protection "in a manner conducive to social and economic welfare," and "to promote the public interest" through domestic measures that "protect public health and nutrition" and promote "socio-economic and technological development."[19] One example is the WTO decision underscoring the legality of the compulsory licensing of expensive HIV/AIDS drugs by developing countries.

Moreover, the WTO rules on standards and technical regulations generally limit local regulations only if they discriminate between and among like traded products, or if they create unnecessary obstacles to international trade or are more trade-restrictive than necessary to fulfill a legitimate objective.[20] Although the trade rules encourage all members of the WTO to participate in international standardizing institutions "with a view to harmonizing technical regulations on as wide a basis as possible," harmonization of standards and technical regulations is not a WTO requirement.[21] The sovereign right to establish national standards and technical requirements for traded products remains intact under the WTO treaty.

Yet, increasingly, protectionism in the twenty-first century is pursued not directly by imposing high tariffs at the border, but indirectly by crafting internal domestic standards and technical requirements to favor domestic over foreign producers of traded products and suppliers of traded services. To help minimize the resulting market distortions and the discriminations from these non-tariff barriers to trade, WTO rules contemplate choosing and following the right line of the "just mean" somewhere "in between" by maximizing legitimate goals for standards and technical regulations while minimizing restrictions on international trade.

Similarly, WTO rules specify that WTO members have the right to take measures that are necessary for the protection of human, animal, or plant life or health.[22] Such "sanitary and phytosanitary" measures must, however, be based on a risk assessment and on scientific principles, and must not be maintained without sufficient scientific evidence.[23] In addition, such local health and safety measures must be applied only to the extent necessary to achieve those purposes; and they must not involve arbitrary or unjustifiable discrimination, or be applied in a manner which constitutes a disguised restriction on international trade.[24]

In their current form, WTO rules may or may not, in each and every instance, be sufficient to support the goals of sustainable development; but, as a whole, these rules can hardly be described as denying WTO members any room at all for discretionary local decisionmaking by imposing strict rules of *laissez faire*. WTO rules assume a whole world full of regulatory actions within an expansive realm of policy space. What is more, these WTO rules have not been *imposed* on any member of the WTO. In agreeing to be bound by the terms of the WTO treaty, all members of the WTO have agreed to all these global rules *voluntarily*.

The WTO is not global coercion; it is global cooperation. The WTO is not a surrender of sovereignty; it is a sharing of sovereignty. It is a pooling of their sovereignty by almost all the countries in the world for the purpose of international cooperation in pursuit of commonly agreed aims in international trade. Any international economic cooperation through multilateralism implies – indeed requires – a sharing of sovereignty that necessitates of every sovereign country a self-imposed limit on the range of its national action.[25] In international trade, in agreeing to be bound by the WTO agreement, every member of the WTO has agreed to accept certain constraints on the domestic exercise of sovereignty – on the extent of local policy space – in exchange for the considerable economic benefits flowing from acceptance of and compliance with the agreed international rules furthering global economic integration.

Dani Rodrik is of the view that WTO rules should be revised to attain his "more moderate form of globalization" by including "[a]n extension of safeguards to cover environmental, labor, and consumer safety standards or developmental practices at home – *with appropriate procedural restraints against abuse.*"[26] In trade parlance, "safeguards" are import restrictions that are imposed without any allegation of an unfair trade practice.[27] Even if erecting new barriers worldwide to trade and investment is not the principal aim of Rodrik's proposed new "safeguards," and even if "procedural restraints" of some sort are put in place, it is politically naïve to think that there would not be "abuse." Soon we would see another coming of a slouching protectionism, newly disguised in the respectable clothes of social concern, and born anew amid the resulting widespread use of such expanded policy space.[28]

Rodrik assures us that "we should not fret too much about a reversal in globalization."[29] Globalists in the late nineteenth century were equally confident that the economic globalization of their time would only accelerate. Then it all fell apart in the bloody slaughter of the First World War. As Rodrik himself explains, it was not until several decades after the Second World War that the extent of economic globalization attained in the last decades before the First World War was attained again.[30] Likewise, the seemingly unstoppable economic globalization of our troubled time is not inevitable. It could well be undermined if there is not sufficient political will worldwide to support it through more international cooperation – and to enhance it through a just transition to a green economy.

As it is, all too many politicians in every part of our unwilling world – and all too many also of the well-intended willing – are ignoring Tocqueville's advice to take the longer and the broader view. They are, instead, backing old and new barriers alike to trade and investment either to advance self-destructive, inward-turning attempts to spur growth and seize markets, or to heed spurious allegations that all traders and investors are somehow bent on harming labor, health, safety, and environment. Thus, in our unwilling world, the continued advance of global economic integration cannot be assumed.

All this said, one of the targets of the Sustainable Development Goals – supported by all the members of the United Nations – is to "[r]espect each country's policy space and leadership to establish and implement policies for poverty eradication and sustainable development."[31] To reach this target, is there need to carve out more policy space in the WTO rules and in the other international economic rules that have an impact on sustainable development?

As the Appellate Body observed in *US – Shrimp* – the WTO shrimp–turtle dispute – the answer to this central question about the meaning of current world trade rules is found in the preamble to the WTO treaty, and in the pledge made there by all the members of the WTO to conduct their "relations in the field of trade and economic endeavor ... with a view to ... the optimal use of the world's resources in accordance with the objective of sustainable development, seeking both to protect and preserve the environment and to enhance the means for doing so in a manner consistent with their respective needs and concerns at different levels of economic development."[32] These must be our constant watchwords in clarifying the meaning of current world trade rules, and also in imagining and reimagining trade, investment, and other international economic rules to help accomplish the Sustainable Development Goals. Given these instructions about our existing international trade rules in these first words of the WTO treaty, our common challenge is clear. WTO rules and all our other international economic rules must leave adequate space for every form of domestic action that advances sustainable development.

Furthermore, these rules must be framed in ways that will not only uphold domestic sustainability actions, but will also actively advance sustainable development *internationally*. Just as, everywhere in the world, we must internalize the costs of carbon emissions into the prices of our products, so too must we proceed, with a shared global urgency, to internalize each of the three "interdependent and mutually reinforcing pillars" of global sustainable development – economic, social, and environmental – into all our international economic rules and institutions.[33] Only in this integrated way will we be able to locate in each instance of rule-making the "in between" of the "just mean" of policy space for local governmental intervention into the workings of the spontaneous order of the market.

At this crossroads for human civilization on climate change, and on so many other severe threats to our global ecosystems, "the rules of ecology are going to have to become rules to live by."[34] Upholding Tocqueville's "principle of interest rightly understood" requires us, in all our international economic undertakings, to discern and draw a line "in between" that fully respects the global reality expressed in Principle 4 of the Rio Declaration in 1992 – the inescapable and the increasingly undeniable economic reality that "to achieve sustainable development, environmental protection shall constitute an integral part of the development process and cannot be considered in isolation from it."[35] A reckoning with this new economic reality must happen simultaneously on a number of global fronts. Some of the reimagining of international economic law in furtherance of finding the right line "in between" for supporting sustainable global development must be in the economic rules themselves. Some of this reimagining, too, must be in how international economic rules relate to international environmental rules and to other international rules that affect trade and investment.

Many of our trade rules affect many of the global connections between economy and environment in which such a reimagining must occur. With each connection, this reimagining of trade law must necessarily draw the right line of policy space at different points somewhere "in between" national and international rule-making. And, with each connection, this reimagining must, wherever possible, enable the empowering of market forces for sustainable development. The first glimpses of how we must blend together the legal connections between economy and environment in this reimagining of trade law have already been seen in some of the first follow-ups to the Paris Agreement on climate change.

POST-PARIS PROGRESS

After Paris, the willing proceeded in earnest to implement and to supplement the Paris Agreement. Added urgency was imparted to their task in October 2016, when climate scientists at Mauna Loa, Hawaii, one of the world's leading "sentinel sites" for monitoring and measuring the amount of carbon dioxide in the atmosphere, announced that CO_2 levels had risen above 400 parts per million and were likely to remain above that elevated level "for the indefinite future."[36] Scientists have suggested that exceeding 400 parts per million makes it all the more difficult to keep global temperatures from rising above the goal of 2 degrees Celsius enshrined in the Paris Agreement – much less the much more ambitious goal envisaged by the willing in Paris of 1.5 degrees Celsius.[37]

By far the most encouraging sign was the groundswell of support from the private sector for the Paris Agreement. The willing engaged in businesses around the world did not even wait to leave Paris before setting forth on a series of bottom-up partnerships formed in furtherance of the Paris climate agreement and the Sustainable Development Goals. Among a great many others, there are regional and sectoral coalitions such as the African Renewable Energy Initiative to increase Africa's capacity for renewable energy, the Renewable Energy Buyers Alliance to build connections between corporate electricity demand and renewable energy supply, and the Partnership for Resilience and Preparedness to harness the data revolution to help local governments access the best available information to manage climate risks.[38]

Worldwide, there is the global climate project of the World Economic Forum, which includes an informal network of seventy-nine global CEOs.[39] There is the Carbon Pricing Leadership Coalition consisting of twenty-one governments and more than ninety global businesses and many global NGOs.[40] There is the global coalition on corporate sustainability led by CEO Paul Polman of Unilever, comprising 376 companies and 183 investors representing $7.9 trillion in revenue and $20.7 trillion in assets.[41] There is the task force on climate-related corporate financial risk disclosures established by Bank of England governor Mark Carney.[42] There is, in addition, the Breakthrough Energy Investment Fund, a $1 billion fund set up by Microsoft founder Bill Gates to fight climate change by investing in clean energy innovation that includes twenty other like-minded investors such as Jack Ma of Ali Baba, Jeff Bezos of Amazon, and former New York City mayor Michael Bloomberg of Bloomberg.[43] The three economic, environmental, and social pillars of sustainable development are the inspirational signposts for innovative public–private partnerships and projects of all kinds locally, regionally, and transnationally which are "unlocking the power of the grassroots efforts of citizens around the world" and are identifying new ideas and new approaches to bottom-up networks that can be shared with the whole world.[44]

In the meantime, the Paris Agreement entered into legal force more than three years ahead of schedule on November 4, 2016, a few weeks after the requisite fifty-five countries representing 55 percent of global emissions had ratified it.[45] Ratifications continued and, later in November 2016, in the midst of increasing populist successes worldwide in protest against the supposed excesses of globalization, COP-22 met in Marrakesh, Morocco, to begin writing the detailed rulebook for implementing the climate deal, and (it was hoped) to accelerate even more the pace of the agreement by ratcheting up the commitments made as part of the deal. The French environment minister, Segolene Royal, explained the process as follows, "The Paris Agreement represents the foundation ... Now we have to raise the walls, the roof of a common home."[46]

Deliberations on the Paris rulebook continued at COP-23 in Bonn in November 2017. Some progress was made there. Delegates debated a uniform format for their climate pledges and how countries should account for them.[47] They deliberated over how much flexibility developing countries should be accorded in fulfilling their transparency, reporting, and review obligations.[48] They discussed how to proceed with the cooperative approaches contemplated under the climate agreement through carbon markets – "internationally transferred mitigation outcomes."[49] They considered how reviews of implementation and compliance will work.[50] They came away with 266 pages of "informal notes" summarizing the various proposals from all the participating countries and a joint commitment to take part in a "Talanoa Dialog" proposed by the Fiji presidency of the COP to employ a Pacific tradition of consensus-building to inform the next round of national climate pledges due in 2020.[51] Yet "[m]ost of the hard decisions about what [the] rule book should look like were put off until 2018," the agreed deadline.[52] Meanwhile, "renewed clashes over perennial issues" reappeared to divide developed and developing countries.[53] Climate campaigners looked ahead to reconvening at COP-24 in Katowice, Poland, in December 2018, to conclude their work on the Paris rulebook.

The missing pages in the Paris rulebook are many. As was fully on display at COP-23, details and decisions are still much needed about how to enhance transparency in national climate actions; how to report, monitor, and verify the keeping of the voluntary national climate pledges; how to measure carbon emissions; how to count, collect, and provide climate finance; how to collaborate in cooperative approaches toward carbon pricing; how to address loss and damage in vulnerable countries; how to structure the "global stocktake"; and a whole lot more. Notably, there is still no agreement in the Paris rulebook on what is and is not a legitimate response measure taken to address climate change. What is more, the climate negotiators have barely grappled with the fact that there is nothing resembling a truly effective and enforceable system of dispute settlement. Deliberations continued throughout 2018 as negotiators set a deadline for completing the rules framework for the Paris Agreement by the conclusion of COP-24 at yearend 2018.

Meanwhile, post-Paris, others of the willing sought to supplement the climate agreement with other needed global actions to battle climate change. In the view of many of the willing, especially in the light of the fact that the national climate pledges under the Paris Agreement fell short of global ambitions, the logical next step was to do even more to curb global emissions by laboring on several climate negotiating fronts that had been omitted from the Paris Agreement. They aimed to prove on these other negotiating fronts that one of the positive influences of the Paris Agreement, "which itself lacks binding enforcement measures, could be its ability to promote and support the conclusion of other, possibly more binding agreements."[54]

Although carbon dioxide is by far the most significant of all the greenhouse gases, it is not the only one. Reducing global carbon dioxide emissions is absolutely essential to fighting climate change because carbon dioxide can linger in the atmosphere for more than five hundred years. But other climate pollutants with shorter life spans are to blame for at least 40 percent of all global warming.[55] These short-lived but highly potent heat-trapping pollutants include the dark soot particles known as "black carbon," methane, lower-atmosphere ozone, and a variety of manmade industrial gases – including the chemical coolants called hydrofluorocarbons (or HFCs).[56]

When scientists discovered a hole forming in the ozone layer over Antarctica in 1984, the world came together to conclude in 1987 the Montreal Protocol on Substances that Deplete the Ozone Layer, which phased out the manmade chemical coolants known as chlorofluorocarbons (CFCs) that were punching the hole in the ozone.[57] Several decades later, scientists have reported that the sizeable seasonal ozone hole over Antarctica is at last shrinking, although elimination of the hole in the ozone layer is not expected until the middle of the century. It is now "only" the size of India.[58] Some recent global researchers have concluded, however, that, while ozone in the upper stratosphere of the atmosphere farthest from the Earth's surface has indeed recovered, the ozone in the lower stratosphere nearest the Earth's surface has slowly, continuously dropped.[59] It may be thinning now over the Earth's most populated latitudes – cause to reexamine and strengthen the Montreal Protocol.[60]

Replacing CFCs as refrigerants in air conditioners and in refrigerators all over the world were HFCs. Unlike CFCs, HFCs do not destroy the ozone layer; but it turns out that, like CFCs, HFCs trap heat and thereby warm the atmosphere. HFCs remain in the atmosphere about fifteen years, only a fraction of the centuries-long persistence of carbon dioxide. Yet, while they remain, "HFCs cause a greenhouse effect between hundreds and thousands of times as powerful as carbon dioxide."[61] Driven especially by the flood of first purchases of air conditioners and refrigerators by the rising new middle classes in India, China, and other emerging economies, estimates are that the contribution of HFCs to greenhouse gas emissions could soar from the current 1 percent to between 9 and 19 percent by 2050.[62]

So it was certainly significant when more than 170 countries meeting in Kigali, Rwanda, in October 2016 concluded an amendment to the Montreal Protocol curbing the worldwide use of HFCs. Different countries in different circumstances are given different targets and timetables in the Kigali Amendment for freezing and then phasing out HFC production and consumption, ranging from 2018 to 2028. The accord includes, too, a financial commitment by the rich countries to help the poor countries pay for the transition to the greener but currently costlier replacement products under development.[63]

The announced goal of the willing had been to avert a full half degree Celsius (0.9 degrees Fahrenheit) of anticipated global warming with the HFC cuts made by the amendment.[64] Scientists reported afterwards that, due mainly to the compromises made at Kigali on the timetables for emissions freezes and cuts, the deal mandates emissions cuts of less than half of that.[65] The new hope now professed by the willing is that the gap in emissions cuts will be filled by – the market. New private investments will be essential to the innovation, production, and worldwide dissemination of new and cheaper refrigerants that will ensure the long-term success of the Kigali Amendment. In many respects, the likely extent and spread of those needed investments will depend on the availability of legal investment protections through effective international investment rules.

To help inspire these needed investments, the Kigali Amendment sends a *signal* to the marketplace. It is a regulatory signal and not a price signal; however, in this market sector, this regulatory signal can serve much the same purposes as a price signal by encouraging a shift by private producers to new, clean technologies, which is what happened previously with CFCs. As with the CFCs, helping the HFC deal along is the fact that this attempt at global regulation involves only one market sector. In contrast to the Paris climate agreement, the goal of the Kigali accord is not to transform the entirety of local economies but, rather, to alter only one sector. This makes the task easier politically; it also suggests that the HFC deal may be a model for transforming other economic sectors as part of the green transition.

Unlike the voluntary climate obligations in the Paris Agreement, the HFC obligations in the Kigali Amendment can be enforced by trade sanctions. Because the HFC agreement is an amendment to the Montreal Protocol, provisions in that protocol for trade sanctions against non-complying countries can be employed.[66] These trade sanctions are intended to be used only as a last resort.[67] So far, the issue of whether such environmentally motivated trade restrictions, when imposed by countries that are parties to the protocol, can be consistent with current WTO law, has yet to be raised in WTO dispute settlement. If the WTO ruling in the shrimp–turtle dispute is any indication, they can be. Most likely, the legal question would not be whether such restrictions are of a kind that could be eligible for an environmental exception to the WTO rules; it would be whether the particular sanctions in dispute had been "applied in a manner which would constitute arbitrary or unjustifiable discrimination."[68]

Like HFCs, international commercial aviation and ocean shipping emissions have been increasing as contributors to overall global emissions.[69] Over the objections of the willing, references to working with the relevant United Nations agencies to curb emissions from international aviation and shipping were deleted from the climate agreement. Thus, post-Paris, while some of the willing went to Kigali to conclude the deal phasing out HFCs, others went to Montreal to try to conclude a long-sought deal to curb international aviation emissions through an arm of the UN, the International Civil Aviation Organization (ICAO). Still others set out to put more pressure on another UN agency, the London-based International Maritime Organization (IMO), to reach a global deal to reduce international shipping emissions.

The potential of sectoral agreements for confronting climate change industry by industry was demonstrated in October 2016, when nearly 200 countries concluded a voluntary agreement by the ICAO in Montreal calling for "carbon neutral growth from 2020" in international aviation emissions, which account for about 2.5 percent of all global carbon emissions and are rapidly rising.[70] The new agreement – backed by the international aviation industry – puts into place a market-based approach that allows airlines to "offset" their emissions from individual flights by using alternative fuels and by reducing emissions elsewhere – outside the aviation industry. This offsetting could be through funding projects that cut carbon pollution in other sectors, including through solar power plants, wind farms, or forest conservation. Some of the willing suspect that the new ICAO deal does not go far enough to achieve carbon neutrality by 2020. Instead of a carbon-offsetting scheme, they would have preferred a tax or another form of carbon pricing.

Yet the mere conclusion of the global pact on international aviation emissions succeeded in putting added pressure on the IMO to conclude a similar agreement on international shipping emissions. Global shipping has a carbon footprint about the size of that of Germany – one that is growing rapidly.[71] Accounting now for about 3 percent of global carbon emissions, shipping emissions are projected by the IMO to rise by as much as 50 percent by 2050, depending on the pace of international trade and the nature of intervening actions.[72] Since 2013, the IMO has imposed mandatory fuel-efficiency regulations on international shipping.[73] These regulations were notable as the first binding global effort to reduce emissions from a single industrial sector. In addition, post-Paris, in London in October 2016, IMO negotiators capped the level of global sulfur in marine fuels, effective in January 2020.[74] Deep sea cargo ships are mostly powered by cheap blends of the residues left over from refining and distilling crude oil for aircraft jet fuel and automotive diesel fuel. These "bunker fuels," high in sulfur, produce toxic sulfur emissions that lead to acid rain and have severe implications for respiratory and heart health. Delaying the shift to low-sulfur fuels could have led to hundreds of thousands more premature deaths worldwide.[75]

Unfortunately, in that same IMO session in London, not even the sense of urgency for climate action inspired by the Paris Agreement could do much to inspire real progress toward reducing carbon emissions from global shipping. The International Transport Forum, an intergovernmental organization within the OECD, has recommended both a carbon tax on shipping and clear targets for cutting carbon emissions from shipping. Despite pressures from the willing, all that the IMO was able to muster post-Paris was an agreement to a mandatory data collection system on fuel oil consumption due to the perceived need to collect more data before taking any action.[76] Throughout 2017 and into 2018, the IMO continued to struggle to make progress on tackling carbon emissions – a task it has been pursuing with scant success for more than two decades.[77]

Compliance with these climate-related agreements will impose new conditions on the conduct of world trade, and could also lead to outright legal restrictions on world trade. The voluntary ICAO pact on international aviation emissions does not yet include an enforcement mechanism; nor is there any indication yet of what, if any, enforcement measures may be contemplated.[78] Enforcement of the international rules of the IMO that relate to ship pollution is allocated among flag, port, and coastal states. In recent years, these rules have been enforced increasingly by the use of the domestic laws of shipping states.[79] To date, neither of these sets of international rules has been addressed by WTO judges. The necessary reimagining of international trade law must include acceptance by the WTO of trade restrictions resulting from any international arrangements aimed at addressing climate change, protecting the environment, and otherwise attaining sustainable development.

After Paris, in addition to climate change, broader issues of sustainable development were considered in the implementation of the other Sustainable Development Goals. In addition to the multitude of multi-stakeholder networks working worldwide to reach the global goals by 2030, national governments are also working to fulfill the commitments they made in New York in 2015. In July 2017, forty-three countries submitted voluntary national reviews of their progress in moving from paper to practice at the UN High-Level Political Forum on Sustainable Development in New York. (The United States was not among them.) Most of these voluntary reviews addressed the full range of national efforts relating to all seventeen of the SDGs.[80]

Global progress was reported by the United Nations in 2017 toward achieving the global goals by 2030.[81] Poverty continued to decline.[82] More children were enrolled in school.[83] The maternal mortality rate continued to drop.[84] The percentage of child marriages declined.[85] And more. Yet an estimated 736 million people worldwide still lived below the line of extreme poverty.[86] About 793 million people still routinely faced hunger.[87] More than a third of girls suffered female genital mutilation in the thirty countries where that unspeakable practice is concentrated.[88] Twenty-nine percent of the people in the world did not have access to a safe drinking water service.[89] "Implementation has begun, but the clock is ticking," warned the new secretary-general of the United Nations, Antonio Guterres, who succeeded Ban Ki-Moon. "This report shows that the rate of progress in many areas is far slower than needed to meet the targets by 2030."[90]

POST-PARIS DISAPPOINTMENT

Despite the initial progress post-Paris on several climate fronts, there was also disappointment from what ought to have been the unlikeliest of places – the United States of America. In what amounted to an ultimate demand for policy space and a total rejection of Tocqueville's "principle of interest rightly understood," in June 2017, the new US president, having previously declared climate change a "hoax," announced that the United States would withdraw from the Paris Agreement.[91] The two lone holdouts in Paris, Nicaragua and Syria, have since joined the Paris Agreement. The aftermath of the latest US presidential decision leaves the

United States as a global climate pariah. "America First" has become America alone in refusing to take part in the global fight against climate change.

"Alternative facts" and the dangerous delusion of a Fortress America that will "Make America Great Again" stoked this US retreat from globalization and from global responsibility. The US decision was framed as a choice of economy over environment, implicitly expressing the view that the two are *not* one and the same. Under the previous president, the United States had pledged leading up to the Paris climate conference to cut its greenhouse gas emissions by 26 to 28 percent below 2005 levels by 2025. The Rhodium Group, an independent thinktank, predicts that, with the announcement of the US withdrawal from the Paris Agreement, US emissions will now decline 15 to 19 percent below 2005 levels by 2025 – significantly short of the US climate pledge made in 2015.[92]

The American climate pledge accounts for 21 percent of all the anticipated emissions cuts in the initial worldwide climate pledges. The immediate global response to the announced US withdrawal was concern that the US decision would increase the anticipated global shortfall in emissions cuts, encourage other countries to join the United States in disavowing or at least diminishing their own climate pledges, and, as a result, make achieving the 2C goal impossible. The World Meteorological Organization estimates that, in the worst case, the US withdrawal could add 0.3 degree Celsius (0.54 degrees Fahrenheit) to global temperatures by the end of the century.[93]

The US withdrawal was not to happen immediately. A country must wait three years from the date the agreement entered into legal force – November 4, 2016 – before formally seeking to leave,[94] and then wait one more year before withdrawing.[95] That would postpone the actual withdrawal until November 4, 2020 – the day following the next American presidential election. While awaiting these formalities, the new US administration disavowed the Nationally Determined Contribution promised by the previous administration; scaled up support for fossil fuels; scaled back support for clean energy; rolled back policies to reduce green-house gas emissions from coal-fired power plants, automobiles, and methane-emitting oil and gas wells; reneged on payment of the remaining $2 billion of the initial $3 billion promised by the United States for the Green Climate Fund to help poor countries deal with climate change; and generally proclaimed, "We are getting out."[96]

Having helped lead the rest of the world toward the successful conclusion of the Paris climate agreement, the United States now did a total aboutface and abandoned the ranks of the willing who are laboring worldwide to make the agreement a success. American leadership was transformed into American obstruction on climate change. After three straight years of declines, US carbon emissions were projected to rise by 1.8 percent in 2018.[97] Thus was it proven anew that the outcome of an election can make a difference, and that, despite what many think, not all politicians are alike.

In the wake of this presidential decision, many Americans quickly rallied to the climate cause. The governor of the State of New York announced a plan to invest $1.65 billion in renewable energy and energy efficiency.[98] The governor of the State of California set out to discuss linking California's carbon market with the national carbon market in the making in China.[99] Former New York mayor Michael Bloomberg announced that a coalition of US states, cities, and businesses would keep the US climate pledge through their own actions, despite the presidential decision.[100] One unintended consequence of the US decision was the seeming opening of new opportunities for "non-state political actors" to participate in the implementing and, conceivably, the making of international law.

Polls at the time showed that a large majority of Americans supported the Paris accord,[101] and the many Americans among the willing pledged to press on, voicing the shared hope that a combination of market forces and non-federal and non-governmental climate actions would keep the United States proceeding along the green path to decarbonization. Independent of any governmental action, market forces have already driven declining emissions in the United States due to a great extent to the shift from coal to natural gas made possible by technological innovations in the energy industry. Natural gas is cheaper than coal and emits about half the CO_2 of coal.[102] Because of this switch from coal to natural gas, greater energy efficiency throughout the US economy, and slower US growth in recent years, energy-related carbon dioxide emissions fell in 2016 to the lowest level since 1992.[103]

In addition, independent of any federal governmental action, many states and cities have been actively engaged for some time in furthering the green transition from the bottom up. Most US states have promised to continue to work to cut emissions even with the announcement of the intent of the federal government to withdraw from the climate agreement. Twenty states and the District of Columbia have adopted their own greenhouse gas emissions targets, some going beyond the US climate pledge.[104] In many places, American cities are doing more than American states to address climate change. Immediately after the withdrawal announcement, 197 US mayors – representing 52 million people – vowed to uphold the climate agreement goals and increase their efforts to cut their greenhouse gas emissions.[105]

Outside the United States, other countries likewise vowed, in the first days following the US decision, to press on with the Paris accord. As some of them noted, a study by the Grantham Research Institute had concluded that the mere existence of the Paris pact had already prodded dozens of countries to enact new clean-energy laws.[106] In the absence of climate leadership by the United States, more of the global burden of leadership fell on the European Union, long in the forefront in facing the realities of climate change. The EU has pledged to cut its emissions 40 percent below 1990 levels by 2030. New voices were heard as well from some new places, such as Fiji, a Pacific island assailed by rising seas, whose prime minister, Josaia Voreqe Bainimarama, reminded us that, in facing climate change, we are all "in the same canoe."[107]

Even before the US withdrawal, there were increasing worries that the global climate canoe was leaking. The European Union is on track to fall significantly short of its goal of cutting emissions 40 percent below 1990 levels by 2030. Germany has struggled with its promised energy transition – its *Energiewende* – aimed at generating 80 percent of its energy from renewable sources by 2050. German emissions rose slightly in 2015 and 2016. Deforestation has nearly doubled in Brazil since the record low in 2012, when Brazil hosted Rio+20. Indonesia, Turkey, and other developing countries are planning new coal-fired power plants to meet growing demands for electricity. Countries that need to add to their climate promises are having a hard time keeping those they have already made.[108]

Against this backdrop, the willing, in search of new climate leadership, turned hopeful eyes to the leaders of China and India. China and India are both on track to overachieve on the targets they set for themselves for limiting their rising greenhouse gas emissions by 2030 in their Nationally Determined Contributions – which could offset to some extent any decline in the US contribution due to the US withdrawal from the climate agreement.[109] Chinese emissions appear to have peaked ten years sooner than the Chinese government promised they would (and "without recourse to statistical sleight of hand"),[110] and India is expected to get 40 percent of its electricity from non-fossil-fuel sources eight years ahead of schedule, by 2022. On top of these advances, China is investing more in green technology than any other country, promising to spend an additional $360 billion by 2030 and to have 7 million electric vehicles on Chinese roads by 2025. At the same time, China and India alike are, despite rapidly rising local energy demands, trying to hold off on the construction of new coal-fired power plants.[111] The Indian government has said that, in another ten years, it may not need any more coal plants, and that, furthermore, by 2030, it hopes to be selling only electric cars.[112] Meanwhile, China is busy building the world's biggest carbon market.[113] Having already experimented with regional markets, China has begun to establish a national carbon market.[114]

Even so, in China, more than 30 million people still live in caves – six times more than lived in caves worldwide during the Stone Age,[115] and, in India, 240 million people still do not have electricity.[116] Although China and India have both made unprecedented economic progress in the past several decades, and hundreds of millions of Chinese and Indians are no longer mired in poverty, both China and India are called "emerging" economies because, in many respects, the two countries are still emerging gradually from centuries of poverty and inwardness. They are both under enormous internal pressures to continue to produce significant growth, and – in the near term – the easiest way to produce growth is to keep pumping out carbon dioxide emissions from coal and from other fossil fuels. Despite these internal pressures, and in part because of competing domestic pressures to reduce air and other forms of pollution, China and India have become two of the global leaders in climate cooperation and in the transition to a low-carbon green economy.

All the same, it is uncertain whether China or India, or, for that matter, any other country, can fill the hole left in the climate framework by the climate flight of the United States.[117] If the United States does not continue to help lead the world in climate action, and if the void in global leadership created by the US withdrawal persists, meeting the goals of the Paris Agreement will be much harder and maybe even impossible.[118] One worry is that, despite their initial vows that they will press on toward higher climate ambitions, the other large emitters will soon back off from such grand ambitions without the example and the presence of the United States and without constant pressure from the United States, in concert with Europe and others, to do more. With their distrust of international cooperation, the anti-globalists in the wealthier countries are helping to facilitate just such a retreat.

Another worry is that, with the US refusal to continue to provide poorer countries with the money they need to address climate change, the flow of global monies to one of the main tools for attaining the Paris goals for climate finance – the Seoul-based Green Climate Fund – will dry up. As of mid 2017, the Green Climate Fund had approved total loans and grants worth only $2.2 billion – and only a paltry $13 million of that sum had been released. The rest was still in the bank.[119] The US reversal on the financial commitments it made in Copenhagen and reaffirmed in Paris could lead other developed countries to back off on their own financial pledges, and could lead many developing countries to back off on the climate actions they have promised on the condition that they get financial help in making needed adjustments to climate change. One estimate is that the abandonment of all the conditional pledges made by developing countries in their voluntary national commitments under the Paris Agreement could result in an increase in annual global emissions of between 1.0 and 2.7 billion tons of carbon dioxide by 2030.[120]

In the hearts of the willing in the world survives and persists the hope that the United States will not, in the end, withdraw from the Paris Agreement, and that, if it does withdraw, it will soon recant its irrational retreat into "economic nationalism," return to its rightful place at the global table, and rejoin the other nations of the world in the urgent necessity of cooperative action on climate change. The most visible contribution of the United States government to COP-23 near yearend 2017 was staging a much-ridiculed side event to promote the use of fossil fuels. Yet, for the most part, the career diplomats who comprised most of the shrunken US delegation worked quietly and constructively on the technical tasks of completing the Paris rulebook.[121] What is more, on the sidelines of the international climate conference, a large number of willing Americans – Congressional, state, city, business, and NGO leaders as well as an assortment of other engaged American citizens – staged dozens of events under the shared banner of "We're Still In."[122] The hope that the United States would soon return to a leadership role endured; but no one was willing to wait for the Americans.

The door will remain open legally to the return of the United States. Any time after its withdrawal takes effect, the United States can change its mind, submit a

notice to the United Nations, and, within thirty days, become once again a party to
the Paris Agreement and submit a new climate pledge.[123] In the meantime, it can be
asked: What will happen if the United States does not report on its climate actions as
required every two years by the Paris Agreement, or does not show up to participate
in the required reviews of its progress toward keeping its climate pledge? Would this
violate the Paris Agreement, and, if so, what would the recourse be, if any, of other
countries under international law? Could other countries impose carbon tariffs or
other carbon trade restrictions to punish the United States as a climate pariah? In the
absence of a climate dispute settlement system, these questions are trade questions
that would be answered by the WTO.

On Food, Forests, Oceans, and Fisheries

All-pervasive as it is, climate change does not by any means comprise the entirety of the environmental dimensions of sustainable development. As the scientists said succinctly in the Report of the Millennium Ecosystem Assessment, "virtually all of Earth's ecosystems have now been significantly transformed through human actions."[1] That was in 2005. The natural resources on which we depend for all else are threatened more and more by the ever-increasing and ever-intensifying burdens imposed by the heedlessness of humanity in interacting with the Earth's ecosystems. These threats are linked. Yet, though they are linked, there is, with each of them, a singular set of climate and sustainability concerns that cannot be resolved without a reimagining of international trade and investment law to unite the economy and the environment in a mutually supportive and enabling framework of international rules. In response to these threats, the members of the WTO in particular must engage in a shared search for just the right line "in between" to ensure just the right balance between the right amount of local policy space and the right amount of international commercial space for freer trade needed to forestall climate change and to secure sustainable development.

FOOD SECURITY AND SUSTAINABLE AGRICULTURE

Like aviation and shipping, agriculture was not addressed specifically in the Paris Agreement on climate change. The word "agriculture" does not appear in the text of the treaty. The silence on this major global economic and environmental issue was due in no small part to the shared concern long voiced by many developing countries that their struggles to feed their ever-growing numbers of people could be hindered if they agreed to limits on their greenhouse gas emissions from agriculture. Goal 2 of the Sustainable Development Goals is to "[e]nd hunger, achieve food security and improved food nutrition and promote sustainable agriculture."[2] The first target under this goal is to, "[b]y 2030, end hunger and ensure access by all people, in particular the poor and people in vulnerable situations, including infants, to safe, nutritious and sufficient food all year round."[3] In one manifestation of the fear of change, many in the developing countries fear they will be left hungry if they try to reduce the greenhouse gas emissions from food production.

Thus, the Paris Agreement refers only indirectly to agriculture, and, understandably, it does so mainly in terms of making certain that people have enough to eat. The policy space envisaged for agriculture in the Paris Agreement is a space for ensuring "food security." The non-binding statements accompanying the climate agreement recognize "the fundamental priority of safeguarding food security and ending hunger, and the particular vulnerabilities of food production systems to the adverse effects of climate change."[4] The binding part of the Paris Agreement states that boosting the world's ability to adapt to those impacts and to foster climate-resilient and low-emissions development should be done "in a manner that does not threaten food production."[5]

Despite the silence on the role of agriculture in the text of the Paris treaty, in their national climate pledges pursuant to the global climate treaty, "[m]ore than 90 percent of countries include the agriculture sectors in their mitigation and/or adaptation contributions."[6] The actual details remain vague. For example, only one country – Rwanda – has included plans to address food waste, which accounts for 8 percent of global GHG emissions.[7] Yet the inclusion of agriculture in these national pledges is unavoidable. "Taken together, agriculture, forestry and land-use change account for about one-fifth of global GHG emissions."[8] Agriculture alone accounts for about 10 percent of global greenhouse gas emissions, and about 50 percent of non-CO_2 global greenhouse gas emissions.[9] "A preliminary reduction target for non-CO_2 emissions mitigation in agriculture compatible with a 2 [degrees] C pathway ... would effectively cap agriculture emissions at just above today's levels. A target compatible with 1.5 [degrees] C would be even more stringent."[10]

All told, agriculture has about the same impact on the planet as energy, and almost every one of the planetary boundaries identified by scientists relates to agriculture.[11] Agriculture has been described as "the most important driver of environmental harms" to the planet caused by runoffs and emissions from nitrogen-based fertilizers, habitat destruction, and greenhouse gas emissions.[12] About half of all the carbon dioxide and other greenhouse gas emissions that originate from agriculture result from cultivation, and about half result from deforestation.

What is more, agriculture is not only causing climate change; it is also threatened by climate change, which is a significant threat to food security. One of the willing, Shenggen Fan, the director general of the respected International Food Policy Research Institute, warns us that, "Climate change is modifying the environment in which agriculture operates by bringing about changes in temperature, precipitation, and weather volatility. It is already having significant negative impacts on crop yields and is expected to decrease yields even more in the coming decades, just as the world requires higher yields to meet future food needs."[13] As he sums up the current state of our global food supply system, "in a context of scarce natural resources and advancing climate change, it is not environmentally sustainable."[14]

According to the United Nations Food and Agricultural Organization (FAO), "Global food demand in 2050 is projected to increase by at least 60 percent above 2006 levels, driven by population and income growth, as well as rapid urbanization ... Without adaptation to climate change, it will not be possible to achieve food security for all and eradicate hunger, malnutrition and poverty."[15] To close the looming gap between the number of people we will have on the planet and the amount of food we will have to feed them, we must transition to sustainable agriculture. A new "Green Revolution" sufficient for the twenty-first century must feed a hungry world *while also diminishing greenhouse gas emissions*. Throughout the world, we must "find new food systems, adapted to local ecological conditions and causing much less ecological damage."[16] In making the willing world, we must embrace a "climate-smart" agriculture that can feed us today and can also sustain the capacity of the planet to keep feeding us for many tomorrows.

All this has profound implications for the fulfillment of the Sustainable Development Goals. In contrast to the Paris climate agreement, agriculture is front and center in the SDGs. In addition to ending hunger by 2030, other decidedly ambitious targets under Goal 2 of the SDGs are to "end all forms of malnutrition";[17] double the agricultural productivity and incomes of small-scale food producers;[18] ensure sustainable agricultural practices that strengthen capacity to adapt to climate change;[19] and maintain genetic diversity in agriculture, all by 2030.[20] Looking beyond this one global goal, more than half of the seventeen agreed global goals for 2030 relate to global food security and nutrition, including the global goals that relate to poverty, gender equality, water and sanitation, responsible production and consumption, and climate change.

On top of all the other food-related targets scattered throughout the SDGs, there is this additional target under Goal 2: "*to correct and prevent trade restrictions and distortions in world agricultural markets*."[21] Underscored there is the need to do so "including through the parallel elimination of all forms of agricultural export subsidies and all export measures with equivalent effect."[22] These are seen as among the essential means of achieving the global goal of ending hunger.[23] In this ambitious global target, the Sustainable Development Goals echo and emphasize a long-sought goal of the world trading system.

As agricultural economist David Blandford explains, "International trade can make a positive contribution to addressing the challenges posed by climate change for the world's food system. Trade can help to provide a buffer against short-term disruption in supplies caused by extreme weather events, such as droughts or floods, which are likely to be more prevalent as global temperatures rise. Through the exploitation of comparative advantage, trade can help to achieve needed structural shifts in world agricultural output as the climate changes. While it may be difficult to reduce total GHG emissions in the face of substantial increases in the demand for food and agriculture raw materials, there is considerable scope for reducing the volume of emissions per unit of agricultural output. Free trade can contribute to this outcome."[24]

Distortions in trade caused by agricultural subsidies raise the costs of food, with particular effect on the poor, and enable land, water, and energy to be used in ways that are less than efficient and are ecologically unsound. These subsidies also often fall most heavily on developing countries, and keep them from enjoying to the extent that they should what ought to be the benefits of their comparative advantage in much agricultural trade. Agricultural subsidies have the same pernicious and protectionist effects on agricultural markets as other governmental subsidies have on other markets. By distorting the global marketplace, agricultural subsidies also distort the search for global climate solutions.

One recent climate study concluded that the Middle East, Africa, and South Asia regions could theoretically reduce climate-related damages to agriculture by half through more liberalized food markets, and could also reduce the costs of food globally.[25] Blandford says, "At the broadest level, an open trading system is perhaps the best guarantee for promoting adaptation and dealing with severe disruptions to economic activity as a result of climate change. As different regions face higher or lower temperatures, rainfall and other climatic changes, trade will allow patterns of production to change over time and will also compensate for local supply disruptions. If droughts and floods are more common, assistance flowing through established trade channels will be more quickly available."[26]

As it is, global protectionism in agriculture far exceeds the protectionism remaining in manufacturing. The agriculture agreement concluded in the Uruguay Round of trade negotiations that established the WTO made something of a start toward freer and less distorted agricultural trade; but, in the more than two decades since, little more has been done to impose additional WTO disciplines on trade-distorting agricultural subsidies. In Nairobi in late 2015, the members of the WTO agreed to end all agricultural *export* subsidies – a significant accomplishment long years in the making and one of the targets of the SDGs.[27] Despite this progress in Nairobi, there was no further progress in Buenos Aires two years later, and nothing has yet been achieved on the principal agricultural item on the WTO agenda: imposing new disciplines on the market distortions of domestic agricultural subsidies. In the meantime, and in many places, these agricultural subsidies continue to increase.

According to the FAO, "In 2015, developed and major developing countries spent more than $560 billion on agricultural production support, including subsidies on inputs and direct payments to farmers."[28] Traditionally, these subsidies have been granted mostly by such major economic powers as Japan, Canada, the European Union, and the United States; but developing countries are now spending more on agricultural support than are developed countries.[29] With agricultural markets extending worldwide, and with so many countries engaged in granting subsidies, the endlessly complicated issue of trade-distorting agricultural subsidies is one trade issue that demands a global solution by the WTO. It cannot be dealt with piecemeal in regional arrangements. It cannot be dealt with bilaterally in deals between just two countries. No one country will be willing to surrender its agricultural subsidies unless all countries do.

In the required reimagining of WTO trade law, sustainability must be central to the global agricultural solution, and therefore must be central to new disciplines on agricultural subsidies. The WTO rules on agriculture already include some limited provisions making allowances for local support through "clearly defined" environmental and conservation programs so long as "they have no, or at most minimal, trade-distorting effects or effects on production."[30] The WTO should build on these rules by blending economy and environment into one in food trade. As part of the global agricultural solution, the members of the WTO should follow the recommendation of the FAO to align trade with sustainability by making the granting of agricultural support by members of the WTO *conditional* upon adoption by local producers of practices that "lower emissions and conserve natural resources."[31] According to the OECD, nearly half of all the agricultural subsidies provided as farm support by the governments of the OECD countries are "potentially the most harmful type of support for the environment" because they create greater demand for chemical fertilizers and fossil fuels and thus lead to more greenhouse gas emissions.[32] This environmental impact should be kept much in mind not only in reimagining trade rules for sustainable development, but also in framing any potential legal claims against trade-distorting agricultural subsidies in WTO dispute settlement. Agricultural dispute settlement in the WTO should not be only about traditional economics; increasingly, it should also be about the new economics of sustainability.

Apart from trade, yet another way to help ensure food security by reducing the growing demands on food production – and thus the pressures for engaging in unsustainable agricultural practices – is to reduce food waste. More than a third of the food we produce – about 1.3 billion tons each year – is not consumed. It is wasted.[33] According to the FAO, if food waste were a country, it would be the world's third-largest greenhouse gas emitter. Food waste and its carbon footprint are likely to increase substantially – if there are no changes.[34]

Developed countries waste much more food per capita than developing countries "partly because in industrialised nations more waste occurs later in the supply chain – at the retail and consumer level – while in developing countries most waste occurs on-farm and during distribution."[35] Perhaps a third of household food waste may be linked to date labels on food products because of consumers confusing the meanings of "use by" and "best before" and discarding food while it is still safe to eat.[36] In addition simply to improving wasteful habits, developed countries should consider "how to alter food labelling requirements to reduce waste while ensuring consumer safety."[37] Meantime, in developing countries, "more efficient storage and distribution systems are needed to reduce on-farm and post-harvest losses."[38] These and other needed innovations could help meet the global target in the SDGs of cutting food waste per capita by 2030.[39]

At COP-23 in Bonn in November 2017, climate negotiators remedied the omission of agriculture from the Paris Agreement by launching a work program on climate and agriculture.[40] About 90 percent of the national climate pledges pertain to agriculture in some way.[41] A whole host of issues relating to sustainable agriculture are to be addressed, ranging from adaptation to resilience to improved water management and to much more.[42] Potentially, one issue that could prove pivotal to securing sustainable agriculture is the relocation of production to more sustainable locales through the freeing of agricultural trade.[43]

ENDANGERED LANDS AND SHRINKING FORESTS

How we make the transition to sustainable agriculture is only one aspect of how we must ensure overall sustainable land use as part of the green transition. There are about 130 million square kilometers of land on the Earth, covering about 28 percent of the Earth's surface.[44] Instilling and following sustainable practices of land use management could contribute much to combating climate change while also providing the increased agricultural productivity that will be necessary globally to meet growing food demands and ensure food security.[45] Promotion of resourceful and far-sighted land use worldwide through the "sustainable use of terrestrial ecosystems" is Goal 15 of the Sustainable Development Goals.[46] One of the most ambitious of the 169 targets of the SDGs is one under this goal: "By 2020, ensure the conservation, restoration and sustainable use of terrestrial and inland freshwater ecosystems and their services, in particular forests, wetlands, mountains and drylands, in line with obliga-tions under international agreements."[47] Our international trade and investment rules must both accommodate and help facilitate the fulfillment of this goal.

Agriculture accounts for about 40 percent of the Earth's land. Forests – ecosystems dominated by trees – account for about 30 percent.[48] Although the pace of forest loss has been cut in half during the past quarter of a century because of the diligent work of the willing, the annual loss of forests due to market and governance failures is still "equivalent in area to Greece."[49] The annual emissions from this forest loss add up to "more than the emissions produced from all the cars, buses, trains, and airplanes in the world."[50] Preserving and restoring the Earth's forests is therefore central to sustainable land use, especially in low-income countries, which are experiencing the largest net losses of forests.[51] Thus, another bold target of Goal 15 is to, "By 2020, promote the implementation of sustainable management of all types of forests, halt deforestation, restore degraded forests and substantially increase afforestation and reforestation globally."[52]

The sustainable use of forests is also a central aim of the Paris climate agree-ment.[53] Forests are natural "sinks" for carbon and, thus, natural defenses against climate change. Forests soak up carbon and store it in trees. About half of the dry weight of a tree consists of stored carbon. Conversely, deforestation causes climate change. The stored carbon in trees is released into the air and adds to the cumulative amount of carbon dioxide in the atmosphere. The destruction of much of the world's native forests by the relentless march of human agriculture and of human industrialization has been a major factor in causing climate change.[54] Our international economic rules must be reimagined to help us accomplish these aims.

Foreshadowed by the conservation writings of Henry David Thoreau, George Perkins Marsh, and John Muir, forest preservation emerged during the last few decades of the twentieth century as a key part of global sustainable development. Intermittent international efforts to negotiate a global forest convention have so far failed;[55] however, various international forest arrangements have been agreed that, increasingly, add up to what is often called "the international forest regime."[56]

One of these arrangements is the International Tropical Timber Agreement of 1983, which binds more than sixty countries.[57] This arrangement has evolved over time from a predominantly commercial agreement to one that allows for at least some modicum of "rhetorical" support for forest conservation and preservation,[58] although, in the ecological eyes of at least some of the willing, it remains mostly a means "to provide trade in tropical timber between the producing and consuming members," with forest protection only a "secondary" objective.[59]

At the Earth Summit of the United Nations in Rio in 1992, a concerted effort to address forest sustainability by launching negotiations on a global forest convention fell short. Despite this setback, the outlines of what would eventually become a global forest consensus were nevertheless agreed in Rio in the form of an aspirational list of "non-legally binding" Forest Principles,[60] including "the need for sustainable forest management"[61] and "the need to balance trade in forest products and forest conservation."[62] On this foundation, the willing have moved forward since then in search of legally binding forest rules. On climate change, their main focus has been on the development of an agreed international "mechanism" on the Reductions of Emissions from Deforestation and Forest Degradation, commonly known as REDD until it was renamed REDD+ when its priorities were expanded to include conservation, sustainable forest management, and enhancement of forest carbon stocks.[63] One of the notable successes at the Paris climate summit in 2015 was the inclusion of the REDD+ mechanism in the Paris climate agreement. The parties decided in the climate agreement that they "should take action to conserve and enhance, as appropriate, sinks and reservoirs of greenhouse gases ... including forests."[64] To "implement and support" this forest ambition, the Paris Agreement made specific reference to "the existing framework ... for... activities relating to reducing emissions from deforestation and forest degradation."[65]

Equally noteworthy is another forest agreement concluded in the run-up to the global agreement on climate change and the adoption of the Sustainable Development Goals. In September 2014, a large group of national governments, subnational governments, companies, indigenous groups, and NGOs came together at the United Nations in a classic example of the bottom-up in action to sign and announce the New York Declaration on Forests. They endorsed ten goals. The first and foremost is to "at least halve the rate of loss of natural forests globally by 2020 and strive to end forest loss by 2030."[66] The governmental and non-state political actors that joined in endorsing the New York Declaration on Forests are now all working to implement the forest aims of the Paris Agreement and the SDGs. At the top of their list is obtaining sufficient forest finance as one component of the billions of dollars needed, all told, for funding climate finance and the estimated trillions of dollars needed, all told, for fulfilling the SDGs. An annual investment of $40 billion is required to halve global deforestation by 2030; much more will be required – and much sooner – to halt deforestation by 2020 as envisaged in the SDGs.[67] Most of this needed money for financing forest preservation must come from more private investment, including a lot more foreign direct investment. This money must be found and invested against a backdrop where – despite all they have promised to do to stop deforestation – some developed and developing countries alike are breaking their promises. In Poland, the government tripled the logging quota in Bialowieza Forest, one of Europe's last primeval forests and a UNESCO World Heritage Site.[68] In the Democratic Republic of Congo, the government broke a moratorium by approving logging concessions for two Chinese companies in 6,500 square kilometers – 2,510 square miles – of the world's second-largest rainforest, in the Congo basin.[69] The Polish forest is home to the world's largest herd of European bison. The Congo forest is home to rare species of forest elephants and dwarf chimpanzees.

International trade can either help or hinder in forest preservation as a part of shaping and sharing in a sustainable global prosperity. Trade can help the prevention of global forest loss if increased trade occurs in a context of efficient forest use management within an enabling framework of WTO and other trade rules that are reimagined to offset and internalize what would otherwise be the costs of environmental harms to forests. Trade can, however, hinder the halt of forest loss if it occurs in a context of governance failure and market failure. Trade that is a part of simply felling forests without thought for future consequences is not sustainable trade.

A telling example is agricultural subsidies, which, by distorting price signals, also distort and misallocate the uses of land. Reimagined WTO rules that cut high agricultural tariffs and halted the flow of the billions of dollars currently spent worldwide on market-distorting and environmentally damaging farm subsidies would not only enhance agricultural sustainability. Those reimagined trade rules would, in addition, help protect forests by "enabling production to be located in areas where resources can be used most efficiently."[70] According to the OECD, "Reducing tariffs as well as subsidies on agricultural products could optimize land use and reduce the overall demand for land, reducing pressure on forested areas."[71] Crops could then be *grown* in those places in the world where arable land and clean water are most bountiful, where there is indeed a natural comparative advantage, and *traded* to those places where food is most needed. With such trade reforms, we would no longer, in effect, be encouraging countries hungry for food and prosperity to rely more and more on stripping and cultivating their forests and their other endangered lands to feed their people.[72]

Because of the direct connection between forest loss and climate change, forest protection should be a part of the WTO climate waiver. In that waiver, WTO rules on governmental purchases should be revised to mandate buying commodities and other goods that have not been produced by deforestation.[73] Worldwide, public procurement affects somewhere between 3 and 20 percent of total timber consumption, depending on the country and the market.[74] The waiver should also specify that WTO rules will uphold local restrictions on the import of wood and other forest products that have been harvested illegally in their country of origin and then traded internationally – such as those in the Lacey Act in the United States and in the similar European Union Timber Regulation.[75] Furthermore, and importantly, the waiver should be broad enough to allow, as noted forest advocate Nigel Purvis has recommended, "banning the importation of commodities grown on lands that were deforested illegally – not just wood and wood products harvested illegally."[76]

What is more, as yet another instance of reimagining WTO rules to enhance sustainability, trade rules should be *interpreted* by the WTO to support the imposition of these existing and potentially extended forest trade restrictions. In addition, global trade rules should support international efforts to use regional trade arrangements to provide more forest protections – such as those in the forest annex to the free trade agreement between the United States and Peru.[77] Where regional arrangements are used as proving grounds for novel approaches to ensuring sustainable forest use management, those arrangements should be seen as consistent with WTO obligations – even if they involve restrictions on trade.

The affirmative participation of the private sector will be essential in all our endeavors to shift agricultural expansion away from forest-clearing and toward the underutilized and degraded lands suitable for agricultural production, to increase the supply of traded commodities free of deforestation, and to ensure more transparency and more traceability in supply chains free of deforestation.[78] WTO rules already permit governmental environmental and other labeling requirements "as they apply to a product, process or production method," so long as they are non-discriminatory and do not create "unnecessary obstacles to international trade."[79] The members of the WTO should affirm anew as part of the climate waiver that private and voluntary non-governmental standards addressing climate change do not fall within the scope of the disciplines of the WTO treaty.[80] These private standards would include the certification schemes involving businesses that have been established with the help of the willing to diminish forest loss.[81]

Furthermore, and even though they often involve national and subnational governments, the lending, financing, regulatory, enforcement, and other collaborative undertakings of the rising bottom-up of innovative and enabling networks of governments, businesses, academics, and NGOs in search of sustainability – such as the forest works of the Tropical Forest Alliance 2020 hosted by the World Economic Forum – should be affirmed by the members of the WTO as beyond the reach of the WTO rules.[82] These collaborations are expressions of the "global partnership for sustainable development" envisaged by Goal 17 of the Sustainable Development Goals.[83]

SAVING A SUSTAINABLE OCEAN

The vast majority of the Earth is covered not by land but by water. The ocean covers more than 70 percent of the Earth's surface.[84] Humanity's dependence on the ocean can hardly be overstated. Every year we derive $2.5 trillion in economic value from the ocean – 5 percent of the world's GDP. The ocean is also "the world's biggest employer, directly supporting the livelihoods of more than three billion people."[85] Over and above its vast economic value, the ocean – as some of the willing remind us – has a value to us that "goes far beyond economics. It provides half the air we breathe, governs our weather, and helps to support peace and prosperity. The ocean's future is the world's future."[86]

The ocean is ground zero for climate change. As human actions continue to add more greenhouse gas emissions to those accumulating in the Earth's atmosphere, almost all the extra carbon dioxide in the air is absorbed by and dissolved in the ocean, moderating what would otherwise have been the atmospheric warming and other climate changes experienced above the water. As a result, CO_2 levels have increased significantly more in the ocean than on land. About one-third of the carbon dioxide produced by human activities and more than 90 percent of the extra heat trapped by greenhouse gases in the atmosphere ends up in the ocean.[87] Pulling this heat from the air, the ocean has warmed by 1 degree Celsius in the past century, with consequences most of us are just now starting to notice. One consequence we have largely overlooked is this: Ocean warming has – so far – shielded us from suffering on land the worst of our own emission excesses.[88]

For the ocean, shielding humanity from even greater impacts from climate change has come at a high price. The International Union for Conservation of Nature and Natural Resources (IUCN) – a global group of scientists from dozens of countries – reports, "Sea surface temperature, ocean heat content, sea-level rise, melting of glaciers and ice sheets, CO_2 emissions and atmospheric concentrations are increasing at an alarming rate with significant consequences for humanity and the marine species and ecosystems of the oceans."[89] The IUCN also warns us that it is uncertain how much longer the ocean can shield the world "from even more rapid changes in climate."[90] In the ocean, climate change is causing a "cocktail of negative effects which we are only just starting to understand," with ultimate consequences for the ocean and for us that cannot yet be foreseen.[91] In many places, lower oxygen levels have created "dead zones" where marine life cannot breathe. These dead zones have approximately doubled every decade since the 1960s, mostly in close proximity to major watersheds and human population.[92]

Another of these effects is the relentlessly rising sea, which is creeping up on vulnerable island states and coastal and low-lying areas all over the world. Warming the water in the ocean makes it expand. Warmer ocean water along with melting polar ice has been causing the sea level to rise by about 3 millimeters per year – about 1.2 inches per decade – since the earliest satellite measurements in 1992.[93] Now the rate of global sea level rise is getting faster.[94] A recent study concluded that between 147 million and 216 million people – more than a quarter of them in China – "live on land that will be below sea level or regular flood levels by the end of the century."[95] Just a small loss of oxygen in coastal waters can cause a complete change in ecosystems.

As WWF International summarizes, "Coastal systems and low-lying areas are ... experiencing adverse impacts from sea level rise – submergence, coastal flooding, and coastal erosion. The loss of coastal ecosystems such as mangroves and seagrass beds increases the vulnerability of coastlines and people to the impacts of climate change." Adding to these coastal losses is fertilizer runoff from farms and residential lawns, which causes eutrophication – "the flourishing of algal blooms that deplete the water's dissolved oxygen and suffocate marine life."[96] This creates more dead zones – as seen, for instance, in the waters of the Indian River Lagoon on the eastern coast of Florida, long home to more than 10,000 species of animal and plants, and the most biodiverse lagoon system in the Northern Hemisphere.[97]

Climate change is also changing the ocean's chemistry. Increasing absorption of carbon dioxide increases the acidity of ocean water – which threatens the survival of all kinds of marine life. One scientific study by 540 analysts from 37 countries concluded that, at the current pace, the seas could become more than 170 percent more acidic than the pre-industrial level by 2100.[98] This would make the pH level – the acid level – of seawater slightly less than that of soap.[99] Methane is one of the most potent of greenhouse gases. Although methane does not linger nearly as long as carbon dioxide in the atmosphere, it is much more efficient than CO_2 at trapping heat and has a comparative impact more than 25 times greater than that of CO_2 over a century. About 2.5 billion tons of frozen methane hydrate are stored in the sea floor. The ocean scientists of IUCN are concerned that "[i]ncreasing water temperature could release this source of carbon into the ocean and ultimately into the atmosphere," with unforeseeable climate consequences.[100]

To the extent that there has been a global focus on the impact of the warming of the oceans, much of that focus has been on the bleaching of the world's coral reefs, which support about a quarter of all marine species and have lost more than half of their reef-building corals in the past thirty years. "Three quarters of the world's coral reefs are currently threatened,"[101] and scientists tell us that almost all coral reefs could vanish by 2050.[102] "[P]opulation sizes of mammals, birds, reptiles, amphibians and fish [in the ocean have fallen] by half on average in just 40 years."[103]

This decline in the amount of life in the ocean is getting ever steeper over time not only due to climate change, but due also to all the other increasing intrusions of humanity on the ocean. High levels of manmade toxins have been found even in tiny crustaceans in the ocean's deepest depths.[104]

These losses cannot be reduced merely to economic calculations. But, in economic terms alone, in addition to the major contribution to jobs and GDP provided annually by the ocean, the total value of the ocean's underpinning assets has been estimated as at least $24 trillion.[105] "More than two-thirds of this value relies on healthy oceans."[106] Without additional cooperative international actions, the cost of harm to the ocean will increase by an additional $22 billion by 2050 – *annually*.[107] Moreover, without immediate and concerted action through more international cooperation, the changes to the ocean may be irreversible. The ocean is dying. If the ocean dies, we will die. Achieving all our other global goals for forestalling climate change and fostering overall sustainable development will be impossible if we do not save the ocean.

Given this threat, it is surprising that the plight of the ocean is mentioned only in passing in the Paris Agreement on climate change – in "a single fleeting reference" in the agreement's preamble to "the importance of ensuring the integrity of all ecosystems, including oceans."[108] Nevertheless, this is a milestone of sorts. It is the first time the ocean has been mentioned in any agreement concluded under the United Nations climate framework – an achievement celebrated in Paris by ocean activists. "This gets us in the game," they said.[109] The ocean is featured much more prominently in the Sustainable Development Goals. One of the seventeen SDGs – Goal 14 – is to "[c]onserve and sustainably use the oceans, seas, and marine resources for sustainable development."[110] A specific target of the SDGs is – by the ambitious date of 2020 – to "sustainably manage and protect marine and coastal ecosystems to avoid significant adverse impacts, including by strengthening their resilience, and take action for their restoration in order to achieve healthy and productive oceans."[111]

The ocean was mentioned only once and only in passing in the Paris Agreement in part because the global climate agreement is an agreement among sovereign states about what they are willing to do *within their own national jurisdictions*. About 64 percent of the ocean lies outside the legal jurisdiction of individual states, and thus is beyond the legal control of any one country. Another way of putting this is: Unlike the sovereign states, nearly two-thirds of the ocean "doesn't have its own negotiator" on climate change.[112] But all of it should. The global commons of the high seas is the common trust of the whole world.

Mindful of this global common trust, nearly two years after approving the Sustainable Development Goals, the members of the United Nations convened in New York in June 2017 and agreed on a fourteen-point "Call for Action" to fulfill Goal 14 and save the ocean.[113] Although it is not legally binding, this Call for Action expresses a shared resolve to move ahead on a number of fronts relating to the ocean.

(Even the United States, by now a climate change pariah, joined in the ocean consensus – but only after reiterating its opposition to the Paris Agreement.)[114]

One UN action call is for more ocean "management tools," including more "marine protected areas" (MPAs), which are geographically defined areas of the ocean in which some or all economic activities – fishing in particular – are restricted or prohibited. Closing off these areas to fishing and to other economic pursuits helps to conserve marine ecosystems, including by protecting threatened and endangered species and unique habitats such as the coral reefs off the shores of Australia and southern Florida. MPAs are also a "potentially important tool in the present and future management of deep-sea eco-systems in the high seas."[115] There are about 7,300 MPAs in the world today covering about 3.4 percent of global marine areas. The vast majority of these MPAs are in national waters, with less than 10 percent in areas outside national jurisdictions.[116]

Marine protected areas are equally needed in the global commons of the high seas. As it stands, less than 1 percent of the high seas has any degree of protection under international law. Numerous scientific studies published during the past generation conclude that, to preserve and restore marine ecosystems, 30 percent of the oceans should be designated as marine protected areas.[117] The target of the SDGs is to conserve at least 10 percent by 2020.[118] The willing are working for even more.

Toward this end, in October 2016, the world's largest marine reserve was established in the Ross Sea, a remote and mostly untouched expanse of the Southern Ocean off the coast of Antarctica more than twice the size of Texas. Twenty-four countries and the European Union agreed to the deal – including Russia and the United States.[119] The Ross Sea is home to 16,000 species and, according to one leading marine biologist, "probably the largest ocean wilderness left on our planet. It is the Serengeti of Antarctica, a wild place full of wildlife such as emperor penguins, leopard seals, minke whales, and killer whales. It's one of those rare places where humans are only visitors and large animals rule."[120]

Another way of accomplishing the Sustainable Development Goal of conserving marine resources is by vastly more international cooperation in preserving our imperiled marine biodiversity. In September 2018, after nearly a decade of deliberations, the United Nations will convene the first of four scheduled rounds of negotiations through mid 2020 on a legally binding international agreement for the sustainable use of marine diversity in the ocean global commons – on the high seas and in the seabed beyond the continental shelves of the coastal states. This proposed agreement is to be negotiated as an annex under the UN Convention on the Law of the Sea – UNCLOS – and will add much to the enabling framework of ocean global governance.

Sixty-four percent of the ocean lies in the global commons beyond all national jurisdictions.[121] As contemplated, this proposed multilateral agreement could deal with numerous aspects of protecting marine biodiversity on the high seas and in deep seabeds, including marine genetic resources, biodiversity loss, environmental impact assessments, marine pollution, capacity-building and the transfer of marine technology, management of deep-sea fisheries, and unsustainable use through overfishing. As the Global Ocean Commission – a global group of the willing – has concluded, such a new agreement could do much to help secure sustainable development of the ocean global commons.[122]

A target under Goal 14 of the SDGs is: "By 2025, prevent and significantly reduce marine pollution of all kinds, in particular from land-based activities, including marine debris and nutrient pollution."[123] In affirming this target, the UN ocean conference gave special attention to the proliferation of plastic debris in the sea. Annual production of plastic has grown exponentially from 1.5 million tons in 1950 to 322 million tons in 2015.[124] Much of this plastic production in our "disposable" economy finds its way to the sea, where an estimated 5 trillion plastic items – most very small – circulate in the surface layer of the ocean.[125] Sea creatures mistake plastic for food, ingest it, and small plastic particles work their way up the food chain. "Microplastic" particles also affect marine algae, "the basic building block of oceanic life," which "are responsible for making about 70 percent of the oxygen we breathe."[126] If no actions are taken to reduce the flow of plastic debris, the weight of the plastic in the ocean may be more than the weight of the fish by 2050.[127] In addition to immediate national actions, more international cooperation and coordination are much needed to do much more to recycle plastics and decouple plastics production from fossil fuels through agreement on a "Global Plastics Protocol" that could also be an annex under UNCLOS.[128]

Another target of Goal 14 is to "[i]ncrease scientific knowledge, develop research capacity and transfer marine technology."[129] New technologies are already making a discernible difference in saving the ocean – such as with ocean drones that offer better and more timely data on ocean conditions and fish stocks at a small fraction of existing costs, and with satellite imagery used to spot illegal fishing. A leading global environmentalist, Jim Leape, of Stanford University, predicts, "The Fourth Industrial Revolution can transform our ability to understand what's happening in the oceans, and manage it."[130] He sees drones, sensors, crowdsourcing, imaging, genomics, genetics, artificial intelligence, and machine learning all as ways "of transforming streams of data into streams of understanding to illuminate sources, interactions, and impacts of stressors" on the ocean.[131]

In addition to a Global Plastics Protocol, other international agreements in other sectors and on other ocean-related issues could hasten ocean salvation. Where these new international agreements are related to the purposes of the International Convention on the Law of the Sea, the proper legal place for them would be as protocols to UNCLOS, which "supplies the overarching legal framework for marine environmental protection" and is already "supplemented by a multitude of other treaties and soft-law instruments."[132] Yet another target of Goal 14 is to "[e]nhance the conservation and sustainable use of oceans and their resources by implementing international law as reflected in UNCLOS, which provides the legal framework for the conservation and sustainable use of oceans and their resources."[133] Specific reference is made in this target to language from the declaration of the Rio+20 Summit in 2012 that expresses the global commitment to apply "an ecosystem approach" and "the precautionary approach" in managing activities impacting the marine environment in accordance with international law and delivering on the economic, environmental, and social dimensions of sustainable development.[134] (The same declaration also urged all UN members to implement their obligations under UNCLOS; regrettably, the United States, despite long years of labors by the willing, has yet to ratify the ocean convention.)[135]

The call to action to rescue the ocean includes a call to enhance "international coordination and coherence throughout the UN system on ocean issues."[136] Concluding an implementing agreement to UNCLOS to protect marine diversity is central to strengthening ocean governance, but it is only part of it. The Global Ocean Commission has stated bluntly that high seas governance is "weak, fragmented and outdated" and faces many risks and uncertainties.[137] The OECD reports "a widely held view that there remains fundamental uncertainty as to where ocean governance is heading," largely because of "legal uncertainty" and a "lack of legal clarity."[138] OECD analysts note that the private sector has long contended that, to attract public and private investment to the opportunities offered by increasing access to the deep sea, "there needs to be a clear, overarching legal regime covering the relations between states as well as the role of private commercial entities."[139]

This legal regime should be the United Nations Convention on the Law of the Sea. Much needed for global sustainable development is a modernized and enhanced UNCLOS with added legal authority to oversee and to adjudicate long-standing and also new and emerging concerns relating to ocean governance. At the heart of this modernization must be the drawing of the right lines "in between" property rights and common responsibilities involving the high seas and the deep seabed. In the absence of this line-drawing, exploitation often prevails over preservation, with dire consequences for sustainability. In further ocean rule-making, the world can no longer afford to swim around the edges of the tension between the freedom of individuals and of individual states to exploit the ocean and the responsibility we all share to sustain it.

All this is not to overlook the centrality here, as everywhere, of bottom-up initiatives relating to sustaining the ocean, including those led by non-state political actors. These global grassroots efforts were much in evidence at the United Nations ocean conference, where more than 1,300 commitments on ocean action were received from business and other parts of civil society,[140] and where British entrepreneur Richard Branson presented a petition with more than 1 million signatures urging governments to preserve at least 30 percent of the world's ocean by 2030.[141] Like the other needed reimaginings of international law for sustainable development, new international ocean agreements will work only if they are based on the true bottom-up of proven practical experience throughout the world in sustaining and thus saving the ocean.

FISHERIES SUBSIDIES AND UNSUSTAINABLE FISHING

Through the centuries, we have assumed that we can dump anything we choose into the ocean and pull anything we choose out of it, and the ocean will roll on as before. In the twenty-first century, we know better. We know now that, although the smooth surface of the ocean swells and subsides in ways that seem to withstand all human actions, the ocean is in fact "a patchwork of habitats and water masses occurring at scales that render them vulnerable to disturbance and depletion."[142] The longstanding tradition of the "freedom of the seas," dating back to the Dutch humanist Hugo Grotius in the seventeenth century, is the very wellspring of international law.[143] Today, this ocean tradition is confronted by the need to internalize our accumulating knowledge of all we must do to save the oceans as part of achieving sustainable development. Sadly, many of our policies and practices still do not reflect this knowledge.

A great number of our unsustainable ocean policies and practices relate to an ocean resource that we value the most and yet are also threatening the most – fish. Worldwide, 3 billion people depend on fish and fish products for up to 15 percent of their daily protein and nutrition.[144] Many of them live in the poorest and least-developed countries. At least 140 million people depend on fisheries for their livelihood.[145] The demand for fish has been growing with a growing – and increasingly prosperous – global population. We each now eat more fish than ever before, an average of 20 kilograms – 44 pounds – every year.[146] We eat more fish than beef.[147]

Meanwhile, the global fish catch has been declining.[148] Nearly 30 percent of the world's global fish stocks are overfished, and more than 60 percent are being fished at the maximum sustainable level. As the world population continues to rise, only about 10 percent of global fish stocks are underfished.[149] The several authors of a study released in the Proceedings of the National Academy of Sciences examined 4,713 fisheries worldwide, accounting for 78 percent of the world's catch. They found that only a third of these fisheries are in good biological condition. Offering hope for change, these scientists also concluded that – if applied globally – modern fisheries management plans can make nearly every fishery in the world healthy by 2050.[150]

But complicating fisheries management is the new reality that, because of warming waters in their traditional habitats, fish are joining sea turtles, seabirds, jellyfish, and other sea species in fleeing to the Earth's poles, where the waters are cooler. Most of the Earth's biological diversity is in the ocean, "life's most expansive habitat,"[151] where ocean species are changing millennia of behavior and moving away from warming climes five times faster than species on land. With equatorial waters warming up, plankton are moving toward the poles, and "[w]here they lead, fish will follow."[152] Fish are moving north at a rate of 30 kilometers – about 18 miles – per year, and, amid this polar exodus, hundreds of marine fishes and invertebrates that are already considered threatened are likely to decline more quickly due to ocean warming.

Little wonder then that the United Nations has made the sustainability of global fisheries a target of the Sustainable Development Goals. One of the ambitious targets under Goal 14 is – by 2020 – to "prohibit certain forms of fisheries subsidies which contribute to overcapacity and overfishing … and refrain from introducing new such subsidies."[153] Another target under the same goal is – again by 2020 – to "end overfishing, illegal, unreported and unregulated fishing and destructive fishing practices and implement science-based management plans."[154] These two targets are a focus of much of the ocean activism of the willing.

Unavoidably, these ambitions involve trade and trade rules. An estimated 37 percent of all the seafood harvested in the world is traded.[155] Developing countries account for most of the world's fisheries exports as measured by both value and volume.[156] Mostly, this involves fishing within the exclusive economic zones (EEZs) of individual countries, which extend 200 nautical miles from their coastlines. Estimates are that 90 percent of the commercially exploited fisheries in the world are within the bounds of these EEZs.[157]

Better trawlers, better mapping, and other technological advances are, however, increasingly enabling fishing beyond the EEZs in the global commons of the high seas, which are defined in international law as part of "the common heritage of mankind," and which span nearly two-thirds of the surface of the ocean.[158] Catches from the high seas are now valued at $16 billion annually.[159] Increasingly, a marine "tragedy of the commons" has been the relentless competition, inspired by the high demand for fish, among those who fish with all too little restriction amid the freedom of the high seas.

Efforts have been made by the United Nations to address the issue of overfishing in the high seas through the UN Convention on the Law of the Sea. One result is the Straddling Fish Stocks Agreement of 1995, which deals with the harvesting of those fish that swim back and forth between national and international waters.[160] But not nearly enough has been done so far to coordinate these UN efforts with those of the WTO on trade; nor has the WTO done much so far to confront the overall issues arising from the trade emerging from the ocean, either within the EEZs or in the global commons of the high seas.

In particular, urgently needed is a reimagining of WTO law to diminish overfishing and otherwise protect ocean ecosystems by prohibiting fisheries subsidies. Worldwide, subsidies contribute to overfishing and depletion of fisheries, add to overcapacity in fishing fleets, and are linked to illegal fishing. Total fisheries subsidies amount to $35 billion – annually. The largest part of these fisheries subsidies – 22 percent – consists of fuel subsidies, which permit trawlers, largely from the wealthier countries, to range farther and farther into the high seas. The global total of fisheries subsidies is between 30 and 40 percent of the landed value generated by wild fisheries worldwide.[161] The Global Ocean Commission has estimated that 60 percent of global fisheries subsidies directly encourage "unsustainable, destructive and even illegal fishing practices." The Commission has recommended that high seas fishing fuel subsidies be capped immediately and then phased out over five years, and that the money saved be redirected into a dedicated "Blue Fund" to implement the SDG targets for saving the ocean.[162]

In one of its few efforts thus far to reimagine trade rules to provide more support for sustainable development, the WTO has, since 2001, tried, as part of the Doha Development Agenda, to "clarify and improve WTO discipline on fisheries subsidies, taking into account the importance of this sector to developing countries."[163] Fearful of lost markets, many countries have long resisted this necessary reform, including many developing countries. They have done so despite the fact that 65 percent of the fisheries subsidies – nearly two-thirds – is provided by such wealthy developed economies as the United States, the European Union, and Japan, now joined also by the rising economic powerhouse of China.[164]

By 2017, spurred at least in part by the SDGs, the issue of imposing global disciplines on fisheries subsidies had moved up on the WTO agenda and was the topic of serious WTO negotiations. As Ricardo Melendez-Ortiz has pointed out, the TPP "contains the first disciplines on fisheries subsidies in any free trade agreement."[165] With the United States on the sidelines, the other eleven countries that have concluded the TPP have resolved to go ahead with a TPP provision barring any TPP party from granting or maintaining subsidies that negatively affect fishing stocks that are overfished, or that are provided to any vessel engaged in illegal, unreported, or unregulated fishing.[166] The TPP is a start toward what must ultimately become a fully multilateral WTO solution. Among those in Buenos Aires for the WTO Ministerial Conference in December 2017 was Peter Thomson, the UN Secretary-General's Special Envoy for the Oceans, who declared, "I'm here in Buenos Aires because I want to hold the WTO accountable for SDG14."[167] The decision there to postpone concluding a deal limiting fisheries subsidies until 2019 left the willing still looking for accountability from the WTO.

As contemplated in the SDGs, equally needed, too, is a reimagining of WTO law to address the global spread of illegal, unreported, and unregulated fishing. According to the "most authoritative" calculation, the global losses from IUU fishing add up to between $10 billion and $23.5 billion annually, meaning that "as many as one in three fish entering international trade could come from IUU fishing."[168] To these economic costs must be added the dire threats posed by IUU fishing to the sustainability of global fisheries and global fish ecosystems. Since the 1990s, the United Nations has sought through a variety of ways to stop IUU fishing, beginning with an international agreement on compliance by fishing vessels with international conservation and management measures concluded under the auspices of the UN Food and Agricultural Organization in 1993.[169]

In 2001, the FAO adopted a voluntary international plan of action to "prevent, deter and eliminate" IUU fishing. In 2009, the FAO adopted the Port State Measures Agreement, which requires foreign vessels to submit to inspection at any port of call, denies port access to vessels that have engaged in IUU fishing, and requires port states to share information on any fishing wrongdoing they discover. In 2015, the United States became the twentieth country to ratify this latest agreement, which will take effect when ratified by twenty-five countries.[170]

The FAO action plan states that trade-related measures intended to combat IUU fishing must be adopted and implemented in accordance with WTO rules, and should be used only in exceptional circumstances and after prior consultation with the targeted countries where other measures have proven unsuccessful. The plan states further: "Unilateral trade measures should be avoided."[171] Despite this admonition, the temptation for those countries most persuaded of the urgency of reducing IUU fishing, when faced with the reluctance of other countries to agree on a global solution, is to seek leverage for securing a global agreement by imposing unilateral trade restrictions.

Like a number of other countries, the United States has succumbed to the temptation to impose unilateral measures. A seafood traceability program to combat IUU fishing and seafood fraud enacted in 2016 includes unilateral trade sanctions. This US measure bans the import of seafood products resulting from IUU fishing or seafood fraud. It also imposes costly new traceability requirements on seafood importers that it does not impose on producers of like domestic seafood products. If challenged, these and other aspects of the seafood traceability program raise considerable doubt as to whether it is consistent with the WTO obligations of the United States.[172]

Unilateral approaches such as this US measure are more likely to lead to retaliation than to cooperation. Some WTO members are already urging the United States and other WTO members to comply with their international obligations when implementing their domestic strategies to combat IUU fishing.[173] Furthermore, fisheries experts have noted that unilateral trade restrictions taken against IUU fishing may not reduce IUU fishing. They may only divert IUU fishing elsewhere.[174]

A global solution would be by far the best solution for stopping IUU fishing on the high seas. The agenda for the upcoming UN negotiations on a new multilateral agreement to preserve marine biodiversity in the global commons should include effective rules and actions to stop IUU fishing. Unquestionably, these rules and actions would be respected by the WTO so long as they were not applied in ways that constituted arbitrary or unjustifiable discrimination or a disguised restriction on international trade. Conceivably, there could be a cooperative global linking of national and regional approaches to combating IUU fishing that could avoid the trade discriminations of unilateral measures.

The regional fisheries management organizations (FRMOs) that have emerged in recent years are textbook examples of Elinor Ostrom's "innovative institutions for collective action" as potential antidotes to the "tragedy of the commons."[175] In the proposed new global agreement on marine biodiversity, the United Nations should encourage the further filling-in of the vital rules framework of governing the commons through more regional fisheries governance by these RFMOs, and through more regular assessment of the performance of RFMOs. More broadly, the UN should also follow through on the recommendation of the Global Ocean Commission that these regional *fisheries* management organizations be transformed into regional *ocean* management organizations "to promote ecosystem-based management of the ocean."[176]

In a new United Nations agreement on marine biodiversity, there should, in addition, be the establishment of global standards for fishing and for fisheries building on the years of work by the FAO. These global standards should not favor trade over sustainability but, rather, should draw the right line "in between" trade and sustainability. Currently, marine fisheries governance is still focused far more on sheer production than it is on issues of sustainability.[177] As with all other types of standards and technical regulations, there is value in such line-drawing in seeking harmonization. Local standards can be helpful, and sovereign countries must retain the right to impose them – if done consistently with the WTO rules. But local standards can also be pretexts for protectionism that become discriminatory non-tariff barriers to trade. Better to draw the right line "in between" through a global standard than to leave this task, too, to WTO judges.

United Nations negotiations should likewise seek new ways to encourage positive private actions that include non-state political actors – such as the increasing efforts of the private sector to find creative solutions to help stop IUU fishing. One such action is the Tuna 2020 Traceability Declaration inspired by the willing affiliated with the World Economic Forum and announced by a coalition of governments, companies, and other civil society groups at the UN ocean conference. They promise in their declaration to help restore the global sustainability of declining tuna stocks by tracking tuna products from vessels to the final buyer and making all tracking information freely available to one and all.[178] To the extent that these actions are only private actions, WTO rules will not apply. To the extent that actions taken pursuant to this declaration are governmental actions that restrict trade, those actions should be upheld by the WTO if they are in fact taken for sustainability reasons and if they do not involve arbitrary or unjustifiable discrimination or a disguised restriction on international trade.

A post-Westphalian reimagination of international law that encompasses more than states is nowhere more appropriate than on the high seas and in the deep seabeds, which are beyond the legal jurisdiction of individual states. The upcoming negotiations on marine biodiversity present an opportunity for a reimagining of part of public international law itself to bring a whole world of innovative private actions further into the collaboration and the cooperation of the public sphere. As with the New York Declaration on Forests, parties in addition to states should be invited by the United Nations to participate in negotiating *and agreeing to* the envisaged marine biodiversity agreement, their certification schemes and other innovative sustainability initiatives should somehow be incorporated into the new international legal arrangements, and they should be bound legally by those arrangements.

Room, too, must be made in the global trade rules to help secure the success of this proposed new UN agreement on marine biodiversity. In parallel and in concert with these proposed UN negotiations, the WTO should likewise confront IUU fishing on a number of fronts. A further delay by the WTO in dealing with the various legal issues arising from the tension between trade and fishing, and between trade and other issues of marine and other biodiversity, will undermine the WTO's goal of promoting sustainable development through trade, and will confront the world with unnecessary collisions between trade and sustainability in WTO dispute settlement.

In these WTO negotiations, the multiplying potpourri of private standards on preventing IUU fishing should be reconciled with the WTO rules on technical barriers to trade. This should be done in ways that will be consistent with the new UN agreement. In addition, on these standards and in other ways, due attention must be paid by the WTO not only to wild-capture fisheries, but also to the spread of aquaculture. Seafood production from aquaculture now exceeds that from wild-capture fisheries, accounting for 58 percent of all the fish we eat.[179] The members of the WTO should address market access for the products of aquaculture and, in particular, should spell out with more clarity when and how questions about the health, safety, and environmental sensitivity of aquaculture products and production will justify a trade restriction.[180]

As with other traded products, we need to draw the right lines, too, with seafood on process and production methods, which are manifested in endless ways that affect sustainability. When is a distinction that is made about a seafood PPM a legitimate environmental measure, and when is it an excuse for protection or arbitrary and unjustified discrimination? Lines of discrimination in the form of such technical barriers to trade have been drawn so far by the WTO in dispute settlement, centered for the most part on "eco-labeling."[181] Seafood and other labeling requirements relating to PPMs are permissible under the WTO rules, but it has been difficult to locate case by case the "just mean" of the "in between."[182] This is yet another trade issue where negotiations on new and reimagined rules should render unnecessary much of what now is likely to end up in dispute settlement.

16

On Water, Biodiversity, and Rules to Protect
Natural Resources

One of the most threatened of the planet's natural resources is the freshwater essential to sustaining human life. Although water is abundant on the Earth, only a small part of it can be used as drinking water and for growing our food. More than 97 percent of all the water on our watery planet is saltwater in the oceans. The freshwater essential to sustaining human life accounts for only 2.4 percent of the planet's water. Moreover, "the vast majority of freshwater – 87 percent – is frozen in solid ice and glaciers, making it inaccessible for human use."[1] So we depend for our drinking water and for our other uses of freshwater on what remains. Only 3 percent of what remains "flows through rivers and streams and rests in lakes."[2] Almost all the freshwater available for human use – 97 percent – is groundwater drawn from increasingly imperiled underground aquifers.[3]

WATER SECURITY IN A HUNGRY AND THIRSTY WORLD

All this said, there is no global shortage of freshwater. "No water is being created or destroyed on Earth."[4] The world has always had exactly the same amount of water because the atmosphere and the ecosystems of the Earth are always recycling water. This natural cycle has existed since eons before the ancient Egyptians irrigated along the Nile, the first Chinese tilled along the Yellow River, the Romans built their aqueducts, and the Byzantines placed their basilica cisterns beneath the streets of what is now Istanbul. Every day, more than 37,000 gallons of freshwater fall from the sky for each and every one of us.[5] The human challenge always and everywhere has been to ensure that the quantity and the quality of water are what we need where and when we need it.

From 1990 through the course of the Millennium Development Goals, 1.9 million people gained access to piped drinking water.[6] With Goal 6 of the Sustainable Development Goals, we aspire now to "[e]nsure availability and sustainable management of water and sanitation for all."[7] This *global* goal is, however, in reality a vastly diverse collection of *local* goals. While local greenhouse gas emissions affect the whole world, local water scarcities usually have only direct local effects. These local effects are best prevented by local actions. In contrast to climate change and the world's air, the security and sustainability of the world's water do not require a *global* solution; they require, instead, many differing *local* solutions that, altogether, add up to a global solution.

Environmental journalist Charles Fishman has explained that, even though there is plenty of freshwater globally, often, locally, "we manage the planet's most abundant and renewable resource so poorly that we sometimes run out of water where and when we need it."[8] Thus, "all water problems are local."[9] At least 1.6 million people in the world, and perhaps many more, already live in circumstances of water stress. If current trends continue and are worsened, as expected, by climate change, nearly 4 billion people will suffer water stress by 2030.[10] By that fast-approaching date, predicts the World Bank, "the world may face a shortfall in water ... with demand exceeding current water supplies by 40 percent."[11] Without vastly improved local water governance, water scarcity – an excess of local demand over locally available supply – will soon be surging worldwide.[12]

We can see this already in how climate change and poor water governance have combined to create water shortages in South Africa, where less rainfall and rising temperatures have led to higher evaporative rates in reservoirs and soils and thus to severe droughts.[13] In Cape Town, a city of nearly 4 million people, residents subjected to water rationing are awaiting "Day Zero" – the date when the city is expected to run out of water.[14] Cape Town is not alone in its thirst. Worldwide, changes in the climate, including changes in the frequency and intensity of extreme weather events, are impacting water supplies and water demands, and, especially when accompanied by inadequate water management, are putting other cities and regions at risk of running dry. Sao Paulo, Melbourne, southern California, and southern Florida could all be the next Cape Town.

Improved water governance is especially needed worldwide in agricultural and energy production. About 70 percent of our freshwater use worldwide is for agriculture – for food production.[15] Developing countries with rising populations of hungry people in need of more food account for more than 70 percent of global water withdrawals – demands that are rapidly rising.[16] Many of these developing countries are directly in the path of climate change, and "climate change with the increase in temperatures in the temperate and arid zones means that there will be less water for the heavily populated areas of the earth."[17] At the same time, 40 percent of the freshwater withdrawals in the United States and in the European Union are for the energy sector and thus are linked also to the exactions of climate change.[18]

The United Nations affirmed the human right to water and sanitation in a resolution in 2010.[19] The "human right to safe drinking water and sanitation" has since been reaffirmed in the Sustainable Development Goals.[20] The first target listed under Goal 6 of the SDGs is to, "[b]y 2030, achieve universal and equitable access to safe and affordable drinking water for all."[21] There is, however, no binding international treaty to help us reach this global target, no "World Water Organiza-tion" – no WWO – akin to the WTO to help us reach it, and no one solution for improved water governance that can prevent water scarcities. Here, too, as in so much of the rest of sustainable development, there is the imperative of building many solutions locally, and often regionally, from the bottom up. One group of the willing has advised of our water worries, "Effective reform will depend ... on the creation of regional, domestic and local coalitions for reform (comprising farmers and agro-businesses, industry, technology, finance, consumers, urban government, media) that will work with finance, planning, and water, food, and energy agencies at the local level. Inclusiveness is essential to drive the political support needed for reform. The crucial decision is a national decision. International cooperation can only support and backstop states that want to make transformations in water resource management."[22]

World trade rules must enhance and not hinder these and other local and bottom-up efforts toward global water security, in part by preserving ample policy space for bottom-up innovations in water governance. International trade can be either a plus or a minus in assuring global water security. Positively, for example, international trade in water-intensive commodities can result in water savings in the countries that import those commodities.[23] For example, "International trade ... reduces global water use in agriculture by 5%."[24] Negatively, international trade may encourage economic actions that are harmful to the local water supply if local regulation and local governance are not sufficient.[25] Thus, whether international trade helps or harms water security can depend on whether there is effective local water use management. Where WTO rules support water security, they must be used and upheld. Where they do not, they must be reimagined as part of the overall reimagin-ing of world trade rules to support sustainable development.

"Trade in water itself is very limited."[26] Water is heavy, and moving water from place to place by any means "other than gravity" can be prohibitively expensive. In natural resources trade, water's sheer weight helps explain why "water, unlike other key resources, is overwhelmingly local."[27] Given this, not surprisingly, at the most basic level, it is unclear under the rules and the rulings of the WTO whether, when, and to what extent water can become subject to the disciplines of the rules of trade. Is water just another widget in world trade?[28] The legal obligations in the WTO goods agreement – the GATT – are obligations owed to internationally traded "products." Can water be a product?

One particular ruling of the WTO Appellate Body in 2004 is relevant to this still-unanswered WTO legal question about the legal status of water and other natural resources. In a long-running dispute between the United States and Canada over alleged Canadian subsidies for softwood lumber production (a dispute that continues still), the WTO judges had to decide whether the concept of "goods" includes trees *before they are harvested*.[29] The Appellate Body ruled there that "goods" for the purposes of the WTO subsidies rules "should not be read so as to exclude tangible items of property, like trees, that are severable from the land."[30] The WTO judges concluded that to have ruled otherwise would have opened a back door to undermining WTO subsidies obligations by permitting financial contributions for subsidies "in a form other than money, such as through the provision of standing timber for the sole purpose of severing it from land and processing it."[31]

This Appellate Body ruling suggests that water (and, by logical extension, other kinds of natural resources, exhaustible and non-exhaustible alike) cannot be excluded automatically from the scope of the application of the WTO rules. Whether water and other natural resources will fall within the bounds of the trade rules will likely be determined by legal line-drawing on a case-by-case basis. If this is so, where is the right line of the "just mean" that is "in between"? Where the natural resource of water is concerned, given the "human right to safe drinking water and sanitation" cited by the United Nations in the Sustainable Development Goals, can water even be an object of the trade rules? Furthermore, if water can be an object of the trade rules, how should the trade rules take into account the legal conflicts between the human right to water and the notion of water as the object of a property right?

The Appellate Body noted in the softwood lumber dispute that the legal question of what is "personal property" or "real property" is a question for municipal law – for the national and other laws of individual members of the WTO.[32] But local laws differ as to what constitutes property and property rights. Should the guarantee of the supposedly universal human right to safe and affordable water depend on the vagaries of local decisionmaking about the meaning of "property"? Legal scholars speak of "the hazy content of the right to water" and question the legal status of this supposed human right.[33] All the same, where there is the expressed recognition by every member of the United Nations, albeit in forms somewhat less than that of full-blown and fully binding treaties, that there *is* a human right, then that human right must not be diminished or denied through means of international commerce or through the parochial conclusions of local decisionmakers about what can and cannot be "property."

Confronted in 1993 by the prospect of a Canadian ban on proposed bulk transfers of water from British Columbia to the United States through diversion of the Canadian water flow, the three parties to the NAFTA – Canada, Mexico, and the United States – faced the threshold legal question of whether water in its natural state is covered by the trade rules. They issued a joint declaration affirming that the "NAFTA creates no rights to the natural water resources of any Party to the Agreement. Unless water, in any form, has entered into commerce and become a good or product, it is not covered by the provision of any trade agreement including the NAFTA."[34] There has, to date, been no similar declaration by the members of the WTO.

There should be one; for, now, fast approaching on the global horizon are a number of difficult water-related trade issues that are likely soon to confront the world trading system with the need to decide whether and under what circumstances water can be considered a good or a product falling within the scope of the WTO trade rules; how trade rules that may apply to water can be reconciled with the professed WTO goal of supporting sustainable development; and how this reconciliation may vary with whether water is still in, or has been removed in some way from, its natural state.

In theory, water could be traded in bulk extensively internationally by means of supertankers, pipelines, or even "giant sealed bags."[35] To date, though, almost all the international trade in water is in bottled water for consumer use as drinking water – trade which raises its own unique issues of sustainability. Studies have shown that three liters of water are needed to produce a single liter of bottled water, and that the production of bottled water burns 17 million barrels of oil per year – equal to the fuel needs annually of 1 million automobiles.[36] Moreover, most of the bottles are made of plastic, posing additional issues of sustainability.

Another rapidly approaching issue for resolution by the WTO is trade in "virtual water" – the transfer of water through trade in an embedded form in goods, mostly in agricultural goods. Virtual water is "virtual" because it is not actually liquid water that can be poured or squeezed from the goods. Rather, "the notion of virtual water represents the quantity of water used in the process of production of a tradable commodity."[37] Because the water is consumed in one country to produce a product that is traded to another country, there is through trade a virtual transfer of water to the importing country.[38] Estimates are that 1,040 billion square meters of virtual water are traded globally every year.[39] About one-fourth of water use "is exported as virtual water."[40]

Here, once more, we are dealing with a PPM – a process and production method; we are dealing not with the product itself but with how it is produced. In this instance, though, the PPM is not automatically harmful to the environment and therefore to sustainability. Whether trade in virtual water is harmful or useful depends on how and where the trade occurs.

To achieve water security, water-scarce countries should import water-intensive products and export products that consume less water in production. Yet, as it is, the very opposite is happening. As one of the willing, Jenny Kehl, from the United States, has pointed out, "Water-scarce regions are overwhelmingly producing and exporting water-intensive products" – especially in agricultural trade.[41] She says that, potentially, trade in "virtual water" could be "reorganized for water-scarce regions to become virtual importers, a reversal of their current net loss, and water-rich regions to become virtual exporters."[42] Trade in water can help save water. "[G]lobal virtual water trade can physically save water if products are traded from countries with high to countries with low water productivity."[43] Indeed, estimates are that the current virtual trade in water allows average savings of 22 percent of the world's water.[44] As two of the willing from the Paris Institute of Political Studies, Alexandre Le Vernoy and Patrick Messerlin, have pointed out, "This figure represents a rough estimate of the opportunity cost of rejecting a WTO-based approach" to trade.[45]

Another issue arising from the connections between trade and water is the extent to which WTO rules on trade in services may require or lead to the "privatization" of the local supply of water services. Those apprehensive of the WTO and of globalization in general have argued that the WTO services rules may require the "privatization" of water distribution services and thus the abolition of public water supply – which currently still accounts for more than 90 percent of the global supply of water and sanitation services.[46] This has been a prominent point of alarm for those who argue broadly that the progressive liberalization of trade in services will result in the privatization of all public services, including water services, for the benefit of supposedly avaricious and nefarious multinational corporations.

These concerns about WTO services rules have no basis. WTO members are required to "privatize" their delivery of services only if they have specifically chosen and committed to other WTO members to do so. Thus far, the number of members of the WTO that have made services commitments on water distribution is – *zero*. Yet misinformation on this – understandably – emotional issue pervades our unwilling world. In its frustration with having to refute such false charges, the WTO Secretariat, as part of its unending Sisyphean struggle to separate fact from fiction in worldwide public perceptions of the WTO, has been reduced to insisting in a published statement, "The WTO is not after your water."[47] This reassurance must be stated clearly in the reimagining of WTO rules.

Creeping ever nearer too to trade deliberations is the potentially explosive issue of putting a *price* on water. Almost nowhere in the world does the price of water reflect the amount of water scarcity. Often there is no charge at all. Often no one even bothers to keep track of how much water is used. Often, too, the provision of water is subsidized "to the point that the signal of scarcity is totally distorted."[48] Moreover, there persists a pervasive belief throughout the world that water should be free, a belief dating back to when the Byzantine emperor Justinian declared in the sixth century that "by natural law" water, like the air we breathe, is "common to all."[49] The notion that water is a human right is but the modern manifestation of this long-held belief.

Yet even with water subsidies, and even with the prevailing predilection that water is and should be "free," millions upon millions of mostly women and children in developing countries spend hours upon hours every day trudging to and from often tainted wells to meet their basic water needs. They have no water security. Many of the willing who are working for water security maintain that putting a price on water is the best way to help those deprived of water security while ensuring water sustainability. They say that, "Water pricing – considering water as an economic good as well as an environmental and social goal – is essential to provide the right incentives to save water and use it wisely," for "currently the incentives often run the wrong way."[50]

As these water specialists among the willing see it, the only truly effective way to ensure water security is by pricing water through the market. One of the willing, economic journalist Steve Solomon, who writes extensively about global water security, speaks for many in arguing that market-based solutions are the best for solving water scarcities "because the market is anchored in a pricing mechanism for valuing water that reflects both the full cost of sustaining ecosystems through externally imposed environmental standards and a social fairness guarantee for everyone to receive at affordable cost the minimum amounts necessary for their basic needs."[51]

As it is, where the market is concerned, and setting aside the proliferation of bottled water (and plastics along with it), generally water still has today, as Adam Smith observed long ago when comparing water to diamonds, a value in *use* but not a value in *exchange*.[52] Nothing is more useful than water, which is essential to life, but cheap. In contrast, diamonds, apart from having some industrial uses, are relatively useless, but nevertheless expensive. Solomon explains, "Smith's answer was that water's ubiquity and the relatively cheap labor required to obtain it accounted for its low price."[53] Several centuries on, we can see more clearly that the value of water in exchange rises as water becomes scarce. We cannot drink diamonds.

Conceivably, under the current WTO rules, unilateral market restrictions in the form of trade restrictions based on unhealthy or unsustainable water use could be eligible for one of the general exceptions to WTO obligations relating to trade in goods. Depending on the facts, this could be so even where such restrictions have an extraterritorial application. For water quality, such restrictions could be justified as "necessary for the protection of human, animal or plant life or health."[54] For water quantity, such restrictions could be justified as "relating to the conservation of exhaustible natural resources."[55]

On the latter, though, there might be the potential hurdle of a threshold legal question. Given that the worldwide supply of water is naturally replenished by rainfall, is water in fact an "exhaustible" natural resource? The Appellate Body has already ruled, in the shrimp–turtle dispute, that living species are exhaustible. Here the WTO judges could find it necessary to rule that there can be a local dimension to exhaustibility because of the local nature of water scarcities. In either case, as with all the general exceptions to the WTO rules, no such restriction would be entitled to this exception or to the health exception if it were "applied in a manner" that constituted "a means of arbitrary or unjustifiable discrimination between countries where the same conditions prevail, or a disguised restriction on international trade."[56]

Some of the willing who work mainly on water security have asked whether, to put a price on water, trade restrictions should be imposed on the basis of the amount of virtual water that is embedded in imported products. The notion of such water-related import restrictions is appealing at first glance as a possible means of promoting water security, but it raises many of the same legal issues under WTO law relating to process and production methods that are raised by proposed import restrictions based on carbon emissions. International trade in goods produced by emitting carbon dioxide and other greenhouse gases is uniformly harmful to the atmosphere. In contrast, trade in virtual water already results in global water savings, and it can result in even more savings if water-scarce regions import and water-rich regions export more virtual water. Thus, there is no need for a water waiver similar to a climate waiver in WTO rules. Instead, WTO rules should be reimagined in ways that, in concert with better local water management, add to the water savings from international trade "by allowing freer trade among undistorted domestic water markets."[57]

One such way would be by water labeling. Through the transparency of water labeling, consumers could be informed of the impacts of producing traded goods on water scarcity and security, including any harmful effects of production on the communities and on the ecosystems that depend on sustainable water systems and supplies.[58] Generally speaking, a water label relating to the quality of water will be legal under WTO rules so long as it does not discriminate and has a sufficient scientific basis,[59] and a water label reporting the quantity of water used in making a product will be legal under the current rules so long as it does not discriminate.[60]

Yet another way of adding to the water savings from international trade would be by revising WTO subsidies rules as they relate to water. On the one hand, as with the connection between agricultural production and climate change, the link between agricultural production and water security should be addressed by making illegal under the trade rules any such production that creates water scarcity or is otherwise damaging to water security. On the other, infrastructure and other investments in improving local water systems and local water management should, as with green subsidies generally, be excused from what would otherwise be the disciplines of WTO subsidies rules.

With water, as with so much else, by far preferable to unilateral actions are multilateral actions, such as global standards on water pricing. In particular, there is urgent need for global standards on the use of water in agriculture, in which the water that goes into food production "is generally hugely underpriced."[61] And certainly, in acknowledgment of the human right to the basic human necessity of water, the pricing in such global standards "should be combined with a minimum water right, in order to prevent poor people in the world not being able to obtain their basic water needs."[62] Once established through international cooperation, such global water standards should be duly recognized and upheld in the deliberations and in the dispute settlement of the WTO.

ENDANGERED SPECIES AND BIODIVERSITY

What is the value of a songbird in the sky? What is the value of a flower in the field? Truly invaluable among all our natural resources are the other species of animal and plant life that share our planet with us. Animals and plants are invaluable in their

countless commercial and other practical uses to us. Much more significant, and
never to be forgotten, is the enduring fact that they are equally and intrinsically
invaluable in their own right. In our hubris, we humans may deign to believe that
nature was made for the sake of man, but do we really believe that a songbird and a
flower have a value limited to our own use and our own perception of them?

In the vastness and the variety of life, the Earth is more marvelous than we know.
The renowned naturalist Edward O. Wilson has rightly reminded us, "[W]e live on
an unknown planet ... The mapping of Earth's biodiversity ... has only begun."[63]
Thus, the planet's natural marvels continue to be revealed, one by one. In 2016,
scientists engaged in the mapping of life on the Earth discovered, in the Greater
Mekong region of Southeast Asia, 163 new species never known before. One is a
rainbow-headed snake. Another is a dragon-like lizard. Still another is a gecko with
pale blue skin.[64] Yet the Earth that is our shared home with so many other species
"is now in the midst of the sixth mass extinction of plants and animals – the sixth
wave of extinctions in the past half-billion years. We're currently experiencing the
worst spate of species die-offs since the loss of the dinosaurs 65 million years ago."[65]

We are losing plant and animal species at 1,000 to 10,000 times the natural rate.[66]
Literally dozens of species are becoming extinct, and forever lost, every day.[67] The
sharp declines in the populations in the ocean are matched by declines on land and
in the air. The willing at the WWF report that, since 1970, there has been a
58 percent decline in the populations of animal wildlife worldwide; and that, if
current trends continue, by 2020, global vertebrate populations may have declined
by an average of 67 percent since 1970.[68] Those at the Royal Botanic Gardens, Kew,
in the United Kingdom report that one in five of the world's 390,000 known species
of plants is at risk of extinction.[69] Unlike the previous mass extinctions, this
unfolding sixth extinction of life on Earth is not caused by a striking asteroid or an
erupting volcano or a natural shift in the climate. It is caused by us.[70]

Economically, environmentally, and socially, a sustainable global development
cannot be secured without saving the biological diversity of the Earth. This too can
be caused only by us. And, this is why one of the most ambitious of all the many
ambitious targets of the Sustainable Development Goals of the United Nations is to
"[t]ake urgent and significant action to reduce the degradation of natural habitats,
halt the loss of biodiversity and, by 2020, protect and prevent the extinction of
threatened species."[71]

Given its pervasiveness, there is a growing tendency to concentrate mainly on
climate change as a threat to the biological diversity of the Earth. Climate change
is indeed a threat to biodiversity. But, as some natural scientists have emphasized,
"by far the biggest drivers of biodiversity decline are overexploitation ... and
agriculture."[72] To preserve biodiversity, not only must we confront climate
change. We must also confront the overexploitation, the unsustainable agricultural
production, and the other causes of habitat destruction that are currently affecting
72 percent of threatened and soon-to-be threatened species.[73] As just one illustration,

logging, mining, and especially land clearing for agriculture have destroyed much of the habitat on the Southeast Asian island of Borneo for orangutans, the largest tree-dwellers on the planet and an endangered species. About half of all the orangutans living on Borneo – an estimated 148,500 – vanished between 1999 and 2015, according to field surveys conducted by 38 international institutions. With some-where between an estimated 105,000 and 148,000 orangutans left, predictions are that more than 45,000 more will die by 2050. A lead researcher explained, "The decline in population density was most severe in areas that were deforested or transformed for industrial agriculture, as orangutans struggle to live outside forest areas."[74]

As with other sustainability concerns, international trade can have either positive or negative effects on biodiversity. Here, too, the outcome depends in part on how trade is conducted. Positively, trade can increase income levels, which in turn can increase demands for habitat conservation, which Wilson says should be a main aim of biodiversity preservation.[75] Also, freer trade reduces trade protection for domestic industries and thus increases the efficiency of those industries in their use of natural resources, which can reduce threats to biodiversity. When conducted within the right lines "in between" of enabling regulation and overall governance, the efficient allocation of resources resulting from trade will preserve biodiversity as one part of promoting sustainability.

Negatively, though, trade will threaten biodiversity if it encourages the over-exploitation of animal and plant species, unsustainable agricultural practices, and habitat loss. Australian scholar Manfred Lenzen maintains that, "in today's increas-ingly globalized economy, international trade chains accelerate habitat destruction far removed from the place of consumption," and that, "in particular, consumers in developed countries cause threats to species through their demand [for] commod-ities that are ultimately produced in developing countries."[76] Whether the effects of trade on biodiversity are positive or negative will therefore depend not only on the conduct of trade. It will depend also on the rules for trade, because the rules for trade will help shape the conduct of trade.

In the Havana Charter of 1948 for a proposed International Trade Organization was a general exception from the newly drafted trade rules for those measures "taken in pursuance of any inter-governmental agreement which relates solely to the conservation of fishery resources, migratory birds or animals."[77] Unfortunately, the GATT alone survived from the Havana conference, to evolve eventually into the WTO. Even so, the general exception provided in the current trade rules for measures "relating to the conservation of exhaustible natural resources" ought to be one international legal means of supporting the conservation of animal and plant species where conservation measures affect international trade. The excep-tional treatment upheld for sea turtles as an endangered species in the WTO shrimp–turtle dispute should certainly be seen by WTO judges to apply equally to other threatened and endangered species.

The WTO has long worked in concert on trade with the United Nations Convention on International Trade in Endangered Species – the CITES.[78] Along with the Montreal Protocol on the ozone layer, the CITES is widely viewed as one of the most successful of all the many multilateral environmental agreements. Since 1973, about 35,000 threatened and endangered species have been "listed" by the CITES for protection against excessive trade and unsustainable exploitation.[79] International commercial trade is prohibited in species that are endangered.[80] Trade is permitted in species that are "listed" as threatened only with a permit.[81]

Tighter controls have been imposed by the CITES, for example, on trade in eight species of pangolin, a small, scaly anteater that bears the unfortunate burden of being the mammal in the world most targeted by illegal trade. It is killed and sent mostly to China, where its scaly skin is roasted for traditional medicine. New controls have also been imposed on trade in a species of wood commonly called "rosewood," which is highly valued commercially in China and other countries in the making of furniture with a deep red glow.

Heightened protections are also underway for the shrinking number of elephants, whose declining populations in Africa have been devastated by rampant poaching.[82] The CITES has banned all commercial trade in ivory from African elephants for decades. The issue has long been effective enforcement of this ban. In recent years, increased efforts have been made to shut down domestic ivory markets and stop the illicit ivory trade. The CITES has sought more effective enforcement at the national level. In 2015, the United States and China both announced plans to prohibit the ivory trade. A Chinese ban entered into force at the beginning of 2018. A month later, lawmakers in Hong Kong – a major crossroads for the illegal ivory trade – voted to outlaw all ivory sales by the beginning of 2022.[83] Meanwhile, in 2017 and into 2018, the new president of the United States equivocated on whether to keep or repeal the US restrictions on importing elephant trophies from Africa.[84]

A rapidly rising challenge is environmental crime, which includes the illegal sale of minerals, trafficking in hazardous waste, carbon credit fraud, and the species crimes that fall within the scope of the CITES, such as illegal logging and illegal fishing. According to Interpol, environmental crime is growing at the "alarming pace" of 5 to 7 percent per year, and is now worth between $91 billion and $258 billion annually. In contrast, the illegal small arms trade is worth around $3 billion annually. Environmental crime is now the fourth most valuable criminal enterprise in the world after drug smuggling, counterfeiting, and human trafficking. One of the 169 targets for 2030 of the UN Sustainable Development Goals is to "[t]ake urgent action to end poaching and trafficking of protected species of flora and fauna and address both demand and supply of illegal wildlife products."[85]

So far, there has been no WTO dispute directly challenging a CITES trade restriction. WTO judges have jurisdiction over only those claims that are made under one or more of the WTO agreements, and not claims made under other international agreements. It has, however, already been shown in the WTO shrimp–turtle dispute that, because it is a part of public international law, the CITES can be relevant to resolving WTO disputes under the WTO treaty. Because all the parties to that dispute were also parties to the CITES, the CITES was relevant there to determining the availability of a general exception to what would otherwise have been a trade obligation.[86] Other multilateral agreements could be relevant to the outcome of future WTO disputes in the same way. (Here, though, there is a legal caveat: An open issue still unresolved in WTO jurisprudence is whether a multilateral agreement that is not a part of the WTO treaty can be found in WTO dispute settlement to be binding on a WTO member that is *not* a party to it.)

One legal issue that has been resolved in WTO dispute settlement is whether WTO members have the policy space to apply trade restrictions to protect animal life. They do. By implication in WTO jurisprudence, they likewise have the policy space to impose limits on trade to protect plant life. This is the legal upshot of the Appellate Body ruling in 2014 in the WTO dispute arising from claims brought by Canada and Norway against the ban imposed by the European Union on importing and marketing seal products.[87] Although the Appellate Body ultimately ruled that the EU ban was not justified because of the arbitrary and unjustifiably discriminatory way in which certain exceptions to the ban were applied, the lasting significance of the ruling is that WTO judges first ruled provisionally that such a ban on seal products could potentially be justified under the general exception in the trade rules for measures "necessary to protect public morals," in this case the public morality of protecting animal welfare.[88]

The members of the WTO should not, however, leave the issue of the legality of national measures protecting animal welfare and other species protections to resolution in WTO dispute settlement. Rather, the resolution of this issue should be part of an overall effort by the WTO to reimagine the trade rules to make certain they are consistent with the aims of sustainable development. A good beginning toward this reimagining would be to borrow and to build on the long-lost language upholding wildlife protection as an exception to trade obligations in the failed Havana Charter of 1948.

Looking beyond the protection of threatened and endangered species of wildlife, the overall challenge of sustaining biodiversity is addressed in the United Nations Convention on Biological Diversity (CBD), which was one of the outcomes of the Rio Summit in 1992.[89] The CBD is intended to help preserve genetic diversity within species, species diversity, and the diversity of ecosystems.[90] The top priority for the CBD in pursuit of the targets of the Sustainable Development Goals is to "mainstream biodiversity into productive sectors, including agriculture, fisheries, tourism, and forests."[91] Two particular concerns relating to this pursuit are the assurance of biosafety and the assurance of fair access to, and a fair sharing of, genetic resources. Two protocols to the biodiversity convention deal with these two concerns, respectively: the Cartagena Protocol on Biosafety, concluded in 2000, and the Nagoya Protocol, on genetic resources, concluded in 2012.[92] Both of these protocols affect international trade and thus give rise to legal issues under the trade rules.

Under the biosafety protocol, the international movement, handling, and use of biotech products are subject to a variety of advance notice requirements. The protocol allows an importing country to use precaution to permit, deny, or impose conditions on the import of the notified product – including when there is a "lack of scientific certainty."[93] It is on the issue of "scientific certainty" that a potential collision awaits between the biosafety protocol and the WTO. The professed objective of the biosafety protocol is to act "in accordance with the precautionary approach in Principle 15" of the Rio Principles announced in 1992.[94] Principle 15 posits "the precautionary approach" in which, "[w]here there are threats of serious or irreversible damage, *lack of full scientific certainty* shall not be used as a reason for postponing cost-effective measures to prevent environmental degradation."[95] There is, though, no definition of "scientific certainty" in the biosafety protocol or in the Rio Principles set out in the Rio Declaration.

The vast majority of scientists tell us that there is no such thing as "scientific certainty." The late Richard Feynman, a Nobel Prize-winning physicist, declared, "All scientific knowledge is uncertain," for "you have to leave the door to the unknown ajar."[96] For his part, as a firm believer that freedom requires living with doubt and with the uncertainty of the unknown, Karl Popper insisted that an idea is "scientific" *only if it is uncertain.* An idea is a "scientific" idea, he taught, only if it is able to be "falsified," only if it can be refuted by further testing by observation through use of the trial and error of the scientific method. Any idea that cannot conceivably be refuted by further use of the scientific method is not "scientific." It is faith. Or it is superstition. Thus, the phrase "scientific certainty" is contradictory; it is an oxymoron.[97] Yet there this phrase is in the binding legal text of the Cartagena Protocol on Biosafety, causing no little consternation for those who cling to the scientific method. Little wonder that there has been so much global debate in legal and other international circles about the meaning and the content of this treaty expression of the precautionary principle, which enshrines the concept of scientific uncertainty as a legal term in an important part of international law.

The Appellate Body has, so far, been able to escape having to define the precautionary principle or to determine whether it has risen now to the level of customary international law. In a WTO dispute involving complaints by Canada and the United States about trade restrictions imposed by the European Union on imports of beef from those two countries treated with a number of growth hormones, the WTO judges concluded that the precautionary approach finds reflection in a WTO rule permitting provisional health safety measures "where relevant scientific evidence is insufficient."[98] But they stopped short of any definitive ruling on the issue.

To be consistent with WTO obligations, national measures protecting human, animal, or plant life or health or safety must be based on a scientific risk assessment, based on "scientific principles," and not "maintained without sufficient scientific evidence."[99] What do these terms mean? No definitions were included in the WTO treaty of "sufficient," of "scientific," or of "evidence," in no small part because the negotiators could not agree on the definitions. Yet the definitions of these treaty terms are often central to seeing where the right lines are denoting the boundaries of the policy space reserved by the WTO rules for national measures on human, plant, and animal health and safety.

Clarifying the meanings of these terms seems to have been left for now to WTO jurists in some future proceeding in WTO dispute settlement. When a ruling becomes necessary, it will not be easily reached. With "genetically modified organisms" (GMOs) and with other biotech products of all kinds, there are, from country to country, contrasting degrees of caution and differing attitudes and approaches to reducing risks to health and safety. WTO members remain free under WTO rules to choose their own "*appropriate* level of . . . protection against risks to human life or health, or to animal and plant life or health."[100] But your view of what is "necessary" and of what is "appropriate" to reduce health and safety risks may differ from mine, and it may depend on where you happen to be. There is resistance everywhere in the world to what is seen as second-guessing by international judges of national decisions about health and safety risks.

One regulatory approach is *not* to allow the marketing of a product *until* it is proven to be *safe*. Another regulatory approach is to allow the marketing of a product *unless* it is proven to be *unsafe*. Both of these contrasting regulatory approaches turn on a view of whether there can be such a thing as scientific certainty. The first approach assumes that there can be scientific certainty; the second assumes that there can never be any such thing because science is always uncertain. Rather than rely on the eventual resolution of this fundamental legal question about the meaning of science in dispute settlement, the members of the WTO would do well to work with their counterparts entrusted with the success of the biodiversity convention and of the biosafety protocol toward a shared solution. In the continued absence of one, the Appellate Body may eventually have to decide whether it agrees with Karl Popper.

An equally compelling concern about biodiversity is the protection of genetic resources. Take, for example, seeds, which have long been seen as part of the "common heritage of mankind." Seeds have, for generations, been free for replanting from the cornucopia of the Earth. Now enters modern science and the genetic modification of seeds. The modern alteration of seeds makes them much more productive. It can also restrict the possibility of replanting. From a common human resource, certain varieties of seeds, in their new, modified manifestations, have been transformed into the legal subjects of property rights. These property rights in genetic resources can inspire further innovations for the benefit of all people everywhere. They can also infringe on the traditional rights and diminish the natural resources of indigenous and other people in the developing countries where most of the Earth's genetic resources are found. Developing countries that have long treated genetic resources as shared resources now find they must respect the proprietary right in innovative new seed varieties that are claimed mainly by the multinational companies that have invented and produced them – often through securing access to the natural resources of those same developing countries.

In trying to draw the exact right line of the "in between" in international rules on genetic resources, the Convention on Biological Diversity agreed on the Nagoya Protocol, which entered into force in 2012. The protocol's titular assertion of the need for "access to genetic resources and the fair and equitable sharing of benefits arising from their utilization" summarizes its scope. In general, the Nagoya Protocol strives to strike a legal balance between, on the one hand, access by innovators to genetic resources and the protection of their intellectual property rights derived from their innovations and, on the other, access to these innovations, and a sharing in the benefits resulting from them.

This line-drawing balance is struck in the Nagoya Protocol by making access to genetic resources conditional on the consent of the country where the resources are located, and, where appropriate, of the "indigenous and local communities" involved.[101] The balance is struck also by requiring the sharing of the benefits derived from those genetic resources with the country from which those resources originate, and, where appropriate, also with "indigenous and local communities," through monetary and non-monetary compensation.[102] The line drawn here is consistent with one of the targets of the Sustainable Development Goals, to "[p]romote fair and equitable sharing of the benefits arising from the utilization of genetic resources and promote appropriate access to such resources, as internationally agreed" – a clear reference to the Nagoya Protocol.[103]

WTO rules are not necessarily inconsistent with the legal lines drawn in the Nagoya Protocol. The trade rules on intellectual property require all WTO members to provide patent protections to products and processes in "all fields of technology."[104] This requirement includes biotechnology. These rules, however, seem to provide an ample amount of policy space in the form of notable exceptions that can apply to biotechnology and its use of genetic resources. WTO members retain the flexibility to "adopt measures necessary to protect public health and nutrition, and to promote the public interest in sectors of vital importance to their socio-economic and technological development."[105] They may exclude from patentability any invention that "is necessary to protect *ordre public* [public policy] or morality, including to protect human, animal or plant life or health or to avoid serious prejudice to the environment."[106] They may also exclude from patentability as well "plants and animals and essential biological processes for the production of plants or animals."[107]

There is, however, much ongoing debate among WTO members about the right reading of these exceptions; and there has been, to date, no WTO jurisprudence fully clarifying their meaning. There is, for instance, no agreement among WTO members on whether current WTO rules require countries to allow patents on gene sequences. Nowhere do the existing WTO rules specifically reference genes or DNA. A global trading system that has, as a whole and despite its rules, still not quite come to terms with the need for the protection of intellectual property as essential to the protection of traded products stands somewhere short of being able to discern and delineate the right legal lines relating to the consequences of gene splicing.

WTO members should not wait and rely on this question – as well as other unanswered questions about the rights and uses of genetic resources – being answered at some unpredictable future date in dispute settlement. They should instead, as part of their reimagining of trade rules to promote sustainable development, negotiate and agree on an understanding on precisely where the legal lines should be drawn in the WTO trading system on genetic resources. In that agreed understanding, they should likewise spell out how these WTO rules relate to the rules in the UN Convention on Biological Diversity and in its Cartagena and Nagoya Protocols.[108]

INTERNATIONAL COMPETITION FOR LIMITED NATURAL RESOURCES

About forty minerals go into the making of a smartphone.[109] One of them is lithium, a crucial ingredient in the minute modern batteries that power smartphones, laptops, and electric cars. Lithium, a silvery-white metal, is – for good reason – called "white gold." A leading source of this precious metal essential to the perpetuation of the modern world is the remote salt flats in some of the poorest parts of the South American triangle connecting the interiors of Bolivia, Chile, and Argentina.[110] There, mining companies use vast volumes of water to suck tiny bits of the metal up through long hoses plunged deep into the salty underground waters. Then they use still more water to sift and to separate those bits of metal into a commercial treasure worth billions of dollars annually that is shipped through extended supply chains to the far corners of the world. Whether this mining is done sustainably, whether the supply chains are sustainable, and whether the impoverished indigenous peoples who own most of the salt flats profit sufficiently from the deals they have made with the mining companies that permit their mining are issues open to much debate.[111]

In addition to lithium, there is also sand. "Usable sand is a finite resource," and we are starting to run out of it. Sand, too, is an "essential ingredient that makes modern life possible." It is, for instance, indispensable to making cement. According to the United Nations Environment Programme, in one recent year alone "the world used enough concrete to build a wall 89 feet high and 89 feet wide around the Equator." In just two recent years alone, a growing China "used more cement than the United States used in the entire 20th century."[112] Not just any sand will do. Desert sand, with little water content, will simply not do for the construction of the buildings, the bridges, and all the rest of the built environment of the twenty-first century. Sand for construction must be wet. Thus, "to get the sand we need, we are stripping riverbeds, floodplains and beaches."[113] The willing of the world who study sand have long maintained that sand mining is causing untold damage to species and to ecosystems and that it should be subject worldwide to more oversight and to more restrictions that would promote sand sustainability.[114]

Lithium and sand are only two among many of the necessary ingredients of our modern human civilization caught up increasingly in an international competition for the world's limited natural resources. Given our need for global growth, and given the extent of global pressures on our natural resources, many of the willing, among them one of the leading authorities on the economic nexus of natural resources with fast-shrinking human "ecosystems services," Bernice Lee, "are predicting a global scramble for natural resources – energy, water, food and minerals – for decades to come, with the struggle taking place against a backdrop of environmental change, economic uncertainty and social unrest."[115]

In the years since the global financial crisis, one widespread expression of the fear of change has been the fear of resource scarcity. As Lee and her colleagues at Chatham House in London concluded just after the crisis, in 2012, "The world is undergoing a period of intensified resource stress, driven in part by the scale and speed of demand growth from emerging economies and a decade of tight commodity markets. Poorly designed and short-sighted policies are also making things worse, not better. Whether or not resources are actually running out, the outlook is one of supply disruptions, volatile prices, accelerated environmental degradation and rising tensions over resource access."[116]

The ups and downs of the global economy in the years since have done nothing to alter this conclusion. Resource competition has intensified, and it is heightened by the fact that natural resources are unevenly distributed among the countries of the world.[117] From this competition, John Gray, the pessimistic British political philosopher, foresees the outbreak of "new wars of scarcity."[118] The ancient Mesopotamians fought over water. The Spanish explorers fought over gold. The European imperialists fought over how to carve up and exploit the rich resources of Africa. Now, he says, "[t]he strategic rivalries of the cold war are being followed," once again, "by resource wars."[119] One of the worst of the fears of the willing is that these commercial wars will become shooting wars.

Today's "resource wars" will differ from those of the past in one crucial respect. There is much less of an abundance of global natural resources to carve up today than before, for we are fast approaching the limits of our natural resources in this new human Age of the Anthropocene. This historical difference may make both commercial wars and shooting wars over diminishing natural resources more likely. Indeed, national defense theorists are so concerned about the potentially dire consequences of resource competition driven by continued unsustainable development that they have coined a phrase denoting a new kind of national security – "natural security."[120] A British thinktank, the Royal United Services Institute, has warned, "If uncontrolled, climate change will have security implications of similar magnitude to the World Wars, but which will last for centuries."[121] This judgment applies to the implications of climate change, and to the implications also of every other facet of humanity's assault on the Earth's ecosystems and natural resources.

International trade is much in the midst of all the rising conflicts worldwide over resources. In fact, international trade has helped make these conflicts more global than ever before. Once, only the most valuable resources could be traded among nations because of the costs involved in shipping. Today, "almost every raw material imaginable" can be shipped afar to foreign shores.[122] With the death of distance, with the spread of far-ranging supply chains, and with the successive lowering of many tariff barriers to resources trade, both the volume and the variety of international trade in natural resources have exploded.

The expansion of international trade in commodities and in other natural resources has led to increasing interdependence among trading nations "at a time when the global economy is more dependent than ever on trade in resources."[123] Interdependence demands international cooperation; but, for some countries, it has led, instead, to a reactive turn inward toward an embrace of partial economic isolation. This turn inward has accelerated with the retreat from globalization since the global financial crisis. Food, fuel, raw materials, strategic minerals and metals – the trade in all these necessary resources has been limited from time to time and from place to place in the name of "self-sufficiency."

Standing out among the trade restrictions imposed with the aim of self-sufficiency have been restrictions on food exports. Nearly one-third of the countries in the world resorted to restrictions on food exports during the global food crisis leading up to the global financial crisis.[124] These food export restrictions did the very opposite of assuring food security. For example, "45% of the price increase in rice during the crisis" has been attributed "to the attempts by countries to insulate their domestic markets, including through the use of export restrictions."[125] Yet, as two of the world's leading trade scholars, Robert Howse and Tim Josling, have pointed out, even with this documented link between food price increases and the use of export restrictions, much of the continuing debate over the expressed "Right to Food" in the United Nations increasingly implies – "regardless of competitiveness, trade distortions, and domestic consumer prices" – a right to self-sufficiency.[126]

Self-sufficiency is an ancient illusion. In ancient Greece, some Athenians extolled the supposed societal virtues of "autarky," the Greek word for self-sufficiency. They foresaw – as Adam Smith did centuries later – the potentially deleterious impacts of specialization on the wholeness of human identity. But where he counseled as a remedy "the education of the people,"[127] they argued for maintaining the economic self-sufficiency of the Greek city-state, insulated from foreign trade. Over time, of course, ancient Athens became anything but an economic autarky. The market in Athens became a crossroads for the maritime trade throughout the Mediterranean and much of the Middle East. Athens, for example, imported most of its grain. Today, what remains of the ancient Athenian agora is still marked by the stone paths of a far-flung trade.[128]

But the appeal of autarky has continued to assail humanity again and again through all the centuries since. Insular medievalists, bullion-hungry mercantilists, Hitler's Germany, Mussolini's Italy, Franco's Spain, communist Albania, Cambodia under the Khmer Rouge – all trumpeted, at one time or another, what they saw as the national benefits of an economic self-sufficiency secured through economic isolation. Many of them coupled with their professed self-sufficiency a "growth strategy" of their own devising that was designed to enable them to profit from exports while also soaking up the natural resources of other, weaker countries by economic exploitation, or by stealing those resources by outright conquest.

All these and many other past experiments with differing versions of a would-be self-sufficiency ultimately failed. Yet, today, many countries, almost all of them members of the WTO, seem to be rediscovering and repeating these old and oft-discredited calls for the autarkic illusion.[129] In their fearful scramble to secure what they see as their fair share of global natural resources, they have turned inward, and some of them have turned to hoarding.[130] About one-third of all WTO members, mostly developing countries, have imposed a whole potpourri of export restrictions on not only food, but also a variety of other traded products.[131]

One fundamental economic truth belies the entirety of the age-old argument for self-sufficiency: No one person and no one country has a sufficient amount or combination of resources to be self-sufficient in everything. This is true of every one of us as individuals. This is equally true of every one of the countries in which we live. Thus, those countries that choose to impose restrictions on exports of one product will surely learn soon enough that, to meet their own needs, they will have to import some other product from one of the countries disadvantaged by their export restriction. Export restrictions make no economic sense. Export restrictions disrupt global supply chains, create economic inefficiencies by distorting the allocation of limited natural resources, and subsidize local producers by lowering the domestic prices of inputs and also by increasing prices for foreign producers. This gives the foreign producers an artificial incentive to move offshore to be closer to their sources of raw materials.

As a development strategy for developing countries especially, a reliance on export restrictions leaves much to be desired. The noted trade economist Claude Barfield observes, "[R]ecent economic research has demonstrated that for some of the important goals – to nurture infant industry, to control inflation, to underpin social policy and income distribution, and to buttress government revenue – export restrictions are less than reliable and must overcome important pitfalls. For instance, without flexible financial markets, efficient and non-corrupt tax systems, and carefully crafted social reforms, developing nations will find it difficult to direct the income from export taxes into socially coherent programs."[132] He goes on to say,

"Further, regarding the infant industry motive, there is the danger (a circumstance often encountered) that the subsidies will result in the maintenance of inefficient companies whose owners are better at rent-seeking from government bureaucrats than constructing an efficient manufacturing process."[133]

But a fearful hoarding of natural resources in furtherance of an illusory self-sufficiency as a part of a national development strategy is not, however, the only motive for the proliferation of export restrictions. There are other reasons for these restrictions that have nothing to do with the "beggar-thy-neighbor" effects of hoarding. Among these other reasons can be the protection of the environment and the preservation of exhaustible natural resources, as well as other dimensions of sustainable development. Export restrictions may not make economic sense; but can they sometimes make sense for sustainability? This is a question for thoughtful consideration by the members of the WTO in the reimagining of the trade rules relating to natural resources.

REIMAGINING INTERNATIONAL TRADE RULES ON NATURAL RESOURCES

The trade rules relating to export restrictions "are overall weaker and less comprehensive than those applicable on import barriers."[134] The rules of the world trading system have always been more about limiting restrictions on imports than on limiting restrictions on exports. When the rules were written, soon after the Second World War, the overriding concern of the trade negotiators doing the writing was to prevent a resurgence of the high tariffs that had deepened and prolonged the Great Depression and contributed to the start of that war. Export restrictions were rare at the time. Moreover, some countries wished to preserve their right to restrict exports in some way during that time of overall global economic uncertainty.

As a general rule, "quantitative restrictions" – measures that limit the quantity of a product that may be imported or exported – are illegal under WTO rules unless they are "duties, taxes, or other charges."[135] These illegal quantitative restrictions on imports or exports are broad in scope and can include such governmental measures as bans, quotas, and import and export licenses, as well as other trade-limiting measures applied through state trading operations, mixing regulations, minimum export price requirements, voluntary export restraints, restrictions on ports of entry, trade balancing requirements, and the like.[136]

For certain exports, there are exceptions to the prohibition on quantitative restrictions. One is the exception for export restrictions applied "temporarily . . . to prevent or relieve critical shortages of foodstuffs or other products essential to the exporting" country.[137] This exception can provide "legal cover" in the existing rules for export restrictions on food – whether or not they make any economic sense.[138] Left, however, to debate and deliberation in dispute settlement by this loophole are the legal definitions of "temporarily," of "critical shortages," and of when a product is "essential" to the exporting country.

Moreover, and significantly, while the WTO rules establish a means for WTO members to agree to limits on tariffs and taxes on *imports*, they do not provide any similar means for limiting tariffs and taxes on *exports*. The WTO rules provide a legal framework for WTO members to make binding concessions on such restrictions on *imports*.[139] Filling in this framework with mutual trade concessions on restrictions on imports has been central to the work of the trading system since its beginning. But no mention is made in the rules of the provision of a comparable framework for making similar concessions on restrictions on *exports*. Nothing in the WTO rules in any way prevents the building by WTO members of a legal framework within the WTO to help facilitate concessions on export restrictions, but one does not exist. This is a missing piece in the enabling rules framework for world trade that is the WTO.

Because of this omission in the trade rules, any country wanting to restrict exports has, since the beginning of the world trading system, been left free to do so under the rules simply by imposing that restriction in the form of a tariff or a tax. No country can discriminate between and among its WTO trading partners in doing so; the basic rule of most-favored-nation treatment applies. All the same, it has long served no purpose for a country affected by any kind of trade-distorting export restriction other than a tariff or a tax to challenge that restriction in dispute settlement – because that restriction could simply be converted into a tariff or a tax and thereby be legalized.[140]

As concerns over export restrictions have risen in recent years, there have been two significant legal rulings by the Appellate Body in disputes relating to export restraints. Both challenged Chinese restrictions on vital mineral exports, and both may be harbingers of many more such disputes that may be on the horizon. In one of the two disputes, the United States, the European Union, and Mexico challenged Chinese restrictions on exports of nine key raw materials vital to the production of steel, aluminum, and certain chemicals.[141] In the other dispute, the United States, the European Union, and Japan challenged Chinese restrictions on exports of the "rare earth elements" that are critical to making magnets, lasers, computer monitors, fiber-optic cables, cell phones, ceramics, stainless steel, low-energy light bulbs, wind turbines, and batteries for hybrid and electric cars. At the time, China mined 93 percent of the total world production of seventeen rare earth elements in the middle of the periodic table.[142]

China lost on the most important legal claims in both of these disputes because China is not bound by the same rules on export taxes as most other WTO members. Upon joining the WTO, China and other newer members, mostly developing countries, have in some instances accepted higher WTO obligations than those that bind other WTO members. In the "accession" agreement China made with other WTO members when it became a member of the WTO in 2001, China agreed not to impose export taxes on a list of eighty-four products. Among these products were all those at issue in the raw materials and rare earths disputes.[143]

Some other countries – including Russia, Croatia, Ukraine, and Vietnam, among others – have made similar commitments on export taxes as a condition of their joining the WTO.[144] The vast majority of WTO members, however, can still freely impose export taxes. (An exception, it should be noted here, is the United States, which is barred by the United States Constitution from imposing taxes on exports.)[145] The countries that have undertaken these additional obligations to gain entry into the WTO did so voluntarily, albeit under pressure from other, existing WTO members. These differing trade obligations do, though, raise real questions of fairness in a trading system founded on principles of non-discrimination.[146]

Conceivably, an export restriction could be excused under one or more of the general exceptions to the current trade rules. It could be "necessary to protect human, animal or plant life or health,"[147] "relating to the conservation of exhaustible natural resources,"[148] or "essential to the acquisition or distribution of products in general or local short supply."[149] But the country claiming the exception must prove that the measure being challenged is one that fits within that specific category of exception. A general defense, for example, that the measure was taken for purposes of sustainable development will not suffice. China did not meet this burden of proof in the raw materials and rare earths disputes. Plus, even if the challenged measure does fit within one of the specified categories of potentially available exceptions, that measure will – as with all claims for general exceptions under the WTO trade rules – be in violation of WTO rules if it is applied in a manner that constitutes "a means of arbitrary or unjustifiable discrimination between countries where the same conditions prevail, or a disguised restriction on international trade."[150]

Recall that Principle 2 of the UN Rio Principles of 1992 declares: "States have, in accordance with the Charter of the United Nations and the principles of international law, the sovereign right to exploit their own resources pursuant to their own environmental and developmental policies, and the responsibility to ensure that activities within their jurisdiction or control do not cause damage to the environment of other States or of areas beyond the limits of national jurisdiction."[151] But where is the right line – the "in between" – of the right balance between fair access for foreign producers to needed local natural resources and the domestic policy space reserved for WTO members to regulate consistently with the stated purpose in the preamble to the WTO treaty of the "optimal use" of resources for sustainable development?

Central to drawing this right line in the reimagining of world trade rules is the legal question of whether a country is free to pollute all it wishes in its own domestic production and in its own chosen use of its own sovereign natural resources – even if its actions cause environmental harm in other countries.[152] The answer under the longstanding international environmental legal principle of no transboundary harm in the balance set out in Rio Principle 2 is "No."[153] This legal principle outlawing transboundary harm is not, however, a WTO obligation. So it cannot support a claim in WTO dispute settlement. Under the current WTO rules, it can be raised only in mounting a defense.

Conceivably, reliance in defense of an *export* restriction in WTO dispute settlement on the legal argument that a restriction is intended to prevent transboundary harm could succeed. A country conscientious about global sustainability may wish to prevent not only the harm to its own country, but also the harm to other countries that could result from a certain type of unsustainable use of its own sovereign natural resources. But here the fate of China in the raw materials and rare earths disputes counsels caution. To prevail, it would have to be proven by the country applying the export restriction that it fit into one of the limited number of specific categories of general exceptions to WTO obligations, and proven also that it had not been applied in a manner that constituted "arbitrary or unjustifiable discrimination" or a "disguised restriction on international trade."

Equally, reliance on the principle of no transboundary harm in defense of an environmentally motivated trade *import* restriction in WTO dispute settlement could arise from a circumstance such as this actual one: Scientists have determined that greenhouse gas emissions from Chinese export industries are being carried by powerful winds within days all the way across the Pacific Ocean. These "imported" GHG emissions are causing "dangerous spikes in contaminants" and a decline in the air quality in the western United States.[154] Could an import restriction applied by the United States be justified under the WTO rules? Here the environmental harm would occur within the territorial boundaries of the United States. Here, too, the same general WTO trade rules and exceptions would apply where products made with the use of natural resources or made with an effect on natural resources are entered into international trade.

What if no environmental harm were done within the territory of the country imposing the import restriction? Under the WTO rules, can a country impose restrictions on imported products because of its environmental and other sustainability concerns *beyond the borders of its own territory*? Does a WTO member have the legal right under the WTO treaty to apply unilateral import restrictions on imported products when those products are produced in ways that cause environmental destruction and pollution – even if that pollution and that destruction do not occur within its own national borders? If a waiver is advised to legalize climate actions that impose import restrictions, then what does this imply about the legality of import restrictions imposed for other environmental and sustainability purposes? All this must be considered by the members of the WTO in reimagining WTO rules to support sustainable development.

Pointedly, the Appellate Body, in its shrimp–turtle ruling, reserved the legal question of whether there is an "implied jurisdictional limitation" in the general environmental exceptions to WTO obligations, "and, if so, the nature and extent of that limitation."[155] More recently, in the seals dispute, the Appellate Body was not faced with ruling on this issue because the defense of the contested measure by the

European Union was based not on protecting animal welfare or exhaustible natural resources, but on upholding local "public morals" – another of the general exceptions to WTO obligations. Although the Europeans did invoke the general exception for measures "necessary to protect ... animal ... life or health," the WTO panel did not rule on this defense.[156] The unresolved issue was not raised by the disputing countries on appeal, and, thus, the Appellate Body was not confronted with the possibility of having to rule on the legality of the arguably extraterritorial aspects of the seal measure on appeal. So the issue of the territorial legal limits of environmentally motivated national actions remains an open question under WTO law.

To meet the target in the Sustainable Development Goals of effecting, by 2030, "the sustainable management and efficient use of natural resources," and as part of blending economy and environment into one in the world trade rules, there must be a reimagining of the trade rules on natural resources.[157] In this needed reimagining, the members of the WTO must strive for a consensus that acknowledges the advantages of their increasing interdependence due to resources trade, and that strikes the right balance between the sovereign use and the cooperative sharing of natural resources through trade. The topic of trade in natural resources is not on the Doha Development Agenda, and thus has not, formally, been on the table in WTO negotiations in this century. Although a number of Doha round and other WTO negotiations have touched on natural resources issues and have had the potential to shape rules relevant to resources trade, WTO members have long been at odds over where and how to draw the line between national sovereignty and market access.[158] This division within the WTO has contributed to the current inadequacies in the trade rules on, for example, export taxes and other export restrictions, and it must be overcome.

This division must be overcome with a "more holistic approach" treating economy and environment as one in the line-drawing on trade and natural resources.[159] Such an approach is necessary to ensure that "trade and economic endeavor" will be conducted consistently with "the optimal use of the world's resources in accordance with the objective of sustainable development," as envisaged in the preamble to the WTO treaty.[160] No longer can economic disputes over natural resources be considered separate and apart from their environmental and other sustainability implications in the WTO. Notable as a potential model for dealing with some of the knottier issues in resources trade is the waiver granted to a large group of WTO members to allow them to restrict trade under the Kimberley Process intended to ban trade in conflict diamonds.[161] These diamonds are called "blood diamonds" because the proceeds of trade in them are often used to finance armed conflicts. The blessing by the WTO of these trade restrictions is a precedent for WTO approval of other trade restrictions that similar coalitions of government, industry, and civil society might embrace to tackle other dark doings in resources trade.

A legal framework should be established in the WTO rules to enable making concessions to limit export tariffs and taxes in much the same way that the rules already enable concessions to limit import tariffs and taxes.[162] This could be done on a product-by-product basis in ways that make sustainability distinctions between and among different metals, minerals, commodities, and other natural resources. As a part of this reimagining of the world trade rules, the inequities should be eliminated in how the rules currently treat the export taxes of different WTO members. Limits on export taxes must no longer apply only to China, Vietnam, and some other new members that have joined the WTO during its first two decades. Limits on export taxes must now apply to all the members of the WTO. (Perhaps China will wish to lead the way in proposing this reform.)

In addition to this new legal framework for facilitating export trade concessions, there could be sectoral agreements in manufacturing, mining, and agricultural industries on the treatment of different types of natural resources. In extractive industries, for instance, as some of the willing have suggested, these sectoral agreements could endorse and perhaps incorporate the private production standards and voluntary principles and guidelines that are proliferating for mining all over the world. Similar agreements could be concluded in steel, cement, and other industries. These agreements could also address the extent to which process and production methods – PPMs – used in extracted products could be accepted as a justification for restricting imports based on the environmental consequences of their production. Promoting and upholding affirmative and internationally coordinated actions to improve sustainability could also be an important part of these agreements.[163]

New efforts should be made, too, to overcome the deep divisions between resource-rich and resource-poor countries by at last drawing the right lines "in between" national sovereignty and market access in new rules on trade in natural resources. These right lines would answer the unanswered questions about the legality of extraterritoriality in national actions to accomplish natural resources and other environmental ends. As of now, the drawing of these lines is not even on the WTO negotiating agenda. It will, to say the least, be extraordinarily difficult to draw these and other lines relating to resources trade in ways that will inspire a consensus of support among all the members of the WTO. But, if a consensus is not reached by the members of the WTO on drawing these new lines in new rules, it will be left, to a great extent, to WTO judges to draw these lines eventually, and unavoidably, in the existing rules during future dispute settlement. Whether the rules they construe are appropriate for drawing these new lines, and whether the lines the judges draw turn out to be right or wrong, this judicial line-drawing will provoke charges of judicial overreaching by those who will not like the ways the lines will be drawn. Better to negotiate than to litigate.

The periodic reviews by the WTO of the trade policies of every WTO member offer an additional opportunity for integrating natural resources and sustainability concerns into the WTO trading system.[164] These reviews are intended to evaluate the entirety of an individual WTO member's trade policies and practices for their impact on the world trading system. Toward fulfillment of the stated WTO aim of trading in ways that promote sustainable development, these reviews should be expanded to evaluate as well the impact of trade policies and practices on sustainability.[165] Special attention should be paid to encouraging sustainability in each of the individual links in global supply chains.

Obviously, such a reimagining of the trade rules affecting natural resources must take into account other rules relating to natural resources in environmental and other international agreements that overlap with trade – such as the Montreal Protocol, the CITES, and, certainly, the Paris Agreement on climate change and the Sustainable Development Goals. The same is true of every other reimagining of the trade rules that may be needed to unite economy and environment into one to attain the global goals for sustainable development. Equally, other international legal frameworks must be more mindful in their line-drawing and rule-writing of the legal framework for trade that has done so much to help lift and liberate the entire world.

What is most needed worldwide toward the accomplishment of our goals relating to the treatment of natural resources, as in all else, is a greatly enhanced appreciation of the merits of Tocqueville's "principle of interest rightly understood." Countries everywhere must find the will and the way to perceive and to pursue their national "self-interest" as viewed – not just here and now – but over the broader and longer term. This enlightened conception of "self-interest" must be reflected in the substance of the rules they write. It must also be reflected in the procedures and the other pieces of the international legal frameworks they build. And yet – as any lawyer anywhere in the world would advise – no matter how enlightened rules may be, rules are fully laws only if there are fair and effective procedures in legal frameworks that uphold and enforce them.

17

On Making and Remaking Enabling Frameworks for Sustainable Development

Consider the traffic light. For a traffic light to work, we must first see the need for lights to tell us when to stop and when to go. We must next believe that other people will all also see the same need to heed the lights when they stop and when they go. If traffic lights are to be anything more than bright adornments at street intersections, we must all be willing to stop when the light is red and go only when the light turns green. Now consider all the red lights and all the green lights of all the international rules that must somehow be agreed together and brought together to work together to achieve global sustainable development. We can write all the right rules. We can draw all the right lines in those rules. We can combine those rules together in international agreements. We can link those international agreements together through still more international agreements. We can call those rules, and we can call those agreements, each and all, "international law." But, if the traffic lights of the rules on which we have agreed in all those interlinked agreements are ignored, then those rules might as well not exist, and they cannot rightly be called "law."

ENABLING FRAMEWORKS FOR SUSTAINABLE DEVELOPMENT

As with the traffic light, there are prerequisites to the existence of something worthy of being labeled "law." Preceding law is the shared perception of the need for law, and preceding law also is the shared willingness to be ruled by law. Will precedes law. Will creates law. Will sustains law. Will upholds and enforces law. If there is no will, if there is no will individually, or if there is no will collectively, to enforce the law, then there will be no willingness by one or by all to follow it. There will be a traffic jam at every crowded intersection. To prevent a paralyzing clog of traffic jams, to progress through all the intersections that threaten to slow us in our travel toward our chosen destination of sustainable development, to make law work for all of us, we must – all of us – be willing to cooperate on the common concerns of humanity.

Law can emerge only from willful cooperation. International law can emerge only from willful international cooperation. Only an enabling framework of international law can liberate us from the chaos and the coercion of a Melian world in which might makes right and in which sustainable development therefore cannot be achieved. Yet, in the pursuit of global sustainable development, and in the pursuit of all else that matters to a struggling and striving humanity, right can prevail over might through the rule of law only as a consequence of willing cooperation. Mutually willed cooperation must begin through a mutual initial commitment to working together to establish the rule of law. Cooperation must then continue, and it must evolve, to enhance and to enforce the law.

The historical evolution of international law has played a central role in the evolution of human civilization. It has truly been an "evolution of cooperation."[1] This long evolution toward an ever-greater reliance on cooperation through the means of law has occurred in parallel with a gradual evolution in our perception of what constitutes our self-interest. It has occurred along with, and has been inspired and spurred by, a concomitant evolution in how each one of us, and how each country and each leader that acts as an agent for some subset of us, has seen our own interests and has seen our best means of serving those interests in an unwilling world.

Here, once more, we meet that proselytizer for law, the rule of law, and the enlightened view of self-interest, the Frenchman Alexis de Tocqueville. Remember, he implores us, from the distance of the early nineteenth century, his "principle of interest rightly understood." It is this principle, this better way of seeing our interest that takes the broader and the longer view, which is the wellspring of the will not only to create law, but also to be ruled by it. In embracing this principle, in taking the broader and the longer view by creating law and by upholding the rule of law, we must each – to be able to progress, to succeed, indeed to survive – choose cooperation over confrontation. We must do so domestically, and, in today's interconnected and interdependent world, we must most certainly do so internationally.

Cooperation or confrontation is forever the choice in all human relations. Human nature being what it is, burdened by the ever-present and unrelenting itch of violence and depravity, cooperation is not always possible. Yet, in any human interaction, cooperation – if possible – is always the better choice. Cooperation spreads and seals the redeeming veneer of civilization that conceals and constrains the worst in human nature that is always lurking somewhere down inside each of us. But it takes only one bully to start a fight in a playground. Cooperation will be chosen over confrontation only if all those who are part of the interaction see that choosing cooperation serves their own interests. This is true of cooperation between you and me. This is equally true of international cooperation between and among sovereign states.

As the Enlightenment philosopher Immanuel Kant taught us, the goal of international cooperation by making and upholding international law is not to subordinate the independent wills of sovereign states. Just the opposite, the goal is to coordinate the joint workings of those independent wills "with a view to maximizing *both* individual freedom of action *and* due respect for the rights of fellow actors, in some kind of combination."[2] The aim, Kant said, is "the maintenance and security of each nation's own freedom, as well as that of the other nations leagued with it" in cooperation and law.[3] Cooperation through making law and upholding the rule of law is not intended to override or subdue the freedom of states. It is intended to preserve and enlarge that freedom, and to add substance to it in a world filled with concerns that ignore the human artifice of political borders.

In Kant's proposed "alternative to the Hobbesian world of anarchy and perpetual conflict," the goal, as Stephen Neff has put it, is "to devise a system in which all of the agents would be left with their freedom – but would *exercise* that freedom in a spirit of self-restraint and mutual respect."[4] The goal, he says, is to fashion "a system in which there is no central authority and no external enforcement mechanism. Order emerges because each actor, on its *own*, in the rational pursuit of its self-interest, sees fit to constrain its *own* behavior in certain ways. Underpinning this system is a shared ethic of rationality and reciprocity – and also of *self*-discipline."[5] As Neff notes, in this insight, the sage of Konigsberg anticipated Robert Axelrod's view of the "evolution of cooperation" by nearly two centuries.

A shared international willingness to cooperate in making enabling international rules is a prerequisite to all that sovereign states seek to achieve together, and it is especially so of the cooperative construction needed to unite economy and environment together as one in advancing global sustainable development. A "carefully constructed institutional architecture" is necessary for this shared task.[6] Still more essential is compliance with the rules we make and, equally, cooperation in revising and adding to those rules as needed over time, no matter the push of passing political pressures. What is more, a shared international willingness to cooperate is required, too, to shape the enabling international frameworks we build in such a way that they can be linked together so as to work together in making the willing world. Indeed, there may not only be a *need* to cooperate. There may also be a *duty* to cooperate. Rafael Leal-Arcas of Queen Mary University of London maintains that, "when it comes to *some* matters of common concern, states are not simply *encouraged* to cooperate; they are in fact *obliged* to do so, in line with their responsibilities under international law."[7]

Two of the willing, Daniel Bodansky and Elliot Diringer, have helpfully summarized "the evolution of multilateral regimes" in their work on international cooperation on climate change: "International regimes rarely emerge in a single step, fully formed. Instead, a regime – as well as the broader set of agreements and institutions addressing an issue area, often referred to as a 'regime complex' – typically evolve over time."[8] As they explain this evolutionary process, first, an international political consensus must form "about whether a problem exists – and, if so, how to address it," which "often takes considerable time to emerge."

Next, "an evolutionary process allows for trial and error." Third, "regimes need to be able to respond in a flexible manner," which is notably the case in environmental regimes, where "there is a particular need for flexibility and evolution, because our understanding of problems is likely to change as science and technology develop." Lastly, "in order to make binding international commitments, states need to have confidence and trust in a regime. Generally, trust emerges only slowly over time, as an institution develops a track record that states can evaluate."[9]

Furthermore, as Bodansky and Diringer say, regimes consisting of international rules in international frameworks can evolve to become deeper, broader, and more integrated over time.[10] In becoming deeper, a rules framework can move incrementally from weaker institutions to more authoritative institutions, from vague and weaker obligations to more precise and stronger obligations, from voluntary arrangements to legally binding arrangements, and also from little or no rules enforcement to "the development of stronger review, dispute settlement, and enforcement mechanisms."[11] In becoming broader, a rules framework can gradually expand to include more members and more subjects, and "can also broaden from regional to global arrangements."[12] In becoming more integrated, a rules framework can shift over time from initially addressing "a problem in a fragmented way, through a number of different instruments, institutions, or procedures" toward gradually becoming "more integrated through institutional consolidation or linkages."[13]

Of course, a common challenge in the evolution of all international rules frameworks is enforcement. Dating back to antiquity, as Neff has recounted, meeting this challenge has been paramount in the process of upholding international law through international agreements.[14] The very first treaties in ancient times were accompanied by cries from the makers of the treaties calling down "supernatural sanctions" in the form of curses from heaven on anyone who was so brazen as to breach the treaties.[15] With the passing of the centuries, the invocation of heavenly curses was succeeded by such substitutes as arbitration, collective security, and – in the case of many contemporary international trade agreements as well as some international environmental and other agreements – trade and other economic sanctions.

The best illustration of how international cooperation can evolve over time is the rules-based world trading system. After more than seven decades, the trade rules regime that began, with a handful of countries, as the GATT and is now, with 164 countries, the WTO deepened, broadened, and integrated to the point where it can be seen in many ways as a model for the creation and the evolution of other needed international rules-based institutions. Additional leading examples of international rules frameworks that have evolved successfully in these ways with time and with experience include the European Court of Justice, the European Court of Human Rights, and the CITES. Other regimes of environmental rules on matters ranging from protection of the wetlands to protection against industrial pollutants have likewise similarly evolved.[16]

In their fondest dreams, the champions of international law share in the idealistic hope for some day creating a "Parliament of man, the Federation of the World," that can do all that, first, the all-too-weak "League of Nations," and, so far, the all-too-divided "United Nations," have not done to unite humanity and to help inspire further human advance.[17] They see the international rule of law as central to the eventual realization of this shared hope. Few, however, of these tribunes for international law seek a world government. Most of them, like Kant, seek instead a willing cooperation among governments, enlightened by a Tocquevillian view of the nature of self-interest. All of them see the international rule of law as the indispensable means to this end. Many of the advocates of international law "envisage a whole system of rules," a system of "rules that are not seen as abstract and formal . . . but instead as fairly specific, concrete, and substantive."[18] Like many others among the willing, they foresee a future where "[a]n overarching rule of law would operate in a continuous fashion to resolve clashes of jurisdiction between substantive norms, and also to deal with abuses of powers and rights."[19]

Toward this bright day, the emergence and the spread of international law in so many international rules agreed in so many international frameworks form the very essence of the true bottom-up. A gradual accumulation of rules permits the testing by trial and error of new and competing ideas.[20] Some will work. Some will not. Those that work locally and regionally can be scaled up over time to work globally. Systemic targets of the Sustainable Development Goals are to "develop effective, accountable and transparent institutions at all levels," to "ensure responsive, inclusive, participatory and representative decisionmaking at all levels," and to "broaden and strengthen the participation of developing countries in the institutions of global governance."[21] Certainly reforms can be instituted at the global level to help reach these targets. These reforms, though, are more likely to be reached if they emerge from the experience of the lessons learned from the practical improvisation of the true bottom-up.

Like the geometric patterns of tessellated tiles, the individual pieces of international law can be put in place separately but can also be fit together collectively over time to comprise a coherent and consistent whole. New and innovative rules frameworks of all kinds arising from everywhere in the world can become the true proving grounds for the varied and the creative ways we need for keeping all the ambitious promises in the Sustainable Development Goals. In shaping and sharing a sustainable global prosperity, ours must not be the top-down of forcing "everyone to conform to a single, static vision" of sustainable development.[22] Ours must be the bottom-up of freeing everyone to cooperate in a manner of their own choosing to define sustainable development by doing it. By competing in finding and in drawing the right lines in separate and different rules frameworks, we can, with experience, learn which rules are best for certain purposes and for certain places, and we can, moreover, learn which rules are best for scaling up to be applied worldwide. In the end, it will be through this global legal version of learning by doing, through this creative competition in legal arrangements in the catalytic mix of the true bottom-up, that we will discover how to achieve and how to ensure the right coherency and the right consistency in all our international rule-making.

This bottom-up rule-making need not be and must not be limited solely to governments. The global sustainable development we seek can emerge in part from networked agreements that include parties that are not governments, and it can result even from such agreements that do not involve governments at all. With good reason, Winnie Byanyima, executive director of Oxfam, has reminded us on climate change that, "[v]oluntary action by the private sector will not be enough on its own. We need strong political leadership and ambitious government regulations to catalyze the global action that both the science and a growing number of people around the world demand."[23] Indeed we do. Yet it is equally true that even the best of political and governmental actions on their own will not be enough to combat climate change and further our other goals for sustainable development.

Onora O'Neill, Baroness O'Neill of Bengarve, the renowned Cambridge philosopher, is among the many worldwide who are increasingly questioning whether the Westphalian system that has prevailed since 1648 – in which states alone make and are bound to comply with international law – must yield to a post-Westphalian approach that extends both the making and the reach of international law beyond states. "[S]tatist approaches to cosmopolitan justice are now implausible," she says. "The initial assumption that states alone are *primary agents of justice* views states, and states alone, as having the will and the capabilities to discharge, delegate or assign all obligations of justice."[24] The answer, she suggests, is to adopt "a more robust view of the plurality of agents of justice that might play some part in institutionalizing cosmopolitan principles of justice" – such as those expressed in the United Nations Sustainable Development Goals.[25]

This task in a post-Westphalian and willing world will necessarily include as "agents of justice" the private sector, NGOs, and other assemblies of civil society. On many matters, these non-state actors should be permitted to sign and to be bound by international agreements in the same way as governments. On some matters which exclusively involve governments, such as arms control and war and peace, it makes sense to continue with exclusively state-to-state agreements. But this is not necessarily so "for issues like trade and climate change, in which many decisionmakers drive actions and outcomes."[26] In the willing world, all those who drive international results must be involved in making international decisions, and they must be bound by and held accountable for them.

We humans are not motivated always and solely by self-interest. It may be that, for all our ineluctable inclination toward violence and depravity, there is nevertheless something in human nature that tends toward justice. It may be that there stands, some distance apart from the mere matter of our self-interest, "the impartial spectator" of Adam Smith's imagining in his "theory of moral sentiments," the quiet watcher within each of us who knows "that to feel much for others, and little for ourselves, that to restrain our selfish, and to indulge our benevolent, affections, constitutes the perfection of human nature."[27] There may be a "universal conscious- ness of justice."[28] But if it exists, "this innate instinct of justice," as Neff concludes, requires "the presence of certain social, economic, political, and religious condi- tions to flourish to its fullest extent."[29]

One of these conditions is the presence of an enabling rules framework that extends the circle of human concern beyond local borders to include the wider world. The intrinsic localism and tribalism of all of humankind have long broken down into "us" and "them." The surpassing challenge in the making of enabling rules in enabling frameworks for sustainable development, and for all the other purposes of international law, is the challenge of seeing an ever-widening circle of "other" people as "us" rather than as "them." This is the challenge of forging what the nineteenth-century British historian and moralist W. E. H. Lecky described as "the enlarging circle of sympathy" that gradually extends beyond the family, the immediate community, the country, and coalitions of countries to include "all humanity."[30]

Throughout history, meeting the challenge of enlarging the circle of human sympathy has never been easy. It is certainly not easy to meet that challenge today when so much of the world is gripped by cultural, ethnic, and economic clashes between the exponents of open and closed societies within each of the world's civilizations. Throughout the world, the circle of human sympathy must be enlarged beyond the current bounds of what is familiar and near to include what is seen now as foreign and far away. Surely our common humanity demands of us that this embracing circle ought to be enlarged. Certainly the sustainability and other global concerns that grip humanity insist that it be enlarged. And it can be enlarged in part through a much wider acceptance of – and a much enhanced expression of – a mutual human sympathy. But this circle of sympathy will not be enlarged if we rely *solely* on sympathy. It will be enlarged only if a wider human sympathy is accompanied in our wider reach by a wider human allegiance to the broader and the longer view of our self-interest "rightly understood."

AN ENABLING FRAMEWORK FOR SUSTAINABLE INVESTMENT

Among the new and different traffic lights we need are some for international investment. Competing visions of self-interest often collide in foreign direct invest- ment, where the circle of human sympathy is not always as large as it should be, and where sustainable development is all too often only an afterthought. During the hot summer of 2017, parents of sick children who live nearby one of Peru's oldest mining pits camped out in protest at the national health ministry in the Peruvian capital, Lima. They demanded help in dealing with the impact of centuries of mining pollution by both local and foreign companies. Lead, zinc, silver, and other metals were mined at Cerro de Pasco in the Andes for more than 400 years. The last mining operation closed there in 2015, but left behind "piles of tailings and traces of contaminants in the soil and water that many blame for ailments ranging from cancer to learning disabilities."[31] The circle of human sympathy throughout centuries of mining at Cerro de Pasco was not wide enough to include the Peruvian children who now have dangerously high levels of lead in their blood.

Throughout the world, such examples of the sometimes-dire risks of foreign direct investment exist side by side with examples of the rich bounties flowing from such investment. Seeing and experiencing these contrasts, those who seek FDI also seek more control over it. As a result, contrasting views of the productive potential and of the perceived perils of foreign direct investment, often voiced in legal disputes between investors and host states, increasingly clash in a cacophony of mutual misunderstanding in our unwilling world. More international cooperation is urgently needed to help prevent these clashes by forging an enabling global framework for sustainable foreign direct investment.

Logically, such international cooperation should lead to the creation of a rule-based global investment system that would be similar to – and would work in concert with – the long-established rule-based global trading system. In fact, China – perhaps incentivized in part by its rising role as an outbound investor – proposed a voluntary multilateral investment framework to the other members of the G20 leading up to the Hangzhou summit in 2016.[32] Ideally, such an enabling global framework for investment would aim to secure and to maintain high standards for the protection of investor rights while also taking fully into account the necessity – as part of countering climate change and of furthering the global green transition – for foreign direct investment always to be *sustainable* investment. A fully global framework for investment rules and investment rulings will not succeed, though, if it is suddenly imparted to the world from the top-down of some global summit through the supposed ideal of some grand global artifice. It will succeed only if it emerges from the global laboratory of the true bottom-up, where we will discover the right balance that must be struck between investor rights and sustainability obligations, and where we will secure that right balance in crafting investment rules and in resolving investment disputes.

From the bottom up, a freestanding, overarching international agreement could emerge with time and with experience on the substance of international investment obligations. This agreement could become a global legal umbrella for all the thousands of current international investment agreements. Such a new, freestanding agreement could help eliminate inefficiencies and distortions in investment by promoting consistency and coherence. In addition, it could set the right balance between investor rights and the regulatory and other public policy rights of host states for furthering sustainable investment. The states that signed and ratified this new agreement would be bound to apply its balanced view of the meaning of common investment obligations in all their existing and future bilateral and other international investment agreements where the parties to those agreements were all likewise each parties to the freestanding agreement. Over time, as with the gradual transformation of the GATT into the WTO, this freestanding agreement could *become* a fully multilateral investment agreement.

As a practical matter, no such overarching agreement on the substance of investment obligations is likely to *begin* as a global agreement. With the traditional divides between capital-exporting and capital-importing countries now blurred, and with many developing countries now exporting as well as importing capital, there is certainly more potential than in the past for international compromise and consensus on a number of long-irreconcilable investment concerns. All the same, global political reality dictates that what could eventually become a fully multilateral framework for investment is more likely to succeed if it starts out as a partial, plurilateral agreement among some but not all the many developed and developing states now engaged in the out-bound and the in-bound of foreign direct investment.

The hopes of the willing for a global investment framework centering on sustainability would also be better served if such a framework began as a partial agreement. In that way, through the substantive and procedural reimagining and the practical experience of learning by doing in the local test tubes of the true bottom-up, the global investment agreement would be more likely to become an agreement that would help make coherent the current incoherence in international investment rules and rulings worldwide. Also, it would be more likely to harmonize the current inconsistent statements of investment obligations across the proliferation of different investment rules frameworks by reconciling them with sustainability. A global investment "framework would have to start from the need to promote sustainable FDI for sustainable investment."[33]

An enabling investment framework that could be built up over time to become a fully multilateral investment agreement could begin and could remain freestanding. It could remain unlinked to any other framework for global governance. A reimagining and harmonizing of investment rules might, for example, begin by being negotiated, incubated, and then gradually scaled up globally through the vehicle of a bilateral investment agreement between two large participants in both in-bound and out-bound investment such as China and the United States or Canada and the European Union. Such an ambitious and politically audacious undertaking in international cooperation would, however, be considerably more likely to succeed if it were, instead, linked to a capable, reliable, and existing international legal framework that could become a firm foundation for the gradual construction of a substantive and procedural multilateral investment framework. Practicality suggests that, if we can, we should build on what already seems to work.

Two options seem the most practical and also the most appealing. The first option would be international cooperation in negotiating an update to the Washington Convention that is the legal underpinning of the enabling administrative framework for investment currently provided by the International Centre for the Settlement of Investment Disputes – the ICSID affiliated with the World Bank. Such an update of the ICSID – "an ICSID II, so to speak"[34] – could add legal substance to this long-valuable facilitative and administrative forum for investment dispute settlement. In this ICSID update, states could address both the imperatives of sustainable investment and the other needed updates of international investment obligations. This reimagining of the ICSID could be applied in all the many cases where the ICSID is employed as a forum for resolving investment disputes.

The other appealing option would be to negotiate an investment framework agreement as a plurilateral agreement within the WTO – as WTO members have already done on information technology and on government procurement. As Gary Hufbauer and Sherry Stephenson, who have proposed this approach, have explained, "[O]nly willing nations would be signatories of the agreement," in which they would agree to substantive investment obligations that are beyond the limited trade-related investment obligations now in the WTO treaty. They add, "Over time, the great majority of WTO members might join this [investment framework agreement] and, at some point, all [its] rights might be extended on an unconditional basis to all WTO members, including the holdouts."[35] In parallel, the WTO could build on the existing agreements on trade-related investment measures and on trade in services "to cover other types of investment and obligations."[36] In this reimagining, the WTO could gradually be transformed into the "World Trade and Investment Organization."[37]

Hufbauer and his colleagues at the Peterson Institute of International Economics studied the impact of an international framework agreement on investment for a mix of twenty-four countries and concluded that the net impact would be a roughly 10 percent increase in inward FDI totaling $1.2 trillion.[38] Richard Baldwin, Simon Evenett, and Patrick Low have added that "getting the WTO into this policy area may be important to ensuring that future developments would remain multilateral-friendly. It would also tend to reduce the hegemonic influence of the large investing nations."[39] In other words, there would, within the WTO, be less chance that, as on Melos long ago, might would make right.

INVESTMENT DISPUTES AND MAKING A GLOBAL
INVESTMENT FRAMEWORK

Whatever our structural approach may be, with foreign direct investment, as with all other forms of international governance, there must be working traffic lights. Once international cooperation has reimagined investment obligations to make them consistent with the objectives of sustainable development, those obligations to "stop" and "go" in FDI must be upheld. When the inevitable disputes arise between investors and host states about the precise meanings of these reimagined obligations, the legal outcomes of those disputes must be consistent, and they must be enforceable. Thus, as with international trade, a framework for international investment will not be fully enabling unless it includes a fair and effective system for dispute resolution. To be fair, and to be effective, such a system must be transparent, accessible, accountable, impartial, and independent of all political influence. Only then will it be viewed as legitimate by all who are affected by its rulings, and only then will it be able to fulfill its fundamental responsibility of upholding the international rule of law.

The challenge confronting the investor–state dispute settlement system (ISDS) that is the centerpiece of dispute resolution in most international investment agreements is that there is insufficient confidence that it meets this standard, which has been endorsed by the G20 in its Guiding Principles for Global Investment Policy-Making.[40] ISDS is a necessary and largely effective tool for protecting investor rights and, thus, a useful means of furthering the foreign direct investment that is essential to sustainable development. But ISDS does not always support sustainable development in the other ways it must to help shape a shared sustainable global prosperity. Moreover, and more generally, ISDS is viewed by many with mounting distrust.

In effect, ISDS amounts to a legal waiver of what would otherwise be the "sovereign immunity" that gives states the legal right not to have their sovereign rights challenged by tribunals outside their own jurisdiction.[41] On top of this, ISDS does not require investors to "exhaust" all their possible remedies through the local courts of the host state before initiating investor–state dispute settlement.[42] In this innovation, the system departs from the general rule in international law that private parties must exhaust all their avenues in local courts before seeking any international redress, and that only states themselves, in acknowledgment of their sovereignty, are not required first to exhaust local remedies.[43] In ISDS, private investors can take their grievances straight to an international tribunal.

ISDS is, thus, a post-Westphalian way of making non-state political actors *parties to* the interpretation of international law. Potentially, ISDS could also pave the way for making non-state political actors – businesses, NGOs, aggrieved groups of citizens, and others – *parties to* international law.[44] The legal learning by doing that could result from such an additional and positive innovation in international investment law could lead also to similar innovations in other areas of international economic law, including in international trade law, and to still other comparable innovations in environmental law and in other domains of what is now exclusively "public" international law. If better framed, ISDS could thus become an affirmative forerunner for the reimagining of international law to include actors in addition to states.

Yet, some countries are withdrawing from the ICSID, others are terminating or revising their international investment agreements, and dozens of countries are revising their model bilateral investment treaties that serve as the basis for their negotiated BITs. As UNCTAD describes it – in an echo of any number of politicians, NGOs, and activists worldwide – more than half a century after its innovative inception as a novel means for private investors to seek redress for harms done to them by sovereign governments, ISDS now has "serious shortcomings."[45] World-wide, today, "inconsistent and unintended interpretations of clauses, unanticipated uses of the system by investors, challenges against policy measures taken in the public interest, [and] limited or no transparency" are "undermining its legitimacy."[46] Given the reflexive public reaction to these "serious shortcomings," business and other advocates of investor–state dispute settlement are on the defensive everywhere amid a global crisis of legitimacy for ISDS.

Meantime, the number of investor–state disputes is increasing and thereby adding to this growing opposition. In 2016, 62 new cases were brought against 41 countries, bringing the total number of "known" arbitrations against host countries to 767.[47] An increasing number of these arbitral cases involve challenges to environmental protection and to the right to regulate. Each time a new case is filed by an investor, there are outcries against the seeming threat that international arbitrators chosen in an obscure and less-than-transparent process will overrule the perfectly legitimate efforts of local officials and national legislators in host countries to protect the public interest by pursuing sustainability. Some of these outcries are heard from some of the willing who seek sustainability and who fear that sustainability concerns will be subordinated to commercial claims in investor–state investment disputes. Others are heard, and most loudly, from anti-globalization activists who stereotype the trading system and the investment system alike as mere fronts for the greedy machinations of oppressive and polluting multinational corporations.

Many of the assertions made in these protests are exaggerated. For example, despite all the rhetoric about the supposed dangers of ISDS to the United States, the fact is, the United States has never lost an ISDS case.[48] Looking more widely at the global picture of ISDS, the fact is, too, that, in more than 90 percent of the several thousand bilateral investment treaties currently in force, no investor has ever claimed there was a breach of a treaty by a host state. True, the total number of investor–state disputes has been rising rapidly, but this rise has been proportional to the parallel rise in recent years in the total global stock of foreign direct investment. Simply put, there are more investors and more capital invested abroad, and, not surprisingly, there are also more investment disputes.

Other widespread assumptions about the supposed overreaching and punitive penalties of investor–state dispute settlement are equally misleading. The fact is, about one-third of these investor–state disputes are settled in advance of an arbitral ruling. Furthermore, these investor disputes are often with states with weak institutions that provide weak investor protections, which has the effect of adding to the frequency of dispute settlement. What is more, "When investors do prevail, awards are a small fraction of the initial claim – on average, less than ten cents on the dollar."[49] (Some studies show that this number is actually two or three cents on the dollar.)[50]

All the same, there *are* significant shortcomings in investor–state dispute settlement, and these shortcomings must be overcome if ISDS is to be a positive part of an enabling framework for sustainable investment. The foremost of these shortcomings is a lack of transparency. We speak of the *"known"* number of investment arbitrations because the actual number of such arbitrations is *unknown*. In most ISDS disputes, little or no information about the dispute is made available to the public, hearings are not open, and third parties are not allowed to intervene in the arbitral proceedings. Commonly, even the notice of arbitration that is filed by an investor is not made public, meaning that often the public does not even know that there is a dispute. Little wonder, then, that these arbitral tribunals are routinely derided as "secret courts."

Some of the newest international investment agreements include rules that try to open up ISDS documents and hearings to more public scrutiny and to more public response. The United States, the European Union, and others have promoted their own models for securing more transparency. Globally, the United Nations has adopted a convention on transparency in treaty-based investor–state arbitration.[51] In addition, the United Nations Commission on International Trade Law has written and promoted transparency rules.[52] Yet, "[w]hile the number of cases for which documents are disclosed is clearly increasing ... many remain completely confidential."[53] Still closed, too, are the arbitral hearings.

The G20 Guiding Principles say that investment dispute settlement must be "open and transparent."[54] In giving practical reality to this central principle, all notifications of investment arbitration must be made public immediately, and all documents must be made public (allowing, of course, for rules that protect and limit access to business confidential information and that relate to national security). All hearings must be open to the public. Ideally, where public rights and interests are at risk in the outcome of an investor–state dispute, there should be livestreaming of all hearings before the tribunal. Certainly, too, all awards and all related arbitral decisions must be made public. Furthermore, this arbitral transparency should happen automatically, without the necessity of the consent of the disputing parties.

Overall, "investor–state" dispute settlement must be reimagined for the future as "investment" dispute settlement. It must not be about investment rights alone. It must also be about sustainable investment. Toward this end, in addition to reimagining substantive investment rules to embrace sustainability, we must also reimagine other ISDS procedures by broadening participation to help enhance sustainability. There must be a better balance in the rights and obligations of all those with a stake in the outcome of an investment dispute, and there must be access for all to remedies.

As reimagined, investment dispute settlement must no longer be limited to claims made by investors against states in dispute settlement proceedings initiated by investors. Others with a demonstrated interest in the outcome must also be allowed to make legal claims for legal remedies. States in particular must be permitted to make counterclaims against investors in such proceedings. Furthermore, states must be permitted to initiate dispute settlement proceedings by making claims against investors, including for actions that are inconsistent with the objectives of sustainable development.

There must also be rules that open up the ISDS process to a wider public engagement by allowing affected citizens, NGOs, and other interested parties from civil society to file *amicus curiae* ("friend of the court") briefs on those legal issues in dispute. Procedural rules for such filings can – as they already do in the United States and in many other domestic courts – help make certain that these *amicus* briefs are accepted only from those who can truly demonstrate legitimate interests. What is more, in this reimagined investment dispute settlement, in addition to having the right to file such *amicus* briefs, citizen groups, business groups, and NGOs should, like investors and states, have legal standing – the legal right to initiate disputes, make legal claims, and participate in tribunal hearings – whenever they can demonstrate that they represent economic or other societal interests with a significant stake in the outcome of the dispute.

Opening up the process and the proceedings in an investment dispute is in the common interest of investors, states, and all those affected by the investment involved. It can help promote more mutual understanding of both rights and obligations. It can help level the legal terrain for all involved, including especially the developing countries and the indigenous peoples who are often at a disadvantage in ISDS. Opening up the legal process to the participation of the wider world can also help encourage acceptance of, and compliance with, arbitral rulings by improving the public perception of the legitimacy of investment dispute settlement. In making the willing world, decisionmaking that affects sustainability cannot be kept secret. Investment dispute settlement must be as transparent as the clearest pane of glass.

The G20 Guiding Principles say, in addition, that investment dispute settlement procedures must have "appropriate safeguards to prevent abuse."[55] The opponents of ISDS question whether sufficient safeguards exist. The (usually) three arbitrators who serve on investor–state tribunals are chosen *ad hoc* in each dispute by the parties to that dispute. They are usually selected from a relatively narrow networked community of specialists in international investment law. Almost all of them are men. Almost all these men are from developed countries. The conclusion of one empirical study is that there is a core group of twenty-five arbitrators, almost half of European nationality, with very few originating from developing countries.[56] This inner circle of frequent arbitrators has widened to some extent lately, but it seems still, to many, to be self-contained, self-referential, and largely closed.

Professor Giorgio Sacerdoti of Italy, a highly regarded arbitrator and a former Member and Chairman of the WTO Appellate Body, contends, "Empirical evidence from the rejection of most disqualifications confirms that the great majority of arbitrators are serious professionals who take care and pride in being independent and professional."[57] Unquestionably, he is correct. But are these highly skilled judges all necessarily the best possible judges of how to balance investor rights with securing sustainability, and do they give sufficient recognition to sustainability in their judgments? These arbitrators may all be expert in investment law, but many of them may not have the same expertise in environmental law or in the rapidly developing law relating to climate change. Moreover, some of these investment experts may sometimes have an unconscious tendency to elevate the protection of investment rights over the fulfillment of other important public policy concerns reflected in national and international law. Furthermore, although these *ad hoc* arbitrators are indeed bound by rules that bar legal conflicts, they are often also practicing lawyers, and thus sometimes vulnerable to being seen as having an interest in achieving certain legal results as arbitrators that may aid them as advocates for their clients elsewhere.

Here we confront again the ever-present question: Who will judge? Public distrust of investment dispute settlement could be diminished and the increasing inconsistencies and the creeping incoherence of investment obligations could be reduced by doing what the members of the WTO did for international trade – by providing for the possibility of appeal. In creating the WTO dispute settlement system, the members of the WTO created the WTO Appellate Body as a final court of appeal in international trade. A comparable final court of appeal could likewise be created for international investment. Establishment of an appellate investment tribunal could help provide the same "security and predictability" for international investment that having the final say of the independent and impartial Appellate Body provides for international trade. Far and away the best way to advance sustainable investment by ensuring the consistency and coherence of rightly balanced investment obligations would be through the legal check and balance of an investment court of final appeal.

Canada and the European Union have cooperated in offering what may prove to be a building block toward an ultimate answer to the shortcomings of investment dispute settlement. While other proposed "mega" regional trade agreements – such as the Trans-Pacific Partnership and the Trans-Atlantic Trade and Investment Partnership – have been assailed in the recent retreat by the unwilling from more international cooperation, Canada and the EU have been steadily moving ahead toward full implementation of their Comprehensive Economic and Trade Agreement (CETA).[58] A notable innovation of CETA is the establishment of standing tribunals of judges to decide investor–state disputes.

CETA establishes two standing investment tribunals – an initial trial tribunal and an appellate tribunal. Decisions made by the first can be appealed to the second for a final and binding decision. The day-to-day administration of both tribunals is to be provided by the ICSID.[59] The qualifications set out by Canada and the EU for the appointed members of both CETA tribunals are very much like those identified in the WTO treaty for the members of the WTO Appellate Body. There are specified ethical obligations barring conflicts[60] and also specified qualifications, including not only expertise in international investment and trade law, but also "demonstrated expertise in public international law," and the possession of "the qualifications required in their respective countries for appointment to judicial office" as "jurists of recognized competence."[61]

Potentially most far-reaching, Canada and the European Union have agreed in CETA to "pursue with other trading partners the establishment of a multilateral investment tribunal and appellate mechanism for the resolution of investment disputes."[62] On top of this, Canada and the EU have also agreed that – upon the creation of such a global investment tribunal – all the investment disputes that arise thereafter under CETA will be decided "pursuant to" that envisaged "multilateral mechanism."[63] Following up, Canada and the EU have been engaged in informal discussions involving more than forty countries on the creation of a World Investment Court.[64] Thus, not only does CETA present the world with a potential model for an entirely new way of judging investment disputes. The creation of the CETA investment tribunal would also lay what could become a cornerstone for an eventual global enabling legal framework for investment. This cornerstone would be laid where it should be laid – at the very base of the framework that needs to be built.

Because the CETA investment tribunal would have independent judges appointed by all the participating countries – with necessary previous assurances of their qualifications and ongoing assurances of their impartiality – dispute settlement under CETA would have more democratic accountability and, thus, more democratic legitimacy than the traditional arbitral approaches under other international investment agreements.[65] As a result, the CETA tribunal would be much more likely than other investment dispute settlement systems to be seen by those affected by it as a *legitimate* judicial forum. On this foundation, CETA could nail the planks into the investment frame of what could ultimately become truly global investment governance. What the Canadians and the Europeans have proposed for the building of an international framework for investment leading to the establishment of a World Investment Court is a legal structural example of the true bottom-up.

How, then, could we build up from this beginning? An appealing and practical option – one perhaps contemplated by some of the Canadians and the Europeans who crafted CETA – would be, first, to build up the cumulative experience and the credibility of the new CETA investment dispute settlement system, and then, over time, broaden its geographical reach. Countries bound by other investment agreements could be invited to "opt in" to the jurisdiction of the CETA appellate tribunal for final appeals in review of judgments by *ad hoc* arbitral panels under those other agreements. In this way, the CETA system, currently regional, could gradually grow and evolve into the "multilateral investment mechanism and appellate tribunal" – the World Investment Court – that is foreseen by Canada and the European Union in CETA as the appropriate global goal.

As one option, such an enhanced global CETA tribunal could eventually be made part of the overarching legal umbrella of a freestanding global framework on investment, covering the legal rights and obligations in all the thousands of other existing and future international investment agreements, and assuring consistency and coherence in all the investment rules and rulings under those many other agreements. As a second option, the CETA tribunal could be made part of an expanded and updated ICSID that would serve the same purposes under the auspices of the ICSID. Or, as a third option, the CETA tribunal could be made part of a plurilateral investment agreement within the WTO that would be used by all those WTO members that agreed to use it. Such a plurilateral WTO agreement could, as with other such WTO agreements, evolve with time and with experience into a fully global agreement. Whichever of these three choices is made for building a global framework, a globally evolved CETA investment tribunal – or, for that matter, any other multilateral investment tribunal we may create – should stand side by side and work in concert with the WTO trade dispute settlement system and its Appellate Body as the two main pillars of dispute settlement under international economic law.

AN ENABLING FRAMEWORK FOR SUSTAINABLE TRADE

We also need to change and add to some of the traffic lights for trade. Many of those who established the World Trade Organization in 1995 as the foremost outcome of the Uruguay Round of global trade negotiations thought that would be the last of the traditional global negotiating rounds, and the last to require a global consensus as a condition of concluding an agreement. They sought, as always, global solutions to trade. They believed, though, that, in an increasingly interconnected and ever-more-rapidly changing world economy, many of those global solutions would best be found by starting with less than fully global agreements. These among the founders of the WTO saw the new international institution as an ongoing forum in which those WTO members that wished to extend the reach and depth of the trading system with more trade liberalization and more economic integration would address an ever-evolving array of trade issues within the WTO as they arose, issue by issue. They foresaw the conclusion of smaller agreements of the willing within the WTO, and the gradual evolution of these smaller agreements into fully global agreements, as had happened with the original GATT "codes" on standards, subsidies, and dumping. They expected the WTO to become an enabling framework in which ambitious and innovative agreements by some WTO members would, over time, expand to include them all.[66]

Those who saw the new WTO in this way were thus surprised when, spurred by the terrorist attacks on September 11, 2001, the members of the WTO launched a ninth round of multilateral trade negotiations, the Doha Development Round. They were even more surprised when, seemingly automatically, WTO members fell back in the new trade round on the all-or-nothing negotiating approach on which they had previously relied. Abandoned was the new negotiating approach the WTO had taken in its first few years that had led to new trade agreements on basic telecommunications services, financial services, and information technology. Resurrected was the rigid "single undertaking" requiring consensus of all WTO members before any agreement of any kind could be reached. Years later, the Doha round was dead, and no global agreement was anywhere in sight.

There has been a transformation in the world economy – not to mention the world ecology in which it is contained – since 1995. A handful of economies no longer comprise most of the world economy. New economies have emerged. Others are emerging. The United States of America remains – for now – the single largest economic power in the world. But the relative balance of economic power between those countries long described as the "haves" and the "have nots" of the world has been forever altered. China, India, Brazil, Indonesia, South Korea, South Africa, and others have now taken their rightful seat at the global table. The World Trade Organization is now truly a *world* trade organization. Along with this new balance of economic power have come new trade and trade-related issues.

Many of these new commercial issues are of pressing concern to some but not yet to all WTO members. Many of them are vastly more complicated, technically and politically, than the mainly tariff issues that preoccupied trade negotiators in the past. Some of these new issues were only dimly foreseen, if at all, as commercial issues back in 1995. Most of them were not included in 2001 on the Doha Development Agenda and are still not on the WTO agenda. A partial list of these new twenty-first century trade issues includes data security, data flows, data storage, the intertwining of services with digital trade, other new dimensions of the outreaching and interconnecting of services trade, embedded services in global value chains, the newest developments in intellectual property rights, the terms of fair competition between private and often subsidized state-owned enterprises, the many overlaps between trade and climate change, and, yes, the utter inescapability of sustainability as an all-pervading *trade* issue.

Despite the many accomplishments of the WTO, "[t]he organization is currently facing what can be called an 'adaptability' crisis."[67] The WTO is a twentieth-century international institution that has yet to adapt to the urgent economic and ecological realities of the twenty-first century. Effective and enduring institutions are flexible, resilient, and ever-evolving to meet new challenges as they arise – just as the world trading system did up until 1995. To remain at the center of international trade, to continue to succeed and add to its success as the fulcrum for a fully *world* trading system, the WTO must be modernized. Instead of retreating from international cooperation and from the WTO, the members of the WTO should be returning to international cooperation and to the WTO. The failure of the Doha round and the arrival of a minatory global populism should revive for WTO members the early vision of what the WTO was originally intended to be by many of those who created it.

Consensus in the negotiation of new world trade rules is always desirable; however, the structuring of WTO trade negotiations as a "single undertaking" in which nothing is agreed unless and until everything is agreed "is no longer a negotiating tool."[68] Instead, it has become a tool of the unwilling against the willing to impede real negotiating. Even more, "[i]t could be argued that the principle has become a way for those countries least willing to take on new commitments to hold the negotiations hostage."[69] While the WTO as a whole largely remains at a standstill on most negotiating fronts in the absence of a required consensus, those members of the WTO that seek a deeper global economic integration – and that would ideally prefer to secure it by modernizing the WTO-based world trading system – are instead compelled by the lack of a consensus within the WTO to go outside the WTO system to craft many of the new rules needed to confront the new trade and trade-related issues of the new world economy.

Hence the resort in the wake of the deadlock in the Doha round to the negotiation of new trade and investment arrangements among self-selected subsets of WTO members *outside* the enabling framework of the WTO. The aim of all these negotiations has been to circumvent the impasse in the WTO by agreeing on WTO-plus rules and arrangements falling outside the legal oversight of the WTO. WTO members that wish to lower more barriers to trade in goods and services and to address together the new trade and trade-related issues of the twenty-first century have had to resort to going outside the rules-based world trading system that they labored so long to create and that, despite these recent circumventions, they mostly continue to support through their stubborn though impeded participation.

These non-WTO deals have offered the prospect of a real reimagining on some of the knottiest of the new issues through creative additional economic integration. In addition to tariff cuts on about 18,000 products, the Trans-Pacific Partnership includes new WTO-plus rules that the United States in particular has long sought on protections for labor and the environment, fair competition with state-owned enterprises, facilitation of digital trade, mutual recognition and harmonization of standards and regulations, non-discrimination in government purchases, and more. Ironically, the United States, which had led the efforts to negotiate the TPP, has now, under new leadership, rejected it. The American people have missed an opportunity through the TPP for advances on many fronts, including trade and sustainable development.

Similarly, negotiations between the United States and the European Union on a proposed Trans-Atlantic Trade and Investment Partnership promised to be a creative exercise in reimagining. The TTIP negotiations aimed, in part, at more harmonization through regulatory convergence, and at improving the legitimacy, the accountability, and the coherence of investor–state dispute settlement – especially with the innovative proposal by the European Union of a standing investment appellate court modeled on the WTO Appellate Body (an idea which has since been largely incorporated into the investment chapter of the CETA between the EU and Canada). But the TTIP remains in limbo because of the protectionist ascendency in the United States.

Conceivably, commitments in such mega-deals that extend beyond those currently in the WTO treaty can be linked to the WTO and scaled up over time to include all WTO members. The obligations in these mega-deals could be transformed into WTO obligations. Yet, as the latest and largest iterations of the ongoing proliferation of hundreds of preferential trade arrangements, such mega-deals can also pose the threat of what Bhagwati has colorfully called "termites in the trading system."[70] Like many others, he fears that non-WTO preferential arrangements are undermining free trade by undermining the non-discrimination principles at the core of the WTO-based world trading system.

Preferential trade arrangements are, Bhagwati reminds us, "inherently discriminatory."[71] An agreement to discriminate in favor of one trading partner is also an agreement to discriminate against another. It is, thus, a violation of the obligation of most-favored-nation treatment. Such discrimination is legally permissible only because of an exception in the WTO trade rules.[72] Bhagwati, along with others among the willing, maintains that such preferential trade arrangements outside the ambit of the WTO do not create more trade but only trade diversion from more cost-efficient to relatively inefficient trading partners in contradiction of what should rightly be the working of comparative advantage. He notes also that these non-WTO arrangements add significantly to the complexities of the arcane trade rules – the rules of origin – used to determine where products are "from" so that it can be determined whether those products are in fact entitled to preferential treatment. In this way, he says, such trade discrimination through trade deals done outside the WTO makes, in yet another of his metaphors, a "spaghetti bowl" of world trade.[73]

The populist opposition to mega-deals and other less than fully multilateral trade arrangements outside the WTO should not lead to a rejection of further trade negotiations. Rather, it should spur a return to the WTO, to renewed global reliance on the non-discriminatory rules of the WTO, and to a reimagination of the WTO as a twenty-first century global framework for trade negotiations, trade oversight, and trade dispute settlement. In part, this reimagining must be done through a collective recollection of the original intent of the WTO as an ever-evolving global forum for confronting the ever-changing realities of global commerce. In part, this must be done, too, as Carolyn Deere Birkbeck has stated, through a collective striving, in reviving and revitalizing the WTO, "to balance issues of fairness and efficiency, with a particular focus on democratization, facilitating attention to development goals, and boosting public transparency and engagement."[74]

Global public perception of the legitimacy of the WTO can be boosted if the members of the WTO turn, as they must, to reimagining WTO rules – to revising existing rules and to devising new rules – consistently with the objective of sustainable development as set out in the United Nations Sustainable Development Goals. In many respects, this reimagining of trade rules for sustainability in the twenty-first century could best be accomplished by the willful cooperation of self-selected "coalitions of the willing" in negotiating and concluding new and inclusive plurilateral agreements *inside* the sheltering and enabling legal framework of the WTO. As Bhagwati contends, when done *outside* the WTO, less-than-global trade deals could turn out to undermine the basic rules of non-discrimination at the heart of the WTO by favoring trade with some countries over trade with others. Such non-WTO trade deals could also be destructive of global economic cooperation by dividing the world economy into rival trading blocs if those deals are not automatically open to the inclusion of new participants willing to comply with their terms in exchange for their benefits.

In contrast, plurilateral deals, when done *inside* the WTO, can be structured in ways that will provide new trade benefits to all WTO members. This can be done from the outset if the deal covers a "critical mass" of the production of and trade in the product or products subject to the deal, and if the negotiating countries therefore decide to extend the benefits of the deal immediately to all other WTO members multilaterally on an MFN basis. An example of such a deal is the WTO Information Technology Agreement. In the alternative, this can be done over time by making the additional trade benefits of the deal available only to those WTO members that agree to the deal – while also providing that the agreement is open to the participation of additional WTO members and that its benefits are available to other WTO members whenever they decide they are willing to assume the new obligations that go along with those benefits. An example of such a deal is the WTO Government Procurement Agreement. Such trade deals, starting out as less than fully global but open to becoming fully global over time, when done *inside* the WTO, do not undermine the WTO. Quite the contrary, they strengthen the WTO, and they can help modernize it.[75]

Foremost among the attractions to the willing of pursuing trade agreements outside the WTO are the opportunities such deals present for legal experimentation in new ways of seeing economy and environment as one, and of thereby connecting trade and sustainable development. There are 285 different types of environmental provisions in 689 trade agreements concluded since 1947.[76] "Recent studies have found strong evidence that environmental clauses in trade agreements can lead to reduced pollution levels. Even clauses that are relatively vague and not subject to a trade dispute settlement mechanism are statistically related to enhanced environmental protection."[77] Experimentation is everywhere. The European Union and the Caribbean Forum have agreed to promote "biodiversity through the establishment of geographical indications" in intellectual property.[78] South Korea has included in several agreements a provision to cooperate on green public purchases.[79] Canada and the European Union have agreed in the CETA that water in its natural state is not a good or a product, and that no country party to the CETA is obliged to permit the commercial use of water for any purpose.[80]

This same bottom-up experimentation can be conducted by the willing *inside* the WTO, and it can be done in ways that will not be limited to a handful of countries but can be scaled up over time to include all 164 members of the WTO. One example would be an agreement to free trade in environmental goods and services. Another would be an agreement to impose disciplines on fisheries subsidies. Still another could be a sustainable energy trade agreement. Other examples could include agreements on trade and water, on trade and deforestation, on trade and biodiversity, on sustainable agriculture, on sectoral standards and supplies, and on export restrictions, excavation restrictions, and other issues interwoven with trade in natural resources. As just two specific illustrations among many, the WTO-plus provisions in the TPP that are meant to combat illegal logging and illegal wildlife trade could be made WTO obligations open to all WTO members that agree to them – with the added benefit that the WTO dispute settlement system would be available to uphold these new trade obligations.

Bhagwati's burrowing "termites in the trading system" could also be exterminated by finding a way to harmonize and globalize all the multitude of trade preferences in the hundreds of bilateral and other free trade agreements that have multiplied in parallel with the impasse in global trade negotiations in the WTO since the turn of the century. One approach would be to negotiate a WTO "code of conduct" – an agreement on the do's and don'ts for concluding new bilateral and regional trade agreements.[81] Such a code of conduct might help improve the global coherence of future agreements. But it would do nothing to make the hundreds of existing agreements any more coherent. A second approach would be to lower global barriers to trade significantly by harmonizing globally all the trade concessions made in those hundreds of existing agreements. A third approach – the one favored by Bhagwati – would be to eliminate much of the economic incentive countries have for entering into preferential arrangements simply by bringing most-favored-nation tariffs down to negligible levels so that "preferences relative to zero would be zero."[82] Some combination of all three of these approaches could be best.

In addition, the positive economic impact of "multilateralizing" the trade concessions in free trade agreements and other preferential trade arrangements should be enhanced by a rollback by the members of the WTO of the protectionist measures they have taken that remain in force in the continuing aftermath of the global financial crisis. Although promises have been made repeatedly at various global summits to stand still and roll back these trade restrictions, the promised rollbacks have not happened, and the G20 leading economies in particular have continued to add to their number of protectionist trade barriers. Between October 2008, at the beginning of the crisis, and October 2016, the numbers of G20-imposed trade restrictions in force increased from 324 to 1,263.[83] Both in globalizing bilateral and regional trade concessions and in rolling back protectionism, special attention must be paid to seeing economy and environment as one in search of sustainability.

The legitimacy of the World Trade Organization as an international institution devoted to trade *and* sustainable development can also be boosted by more "transparency" in the WTO – by opening the doors of the WTO wider to public observation and to public participation.[84] There are, of course, limits to transparency. The back and forth and give and take of trade negotiations toward the conclusion of an agreement satisfactory and advantageous to all those negotiating it is not conducive to public observation. Negotiators for many countries would surely be unwilling to incur the immediate political wrath back home of being seen to offer tentative and conditional trade concessions on domestically sensitive trade issues across the negotiating table without knowing yet what they might get in return from other countries. Yet without such conditional offers as ways of enticing reciprocal concessions, there would be no prospect of the mutual balance of concessions that alone can be the makings of a mutually satisfactory and mutually advantageous trade deal.

This said, WTO negotiations on reimagining trade rules must be much better informed through reimagined rules on transparency ensuring that the ongoing voice of the public is heard worldwide. This begins with access to the negotiating process for the chosen representatives of the people in governments worldwide, but it does not end there. In every country, there must be guarantees that individual citizens and interested and affected citizen groups of all kinds have their fair say in shaping the negotiating agenda and advancing the progress of the negotiating process. Meanwhile, in Geneva, at the global seat of the WTO, meetings of all WTO councils and committees – including the WTO Dispute Settlement Body – must be opened to public observation and scrutiny. Moreover, the considerable efforts made in recent years to engage in outreach to citizens and to citizen groups worldwide – such as through the soapbox of the annual WTO Global Forum – must be continued and significantly increased.

One transparent process should be the trade policy reviews that the WTO members undertake of other WTO members on a regular and rotating basis.[85] The WTO has conducted hundreds of such reviews of almost all WTO members since 1995. When problems are found in the trade policies of WTO members, improvements are recommended. These reviews are not "hard law." They are somewhere short of "soft law." There are no legal penalties; there are no economic sanctions for not complying with these review recommendations. Penalties become possible only when questions of inconsistencies with WTO obligations are taken to dispute settlement by a WTO member or WTO members. Nevertheless, the "name and shame" of these peer reviews serves to highlight trade shortcomings and can also serve to cause them to be corrected over time through the cumulative power of collective suasion.

Steve Charnovitz has noted that this review process "could be adapted more broadly to deal with issues beyond trade."[86] Certainly it could – and should – be extended to include an assessment by the WTO of whether a WTO member is trading in ways that further the objective of sustainable development. As Carolyn Deere Birkbeck has contended, "[T]he scope of the WTO's Trade Policy Review process could be expanded to serve as a tool to help governments integrate sustainable development considerations into trade decision-making."[87] At a minimum, this should include the added transparency of opening up the review process to public observation. More than this, Birkbeck suggests, reform of the trade review process should also include opening up the process to public participation, such as by involving interested citizens and citizen groups in preparing reports at the national level, and seeking input from recognized international experts and other interested national and international parties into the final WTO report.[88]

These same suggestions about transparency and participation should be applied equally to WTO dispute settlement.

18

On Resolving Disputes and Linking Enabling Frameworks Through the International Rule of Law

The WTO calls its dispute settlement proceedings "confidential."[1] The rest of the world calls them "secret." It is only because the doors are closed to the dispute settlement hearings in the WTO that the critics of the WTO can claim any credibility in castigating the organization as a star chamber or as a kangaroo court. Keeping the doors closed to dispute settlement proceedings feeds the unfounded and far-fetched paranoia about the organization that prevails among many of the anti-globalists and that helps fuel the global reaction against trade and globalization. It plays, too, into the political ploys of the hardcore protectionists, statists, crony capitalists, economic nationalists, and all the others who oppose what WTO rules represent and what WTO members are trying to accomplish for all the world. The Sustainable Development Goals aim for "effective, accountable and transparent institutions at all levels."[2] Toward this end, in trade, continue to conduct the deliberations and decisionmaking of WTO panels and the WTO Appellate Body behind closed doors – just like every other court in the world that upholds the rule of law. Continue to keep confidential business information and national security matters confidential – just as the WTO has always done. But, apart from that, *open the doors to the* WTO. Televise and livestream WTO dispute settlement and other WTO proceedings worldwide. Show the world willful international cooperation and the rule of law in action. Let the "sunshine" in to global trade governance.

AN ENHANCED FRAMEWORK FOR WTO DISPUTE SETTLEMENT

In addition to letting the wider world *see* what is happening in WTO dispute settlement, the WTO should also let the wider world *participate* in WTO dispute settlement. Disputes in the WTO are disputes between and among states. States alone are the legal parties to WTO disputes. States alone have the legal right – what lawyers call "standing" – to initiate WTO disputes. But in our post-Westphalian world, where many parties other than states are increasingly active participants alongside states in the efforts that make and that uphold international law, we have now reached the point where, in the interests of transparency and of informed judgment, parties in addition to states should be allowed to participate in some respects in WTO dispute settlement.

The most obvious means for parties other than states to participate is to do so through the filing of *amicus curiae* briefs in the panel and appellate proceedings in individual state-to-state disputes. *Amicus curiae* briefs appear to a limited extent already in WTO dispute settlement.[3] Such outside briefs have been supported by some countries but opposed by many developing countries fearful of being elbowed aside in the WTO by well-funded, well-informed NGOs – as has happened in some other international settings. *Amicus* briefs can, however, be helpful in WTO dispute settlement in numerous ways, including informing the judgment of WTO jurists on how best the WTO rules can be clarified in a particular dispute consistently with the objective of sustainable development. After consulting with WTO members, the Appellate Body should issue procedural rules on *amicus* briefs under its authority to establish its own working procedures.[4] In all likelihood, WTO panels would follow suit consistently with the appellate rule.

In addition to more transparency and more participation, additional reforms are much needed through further reimagining of the WTO dispute settlement system.[5] Disputes are being taken to the WTO in increasing numbers. The complexity of these disputes is increasing as well. The resolution of these disputes demands more time, more work, and more expertise from those who judge them. Today, exceedingly complicated disputes involving billions of dollars in subsidies for large commercial aircraft, thick slices of global food trade, highly emotional health and safety issues affecting many millions of consumers and citizens, and even the very meaning of what it is to have a "market" economy are being resolved in WTO dispute settlement. Trade disputes still involve tariffs, but now usually they involve much more. Moreover, the sheer economic – and thus political – stakes of the legal outcomes of these WTO disputes are enormous. Through yearend 2014, the WTO had already handled disputes affecting $1 trillion in trade flows, and that sum continues to rise.[6]

Other factors are also increasing the burden on the WTO dispute settlement system. With WTO members unable to agree on revising existing rules and on establishing new rules through rule-making, more and more of the difficult new issues are being diverted from trade negotiations into legal claims made in dispute settlement. Some of these legal claims can be resolved within the capaciousness of the existing rules and the capacity of the dispute settlement system. Others are much harder to fit within an existing WTO rulebook that is not yet modernized and "fit to purpose" for all the multiplying disputes over all the new trade and trade-related issues of the current century. In their abiding desire for "security and predictability" and a positive solution to every trade dispute, the WTO members are sometimes tempted to implore WTO jurists to read more into the existing rules than is there.[7] WTO jurists have resisted and are right to resist. The dispute settlement rules rightly require that in their findings and recommendations, the panel and the Appellate Body cannot add to or diminish the rights and obligations provided in the covered agreements in the WTO treaty.[8] But in the absence of a reimagining of the rules, where does that leave the usefulness and the effectiveness of the WTO-based world trading system in the ever-changing modern world?

Amid a proliferation of trade rules outside the WTO, ensuring that the trade rules of the WTO "remain relevant and impactful in the global trading system" is a challenge that must be met and that can, in many ways, best be met by "[o]ffering a venue for plurilaterals" within the WTO as one part of reimagining the WTO trading system.[9] Ideally, the sectoral and other WTO-plus trade and investment arrangements that are being sought elsewhere should be brought within the WTO framework. Ideally, too, these agreements should be subject to WTO dispute settlement. All this would help keep the WTO at the center of global trade governance.

In addition, the jurisdiction of the WTO dispute settlement system could be expanded to include appeals to the WTO from dispute settlement rulings under the regional trade agreements (RTAs) that have proliferated since the turn of the century. As Henry Gao and Chin Leng Lim have contended, "[B]y using the WTO dispute settlement system for some RTA disputes, the Members [of the WTO] will be able to develop, albeit gradually, incrementally, and pragmatically, a body of 'common law' on RTAs. Such a body of common principles could form the basis of multilateral rules on RTAs or harmonize RTA rules. This could minimize the harmful effect of RTAs."[10] Thus, by "contracting out" the services of WTO jurists in this way (and by making those other systems pay for those services), even more could be done to maintain the centrality of the WTO and to secure "security and predictability" in world trade through WTO dispute settlement.

The striking imbalance in the WTO system occasioned by too much reliance on rule interpretation and by too little reliance on rule-making cannot last forever. Expediency will continue to tempt disputing WTO members to push the existing rules beyond where they were meant to go. On top of this, while the overall rate of compliance with WTO dispute settlement rulings remains somewhere between 85 and 95 percent, the willingness of some countries that lose WTO cases to comply with adverse WTO rulings seems to some extent to be waning. This is evidenced, as Giorgio Sacerdoti has said, by the fact that "effective implementation, while usually performed, requires on average more time."[11]

The effectiveness of the WTO dispute settlement system can be improved through some basic reforms. Standard rules of evidence should be adopted by the members of the WTO for WTO dispute settlement. As it is, what is and is not evidence depends entirely on the subjectivity of the judges in any given dispute. Although there is more coherence than might be anticipated with such unlimited judicial discretion, the fact remains, what may be considered evidence by one WTO panel will not be considered evidence by another.[12] Likewise, WTO members should adopt standard working procedures for WTO panels to match those instituted from the beginning for appeals pursuant to their treaty authority by the Appellate Body.

Moreover, the legal consistency and coherence of the system would be served by narrowing the potential list of WTO panelists to something less than the more than 7 billion people in the world. Several hundred men and women have served as panelists since the establishment of the WTO – providing the WTO with a breadth of views and of expertise to call upon in rendering legal judgments. At the same time, not a few of these panelists have come to those panels without much experience with the WTO and without much knowledge of WTO rules and other international law.

Early in the Doha round, the European Union suggested the creation of a previously vetted and "standing panel body" similar to the standing Appellate Body as the sole source of panelists in WTO dispute settlement. The advantage of a standing panel body would be the security and predictability – the legal consistency – it could bring to WTO panel judgments. The disadvantage of a standing panel body is that limiting the number of candidates for panelists would limit also the amount and variety of expertise on which WTO members could draw for reaching reasoned judgments. A standing panel body of, say, fifteen, might include one or perhaps two specialists vetted and available on each of international health law, international labor law, intellectual property law, competition law, and environmental and sustainability law. But, where there are many specialists all over the world in a single field, why limit the members of the WTO to the potential services of only one or two? As a compromise, a standing body of panel chairs could be selected from among the most reliable and experienced of WTO jurists. The chair of the panel in a dispute could be chosen from among this standing body of panel chairs, and the two other panelists could be identified and selected case by case in a worldwide search for the right combination of experience and expertise needed to resolve a particular dispute. This selection process should of course include panelists with an extensive knowledge not only of international trade law, but also of the law and the goals of sustainable development.

The effectiveness of the WTO dispute settlement system could be improved as well by providing speedier trade justice for the members of the WTO. Toward this end, for developing countries, and particularly for the least-developed countries, more must be done also to develop the largely neglected option of "good offices, conciliation, and mediation" in the trade rules as an alternative to lengthy and expensive dispute resolution.[13] This hastening of dispute resolution could be accomplished in part by creating the WTO equivalent of a "small claims" court that would provide due process and dispute resolution in smaller disputes without all the legal bells and whistles of the full and prolonged panoply of most WTO dispute settlement.[14]

For speedier trade justice, more must also be done to help resolve disputes without lengthy and expensive dispute settlement through the consultations that are a prerequisite to dispute settlement.[15] As it is, many disputes are indeed resolved through these mandated consultations (a largely unnoted success of the trading system). But often the consultations are viewed by the disputing parties primarily as an opportunity for factual "discovery" of useful information in prelude to the initiation of dispute settlement through the filing of a formal legal complaint. Clearly, some disputes can be resolved only after a legal judgment. This said, the requirement of consultations must be seen foremost as an opportunity to cooperate in resolving the dispute *through consultations*.

Next, more must be done to speed up panel proceedings. Although the WTO treaty says that panel proceedings "shall, as a general rule, not exceed six months,"[16] usually panel proceedings take a year or more. With the ever-growing dispute caseload, panel proceedings are stretching even longer. Most of these delays are due to the growing weight on the system of the numbers and the complexities of trade disputes. More human and financial resources must be provided by the members of the WTO to shorten overall time frames and provide speedier trade justice. Also, where disputing parties cannot agree on panelists within an agreed and limited time, the Director General of the WTO should be empowered to intervene and appoint panelists without the parties first requesting it.[17]

Furthermore, changes are needed in how some of the rules involving implementation of dispute settlement rulings are viewed. The rules say that, if it is not practical to comply "immediately" with an adverse ruling, then a WTO member in breach of its WTO obligations "shall have a reasonable period of time in which to do so."[18] A guideline in the rules is that such a "reasonable period of time . . . should not exceed 15 months" from the date when the report was adopted.[19] Yet WTO arbitrators have routinely bowed to the procrastinations of WTO members and have thus prolonged their illegal actions by deciding that periods much longer than fifteen months amount to a "reasonable period of time." In effect, they have written the word "immediately" out of the rule. Shorter time periods for implementation of WTO rulings are needed to help protect the integrity and the efficacy of the WTO dispute settlement system.

There is likewise need to reimagine some of the ways in which economic suasion is used to uphold WTO rulings. Under the current rules, when the "last resort" of economic sanctions is employed by a complaining country because a defending country has chosen not to comply with an adverse WTO ruling, a calculation is made by a WTO arbitrator of the trade damages to the complaining country, and the complaining country is then authorized to withhold previously granted trade concessions in the amount of those damages.[20] Yet Jack Goldsmith and Eric Posner rightly explain, "The bilateralism of trade sanctions implies that weak states cannot credibly commit to sanction powerful states, and that powerful states will in general have more freedom of action than weaker states."[21] Those in the United States who believe WTO rules are rigged against them overlook how these WTO rules on economic sanctions are structured to favor them and those in other large trading countries. To counter this imbalance in the existing rules, the WTO rules on damages must be reimagined.

Some have suggested simply providing complaining countries with monetary compensation for WTO offenses.[22] This approach, however, preserves protectionism while making the taxpayers in the country defending the protectionism pay twice for it, first in higher local prices, and second in higher taxes to support higher government spending. This is what happened when the United States and Brazil agreed that the United States would pay Brazil an agreed annual sum rather than repeal its illegal cotton subsidies.[23] What is more, larger and wealthier countries such as the United States are more likely than smaller and poorer countries to have the means to pay cash to preserve their protectionism. Rich countries should not be permitted simply to write a check to excuse their ongoing violation of WTO rules.

A better approach would be to change the economic balance between large and small countries by allowing those developing countries that are not yet numbered with China, India, and the other major emerging economies to receive "treble damages" in their disputes with more prosperous countries, perhaps including not only the OECD developed countries, but also the major emerging economies. In addition, in all WTO disputes, the amount of damages should be determined not prospectively, as now, but retroactively, from the date of the application of an unlawful measure. For all WTO members, including the largest trading countries, the prospect of paying treble and retroactive damages would be a powerful new incentive not to act inconsistently with their WTO obligations.

As James Flett of the European Union, among the most experienced and insightful of all WTO legal advocates, has suggested, yet another approach to enhancing the likelihood of speedy compliance with WTO rulings by countries found to have applied illegal trade measures "would be to multilateralize the compliance process" by having "every case ... brought by the entire Membership as a sort of class action."[24] This would greatly magnify the prospect of damages and thus make for an even more potent incentive for treaty compliance. As Flett points out, the dispute settlement rules "already foresee this" to some extent by providing the option of multiple complainants in individual trade disputes.[25]

Flett has also recommended speeding up compliance by having panels and the Appellate Body begin to make suggestions about how their legal rulings could be implemented.[26] Under the existing rules, panels and the Appellate Body "may suggest ways in which Members concerned could implement the recommendations."[27] Both panels and the Appellate Body have, however, been reluctant to use this legal authority, thinking it best for the disputing members to reach their own resolution of their dispute based on a legal ruling. But the increase in evasive foot-dragging and in pretended compliance with adverse rulings by some WTO members may now be reason for panels and the Appellate Body to reconsider their reluctance to make suggestions about how their rulings could be implemented.

MAINTAINING THE RULE OF LAW IN WTO DISPUTE SETTLEMENT

The sturdiest pillars in the enabling legal framework of WTO dispute settlement have been those raised by the rulings of the WTO Appellate Body. The Appellate

Body has a unique and unprecedented authority for an international legal tribunal. Yet its authority remains fragile, and it remains dependent on the willingness of all WTO members to comply with the rule of law and otherwise to uphold the rule of law.[28] The Appellate Body must continue to have the strong support of the members of the WTO against those both within the WTO and without who would undermine the exercise of its necessary authority in service to the members of the WTO. And it must be strengthened to the task of continuing to serve the members of the WTO in meeting the new challenges facing the world trading system in the twenty-first century.

Before establishing a standing body of chairs for WTO panels, the members of the WTO should first make the standing WTO Appellate Body a full-time instead of a nominally part-time tribunal. Serving on the Appellate Body has never really been a part-time job. It is certainly not one now. As full-time jurists on the highest court of world trade, Members of the Appellate Body should be given compensation, benefits, and appropriate assistance befitting their service on an international tribunal dealing with trillions of dollars in trade disputes. The Appellate Body should continue to be based in Geneva at the WTO; however, given the nature of their work, the Members of the Appellate Body need not necessarily be resident full-time in Geneva. As now, when officially full-time, they will need to be in Geneva only for hearings and deliberations. (A legal brief and a panel record can be read anywhere.) Not least, they should be provided with ample support staff and the other resources they need to do the job they are entrusted with doing.

The biggest threat to the continued success of the Appellate Body is a design flaw in the Appellate Body – the fact that, once appointed for an initial term of four years, Appellate Body Members are eligible to be reappointed for a second term of four years. Apparently overlooked in the Uruguay Round of trade negotiations that created the Appellate Body along with the WTO was that this beckoning possibility of reappointment puts those Members of the Appellate Body who have not yet been reappointed in the highly uncomfortable position of sitting in judgment on appeals involving countries whose support they need to help make the consensus that is required for their reappointment.[29] This provides every Member of the WTO with the potential of employing the leverage of its right to veto a reappointment as a tool for trying to influence the actions of Members of the Appellate Body desirous of reappointment. There is no evidence whatsoever that any Member of the Appellate Body has ever ruled in a certain way because of the press of any such influence. But human nature is human nature. One who has an appointment will tend to want to keep it. One who has leverage will be tempted to use it.

During the first decade of the WTO, reappointments to the Appellate Body were more or less automatic. Despite the inevitable disappointments of some WTO members with some Appellate Body judgments that went against them, not one member of the WTO during that time interjected such disappointments into the reappointment process. The design flaw in the structure of the Appellate Body seemed not to exist while WTO members acted as if it did not. No Appellate Body Member has a right to reappointment. That is a discretionary decision reserved in the WTO treaty exclusively for the members of the WTO. And yet, in exercising this discretion, the members of the WTO wisely decided during that first decade of the WTO – in the absence of any indication of any bias, incompetence, or inattention – to reappoint all those sitting Members of the Appellate Body who sought reappointment. This show of mutual self-restraint for the sake of the entire cooperative enterprise of the WTO contributed much to the establishment of the legitimacy and credibility of the WTO dispute settlement system worldwide. Every member of the WTO knew it could get a legal verdict from the Appellate Body independent of any political influence.

Since then, as the economic stakes in WTO disputes have grown and as the political pushback against politically unwelcome WTO rulings has grown as well, the possibility provided by the WTO treaty for reappointment to a second four-year term has increasingly exposed individual Members of the Appellate Body to subtle (and not so subtle) intimidation through the implicit threat that they will not be reappointed if they rule in any one dispute against a particular country. Sadly, and ironically, the country engaging in this intimidation has been the country that has long been among the most insistent on an independent judiciary as the foundation for the rule of law – the United States of America.[30]

Responding to mounting protectionist pressures back home, and politically distressed by repeated WTO rulings against US anti-dumping and other trade remedies applied inconsistently with WTO rules, the past three American administrations have embarrassed supporters of the rule of law in the United States and appalled those elsewhere by engaging in increasingly transparent attempts to intimidate incumbent WTO judges into ruling in favor of the United States. Initially, this pressure was applied by vetoing the reappointment of sitting judges. More recently, it has been applied by delaying the appointment of new ones.[31] Although these attempts at judicial intimidation began early during the second decade of the WTO, starting around 2007, they have intensified under the current US administration. The current, protectionist president of the United States and those who serve him have seized on this preexisting pretext as a convenient cover for their systemic assault against rules-based multilateralism and dispute settlement. Their challenge to the Appellate Body has been described correctly as a "stealth war" against the WTO, cleverly disguised as an arcane procedural spat.[32] At first simply shocked by this unwelcome turn of events, increasingly, WTO members have opposed these pressure tactics by the United States. In fact, based on press accounts of what has transpired in sessions behind closed doors in Geneva, not even one other WTO member seems to have sided with the United States.[33]

Although motivated mostly by its animus against the Appellate Body arising from adverse rulings in a long series of trade remedies disputes, the United States has largely not mentioned those lost disputes in its formal criticisms of the Appellate

Body. This may be in part because the United States may be the only one of the 164 WTO members that has expressed any concern about most of those legal rulings. By far the greater concern of other members would be if those rulings had gone the other way. Instead, the United States has leveled more general criticisms about what it alleges has been increasing legal "overreaching" by the Appellate Body beyond the limited extent of its treaty mandate.[34] While some other WTO members likewise continue to lick their wounds over lost WTO cases, the United States has been alone in insisting that the Appellate Body has routinely exceeded its jurisdiction.

The Appellate Body may be right or wrong in the eyes of others in any given judgment. No one argues for the infallibility of the Appellate Body – least of all those who have served on it. WTO rules, however, do not give the Appellate Body the option of not judging an appeal by refusing to take it or of refusing to rule on a legal issue when it is raised in an appeal. When a legal issue is appealed claiming a violation of a WTO obligation, the Appellate Body must render a judgment clarifying the meaning of that obligation even when the trade negotiators who wrote it may have left its meaning less than crystal-clear.[35] The appellate judges can rule only on those legal issues that are appealed. They cannot wander from those legal issues into mere conjecture on others that have not been appealed. Their job is to answer the legal questions they are asked – nothing more, and nothing less.

The Appellate Body fulfills this responsibility by endeavoring to discern – in strict accordance with the customary rules of interpretation of public international law – the ordinary meaning of the words in the WTO obligation in their context in the treaty and in the light of their object and purpose as reflected in the treaty.[36] These interpretive rules not only assume that treaty obligations have a meaning; they also assume that treaty obligations have one meaning – a single meaning which must be "clarified" by the Appellate Body when a legal issue is appealed that requires a judgment on the meaning of an obligation. This is not overreaching. This is just the Appellate Body doing its job. This is precisely what the Appellate Body has been instructed to do by the members of the WTO in the WTO treaty.[37]

Despite their increasingly vocal concern, the other WTO members – constrained by the consensus rule and uncertain of how to react to the blatant bullying of the United States – have had difficulty in summoning the willingness to stand up to this US intimidation of independent judges and to the threat it poses to the continued success of the WTO dispute settlement system. Unwillingness will not do. The rule of law is only as strong as our willingness to stand up for it. In 2016, these embarrassing actions by the United States inspired an extraordinary letter from the current Members of the Appellate Body warning of the dangers to the system of tying the reappointment of any Member of the Appellate Body "to interpretations in specific cases," which have, in any event, almost always been by consensus, and in which it is impossible to discern the individual interpretation of any one Appellate Body Member from the consensus opinion.[38] That same year, these US actions also provoked an unprecedented letter of caution written and signed by all thirteen living former Members of the Appellate Body.[39]

But to no avail. The United States blocked the required consensus to reappoint one of the Members of the Appellate Body in 2016 and then employed similar stonewalling tactics in 2017 and 2018 to prevent the selection of new Appellate Body Members to fill vacancies due to retirements. This US tactic left the Appellate Body with fewer than its full treaty complement of seven judges, further slowed the pace of WTO dispute settlement, and fueled widespread apprehension that, with additional anticipated retirements, soon the Appellate Body would not have the minimum of three judges it needs to decide an appeal.[40]

The thirteen living former Members of the Appellate Body summed up the stakes in this way in their cautionary letter to the members of the WTO: "The unquestioned impartiality and independence of the Appellate Body has been central to the success of the WTO dispute settlement system, which has in turn been central to the overall success of the WTO. Undermining the impartial independence of the Appellate Body now would not only call into question for the first time the integrity of the Appellate Body; it would also put the very future of the WTO trading system at risk."[41] What remains essential, the thirteen former WTO judges wrote, is "the unflinching independence of the Members of the Appellate Body in fulfilling their pledge to render impartially what they see as the right judgments in each dispute by upholding the trade rules on which all WTO Members have agreed."[42]

Because will precedes law and law builds institutions, will must sustain the law and the institutions. An indispensable part of such will is the show of restraint. Mutual self-restraint is the underpinning of the framework of law and of the institutions that make and aim to uphold law through the rule of law. The ultimate test of the expression of such self-restraint in a system dedicated to the resolution of international disputes is when a dispute is *lost*. A legal loss in any one dispute, or even in a series of disputes, should never lead a country to undermine the upholding of the rule of law that is the transcending purpose of a dispute settlement system and that is in the "interest rightly understood" of every country. Real respect for the rule of law is shown by what you do not when you win, but when you lose.

The United States has long been the first to preach the rule of law to others. The United States should also be the first to practice it. It can be hoped that those entrusted with leading the American people will remember in time why the United States has long supported a rule-based world trading system and the rule of law in world trade. Instead, the current United States Trade Representative has been quoted as saying that "an unthinking, simplistic and slavish dedication to the mantra of 'WTO-consistency' . . . makes little sense."[43] The underlying implication in this statement is that compliance with international law is optional.

The message is that the United States will choose whether to comply with its WTO obligations only when it sees fit and only to the extent that it sees fit. What if other countries heed this message and do the same? This is reasoning that can unravel all that has been accomplished by the WTO toward establishing the international rule of law in trade and toward demonstrating as well that there truly can be such a thing as the international rule of law. This is the might-makes-right reasoning of the Athenian generals on ancient Melos.

Neither trade nor sustainable development can be advanced without an unwavering adherence to the international rule of law. No one should have to explain this to any WTO member, least of all to the United States of America. Still, it may be best for the WTO simply to eliminate the temptation for the United States or any other WTO member to engage in such intimidation. The long-term solution is obvious: The possibility of reappointment for Appellate Body Members should be eliminated. This one change in the dispute settlement rules would put an end to this form of intimidation and would reinforce the independence and the impartiality of the Appellate Body going forward. Further, it could be part of a constructive restructuring of the Appellate Body that would enable it better to fulfill its mandate of service to all the members of the WTO.

Two options seem most attractive. There could continue to be seven Members of the Appellate Body, but with each appointed for a single seven-year term, and with one of the seven completing a term each year. Or, as an alternative, the size of the Appellate Body could be increased to nine Members, with each appointed for a single nine-year term, and with one of the nine departing each year.[44] The first option, by preserving the current number of seven judges, would do more to ensure the continued collegiality of the Appellate Body in working toward a desired consensus in each dispute. The second option, by adding two more judges, would do more to make the Appellate Body broadly representative of the membership of the WTO as a whole, given that there are many more members of the WTO now than when it was established in 1995. With either option, the possibility of reappointment would be eliminated. No longer could a country be tempted by a looming judicial appointment or reappointment to descend to the global disgrace of undermining the rule of law by trying to intimidate international judges.

AN ENABLING FRAMEWORK FOR CLIMATE, ENVIRONMENT, AND SUSTAINABLE DEVELOPMENT

We have too few traffic lights for climate, environment, and sustainable development. We need more. The year the Second World War ended – 1945 – was a "charter moment" for reimagining global governance. The United Nations was founded. The Bretton Woods and numerous other international institutions were established. Human rights were asserted and new forms of international cooperation were pursued. The world was made new. This should be another charter moment, a moment for structuring and restructuring global governance for sustainability, a moment when we consider anew the number and placement of all our traffic lights through "transformative change of sustainability governance."[45] As one group of the willing has explained, "While incremental changes have enabled certain progress towards sustainability, the current system governing sustainable development is no longer sufficient given the number, impact, interdependence and complexity of problems associated with global change. Governance for sustainability requires transformative reforms with clear vision."[46] Once again, we must make the world new, and, as before, we must do so with "new types of governance."[47] We must have state-driven institutions. We must have new institutions that are not driven by states. We must have new institutions built on endeavors that extend global governance "beyond the state" to include the active participation in governance of many more of the willing of the world.

First and foremost, on climate change, sheer urgency requires international traffic lights that send the right stop and go signals immediately. Whether we send the right climate signals will depend in no small part on whether we succeed in implementing agreed climate rules, accelerating and adding to climate commitments, and upholding the terms of the Paris climate agreement. The unique challenge of climate governance is that, in constructing such coordination on a global scale, there is simply not time enough left for the steady, slow but sure, trial and error of ordinary incrementalism. Climate change will not wait.

A shared understanding of the urgency of speeding up the usual pace of rule and structural reform must underlie, inform, and motivate all our efforts toward implementing, accelerating, supplementing, and upholding the Paris Agreement. Thus, the first priorities under the Paris Agreement must be to hasten the completion of the unfinished Paris climate rulebook and to ramp up, along with this rule-making, the addition of much more ambitious national climate pledges than those made in the run-up to the Paris summit in 2015. Such a hastening of heightened global climate action can be accomplished only within an enabling and mutually reinforcing climate framework – one that encourages speed and that discourages continued denial and recalcitrance in confronting the realities of climate change, both nationally and internationally.

In pondering the "pathways forward" for such governance, another group of the willing has advised, "[t]he development of a Paris Agreement 'rulebook' must be completed as fast as possible, to ensure accountability and proper reporting. At the same time, tailored national compliance systems will have to be put in place. The Paris Agreement also puts greater emphasis on the role of domestic and transnational non-state actors. More than ever, mitigation initiatives and policies must *trickle down from governments* through to businesses, financial services, investors, NGOs, and the broader civil society."[48] This is emphatically true in most respects. Motivating mechanisms for monitoring, reviewing, and spurring national climate actions are some of the most important missing pages that must be written into the Paris climate rulebook. Yet, apart from the necessity of enabling the right actions by sending the right signals, there is a limit to how much the unfolding Paris climate framework should cause climate initiatives and policies to *trickle down from governments*.

Instead of trickling from the top down, most needed climate policies and initiatives, to be successful in advancing and accelerating global climate action, must *flow up from the true bottom-up* to motivate and to move often-hesitant governments into taking decisive climate actions. As with all the rest of what will go into making global sustainable development, climate experiments must be tried to be true through "learning by doing" at the grassroots of the world, and then shaped and scaled up to serve the wider world. Workable policies and initiatives must rise up from local and regional public, private, and public/private initiatives and other networks of the willing that often come together outside the usual lines of government in successful collaborative climate actions that cannot ultimately be ignored by even the most reluctant of governments. The press of cumulative success from outside governments can help push governments toward climate successes of their own. Indeed, it can help create a political atmosphere in which such successes are demanded of governments. When accompanied by effective national policies for a "just transition," the outside press of climate success can also transform the current political equation by causing politicians to conclude that they will be rewarded by voters if they take needed climate actions – and rejected by voters if they do not.

To pass the ultimate test of spurring more ambitious climate actions, the implementation and compliance arrangements in the Paris Agreement must yield more positive effects sooner than the usual "name-and-shame" processes of mutual peer pressure that promote compliance in most multilateral environmental agreements. Climate rules must ensure full implementation of the national climate pledges, discourage non-compliance with those pledges, and encourage the ratcheting-up of those pledges to accelerate action against climate change. In the absence of sanctions and of WTO-like dispute settlement, the combined pressure for universal climate compliance from all the countries that have ratified the Paris climate agreement must be unwavering and unparalleled in support of the "transparent, non-adversarial and non-punitive" actions of the "facilitative compliance mechanism" that is the closest climate negotiators could come in Paris to a climate dispute settlement system.[49]

This "expert-based" climate committee is to consist of "12 members with recognized competence in relevant scientific, technical, socio-economic, or technical fields" who are to be selected with an eye to both "equitable geographical representation" and "gender balance."[50] In their endeavors to "facilitate implementation of" and "promote compliance with" the Paris Agreement, these dozen experts are supposed to "pay particular attention to the respective national capabilities and circumstances" of different countries.[51] Beyond this, they have been given no instructions in the climate agreement. "Despite lengthy negotiations in Paris," the climate negotiators could not agree on any further instructions for them.[52] Left unanswered in Paris were numerous questions about the scope of the committee's work, how an issue will get to the committee, what it will do with an issue, and how it will work.[53] One question is: How will committee action be initiated? By a party to the treaty with respect to itself? By another treaty party? By the committee on its own initiative? Another question is: What will be the outcome of committee action? Advice? Access to technical assistance? Other help in implementation and compliance? A formal statement of "compliance" or "non-compliance"? All of the above?[54] The answers to these and other questions when completing the Paris rulebook must afford the broadest range for committee action if this facilitative compliance mechanism is to succeed.

Precisely how this facilitative climate committee will proceed in practice remains an open question while the work on the climate rulebook continues. Until countries are required to begin to implement their climate pledges in earnest, there will be no need to monitor implementation or evaluate compliance. In considering how best to structure this climate mechanism, Christina Voigt of the University of Oslo has suggested that the facilitative committee's work could be divided between two separate branches, one devoted to implementation and the other to compliance. Over time, she adds, additional structures could be added to the committee architecture, such as one for fact-finding.[55]

As Voigt states what should be the obvious but, for some reason, does not seem to be obvious to everyone about international agreements, "[p]articipation and ambition alone are of little value as long as parties do not do what they said they would do and refrain from complying with their obligations. Compliance of parties with their international obligations set out in an agreement is therefore an important determinant of effectiveness. It is also an indispensable requirement to establish trust and confidence among parties. And trust, again, feeds back to increasing participation and ambition."[56] Whether a country decides to comply with its treaty obligations on the basis of a rational calculation of its self-interest (preferably its self-interest "rightly understood"), or whether it simply complies because it does not wish to be seen by the rest of the world as a pariah and a scofflaw that does not keep its word or its commitments, the mutually reinforcing feedback loop of mutual trust is crucial to effective treaty compliance.[57]

One page of mutual trust that has yet to be completed in the climate rulebook is the page on the actions taken in response to climate change called response measures.[58] What precisely are these response measures, and when can they justify trade, investment, and other commercial restrictions? Unanswered in the Paris climate agreement, these questions must be answered in the rulebook for the agreement. As a protocol to the United Nations Framework Convention on Climate Change, the Paris Agreement is governed by the WTO-like admonition in the UNFCCC that "[m]easures taken to combat climate change, including unilateral ones, should not constitute a means of arbitrary or unjustifiable discrimination or a disguised restriction on international trade."[59] More, in combating climate change, countries "should cooperate to promote a supportive and open international economic system."[60] But where is the line to be drawn? And who will draw that line – the climate regime or the trade regime?

Long a topic in climate talks, response measures have evolved as a concept from, first, the demands of oil-rich countries to be compensated for their losses from a shift to a low-carbon economy to, today, an entirely different and vastly broader discussion on the ways in which countries should take climate actions. Particular attention – and rightly so – in this current discussion is being given to the plight of the island states and the least-developed countries in acquiring the capacity and in securing the wherewithal to adjust to the impacts of climate change. In these ongoing talks in the aftermath of the Paris Agreement, "[t]he issue of response measures is now starting to be seen in the context of sustainable development, and especially in the context of a sustainable transition to a low-GHG economy ... Currently the focus is on economic diversification and the just transition of the workforce, which is another way to look at the economic and social pillars of sustainable development and a sustainable transition."[61]

This is certainly the right focus for filling in some of the blanks in the climate rulebook. But some definition is needed of when a response measure that restricts trade is truly a climate measure that ought to be justified as a legal derogation from WTO trade rules. In the absence of a climate dispute settlement system, and in the absence of any definitive statement by those implementing the Paris climate agreement about the meaning of a response measure, these necessary lines will be drawn either in dispute settlement in the WTO or – preferably – in rule-making by the WTO.

In crafting a WTO climate waiver, the members of the WTO, as countries that are also parties to the Paris Agreement, would doubtless defer to the COP climate regime in delineating the boundaries of legitimate and truly climate-motivated response measures that restrict trade. If the climate regime does not draw those lines, and if the WTO does not draw them in a climate waiver or in some broader version of rule revision, then they will end up being drawn by jurists in WTO dispute settlement. Likewise, with other issues relating to compliance with Paris climate promises – such as the metrics for measuring whether those promises have been kept – inaction by the climate regime will, in the eventual occurrence of a climate-related trade dispute, lead inexorably to line-drawing by WTO judges.

As with response measures taken in the context of addressing climate change, the right stop and go signals must also be sent in taking all those measures that fall within the legal scope of the hundreds of existing multilateral environmental agreements of all kinds. All these governmental actions must be seen in the context of securing sustainable development and, specifically, of the common task of accomplishing the United Nations Sustainable Development Goals. The number of environmental treaties – now totaling more than five hundred – continues to grow, there is evidence that many of them are succeeding, and there are sound suggestions for the negotiation of still more such treaties to meet ever-changing environmental needs.[62]

Potentially significant especially is a proposal backed by French president Emmanuel Macron, former UN secretary-general Ban Ki-Moon, former California governor Arnold Schwarzenegger, and others of the willing for a global treaty to protect the human right to a clean and healthy environment. This treaty would be framed as the third United Nations covenant on human rights, joining two earlier covenants – one on civil and political rights and one on social, economic, and cultural rights – which were adopted in 1966 and entered into force in 1976. Both followed the adoption by the United Nations General Assembly of the Universal Declaration of Human Rights in 1948.[63]

In concept, this new global human rights agreement would impose legally binding obligations on the countries that signed it and would also provide for reparations when treaty obligations are breached.[64] As conceived, it would enshrine the polluter-pays principle and other customary environmental principles into treaty law. Like other dimensions of human rights, environmental human rights would need to be upheld through the rule of law. The preamble to the Universal Declaration of Human Rights of 1948 states, "[I]t is essential, if man is not to be compelled to have recourse, as a last resort, to rebellion against tyranny and oppression, that human rights should be protected by the rule of law."[65] One of the willing, Daniel Magraw, lists the environmental aspects of the rule of law as including: "environmental law must be available; environmental law must be enforceable and enforced; environmental law applies to everyone, including the state and non-state parties; and environmental law must have sufficient authority to be observed. In addition, the regulatory environment must allow full non-state stakeholder participation, and observance of the environmental rule of law [as] the primary task of the courts."[66] These assurances should be included in any human rights agreement on the environment.

A test of this proposed new agreement will be whether it imposes top-down obligations – such as by trying to compel countries on pain of penalty to adopt green laws – or whether it embraces the logic of the true bottom-up. Unless it proceeds from the bottom up, it is unlikely to succeed. The adoption of any new global human rights agreement centered on the environment must be consonant with the creative and catalytic bottom-up experimentation necessary to meet the many discrete challenges of safeguarding the Earth's fragile ecosystems.

So too with the continued multiplication of multilateral environmental agreements of all kinds, shapes, and sizes. The planet's numerous superficially discrete environmental challenges are not discrete; they are all connected. There is increasing need for coordination in confronting these linked challenges among those entrusted with overseeing different environmental agreements. The Earth is one, even as the economy and the environment are one. Our response to the oneness of the Earth must be the forging of a greater unity in how we strive to save the Earth while advancing our own future on it; otherwise we will never achieve our goals for sustainable development.

Because all our environmental challenges are linked, all the hundreds of our international environmental agreements must therefore be *linked* within an enabling global framework for sustainable development.[67] On this, John Scanlon, the secretary-general of the CITES, has summed up the prevailing global view: "[T]here is general agreement that: the international environmental governance system is not adequately fulfilling its objectives and functions; environmental governance reform should be addressed in the broader context of environmental sustainability and sustainable development; and the status quo is not an option."[68] He said this in 2012. Since then, the worldwide search has continued for how best to get from here to there in coordinating the protection and preservation of the global environment.

In an endeavor known as "the Belgrade Process," the willing debated from 2009 to 2010 how best to bring together the multitude of international environmental arrangements to help make all of them more effective through global environmental governance.[69] In the end, they settled on what they saw as five global options: enhancing the United National Environment Programme; establishing a new umbrella organization for sustainable development; establishing a specialized agency such as a world environment organization; reforming the United Nations Economic and Social Council and the United Nations Commission on Sustainable Development; and enhancing institutional reforms and streamlining existing struc- tures. At the Rio+20 conference in 2012, continued debate about the reform of the institutional structure of environmental governance narrowed and centered on a choice between the first of these options – enhancing UNEP – and the third – establishing a specialized agency such as a world environment organization. In the rain at Rio, the assembled governments ultimately rejected both of these choices and decided to maintain the original mandate of UNEP while giving it some additional authority and some more money.[70]

Under the first option, a strengthened UNEP would remain a subsidiary arm of the United Nations, linked directly to the UN and to its other subsidiary arms, and linked through the UN to the wider agenda of the Sustainable Development Goals. Under the third option, the current responsibilities of UNEP would be folded in some fashion into a specialized agency separate and distinct from the United Nations, much like the World Bank, the World Health Organization, the Inter- national Labor Organization, the Food and Agricultural Organization, and (outside the legal framework of the UN) the WTO. Enhancing UNEP could easily be done through a resolution of the United Nations General Assembly. Establishing a new specialized international agency would be more difficult because it would require the negotiation of a new and freestanding international agreement.[71]

The negotiation of a new international agreement creating a new specialized international agency is necessary if we are to respond as we must to the urgency of the environmental challenges we face together in the twenty-first century. This new agency should not, however, be solely an agency for global stewardship of the environment. As contemplated in one of the other options identified in the Belgrade Process, it should, more broadly, be a specialized international agency that would serve as an umbrella organization for ensuring that all our international environ- mental arrangements function consistently with their own environmental purposes and also with the United Nations Sustainable Development Goals. It should be a World Sustainability Organization.

As with the reimagining of international trade rules and of international investment rules, the international environment must also be seen through the lens of sustainable development. In this new World Sustainability Organization, this line of sight must include all three dimensions of sustainable development – not only the environment but also the economy that is contained within the environment and the social impacts of environmental decisions. Just as the international institutions on trade and investment must be mindful of their impacts on the environment and on society, so too must this new specialized agency be mindful of the many economic and social dimensions of the Sustainable Development Goals and how they relate to the environment. In particular, as Maria Ivanova, a leading thinker on global environmental governance, reminds us, "At the core of the challenge ... stands the persistent false dichotomy of the environment and the economy."[72]

This dichotomy is not always false. Sometimes the irreplaceable treasures of the global environment must simply be protected and preserved – even at the cost of short-term economic opportunities. So it is with the coral reefs of Australia, the pristine forests of the Amazon, and the wild elephants of the African plain. And so it is with the river of grass in the Everglades and with the mild-mannered manatees in the coastal channels and the nesting sea turtles on the beaches of Florida. The list goes on of instances everywhere in which economic demands must simply yield to the urgencies of preserving the Earth's enveloping ecosystems. Yet, in many other instances, the true challenge in advancing toward sustainable development is in finding, wherever we can, solutions that will work both economically and environmentally. In discovering those solutions, and in drawing the right lines "in between" in the rules that will secure them, often we must ask: When is a public or a private action that falls within the scope of any of the hundreds of multilateral environmental agreements consistent with the obligations in those agreements and also with the Sustainable Development Goals? And who will decide?

There is, at this time, no ultimate global source or recourse for the answers to these vital questions. To the extent that dispute settlement systems are used to enforce these environmental agreements, their effectiveness is uneven and their jurisdiction does not extend beyond the legal limits of their own treaty terms. Furthermore, as with international investment law, the proliferation of international environmental agreements and the consequent accumulation of international environmental law can sometimes result in different legal answers to the same questions. There is mounting need to ensure that general international environmental rules are interpreted consistently by different international environmental treaty regimes. There is likewise increasing need to ensure that environmental rules and rulings are interpreted consistently with all three pillars of sustainable development.

Thus, the new World Sustainability Organization should have a new dispute settlement system, which should feature a new global tribunal on sustainable development structured much like the WTO Appellate Body and like the planned CETA investment tribunal. Appeals on sustainability issues could be taken by legal right by disputing parties to this new World Sustainability Court from decisions made by the dispute settlement systems of all multilateral environmental agreements, ITLOS and other ocean tribunals, and dispute panels under regional international environmental arrangements. The verdicts of the World Sustainability Court on sustainability issues should be recognized legally both by the WTO Appellate Body and by the CETA investment tribunal – and by any World Investment Court that may emerge from the further development of the CETA tribunal or otherwise.

The jurisdiction of the new World Sustainability Court should include those legal issues relating to whether particular judgments by environmental tribunals are consistent with the three social, economic, and environmental pillars of sustainable development as agreed and expressed in the United Nations Sustainable Development Goals. An appeal, for example, could concern whether a ruling has struck the right balance by drawing the right lines along the nexus of social, economic, and environmental concerns. Rulings by the World Sustainability Court in review of previous legal rulings on sustainability issues by environmental tribunals would give needed primacy to sustainable development, and would also help ensure much-needed consistency and coherence in the interpretation of the rules of the highly fragmented environmental treaty system.

In addition, WTO panels and investment arbitral tribunals – and also their respective appellate tribunals – could be authorized to seek advisory opinions from the World Sustainability Court on particular sustainability issues in advance of their own rulings, and could also be bound by those opinions. In the WTO, this would be a significant elaboration on the current right of a panel "to seek information and technical advice from any individual or body which it deems appropriate."[73] In this way, rulings by the World Sustainability Court could also help ensure consistency and coherence within the broader context of the global pursuit of the objective of sustainable development as set out in the United Nations Sustainable Development Goals.

Ideally, this new World Sustainability Court would also hear appeals from the decisions of the facilitative committee under the Paris Agreement. Climate change is all-pervasive. Yet climate change, like all else environmentally and economically, must be viewed within the all-embracing context of sustainable development. The process set out in the climate agreement for global review of implementation and of compliance with national climate pledges is to be "non-adversarial and non-punitive."[74] All the same, countries should be able to appeal any decisions made by the climate regime on their implementation of, and their compliance with, their national climate pledges if they think those decisions are inconsistent with the broader global goals for sustainable development, which extend beyond climate change. Thus, in practical effect, there would be a climate dispute settlement system. The World Sustainability Court would also be a world climate court.

LINKING ECONOMIC AND ENVIRONMENTAL FRAMEWORKS
THROUGH THE INTERNATIONAL RULE OF LAW

Lastly, we must link all our enabling economic and environmental frameworks for global governance by coordinating each "stop" and each "go" of all their traffic lights. Just as traffic lights must be coordinated to ensure the smooth flow of traffic, our international rules for the economy and the environment must be coordinated to ensure they advance our global goals for sustainable development. To be able to call all the complex mix of fragmented international rules in the multitude of international agreements "laws," those rules must be coordinated within a multilevel global institutional architecture that enables the true bottom-up and that evolves over time toward a fullness of willful international cooperation through mutual reliance on Tocqueville's "principle of interest rightly understood." The logic of such international cooperation in making international law leads straight to the centrality and to the indispensability of upholding the rules we make through strict adherence to the international rule of law.

To be successful, such a global institutional architecture may necessarily be to some extent vertical and hierarchical; but it cannot be top-down. It must be decentralized, and it must be multilevel. It must be comprised, as Ernst Ulrich Petersmann puts it, of "'overlapping,' self-governing local, national, and trans-national polities responsible for multilevel protection of transnational [public goods] that are necessary conditions for human autonomy and well-being."[75] No one institution or group of institutions should dictate global governance from up above. Rather, global governance must be constructed and must emerge from down below through innovative experiments in providing for human flourishing by sustainable development. Globally, what must be done is to ensure that an atmosphere exists in which such experiments can happen.[76]

Political theorists speak of this as "polycentric governance" – which is just a fancy way of describing the rules frameworks resulting and emerging from the true bottom-up.[77] The fragmentation of international law and, thus, of global governance that causes anxiety for some legal theorists should rightly be seen instead as its greatest potential strength. Decentralization – not centralization – is the better approach toward more effective global governance. Decentralization allows for local initiative in organization, tailored attention to local conditions, the facilitation of learning by doing, and the building of invaluable mutual trust through mutual and reiterative local cooperative action.[78] Much of this useful experience and this useful knowledge can then be refined and scaled up over time as a model for meeting wider needs.

Elinor Ostrom, whose empirical research into the wellsprings of actual coopera-tive action led her to become one of the pioneering exponents of polycentric governance, stressed that her research "repeatedly identified a necessary core of trust and reciprocity among those involved that is associated with successful levels of collective action."[79] This "necessary core of trust and reciprocity" is most likely to emerge from the cumulative shared experience of working closely together over a period of time in facing common challenges. In short, cooperation for just and effective governance can be learned by doing.

This process of trust-building for just and effective governance can happen locally – as any local elected official from anywhere in the world will readily attest. When local people work cooperatively on solutions that will directly affect them, trust and reciprocity are established that can provide the confidence for finding additional solutions locally and also for a scaling of local governance to find broader solutions to broader problems that affect many more people. This same process can also happen globally – as has happened with the determined consensus-building around the table of the WTO Appellate Body.

Although it must be decentralized, the overall architecture we need for global governance can deliver scaled global solutions only if it *links* all our decentralized endeavors pursuant to all our thousands of international economic and environmental agreements much more effectively through an enhanced coordination aimed at achieving sustainable development. Links are needed between levels and "across scales, issues, and institutions."[80] Some of the existing links are formal – such as the productive link established by the CITES and the WTO to help combat illegal trade in endangered species. Most current links, however, are informal. Most are also the exception and not the rule.

This must be reversed. Adam Smith would advise us that, with institutions as with markets, we can benefit by creating more – and more effective – divisions of labor. With international institutions, this must mean shared information, shared experiences, joint research, joint projects, and joint sessions on overlapping concerns. It must mean collaborative monitoring, reporting, and verification of implementation and compliance with separate rules frameworks that are facing overlapping concerns. Above all, it must mean drawing from the work of the willing in voluntary networks committed to sustainable development worldwide. All of this together will add up to cooperative accomplishment toward the willing world.

Some of these links exist now. More are being made. People *are* trying to work together. Yet there are not nearly enough links. Why not, for example, have the national delegates to the WTO and the national delegates to the UN climate COP meet jointly to try to develop together a common understanding and a common approach on the crucial nexus between trade and climate change? These emissaries from the "two different planets" of economy and environment could seek common agreement on how to measure the carbon emissions from making a product, on how to define a climate response measure, and on how best and where best to establish the parameters of a WTO climate waiver. By pooling and sharing the best of our currently separate institutional efforts under separate international legal umbrellas, we can shelter the economy and the environment alike much more successfully under the overarching umbrella of sustainable development.

These links must extend to international dispute settlement. In *US – Shrimp* – the WTO shrimp–turtle dispute on the line between trade and the environment – the WTO Appellate Body had the legal authority to rule only on whether legal obligations under the WTO treaty were being fulfilled. The WTO judges had no legal authority to rule on whether the obligations in the environmental treaty relevant to the dispute – the CITES – were likewise being fulfilled. All the countries engaged in that landmark WTO dispute were also parties to the CITES and were therefore legally bound by the CITES to protect endangered sea turtles. No country contended in the WTO dispute that the contested United States measure requiring the use of turtle-excluder devices by fishing vessels when fishing for shrimp was *not* consistent with the CITES.

But what if one or more of those countries had done so? Surely the Appellate Body would have respected and followed any ruling by the CITES that answered that legal question. There was, though, no established legal means for the Appellate Body to seek such a ruling from the CITES. What is more, despite its links with the WTO, there was no established way for the CITES as an institution to intervene in the WTO proceedings and offer such a ruling. In these circumstances, without a CITES ruling, how then would the Appellate Body have responded? The Appellate Body would have been left with the need to interpret the environmental agreement itself in order truly to resolve the international trade and environment dispute – but without the legal authority to find that a WTO member was acting inconsistently with its WTO obligations because it was acting inconsistently with the CITES.

As so often, it comes down to this: Who will judge?

With the reimagining of trade and investment law to achieve sustainable development, with the continued spread of environmental law, with the accumulation of what is quickly becoming climate change law, with the advent of what could in time become an all-embracing law of sustainable development, and with the intertwining and interacting of the complicated rules and rules frameworks that comprise all these forms of international law, the question of who will judge becomes paramount. The site of the source of a final independent and impartial judgment is at the very heart of the assurance of the rule of law. That legal source must have the legitimacy, the credibility, the accountability, and, thus, the authority to make a judgment – and to make it stick.

The WTO Appellate Body has largely acquired – but must be ever diligent to maintain – the authority to rule on trade and trade-related issues under the WTO treaty as, in effect, a world trade court. A World Investment Court does not yet exist. Likewise, a World Sustainability Court does not yet exist. The making and shaping of these necessary tools for upholding international rules as centerpieces of enabling rules frameworks must include the establishment of legal links between and among them. On trade, on investment, and on the intertwining of environment, climate, and sustainability, each of these three separate current and imagined international dispute settlement systems must have the means of making legal decisions that have real and general effect. They must be able to seek advisory opinions and other preliminary rulings from the two others that may affect their own decisions. And, once made, the decisions of each of the three within its own scope of jurisdiction must be binding on the two others.

To achieve these ends, it will be essential to have mutually negotiated and mutually binding rules in an agreement among these three separate systems that establishes clearly the jurisdictional lines of which system will deal with which legal issues, and that sets out also a mutual understanding of which system will decide whenever there are the inevitable conflicts about jurisdiction. Even with such an agreement in place among the three systems, there will undoubtedly be times when there will be disagreements among disputants and also among systems about which dispute settlement system should judge, and on what. In instances involving successive treaties, the customary rules of international law on treaties will often provide the answer; but more specific understandings will also be needed.[81]

Recall the *Swordfish Stocks* case between Chile and the European Union, when Chile banned from Chilean ports fishing vessels from Spain targeting swordfish near Chilean waters.[82] The European Union initiated trade consultations in the WTO, and, at the same time, Chile commenced proceedings in UNCLOS under the law of the sea. Both institutions had jurisdiction over particular aspects of the dispute. Conceivably, in the end, the two institutional results could have been consistent and complementary. But "it was possible that the two separate dispute settlement systems might have reached divergent conclusions on some legal issues, and upon factual matters, a clearly undesirable result."[83] With such an outcome, who would have judged? As it turned out in the *Swordfish Stocks* case, Chile and the European Union resolved their dispute without need for legal rulings by either the WTO or the International Tribunal on the Law of the Sea. Even so, their dispute underscores the need for an agreement among the international economic and environmental institutions on how to deal with their inevitable conflicts over jurisdiction.[84]

Jurisdictional conflicts can be avoided by the conclusion of a jurisdictional agreement among international institutions with separate and different international legal frameworks. In addition to such an agreement, mutual understanding, mutual respect, and, not least, mutual restraint would go a long way toward making the legal links among the WTO Appellate Body, a World Investment Court, and a World Sustainability Court mutually advantageous and also mutually reinforcing. So too would having, in each of these systems, jurists and other decisionmakers who do not think in terms of separate silos, who are not solely specialists in their own legal provinces, but who range, in their experience, in their expertise, and, above all, in their insight, into the broader vistas of the entire terrain of international law. More than that, in our shared pursuit of sustainable development, we must have international judges who fully understand the urgency of sustainable development.

Jurists must never roam beyond the bounds of their jurisdiction. They must not invent obligations where they are not there. Customary rules of interpretation of public international law require them – and rightly so – to render their interpretations "in good faith according to the ordinary meaning given to the terms of the treaty in their context and in the light of its object and purpose."[85] There is much to be said in international dispute settlement among sovereign states for taking a conservative view of legal jurisdiction and for applying a strict construction to international rules.

This does not mean, however, that international jurists – whether they happen to be ruling on trade, investment, climate, environment, or anything else – should be heedless of the wider world beyond the echo chambers of their own specialized silos. In particular, the right legal decision in any kind of international dispute will not be a decision made while wearing parochial blinders that conceal the urgency of global sustainability. The legal linking of dispute settlement systems must begin to remove any such blinders. Working within the rule of law, the vision of judges must do the rest.

There will be no sustainable development without the rule of law. As it is within each separate domain of dispute settlement, the links between and among these three current and envisaged international dispute settlement frameworks for trade, investment, and sustainability will be strong enough to work, to evolve, and to last only if they are connected by a common adherence to the rule of law. Because almost all we do in the world is related in some way to sustainable development, the legal decisions in each of them will affect all of them. These legal decisions will have the impact of "law" only if they are made by jurists who are impartial and independent of all political influence, and only if they are backed by economic sanctions or by other effective forms of securing and ensuring compliance. The rule of law depends on those who are entrusted with upholding it, and on the means provided to uphold it.

Without the rule of law, the traffic lights of international law will not work. We will not "stop" and we will not "go" when we should, and we will not get to where we must go. Our progress will come to a halt. The big will push aside the small. The strong will leave the weak behind to suffer. Yet, no matter how much they may cut off and crowd out the small and the weak, the big and the strong will themselves also end up worse off than they would have been if all the traffic lights had worked.

Without the rule of law, we will all be back again on the island of Melos, millennia ago, when the strong did what their power permitted them to do, and the small and the weak suffered – but when, in the end, the bullies of Athens discovered that there are limits to might making right, and Athens ended up losing the Peloponnesian War. Our long voyage of more than two thousand years away from Melos must continue to take us in the opposite direction, toward the rule of law, toward sustainable development, and toward the willing world.

But, to reach the willing world, we must first summon the willingness to go there.

Conclusion: The Willing World

Willingness can be witnessed at Cape Canaveral on the "Space Coast" of Florida. Commanding the shore there at Kennedy Space Center are launch pads 39A and 39B, where humanity has left in rockets for the International Space Station and for the Moon.[1] The Atlantic Ocean is less than a quarter of a mile away from both pads – and it is getting closer. The beach fronting the space center "has thinned and moved inland by as much as 200 feet," and "shrinking dunes and damaged shoreline [are] just a stone's throw from the launch pads." The rocket scientists are "watching waters rise right outside the front door."[2] In a "managed retreat" from the advancing shoreline, the National Aeronautics and Space Administration (NASA) has built manmade dunes to replace the natural dunes that had long provided shelter, and has otherwise reinforced the nearby beach to protect the launch pads from the rising sea.[3]

The sea is rising there like the sea is rising everywhere. Climate models cited by NASA project that the sea along the Florida Space Coast will rise 5 to 8 inches by the 2050s, and 9 to 15 inches by the 2080s. Those estimates will multiply several times over if ice sheets in Greenland and Antarctica continue to melt at their current accelerating pace – to 21 to 24 inches by the 2050s and 43 to 49 inches by the 2080s.[4] Worldwide, according to NASA, "The rate of sea level rise is faster now than at any time in the past 2,000 years, and that rate has doubled in the past two decades."[5] Even if we meet the goal in the Paris Agreement of cutting greenhouse gas emissions to net zero in the second half of this century, sea levels will continue to rise for the next two centuries. Every five years of delay beyond 2020 in peaking global emissions will result in an extra 20 centimeters – 8 inches – of sea level rise by 2300.[6]

The relentless rise of the seas is an irrepressible reminder, if we need one, that concerted global actions on climate change and on sustainability are needed – and needed now. Other new signs of the arrival of ecological upheaval appear daily. Parts of Antarctica are turning "green and likely to be getting greener" as vast expanses of melting ice sheets crack and threaten to break off into the sea.[7] Climate change has altered the patterns of songbirds so that once again we confront the prospect of silent springs.[8] Several hundred miles south of Kennedy Space Center on Florida's eastern coastline, researchers with the US Geological Survey have discovered that the floor of the ocean around the degrading coral reefs in the Florida Keys is eroding and sinking because of climate change, pollution, and other human actions. The natural processes that once replenished the ocean floor as coral reefs grew are – now that coral growth has slowed – no longer working.[9]

The launch pads near the shore at Kennedy Space Center are enduring monuments to all that human imagination can accomplish. The seawaters rising slowly toward those launch pads are reminders of what can best be described as our "failure of imagination" so far on climate change and the rest of sustainable development.[10] In the WTO treaty, in the Paris Agreement, in the Sustainable Development Goals, and in many other ambitious expressions of international cooperation, the willing of the world have imagined our shared goals. Many of us are busy now imagining how best to pursue them as we strive to achieve them. Yet, so far, ours has been a failure of imagination in figuring out how we can add sufficiently – and soon enough – to the numbers of the willing to be able to summon and inspire the worldwide willingness necessary to reach all our goals.

Time and again in the history of our aspiring but endlessly struggling species, we have suffered from a failure of imagination. Sometimes this has led to war.[11] The Spartans and the Athenians could not imagine how they could coexist in ancient Greece. The Allies and the Central Powers could not imagine how they could avoid conflict a century ago following an assassination in Sarajevo. At other times, the failure of imagination has led to other forms of human destruction that have often been accompanied by ecological devastation, ranging across the world and across history, from famines to nuclear fallout to the fall and disappearance of once-great civilizations due to shrinking natural resources.[12] The solemn stone statues on Easter Island, sinking slowly into the sea, are abiding testimony to the connections between societal collapse and "self-inflicted environmental damage."[13]

At all times, the human failure of imagination has been caused by a refusal to see the world through different eyes and to act in the world in new ways. In our time, we can – enough of us – imagine a world in which we travel to the stars. So we have gone to the Moon, and we speak now of returning to the Moon and going on to Mars and beyond. Our space telescopes peer into the deepness of the universe in search of new planets. Yet imagination fails all too many of us when it comes to acting together to hold back the rising seas and halt all the other looming calamities of climate change and other unsustainable developments here on this planet. Not enough of us are willing to see the world as it truly has become in this Anthropocene Age, and to see the future as necessarily proceeding from this changed world to sustainable development. From time to time – such as in New York and in Paris in 2015 – we can catch glimpses of the willing world, but we cannot truly see it and imagine how we must proceed from now to the then of making it. So ours remains an unwilling world.

To create the willing from our unwilling world, we must first be able to imagine it. Some of my own imaginings of how we can shape and share a sustainable global prosperity have been set out in the preceding pages. Others of the willing have other imaginings equal to or better than mine. Admittedly, at this writing, most of these imaginings have virtually no global constituency other than some of the most ardent of the willing. It may seem folly to some to offer such optimistic imaginings at a time of paralyzing pessimism. Given the seeming gulf between now and the then we are seeking, can we really expect to come together to put a price on carbon, discipline fossil fuel subsidies, define legitimate climate response measures, further free trade and investment, and create a World Investment Court and a World Sustainability Court? Many will think it foolish even to try.

This much we know: If we do not try, all we imagine of the willing world will remain mere imaginings. Only if we do try can our imaginings help us reach the willing world. But a sufficiency of the needed willingness to try is everywhere missing; for missing also are some of the essential sparks needed to enable us first to imagine the willing world and then work together to shape and share it.

Missing is confidence. Missing in many parts of the world is the necessary belief among millions of fearful people that they can survive the ordeal of change, make the green transition, and succeed in a new low-carbon economy. More – and more effective – domestic actions are imperative everywhere in the world to ease and further this transition by helping these people get through it and have every opportunity to prosper from it. The fearful must see in their own lives that globalization and technological change can deliver a shared prosperity – and that the right lines can be drawn in the right combination of market and governmental actions to provide transitional solutions and sustainable growth. Only then will they be able to find anew the courage to confront the uncertainties of the open-endedness of freedom in an open society. Only then will their fear begin to yield to the confidence needed to trust that the green transition will be a just transition.

Missing is trust. Missing in many places in the world is the trust that this transitional help will arrive and will secure solutions. Untold millions – many of them with good reason – simply do not trust their own government. They do not feel they are heard. They do not feel they are represented. They do not feel their fate is considered when governmental decisions are made that affect their lives. They believe their government belongs to and speaks for someone else, and they have been discarded, abandoned, and left on their own. The ultimate source of much of the disorder in the world is this widespread popular distrust of government and everyone involved in it. Creating new and renewed trust will help create confidence. Such trust will be inspired by more transparency, more accountability, more responsiveness, and – most of all – more truly representative democracy. More true democratic representation *nationally* can diminish the unwillingness of people everywhere. It can in turn instill more legitimacy into all that is done *internationally* to try to find the right global solutions through the right kind of leadership.

Missing is leadership. True democratic representation is not just a rote reflection of the popular majority of the moment. Leaders owe those they represent not their finger in the wind of political "tracking" polls and passing public opinion, but their judgment.[14] Especially with the flood of disinformation amid the fog of our "post-factual" world, those who would lead us must base their judgments on demonstrated facts about the world as it truly is – including scientific facts – and not on fantasies about the world now or as it used to be. To create, and to serve in, a political atmosphere receptive to sound and enlightened judgment, leaders also must never stoop to pandering to the people. Those who would truly lead us must always tell us what we need to hear, and not only what we may seem to want to hear at the moment. Always they must do their best to try to educate us – even as they strive to be educated by us.

By being honest and straightforward with the people about the facts of the global realities and of the global choices before us, leaders will acquire the credibility they now lack to help pry open the political door to the political will needed to deliver results to the people that will help improve their lives and their future. Such results will be possible only if leaders appeal to the best in us, not the worst, and to our hopes, not our fears. People who are shown a future they can hope for are more likely to support leaders who are trying to get them there. Democratic representation must earn trust by offering the people not a lament for a lost and illusory past but a vision of a brighter future. The sight of such a vision on the horizon can help quell the fear of change and can help inspire the confidence to confront change with shared hope for a shining tomorrow.

Missing is vision. Missing in the pessimism of our retreat from the world is the optimism of the Enlightenment, the lost optimism that, found again, can give new birth to a vision that will beckon us to embrace the changing world. To make the willing world, we must recommit ourselves to the ideals of the Enlightenment that are the generators of open societies where progress is possible for one and all. As Steven Pinker, one of the most optimistic of the willing, reminds us, "Progress is a gift of the ideals of the Enlightenment and will continue to the extent that we rededicate ourselves to those ideals."[15] To be sure, there remains much amiss in our unwilling world. There is much to which pessimists can point to justify their pessimism. There always has been. There always will be. Yet, look how far we have come toward human flourishing since the eighteenth century. How much more flourishing can there be for humanity if we employ the Enlightenment ideals of rational thought, free inquiry, testing by observation, reliance on experience, adherence to science and to fact, and an ever-open and never-ending search for truth, to achieve sustainable development? And how much more can be achieved toward that goal if the employment of these ideals is framed within the Enlightenment notion of a mutual human sympathy that extends to include all humanity?

The enlightened vision that seems to be missing is there for all to see in the United Nations Sustainable Development Goals – if we choose to see it. It is there too in the specific proposals of the willing to fulfill those global goals – if we choose to pursue them. Yet, to achieve those goals, this vision given voice by the United Nations of a global sustainable prosperity we all can shape and share must not be seen only at global summits. It must be seen everywhere. It must be shared by everyone in the world so that all those who seek a shining tomorrow will see it on the horizon.

In the making of willingness, the top-down of concerted global actions at the summits of the world must be linked to the true bottom-up of creative and collaborative human actions down at the grassroots of the world. Those who would lead the world and those who would shape the world sustainably must communicate their vision with all at the global grassroots so that all of us everywhere can make that vision our own. Far more important, all of us at the global grassroots must communicate our vision of a shining tomorrow from the bottom up to all those who would lead us nationally and internationally. To achieve our global goals, the scaling up and linking up of successful local and regional experimentation and improvisation must help frame the architecture and help fill in the blanks for attaining global sustainable development.

The spark of imagination we need everywhere in the world cannot be lit from the top down. It can only be ignited from the true bottom-up. It can only emerge from the individual and collective endeavors of each one of the willing – whoever and wherever we may be in the world, and however we may be working together toward the economic, environmental, and social goals of sustainable development. Enlisting the endless energies and the boundless imagination of all the multitude of voluntary action networks and other partnerships throughout the world engaged in the true bottom-up is the only way we can – all of us – begin to understand how to make the global vision of the Sustainable Development Goals a global reality.

Missing is understanding. Against all evidence, much of the world persists in seeing the economy and the environment as separate and apart, and as therefore requiring rules and rules frameworks that are likewise separate and apart. Much of the world fails to see that the economy is *within* the environment, and that the broad and lasting prosperity we seek can be achieved only if we are proper stewards of the Earth's endangered ecosystems. Keeping the economy and the environment separate and apart in the rules and in the frameworks with which we address them will keep us from reaching our Sustainable Development Goals. Thus, in all we do, we must for the first time see and treat the economy and the environment as one, most of all by uniting them as one in discerning and drawing the right lines of the "just mean" that is "in between" in all our cooperative international rule-making.

Missing is cooperation. Starting now, and rising up from the bottom up, our confidence, our trust, our leadership, our vision, and our understanding must all combine at every level of global endeavor to end the retreat from globalization and begin a new and enduring era of international cooperation founded on the international rule of law. In a shared expression of our self-interest "rightly understood," we must combine across all the lines that would divide us to work together not only for the few, and not only for now, but for all and for all time. The myopic insularity of the recent withdrawal from international cooperation must be overcome and transformed into the solidarity that can come from uniting in a common purpose to accomplish common goals.[16]

Lastly, missing is purpose. Missing is a shared sense of purpose to inspire the unwilling to enlist with the willing to achieve our global goals. And missing even among many of the willing is the sense that their purpose is part of a larger purpose that must motivate all humanity. We may be working toward some economic, environmental, or social goal here at home; but what does this have to do with what others are experiencing and doing on the far side of the world?

The rocket launches from Cape Canaveral have given us the chance for the first time to see the world from afar. They have given us the opportunity to see the oneness of humanity on this small planet, "the human species at a human scale, intimately connected, even embedded, in its home. The more distant our perspective, seemingly the more intimate."[17] We must see our world now as we have seen it from space. We must see our world as one, and we must see ourselves as one.

Seeing in this new way can inspire us to act in new ways – including by striving to save our planet and our future on it. The weather satellites and remote sensing satellites we have launched from Cape Canaveral have revealed the changes we have made to the climate and the ecology of the Earth. Over time, they have shown the unrelenting unfolding of a heat wave moving across the surface of the planet. Each and every one of us is already affected or soon will be. It is only a matter of time.

In an open society, we have the freedom to choose. We are not told what to choose. We have the open-endedness of freedom. We have the uncertainty that comes with being free to make our own choice among the endless choices living in an open society offers us. Confronted with this open-endedness, confronted with this uncertainty, many people do not know what to choose. They do not know what to do with their freedom. So they are left without meaning or direction in their lives. They drift aimlessly. They live only on the surface. They do not have purpose.

For all of us, life has the purpose we choose to give it. What is our freedom *for*? Each one of us must answer this question for ourselves. In answering it, we can choose to be optimists, not pessimists. We can choose to believe that, through the exercise of our freedom, and despite all, tomorrow can be better than today – for all of us. We can choose also to use our freedom for something more than merely ourselves and our own material gain. We can choose to pursue our own lives while taking the broader and longer view of the "principle of interest rightly understood." We can choose to be willing. We can choose to serve.

Through willing service, we can each find purpose. Through willing service together, we can find even more. Enlightened purpose can be found for freedom by seeing humanity as one and making it into one by shaping and sharing a sustainable global prosperity in which economy and environment are seen and treated as one. The common pursuit of sustainable development can unite humanity in a shared sense of purpose.

All of us must participate in this pursuit all over the world. A special responsibility falls to the older among us who have tried and, so far, largely failed to convince the vast majority of humanity to see their future from the perspective of those we have launched into space and, thus, through the global lens of sustainable development. We must do much more. A special opportunity beckons to the younger among us who have not yet discovered a shared sense of purpose, and who will, without willingness, have to live in a world vastly changed by climate change and other ecological destruction. The young, above all, must be foremost among the willing.

In agreeing to the Sustainable Development Goals, the United Nations declared, "The future of humanity and of our planet lies in our hands. It lies also in the hands of today's younger generation who will pass the torch to future generations ... Children and young women and men are critical agents of change and will find in the new Goals a platform to channel their infinite capacities for activism into the creation of a better world."[18] We must all be among the willing, but the youngest of us must lead the way.

With a shared sense of purpose born of seeing humanity as one and the world as one, we will find, at last, the courage to face as one throughout the world the challenge of sustainable development. We will confront and complete the historic human mission of securing a global prosperity we all can shape and share. We will do so through an overflowing of imagination and cooperation. Together, with our failure of imagination behind us, with our tools of cooperation beside us, and with the vision of a bright future before us, we will summon the will we must have to put our unwillingness behind us and transform our unwilling into the willing world.

I am one of the willing. Join us.

Notes

PREFACE

1 David G. Victor, *Global Warming Gridlock: Creating More Effective Strategies for Protecting the Planet* (Cambridge: Cambridge University Press, 2011), 236.
2 James Bacchus, *Trade and Freedom* (London: Cameron May, 2004).

INTRODUCTION

1 Andrew Browne, "Xi Jinping's Trump Moment," *Wall Street Journal* (October 22, 2016).
2 Ruchir Sharma, "When Borders Close," *New York Times* (November 13, 2016).
3 Shawn Donnan, "Global Warning," *Financial Times* (December 24, 2016).
4 Max Ehrenfreund, "At the World Economic Forum, Talk of Equitable Capitalism," *Washington Post* (January 20, 2017).
5 Quoted in Donnan, "Global Warning."
6 Angus Deaton, "It's Not Just Unfair: Inequality Is a Threat to Our Governance," *New York Times* (March 26, 2017).
7 Quoted in Donnan, "Global Warning."
8 OECD, "Key Issues Paper," Meeting of the OECD Council at Ministerial Level (Paris: OECD, June 7–8, 2017), 3.
9 Ibid.
10 Gretchen Morgensen, "How Letting Bankers off the Hook May Have Tripped the Election," *New York Times* (November 13, 2016).
11 "G20 Business Leaders Reject Protectionism," Environment News Service (May 5, 2017), http://ens-newswire.com/2017/05/05/business-leaders-reject-protectionism.
12 Griff White and Emily Rauhala, "After Trump's Win, a Worldwide Populist Surge," *Washington Post* (November 14, 2016).
13 WEF, "Outlook on the Global Agenda 2015" (Geneva: World Economic Forum, 2015).
14 UNDP, "Human Development Report 2014" (Vienna: United Nations Development Programme, 2014), 41.
15 Ibid., 19.

16 Ibid.

17 Ibid.

18 Shannon K. O'Neil, "The UN's Third Financing for Development Conference: After Growth & Aid, What Comes Next?," Development Channel, Council on Foreign Relations (July 16, 2015).

19 World Bank and WTO, "The Role of Trade in Ending Poverty" (Geneva: World Bank and World Trade Organization, July 2015), 7.

20 Ibid., 15. These are the most recent numbers, from 2011. For details, see World Bank and IMF, "Global Monitoring Report 2014/2015: Ending Poverty and Sharing Prosperity" (Washington, D.C.: World Bank and International Monetary Fund, 2015).

21 World Bank and WTO, "The Role of Trade in Ending Poverty," 7.

22 Rakesh Kochbar, "A Global Middle Class Is More Promise than Reality: From 2001 to 2011, Nearly 700 Million Step Out of Poverty, But Most Only Barely," Pew Research Center (Washington, D.C., July 2015). See also Somini Sengupta, "Study Finds Low Incomes Constrain Half of World," *New York Times* (July 8, 2015); Shawn Donnan and Sam Fleming, "Data Point to Poorer Global Middle Class," *Financial Times* (July 9, 2015).

23 Kochbar, "A Global Middle Class Is More Promise than Reality."

24 Facundo Alvaredo et al., "World Inequality Report 2018" (Paris: World Inequality Lab, Paris School of Economics, 2017), Executive Summary.

25 World Bank and WTO, "The Role of Trade in Ending Poverty," 7.

26 Ibid., 8.

27 Svante Arrhenius, "On the Influence of Carbonic Acid in the Air Upon the Temperature of the Ground," *Philosophical Magazine and Journal of Science*, Vol. 5, No. 41 (1896), 237–76.

28 UN IPCC, Summary for Policymakers, "Climate Change 2013: The Physical Science Basis" (New York: United Nations, September 27, 2013), 13, 15.

29 On all that follows about climate change facts and predictions, see the various working party reports comprising the Fifth Assessment of the United Nations Intergovernmental Panel on Climate Change, and especially the Summary for Policymakers of the Synthesis Report (New York: United Nations, November 2, 2014).

30 UN IPCC, Summary for Policymakers, "Climate Change 2013: The Physical Science Basis," 2.

31 Melissa Davey, "Humans Causing Climate to Change 170 Times Faster than Natural Forces," *Guardian* (February 12, 2017).

32 NASA and NOAA, "NASA, NOAA Data Show 2016 Warmest Year on Record Globally" (Washington, D.C.: National Aeronautics and Space Agency and National Oceanic and Atmospheric Administration, January 18, 2017).

33 Dana Nuccitelli, "2017 Was the Hottest Year on Record Without El Nino, Thanks to Global Warming," *Guardian* (January 2, 2018).

34 Alister Doyle, "Warming Set to Breach Paris Accord's Toughest Limit by Mid Century: Study," Reuters (January 12, 2018) (reporting on the most recent findings by the IPCC).

35 Chris Mooney, "New US View of Climate Accord Apparent in Bonn Delegation," *Washington Post* (May 9, 2017).

36 World Bank, "Turn Down the Heat: Confronting the New Climate Normal" (Washington, D.C.: World Bank, 2014), xvii.

37 Coral Davenport, "Championing Environment, Francis Takes Aim at Global Capitalism," *New York Times* (June 19, 2015).

38 Ibid.

39 Pope Francis, Encyclical Letter "Laudato Si'" of the Holy Father Francis on Care for Our Common Home (June 2015).

40 Ibid.

41 Daniel W. O'Neill, Andrew L. Fanning, William F. Lamb, and Julia K. Steinberger, "A Good Life for All Within Planetary Boundaries," *Nature Sustainability*, Vol. 1 (February 2018), 88–95.

42 John Schwartz, "Providing for 7 Billion. Or Not," *New York Times* (February 14, 2018).

43 Ibid.

44 Ibid.

CHAPTER 1

1 UN, "Report of the United Nations Commission on Environment and Development: Our Common Future" (1987) (the "Brundtland Report"), www.un-documents.net/our-common-future.pdf.

2 Joel Mokyr, *The Lever of Riches: Technological Creativity and Economic Progress* (New York and Oxford: Oxford University Press, 1990), 5.

3 Adam Smith, *An Inquiry into the Nature and Causes of the Wealth of Nations* (New York: Modern Library, 1994) [1776].

4 Dwight H. Perkins, Steven Radeler, Donald R. Snodgrass, Malcolm Gillis, and Michael Roemer, *Economics of Development* (New York: W. W. Norton, 2001, 5th edn.), 8–9 (emphasis in original).

5 See generally World Bank, "What Is Development?," in Tatyana P. Soubbotina, *Beyond Economic Growth: An Introduction to Sustainable Development*, WBI Learning Resource Series 24894, 2nd edn. (Washington, D.C.: World Bank, 2004), 7–10; H. W. Arndt, *Economic Development: The History of an Idea* (Chicago: University of Chicago Press, 1989); and G. Meier, *The Biography of a Subject: An Evolution of Development Economics* (New York: Oxford University Press, 2004).

6 According to the UNDP's "Human Development Report 1996" (New York and Oxford: Oxford University Press, 1996), "human development is the end – economic growth a means."

7 Simon Dresner, *The Principles of Sustainability* (London: Earthscan, 2004), 68 [2002]. The concept of "gross national product" had been invented by economist Simon Kuznets in 1937, during the New Deal, to gauge recovery in national production from the depths of the Great Depression: Jeremy L. Caradonna, *Sustainability: A History* (London: Oxford University Press, 2014), 129.

8 William Easterly, *The Tyranny of Experts: Economists, Dictators, and the Forgotten Rights of the Poor* (New York: Basic Books, 2013), 6.

9 Ibid., 7.

10 Ibid.

11 Dresner, *The Principles of Sustainability*, 69.

12 Ibid.

13 Wilfred Beckerman, "The Chimera of 'Sustainable Development,'" *Electronic Journal of Sustainable Development*, Vol. 1, No. 1 (2007), 17.

14 For example, the psychologist Abraham Maslow established a "hierarchy of needs" consisting "of a motivational hierarchy based on universal predispositions": Alizan Mazadi, "Adopting the Capabilities Approach in Developing a Global Framework for Sustainable Development" (Master's Thesis, Uppsala University, Sweden, 2012), 5.

15 See UNDP, "Reflecting on the Human Development Approach: Past, Present and Future" (Vienna: UN Development Programme, August 7, 2015), www.et.undp.org/content/ethiopia/en/home/presscenter/articles/2015/08/07/reflecting-on-the-human-development-approach-past-present-and-future.html; and see Michael J. Trebilcock and Mariana Mota Prado, *Advanced Introduction to Law and Development* (Cheltenham, UK: Edward Elgar, 2014), 9.

16 Amartya Sen, *Development as Freedom* (New York: Random House, 1999).

17 Ibid., xii.

18 Ibid.

19 Ibid., 3.

20 Ibid., 18.

21 Peter Bauer, *Economic Analysis and Policy in Underdeveloped Countries* (Durham, N.C.: Duke University Press, 1957), 113; for a discussion, see James A. Dorn, "Sustainable Development: A Market-Liberal Vision," *Electronic Journal of Sustainable Development*, Vol. 1, Issue 1 (2007).

22 Karl Popper, "Immanuel Kant: Philosopher of the Enlightenment," in Karl Popper, *In Search of a Better World: Lectures and Essays from Thirty Years* (London and New York: Routledge, 1996), 134.

23 Karl R. Popper, *The Open Society and Its Enemies* (Princeton: Princeton University Press, 1971), Vol. I, 173 [1962]. See my previous discussion of Popper's view of freedom in Bacchus, *Trade and Freedom*, 133–37, and see an interview in 2016 in which I expressed my view that, "The struggle in the world today is not a struggle along the tired truisms of left and right. The real struggle is between open and closed societies": Mark Howard, "Trading in Ignorance," *Florida Trend* (September 2016).

24 Popper, *The Open Society and Its Enemies*.

25 Ibid.

26 Ibid., 188.

27 Ibid., 198. I made these same points in Bacchus, *Trade and Freedom*, 190–91.

28 Article 1.1, United Nations Declaration on the Right to Development (December 4, 1986), A/RES/41/128.

29 Article 1.2, United Nations Declaration on the Right to Development.

30 See Jared Diamond, *Collapse: How Societies Choose to Fail or Succeed* (New York: Penguin Books, 2006).

31 René Descartes, *Discourse on the Method of Rightly Conducting One's Reason, and Seeking the Truth in the Sciences* [1637], www.gutenberg.org/files/59/59-h/59-h.htm.

32 Francis Bacon, *Novum Organum* [1620], www.earlymoderntexts.com/assets/pdfs/bacon1620.pdf.

33 Caradonna, *Sustainability: A History*, 33. See pp. 33–41.

34 Leslie Paul Thiele, *Sustainability* (Cambridge: Polity Press, 2013), 16.

35 See Caradonna, *Sustainability: A History*, 35–38.

36 John Gray, *Enlightenment's Wake: Politics and Culture at the Close of the Modern Age* (London and New York: Routledge, 2008) [1995].

37 J. B. Bury, *The Idea of Progress: An Inquiry Into Its Origin and Growth* (London: Macmillan and Co., 1920), 2.

38 Ibid., 216.

39 Steven J. Pinker, *Enlightenment Now: The Case for Reason, Science, Humanism and Progress* (New York: Penguin Random House, 2018); Steven J. Pinker, "The Enlightenment Is Working," *Wall Street Journal* (February 10, 2018).

40 Stephen Eric Bronner, *Reclaiming the Enlightenment: Toward a Politics of Radical Engagement* (New York: Columbia University Press, 2004), 158.

41 Joel Mokyr, *The Enlightened Economy: An Economic History of Britain 1700–1850* (New Haven and London: Yale University Press, 2009), 33, quoting Eric Hobsbawm, "Barbarism: A User's Guide," in Eric Hobsbawm, *On History* (New York: New Press, 1997), 263–65.

42 Gray, *Enlightenment's Wake*, 217.

43 Ibid., 266.

44 Ibid., 272.

45 Mokyr, *The Enlightened Economy*, 33.

46 See Peter Laslett, *The World We Have Lost: England Before the Industrial Age* (London: Routledge, 1983) [1965].

47 Mokyr, *The Enlightened Economy*, 62.

48 Pinker, "The Enlightenment Is Working."

49 Mokyr, *The Enlightened Economy*, 30, citing Richard Rorty, "The Continuity Between the Enlightenment and 'Postmodernism'," in Keith Michael Baker and Peter Hans Reill, eds., *What's Left of the Enlightenment?* (Stanford: Stanford University Press, 2001), 19–36.

50 Mokyr, *The Enlightened Economy*, 30.

51 Ibid., 31.

52 Peter Gay, *The Enlightenment*, Vol. II, *The Science of Freedom* (New York: Norton, 1969), 360, 368.

53 Smith, *The Wealth of Nations* (1776), Book I, Chapter II.

54 Ibid., Book I, Chapter IV.

55 Ibid., Book IV, Chapter II.

56 Emma Rothschild, *Economic Sentiments: Adam Smith, Condorcet, and the Enlightenment* (Cambridge, MA: Harvard University Press, 2001), 8. For my own broader discussion of this topic, see "Smith's Hand" in Bacchus, *Trade and Freedom*, 148–55.

57 Smith, *The Wealth of Nations*, Book IV, Chapter II.

58 Ibid., Book II.

59 Ibid., Book IV, Chapter IX.

60 Ibid., Book IV, Chapter III, Part I.

61 Norman Hampson, *The Enlightenment: An Evaluation of Its Assumptions, Attitudes and Values* (London: Penguin Books, 1990), 118 [1968].

62 This discussion of Ricardo's theory of "comparative advantage" repeats much of what I wrote previously in the passage on "Ricardo's Insight" in Bacchus, *Trade and Freedom*, 175–83.

63 David Ricardo, *The Principles of Political Economy and Taxation* (New York: Everyman's Library, 1977), 81 [1817]; Douglas A. Irwin, *Against the Tide: An Intellectual History of Free Trade* (Princeton: Princeton University Press, 1996), 177–78.

64 Donald Worster, *Nature's Economy: A History of Ecological Ideas*, 2nd edn. (Cambridge: Cambridge University Press, 1994), 53 [1977].

65 Ibid., 52.

66 Ibid.

67 Ibid., 53.

68 William Wordsworth, "Lines Written a Few Miles Above Tintern Abbey, on Revisiting the Banks of the Wye During a Tour. July 13, 1798" [1798], in *The Poetical Works of William Wordsworth* (London: Oxford University Press, 1960), 163.

69 J. E. de Steiguer, *The Origins of Modern Environmental Thought* (Tucson: University of Arizona Press, 2006), 9.

70 George Perkins Marsh, *Man and Nature, or, Physical Geography as Modified by Human Action* (Seattle: University of Washington Press, 2003), 37 [1864]. See also John Elder, *Pilgrimage to Vallombrosa: From Vermont to Italy in the Footsteps of George Perkins Marsh* (Charlottesville and London: University of Virginia Press, 2006).

71 Marsh, *Man and Nature*.

72 Thiele, *Sustainability*, 16.

73 Severin Carrell, "Scotland's Historic Sites at High Risk from Climate Change, Report Says," *Guardian* (January 15, 2018).

74 United Nations Resolution 2398 (XXIII) of the General Assembly (3 December 1968).

75 Ibid.

76 Ibid.

77 See the helpful account in Ulrich Grober, *Sustainability: A Cultural History* (Totnes, UK: Green Books, 2012), 161–62 [2010].

78 United Nations, "Declaration of the United Nations Conference on the Human Environment" (Stockholm: United Nations, June 16, 1972), Proclamation 6 (the "Stockholm Declaration").

79 Donella H. Meadows, Dennis L. Meadows, Jorgen Randers, and William W. Behrens III, *The Limits to Growth* (New York: Universe Books, 1972).

80 Ibid., 23–24.

81 Bill McKibben, *Enough: Making a Life on a Tough New Planet* (New York: Henry Holt, 2010), 90.

82 Grober, *Sustainability: A Cultural History*, 155.

83 See Philip Shabecoff, *A New Name for Peace: International Environmentalism, Sustainable Development, and Democracy* (Lebanon, N.H.: University Press of New England, 1996), 64.

84 Ibid.

85 Quoted in Jeffrey D. Sachs, *The Age of Sustainable Development* (New York: Columbia University Press, 2015), 5 (emphasis added).

86 Ibid.

87 Caradonna, *Sustainability: A History*, 136.

CHAPTER 2

1 Thiele, *Sustainability*, 144.

2 Smith, *The Wealth of Nations*, Book I, Chapter III.

3 Matthew Ridley, *The Rational Optimist: How Prosperity Evolves* (New York: Harper Collins, 2010), 7.

4 Wendell Berry, *The Unsettling of America: Culture and Agriculture* (San Francisco: Sierra Club Books, 1977), 21.

5 Smith, *The Wealth of Nations*, Book V, Chapter I, Part III.

6 Ridley, *The Rational Optimist*, 12.

7 Virginia Postrel, *The Future and Its Enemies: The Growing Conflict over Creativity, Enterprise, and Progress* (New York: Touchstone, 1998), 153 and 91.

8 Peter Foster, *Why We Bite the Invisible Hand: The Psychology of Anti-Capitalism* (Toronto: Pleasaunce Press, 2014), 28.

9 Smith, *The Wealth of Nations*, Book I, Chapter X.

10 Adam Smith, *The Theory of Moral Sentiments* (Amherst, N.Y.: Prometheus Books, 2000), 265 [1759].

11 Ibid., 264.

12 Quoted in Michael Brodie, *The Secret Chain: Evolution and Ethics* (Albany, N.Y.: SUNY Press, 1994), 41.

13 Douglas A. Irwin, "The Ultimate Global Antipoverty Program," *Wall Street Journal* (November 2, 2014).

14 Quoted in Douglas Coate, "Improving the GOP's Free-Market Pitch," *Wall Street Journal* (March 10, 2015).

15 Edward P. Lazear, "Want to Reduce Inequality? Consult China, Vietnam and India," *Wall Street Journal* (April 1, 2015).

16 Irwin, "The Ultimate Global Antipoverty Program." (These are the most recent official numbers available.)

17 Ibid. (These, too, are the most recent official numbers available.)

18 UN, High-Level Panel of Eminent Persons on the Post-2015 Development Agenda, "A New Global Partnership: Eradicate Poverty and Transform Economies Through Sustainable Development" (New York: United Nations, 2014), Annex II, 32.

19 Irwin, "The Ultimate Antipoverty Program."

20 Ibid.

21 Ibid. See also Richard McGregor, "China Takes On Its New Tycoons," *Wall Street Journal* (October 14, 2017).

22 Alan S. Blinder, "What's the Matter with Economics?," *New York Review of Books* (December 18, 2014).

23 Jasson Urbach, "SA Policy Should Rather Seek to Focus on Equality of Opportunity," www.businesslive.co.za/bd/opinion/2015-03-02-sa-policy-should-rather-seek-to-focus-on-equality-of-opportunity/.

24 Ibid.

25 UN, High-Level Panel of Eminent Persons on the Post-2015 Development Agenda, "A New Global Partnership," Annex II, 32.

26 Dresner, *The Principles of Sustainability*, 28.

27 Jack M. Hollander, *The Real Environmental Crisis: Why Poverty, Not Affluence, Is the Environment's Number One Enemy* (Berkeley: University of California, 2003).

28 Ridley, *The Rational Optimist*, 7.

29 "Our Common Future," Ch. 2, Para. 10.

30 Specifically, Malthus was writing in reaction to William Godwin, William Paley, and the Marquis de Condorcet.

31 Thomas Malthus, *An Essay on the Principle of Population and A Summary View of the Principle of Population* (London: Penguin Books, 1970) [1798, 1830].

32 Parenthetically, he adds, "(notwithstanding the reductions in life expectancy experienced by the urban poor during the nineteenth century)": Julian Morris, "The Persistence of Population Pessimism," *Electronic Journal of Sustainable Development*, Vol. 1, No. 3 (2009).

33 Sachs, *The Age of Sustainable Development*, 183.

34 Quoted in Postrel, *The Future and Its Enemies*, 64.

35 Ibid.

36 Ibid.

37 Jerry Taylor, "Sustainable Development: A Model for China?," in James A. Dorn, ed., *China in the New Millennium: Market Reforms and Social Development* (Washington, D.C.: Cato Books, 1998), 382.

38 Ibid., 381. For more on this "functional" view of resources, see William M. Dugger and James T. Peach, *Economic Abundance: An Introduction* (London and New York: Routledge, 2015), 61–62 [2009]. The disagreement over the meaning of "resources" finds further reflection in the differing concepts of, in the jargon, "strong" and "weak" sustainability. As Taylor explains, in "strong" sustainability, the base of natural resources is not allowed to deteriorate. In "weak" sustainability, the base of natural resources is allowed to deteriorate as long as biological resources are maintained at a minimum critical level and the wealth generated by the exploitation of natural resources is preserved for future generations: Taylor, "Sustainable Development: A Model for China?," 380.

39 See James Bacchus, "Is Progress Still Possible in This Heat?," *Huffington Post* (August 3, 2010).

40 Johan Rockstrom et al., "Planetary Boundaries: Exploring the Safe Operating Space for Humanity," *Ecology and Society*, Vol 14, Issue 2 (2009), 32, https://ecologyandsociety.org/vol14/iss2/art32.

41 See Johan Rockstrom et al., "A Safe Operating Space for Humanity," *Nature*, Vol. 461 (2009), 472–75.

42 Will Steffen et al., "Planetary Boundaries: Guiding Human Development on a Changing Planet," *Science* (January 15, 2015), 1.

43 Rockstrom et al., "A Safe Operating Space for Humanity."

44 Steffen et al., "Planetary Boundaries," 1.

45 Barry M. Brook et al., "Does the Terrestrial Biosphere Have Planetary Tipping Points?," *Trends in Ecology and Evolution*, Vol. 20 (2012), 1–6.

46 "Boundary Conditions," *Economist* (June 16, 2012).

47 Brook et al., "Does the Terrestrial Biosphere Have Planetary Tipping Points?"

48 Geographer Lionel Bomqvist, quoted in David Biello, "Walking the Line: How to Identify Safe Limits for Human Impacts on the Planet," *Scientific American* (June 13, 2012), https://scientificamerican.com/article/do-planetary-boundaries-help-humanity-manage-environmental-impacts/.

49 Ibid.

50 Andrew C. Revkin, "Can Humanity's 'Great Acceleration' Be Managed, and If So, How?", *New York Times* (January 15, 2015).

51 Ibid.
52 Ibid.
53 Ibid.
54 Sachs, *The Age of Sustainable Development*, 193.
55 For a different view, see Naomi Klein, *This Changes Everything: Capitalism vs. the Climate* (New York: Simon & Schuster, 2014).
56 Ibid.
57 Adam Smith, "History of Astronomy," in W. P. D. Wightman and J. C. Bryce, eds., *Adam Smith: Essays on Philosophical Subjects* (Oxford: Clarendon Press, 1980), 105. Here Smith was referring specifically to the astronomical theories of Sir Isaac Newton.
58 Bury, *The Idea of Progress*.
59 Ibid., 2.
60 Ibid.
61 Smith, *The Wealth of Nations*, Book I, Chapter I.
62 Smith, *The Theory of Moral Sentiments*, Part VI, Section II.
63 See Friedrich A. Hayek, "The Results of Human Action But Not of Human Design," in his *Studies in Philosophy: Politics and Economics* (London: Routledge and Kegan Paul, 1967), 96–105; Scott A. Boykin, "Hayek on Spontaneous Order and Constitutional Design," *Independent Review*, Vol. 15, No. 1 (Summer 2010), 19–34; and Norman Barry, "The Tradition of Spontaneous Order," *Literature of Liberty*, Vol. 5, No. 2 (Summer 1982), 7–58.
64 Barry, "The Tradition of Spontaneous Order," 10.
65 Andrew Gamble, *Hayek: The Iron Cage of Liberty* (Boulder, Col.: Westview Press, 1996), 67; see also Friedrich A. Hayek, "The Use of Knowledge in Society," *American Economic Review*, Vol. 55, No. 4 (1945), 519–30.
66 Christian Petsoulas, *Hayek's Liberalism and Its Origins: His Idea of Spontaneous Order and the Scottish Enlightenment* (London: Routledge, 2001), 2.
67 Kenneth Arrow, "The Economic Implications of Learning by Doing," *Review of Economic Studies*, Vol. 29, No. 3 (1962), 155–73.

CHAPTER 3

1 Paul J. Crutzen and Eugene F. Stoermer, "The Anthropocene," *International Geosphere-Biosphere Programme Newsletter*, Vol. 41 (2000), 17.
2 Paul J. Crutzen, "Geology of Mankind," *Nature* (January 3, 2002), 23. The "Anthropocene" geological era would succeed the "Helocene" era – the warm period of the past 10,000 to 12,000 years.
3 Dipesh Chakrabarty, "The Climate of History: Four Theses," *Critical Theory*, Vol. 35 (Winter 2009), 208.
4 Ibid.
5 Ibid., 206.
6 Ibid., 210.
7 Jedediah Purdy, "Imagining the Anthropocene," *Aeon* (March 31, 2015), http://aeon.co/magazine/science/should-we-be-suspicious-of-the-anthropocene/.
8 Chakrabarty, "The Climate of History: Four Theses," 210.

9 Nathan Glick, "The Last Great Critic," *Atlantic Monthly* (July 2000), www.theatlantic
.com/magazine/archive/2000/07/the-last-great-critic/378281.

10 Jagdish Bhagwati, *In Defense of Globalization* (Oxford: Oxford University Press, 2004), 140.

11 WTO, "World Trade Report 2013: Factors Shaping the Future of World Trade" (Geneva: World Trade Organization, 2013), 238.

12 Jagdish Bhagwati, "The Case for Free Trade," *Scientific American*, Vol. 269 (November 1993), 42.

13 Michael Jacobs, *The Green Economy: Environment, Sustainable Development and the Politics of the Future* (London: Pluto Press, 1991), Chapter 3.

14 See Perkins et al., *Economics of Development*, 199.

15 "Our Common Future," Ch. 3, Para. 54.

16 Perkins et al., *Economics of Development*, 197.

17 Ibid.

18 Gernot Wagner and Martin L. Weitzman, *Climate Shock: The Economic Consequences of a Hotter Planet* (Princeton: Princeton University Press, 2015), 37.

19 Perkins et al., *Economics of Development*, 199.

20 Garrett Hardin, "The Tragedy of the Commons," *Science*, Vol. 162, No. 3859 (December 13, 1968), 1243–48.

21 Thiele, *Sustainability*, 44.

22 Elinor Ostrom, *Governing the Commons: The Evolution of Institutions for Collective Action* (Cambridge: Cambridge University Press, 1990).

23 This was the subtitle of her book.

24 Luca de Biase, "The Tragedy of the Commons," in John Brockman, ed., *This Idea Must Die: Scientific Theories That Are Blocking Progress* (New York: Harper, 2015), 338–40.

25 Principle 4, Rio Declaration on Environment and Development, UN Doc A/CONF.151/ 26(vol. 1); 31 ILM 874 (1992) (the "Rio Declaration").

26 Bhagwati, "The Case for Free Trade," 42.

27 Ibid.

28 Wagner and Weitzman, *Climate Shock*, 46.

29 My son, Joe, the ultimate utilitarian, maintains that we all always weigh costs and benefits in all we do.

30 See, for example, http://knowledge.allianz.com/search.cfm?2967/The-price-tag-on-earths-ecosystem-services.

31 "Our Common Future," Ch. 2, Para. 1.

32 Principle 3, Rio Declaration on Environment and Development.

33 Wagner and Weitzman, *Climate Shock*, 68.

34 Ibid.

35 Ibid., 69.

36 Edmund Burke, *Reflections on the Revolution in France* (New York: Penguin Classics, 1987), 194–95 [1790].

37 Ibid., 192.

38 Ibid., 193.

39 Thiele, *Sustainability*, 23.

40 Shabecoff, *A New Name for Peace*, 112.

41 Rachel Carson, *Silent Spring* (Boston: Houghton Mifflin, 1962).

42 Peter Christoff and Robyn Eckersley, *Globalization and the Environment* (Plymouth: Rowman & Littlefield, 2013), 7.

43 R. Hooke and J. F. Martin-Duque, "Land Transformation by Humans: A Review," *GSA Today*, Vol. 22, Issue 12 (2012), 4–10.

44 Christoff and Eckersley, *Globalization and the Environment*, 7.

45 UNCTAD, "UN System Task Team on the Post-2015 UN Development Agenda: Trade and Development and the Global Partnership Beyond 2016," unpublished paper (UN Conference on Trade and Development, January 2013), 3.

46 Frank J. Garcia, *Trade, Inequality, and Justice: Toward a Liberal Theory of Just Trade* (Ardsley, N.Y.: Transnational, 2003), 107.

47 Rob Nixon, *Slow Violence and the Environmentalism of the Poor* (Cambridge, Mass.: Harvard University Press, 2011).

48 Smith, *The Wealth of Nations*, Book I, Chapter II.

49 Peter Newell, *Globalization and the Environment: Capitalism, Ecology and Power* (Cambridge, UK: Polity Press, 2012), 68.

50 Ibid.

51 Ibid.

52 D. Crawford-Brown et al., "Acceptance of Consumption-Based Climate Policy Instruments and Implementation Challenges," Carbon-Cap Policy Brief 2 (Geneva: International Centre for Trade and Sustainable Development, 2016).

53 WTO and UNEP, "Trade and Climate Change" (Geneva: World Trade Organization and UN Environment Programme, 2009), 58–59.

54 See Carol McAusland, "Globalisation's Direct and Indirect Effects on the Environment" (paper presented at the Global Forum on Transport and Environment in a Globalising World, November 10–12, 2008, Guadalajara, Mexico), 18.

55 See WTO and UNEP, "Trade and Climate Change," 60; and UNEP, "Trade and Environment Briefings: International Transport" (Nairobi: UN Environment Programme, June 2012). Different official reports give slightly different percentages.

56 Costas Paris, "The State of Global Shipping in Three Charts," *Wall Street Journal* (June 8, 2017).

57 UNEP, "Trade and Environment Briefings: International Transport," 1.

58 Anca Cristea, David Hummels, Laura Puzzello, and Misak Avetisyan, "Trade and the Greenhouse Gas Emissions from International Freight Transport," NBER Working Paper No. 17117 (Cambridge, Mass.: National Bureau of Economic Research, June 2011).

59 UNEP, "Trade and Environment Briefings: International Transport," 4.

60 WTO, "World Trade Report 2013," 241.

61 Bhagwati, "The Case for Free Trade," 43.

62 Grant Aldonas, ed., *Rethinking the Global Trading System: The Next Frontier* (Washington, D.C.: Center for Strategic and International Studies, 2009), 24.

63 Bhagwati, "The Case for Free Trade," 43.

64 Thiele, *Sustainability*, 162. See, in particular, John Antle and Gregg Heidebrink, "Environment and Development: Theory and International Evidence," *Economic Development and Cultural Change*, Vol. 43 (April 1995), 603–25.

65 WTO, "World Trade Report 2013," 240.

66 Ibid.

67 Economists call this notion the "pollution haven hypothesis." See, for example, Brian R. Copeland, "International Trade and Green Growth" (Washington, D.C.: World Bank, 2012), 3.

68 Edward M. Graham, *Fighting the Wrong Enemy: Antiglobal Activists and Multinational Enterprises* (Washington, D.C.: Institute for International Economics, 2000), 141.

69 David Collins, *An Introduction to International Investment Law* (Cambridge: Cambridge University Press, 2017), 257, citing A. Harrison, "Do Polluters Head Overseas: Testing the Pollution Haven Hypothesis," ARE Update (University of California Gianni Foundation of Agricultural Economics, December 2002).

70 Harrison, "Do Polluters Head Overseas." The World Bank does note that there is more evidence thus far from developed than from developing countries. For a similar conclusion and additional empirical evidence, see also Gary Clyde Hufbauer and Kati Suominen, *Globalization at Risk: Challenges to Finance and Trade* (New Haven and London: Yale University Press, 2010), 14–15.

71 Daniel W. Drezner, "Bottom Feeders," *Foreign Policy* (November 19, 2009).

72 Ibid.

73 UNCTAD, "World Investment Report 2013. Global Value Chains: Investment and Trade for Development" (Geneva: UN Conference on Trade and Development, 2013), 162.

74 See WTO and UNEP, "Trade and Climate Change," 49–54; and WTO, "World Trade Report 2013," 240–42. This analytical approach originated with Gene M. Grossman and A. B. Krueger, "Environmental Impacts of a North American Free Trade Agreement," in P. M. Garber, ed., *The US–Mexico Free Trade Agreement* (Cambridge, Mass.: MIT Press, 1993), 13–56.

75 This is "the composition effect."

76 This is "the scale effect."

77 This is "the technique effect."

78 This is "the product effect."

79 This is "the income effect."

80 UNEP, "Green Economy: Briefing Paper: Trade" (Nairobi: UN Environment Programme, 2017).

81 A "foreign direct investment" is usually thought to be at least 10 percent of the voting shares in a firm. Anything less is generally seen as a "portfolio investment" lacking in direct personal management and control of a firm, such as a market purchase by an individual investor of stock in a large company through a stock exchange. See IMF, "Glossary of Selected Financial Terms and Definitions" (Washington, D.C.: International Monetary Fund, October 31, 2006).

82 Pasquale Pazienza, *The Relationship Between FDI and the Natural Environment: Facts, Evidence and Prospects* (New York: Springer, 2014), 7. See generally Jorge E. Vinuales, *Foreign Investment and the Environment in International Law* (Cambridge: Cambridge University Press, 2012).

83 Michael J. Trebilcock and Mariana Mota Prado, *Advanced Introduction to Law and Development* (Cheltenham, UK: Elgar, 2014), 194.

84 Roberto Echandi and Pierre Sauve, "Introduction and Overview," in Roberto Echandi and Pierre Sauve, eds., *Prospects in International Investment Law and Policy* (Cambridge: Cambridge University Press, 2013), 1.

85 ICC, "ICC Guidelines for International Investment" (Paris: International Chamber of Commerce, 2012, 2016), 5. I chaired the ICC task force that prepared these guidelines.

86 Collins, *An Introduction to International Investment Law*, 23.

87 USCIB, "USCIB Policy Pillars on Foreign Direct Investment" (Washington, D.C.: United States Council for International Business, October 2014). I am a member of the USCIB and was one of many members involved in preparing this policy statement.

88 Mary E. Footer, "On the Laws of Attraction: Examining the Relationship Between Foreign Investment and International Trade," in Echandi and Sauve, eds., *Prospects in International Investment Law and Policy*, 105.

89 S. Picciotto, "Linkages in International Investment Regulation: The Antinomies of the Draft Multilateral Agreement on Investment," *University of Pennsylvania Journal of International Economic Law*, Vol. 19, No. 3 (1998), 744.

90 Footer, "On the Laws of Attraction," 1.

91 Newell, *Globalization and the Environment*, 91.

92 Nick Mabey and Richard McNally, "Foreign Direct Investment and the Environment: From Pollution Havens to Sustainable Development" (London: World Wildlife Fund-UK, August 1999), 43.

93 WTO, "World Trade Report 2014. Trade and Development: Recent Trends and the Role of the WTO" (Geneva: World Trade Organization, 2014), 111.

94 Facundo Albornoz, Matthew A. Cole, Robert J. R. Elliott, and Marco G. Ercolani, "In Search of Environmental Spillovers," *World Economy* (2009), 136.

95 WTO, "World Trade Report 2013," 242.

96 Ibid., 111.

97 World Bank, "Trade and Climate Change," in *World Development Report: Development and Climate Change* (Washington, D.C.: World Bank, 2010), 251–56.

CHAPTER 4

1 John H. Finley, Jr., *Thucydides* (Cambridge, Mass.: Harvard University Press, 1942), 210; see also Donald Kagan, *The Peloponnesian War* (New York: Penguin Books, 2003), 247–49.

2 Kagan, *The Peloponnesian War*, 147.

3 Robert B. Strassler, ed., *The Landmark Thucydides* (New York: Free Press, 1996), 351.

4 Ibid., 352.

5 Ibid., 353.

6 Finley, *Thucydides*, 209.

7 Ibid., 211.

8 G. R. Grundy, *Thucydides and the History of His Age*, Vol. II (Oxford: Basil Blackwell, 1942), 42.

9 Ibid., 61.

10 Simon Chesterman, "An International Rule of Law?," *American Journal of Comparative Law*, Vol. 56 (2008), 342.

11 This description in this paragraph paraphrases the classic definition offered in Roscoe Pound, "Law in Books and Law in Action," *American Law Review*, Vol. 44 (1910), 12–36; see also A. W. Bradley and K. D. Ewing, *Constitutional and Administrative Law*, 12th edn. (New York: Longman, 1997), 105.

12 Anne-Marie Slaughter, "International Law in a World of Liberal States," *European Journal of International Law*, Vol. 6 (1995), 511 n. 18.

13 Smith, *The Wealth of Nations*, Book V, Chapter I, Part II.

14 John Locke, *Second Treatise of Government*, Chapter 7, Paragraph 87 [1689], in Mark Goldie, ed., *John Locke: Two Treatises of Government* (London: Everyman, 1993), 158.

15 Baron de Montesquieu, *The Spirit of the Laws* [1748], as quoted in Number 78, Federalist Papers [1787], *The Federalist: A Commentary on the Constitution of the United States* (New York: Modern Library, n.d.), 502.

16 Number 78, Federalist Papers.

17 United Nations, "The Rule of Law and Transitional Justice in Conflict and Post-Conflict Societies: Report of the Secretary General," Report S/2004/616, 4. See also World Bank, "World Development Report 2017: Governance and the Law" (Washington, D.C.: World Bank, 2017), 83–97.

18 I first explored this point in James Bacchus, "The Rule of Law: Reflections on Thucydides and the World Trade Organization," *Vanderbilt Magazine* (Winter/Spring, 2000), 16.

19 Gamble, *Friedrich A. Hayek: The Iron Cage of Liberty*, 136. As Gamble observes, Hayek saw the origins of the classical Greek notion of the rule of law in their concept of "isonomy": Friedrich A. Hayek, *The Constitution of Liberty* (Chicago: University of Chicago Press, 1960), 164.

20 Josiah Ober, *The Rise and Fall of Classical Greece* (Princeton and Oxford: Princeton University Press, 2015), 11ff.

21 Christian Meier, *A Culture of Freedom: Ancient Greece and the Origins of Europe* (Oxford: Oxford University Press, 2011), 222.

22 Ober, *The Rise and Fall of Classical Greece*, 110.

23 Ibid.

24 Ibid., 1. See also James Romm, "Greeks and Their Gifts," *Wall Street Journal* (May 23, 2015).

25 Ibid.

26 Hayek, *The Constitution of Liberty*, 162. Even Hayek concedes the role of the Dutch Republic and others in the establishment of liberty, albeit in a footnote.

27 Locke, *Second Treatise of Government*, Section 57, 142.

28 Bronner, *Reclaiming the Enlightenment*, 39, 106; citing Gay, *The Enlightenment*, Vol. II, 441.

29 Mokyr, *The Enlightened Economy*, 413.

30 See David Trubek, "Max Weber on Law and the Rise of Capitalism," *Wisconsin Law Review* (1972), 720.

31 This is the phrase of Professor Jerry Z. Muller in Muller, *Adam Smith in His Time and Ours: Designing the Decent Society* (Princeton: Princeton University Press, 1993), 140.

32 Ibid.

33 Jerry Z. Muller, *The Mind and the Market: Capitalism in Modern European Thought* (New York: Alfred A. Knopf, 2002), 152.

34 Muller, *Adam Smith in His Time and Ours*, 140.

35 Nicholas Phillipson, *Adam Smith: An Enlightened Life* (New Haven: Yale University Press, 2010), 231.

36 Smith, *The Wealth of Nations*, Book V, Chapter I, Part II.

37 Muller, *The Mind and the Market*, 392.

38 Postrel, *The Future and Its Enemies*, 111.

39 Alan Ebenstein, *Friedrich Hayek: A Biography* (Chicago and London: University of Chicago Press, 2001), 224.

40 Hayek, *The Constitution of Liberty*, 208.

41 Friedrich A. Hayek, *Law, Legislation and Liberty: A New Statement of the Liberal Principles of Liberty and Political Economy*, Vol. I, *Rules and Order* (Chicago: University of Chicago Press, 1973), 45–46.

42 Postrel, *The Future and Its Enemies*, 116.

43 Mokyr, *The Enlightened Economy*, 8–9.

44 This emphasis on institutions flows from the work of economist Douglass North; see, for example, Douglass North, *Institutions, Institutional Change, and Economic Performance* (Cambridge: Cambridge University Press, 1990).

45 D. Rodrik, A. Subramanian, and F. Trebbi, "Institutions Rule: The Primacy of Institutions over Geography and Integration in Economic Development," *Journal of Economic Growth*, Vol. 9 (2004), 131.

46 Trebilcock and Prado, *Advanced Introduction to Law and Development*, 35.

47 Douglass North, "The New Institutional Economics and Third World Development," in J. Harris, J. Hunter, and C. M. Lewis, eds., *Economics and Third World Development* (London: Routledge, 1995), 17; see generally North, *Institutions, Institutional Change, and Economic Performance*, in general and especially p. 3.

48 I am, of course, a lawyer.

49 2005 World Summit Outcome Document, UN Doc. A/RES/60/1 (16 September 2005), para. 134.

50 UNCLEP and UNDP, "Making the Law Work for Everyone," Vol. I (New York: UN Commission on Legal Empowerment of the Poor and UN Development Programme, 2008), 4.

51 Declaration of the High-Level Meeting of the General Assembly on the Rule of Law at the National and International Levels, UN Doc. A/RES/67/1 (2012).

52 2012 Outcome Document of the Rio+20 Conference on Sustainable Development, "The Future We Want," A/RES/66/288 (September 11, 2012).

53 "Economics and the Rule of Law: Order in the Jungle," *Economist* (March 13, 2008).

54 Ibid.

55 Zhao Jun, "Rule of Law at the National and International Levels: A Review from the Global Governance Perspective," *Social Sciences in China*, Vol. 37, No. 2 (2016), 45.

56 Jeremy Bentham, *An Introduction to the Principles of Morals and Legislation*, J. H. Burns and H. L. A. Hart, eds. (London: Athlone Press, 1970), 6 [1789]; see M. W. Janis, "Jeremy Bentham and the Fashioning of 'International Law,'" *American Journal of International Law*, Vol. 78, No. 2 (April 1984), 405–18.

57 John Austin, *The Province of Jurisprudence Determined*, Wilfrid E. Rumble, ed. (Cambridge: Cambridge University Press, 2009), Lectures I and V [1832].

58 H. L. A. Hart, *The Concept of Law* (Oxford: Clarendon Press, 1961).

59 Ibid.

60 Jens David Ohlin, *The Assault on International Law* (Oxford: Oxford University Press, 2015), 57. As Ohlin notes there, for Hart, "Other important secondary rules are the rule of change, which dictates how laws might be amended or appealed, and the rule of adjudication, which governs how laws are applied and enforced when violations occur."

61 See Article 38(1) of the Statute of the International Court of Justice. The ICJ Statute governs only the ICJ, but it is the only text in which states have expressly recognized general international lawmaking procedures. Although his assertion is a matter of ongoing debate among legal scholars, according to Ian Brownlie, "Article 38 is generally regarded as a complete statement of the sources of international law": Ian Brownlie, *Principles of Public International Law*, 5th edn. (Oxford: Clarendon Press, 1998), 3 [1966].

62 Ibid.

63 This is known as *opinio juris*. See Nicaragua v. United States, ICJ Reports (1986), 97.

64 Brownlie, *Principles of International Law*, 12.

65 Article 102, Charter of the United Nations (24 October 1945), 1 UNTS XVI.

66 Ibid.

67 See www.treaties.un.org.

68 Louis Henkin, *How Nations Behave: Law and Foreign Policy* (New York: Praeger, 1968).

69 See Abram Chayes and Antonia Chayes, "On Compliance," *International Organization*, Vol. 47 (1993), 176.

70 It has been said that there is a growing "subfield" of international law devoted to issues of compliance. See William Bradford, "International Legal Compliance: Surveying the Field," *Georgetown International Law Journal*, Vol. 36 (2005), 495–536.

71 See Article 26, Vienna Convention on the Law of Treaties (27 January 1980), 1155 UNTS 331 ("Every treaty is binding upon the parties to it and must be performed by them in good faith").

72 This "managerial approach" is identified with Abram Chayes and Antonia Handler Chayes and is elaborated most fully in Abram Chayes and Antonia Chayes, *The New Sovereignty: Compliance with International Regulatory Agreements* (Cambridge, Mass.: Harvard University Press, 1995).

73 This "legitimacy theory" or "fairness approach" is identified with Thomas M. Franck and is spelled out in Thomas M. Franck, *Fairness in International Law and Institutions* (Oxford: Clarendon Press, 1995) (quote, 706).

74 This "transnational legal process" theory is identified with Harold Koh. See Harold H. Koh, "Transnational Legal Process," *Nebraska Law Review*, Vol. 75 (1994), 206; and Harold H. Koh, "Why Do Nations Obey International Law?," *Yale Law Journal*, Vol. 106 (1997), 2651.

75 Koh, "Why Do Nations Obey International Law?," 2651.

76 Andrew T. Guzman, "A Compliance Based Theory of International Law," *California Law Review*, Vol. 90 (2002), 1823–87.

77 See Scott J. Shapiro and Oona A. Hathaway, "Outcasting: Enforcement in Domestic and International Law," *Yale Law Journal*, Vol. 121 (2011), 252–349.

78 See Slaughter, "International Law in a World of Liberal States"; and Anne-Marie Slaughter, "Law Among Liberal States: Liberal Internationalism and the Act of State Doctrine," *Columbia Law Review*, Vol. 92 (1992), 1920–21.

79 Koh, "Why Do Nations Obey International Law?," 2633. See also the articles cited on that same page in n. 178.
80 Easterly, *The Tyranny of Experts*, 6.
81 Jack L. Goldsmith and Eric A. Posner, *The Limits of International Law* (Oxford: Oxford University Press, 2005), 200.
82 Aristophanes, "The Clouds," in F. L. Lucas, *Greek Drama for Everyman* (London: J. M. Dent & Sons Ltd., 1954), 384.
83 Goldsmith and Posner, *The Limits of International Law*, 202.
84 Ibid., 3.
85 Ibid., 13.
86 Ibid., 167.
87 Ohlin, *The Assault on International Law*, 143.
88 Ibid., 143–44.
89 Ibid., 144.
90 Alexis de Tocqueville, "The Americans Combat Individualism by the Principle of Interest Rightly Understood," *Democracy in America* (New York: Colonial Press, 1899), Volume II, Book II, Chapter VIII, 129–32 [1840].
91 See Bacchus, *Trade and Freedom*, 133.
92 Tocqueville, *Democracy in America*, Volume II, 130, 131.
93 Cited in Joshua Mitchell, *The Fragility of Freedom: Tocqueville on Religion, Democracy, and the American Future* (Chicago and London: University of Chicago Press, 1995), 197–202.
94 Tocqueville, *Democracy in America*, Volume II, Book II, Chapter XVII, 158, 159.
95 Mitchell, *The Fragility of Freedom*, 201.
96 Tocqueville, *Democracy in America*, Volume II, 159–60.
97 Ibid.
98 Goldsmith and Posner, *The Limits of International Law*, 14.

CHAPTER 5

1 As previously noted, this is consistent with the view of freedom of Karl Popper.
2 Global Agenda Councils on Trade and FDI and on Competitiveness, "The Case for Trade and Competitiveness" (Geneva: World Economic Forum, 2015). I am a member of this particular group of the willing, and am one of those who signed this report.
3 Ibid., 4.
4 Commission on Growth and Development, "The Growth Report: Strategies for Sustained Growth and Inclusive Development" (Washington, D.C.: World Bank, 2008), 21.
5 Ibid.
6 Ibid.
7 WTO, IMF, and World Bank, "Making Trade an Engine of Growth for All: The Case for Trade and for Policies to Facilitate Adjustment" (Washington, D.C.: World Trade Organization, International Monetary Fund, and World Bank, March 2017), 5.
8 Paul Samuelson, *Economics*, 11th edn. (New York: McGraw Hill, 1980), 651; on the gains from trade, this passage repeats much I summarized previously in Bacchus, *Trade and Freedom*, 168–70.

9 John Stuart Mill, *Principles of Political Economy* (London: Longmans, 1909), 58off. [1848].
10 Douglas A. Irwin, *Free Trade Under Fire* (Princeton: Princeton University Press, 2002), 30.
11 Ibid., 32.
12 Ibid., 32–33.
13 Editorial, "Trade Deficit Myths," *Wall Street Journal* (July 9, 2015).
14 Anne Krueger, "How Imports Boost Employment" (March 17, 2017), https://project-syndi cate.org/commentary.
15 Paul Krugman, *The Age of Diminishing Expectations* (Cambridge, Mass.: MIT Press, 1997), 11.
16 Mill, *Principles of Political Economy*, 581.
17 Peter Green, *The Greco-Persian Wars* (Berkeley and Los Angeles: University of California Press, 1996), 11.
18 Ibid., 11–12. See also Bacchus, *Trade and Freedom*, 172–73.
19 Popper, *The Open Society and Its Enemies*, Vol. I, 175. See also Bacchus, *Trade and Freedom*, 184.
20 Popper, *The Open Society and Its Enemies*, 177.
21 Ibid.
22 Ibid.
23 Global Agenda Councils on Trade and FDI and on Competitiveness, "The Case for Trade and Competitiveness," 4.
24 OECD, "Towards a More Open Trading System and Jobs Rich Growth" (Paris: Organisation for Economic Co-operation and Development, 2012), 2.
25 Global Agenda Councils on Trade and FDI and on Competitiveness, "The Case for Trade and Competitiveness," 5.
26 Eric Hoffer, *The Ordeal of Change* (New York: Harper and Row, 1952).
27 Michael Spence, *The Next Convergence: The Future of Economic Growth in a Multispeed World* (New York: Farrar, Straus and Giroux, 2011), 67. In this assertion, Spence echoes the famous notion of the "creative destruction" of capitalism advanced by the twentieth-century Austrian economist, Joseph Schumpeter. See Joseph Schumpeter, *Capitalism, Socialism, and Democracy*, 3rd edn. (New York: Harper Perennial, 2008) [1942].
28 Spence, The Next Convergence, 67.
29 Commission on Growth and Development, "The Growth Report," 8.
30 Ibid.
31 Spence, *The Next Convergence*, 68.
32 Ibid., 66.
33 On comparative advantage, see Robert M. Stern, *Comparative Advantage, Growth, and the Gains from Globalization: A Festschrift in Honor of Alan V. Deardorff* (Hackensack, N.J.: World Scientific, 2011).
34 Spence, *The Next Convergence*, 67.
35 For an illuminating discussion of this overall issue in the context of US manufacturing jobs in the United States, see Lawrence Edwards and Robert Z. Lawrence, *Rising Tide: Is Growth in Emerging Economies Good for the United States?* (Washington, D.C.: Peterson Institute for International Economics, 2013).
36 Robert Z. Lawrence and Lawrence Edwards, "Shattering the Myths About US Trade Policy," *Harvard Business Review* (March 2012), 2901–02.

37 Douglas A. Irwin, "The Truth About Trade: What Critics Get Wrong About the Global Economy," *Foreign Affairs* (July/August 2016), 89. See WTO, "WTO Report 2017" (Geneva: World Trade Organization, 2017), 9.

38 Michael J. Hicks and Srikant Devaraj, "The Myth and the Reality of Manufacturing" (Muncie, Ind.: Center for Business and Economic Research, Ball State University, June 2015), https://conexus.cyberdata.org/files/MfgReality.pdf. For a contrasting view, see Adams Nager, "Trade vs. Productivity: What Caused US Manufacturing's Decline and How to Revive It" (Washington, D.C.: Information Technology & Innovation Foundation, February 2017).

39 Lawrence and Edwards, "Shattering the Myths About US Trade Policy," 2902.

40 Daren Acemoglu, David Autor, David Dorn, Gordon H. Hanson, and Brendan Price, "Import Competition and the Great US Employment Sag of the 2000s," *Journal of Labor Economics*, Vol. 34, No. 51 (Part 2, January 2016), 5141–98; David H. Autor, David Dorn, and Gordon H. Hanson, "The China Syndrome: Local Labor Market Effects of Import Competition in the United States," NBER Working Paper 18054 (Washington, D.C.: National Bureau of Economic Research, 2012).

41 Paul Krugman, "Trade and Jobs: A Note," *New York Times* (July 3, 2016).

42 Scott Sumner, "Does Trade with China Cost Jobs?," *Library of Economics and Liberty* (April 16, 2017), http://econlog.econlib.org/cgi-bin/printblog.pl.

43 Jonathan Rothwell, "Cutting the Losses: Reassessing the Costs of Import Competition to Workers and Communities" (March 22, 2017), https://papers.ssrn.com/sol3/papers.cfm?abstract_id=2920188.

44 Ildiko Magyari, "Firm Reorganization, Chinese Imports, and US Manufacturing Employment," Job Market Paper (January 16, 2017), www.columbia.edu/~im2348/JMP_Magyari.pdf.

45 Editorial, "The Truth About the China Trade Shock," *Wall Street Journal* (April 2, 2017).

46 Paul Krugman, "Publicity Stunts Aren't Policy," *New York Times* (April 10, 2017).

47 Gary Clyde Hufbauer and Zhiyao (Lucy) Liu, "The Payoff to America from Globalization: A Fresh Look with a Focus on Costs to Workers," Policy Brief 17–16 (Washington: Peterson Institute of International Economics, May 2017), 2, 14, 21, 25.

48 Ibid., 21.

49 Mokyr, *The Enlightened Economy*, 421–22.

50 Ibid.

51 See, for example, Executive Office of the President, "Artificial Intelligence, Automation, and the Economy" (Washington, D.C.: White House, December 2016), 18–19.

52 See Claire Cain Miller, "Evidence That Robots Are Winning the Race for American Jobs," *New York Times* (March 28, 2017); see also the collection of thoughtful articles on this topic in the July/August 2015 issue of *Foreign Affairs*.

53 Thomas Babington Macaulay, "On Mitford's History of Greece," in *Essays and Poems* (Boston: Dana Estes and Company), Vol. I, 180 [1824].

54 Article 3.2, WTO Understanding on Rules and Procedures Governing the Settlement of Disputes (the "Dispute Settlement Understanding" or "DSU").

55 Daron Acemoglu, Simon Johnson, and James Robinson, "The Rise of Europe, Institutional Change and Economic Growth," *American Economic Review*, Vol. 95, No. 3 (June 2005), 546–79.

56 Easterly, *The Tyranny of Experts*, 139.

57 WTO, "The WTO in Brief," www.wto.org/english/thewto_e/whatis_e/inbrief_e/inbroo_e.htm.

58 "Bosnia and Herzegovina near Finish Line in WTO Accession Talks, Officials Say," *Bridges*, Vol. 22, No. 5 (February 15, 2018), 14–15.

59 On the Bretton Woods conference, see Benn Steil, *The Battle of Bretton Woods: John Maynard Keynes, Harry Dexter White, and the Making of the New World Order* (Princeton: Princeton University Press, 2014); and Ed Conway, *The Summit: Bretton Woods, 1944: J. M. Keynes and the Reshaping of the Global Economy* (New York: Pegasus, 2014).

60 Theodore Phalan, Deema Yazigi, and Thomas Rustici, "The Smoot–Hawley Tariff and the Great Depression," Foundation for Economic Education (February 29, 2012), fee.org/articles/the-smoot-hawley-tariff-and-the-great-depression.

61 Spence, *The Next Convergence*, 28–29.

62 Angus Maddison, *The World Economy: A Millennial Perspective* (Paris: Organisation for Economic Co-operation and Development, 2001), 125.

63 OECD, "Towards a More Open Trading System and Jobs Rich Growth," 3.

64 WTO and World Bank, "The Role of Trade in Ending Poverty," 13.

65 WTO, "World Trade Report 2014," 44.

66 Ibid.

67 Ibid.

68 Hufbauer and Liu, "The Payoff to America from Globalization," 21. These calculations are based on an average household of 2.64 persons.

69 On Frederic Bastiat, see George Roche, *Free Markets, Free Men: Frederic Bastiat, 1801–1850* (Hillsdale, Mich.: Hillsdale College Press and Foundation for Economic Education, 1993) [1971].

70 Article I.1, General Agreement on Tariffs and Trade 1994, April 15, 1994, 1867 UNTS 154, 33 ILM 1144 (1994) (the "GATT").

71 Whether such an agreement is in fact a "free trade agreement" entitled to this exception can be a matter of legal dispute under Article XXIV, General Agreement on Tariffs and Trade.

72 Article III, General Agreement on Tariffs and Trade.

73 For much more about the WTO dispute settlement system, and about its overall significance, see Chapter 9.

74 Rosalyn Higgins et al., eds., *Oppenheim's International Law*, Vol. 1, Sec. 51 (Oxford: Oxford University Press, 2017) [1905].

75 Guzman, "A Compliance Based Theory of International Law," 1826.

76 Appellate Body Report, EC – Hormones, DS26, WT/AB/R (1998), para. 187.

77 Robert Axelrod, *The Evolution of Cooperation*, rev. edn. (Cambridge, Mass.: Perseus, 2006), 3 [1984].

78 Ibid., 6.

79 Ibid., 7–8.

80 Ibid., 12.

81 Ibid., 126–34.

82 Ibid., 7.

83 Ibid., 126, 129.

84 John Ikenberry, *Liberal Leviathan* (Princeton: Princeton University Press, 2011), 340.

CHAPTER 6

1 Daniel W. Drezner, *The System Worked: How the World Stopped Another Great Depression* (Oxford: Oxford University Press, 2014).

2 "Signs of Life," *Economist* (November 15, 2014); see Simon J. Evenett, "The Global Trade Disorder: The 16th GTA Report," Global Trade Alert (London: Centre for Economic Policy Research, November 12, 2014).

3 Simon J. Evenett, "What Restraint? Five Years of G20 Pledges on Trade: The 14th GTA Report," Global Trade Alert (London: Centre for Economic Policy Research, 2013), 2, 7.

4 Daniel W. Drezner, "As It Turns Out America First Does Equal America Alone," *Washington Post* (June 10, 2017).

5 Robert E. Lighthizer, Testimony Before the US–China Economic Security and Review Commission, "Evaluating China's Role in the World Trade Organization Over the Past Decade" (June 9, 2010), 33, 35, https://uscc.gov/sites/default/files/6.9.10Lighthizer.pdf.

6 Damien Paletta and Ana Swanson, "Trump Suggests Ignoring World Trade Organization in Major Policy Shift," *Washington Post* (March 1, 2017); Editorial, "Trump Threatens to Tear Up the Trade Rule Book," *Washington Post* (February 27, 2017); Shawn Donnan and Demetri Sevastopulo, "Trump Team Looks to Bypass WTO Dispute System," *Financial Times* (February 27, 2017); Alex Lawson, "Trump Will Not Comply With Adverse WTO Rulings," Law360 (March 1, 2017).

7 James Bacchus, "Trump's Challenge to the WTO," *Wall Street Journal* (January 4, 2017).

8 See Kym Anderson, "Trade Assessment Paper: Benefits and Costs of the Trade Targets for the Post-2015 Development Agenda" (Copenhagen: Copenhagen Consensus Center, October 10, 2014), www.copenhagenconsensus.com/sites/default/files/trade_assessment_-_anderson_-_trade_final_101514.pdf; AFP, "WTO Doha Deal Would Make World $11-Trillion Richer by 2030: Economists," *Economic Times* (October 21, 2014).

9 Article IX.1 and footnote 1, Marrakesh Agreement Establishing the World Trade Organization (the "WTO Agreement").

10 Ibid., footnote 1.

11 "Prospects Dim for WTO Work Programme as July Deadline Approaches," *Bridges Weekly*, Vol. 19, No. 26 (July 16, 2015).

12 Hufbauer and Liu, "The Payoff to America from Globalization," 7.

13 Agreement on Trade Facilitation, opened for acceptance 27 November 2014, entered into force 22 September 2017.

14 Gary Hufbauer and Jeff Schott, "Payoff from the World Trade Agenda 2013," Report to the ICC Research Foundation (Washington, D.C.: Peterson Institute of International Economics, April 2013), 11–13.

15 WTO, "World Trade Report 2015. Speeding Up Trade: Benefits and Challenges of Implementing the WTO Trade Facilitation Agreement" (Geneva: World Trade Organization, 2015).

16 Ibid.

17 Ibid., 8. See "Implementation of Trade Facilitation Deal Could Yield Major Benefits, WTO Report Says," *Bridges Weekly*, Vol. 19, No. 36 (October 29, 2015).

18 Editorial, "The Doha Round Finally Dies a Merciful Death," *Financial Times* (December 21, 2015).

19 "WTO Members Clinch Agriculture Export Competition Deal, Weigh Next Steps for Negotiating Future," *Bridges Daily Update* (December 19, 2015).

20 Article II.3 and Annex 4, WTO Agreement.

21 Bruce Baschuk, "WTO to Finalize IT Tariff Cutting Deal," Bloomberg BNA (July 23, 2015).

22 "Technology Trade Deal Reached at Nairobi WTO Ministerial," *Bridges Daily Update* (December 16, 2015).

23 "WTO Ministerial: In Landmark Move, Country Coalitions Set Plans to Advance on New Issues," *Bridges Special Update* (December 13, 2017).

24 Ibid., 1.

25 Alex Lawson, "The WTO May Have Reached Its Breaking Point," Law360 (December 14, 2017); Megan Cassella, "It's the End of the WTO as We Know It – and Trump Feels Fine," Politico (December 14, 2017).

26 "The WTO Remains Stuck in Its Rut," *Economist* (December 14, 2017).

27 "WTO Ministerial: In Landmark Move, Country Coalitions Set Plans to Advance on New Issues," 2.

28 Ernesto Londono and Motoko Rich, "US Allies Sign Sweeping Trade Deal in Challenge to Trump," *New York Times* (March 8, 2018).

29 Chs. 14, 15, 17, 19, and 20, Trans-Pacific Partnership, https://ustr.gov/trade-agreements/free-trade-agreements/trans-pacific-partnership/tpp-full-text. See Tania Voon, ed., *Trade Liberalization and International Cooperation: A Legal Analysis of the Trans-Pacific Partnership* (Cheltenham, UK: Edward Elgar, 2013); and C. L. Lin, Deborah Elms, and Patrick Low, eds., *The Trans-Pacific Partnership: A Quest for a Twenty-First Century Trade Agreement* (Cambridge: Cambridge University Press, 2012).

30 See Jagdish Bhagwati, *Termites in the Trading System: How Preferential Agreements Undermine Free Trade* (New York: Oxford University Press, 2008).

31 Ibid.

32 Bernard Hoekman, "Trade and Growth – End of an Era?," VOX, Policy Portal of Centre for Economic Policy Research (June 24, 2015), www.voxeu.org.

33 Hufbauer and Liu, "The Payoff to America from Globalization," 7.

34 See Cristina Constantinescu, Aaditya Mattoo, and Michele Rota, "The Global Trade Slowdown: Cyclical or Structural?," IMF Working Paper WP/15/6 (Washington, D.C.: International Monetary Fund, January 2015).

35 See Uri Dadush, "What Should Be Done About the Great Trade Slowdown?," *The Hill* (August 18, 2015).

36 See Patrice Olivaud and Cyrille Schwellnus, "Does the Post-Crisis Weakness of Global Trade Solely Reflect Weak Demands?," OECD Economics Department Working Papers, No. 1216 (Paris: Organisation for Economic Co-operation and Development, 2015).

37 Shawn Donnan, "World Trade back to Crisis Levels as EM Demand Slides," *Financial Times* (February 26, 2016).

38 Amgad Shehata, "Bold Political Leadership and Vision Can Unlock Global Trade Growth," in Bernard Hoekman, ed., *The Global Trade Slowdown: A New Normal?* (London: CEPR Press, 2015), 329.

39 E15 Expert Group on Services, "Rethinking Services in a Changing World: Synthesis of the Policy Options," E15 Initiative (Geneva: International Centre for Trade and

Sustainable Development and World Economic Forum, 2016), 2. See also Pierre Sauve, "To Fuse or Not to Fuse? Assessing the Case for Convergent Disciplines on Goods and Services Trade," E15 Initiative (Geneva: International Centre for Trade and Sustainable Development and World Economic Forum, 2015).

40 Hildegunn K. Nordas and Dorothee Rouzet, "The Impact of Services Trade Restrictiveness on Trade Flows: First Estimates," OECD Trade Policy Papers No. 178 (Paris: Organisation for Economic Co-operation and Development, 2015), 6.

41 Ibid.; see Daniel Pruzin, "OECD Cites Widespread Barriers, Opportunities in Global Services Trade," *Inside US Trade* (March 7, 2014); see also OECD, *Services Trade Policies and the Global Economy* (Paris: Organisation for Economic Co-operation and Development, 2017).

42 OECD, "Trade Policy Implications of Global Value Chains" (Paris: Organisation for Economic Co-operation and Development, May 2013), 3.

43 "Embodied" services are delivered *within* the final product. "Embedded" services are delivered *alongside* the final product.

44 In contrast to the "positive list" approach in current WTO services rules, in which concessions on national treatment are made only if they are listed, the negotiations conducted on the sidelines of the WTO on the proposed Trade in Services Agreement have been conducted on a "negative list" approach, requiring each participant to provide national treatment for all services and services suppliers of other participants, subject to any agreed reservations in its schedule of concessions. See Amy Porges and Alice Enders, "Data Moving Across Borders: The Future of Digital Trade Policy," E15 Initiative (Geneva: International Centre for Trade and Sustainable Development and World Economic Forum, April 2016), 11.

45 Rana Forooher, "Trump's Trade Policies Won't Help My Town," *Financial Times* (March 6, 2017).

46 UNCTAD, "Information Economy Report 2015" (Geneva: Organisation for Economic Co-operation and Development, 2015); see also Joshua Meltzer, "Maximizing the Opportunities of the Internet for International Trade," E15 Initiative, E15 Expert Group on the Digital Economy, Policy Option Paper (Geneva: International Centre for Trade and Sustainable Development and World Economic Forum, 2016).

47 UNCTAD, "Information Economy Report" (Geneva: Organisation for Economic Co-operation and Development, 2009), xvii.

48 Meltzer, "Maximizing the Opportunities of the Internet for International Trade," 2.

49 "IBM Report: Technology Holds the Key to Economic and Social Reform in Accra, Ghana" (2013), www-03.ibm.com/press/us/en/pressrelease/40817.wss; John Gantz and David Reinsel, "The Digital Universe in 2020: Big Data, Bigger Digital Shadows, and Biggest Growth in the Far East," International Data Corporation (December 2012), www.emc.com/collateral/analyst-reports/idc-the-digital-universe-in-2020.pdf.

50 Andrew McAfee and Erik Brynjolfsson, "Big Data: The Management Revolution," *Harvard Business Review* (September 2012), https://hbr.org/2012/09/big-datas-management-revolutio.

51 See Dan Ciuriak and Maria Ptashkina, "The Digital Transformation and the Transformation of International Trade," RTA Exchange (Geneva: Inter-American Development Bank and International Centre for Trade and Sustainable Development, January 2018).

52 For these and other possible reforms relating to digital trade, see Joshua P. Meltzer, "A New Digital Trade Agenda," E15 Initiative, E15 Expert Group on the Digital Economy, Overview Paper (Geneva: International Centre for Trade and Sustainable Development and World Economic Forum, 2015); and Meltzer, "Maximizing the Opportunities of the Internet for International Trade."

53 See Porges and Enders, "Data Moving Across Borders," 5–9.

54 "WTO Ministerial: In Landmark Move, Country Coalitions Set Plans to Advance on New Issues," 2.

55 Joshua P. Meltzer, "The Internet and International Data Flows in the Global Economy" (Geneva: International Centre for Trade and Sustainable Development, May 27, 2016), www.ictsd.org/opinion/the-internet-and-international-data-flows-in-the-global-economy.

56 ICC, "ICC Guidelines for International Investment," 5. As previously mentioned, I chaired the ICC task force that prepared these guidelines.

57 James Zhan, "G20 Guiding Principles for Global Investment Policymaking: A Facilitator's Perspective," E15 Initiative (Geneva: International Centre for Trade and Sustainable Development and World Economic Forum, December 2016), 1.

58 Ibid.

59 UNCTAD, "World Investment Report 2011: Non-Equity Modes of International Production and Development" (Geneva: UN Conference on Trade and Development, 2011), xvi.

60 WTO, "World Trade Report 2013," 138.

61 Hufbauer and Schott, "Payoff from the World Trade Agenda 2013," 11.

62 WTO, "World Trade Report 2013," 135, 141.

63 OECD, "The Trade and Investment Nexus: Maximizing the Benefits from Trade and Investment" (Paris: Organisation for Economic Co-operation and Development, April 17, 2015).

64 Trebilcock and Prado, *Advanced Introduction to Law and Development*, 195.

65 Tomer Broude, "Investment and Trade: The 'Lottie and Lisa' of International and Economic Law?," in Echandi and Sauve, eds., *Prospects in International Investment Law and Policy*, 141.

66 Agreement on Trade-related Investment Measures, April 15, 1994, Marrakesh Agreement Establishing the World Trade Organization, Annex 1A, 1867 UNTS 187, 33 ILM 1153 (1994) (the "TRIMS" Agreement).

67 Stephan W. Schill, *The Multilateralization of International Investment Law* (Cambridge: Cambridge University Press, 2009), 25.

68 Collins, *An Introduction to International Investment Law*, 9 (emphasis added).

69 Schill, *The Multilateralization of International Investment Law*, 29–30.

70 I owe this thought to one of the willing, my friend Steve Charnovitz.

71 Schill, *The Multilateralization of International Investment Law*, 26–27.

72 Ibid. See also Rudolf Dolzer and Christoph Schreuer, *Principles of International Investment Law* (New York: Oxford University Press, 2008), 12.

73 Ibid. (emphasis added).

74 Schill, *The Multilateralization of International Investment Law*, 26–27.

75 Collins, *An Introduction to International Investment Law*, 157.

76 Dolzer and Schreuer, *Principles of International Investment Law*, 89.

77 Ibid., 91.

78 Collins, *An Introduction to International Investment Law*, 162.

79 Ibid., 124.

80 Ibid., 128.

81 Ibid., 135.

82 Ibid.

83 Article 2.1, TRIMS Agreement.

84 Annex (1), TRIMS Agreement.

85 Article 1, TRIMS Agreement.

86 Article I.2(c) (what is commonly called "Mode 3" of the supply of services), General Agreement on Trade in Services, April 15, 1994, Marrakesh Agreement Establishing the World Trade Organization, Annex 1C, 1869 UNTS 299, 33 ILM 1167 (1994) (the GATS).

87 Schill, *The Multilateralization of International Investment Law*, 33; and see pp. 33–35 on the Havana Conference and its aftermath.

88 Ibid., 49–60.

89 UNCTAD, "World Investment Report 2017: Investment and the Digital Economy" (Geneva: UN Conference on Trade and Development, 2017), xii.

90 Simon Lester, "Rethinking the International Investment Law System," *Journal of World Trade*, Vol. 49, No. 2 (2015), 214; see Jason Webb Yackee, "Bilateral Investment Treaties, Credible Commitment, and the Rule of (International) Law: Do BITs Promote Foreign Direct Investment?," *Law and Society Review*, Vol. 42 (2008), 805–32, and Jason Webb Yackee, "Do Bilateral Investment Treaties Promote Foreign Direct Investment? Some Hints from Alternative Evidence," *Virginia Journal of International Law*, Vol. 51 (2010), 397–442.

91 Gary Hufbauer et al., "From Drift to Deals: Advancing the WTO Agenda," Report to the ICC World Trade Agenda (Washington, D.C.: Peterson Institute for International Economics, June, 2015), 44.

92 UNCTAD, "World Investment Report 2011," xvii.

93 Richard Baldwin, *The Great Convergence: Information Technology and the Next Globalization* (Cambridge, Mass.: Harvard University Press, 2016), 6.

94 "The Slowdown in World Trade," Remarks by Angel Gurria, Secretary-General to the OECD, to the Istanbul G20 Trade Ministers Meeting, Istanbul, Turkey (October 26, 2015), www.oecd.org/about/secretary-general/istanbul-g20-trade-ministers-meeting-remarks-at-session-on-the-slowdown-in-global-trade.htm.

95 World Bank, "Global Value Chains: The Basics," https://olc.worldbank.org/content/global-value-chains-basics.

96 OECD, "Towards a More Open Trading System and Jobs Rich Growth," 8.

97 WTO, "World Trade Report 2014," 78.

98 WTO and World Bank, "The Role of Trade in Ending Poverty," 14.

99 WTO and OECD, "Aid for Trade at a Glance 2015: Reducing Trade Costs for Inclusive, Sustainable Growth" (Geneva and Paris: World Trade Organization and Organisation for Economic Co-operation and Development, July 2015), 166.

100 Constantinescu, Mattoo, and Ruta, "The Global Trade Slowdown: Cyclical or Structural?," 26–27.

101 Ibid.

102 Ibid.

103 Cecilia Malmstrom, "Modernising Trade Policy – Effectiveness and Responsibility," Speech to the International Trade Committee of the European Parliament (July 13, 2015), http://trade.ec.europa.eu/doclib/docs/2015/july/tradoc_153621.pdf.

104 WEF, "Enabling Trade: Valuing Growth Opportunities," Executive Summary (Geneva: World Economic Forum, 2013).

105 Ibid.

106 Ibid.

107 UNCTAD, "World Investment Report 2013," 162.

108 Victor, *Global Warming Gridlock*, 236.

CHAPTER 7

1 For more detail, see IPCC, "Climate Change 2014 Synthesis Report," Summary for Policymakers.

2 I have borrowed this phrase from the title of Philippe Sands, ed., *Greening International Law* (New York: New Press, 1994).

3 Edward O. Wilson, "The Global Solution to Extinction," *New York Times* (March 13, 2016).

4 Millennium Ecosystem Assessment, "Ecosystems and Human Well-Being: Synthesis" (Washington, D.C.: Island Press, 2005).

5 Ibid., 1.

6 Ibid.

7 Ibid.

8 Ibid.

9 Ibid., 11.

10 Ibid.

11 Ibid., 1.

12 Ibid., 2.

13 Ibid.

14 Ibid., 95–97.

15 Ibid., 95.

16 Ibid.

17 Ibid.

18 Ibid., 20.

19 Constantinescu, Mattoo, and Ruta, "The Global Trade Slowdown: Cyclical or Structural?," 26–27.

20 This is the count, as of August 2015 by the IEA Database Project of the University of Oregon. For the latest count, see http://iea.uoregon.edu.

21 Daniel Bodansky, *The Art and Craft of International Environmental Law* (Cambridge, Mass.: Harvard University Press, 2009), 18.

22 Ibid., 19.

23 Ibid.

24 Sindya H. Bhanoo, "Climate Change Could Harm British Butterflies," *New York Times* (August 11, 2015).

25 Bodansky, *The Art and Craft of International Environmental Law*, 19.

26 Sands, *Greening International Law*, xxiv.

27 Bodansky, *The Art and Craft of International Environmental Law*, 19.

28 Steinar Andresen and Jon Birger Skjaerseth, "Science and Technology: From Agenda Setting to Implementation," in Daniel Bodansky et al., eds., *The Oxford Handbook of International Environmental Law* (Oxford: Oxford University Press, 2010), 183–87 [2007].

29 I have previously explored Popper's view of the connection between science and freedom at more length in Bacchus, *Trade and Freedom*, 190–92.

30 Popper, *The Open Society and Its Enemies*, Vol. I.

31 Eliezer J. Sternberg, "Objective Reality vs. What Our Brain Perceives," *Washington Post* (June 11, 2017).

32 Karl Popper, *Unended Quest: An Intellectual Autobiography* (London and New York: Routledge, 1992), 88 [1974].

33 Gerhard von Glahn and James Larry Taulbee, *Law Among Nations: An Introduction to Public International Law*, 8th edn. (New York: Pearson, 2007), 558.

34 Sands, *Greening International Law*, xxxi; Timo Koivurova, *Introduction to International Environmental Law* (New York: Routledge, 2014), 105–06.

35 Principle 2, Rio Declaration on Environment and Development.

36 Ibid.

37 Rafael Leal-Arcas, "Sustainability, Common Concern, and Public Goods," *George Washington International Law Review*, Vol. 49, No. 4 (2017), 807.

38 This is the legal test for establishing custom as international law. "Customary international law results from a general and consistent practice of states followed by them from a sense of legal obligation": Restatement (Third) of the Foreign Relations Law of the United States, Section 102(2) (1987); Asylum Case (Colombia v. Peru), International Court of Justice Reports of Judgments, Advisory Opinions and Orders (ICJ) 1950), 266–389, at 277.

39 Peter H. Sand, "The Evolution of International Environmental Law," in Bodansky et al., eds., *Oxford Handbook of International Environmental Law*, 35.

40 Convention on the Prevention of Marine Pollution by Dumping of Hazardous Wastes and Other Matter, adopted December 29, 1972, 26 UST 2403, 1046 UNTS 138 (the "London Convention").

41 Convention for the Protection of the World Cultural and Natural Heritage, adopted November 16, 1972, 27 UST 37, 1037 UNTS 151 (the "World Heritage Convention").

42 Convention on International Trade in Endangered Species of Wild Fauna and Flora, adopted March 2, 1973, 27 UST 1087, 993 UNTS 243 (the "CITES").

43 Convention on Wetlands of International Importance Especially as Waterfowl Habitat, Ramsar, Iran, adopted February 2, 1971, 1976 UNTS, 11 ILM 969 (the "Ramsar Convention").

44 Long-Range Transboundary Air Pollution Convention, adopted November 13, 1979, 1302 UNTS 217, 18 ILM 1442 ("LRTAP").

45 United Nations Convention on the Law of the Sea, December 10, 1992, 1833 UNTS 3. See generally Donald R. Rothwell and Tim Stephens, *The International Law of the Sea* (Oxford and Portland, Ore.: Hart Publishing, 2010).

46 Montreal Protocol on Substances that Deplete the Ozone Layer, adopted September 16, 1987, 1522 UNTS 3, 26 ILM 1550 (the "Montreal Protocol").

47 Thomas Hobbes, *Leviathan* (London: Penguin Books, 1985), 188 [1651].

48 Ibid.

49 Non-legally Binding Authoritative Statement of Principles for a Global Consensus on the Management, Conservation and Sustainable Development of All Types of Forests (1992), UN Doc. A/CONF. 151/26, v. 3.

50 Peter Malanczuk, *Akehurst's Modern Introduction to International Law*, 7th rev. edn. (London and New York: Routledge Press, 1987), 248 [1870].

51 Convention on Biological Diversity, adopted June 5, 1992, 1760 UNTS 79 (the "Biodiversity Convention").

52 United Nations Framework Convention on Climate Change, adopted May 9, 1992, 1771 UNTS (the "UNFCCC").

53 Convention to Combat Desertification in those Countries Experiencing Serious Drought and/or Desertification, Particularly in Africa, adopted June 17, 1994, 33 ILM 1328 (the "Desertification Convention").

54 Agreement for the Implementation of Provisions of UNCLOS Relating to the Conservation and Management of Straddling Fish Stocks and Highly Migratory Fish Stocks, adopted December 4, 1995, 34 ILM 1542 (the "Fish Stocks Agreement").

55 Cartagena Protocol on Biosafety to the Convention on Biological Diversity, adopted January 29, 2000, 39 ILM 1027 (the "Biosafety Protocol").

56 International Treaty for Plant Genetic Resources for Food and Agriculture, adopted November 3, 2001, 2001 IELMT 28.

57 Stockholm Convention on Persistent Organic Pollutants, adopted May 22, 2001, 40 ILM 532 (the "POPs Convention").

58 International Tropical Timber Agreement, adopted January 27, 2006, UN Doc. TD/TIMBER 3/12 (the "Tropical Timber Agreement").

59 Article XX, General Agreement on Tariffs and Trade.

60 Principle 12, Rio Declaration on Environment and Development.

61 Separate Opinion by Judge Christopher Weeramantry, Gabcikova-Nagymaros Project (Hungary/Slovakia), Judgment, September 25, 1997, 95.

62 As it is, most of these principles have an evolving and elusive legal status that the distinguished Egyptian jurist Georges Abi-Saab, a former member of the WTO Appellate Body, has aptly described as "muffled": Georges Abi-Saab, "Eloge du 'droit assourdi.' Quelques réflexions sur le rôle de la *soft-law* en droit international contemporain," in *Nouveaux itineraires en droit. Hommage A. F. Rigaux* (Brussels: Bruylant, 1993), 60.

63 Ulrich Beyerlin, "Different Types of Norms in International Environmental Law: Policies, Rules, and Principles," in Bodansky et al., eds., *Oxford Handbook of International Environmental Law*, 427–28.

64 Dinah L. Shelton, "Soft Law," in David Armstrong, ed., *Routledge Handbook of International Law* (London and New York: Routledge, 2008), 68.

65 See Malcolm N. Shaw, *International Law*, 5th edn. (Cambridge: Cambridge University Press, 2003), 754–55. Shaw makes this point about environmental damages, but it applies generally. See also Wolfgang Friedmann, *The Changing Structure of International Law* (New York: Columbia University Press, 1964).

66 Daniel Bodansky, "The History of the Global Climate Change Regime," in Urs Luterbacher and Detlef F. Sprinz, eds., *International Relations and Global Climate Change* (Cambridge, Mass.: MIT Press, 2001), 23.

67 For an illuminating overview, see Jutta Brunnee, "Common Areas, Common Heritage, and Common Concern," in Bodansky et al., eds., *Oxford Handbook of International Environmental Law*, 550–73.

68 Judge Christopher Weeramantry, Separate Opinion, C(c).

69 First Recital, Preamble, UNFCCC.

70 Protection of Global Climate for Present and Future Generations of Mankind, UN General Assembly Res. 43/53 (1988).

71 Article 2, UNFCCC.

72 Kyoto Protocol to the United Nations Framework Convention on Climate Change, adopted December 10, 1997, 2302 UNTS 148, 37 ILM 22 (the "Kyoto Protocol").

73 Andrei Marcu and Wijnand Stoefs, "The Role of Response Measures in Ensuring the Sustainable Transition to a Low-GHG Economy" (Geneva: International Centre for Trade and Sustainable Development, January 2017), 3.

74 Article 12, Kyoto Protocol.

75 Bali Action Plan, UNFCCC, Decision 1/CP.13 2008.

76 Copenhagen Accord, UNFCCC, Decision 2/CP.15 2010.

77 Cancun Agreements, UNFCCC, Decision 1/CP.16 2011.

78 Durban Platform, UNFCCC, Decision 1/CP.17 2012.

79 See Articles 15:3 and 18:1, UNFCCC.

80 Article 3:1, UNFCCC. See also Article 3:2, UNFCCC, which requires the "full consideration" of the "specific needs and circumstances" of those developing countries that are "particularly vulnerable" when apportioning the burden of the responsibilities of the convention.

81 These same divisions have been observed and noted by others. See, for example, Daniel Bodansky and Lavanya Rajamani, "The Evolution and Governance Architecture of the United Nations Climate Change Regime," in Delief Sprinz and Urs Luterbacher, eds., *International Relations and Global Climate Change: New Perspectives*, 2nd edn. (Cambridge, Mass.: MIT Press, 2016), http://ssrn.com/abstract=2168859.

82 See Alister Doyle and Barbara Lewis, "With Landmark Climate Accord, World Marks Turn from Fossil Fuels," Reuters (December 12, 2015).

83 Coral Davenport, "Nations Approve Landmark Climate Accord in Paris," *New York Times* (December 13, 2015).

84 Paris Agreement, FCCC/CP/2015/L.9 (December 12, 2015).

85 Ibid.

86 Decision 1, Paris Agreement.

87 Article 2.1(a), Paris Agreement.

88 Article 4.1, Paris Agreement.

89 Article 4.2, Paris Agreement.

90 David G. Victor, "America Heads to the Exit: What Trump Got Wrong About Paris," Yale Environment 360 (June 2, 2017).

91 Article 4.2, Paris Agreement.

92 Article 4.12, Paris Agreement.

93 Article 4.8, Paris Agreement.

94 Mark Landler, Brad Plumer, and Linda Qui, "Trump, Prioritizing Climate over Economy, Cites Disputed Premises," *New York Times* (June 1, 2017).

95 UNEP, "The Emissions Gap Report 2017: A UN Environment Synthesis Report" (Nairobi: UN Environment Programme, November 2017).

96 "Synthesis Report on the Aggregate Effect of the Intended Nationally Determined Contributions," Conference of Parties, United Nations Framework Convention on Climate Change (October 30, 2015), FCCC/CP/20157; see also Sewell Chan and Melissa Eddy, "Leaders Move to Convert Paris Climate Pledges into Action," *New York Times* (December 13, 2015).

97 Article 4.4, Paris Agreement.

98 Article 2.2, Paris Agreement.

99 Article 4.4, Paris Agreement.

100 Article 3, Paris Agreement.

101 Chris Mooney, "New US View of Climate Accord Apparent in Bonn Delegation," *Washington Post* (May 9, 2017).

102 Article 3, Paris Agreement.

103 Article 4.2, Paris Agreement.

104 Article, 4.4, Paris Agreement.

105 Article 4.11, Paris Agreement. Whether such adjustments can be made to reduce climate ambitions as well as to enhance them has been debated. The better argument seems to be that NDCs can either be reduced or enhanced over time under the terms of the agreement. See Daniel Bodansky and Susan Biniaz, "Legal Issues Related to the Paris Agreement," Center for Climate and Energy Solutions (Arlington, Va.: May 2017), https://c2es.org/site/assets/uploads/2017/05/legal-issues-related-paris-agreement.pdf.

106 Article 4.9, Paris Agreement. Countries whose initial pledges go out to 2025 will be required to update them (and to up their ambition) in 2020, and countries whose initial pledges go out to 2030 will be required to do the same.

107 Decision 20; Article 14.2, Paris Agreement.

108 Article 13, Paris Agreement.

109 Articles 13.1 and 13.7, Paris Agreement.

110 Article 7, Paris Agreement.

111 Article 8, Paris Agreement. See "Explainer: Dealing with the 'Loss and Damage' Caused by Climate Change," Carbon Brief (May 15, 2017), www.carbonbrief.org/explainer-dealing-with-the-loss-and-damage-caused-by-climate-change.

112 Decision 52, Paris Agreement.

113 Article 10, Paris Agreement.

114 Article 10.1, Paris Agreement.

115 Article 10.4, Paris Agreement.

116 Article 10.5, Paris Agreement.

117 Article 11, Paris Agreement.

118 Article 9, Paris Agreement.

119 Decision 54, Paris Agreement.

120 Ibid.

121 Article 9.3, Paris Agreement.

122 Article 9.2, Paris Agreement.

123 Article 9.3, Paris Agreement (emphasis added).

124 "Climate Governance after the Paris Agreement," Workshop Report, University College of London Global Governance Institute (November 25, 2016), 13.

125 Articles 6.1 and 6.2, Paris Agreement.

126 Article 6.8, Paris Agreement.

127 Decision 137, Paris Agreement.

128 Article 5 and Article 2.1(b), Paris Agreement.

129 Preamble, Paris Agreement.

130 Clara Brandi, "Strengthening Climate-Friendly Trade Elements in Future Nationally Determined Contributions" (Geneva: International Centre for Trade and Sustainable Development, May 10, 2017).

131 Clara Brandi, "Trade Elements in Countries' Climate Contributions Under the Paris Agreement," Issues Paper (Geneva: International Centre for Trade and Sustainable Development, March 2017), vii; see also the analysis in Rana Elkahwagy, Vandana Gyanchandani, and Dario Piselli, "UNFCCC Nationally Determined Contribution: Climate Change and Trade," CTEI Working Papers, CTEI-2017-2 (Geneva: UN Conference on Trade and Development, 9 January 2017).

132 Preamble, Paris Agreement.

133 Decision 95(f), Paris Agreement.

134 Article 4.15, Paris Agreement.

135 Article 3.5, UNFCCC.

136 Article 24, Paris Agreement.

137 Article 14, UNFCCC.

138 Article 15.1, Paris Agreement.

139 Article 15.2, Paris Agreement.

140 Tom Bawden, "COP21: Paris Deal Far Too Weak to Prevent Devastating Climate Change, Academics Warn," *Independent* (January 8, 2016).

141 Oliver Milman, "James Hansen, Father of Climate Change Awareness, Calls Paris Talks 'a Fraud'", *Guardian* (December 12, 2015).

142 This is the title of his popular book: Bjorn Lomborg, *The Skeptical Environmentalist: Measuring the Real State of the World* (Cambridge: Cambridge University Press, 2006).

143 Bjorn Lomborg, "The Paris Deal Won't Even Dent Global Warming," *New York Post* (February 22, 2016); Bjorn Lomborg, "A Climate Agreement Powered by Hypocrisy," Project Syndicate (December 17, 2015), www.project-syndicate.org; Bjorn Lomborg, "COP21 Climate Talks; Wasting Trillions on Carbon Curbs Is Immoral," *Wall Street Journal* (November 30, 2015).

144 Lomborg, "The Paris Deal Won't Even Dent Global Warming."

145 WEF, "The Global Risks Report 2016: 11th Edition" (Geneva: World Economic Forum, 2016), 14.

146 Davenport, "Nations Approve Landmark Climate Accord in Paris."

CHAPTER 8

1 Norichika Kanie and Frank Biermann, eds., *Governing Through Goals: Sustainable Development Goals as Governance Innovation* (Cambridge, Mass.: MIT Press, 2017), 5.

2 United Nations, "Transforming Our World: The 2030 Agenda for Sustainable Development" (September 2015), A/RES/70/1. See also Somini Sengupta, "UN Adopts Ambitious Global Goals After Years of Negotiations," *New York Times* (September 26, 2015).

3 "Transforming Our World," heading to para. 49.

4 Ibid., para. 18.

5 Ibid., paras. 18 and 39.

6 Ibid., para. 55.

7 "Global Goals Received with Rapture in New York – Now Comes the Hard Part," *Guardian* (September 26, 2015).

8 "Transforming Our World," para. 7.

9 Ibid., para. 2.

10 Sengupta, "UN Adopts Ambitious Global Goals After Years of Negotiations."

11 "Global Goals Received with Rapture in New York – Now Comes the Hard Part."

12 Four of the twenty-two targets were added by the UN General Assembly in 2005: United Nations, World Summit Outcome, UN General Assembly A/60/1 (2005).

13 John W. MacArthur, "The Origin of the Millennium Development Goals," *SAIS Review*, Vol. 34, No. 2 (Summer–Fall 2014), 6–7.

14 John W. MacArthur, "Own the Goals: What the Millennium Development Goals Wave Accomplished," Brookings Institute (February 21, 2013), https://brookings.edu/articles/own-the-goals-what-the-millennium-goals-have-accomplished.

15 Ibid.

16 Ibid. See United Nations, "Monterrey Consensus on Financing for Development Goals," the final text of agreements and commitments adopted at the International Conference on Financing for Development, Monterrey, Mexico (March 18–22, 2002).

17 See United Nations, "Doha Declaration on Financing for Development: Outcome Document of the Follow-Up International Conference on Financing for Development to Review the Implementation of the Monterrey Consensus" (Doha, Qatar, November 29–December 2, 2008).

18 Robert Muggah, research director of the Igarape Institute, quoted in Bilyana Lilly, "Global Development Baton Passes from MDGs to SDGs," *Washington Diplomat* (August 27, 2015), www.washdiplomat.com/index.php?option=com_content&view=article&id=12291:global-development-baton-passes-from-mdgs-to-sdgs&catid=1535&Itemid=428.

19 Professor Sakiko Fukuda-Farr, of the New School in New York, quoted ibid.

20 Lord Malloch-Brown has confirmed this suspicion: "How to Eliminate Poverty in 169 Not-So-Easy Steps," National Public Radio (July 7, 2015).

21 UN, "The Millennium Development Goals Report 2015" (New York: United Nations, 2015), Foreword, 3.

22 Ibid., 4.

23 Ibid. See "Millennium Hunger Target Achieved, New FAO Data Indicates," *Bridges Weekly* (June 11, 2015).

24 "The Millennium Development Goals Report 2015," Foreword, 4.

25 John W. MacArthur, "15 Million Success Stories Under the Millennium Development Goals," Brookings Brief (September 24, 2015).

26 Lilly, "Global Development Baton Passes from MDGs to SDGs."

27 Ibid., 7.

28 Ibid.

29 Paragraph 245, "The Future We Want."

30 Paragraph 246, "The Future We Want."

31 "Transforming Our World," 3.

32 Paragraphs 2, 4, and 5, "Transforming Our World."

33 Sengupta, "UN Adopts Ambitious Global Goals After Years of Negotiations."

34 An asterisk to this goal adds: "Acknowledging that the United Nations Framework Convention on Climate Change is the primary international, intergovernmental forum for negotiating the global response to climate change."

35 Target 1.1, SDGs.

36 Target 1.2, SDGs.

37 Paragraphs 14 and 24, "Transforming Our World."

38 Paragraphs 2 and 5, "Transforming Our World."

39 Paragraph 5, "Transforming Our World."

40 "A Multi-Stakeholder Message: Key Principles in the Formulation of Sustainable Development Goals" (Geneva: World Economic Forum, 2014). I was among those who signed this "multi-stakeholder message."

41 "The UN Obsession with Global Targets for Poverty," *Financial Times* (September 26, 2015).

42 "The 169 Commandments," *Economist* (March 28, 2015).

43 Bjorn Lomborg, "What Should the World Focus on for the Next 15 Years?," *Washington Post* (November 23, 2014).

44 George Russell, "Exclusive: UN Ignores Science Council Warnings in Creating Vast Sustainable Development Goals," Fox News (September 29, 2015).

45 Glen David Kuecker, "UN Sustainable Development Goals: The Matrix Reloaded" (October 4, 2015), www.telesurtv.net/english/opinion/. For similar sentiments, see Jason Hickel, "The Problem with Saving the World," *Jacobin Magazine* (August 2015), www.jacobinmag.com/2015/08/global-poverty-climate-change-sdgs/.

46 Scott Wisor, "The Impending Failure of the Sustainable Development Goals," *Ethics and International Affairs* (September 29, 2014), www.ethicsandinternationalaffairs.org/. . ./the-impending-failure-of-the-sustainable-development-goals/.

47 Ibid.

48 International Council for Science and International Social Science Council, "Review of Targets for the Sustainable Development Goals: The Science Perspective" (2015), www.icsu.org/publications/review-of-targets-for-the-sustainable-development-goals-the-science-perspective-2015.

49 "Sustainable Agriculture Is the Key," www.cattlesite.com (September 30, 2015).

50 Eric A. Hanushek and Ludger Woessman, "Teach the World: Why the UN Sustainable Development Goals Should Focus on Education," *Foreign Affairs* (August 20, 2015).

51 "Environmental Protection Decisive to Sustainable Development: PM," www.vietnam.net (October 1, 2015).

52 Jose Graziano de Silva, "Much More Than Trees: Forests are Key to Sustainable Development," http://foodtank.com (September 8, 2015).

53 Magdalena Mis, "Water Management Key to Achieving Sustainable Development Goals – World Bank," Reuters (August 24, 1015).

54 Jamie McAuliffe, "What to Do With the World's NEETS?," *Huffington Post* (September 11, 2015).

55 Phumzile Miambo-Ngkuka, "Why Gender Equality Is the Most Critical of All the Global Goals," *Huffington Post* (September 8, 2015).

56 Michael W. Doyle and Joseph E. Stiglitz, "Eliminating Extreme Inequality: A Sustainable Development Goal, 2015–2030," *Ethics and International Affairs* (March 20, 2014).

57 Risa Edelman, "Weaning Ourselves off of Fossil Fuels," *Huffington Post* (September 10, 2015).

58 Lisa Witter, "The One Goal That Could Spell Disaster for All the Rest," Toplink, https://toplink.weforum.org (September 25, 2015).

59 Chris Arsenault, "Kale or Steak? Change in Diet Key to UN Plan to End Hunger by 2030," Reuters (September 11, 2015).

60 "Transforming Our World," 27.

61 *Earth Negotiations Bulletin*, Vol. 33, No. 36 (July 22, 2017), 15–17. See UN, "Sustainable Development Report 2017" (New York: United Nations, 2017).

62 *Earth Negotiations Bulletin*, Vol. 33, No. 36 (July 22, 2017), 15–17.

63 Ibid.

64 Ellen Wulfhorst, "Leaders Call for 'Less Conversation, More Action' After Adopting UN Global Goals," Reuters (September 26, 2015).

65 Target 3.3, "Transforming Our World."

66 Ariana Eunjieng Cha, "Millions Could Get Drugs for Early Treatment of HIV," *Washington Post* (October 1, 2015).

67 Michael Gerson, "Today's Golden Age of Aid," *Washington Post* (September 29, 2015).

68 Ferdinando Gugliano, "Nobel Prize Winner Angus Deaton Shares 3 Big Ideas," *Financial Times* (October 12, 2015).

69 UN, High-Level Panel of Eminent Persons on the Post-2015 Development Agenda, "A New Global Partnership," Executive Summary and 23.

70 Ibid., Executive Summary.

71 Paragraph 48, "Transforming Our World."

72 United Nations, "Spotlight on Sustainable Development Goal 5: Achieve Gender Equality and Empower All Women and Girls," UN Women, www.unwomen.org/en/digital-library/multimedia2017/7/infographic-spotlight-on-sdgs.

73 Francisco Ferreira, "The International Poverty Line Has Just Been Raised to $1.90 a Day, But Global Poverty Is Basically Unchanged. How Is That Even Possible?," http://blogs.worldbank.org/developmenttalk/ (October 4, 2015).

74 "World Bank Forecasts Global Poverty to Fall Below 10% for First Time; Major Hurdles Remain in Goal to End Poverty by 2030," www.worldbank.org (October 4, 2015); Tim Worstall, "World Bank: Less Than 10% of the World Will Be Poor This Year," *Forbes* (October 5, 2015).

75 Justin Sandehur, "Nobel Prizes, Poverty Numbers, and Tales of Mythical Creatures" (Washington, D.C.: Center for Global Development, October 14, 2015).

76 Sustainable Development Solutions Network, "Data for Development: An Action Plan to Finance the Data Revolution for Sustainable Development" (New York: United Nations, 2015); Sustainable Development Solutions Network, "Indicators and a Monitoring Framework for the Sustainable Development Goals: Launching a Data Revolution for the SDGs" (New York: United Nations, 2015); CIGI and KDI, "Post-2015 Development Agenda: Goals, Targets, and Indicators" (Waterloo, Canada: Centre for International Governance Innovation and Korea Development Institute, 2012).

77 Alister Doyle, "World Risks Spending $250 Billion Just to Monitor UN Development Goals," Reuters (September 25, 2014); Morten Jerven, "Data for Development Assessment:

Benefits and Costs of the Data for Development Targets for the Post-2015 Development Agenda" (Copenhagen: Copenhagen Consensus Center, September 16, 2014).

78 United Nations General Assembly, A/69/315 (August 15, 2014).

79 Ibid.

80 "Who Funds the Trillion Dollar Plan of the UN's Sustainable Development Goals?," Reuters (September 27, 2015); Malaka Gharib, "It's Up to the World: Pay for the Global Goals or Buy Everyone a Latte," www.npr.org (September 29, 2015).

81 Target 17.2, "Transforming Our World."

82 Shannon K. O'Neill, "The UN's Third Financing for Development Conference: After Growth & Aid, What Comes Next?," http://blogs.cfr.org/development-channel/ (July 16, 2015).

83 OECD, "Development Aid Stable in 2014, But Flows to Poorest Countries Still Falling" (Paris: Organisation for Economic Co-operation and Development, August 4, 2015); UNCTAD, "World Investment Report 2015: Reforming International Investment Governance" (Geneva: UN Conference on Trade and Development, 2015); World Bank, "Remittance Growth to Slow Sharply in 2015, as Europe and Russia Stay Weak; Pick Up Expected Next Year" (Washington, D.C.: World Bank, April 13, 2015).

84 World Bank et al., "From Billions to Trillions: Transforming Development Finance: Post-2015 Financing for Development: Multilateral Development Finance" (Washington, D.C.: World Bank, April 2, 2015).

85 "The Addis Ababa Action Agenda of the Third International Conference on Financing for Development" in Addis Ababa, Ethiopia, Resolution A/69/313 (July 15, 2015); paragraphs 40 and 62, "Transforming Our World."

86 Addis Ababa Action Agenda, II–C.

87 Addis Ababa Action Agenda, I and II-B.

88 Paragraph 35, Addis Ababa Action Agenda.

89 "Third FfD Failing to Finance Development: Civil Society Response to the Addis Ababa Action Agenda on Financing for Development," Addis Ababa, Ethiopia (July 16, 2015), http://ifp-fip.org/en/resource/third-ffd-failing-to-finance-development/.

90 Clar Ni Chonghaile, "Addis Ababa Outcome: Milestone or Millstone for the World's Poor?," *Guardian* (July 15, 2015).

91 Paragraph 123, Addis Ababa Action Agenda; paragraph 70, "Transforming Our World."

92 Paragraph 70, "Transforming Our World."

93 Targets 12 and 13, MDGs; Alice Tipping, "Trade Policy and the Post-2015 Agenda," *BioRes*, Vol. 8, No. 1 (February 7, 2014).

94 Targets 17.10 and 17.11, "Transforming Our World."

95 Targets 17.10 and 17.12, "Transforming Our World."

96 Target 8.a, "Transforming Our World."

97 Target 2.b, "Transforming Our World."

98 Target 3.b, "Transforming Our World."

99 Target 10.a, "Transforming Our World."

100 Target 14.6, "Transforming Our World."

101 Target 12.c, "Transforming Our World."

102 Paragraph 68, "Transforming Our World."

103 Paragraph 79, Addis Ababa Action Agenda.

104 Paragraph 82, Addis Ababa Action Agenda.

105 Paragraph 30, "Transforming Our World" (emphasis added).

106 "Third FfD Failing to Finance Development."

107 Deborah James, "Some Changes That Must Be Made to Global Trade Rules to Achieve the Sustainable Development Goals (SDGs) of the Post-2015 Development Agenda," Center for Economic and Policy Research (July 19, 2014), www.ourworldisnotforsale.org/en/node/24387.

108 "The Economics of Optimism," *Economist* (January 24, 2015).

109 Anderson, "Trade Assessment Paper: Benefits and Costs for the Post-2015 Development Agenda."

110 Ibid.

111 Patrick Low, "Trade Perspective Paper: Benefits and Costs of the Trade Targets for the Post-2015 Development Agenda" (Copenhagen: Copenhagen Consensus Center, September 30, 2014), www.copenhagenconsensus.com/sites/default/files/trade_perspective_-_low.pdf.

112 Bernard Hoekman, "Trade Perspective Paper: Benefits and Costs of the Trade Targets for the Post-2015 Development Agenda" (Copenhagen: Copenhagen Consensus Center, September 30, 2014), www.copenhagenconsensus.com/sites/default/files/trade_perspective_-_hoekman_0.pdf.

113 Vinaye Ancharaz, "Trade Viewpoint Paper: Benefits and Costs of the Trade Targets of the Post-2015 Development Agenda" (Copenhagen: Copenhagen Consensus Center, September 30, 2014), www.copenhagenconsensus.com/sites/default/files/trade_viewpoint_-_ancharaz.pdf. For a similar view, see ODI, "Trade and the Post-2015 Agenda: From Millennium Development Goals to Sustainable Development Goals," Briefing 89 (London: Overseas Development Institute, June 2014).

114 Ancharaz, "Trade Viewpoint Paper: Benefits and Costs of the Trade Targets of the Post-2015 Development Agenda"; see also Bjorn Lomborg, "How Free Trade Might Be the Best Option," *Huffington Post* (August 16, 2013).

115 Karl P. Sauvant and Khalil Hamdani, "How to Boost Sustainable Investment for a Post-2015 Development Agenda," *BioRes*, Vol. 9, No. 7 (September 18, 2015), www.ictsd.org/bridges-news/biores/news/how-to-boost-sustainable-investment-for-a-post-2015-development-agenda.

116 UNCTAD, "World Investment Report 2014: Investing in the SDGs: An Action Plan" (Geneva: UN Conference on Trade and Development, 2014), Chapter IV, http://unctad.org/en/PublicationsLibrary/wir2014_en.pdf.

117 UNCTAD, "Investment Policy Framework for Sustainable Development" (Geneva: UN Conference on Trade and Development, 2015).

118 UNCTAD, "The Latest FDI Trends and Policy Developments: An Action Plan for Investment in Sustainable Development" (Geneva: UN Conference on Trade and Development, June 24, 2014).

119 Ibid.

120 Target 17.16, "Transforming Our World."

121 Target 17.17, "Transforming Our World."

122 "From Aspiration to Achievement: Breaking Down the UN Sustainable Development Goals," PYXERA Global (2015), www.pyxeraglobal.org/wp-content/uploads/2015/08/SDGs-VENN-DIAGRAM.pdf.

123 Paragraph 283, "The Future We Want."
124 See https://sustainabledevelopment.un.org/partnerships.
125 Paragraph 67, "Transforming Our World."
126 Robert Ellison, "The Only UN Sustainable Development Goal Needed Is Economic Freedom," *American Thinker* (June 17, 2015).
127 Oran R. Young, "Conceptualization: Goal Setting as a Strategy for Earth System Governances," in Kanie and Biermann, eds., *Governing Through Goals*, 31, 48.

CHAPTER 9

1 Goal 16, "Transforming Our World."
2 Ambassador Samantha Power, "Remarks at a Reception on the Eve of the UN Summit to Adopt the 2030 Agenda: Delivering on the Promise of Goal 16," New York City (September 25, 2015), https://2009-2017-usun.state.gov/remarks/6835.
3 Smith, *The Theory of Moral Sentiments*, 335–36 (emphasis added).
4 Cesare Romano, "The Shift from the Consensual to the Compulsory Paradigm in International Adjudication: Elements for a Theory of Consent," *New York University Journal of International Law and Politics*, Vol. 39 (2007), 868.
5 The 500th complaint was filed by Pakistan against South Africa in a dispute over anti-dumping duties on Portland cement on November 9, 2015. See World Trade Organization, "WTO Disputes Reach 500 Mark," *WTO News* (November 10, 2015).
6 World Trade Organization, "Dispute Settlement," Press Release (November 6, 2009).
7 David Hume, "Of the Jealousy of Trade," in Eugene F. Miller, ed., *Essays, Moral, Political, and Literary* (Indianapolis: Liberty Fund, 1987), 334–38 [1759]. For more, see Istvan Holt, *Jealousy of Trade: International Competition and the Nation-State in Historical Perspective* (Cambridge, Mass., and London: Belknap Press of Harvard University Press, 2005).
8 Article 3.10, WTO Dispute Settlement Understanding.
9 Article 23.1, WTO Dispute Settlement Understanding.
10 Ibid.
11 See http://wto.org.
12 See Articles 3.7, 21, 22, and 23 of the WTO Dispute Settlement Understanding.
13 Article 17.3, WTO Dispute Settlement Understanding.
14 Here they follow the example of the American nativist and populist Patrick Buchanan in his 1996 campaign for the Republican presidential nomination in the United States. See William K. Tabb, *Economic Governance in the Age of Globalization* (New York: Columbia University Press, 2004), 315–16; Michael Veseth, ed., *The Rise of the Global Economy* (Chicago and London: Fitzroy Dearborn, 2002), 33.
15 Article 3.2, WTO Dispute Settlement Understanding. It may be worth noting here that I was appointed by consensus of the members of the WTO as one of the seven original members of the Appellate Body in 1995, was reappointed by consensus in 1999, and served for the maximum of eight years permitted by the WTO treaty, through yearend 2003, including two terms as chairman of the Appellate Body, in 2002 and 2003.
16 Articles 16.4 and 17.14, WTO Dispute Settlement Understanding.

17 David Sanger, "US Defeated in Its Appeal of Trade Case," *New York Times* (April 30, 1996), D-1.

18 Philippe Sands, *Lawless World: America and the Making and Breaking of Global Rules* (London: Allen Lane, 2005), 99.

19 Article 17.3, WTO Dispute Settlement Understanding.

20 WTO Rules of Conduct, http://wto.org.

21 Michael M. Weinstein, "Economic Sense: Should Clinton Embrace the China Deal?," *New York Times* (September 9, 1999).

22 Article 17.12, WTO Dispute Settlement Understanding.

23 Steve Charnovitz, "An Introduction to the Trade and Environment Debate," in Kevin P. Gallagher, ed., *Handbook on Trade and Environment* (Cheltenham, UK: Edward Elgar, 2008), 237.

24 Ibid., citing 102 BFSP 969, art. 2 (no longer in force).

25 Ibid., citing 97 LNTS 391, art. 4, ad art. 4 (not in force).

26 Ibid., 238.

27 Article 3.7, WTO Dispute Settlement Understanding.

28 See Article 6, WTO Dispute Settlement Understanding.

29 Appellate Body Report, European Communities – Regime for the Importation, Sale and Distribution of Bananas, WT/DS27/AB/R (1997).

30 Article 59, Statute of the International Court of Justice.

31 Article 3.2, WTO Dispute Settlement Understanding.

32 The task in WTO dispute settlement is to "clarify" the provisions of the various international agreements comprising the WTO treaty: Article 3.2, WTO Dispute Settlement Understanding.

33 Appellate Body Report, United States – Standards for Reformulated and Conventional Gasoline, WT/DS2/AB/R (1996) ("US – Gasoline").

34 Appellate Body Report, European Communities – Measures Concerning Meat and Meat Products (Hormones), WT/DS26/AB/R (1998) ("EC – Hormones").

35 Appellate Body Report, United States – Import Prohibition of Certain Shrimp and Shrimp Products, WT/DS58/AB/R (1998) ("US – Shrimp").

36 Appellate Body Report, Brazil – Measures Affecting Imports of Retreaded Tyres, WT/DS332/AB/R (2007) ("Brazil – Retreaded Tyres").

37 Appellate Body Report, European Communities – Measures Affecting Asbestos and Asbestos Containing Products, WT/DS135/AB/R (2001) ("EC – Asbestos").

38 Panel Report, European Communities – Measures Affecting the Marketing and Approval of Biotech Products, WT/DS291/R (2006) (not appealed) ("EC – Biotech Products").

39 Appellate Body Report, Measures Relating to the Feed-in Tariffs Program, WT/DS426/AB/R (2013) ("Canada – Feed-in Tariffs").

40 Appellate Body Report, United States – Countervailing Duties on Certain Products from China, WT/DS437/AB/R (2015) ("US – CVD").

41 Appellate Body Report, European Communities – Measures Prohibiting the Importation and Marketing of Seal Products, WT/DS400/AB/R (2014) ("EC – Seals").

42 Appellate Body Report, United States – Measures Concerning the Importation, Marketing, and Sale of Tuna and Tuna Products, WT/DS381/AB/RW (Article 21.5) (2015) ("US – Tuna").

43 US – Gasoline, 17.

44 Peter Van den Bossche and Werner Zdouc, *The Law and Policy of the World Trade Organization*, 3rd edn. (Cambridge: Cambridge University Press, 2013), 61. See James Bacchus, "Not in Clinical Isolation," in Gabrielle Marceau, ed., *A History of Law and Lawyers in the GATT/WTO: The Development of the Rule of Law in the World Trading System* (Cambridge: Cambridge University Press, 2015), 507–16.

45 Sands, *Lawless World*, 110.

46 US – Gasoline, 30.

47 Ibid.

48 Ibid., 20–21.

49 Article XX (b) and (g), General Agreement on Tariffs and Trade .

50 Chapeau (introductory paragraph), Article XX, General Agreement on Tariffs and Trade.

51 Tim Stephens, *International Courts and Environmental Protection* (Cambridge: Cambridge University Press, 2009), 326.

52 US – Shrimp, para. 121 (emphasis added).

53 See the discussion in Chapter 5.

54 See, for example, for a helpful discussion, Van den Bossche and Zdouc, *The Law and Policy of the World Trade Organization*, 325–31.

55 US – Shrimp, para. 133.

56 See Van den Bossche and Zdouc, *The Law and Policy of the World Trade Organization*, 551.

57 Article 3.2, WTO Dispute Settlement Understanding.

58 US – Shrimp, para. 131.

59 See Articles 14 and 15 of the North American Agreement on Environmental Cooperation (1994); see also Sierra Club et al., "NAFTA: 20 Years of Costs to Communities and the Environment" (Washington, D.C.: Sierra Club, March 2014), 9–10. It should perhaps be noted here that, while serving as a Member of the Congress of the United States, I supported and voted for the NAFTA.

60 Articles 1105, 1106, and 1110, North American Free Trade Agreement, Canada-Mexico-United States (December 17, 1992), 32 ILM 289 (1993) (the "NAFTA").

61 See Roderick Abbott et al., "Demystifying Investor–State Dispute Settlement (ISDS)," ECIPE Occasional Paper No. 5/2014 (Brussels: European Centre for International Political Economy, May 2014), 4.

62 Tim Stephens, *International Courts and Environmental Protection* (Cambridge: Cambridge University Press, 2009), 80.

63 Annette Magnusson, "How the Investment Protection Regime Can Contribute to a Better Environment," Speech to Roundtable: Challenges and Future of Investment Arbitration in Warsaw, Poland (May 29, 2015).

64 Howard Mann and Konrad Von Moltke, "NAFTA's Chapter 11 and the Environment: Addressing the Impacts of the Investor–State Process on the Environment" (Winnipeg, Canada: International Institute for Sustainable Development, 2000), 2.

65 Metalclad Corporation v. The United States of Mexico, 25 August 2000, 40 ILM 35 (2001); Ethyl Corporation v. Canada, Jurisdictional Phase, 38 ILM 708 (1999); S.D. Myers, Inc. v. Canada, Partial Award (Decision on the Merits), November 2000.

66 Bilcon of Delaware Inc. v. Canada, PCA, UNCITRAL, Award on Jurisdiction and Liability (17 March 2015).

67 Ibid., 49 (Dissenting Opinion).
68 Windstream Energy LLC v. Canada, PCA, UNCITRAL, Award (27 September 2016), 515(b).
69 Ibid., 7.
70 Kate Miles, *The Origins of International Investment Law: Empire, Environment, and the Safeguarding of Capital* (Cambridge: Cambridge University Press, 2013), 154, 170.
71 Azurix Corp. v. Republic of Argentina (ICSID Case No. ARB/01/12, Award of July 14, 2006).
72 Compania del Desarrollo de Santa Elena S.S. v. The Republic of Costa Rica, (2000), 39 ILM 1317.
73 For one who sees no "chill," see Stephan Schill, "Do Investment Treaties Chill Unilateral State Regulation to Mitigate Climate Change?," *Journal of International Arbitration*, Vol. 24, No. 5 (2007), 469–77; for one who does see a "chill," see Kyla Tienhaara, *The Expropriation of Environmental Governance* (Cambridge: Cambridge University Press, 2009), 262.
74 Among the dozens of such cases filed with the ICSID, see, for example, Eskonol, ARB/15/50; Landesbank Baden-Wurttemberg, ARB/15/45; Watkins Holdings, ARB 15/44; Hydro Energy, ARB/15/42; and Silver Ridge Power, ARB/15/37. See generally Tom Jones, "Spain Wins First Solar Case," *Global Arbitration Review* (January 28, 2016).
75 Philippe Sands, "Search for Balance: Concluding Remarks," *NYU Environmental Law Journal*, Vol. 11 (2002), 198–207.
76 Peter H. Sand, "Evolution of International Environmental Law," in Bodansky et al., eds., *Oxford Handbook of International Environmental Law*, 35.
77 Stephens, *International Courts and Environmental Protection*, 21.
78 Ibid.
79 Ibid., 27. The total of the global number of international tribunals is taken from the count in 2004 by the Project on International Courts and Tribunals. See www.pict.org/publica tions/synoptic_chart/synop_c4.pdf.
80 Christoff and Eckersley, *Globalization and the Environment*, 165, citing the International Environmental Agreements Database Project. See www.iea.uoregon.edu.
81 See, for example, Shelton, "Soft Law"; H. Hillgenberg, "A Fresh Look at Soft Law," *European Journal of International Law*, Vol. 10, No. 3 (1999), 499–515; and Jan Klabbers, "The Undesirability of Soft Law," *Nordic Journal of International Law*, Vol. 47, No. 7 (1998), 381–91.
82 See Koivurova, *Introduction to International Environmental Law*, 69–73.
83 Marcos A. Orellana, "The Swordfish Dispute Between the EU and Chile at the ITLOS and the WTO," *Nordic Journal of International Law*, Vol. 71 (2002), 55–81.
84 Koivurova, *Introduction to International Environmental Law*, 195–96.
85 Gabcikovo-Nagymaros Dam Project (Hungary v. Slovakia), ICJ Rep 92 (23 September 1997) (Separate Opinion of Vice-President Weeramantry).
86 Request for an Examination of the Situation in Accordance With Paragraph 63 of the Court's Judgment of 20 December 1974 in the Nuclear Tests (New Zealand v. France) case, ICJ Rep 288 (1995), Dissenting Opinion of Judge Weeramantry, 345.
87 Stephens, *International Courts and Environmental Protection*, 38–40.
88 Ibid., 39–40.

89 Francisco Orrego Vicuna, *International Dispute Settlement in an Evolving Global Society* (Cambridge: Cambridge University Press, 2004), 83–84.

90 See, e.g., Pulp Mills on the River Uruguay (Argentina v. Uruguay), ICJ Rep 2010 (20 April 2010); Aerial Herbicide Spraying (Ecuador v. Colombia), ICJ Rep 2013 (13 September 2013); Whaling in the Antarctic (Australia v. Japan, New Zealand Intervening), ICJ Rep 2014 (31 March 2014); and Joint Statement by Leaders of Pacific Islands Forum, UN Secretary-General, 10 October 2012, SG/219.

91 Territorial Jurisdiction of the International Commission of the River Oder (United Kingdom, Czechoslovakia, Denmark, France, Germany, Sweden/Poland) [1929] PCIJ (ser. A), no. 23, 5; Corfu Channel (United Kingdom of Great Britain and Northern Ireland v. Albania), Judgment of 9 April 1949, ICJ Reports 1949, 2; Pulp Mills on the River Uruguay, at para. 204.

92 Gabcikovo-Nagymaros Dam Project, at para. 140.

93 Ibid. (Separate Opinion of Vice-President, Judge Weeramantry).

94 Arthur Neslen, "Dutch Government Ordered to Cut Carbon Emissions in Landmark Ruling," *Guardian* (June 24, 2015).

95 Eric Holthaus, "Children Sue over Climate Change," *Slate* (November 16, 2015).

96 "Nine-Year-Old Sues Indian Government over Climate Change Inaction," Reuters (April 4, 2017).

97 "Climate Change Court Cases on the Rise Globally, Majority in US," Reuters (May 23, 2017) (citing a study by UN Environment and the Columbia Law School's Sabin Center for Climate Change Law).

98 I have made this same point, and have elaborated on it, on behalf of the E15 Expert Group that studied the nexus of trade and climate change. See James Bacchus, "Global Rules for Mutually Supportive and Reinforcing Trade and Climate Regimes," E15 Initiative, E15 Expert Group on Measures to Address Climate Change and the Trade System, Policy Options Paper (Geneva: International Centre for Trade and Sustainable Development and World Economic Forum, 2016), 14.

99 Article 3.5, UNFCCC.

CHAPTER 10

1 McKinsey Global Institute, "Global Flows in a Digital Age: How Trade, Finance, People, and Data Connect the World Economy" (April 2014), 4, www.mckinsey .com/~/media/McKinsey/Global%20Themes/Globalization/Global%20flows%20in%20a %20digital%20age/MGI%20Global%20flows%20in%20a%20digial%20age%20Executive %20summary.ashx.

2 Quoted in Gianni Riotta, "Was Genghis Khan Really a Driver of Globalization?," *Wall Street Journal* (March 27, 2016).

3 Martin Wolf, "Worlds Apart," *Financial Times* (April 16, 2016); see Branko Milanovic, *Global Inequality: A New Approach for the Age of Globalization* (Cambridge, Mass.: Harvard University Press, 2016); and Francois Bourguignon, *The Globalisation of Inequality* (Princeton: Princeton University Press, 2015).

4 Milanovic, *Global Inequality*, 161–76.

5 Spence, *The Next Convergence*.

6 Milanovic, *Global Inequality*, 24–25. These numbers, produced in 2015, are from 1988 through 2008.

7 Ibid., 36.

8 Ibid., 41–42.

9 Tyler Cowen, "Why There's Hope for the Middle Class (with Help from China)," *New York Times* (April 17, 2016).

10 Barney Jopson and Hannah Murphy, "US Views on Climate Change Pose Test for 2016 Candidates," *Financial Times* (December 30, 2015).

11 Ibid.

12 Hoffer, *The Ordeal of Change*.

13 Ibid., 3.

14 Ibid.

15 Ibid.

16 Zygmunt Bauman, *Liquid Modernity* (Cambridge, UK: Polity Press, 2012) [2000].

17 This, of course, is a paraphrase of Karl Marx and Friedrich Engels in *The Communist Manifesto*, where they said, "All that is solid melts into air": Marx and Engels, *The Communist Manifesto* (London: Penguin Books, 1985), 83 [1848].

18 Ronald Syme, *The Roman Revolution* (Oxford and New York: Oxford University Press, 1939).

19 Davenport, "Nations Approve Landmark Climate Accord in Paris."

20 IEA, "Energy and Climate Change: World Energy Outlook Special Briefing for COP21" (Paris: International Energy Agency, December 2015).

21 Coral Davenport, "Key to Success of Climate Pact Will Be Its Signal to Global Markets," *New York Times* (December 9, 2015).

22 IEA, "World Energy Outlook Special Report: Energy and Climate Change" (Paris: International Energy Agency, 2015).

23 UNEP, "The Emissions Gap Report 2017: A UN Environment Synthesis Report" (Nairobi: UN Environment Programme, November 2017), xvii.

24 Nina Chestney and Barbara Lewis, "For Big Business Seeking CO_2 Emissions Price, a Ray of Hope from Paris," Reuters (December 13, 2015).

25 Decision 137, Paris Agreement.

26 Article 6.2, Paris Agreement.

27 Justin Gillis and Coral Davenport, "Leaders Roll Up Their Sleeves on Climate, But Experts Say Plans Don't Pack a Wallop," *New York Times* (April 21, 2016).

28 Ibid., citing UNEP and Bloomberg New Energy Finance, "Global Trends in Renewable Energy Investment 2016" (Nairobi: UN Environment Programme, 2016), 11. These numbers are for 2015.

29 Ibid.; Coral Davenport, "Signs Are Promising That Economies Can Rise as Carbon Emissions Decline," *New York Times* (April 5, 2016).

30 IEA, "IEA Finds CO_2 Emissions Flat for Third Straight Year Even as Global Economy Grew in 2016" (Paris: International Energy Agency, March 17, 2017); Nate Aden, "The Roads to Decoupling: 21 Countries Are Reducing Carbon Emissions While Growing GDP," World Resources Institute (April 5, 2016), www.wri.org/blog/.

31 "BP Statistical Review of World Energy June 2017," 66th edn., Statistical Review 2017 slidepack, www.bp.com/content/dam/bp/en/corporate/pdf/energy-economics/statistical-review-2017/bp-statistical-review-of-world-energy-2017-full-report.pdf.

32 Nina Chestney and Susana Twidale, "Investors Aware of Climate Change Risks But Still Slow to Act," Reuters (April 15, 2016).

33 Jeffrey Ball, "Who Will Pay for Climate Change?," *New Republic* (November 3, 2015).

34 "Half of Leading Investors Ignoring Climate Change: Study," Reuters (May 2, 2016), citing a report by the Asset Owners Disclosure Project, a not-for-profit organization aimed at improving the management of climate change.

35 Ibid.

36 Robert Stavins, "Paris Agreement – A Good Foundation for Meaningful Progress," *Huffington Post* (January 2, 2016).

37 See Decisions 118, 119, 120, 134, and 135, Paris Agreement.

38 Decision 135, Paris Agreement.

39 Decision 119, Paris Agreement.

40 Paragraph 39, "Transforming Our World."

41 UN, High-Level Panel of Eminent Persons on the Post-2015 Development Agenda, "A New Global Partnership: Eradicate Poverty and Transform Economies Through Sustainable Development."

42 UN Development Group, "Delivering the Post-2015 Development Agenda: Opportunities at the National and Local Levels" (Vienna: UN Development Group, 2014), 5.

43 Target 17.16, "Transforming Our World."

44 Goal 17, "Transforming Our World."

45 Peter Orebech and Martin Chanock, "Towards Sustainability: The Basis in International Law," in Peter Orebech et al., *The Role of Customary Law in Sustainable Development* (Cambridge: Cambridge University Press, 2010), 389 [2005].

46 Andrew Reskin, "The Climate Path Ahead," *New York Times* (December 13, 2015).

47 Dale Jamieson, *Reason in a Dark Time: Why the Struggle Against Climate Change Failed – And What It Means for Our Future* (Oxford: Oxford University Press, 2014), 193–94 (emphasis added).

48 Bret Stephens, "The Tyranny of a Big Idea," *Wall Street Journal* (November 3, 2015).

49 David Warsh, *Knowledge and the Wealth of Nations: A Story of Economic Discovery* (New York and London: Norton, 2006), 65.

50 Barry Norman, "The Tradition of Spontaneous Order," *Literature of Liberty: A Review of Contemporary Liberal Thought*, Vol. 5, No. 2, 7–58.

51 Hayek, *The Constitution of Liberty*, 24, 41.

52 Adam Ferguson, *An Essay on the History of Civil Society* (Edinburgh: Edinburgh University Press, 1966), 122 [1767].

53 Cesar Hidalgo, *Why Information Grows: The Evolution of Order, from Atoms to Economies* (New York: Basic Books, 2015).

54 Ibid., 8.

55 Matt Ridley, "Don't Dismiss the Materialist Expansion," in *Bourgeois Dignity: The Virtue of the Modern World*, Cato Unbound (October 8, 2010), www.cato-unbound.org/2010/10/08/matt-ridley/dont-dismiss-materialist-explanation.

56 Hayek, *Law, Legislation and Liberty*, Vol. I, *Rules and Order*, 46.

57 Quoted in Glick, "The Last Great Critic."

58 Thomas Babington Macaulay, Speech in the House of Commons in support of the Ten Hour Bill (May 22, 1846), in Thomas Babington Macaulay, *The Works of Lord Macaulay*

Complete, Vol. VIII (London: Longman, Green and Co., 1871), 361; see also J. T. Ward, ed., *The Factory System*, Vol. II, *Birth and Control* (New York: Barnes & Noble, 1970), 172.

59 Deirdre Nansen McCloskey, *Bourgeois Equality: How Ideas, Not Capital or Institutions, Enriched the World* (Chicago: University of Chicago Press, 2016), xxi.

60 Ibid., xxxi.

61 Ibid., xix.

62 Diane Coyle, "Immaterial World," *Financial Times* (April 8, 2016).

63 See Lawrence E. Harrison and Samuel P. Huntington, *Culture Matters: How Values Shape Human Progress* (New York: Basic Books, 2000).

64 Marc Gunther, "This Idea to Change the World Was Half-Baked," *Washington Post* (November 1, 2015).

65 Target 4.7, "Transforming Our World."

66 David Wootton, *The Invention of Science: A New History of the Scientific Revolution* (New York: Harper, 2015).

67 Scott Russell Sanders, "What Does It Mean to Live a Good Life?," *Washington Post* (May 8, 2016).

68 Wootton, *The Invention of Science*, 421.

69 Ibid.

70 Steven W. Popper, Robert J. Lempert, and Steven C. Bankes, "Shaping the Future," *Scientific American*, Vol. 292 (2005), 66–71.

71 Emma Marris, "Humility in the Anthropocene," in Ben A. Minter and Stephen J. Pyne, eds., *After Preservation: Saving American Nature in the Age of Humans* (Chicago: University of Chicago Press, 2015), 41.

72 Ibid., 44.

73 Popper et al., "Shaping the Future," 66.

74 Ibid.

75 Ibid.

76 Edward O. Wilson, *Half-Earth: Our Planet's Fight for Life* (New York and London: W.W. Norton and Company, 2016), 193.

77 Hoffer, *The Ordeal of Change*, 102.

78 Wilson, *Half-Earth*, 14, 173.

79 WEF, "A Message from the Friends of Rio+20" (Davos: World Economic Forum, June 2012), Paragraph 7. I was a member of the Friends of Rio+20 and one of the drafters of this message.

80 See WEF, "Annex to the Message of the Friends of Rio+20" (Davos: World Economic Forum: June 2012); WEF, "A Message from the Friends of Rio+20."

81 See https://sustainabledevelopment.un.org/index.php?menu=1348.

82 See www.un.org/esa/ffd/ffd3/commitments.html.

83 I should disclose that I was on a panel of advisers to the Peruvian presidency of the COP at the time.

84 See http://climateaction.unfccc.int. I was an appointed member of the High-Level Advisory Panel to the Peruvian presidency of the COP, and joined with many others preceding the Paris climate summit in urging that this process be put in place.

85 Ram Nidumolu, C. K. Prahalad, and M. K. Rangaswami, "Why Sustainability Is Now the Key Driver of Innovation," *Harvard Business Review* (September 2009), https://hbr.org/2009/09/why-sustainability-is-now-the-key-driver-of-innovation.

86 I owe this thought to my friend Peter Robinson, president of the United States Council for International Business.

87 Yale Climate Dialogue, "Lifting the Ambition of the Paris 2015 Agreement: An Agenda for Lima" (New Haven: Yale Center for International Law and Policy, November 2014).

88 Tocqueville, "The Americans Combat Individualism by the Principle of Interest Rightly Understood."

89 Alexis de Tocqueville, "Of the Use Which the Americans Make of Public Associations in Civil Life," *Democracy in America*, Vol. II, Book II, Chapter 5, 114.

90 Ibid.

91 Ibid., 115.

92 Ibid., 116.

93 Ibid., 117.

94 Ibid.

95 Ibid.

96 For a broader discussion of this point, see Alan Ryan, *On Politics: A History of Political Thought – From Herodotus to the Present* (New York: W. W. Norton, 2012), 768; see also Larry Siedentop, *Tocqueville* (Oxford and New York: Oxford University Press, 1994), 86–95.

CHAPTER 11

1 A sampling of these imaginings includes: Global Redesign Initiative (Davos: World Economic Forum, 2010) (I was one of those participating in this worldwide WEF initiative); Pathways to Deep Decarbonization (Sustainable Development Solutions Network and Institute for Sustainable Development and International Relations, July 2014); David King, John Browne, Richard Layard, Gus O'Donnell, Martin Rees, Nicholas Stern, and Adair Turner, "A Global Apollo Programme to Combat Climate Change" (June 2015), http://cep .lse.ac.uk/pubs/download/special/Global_Apollo_Programme_Report.pdf; The New Climate Economy, "Better Growth, Better Climate: The New Climate Economy Report" (Washington, D.C.: Global Commission on the Economy and Climate, 2014); E15 Initiative, "Strengthening the Global Trade and Investment System in the 21st Century: Synthesis Report" (Geneva: International Centre for Trade and Sustainable Development and World Economic Forum, 2016) (I was one of the "participating experts" in the E15 Initiative); "Green Economy Roadmap: A Guide for Business, Policymakers and Society" (Paris: International Chamber of Commerce, 2012) (I was among the many volunteers participating in the shaping of this ICC proposal); WBCSD, "Vision 2050: The New Agenda for Business" (Geneva: World Business Council for Sustainable Development, 2010); "Introducing the Breakthrough Energy Coalition," http://breakthroughenergycoalition.com/en/ index.html; numerous Business 20 (B20) task force reports on trade, investment, and other issues are available on the website of the International Chamber of Commerce at http:// www.iccwbo.org (I have been a member of some of these business task forces advising the G20 group of leading economies); "American Climate Prospectus: Economic Risks in the United States," prepared as input to the Risky Business Project (New York: Rhodium Group, October, 2014). See Burt Helm, "Climate Change's Bottom Line," *New York Times* (February 1, 2015).

2 UNEP, "Towards a Green Economy: Pathways to Sustainable Development and Poverty Eradication. A Synthesis for Policy Makers" (St. Martin-Bellevue, France: UN Environment Programme, 2011), 2.

3 McCloskey, *Bourgeois Equality.*

4 Deirdre McCloskey, "How the West (and the Rest) Got Rich," *Wall Street Journal* (May 21, 2016).

5 See the Declaration of Independence of the United States of America.

6 Smith, *The Wealth of Nations*, Book IV, Chapter IX.

7 Fiona Harvey, "Humans Damaging the Environment Faster Than It Can Recover, UN Finds," *Guardian* (May 19, 2016).

8 Brady Dennis, "Humanity Blinded by the Light," *Washington Post* (June 11, 2016), citing a report in the journal *Science Advances.*

9 Chris Mooney, "Nothing Pristine: Humanity's Patina Envelops the Globe," *Washington Post* (June 7, 2016), citing a study published in the *Proceedings of the National Academy of Sciences* on June 6, 2016.

10 UNEP, "Global Environmental Outlook: Regional Assessments" (Nairobi: UN Environment Programme, May 2016) ("GEO-6").

11 For a broader discussion of this point, see Bacchus, *Trade and Freedom*, 172.

12 The New Climate Economy, "Better Growth, Better Climate," 40.

13 Easterly, *The Tyranny of Experts*, 278–79.

14 Dan Turello, "Climate Change Actions? It's Not the Data That's Missing, It's Our Ability to Imagine," *Huffington Post* (May 5, 2015).

15 Ibid.

16 Wilson, *Half-Earth*, 185.

17 Ibid., 192.

18 "An Ecomodernist Manifesto" (April 2015), www.ecomodernism.org. See Michelle Nijhuis, "Is the 'Ecomodernist Manifesto' the Future of Environmentalism?," *New Yorker* (June 2, 2015).

19 Ibid., 6.

20 Ibid.

21 Ibid., 17.

22 Jennifer Clapp and Peter Dauvergne, *Paths to a Greener World: The Political Economy of the Global Environment*, 2nd edn. (Cambridge, Mass.: MIT Press, 2011), 40 [2005].

23 Ibid., 44.

24 William J. Broad, "Potential Eyes in the Sky on Greenhouse Gases," *New York Times* (May 9, 2016).

25 Jacques Leslie, "Eyes in the Sky: Green Groups Are Harnessing Data from Space," Yale Environment 360 (January 11, 2016), www.e360.yale.edu.

26 Target 17.6, "Transforming Our World."

27 OECD and IEA, "Energy Technology Perspectives 2017" (Paris: Organisation for Economic Co-operation and Development and International Energy Agency, June 2017); Nina Chestney, "World's Energy System Not on Track to Meet Climate Goals," Reuters (June 6, 2017).

28 OECD, "Reframing Climate and Competitiveness: Is There a Need for Co-operation on National Climate Change Policies?," 31st Roundtable on Sustainable Development (Paris: Organisation for Economic Co-operation and Development, February 2–3, 2015), 96.

29 I owe this observation to my colleague at the University of Central Florida, Professor Kate Mansfield, who leads the UCF Marine Turtle Research Group.

30 Pilita Clark, "*Climate Shock: The Economic Consequences of a Hotter Planet,* by Germot Wagner and Martin Weitzman" (review), *Financial Times* (March 30, 2015). See Steven Levitt and Stephen J. Dubner, *SuperFreakonomics: Global Cooling, Patriotic Prostitutes, and Why Suicide Bombers Should Buy Life Insurance* (New York: William Morrow, 2009).

31 Nina Chestney, "CO_2 Removal 'No Silver Bullet' to Fighting Climate Change – Scientists," Reuters (January 31, 2018).

32 Ibid.

33 Clark, "*Climate Shock.*"

34 Joel Mokyr, *The Gifts of Athena: Historical Origins of the Knowledge Economy* (Princeton and Oxford: Princeton University Press, 2002), 244–45.

35 Amy Harmon, "Species-Wide Gene Editing, Applauded and Feared, Gets a Push," *New York Times* (June 9, 2016).

36 Mokyr, *The Gifts of Athena,* 246.

37 *Economist* (September 8, 1990), 25.

38 Marianne Fay, Stephane Hallegatte, Adrien Vogt-Schib, Julie Rozenberg, Ulf Narloch, and Tom Kerr, "Decarbonizing Development: Three Steps to a Zero-Carbon Future," Climate Change and Development (Washington, D.C.: World Bank, 2015), 96.

39 Mokyr, *The Gifts of Athena,* 246.

40 Edward Tenner, *Why Things Bite Back: Technology and the Revenge of Unintended Consequences* (New York: Knopf, 1997).

41 Anastasia Moloney, "Panama Indigenous Tribes Launch Drones to Fight Deforestation," Reuters (June 2, 2016).

42 OECD, "Aligning Policies for a Low-Carbon Economy" (Paris: Organisation for Economic Co-operation and Development, 2015), 125.

43 E15 Initiative, "Trade and Innovation: Policy Options for a New Innovation Landscape. Synthesis of the Policy Options" (Geneva: International Centre for Trade and Sustainable Development and World Economic Forum, 2016), 5.

44 Daniela Benavente, "Measurement of Trade and Innovation: Issues and Challenges," E15 Initiative (Geneva: International Centre for Trade and Sustainable Development and World Economic Forum, 2014); see N. Kiriyana, "Trade and Innovation: Synthesis Report, OECD Trade Policy Papers, No. 135 (Paris: Organisation for Economic Co-operation and Development, 2012).

45 Matt Ridley, *The Evolution of Everything: How New Ideas Emerge* (New York: HarperCollins, 2015), 111.

46 See The New Climate Economy, "Better, Growth, Better Climate," 212–32.

47 Goal 9, "Transforming Our World."

48 Sherry Stephenson, "Trade Governance Frameworks in a World of Global Value Chains: Policy Option," E15 Initiative (Geneva: International Centre for Trade and Sustainable Development and World Economic Forum), 5.

49 Kristina M. Lybecker and Sebastian Lohse, "Innovation and Diffusion of Green Technologies: The Role of Intellectual Property and Other Enabling Factors" (Geneva: World Intellectual Property Organization, June 2016), 29.

50 Hidalgo, *Why Information Grows,* 50.

51 OECD, "Taxing Energy Use 2018" (Paris: Organisation for Economic Co-operation and Development, February 14, 2018); Nina Chestney, "OECD Says Energy Taxes in Developed Economies Too Low to Fight Climate Change," Reuters (February 14, 2018).

52 The New Climate Economy, "Better Growth, Better Climate," 172.

53 Ibid.

54 James Rydge, "Implementing Effective Carbon Pricing: Contributing Paper for Seizing the Global Opportunity. Partnerships for Better Growth and a Better Climate," Working Paper (London and Washington: New Climate Economy, 2015), 3.

55 Editorial, "The Carbon Tax Chimera," Wall Street Journal (February 25, 2017).

56 "Marketing Mechanisms: Understanding the Options" (Arlington, Va.: Center for Climate and Energy Solutions, April 2015), 1.

57 Sir Nicholas Stern, in The New Climate Economy, "Better Growth, Better Climate," 12.

58 Ibid., 34.

59 IMF Staff Discussion Note, "After Paris: Fiscal, Macroeconomic, and Financial Implications of Climate Change" (Washington, D.C.: International Monetary Fund, January 2016), 5.

60 IRENA, "Accelerating the Energy Transition Through Innovation," Working Paper (Paris: International Renewable Energy Agency, June 2017).

61 Jonathon Camuzeaux, Dirk Forrister, Nathaniel Keohane, Ruben Lukowski, Jeremy Proville, Jeff Swartz, and Derek Walker, "Doubling Down on Carbon Pricing: Laying the Foundation for Greater Ambition" (Washington, D.C., and Geneva: Environmental Defense Fund and International Energy Trading Association, April 2016), 7.

62 Jada F. Smith, "US Bans Commercial Trade of African Elephant Ivory," New York Times (June 2, 2016).

63 See the discussion on environmental crimes and threatened and endangered species in Chapter 16.

64 Sebastian Rausch and Valerie J. Karplus, "Markets Versus Regulation: The Efficiency and Distributional Impacts of US Climate Policy Proposals," Joint Program Report Series Report No. 263, MIT Joint Program on the Science and Policy of Global Change (May 2014), Abstract/Summary, https://globalchange.mit.edu/publication/15897. This 2014 study modeled how a United States cap-and-trade policy would compare to a variety of regulatory options, including a federal renewable portfolio standard, a clean energy standard, and fuel economy standards.

65 Ibid., 9. See also IMF Discussion Note: "After Paris: Fiscal, Macroeconomic, and Financial Implications of Climate Change," 15–16.

66 Eduardo Porter, "US Leaves the Markets Out in the Fight Against Carbon Emissions," New York Times (June 30, 2015), citing Rausch and Karplus, "Markets Versus Regulation."

67 International Emissions Trading Association, "Why Emissions Trading Is More Effective than Comand and Control," www.ieta.org/Three-Minute-Briefings/3891688.

68 "Market Mechanisms: Understanding the Options," 3.

69 Ibid.

70 Ibid.

71 Principle 16, Rio Declaration on Environment and Development.

72 See, for example, Joseph E. Stiglitz, Making Globalization Work (New York and London: W. W. Norton, 2006), 181–84.

73 World Bank, "Carbon Pricing Watch 2017" (Washington, D.C.: World Bank, May 23, 2017), 2.

74 EDF and IETA, "Carbon Pricing: The Paris Agreement's Key Ingredient" (Washington, D.C., and Geneva: Environmental Defense Fund and International Energy Trading Association, April 2016), 2.

75 International Institute for Sustainable Development, "Carbon Pricing and Markets Update: Year Closes on Chinese Carbon Market Launch" (January 9, 2018), http://sdg .iisd.org/new-carbon-pricing-and-markets-update-year-close-on-chinese-carbon-market-launch.

76 World Bank, "Carbon Pricing Watch 2017," 3.

77 EDF and IETA, "Carbon Pricing: The Paris Agreement's Key Ingredient"; see also Rydge, "Implementing Effective Carbon Pricing," 4.

78 "The EU Emissions Trading System (EU ETS)," https://ec.europa.eu/clima/policies/ets_en.

79 "European Parliament Backs Post-2020 Carbon Market Reform," *Bridges Weekly*, Vol. 22, No. 4 (February 8, 2018).

80 EDF and IETA, "Carbon Pricing: The Paris Agreement's Key Ingredient"; IETA Press Release, "IETA Welcomes Ontario Law Establishing a Carbon Market" (International Energy Trading Association, May 18, 2016).

81 World Bank, "Carbon Pricing Watch 2017," 2.

82 Corbett Grainger and Charles Kolstad, "How Regressive Is a Price on Carbon?," NBER Working Paper No. 15239 (Cambridge, Mass.: National Bureau of Economic Research, June 8, 2017).

83 IMF Staff Discussion Note, "After Paris: Fiscal, Macroeconomic, and Financial Implications of Climate Change," 20.

84 The New Climate Economy, "Better Growth, Better Climate," 173.

85 World Bank, "Statement: Putting a Price on Carbon" (Washington, D.C.: World Bank, 2014).

86 CDP, "Embedding a Carbon Price into Business Strategy" (London: CDP, September 2016).

87 EDF and IETA, ""Carbon Pricing: The Paris Agreement's Key Ingredient," 2.

88 Camuzeaux et al., "Doubling Down on Carbon Pricing," 4.

89 Article 6, Paris Agreement.

90 See, for example, The New Climate Economy, "Better Growth, Better Climate," 8; Fay et al., "Decarbonizing Development," 4; and OECD, "Aligning Policies for a Low-Carbon Economy," 17–19.

91 This phrase is borrowed from The New Climate Economy, "Better Growth, Better Climate," 167.

92 Ibid., 185; see also Rydge, "Implementing Effective Carbon Pricing," 11.

93 WEF, "The Global Risks Report 2016: 11th Edn.," 33. I participated in the preparation of this annual report.

94 Ibid.

95 See the earlier discussion in Chapter 5.

96 Editorial, "What President Trump Doesn't Get About America," *New York Times* (January 20, 2017), citing BLS Working Paper No. 493 (Washington, D.C.: US Bureau of Labor Statistics, 2016).

97 Eduardo Porter, "Jobs Threatened by Machines: A Once 'Stupid' Concern Gains Respect," *New York Times* (June 8, 2016).

98 See, for example, Robin Hanson, *The Age of Em* (Oxford and London: Oxford University Press, 2016).

99 ITUC, "Growing Green and Decent Jobs," Millennium Institute (Brussels: International Trade Union Confederation, 2012), www.ituc-csi.org/growing-green-and-decent-jobs,11011.

100 World Bank, "Inclusive Green Growth: The Pathways to Sustainable Development" (Washington, D.C.: World Bank, 2012), 92.

101 Citi Global Perspectives and Solutions, "Energy Darwinism II: Why a Low Carbon Future Doesn't Have to Cost the Earth" (New York: Citigroup, August 2015).

102 IEA and IRENA, "Perspectives for the Energy Transition: Investment Needs for a Low-Carbon Energy System," Executive Summary (Paris: International Energy Agency and International Renewable Energy Agency, 2017), 10.

103 Ibid.

104 Ibid.

105 OECD, "Investing in Climate, Investing in Growth" (Paris: Organisation for Economic Co-operation and Development, May 23, 2017).

106 OECD, "Employment Implications of Green Growth: Linking Jobs, Growth, and Green Policies," OECD Report for the G7 Environment Ministers (Paris: Organisation for Economic Co-operation and Development, June 2017).

107 Quoted in Duncan Kelly, "Obey the Great Law," *Times Literary Supplement* (April 29, 2016).

108 See Global Agenda Councils on Competitiveness and Trade and FDI, "The Case for Trade and Competitiveness." As previously noted, I participated in the writing of this report.

109 Alvaredo et al., "World Inequality Report 2018," Executive Summary.

110 Christopher Ingraham, "Study: Richest 1% Own 40% of Country's Wealth," *New York Times* (December 7, 2017).

111 Alvaredo et al., "World Inequality Report 2018," Executive Summary.

112 Oxfam International, "Reward Work, Not Wealth" (London: Oxfam International, January 2018), 2.

113 Ibid.

114 Eduardo Porter and Karl Russell, "It's an Unequal World: It Doesn't Have to Be," *New York Times* (December 14, 2017).

115 Goal 10, "Transforming Our World."

116 Mark Goldring, "Eight Men Own More Than 3.6 Billion People Do: Our Economics Is Broken," *Guardian* (January 16, 2017).

117 Max Ehrenfreund, "At the World Economic Forum, Talk of Equitable Capitalism," *Washington Post* (January 20, 2017).

118 Robert Atkinson, "The Trouble with Progressive Economics," *Breakthrough* (Summer 2011), https://thebreakthrough.org/index.php/journal/past-issues/issue-1/the-trouble-with-progressive-economics.

119 Ibid., 7; see Paragraph 82, Addis Ababa Action Agenda.

120 See the helpful discussion in Rafael Leal-Arcas, *Climate Change and International Trade* (Cheltenham, UK, and Northampton, Mass.: Edward Elgar, 2013), 135.

121 The New Climate Economy, "Better Growth, Better Climate," 187.

122 Ibid.

123 "Environmental Policies Don't Have to Hurt Productivity," OECD Observer No. 301 Q4 (2014), 9.

124 Fay et al., "Decarbonizing Development," 17.

125 The New Climate Economy, "Better Growth, Better Climate," 187, citing S. Bassi and D. Zenghelis, "Burden or Opportunity? How UK Emissions Reduction Policies Affect the Competitiveness of Business," Policy Paper, Grantham Research Institute on Climate Change and the Environment, LSE (London: London School of Economics, 2014).

126 The New Climate Economy, "Better Growth, Better Climate," 187, citing Bassi and Zenghelis, "Burden or Opportunity."

127 For an early warning of this looming collision, see Ad Hoc Working Group on Trade and Climate Change, "From Collision to Vision: Climate Change and World Trade: A Discussion Paper" (Geneva: World Economic Forum, November 2010). I chaired the *ad hoc* working group that produced this report.

128 Article II:2(a), General Agreement on Tariffs and Trade.

129 GATT Working Party Report, Border Tax Adjustments, BISD 18S, 97 (1970).

130 For one of the best explanations, among many, see Aaron Cosbey et al., "A Guide for the Concerned: Guidance on the Elaboration and Implementation of Border Carbon Adjustment," Entwined, Policy Report 03 (November 2012).

131 For one excellent discussion, see Joel P. Trachtman, "WTO Law Constraints on Border Tax Adjustment and Credit Tax Mechanisms to Reduce the Competitive Effects of Carbon Taxes," Discussion Paper RFF DP 16–03 (Washington, D.C.: Resources for the Future, January 2016).

132 I have made these same points in James Bacchus, "Triggering the Trade Transition: The G20's Role in Reconciling Rules for Trade and Climate Change," White Paper (Geneva: International Centre for Trade and Sustainable Development, February 2018), 11.

133 Ibid., 10–11.

134 See Bacchus, "Global Rules for Mutually Supportive and Reinforcing Trade and Climate Regimes," 17.

135 Article IX:2, WTO Agreement.

136 Ibid.

137 Ibid., 14.

138 Jacob Bronowski, *The Common Sense of Science* (Cambridge, Mass.: Harvard University Press, 1978), 22.

139 Ibid., 21.

140 Ibid., 22.

141 See Appellate Body Report, Japan – Measures Affecting the Importation of Apples, WT/DS245/AB/R (2003).

142 See Appellate Body Report, Japan – Alcoholic Beverages II, WT/DS11/AB/R (1996), 114.

143 Ibid. I was one of the Members of the Appellate Body who judged in this dispute.

144 See Van den Bossche and Zdouc, *The Law and Policy of the World Trade Organization*, 325–28. See also the related discussion in Chapter 9.

145 Appellate Body Report, European Communities – Measures Affecting Asbestos and Asbestos Containing Products, WT/DS135/AB/R (2001), paras. 90–122; see especially paras. 101 and 117.

146 Appellate Body Report, Canada – Feed-in Tariffs Program, WT/DS426/AB/R (2013), para. 5.63. This passing observation was made by the Appellate Body in the context of determining the scope of the limitation of the exception to the national treatment obligation for government procurement under Article III:8(a), General Agreement on Tariffs and Trade.

147 See Article XX, General Agreement on Tariffs and Trade, and Article XIV, General Agreement on Trade in Services.

148 Article 17.12, WTO Dispute Settlement Understanding.

149 Bhagwati, *In Defense of Globalization*, 154–55.

150 GATT Panel Report, Belgium – Family Allowances, (BISD 1S) (1952), 9. See Steve Charnovitz, "Belgian Family Allowances and the Challenge of Origin-Based Discrimination," in Steve Charnovitz, *The Path of World Trade Law in the 21st Century* (London and Hackensack, N.J.: World Scientific Publishing, 2015), 249–78.

151 Ibid.

152 Ibid.

153 See my longer discussion and analysis of the proposal for a WTO climate waiver in James Bacchus, "The Case for a WTO Climate Waiver," Special Report (Waterloo, Canada: Center for International Governance Innovation, November 2, 2017).

154 For HIV and other drugs, see General Council Decision of 30 August 2003, WT/L/540, dated 2 September 2003; for conflict diamonds, see General Council Decision of 15 December 2006, WT/L/676, dated 19 December 2006.

155 Article IX:3, WTO Agreement; see the General Council Decision of 15 November 1995 on "Decision-Making Procedures under Articles IX and XII of the WTO Agreement," WT/L/93, dated 24 November 1995, first paragraph; and see Van den Bossche and Zdouc, *The Law and Policy of the World Trade Organization*, 140.

156 For additional details on this process, see Bacchus, "The Case for a WTO Climate Waiver."

CHAPTER 12

1 Preamble, WTO Agreement.

2 Preamble, General Agreement on Tariffs and Trade.

3 Appellate Body Report, United States – Shrimp I, WT/DS59/AB/R (1998), paras. 152–53.

4 Article 3.2, WTO Dispute Settlement Understanding; Article 31.1, Vienna Convention on the Law of Treaties.

5 Article 31.2(c), Vienna Convention on the Law of Treaties.

6 Christina Voigt, *Sustainable Development as a Principle of International Law: Resolving Conflicts between Climate Measures and WTO Law* (Leiden and Boston: Martinus Nijhoff, 2009). See Arbitration Regarding the Iron Rhine ("Ijzeren Rijn") Railway between the Kingdom of Belgium and the Kingdom of the Netherlands, Arbitral Tribunal of the PCA, The Hague, 24 May 2005.

7 WTO Decision on Trade and Environment, GATT Doc. MTN/TNC/45/MIN (15 December 1993).

8 Ibid.

9 To date, the closest the Committee on Trade and Environment has come to any such decision had been to make recommendations to the General Council of the WTO on what items should be on the committee's agenda.

10 Paragraphs 31 and 32, Doha Declaration, WT/MIN(01)/DEC/1 (20 November 2001), adopted 14 November 2001.

11 Paragraph 51, Doha Declaration.

12 Paragraph 79, Addis Ababa Action Agenda.

13 Paragraph 82, Addis Ababa Action Agenda.

14 Appellate Body Report, United States – Shrimp I, para. 153.

15 John H. Jackson, "Justice Feliciano and the WTO Environmental Cases: Laying the Foundation of a 'Constitutional Jurisprudence' with Implications for Developing Countries," in Steve Charnovitz, Debra P. Steger, and Peter van den Bossche, eds., *Law in the Service of Human Dignity* (Cambridge: Cambridge University Press, 2005), 40.

16 Article 6.1, Paris Agreement.

17 Article 6,2, Paris Agreement.

18 Article 6.4, Paris Agreement.

19 IETA, "A Vision for the Market Provisions of the Paris Agreement" (Geneva: International Energy Trading Association, May 2016), 3, www.ieta.org/resources/UNFCCC/IETA_Article_6_Implementation_Paper_May2016.pdf.

20 Matthew Carr and Joe Ryan, "Tough to Keep the World from Warming When Carbon Is This Cheap," *Bloomberg News* (July 7, 2016).

21 IETA, "A Vision for the Market Provisions of the Paris Agreement," 4.

22 Ibid.

23 Robert N. Stavins, "Linkage of Regional, National, and Sub-National Policies in a Future International Climate Agreement," 286, https://voxeu.org/sites/default/files/file/stavins.pdf.

24 Camuzeaux et al., "Doubling Down on Carbon Pricing," 4.

25 Ibid.

26 David G. Victor, "Three-Dimensional Climate Clubs: Implications for Climate Cooperation and the G20" (Geneva: International Centre for Trade and Sustainable Development, August 2017).

27 E. Arcese and J. McDonald, "Multijurisdictional Approaches to Carbon Pricing: Integrating Design Elements for a Low Carbon Club," Workshop Report, Stanley Foundation (April 2016), 2.

28 Victor, "Three-Dimensional Climate Clubs."

29 Nigel Purvis, Samuel Grausz, and Andrew Light, "Carbon Market Crossroads: New Ideas for Harnessing Global Markets to Confront Climate Change" (Washington, D.C.: Center for American Progress, April 2013), 32.

30 See N. Keohane, A, Petsonk, and A. Hanafi, "Toward a Club of Carbon Markets" (October 15, 2015), https://link.springer.com/content/pdf/10.1007%2Fs10584-015-1506-z.pdf; and David G. Victor, "A Case for Climate Clubs," E15 Initiative, E15 Expert Group on Measures to Address Climate Change and the Trade System (Geneva: International Centre for Trade and Sustainable Development and World Economic Forum, October 2014).

31 See Article 7.2(c), UNFCCC.

32 See Keohane et al., "Toward a Club of Carbon Markets," and Victor, "A Case for Climate Clubs."

33 William D. Nordhaus, "A New Solution: The Climate Club," *New York Review of Books* (June 4, 2015).

34 Ibid.; see also William D. Nordhaus, "Climate Clubs: Overcoming Free-Riding in International Climate Policy," *American Economic Review*, Vol. 105, No. 4 (April 2015), 1339–70.

35 Nordhaus, "A New Solution: The Climate Club."

36 Eduardo Porter, "Climate Deal Badly Needs a Big Stick," *New York Times* (June 3, 2015).

37 For a thorough analysis of this threshold legal issue, see Felicity Deane, *Emissions Trading and WTO Law: A Global Analysis* (Cheltenham, UK, and Northampton, MA: Edward Elgar, 2015), chs. 4 and 5.

38 Rob Howse, "Securing Policy Space for Clean Energy Under the SCM Agreement: Alternative Approaches," E15 Initiative, E15 Clean Energy and the Trade System Group: Proposals and Analysis (Bali: International Centre for Trade and Sustainable Development and World Economic Forum, December, 2013), 50, 53.

39 Macaulay, Speech in the House of Commons in Support of the Ten Hour Bill. See the related discussion in Chapter 10.

40 Victor, *Global Warming Gridlock*, 28.

41 See Nicholas Stern, *The Economics of Climate Change: The Stern Review* (Cambridge: Cambridge University Press, 2007).

42 See Smith's discussion of "bounties" and especially of Scottish herring bounties: Smith, *The Wealth of Nations*, Book IV, Chapter V.

43 Ibid., Book IV, Chapter V.

44 Gary Horlick and Peggy A. Clarke, "Rethinking Subsidies Disciplines for the Future," E15 Initiative (Geneva: International Centre for Trade and Sustainable Development and World Economic Forum, 2016), 9.

45 I made these same observations in much the same words previously in James Bacchus, "World Trade Rules Need an Exemption for Green Energy," *International Business Times* (November 2, 2012), and in James Bacchus, "The Case for Clean Subsidies," *Harvard Business Review* (November 13, 2012).

46 Michael J. Trebilcock and Robert Howse, *The Regulation of International Trade* (London and New York: Routledge Press, 1995), 148.

47 Steve Charnovitz, "Green Subsidies and the WTO," Policy Research Working Paper 7060 (Washington, D.C.: World Bank, October 2014), 6.

48 Agreement on Subsidies and Countervailing Measures, April 15, 1994, Marrakesh Agreement Establishing the World Trade Organization, Annex 1A, 1869 UNTS 14 (1994).

49 Fay et al., "Decarbonizing Development," 80.

50 "Tackling the Folly of Fossil Fuel Subsidies," OECD Observer No. 304 (Paris: Organisation for Economic Co-operation and Development, November 2015).

51 Michael Kavanaugh, "Subsidy Support for 'Dirty' Fuels Across the World Still Exceeds That for Renewables," *Financial Times* (July 26, 2016).

52 World Bank, "Decarbonizing Development," 82, citing Arze del Granado, E. J. D. Coady, and R. Gillingham, "The Unequal Benefits of Fuel Subsidies: A Review of Evidence for Developing Countries," *World Development*, Vol. 40 (2012), 2234–48.

53 The New Climate Economy, "Better Growth, Better Climate," 178.

54 This IMF report is summarized in David Wessel, "Rethinking Energy Subsidies," *Wall Street Journal* (March 27, 2013).

55 Ibid.

56 "Tackling the Folly of Fossil Fuel Subsidies."

57 Damian Carrington, "Fossil Fuels Subsidized by $10m a Minute, Says IMF," *Guardian* (May 18, 2015).

58 David Wessel, "Rethinking Energy Subsidies," *Wall Street Journal* (March 27, 2013).

59 Goal 12, "Transforming Our World."

60 Target 12.c, "Transforming Our World."

61 The individual member states of the European Union were unable to sign because, under EU rules, they do not have the legal competence to do so.

62 Gary Horlick, "The WTO Subsidies Agreement Can Be Changed to Discipline Fossil Fuel Subsidies" (Geneva: International Centre for Trade and Sustainable Development, August 22, 2017).

63 Article 3, WTO Agreement on Subsidies and Countervailing Measures.

64 See Bacchus, "Global Rules for Mutually Supportive and Reinforcing Trade and Climate Regimes," 17. See also Joel P. Trachtman, "Fossil Fuel Subsidies and the World Trade Organization" (Geneva: International Centre for Trade and Sustainable Development, October 27, 2017).

65 Carbon Brief, "New BP Data Shows Emissions Flat in 2016 with Record Rise in Renewables" (June 15, 2016).

66 UNEP and Bloomberg New Energy Finance, "Global Trends in Renewable Energy Investment 2016," 11.

67 Ibid.

68 Carbon Brief, "New BP Data Shows Emissions Flat in 2016 with Record Rise in Renewables"; BP Statistical Review of World Energy 2017, www.bp.com/en/global/corporate/energy-economics/statistical-review-of-world-energy.html.

69 The New Climate Economy, "Better Growth, Better Climate," 141.

70 "Global Power Sector Emissions to Peak in 2026: Report," Reuters (June 16, 2016), citing Bloomberg New Energy Finance, "BNEF – New Energy Outlook 2017" (June 2017).

71 Michael Kavanaugh, "Subsidy Support for 'Dirty' Fuels Across the World Still Exceeds That for Renewables," *Financial Times* (July 26, 2016).

72 International Energy Agency, "World Energy Outlook 2014 Factsheet," www.worldenergyoutlook.org/media/weowebsite/2014/141112_WEO_FactSheets.pdf.

73 See Charnovitz, "Green Subsidies and the WTO," 17.

74 I owe the framing of this distinction in this way to one of the most insightful of the willing, Aaron Cosbey of the International Institute for Sustainable Development in Canada.

75 As prices of wind, solar, and other renewable energy sources continue to decline, the persuasiveness of this logic will diminish.

76 Irwin, *Against the Tide*, 117.

77 Ibid., 121.

78 Ibid., 128–30.

79 Article XVIII:4 and Sections A and D, General Agreement on Tariffs and Trade.

80 Quoted in Irwin, *Against the Tide*, 130.

81 Article 8, WTO Agreement on Subsidies and Countervailing Measures.

82 Article 6.1(c), WTO Agreement on Subsidies and Countervailing Measures.

83 See Appellate Body Report, Canada – Feed-in Tariff Program, WT/DS426/AB/R (2013).

84 See Gary Clyde Hufbauer et al., "Local Content Requirements: A Global Problem," in *Policy Analyses in International Economics* (Washington, D.C.: Peterson Institute of International Economics, 2013).

85 Thomas Cottier, "Renewable Energy and WTO Law: More Policy Space or Enhanced Disciplines?" E15 Initiative (Geneva: International Centre for Trade and Sustainable Development and World Economic Forum, 2015).

86 Howse, "Securing Policy Space for Clean Energy under the SCM Agreement," 50.

87 Fay et al., "Decarbonizing Development," 157.

88 See the discussion in Deane, *Emissions Trading and WTO Law*, 133–74.

89 "European Parliament Backs Post-2020 Carbon Market Reform," *Bridges Weekly*, Vol. 22, No. 4 (February 8, 2018).

90 Article 6.3, WTO Agreement on Subsidies and Countervailing Measures.

91 Whether Article XX of the GATT applies to the WTO subsidies agreement has not yet been clarified in WTO dispute settlement; negotiations contemplated on subsidies for services by Article XV of the GATS have not yet been pursued. See Deane, *Emissions Trading and WTO Law*, 171–73. See also Bacchus, "Global Rules for Mutually Supportive and Reinforcing Trade and Climate Regimes," 17.

92 See Article XX, General Agreement on Tariffs and Trade, and Article XIV, General Agreement on Trade in Services.

93 Michael Trebilcock and James S. F. Wilson, "Policy Analysis: The Perils of Picking Technological Winners in Renewable Energy Policy," Energy Probe (February 28, 2010).

94 Ibid., 31.

95 Ibid., 3–4.

96 Ibid., 27.

97 Ibid.

98 Ibid., 21–25.

99 Ibid., 22.

100 See Article 10.1, Paris Agreement, and Target 17.7, "Transforming Our World."

101 OECD, "Reframing Climate and Competitiveness: Is There a Need for Cooperation on National Climate Change Policies?" Background Paper for the 31st Round Table on Sustainable Development (Paris: Organisation for Economic Co-operation and Development, February 2–3, 2015), 17.

102 Report by the MIT Committee to Evaluate the Innovation Deficit, "The Future Postponed: Why Declining Investment in Basic Research Threatens a US Innovation Deficit" (Cambridge, Mass.: MIT, April 2015), v, ix.

103 "Our Common Future," Overview, Para. 58.

104 Peter Voser, "Energy for Economic Growth" (Davos: World Economic Forum, 2012), Preface, 2.

105 Rafael Leal-Arcas and Andre Filis, "The Fragmented Governance of the Global Energy Economy: A Legal-Institutional Analysis," *Journal of World Energy Law and Business*, Vol. 6 (July 19, 2013), 2, 4.

106 Rafael Leal-Arcas, "Trade Redemption: How Trade Agreements Can Help Decarbonise the Economy," Queen Mary University of London, School of Law Legal Research Paper No. 271/2018 (January 19, 2018), https://papers.ssrn.com/sol3/papers.cfm?abstract_id=3101665.

107 Ricardo Melendez-Ortiz, "Enabling the Energy Transition and Scale-Up of Clean Energy Technologies: Options for the Global Trade System," E15 Initiative, E15 Expert Group on Clean Energy Technologies and the Trade System, Policy Options Paper (Geneva: International Centre for Trade and Sustainable Development and World Economic Forum, January 2016), 5.

108 Ibid., 13.

109 Article 2b, Paris Agreement.

110 Goal 7, "Transforming Our World."

111 Target 7.2, "Transforming Our World."

112 I have also explored this possibility in Bacchus, "Triggering the Trade Transition."

113 The New Climate Economy, "Better Growth, Better Climate," 42.

114 These estimates by the International Finance Corporation were for 2012: Hari Manoharan and Madhavan Nampoothiri, "Using Trade Policy to Address Renewable Energy Access Challenges in Africa," *BioRes*, Vol. 8, No. 5 (June 2014), 16.

115 Leal-Arcas, "Trade Redemption," 5.

116 Amartya Sen, "Reducing Emissions Is Not Enough," *New Republic* (August 25, 2014).

117 Ibid.

118 See Melendez-Ortiz, "Enabling the Energy Transition and Scale-Up of Clean Energy Technologies."

119 Sonja Hawkins, "Use Trade Policy to Achieve the Benefits of Low Emission Development," LEDS in Practice (Geneva: International Centre for Trade and Sustainable Development, June 2016), 1–2.

120 See, in part for a slightly different view, Bernhard Potter, "TTIP in Green: Free Trade for Ostensibly Eco-Goods," *Green European Journal* (June 24, 2016).

121 Melendez-Ortiz, "Enabling the Energy Transition and Scale-Up of Clean Energy Technologies," 20.

122 Ibid., 9.

123 James Bacchus, "A Common Gauge: Harmonization and International Law," *Boston College International and Comparative Law Review*, Vol. 37, No. 1 (Winter 2014), 1–18.

124 OECD, "Reframing Climate and Competitiveness: Is There a Need for Cooperation on National Climate Change Policies?" Background Paper for the 31st Round Table on Sustainable Development (Paris: Organisation for Economic Co-operation and Development, February 2–3, 2015), 12. I was a participant in this roundtable discussion at the OECD.

125 Aaron Cosbey, "Are There Downsides to a Green Economy? The Trade, Investment, and Competitiveness Implications of Unilateral Green Economy Pursuit," Background Paper for Ad Hoc Expert Meeting on the Green Economy: Trade and Sustainable Development Implications (Geneva: UN Conference on Trade and Development, October 2010).

126 Agreement on Technical Barriers to Trade, April 15, 1994, Marrakesh Agreement Establishing the World Trade Organization, 1868 UNTS 120 (1994) (the "TBT Agreement").

127 Article 2.1 and 2.2, TBT Agreement.

128 Article 2.6, TBT Agreement.

129 Melendez-Ortiz, "Enabling the Energy Transition and Scale-Up of Clean Energy Technologies," 21; for a detailed discussion, see Yulia Selivanova, "Clean Energy and Access to Infrastructure: Implications for the Global Trade System," E15 Initiative (Geneva:

International Centre for Trade and Sustainable Development and World Economic Forum, 2015).

130 Lybecker and Lohse, "Innovation and Diffusion of Green Technologies," 10.

131 Ibid.

132 Agreement on Trade-Related Aspects of Intellectual Property Rights, April 15, 1994, Marrakesh Agreement Establishing the World Trade Organization, Annex 1C, 1869 UNTS 299, 33 ILM 1197 (1994) (the "TRIPS" Agreement). The TRIPS Agreement was concluded as one of the Uruguay Round trade agreements comprising the WTO treaty.

133 Article 7, TRIPS Agreement

134 Article 66.2, TRIPS Agreement. See Yulia Sulevinova, "The WTO and Energy: WTO Rules and Agreements Relevant to the Energy Sector," Issue Paper Number 1 (Geneva: International Conference on Trade and Sustainable Development, 2007), 24.

135 Helene de Coninck and Shikha Bhasin, "Meaningful Technology Development and Transfer: A Necessary Condition for a Viable Climate Regime," in Scott Barrett, Carlo Carraro, and Jaime de Melo, eds., *Towards a Workable and Effective Climate Regime* (London: Centre for Economic Policy Research and Ferdi, 2015), 451, 453, citing J. Haselip, U. Hansen, D. Puig, S. Traerup, and S. Dhar, "Governance, Enabling Frameworks and Policies for the Transfer and Diffusion of Low Carbon and Climate Adaptation Technologies in Developing Countries," Climatic Change, Vol. 131, Issue 3 (2015), 363–70.

136 World Trade Organization, "Telecommunications Services: Reference Paper. Negotiating Group on Basic Telecommunications Services" (April 24, 1996), https://www.wto.org/english/tratop_e/serv_e/telecom_e/tel23_e.htm.

137 Agreement on Government Procurement, revised (February 7, 2014), www.wto.org/english/tratop_e/gproc_e/gp_gpa_e.htm (the "Government Procurement Agreement").

CHAPTER 13

1 Klaus Schwab, *The Fourth Industrial Revolution* (Geneva: World Economic Forum, 2016), 6–7.

2 Ibid.

3 Ibid.

4 See the earlier discussion on global value chains in Chapter 6.

5 See Hubert Escaith, "Trade in Tasks and Global Value Chains: Stylized Facts and Implications" (Geneva: World Trade Organization, January 16, 2013); for some of the implications of the trade in tasks for international trade statistics, see Alejandro Jara, Keynote Speech to the World Input–Output Database Conference, in Vienna, Austria (May 26, 2010), https://wto.org/english/news_e/news10_e/devel_26may10_e.htm.

6 Smith, *The Wealth of Nations*, Book I, Chapter I.

7 See Sherry Stephenson, "Global and Regional Supply Chains: The Services Dimensions," United States Agency for International Development (USAID) Support for Economic Analysis Development in Indonesia (SEADI) Project and Nathan Associates (Washington, D.C.: USAID, April 2013); see also Patrick Low, "Rethinking Services in a Changing World," E15 Initiative, E15 Expert Group on Services, Policy Options Paper (Geneva:

International Centre for Trade and Sustainable Development and World Economic Forum, 2016).

8 Ronald Steenblik and Massimo Geloso Grosso, "Trade in Services Related to Climate Change: An Exploratory Analysis," OECD Trade and Environment Working Papers 2011/03 (Paris: Organisation for Economic Co-operation and Development, 2011).

9 Schwab, *The Fourth Industrial Revolution*, 64–66.

10 WTO, "World Trade Report 2015."

11 UNCTAD, "World Investment Report 2017," xiv.

12 Green Growth Action Alliance, "The Green Investment Report: The Ways and Means to Unlock Private Finance for Green Growth" (Geneva: World Economic Forum, 2013), 6.

13 Ibid., 11.

14 The New Climate Economy, "Seizing the Global Opportunity: Partnerships for Better Growth and a Better Climate" (Washington, D.C.: Global Commission on the Economy and Climate, July 2015), 43.

15 Ibid.

16 Editorial, "Many Countries Will Need Help Adapting to Climate Change," *New York Times* (August 8, 2016). See also Dino Grandoni, "How Much Investment Is Needed to Slow Global Warming? We're Not Even Close?," *Washington Post* (November 1, 2017).

17 "Battered by Climate Change, Small Islands Turn to Selling Passports," *Caribbean News* (July 24, 2016).

18 OECD, "Developing Co-operation Report 2016: The Sustainable Development Goals as Business Opportunities" (Paris: Organisation for Economic Co-operation and Development, 2016), 17.

19 Ibid., 17.

20 Homi Kharas and John MacArthur, "Mobilizing Private Investment for Post-2015 Sustainable Development: A Large Scale Task," Brookings (May 28, 2014).

21 Henry M. Paulson, Jr., "How to Raise Trillions for Green Investments," *New York Times* (September 20, 2016).

22 UNCSD Secretariat, "Finance for the Transition to a Green Economy in the Context of Sustainable Development and Poverty Eradication," Rio 2012 Issues Briefs No. 16 (New York: UN Commission on Sustainable Development, August 2012), 1.

23 Kharas and MacArthur, "Mobilizing Private Investment for Post-2015 Sustainable Development."

24 Ryan Dube, "The Andean Town at the Center of Peru's Pollution Dilemma," *Wall Street Journal* (July 31, 2016).

25 Smith, *The Wealth of Nations*, Book I, Chapter X. See the earlier discussion in Chapter 2.

26 Bhagwati, *In Defense of Globalization*, 149–50.

27 Renee Karunungan, "Who Gets to Influence the Climate Negotiations?," *Ecologist* (June 10, 2016); see also "Conflict of Interest: Private Companies in Climate Negotiations," *Climate Tracker* (May 25, 2016).

28 Karunungan, "Who Gets to Influence the Climate Negotiations?."

29 Ibid.

30 Karl P. Sauvant and Howard Mann, "Towards an Indicative List of FDI Sustainability Characteristics," E15 Initiative (Geneva: International Centre for Trade and Sustainable Development and World Economic Forum, February 2017), 2.

31 Ibid.

32 Principles 2 and 3, G20 Guiding Principles for Global Investment Policymaking.

33 UNCTAD, "Investment Policy Framework for Sustainable Development" (Geneva: UN Commission on Trade and Development, 2015), 30.

34 Ibid.

35 Ibid., 28.

36 Karl P. Sauvant, "The Evolving International Investment Law and Policy Regime: Ways Forward. Synthesis of the Policy Options," E15 Initiative (Geneva: International Centre for Trade and Sustainable Development and World Economic Forum, 2016), 5.

37 See OECD, "Policy Framework for Investment" (Paris: Organisation for Economic Co-operation and Development, 2015), 3, 11.

38 Howard Mann, "Reconceptualizing International Investment Law: Its Role in Sustainable Development," *Lewis and Clark Law Review*, Vol. 17, No. 2 (2013), 532.

39 Ibid.

40 UNCTAD, "Investment Policy Framework for Sustainable Development," 69.

41 See, for example, the discussion of the Santa Elena dispute in Costa Rica in Chapter 9.

42 Principle 3, G20 Guiding Principles for Global Investment Policymaking.

43 Collins, *An Introduction to International Investment Law*, 5; see Quiborax v. Bolivia, ICSID Case No. ARB/06/2, Decision on Jurisdiction (29 September 2012).

44 Mann, "Reconceptualizing International Investment Law," 534 (emphasis added). See Marie-Claire Condonnier Segger, Markus Gehring, and Andrew Newcombe, eds., *Sustainable Development in International Investment Law* (The Hague: Kluwer Law International, 2015).

45 Miles, *The Origins of International Investment Law*, 359. See Olivier de Schatter, Johann Swinnen, and Jan Wouters, eds., *Foreign Direct Investment: The Law and Economics of International Investment Agreements* (New York: Routledge Press, 2013).

46 Frank J. Garcia, "Investment Treaties Are About Justice," Columbia FDI Perspectives, No. 185 (October 24, 2016).

47 Ibid.

48 Saurabh Garg, "The Next Phase of IIA Reforms," Columbia FDI Perspectives, No. 200 (May 22, 2017).

49 ICC, "ICC Guidelines for International Investment," 18. As previously noted, I chaired the ICC group that drafted these guidelines.

50 Ibid., 7, 15.

51 Ibid., 15.

52 OECD, "OECD Guidelines for Multinational Enterprises" (Paris: Organisation for Economic Co-operation and Development, 2008); UN, "United Nations Global Compact" (New York: United Nations, 1999).

53 The Friends of the Earth, a leading environmental NGO, proposed their version of such an agreement in 2002, "Towards Binding Corporate Accountability," www.foei.org/en/corporate/accountability.html.

54 See Lorenzo Cotula, "Investment Treaties, Natural Resources and Regulatory Space: Technical Issues and Political Choice in International Investment Law," in Celine Tan and Julio Faundez, eds., *Natural Resources and Sustainable Development: International Economic Law Perspectives* (Cheltenham, UK, and Northampton, Mass.: Edward Elgar, 2017), 8–27.

55 Sauvant, "The Evolving International Investment Law and Policy Regime," 5.
56 Vinuales, *Foreign Investment and the Environment in International Law*, 341, citing Parkerings-Compagniet AS v. Republic of Lithuania, ICSID Case No. ARB/05/8, Award (11 September 2007), para. 332.
57 Mann, "Reconceptualizing International Investment Law," 532.
58 For a view that there *is* a "chilling effect," see Kyla Tienhaara, *The Expropriation of Environmental Governance* (Cambridge: Cambridge University Press, 2009), 262; for a view that there *is not* a "chilling effect," see Stephan Schill, "Do Investment Treaties Chill Unilateral State Regulation to Mitigate Climate Change?," *Journal of International Arbitration*, Vol. 24, No. 5 (2007), 469–77.
59 Vinuales, *Foreign Investment and the Environment in International Law*, 542. For a different view on current international investment agreements and the "right to regulate," see Kenneth J. Vandevelde, "IIA Provisions, Properly Interpreted, Are Fully Consistent with a Robust Regulatory State," Columbia FDI Perspectives, No. 216 (January 1, 2016).
60 As in Article 1114(2), NAFTA.
61 As in, for example, the Norwegian Model BIT, Article 24, Ministry of Trade and Industry, Norway (2008).
62 Principle 7, G20 Guiding Principles for Global Investment Policymaking.
63 "Creating Benefits for All: Driving Inclusive Growth Through Trade and Investment," B20 Taskforce, Trade and Investment, Policy Paper 2017, presented to the G20 at the G20 summit in Hamburg, Germany in July, 2017, 33. I have served as one of the B20 business advisers to the G20 group of leading economies on issues relating to trade and investment.
64 Ibid.
65 Karl P. Sauvant and Khalil Hamdani, "An International Support Programme for Sustainable Investment Facilitation," E15 Initiative, E15 Task Force on Investment Policy (Geneva: International Centre for Trade and Sustainable Development and World Economic Forum, July 2015), 3.
66 Ibid., 4.
67 "WTO Ministerial: In Landmark Move, Country Coalitions Set to Advance on New Issues," 2.
68 "Brazil Circulates Proposal for WTO Investment Facilitation Deal," *Bridges Weekly*, Vol. 22, No. 4 (February 8, 2018), Communication from Brazil, Structural Discussions on Investment Facilitation, WTO/JOB/GC/169 (February 1, 2018).
69 See Asa Romson, *Environmental Policy Space and International Investment Law* (Stockholm: Stockholm University Press, 2012), 243–82; Mann, "Reconceptualizing International Investment Law," 538–39; IISD, "Investment Treaties and Why They Matter to Sustainable Development: Questions and Answers" (Winnipeg, Canada: International Institute for Sustainable Development, 2012), 15; and Collins, *An Introduction to International Investment Law*, 161–68.
70 UNCTAD, "Investment Policy Framework for Sustainable Development," 79.
71 See Dolzer and Schreuer, *Principles of International Investment Law*, 186–90.
72 Collins, *An Introduction to International investment Law*, 97.
73 Ibid.
74 See the discussions on "likeness" under trade law in Chapters 9 and 11.

75 Vinuales, *Foreign Investment and the Environment in International Law*, 325. See also Miles, *The Origins of International Investment Law*, 355–56; and Howard Mann et al., "Model International Agreement on Investment for Sustainable Development" (Winnipeg, Canada: International Institute for Sustainable Development, 2005), Article 5 (E).

76 Dolzer and Schreuer, *Principles of International Investment Law*, 124–25.

77 Ibid., 119.

78 Romson, *Environmental Policy Space and International Investment Law*, 166; UNCTAD, "Investment Policy Framework for Sustainable Development," 80.

79 On the issue of "legitimate expectations," see Vinuales, *Foreign Investment and the Environment in International Law*, 350; and see Dolzer and Schreuer, *Principles of International Investment Law*, 124.

80 "G20 Leaders' Communique, Hangzhou Summit, 4–5 September 2016," www.fsb.org/wp-content/uploads/G20-Hangzhou-Leaders-Summit-Communique.pdf; "G20 Trade Ministers, Statement, 9–10 July 2016, Shanghai," http://trade.ec.europa.eu/doclib/docs/2016/july/tradoc_154788.pdf, Annex III, G20 Guiding Principles for Global Investment Policy-Making, www.oecd.org/direct/investment-policy/G20-Trade-Minister-Statement-July-2016.pdf.

81 Zhan, "G20 Guiding Principles for Global Investment Policymaking," 3. See also Rodrigo Polanco Lazo, "G20 International Investment Agreements and Guiding Principles for Global Investment Policymaking," E15 Initiative (Geneva: International Centre for Trade and Sustainable Development and World Economic Forum, November 2017).

82 Anna-Joubin Bret and Cristian Rodriguez Chiffelle, "G20 Guiding Principles for Global Investment Policy-Making: A Stepping Stone for Multilateral Rules on Investment," E15 Initiative (Geneva: International Centre for Trade and Sustainable Development and World Economic Forum, January 2017).

83 Preamble, G20 Guiding Principles for Global Investment Policy-Making.

84 Principles 1, 2, 3, and 4, G20 Guiding Principles for Global Investment Policy-Making.

85 Preamble, G20 Guiding Principles for Global Investment Policy-Making.

86 Principle 5, G20 Principles for Global Investment Policy-Making.

87 Concluding Paragraph, G20 Guiding Principles for Global Investment Policy-Making.

88 Sauvant and Mann, "Towards an Indicative List of FDI Sustainability Characteristics," 17; see also Daying Yan, "Performance Criteria for Sustainable FDI," E15 Initiative (Geneva: International Centre for Trade and Sustainable Development and World Economic Forum, February 2017).

89 Sauvant and Mann, "Towards an Indicative List of FDI Sustainability Characteristics," 6, 11.

90 "Transforming Our World."

91 Preface and Principle 5, G20 Guiding Principles for Global Investment Policy-Making.

92 See the earlier discussion of each of these aspects of investment obligations in Chapter 11. See also Schill, *The Multilateralization of International Investment Law*.

93 See Business and Industry Advisory Committee to the OECD (BIAC), "A Proactive Investment Agenda for 2016" (Paris: Organisation for Economic Co-operation and Development, 2016). I have been a participant in BIAC.

CHAPTER 14

1 See, for example, Alisa di Caprio and Kevin P. Gallagher, "The WTO and the Shrinking of Development Space: How Big Is the Bite?," *Journal of World Investment and Trade*, Vol. 7, No. 5 (October 2006), 781–804; Nagesh Kumar and Kevin P. Gallagher, "Relevance of 'Policy Space' for Development: Implications for Multilateral Trade Negotiations," RIS Discussion Paper, No. 120 (New Delhi: Research and Information System for Developing Countries, March 2007); Kevin P. Gallagher, ed., *Putting Development First: The Importance of Policy Space in the WTO and IFIs* (Chicago: Zed Books, 2005).

2 Dani Rodrik, "Put Globalization to Work for Democracies," *New York Times* (September 17, 2016). For extended expressions of his views, see Dani Rodrik, *Straight Talk on Trade: Ideas for a Sane World Economy* (Princeton: Princeton University Press, 2018), and Dani Rodrik, *The Globalization Paradox: Democracy and the Future of the World Economy* (New York: W. W. Norton, 2011). For a thoughtful critique, see Simon Lester, "Review of Dani Rodrik, 'The Globalization Paradox: Democracy and the Future of the World Economy,'" *World Trade Review*, Vol. 10 (2011), 409–17.

3 Rodrik, "Put Globalization to Work for Democracies."

4 Dani Rodrik, "Deglobalization Is a Chance to Make Good an Imbalance," *Financial Times* (October 6, 2016).

5 Ibid.

6 WTO, "World Trade Report 2010: Trade and Natural Resources" (Geneva: World Trade Organization, 2010), 69.

7 Robert Gilpin, *The Challenge of Global Capitalism: The World Economy in the 21st Century* (Princeton: Princeton University Press, 2000), 34.

8 Ibid., 35.

9 Ibid.

10 Quoted in "Dani Rodrik on Policy Space," Trade and Economic Law and Policy Blog, http://worldtradelaw.typepad.com/ielblog/2008/12/rodrik-on-policy-space.html.

11 On domestic-content requirements for energy, for instance, see OECD, "Aligning Policies for a Low-Carbon Economy," 131.

12 Dani Rodrik, "Straight Talk on Trade" (November 15, 2016), www.project-syndicate.org/commentary.

13 E15 Initiative, "Strengthening the Global Trade and Investment System in the 21st Century," 119.

14 Ibid. See notes 119 and 120 of this E15 report for a long list of empirical studies confirming this conclusion.

15 Ibid.

16 Ibid.

17 Article I and Article III, General Agreement on Tariffs and Trade 1994.

18 Paragraph 2, Annex on Financial Services, General Agreement on Trade in Services.

19 Articles 7 and 8, WTO TRIPS Agreement.

20 Article 2.1 and Article 2.2, WTO Agreement on Technical Barriers to Trade.

21 Article 2.6, WTO Agreement on Technical Barriers to Trade.

22 Article 2.1, WTO Agreement on the Application of Sanitary and Phytosanitary Measures, April 15, 1994, Marrakesh Agreement Establishing the World Trade Organization, Annex 1A, 1867 UNTS 493 (1994) (the "SPS Agreement").

23 Article 2.2 and Article 5.1, WTO Agreement on the Application of Sanitary and Phytosanitary Measures.

24 Article 2.3, WTO Agreement on the Application of Sanitary and Phytosanitary Measures.

25 ODI, "Policy Space: Are WTO Rules Preventing Development?," Briefing Paper 14 (London: Overseas Development Institute, January 2007), 1.

26 Rodrik, The Globalization Paradox, 255 (emphasis added).

27 Agreement on Safeguards, April 15, 1994, Marrakesh Agreement Establishing the World Trade Organization, Annex 1A, 1869 UNTS 154 (1994) (the "Safeguards Agreement").

28 Homage is due here to William Butler Yeats in his poem "The Second Coming." See Helen Gardner, ed., The New Oxford Book of English Verse, 1250–1950 (Oxford: Oxford University Press, 1972), 820–21.

29 Dani Rodrik, "There Is No Need to Fret About Deglobalisation," Financial Times (October 4, 2016).

30 Rodrik, The Globalization Paradox, 24–46.

31 Target 17.15, "Transforming Our World."

32 Preamble, WTO Agreement.

33 Report of the World Summit on Sustainable Development, 4 September 2002. A/CONF.199/20, Chapter I, item 1 Political Declaration, para. 5.

34 Sean B. Carroll, The Serengeti Rules: The Quest to Discover How Life Works and Why It Matters (Princeton: Princeton University Press, 2016), "Afterword: Rules to Live by," 204.

35 Principle 4, Rio Declaration on Environment and Development. See V. Baral and P.-M. Dupuy, "Principle 4: Sustainable Development Through Integration," in L.-A. Duvic Paoli and J. E. Vinuales, The Rio Declaration on Environment and Development: A Commentary (Oxford: Oxford University Press, 2015), 157–79.

36 John Schwartz, "A Milestone for Carbon Dioxide in the Atmosphere," New York Times (October 3, 2016).

37 Ibid.

38 United Nations, "Marrakech: Private Sector Commits to Actions on Sustainable Energy for a Just Climate Future for All" (November 11, 2016), https://news.un.org/en/story/2016/11/545132-marrakech-private-sector-commits-actions-sustainable-energy-just-climate-future; World Resources Institute, "New Public–Private Partnership Launched to Help Communities Bridge Gap Between Climate Data and Resiliency Planning" (September 26, 2016), wri.org/2016/9.

39 See www.weforum.org.

40 World Bank, "Carbon Pricing Leadership Coalition: Release of Official Work Plan" (January 29, 2016), www.worldbank.org/en/topic/climatefinance/brief/carbon-pricing-leadership-coalition.

41 Rida Bilgrami, "The Evolving Private Sector Response to Climate Change Post-Paris Agreement" (June 30, 2016), http://sustainability.com/our-work/insights/.

42 Ibid.

43 "Bill Gates Launches $1 Billion Breakthrough Energy Investment Fund," Forbes (December 12, 2016).

44 WEF, "The Global Risks Report 2016: 11th Edition," 46.

45 Byron Tau and Amy Harder, "Paris Climate Treaty to Take Effect in November," Reuters (October 5, 2016).

46 Alister Doyle, "Governments Seek Rules for Paris Climate Deal; Temperatures Soar," Reuters (May 16, 2016).

47 See Article 4, Paris Agreement.

48 See Article 13, Paris Agreement.

49 See Article 6, Paris Agreement.

50 See Article 15, Paris Agreement.

51 Center for Climate and Energy Solutions, "Outcomes of the UN Climate Change Conference in Bonn" (Arlington, Va.: CCES, November 2017).

52 Brad Plumer, "At Bonn Climate Talks, Stakes Get Higher in Gamble on Climate's Future," *New York Times* (November 19, 2017).

53 Ibid.

54 This point was made by Jacob Werksman, the lead European climate negotiator in Paris, at a conference sponsored in London by the Global Governance Institute of University College London on November 25, 2016.

55 David G. Victor, Charles F. Kennel, and Veerabhadran Ramanathan, "The Climate Threat We Can Beat: What It Is and How to Deal With It," *Foreign Affairs* (May/June, 2012), 113. See also, on aerosols, Veerabhadran Ramanathan, Jessica Seddon, and David G. Victor, "The Next Front on Climate Change: How to Avoid a Dimmer, Drier World," *Foreign Affairs* (March/April 2016), 135–42.

56 "The Montreal Protocol: To Coldly Go," *Economist* (September 24, 2016).

57 1522 UNTS 28 (16 September 1987).

58 Henry Fountain, "Ozone Hole Shows Signs of Shrinking, Scientists Say," *New York Times* (June 30, 2016).

59 Annie Sneed, "Wait – the Ozone Layer Is Still Declining?," *Scientific American* (February 6, 2018), www.scientificamerican.com/article/wait-the-ozone-layer-is-still-declining1/.

60 Robert Lee Hotz, "Ozone Layer May Be Thinning over Earth's Heavily Populated Areas," *Wall Street Journal* (February 6, 2018).

61 "The Montreal Protocol: To Coldly Go." See an international study published in June 2016, in the journal *Science* http://science.sciencemag.org/content/early/2016/06/30/science.aae0061.

62 See www.pnas.org/content/106/27/10949. See also "Why a UN Climate Deal on HFCs Matters," Carbon Brief (October 10, 2016), https://carbonbrief.org/explainer.

63 Coral Davenport, "Nations, Fighting Powerful Refrigerant That Warms Planet, Reach Landmark Deal," *New York Times* (October 15, 2016); Chris Mooney, "The World Just Took Another Huge Step Forward on Fighting Climate Change," *Washington Post* (October 15, 2016).

64 These are the projections of the National Resources Defense Council. See Davenport, "Nations, Fighting Powerful Refrigerant That Warms the Planet, Reach Landmark Deal."

65 Alister Doyle, "Benefits of Greenhouse Gas Pact May Fall Short of High Hopes," Reuters (October 16, 2016).

66 Article 4, Montreal Protocol on Substances that Deplete the Ozone Layer, 16 September 1987, 1522 UNTS 29; Ellen Hey, "International Institutions," in Bodansky et al., eds., *Oxford Handbook of International Economic Law*, 749–66.

67 For an excellent explanation of the trade sanctions in the Montreal Protocol, and of their relationship with WTO trade obligations, see Scott Barrett, "Climate Change and International Trade: Lessons on Their Linkage from International Environmental Agreements," a paper delivered at a conference on "Thinking Ahead on International Trade" held at the World Trade Organization, Geneva, Switzerland, June 16–18, 2010.

68 Article XX, General Agreement on Tariffs and Trade.

69 See the earlier discussion of international aviation and shipping emissions in Chapter 3.

70 ICAO, "Carbon Offsetting and Reduction Scheme for International Aviation (CORSIA)" (October 6, 2016). See the earlier discussion in Chapter 3.

71 Megan Darby, "Offshore Carbon: Why a Climate Deal for Shipping Is Sinking," *Climate Change News* (July 15, 2016).

72 Jonathan Saul, "Shipping Braces for Pollution Tax After Paris Talks," Reuters (November 2, 2015). See the earlier discussion in Chapter 3.

73 Adopted in 2011 and entering into force in 2013, the regulations are in the form of amendments to the International Convention for the Prevention of Pollution from Ships (MARPOL) and are set out in a new chapter of MARPOL, Annex VI.

74 Spencer Jakab, "An Energy Shock from the High Seas," *Wall Street Journal* (June 7, 2017).

75 Arthur Nelsen, "Delay to Curbs on Toxic Shipping Emissions Would Cause 200,000 Extra Premature Deaths," *Guardian* (October 7, 2016) (citing an unpublished IMO study).

76 "UN Shipping Agency Announces Plans for Developing Emissions Reduction Strategy," *Bridges Weekly*, Vol. 20, No. 37 (November 3, 2016), 7–9.

77 Aldo Chircop and Meinhard Doelle, "Is the Shipping Industry Doing Its Fair Share in the Global Response to Climate Change" (Waterloo, Canada: Centre for International Governance Innovation, October 4, 2017).

78 ICAO, "Carbon Offsetting and Reduction Scheme for International Aviation (CORSIA)."

79 Pierre-Marie Dupuy and Jorge E. Vinuales, *International Environmental Law* (Cambridge: Cambridge University Press, 2015), 101.

80 High-Level Political Forum on Sustainable Development, "2017 Voluntary National Reviews: Synthesis Report" (New York: United Nations, February 2018), vi.

81 United Nations, "The Sustainable Development Goals Report 2017" (New York: United Nations, July 2017).

82 Ibid., 1.

83 Ibid., 3.

84 Ibid., 2.

85 Ibid., 3.

86 Ibid., 1.

87 Ibid., 2.

88 Ibid., 3.

89 Ibid., 4.

90 Ibid., Foreword, i.

91 Michael D. Shear, "Trump Will Withdraw US from Paris Climate Agreement," *New York Times* (June 1, 2017); Elle Hunt, "Paris Climate Agreement: World Reacts as Trump Pulls Out of Global Accord – As It Happened," *Guardian* (June 2, 2017).

92 Brad Plumer, "The US Can't Leave the Paris Climate Deal Just Yet," *New York Times* (June 8, 2017).

93 John Wagner, "By Upending Paris Accord, Trump Buoys His Base," *Washington Post* (June 4, 2017).

94 Article 28.1, Paris Agreement.

95 Article 28.2, Paris Agreement.

96 Statement of the President of the United States in the Rose Garden of the White House (June 1, 2017).

97 EIA, "US Energy-Related CO$_2$ Emissions Expected to Rise Slightly in 2018, Remain Flat in 2019" (Washington, D.C.: US Energy Information Administration, February 8, 2017), www.eia.gov/todayinenergy/detail.php?id=34872.

98 Steven Mufson, "States, Firms Vow to Press Ahead with Climate Policies," *Washington Post* (June 2, 2017).

99 Peter Henderson, "California to Discuss Linking Carbon Market with China," Reuters (June 2, 2017).

100 Alejandro Lazo, "US States Defy Trump's Climate Pact Withdrawal," *Wall Street Journal* (June 3, 2017).

101 Wagner, "By Upending Paris Accord, Trump Buoys His Base."

102 Union of Concerned Scientists, "Environmental Impacts of Natural Gas," www.ucsusa.org/clean-energy/coal-and-other-fossil-fuels/environmental-impacts-of-natural-gas#.WpoVciOcZBw.

103 EIA, "US Energy-Related Carbon Dioxide Emissions, 2016" (Washington, D.C.: US Energy Information Administration, 2017), 2.

104 Wagner, "By Upending Paris Accord, Trump Buoys His Base."

105 Ed Crooks, "Trump Paris Deal Pullout Faces US States' Backlash," *Financial Times* (June 5, 2017).

106 Brad Plumer, "Q & A: The Paris Climate Accord," *New York Times* (June 1, 2017).

107 Fiji: H.E. Mr. Josaia Voreqe Bainimarama, Prime Minister, "General Assembly of the United Nations" (September 20, 2017), https://gadebate.un.org/en/72/fiji.

108 For an excellent overview, see Brady Dennis and Chris Mooney, "Countries Made Only Modest Climate-Change Promises in Paris: They're Falling Short Anyway," *Washington Post* (February 20, 2018).

109 "Action by China and India Slows Emissions Growth, President Trump's Policies Likely to Cause US Emissions to Flatten," Report by Climate Action Tracker (May 15, 2017), http://climateactiontracker.org/assets/publications/briefing_papers/CAT_2017-05-15_Briefing_India-China-USA.pdf.

110 Fred Pearce, "With the US out of Paris, What Is the Future for Global Climate Fight?," Yale Environment 360 (June 8, 2017).

111 Annie Gowen and Simon Denyer, "China and India Have the Will – But Not the Resources – to Lead on Climate," *Washington Post* (June 2, 2017).

112 Somini Sengupta, Melissa Eddy, and Chris Buckley, "As Trump Exits Paris Agreement, Other Nations Are Defiant," *New York Times* (June 2, 2017).

113 Stian Reklev, "China Finalizes Allowance Allocation Plans for World's Biggest Carbon Market," Reuters (October 24, 2016); Chris Buckley, "Xi Jinping Is Set for a Big Gamble with China's Carbon Trading Market," *New York Times* (June 23, 2017).

114 Edward Wong, "China Poised to Take Lead on Climate After Trump's Move to Undo Policies," *New York Times* (March 30, 2017); Brad Plumer, "At Bonn Climate Talks, Stakes Are Higher in Gamble on Planet's Future," *New York Times* (November 19, 2017).

115 Barbara Demick, "In China, Millions Make Themselves at Home in Caves," *Los Angeles Times* (March 18, 2012); "Six Times More People Currently Live in Caves in China Alone Than Lived in Caves All over the World During the Stone Age," *Washington's Blog* (February 24, 2015).

116 Gowen and Denyer, "China and India Have the Will – But Not the Resources – to Lead on Climate."

117 Climate Action Tracker, "Improvement in Warming Outlook as India and China Move Ahead, But Paris Agreement Gap Still Looms Large" (November 2017), http://climateac tiontracker.org/news/287/Improvement-in-warming-outlook-as-India-and-China-move-ahead-but-Paris-Agreement-gap-still-looms-large.html.

118 Brad Plumer, "Meeting the Paris Climate Goals Was Always Hard: Without the US, It Is Far Harder," *New York Times* (June 3, 2017).

119 Heckyong Yang, Jane Chung, and Alister Doyle, "Climate Fund Criticized by Trump Has Slow, Complex Start," Reuters (June 13, 2017).

120 Fred Pearce, "With the US out of Paris, What Is the Future for the Climate Fight?," Yale Environment 360 (June 8, 2017) (citing a study by Joeri Rogelj of the International Institute for Applied Systems Analysis in Austria).

121 Brad Plumer, "At Bonn Climate Talks, Stakes Get Higher in Gamble on Planet's Future," *New York Times* (November 19, 2017).

122 Ibid.

123 Articles 20 and 21, Paris Agreement.

CHAPTER 15

1 Millennium Ecosystem Assessment, "Ecosystems and Human Well-Being," Synthesis (Washington, D.C.: Island Press, 2005), 26.

2 Goal 2, "Transforming Our World."

3 Target 2.1, "Transforming Our World."

4 Preface, Paris Agreement.

5 Article 2.1(b), Paris Agreement.

6 FAO, "The State of Food and Agriculture: Climate Change, Agriculture and Food Security" (Rome: UN Food and Agriculture Organization, 2016), 93.

7 Georgina Gustin, "2017: Agriculture Begins to Tackle Its Role in Climate Change," *Climate Change News* (January 4, 2017).

8 FAO, "The State of Food and Agriculture," xiii.

9 "What's on the Table? Mitigating Agricultural Emissions While Achieving Food Security," Climate Action Tracker (January 2018), 1, http://climateanalytics.org/publications/2018/whats-on-the-table-mitigating-agricultural-emissions-while-achieving-food-security.html.

10 Ibid.

11 Sachs, *The Age of Sustainable Development*, 205.

12 Ibid., 339; Sustainable Development Solutions Network Thematic Group on Sustainable Agriculture and Food Security, "Solutions for Sustainable Agriculture and Food Systems:

Technical Report for the Post-2015 Development Agenda" (New York: Sustainable Development Solutions Network, 2013).

13 See Shenggen Fan, "Food Policy in 2015–2016: Reshaping the Global Food System for Sustainable Development," in "Global Food Policy Report 2016" (Washington, D.C.: International Food Policy Research Institute, 2016), 7.

14 Ibid., 6.

15 FAO, "The State of Food and Agriculture," xi.

16 Sachs, *The Age of Sustainable Development*, 207.

17 Target 2.2, "Transforming Our World."

18 Target 2.3, "Transforming Our World."

19 Target 2.4, "Transforming Our World."

20 Target 2.5, "Transforming Our World."

21 Target 2.b, "Transforming Our World" (emphasis added).

22 Ibid.

23 Ibid.

24 David Blandford, "Climate Change Mitigation and Adaptation," E15 Initiative, E15 Agriculture and Food Security Group: Proposals and Analysis (Bali: International Centre for Trade and Sustainable Development and World Economic Forum, December 2013), 69.

25 Anne Biewald et al., "The Impact of Climate Change on Costs of Food and People Exposed to Hunger at Subnational Scale," PIK Report No. 128 (Potsdam: Potsdam Institute for Climate Impact Research, October 2015), 42, 55. It should be noted that the authors of the study went on to say, "However, our results show that trade liberalization could have some negative local effects. In such regions, international trade liberalization should be accompanied by national policy measures, e.g. food aid or favorable terms for agricultural exports" (ibid., 42). As they acknowledged, this has already been agreed by the members of the WTO in the "Decision on Measures Concerning the Possible Negative Effects of the Reform Programme on Least-Developed and Net Food-Importing Developing Countries," which is part of the WTO treaty.

26 Blandford, "Climate Change Mitigation and Adaptation," 69–70.

27 Target 2.b, "Transforming Our World."

28 FAO, "The State of Food and Agriculture," xvi.

29 Jean-Christophe Bureau and Sebastien Jean, "Do Yesterday's Disciplines Fit Today's Farm Trade?," E15 Initiative, E15 Agriculture and Food Security Group: Proposals and Analysis (Bali: International Centre for Trade and Sustainable Development and World Economic Forum, December 2013), 18, 27; in 2015, the OECD countries spent $211 billion, and the non-OECD countries spent $352 billion on agricultural subsidies: FAO, "The State of Food and Agriculture," 96.

30 Agreement on Agriculture, April 15, 1994, Marrakesh Agreement Establishing the World Trade Organization, Annex 1A, 1867 UNTS 410 (1994) (the "Agriculture Agreement"), Annex 2, paragraphs 1 and 12.

31 FAO, "The State of Food and Agriculture," xvi.

32 OECD, "Aligning Policies for a Low-Carbon Economy," 213–14.

33 FAO, "Food Wastage Footprint: Impacts on Natural Resource. Summary Report" (Rome: UN Food and Agriculture Organization, 2013), www.fao.org/docrep/018/i3347e/i3347e.pdf.

34 Ceren Hic, Diego Rybski, Prajal Pradhan, and Jurgen P. Kropp, "Food Surplus and Its Climate Burdens," *Environmental Science and Technology*, Vol. 50, No. 8 (2016), 4269–77.

35 "What's on the Table?," 5–6.

36 European Commission, "European Commission Date Marking Infographic" (2016), https://ec.europa.eu/food/sites/food/files/safety/docs/fw_eu_actions_date_marking_infographic_en.pdf.

37 "What's on the Table?," 6.

38 Ibid.

39 Target 12.3, "Transforming Our World."

40 "In Landmark Shift, New UN Work Programme to Address Agriculture Emissions Under Climate Action Framework," *Bridges Weekly*, Vol. 21, No. 41 (December 7, 2017), 6–10.

41 Ibid., 10.

42 Ibid., 9.

43 Ibid.

44 Sachs, *The Age of Sustainable Development*, 328.

45 OECD, "Aligning Policies for a Low-Carbon Economy," 206.

46 Goal 15, "Transforming Our World."

47 Target 15.1, "Transforming Our World."

48 Sachs, *The Age of Sustainable Development*, 328.

49 The New Climate Economy, "Better Growth, Better Climate," 108.

50 Nigel Purvis, "Breaking the Link Between Commodities and Climate Change" (Washington, D.C.: Climate Advisers, 2013), 1.

51 FAO, "State of the World's Forests 2016" (Rome: UN Food and Agriculture Organization, 2016), 14.

52 Target 15.2, "Transforming Our World."

53 Article 5, Paris Agreement.

54 James Bacchus, "Indonesian Forest Plan May Be Breakthrough on Climate Change," *Huffington Post* (May 24, 2011).

55 Anja Eikermann, *Forests in International Law: Is There Really a Need for an International Forest Convention?* (London: Springer, 2015).

56 David Humphreys, *Logjam: Deforestation and the Crisis of Global Governance* (London: Routledge, 2006), 213.

57 International Tropical Timber Agreement (1983), adopted in Geneva, 18 November 1983, and entered into force 1 April 1985, 1393 UNTS 671. The most recent iteration is International Tropical Timber Agreement (2006), adopted in Geneva, 27 January 2006, entered into force 7 December 2011, UN Doc. TD/TIMBER.3.12 (ITTA 2006).

58 Article 1(a), International Tropical Timber Agreement.

59 Eikermann, *Forests in International Law*, 77–78.

60 Report of the UN Conference on Environment and Development, Rio de Janeiro, 3–14 June 1992, Annex III: Non-Legally Binding Authoritative Statement of Principles for a Global Consensus on the Management, Conservation and Sustainable Development of all Types of Forests, UN Doc. A/CONF.151.26 (Vol. III), 14 August 1992 (the "Forest Principles").

61 Principle 2(b), the Forest Principles.

62 Principle 13, the Forest Principles.

63 Eikermann, *Forests in International Law*, 121–26.

64 Article 5.1, Paris Agreement.

65 Article 5.2, Paris Agreement.

66 Goal 1, New York Declaration on Forests (September 2014), Section 1, www.un.org/climatechange/summit/wp-content/uploads/sites/2/2014/07/New-York-Declaration-on-Forest—Action-Statement-and-Action-Plan.pdf.

67 Richard Saines and Marisa Martin, "REDD+ Market and the Road to Paris," in IETA, "2014 Report: Markets Matter" (Washington, D.C.: International Emissions Trading Association, 2014), 34.

68 Robert-Jan Bartunek and Agnieszka Barteczko, "EU Court Advisers Back Commission in Forest Dispute with Poland," Reuters (February 21, 2018).

69 "Congo Approves Logging near Carbon-Rich Peatlands," Reuters (February 21, 2018).

70 OECD, "Aligning Policies for a Low-Carbon Economy," 217.

71 Ibid.

72 Eikermann, *Forests in International Law*, 82.

73 Lars H. Gulbrandsen and Ole Kristian Fauchald, "Assessing the New York Declaration on Forests from a Trade Perspective," *BioRes*, Vol. 9, No. 4 (May 2015), 4–7; Purvis, "Breaking the Link Between Commodities and Climate Change," 6.

74 Gulbrandsen and Fauchald, "Assessing the New York Declaration on Forests from a Trade Perspective," 5.

75 See The New Climate Economy, "Better Growth, Better Climate," 108; Paige McClanahan, "The Lacey Act: Timber Trade Enforcement Gets Some Teeth," *BioRes*, Vol. 4, No. 1 (March 22, 2010), 11–12; and the Forest Legality Alliance website, www.forestlegality.org.

76 Purvis, "Breaking the Link Between Commodities and Climate Change," 7.

77 Ibid., 5–6; see also McClanahan, "The Lacey Act."

78 Purvis, "Breaking the Link Between Commodities and Climate Change," 7–12.

79 Article 2.1, Article 2.2, and Annex 1.1, Agreement on Technical Barriers to Trade.

80 Annex 1.2, Agreement on Technical Barriers to Trade.

81 These certifications include those of the Forest Stewardship Council (FSC), the Programme for the Endorsement of Forest Certification (PEFC), and the Roundtable on Sustainable Palm Oil (RSPO). These private and "multi-stakeholder" certification efforts have not, however, escaped criticism. They have sometimes been accused of not going far enough or fast enough in slowing deforestation. For example, on the RSPO, see Oliver Blach, "Sustainable Palm Oil: How Successful Is RSPO Certification?," *Guardian* (July 4, 2013).

82 The New Climate Economy, "Better Growth, Better Climate," 286–87. See http://www.tfa2020.com.

83 Goal 17 and Targets 17.16 and 17.17, "Transforming Our World."

84 More precisely, 70.8 percent.

85 Jose Marie Figueres, Pascal Lamy, and John D. Podesta, "Our Oceans Need Protecting: This Is How We Can Help" (Geneva: World Economic Forum, February 17, 2017), www.weforum.org/agenda/2017/02.

86 Ibid.

87 WWF International, "Living Blue Planet Report: Species, Habitats and Human Well-Being" (Gland, Switzerland: WWF International, 2015), 33; Carbon Brief (March 15, 2017), www.carbonbrief.org/rate-ocean-warming-quadrupled-since-late-twentiteth-century.

88 F. Whitmarsh, J. Zika, and A. Cazaja, "Ocean Heat Uptake and the Global Surface Temperature Record," Grantham Institute on Climate Change and the Environment, Imperial College London, Briefing Paper No. 14 (London: Grantham Institute, 2015).

89 D. Laffoley and J. M. Baxter, "Explaining Ocean Warming: Causes, Scale, Effects and Consequences" (Gland, Switzerland: International Union on the Conservation of Nature and Natural Resources, September 2016), 10. See Oliver Milman, "Soaring Ocean Temperature Is 'Greatest Hidden Challenge of Our Generation,'" *Guardian* (September 5, 2016); Alister Doyle, "Global Warming Disrupts Oceans, Seen Lingering in Their Depths," Reuters (September 5, 2016).

90 Laffoley and Baxter, eds., "Explaining Ocean Warming," 17.

91 Ibid., 10.

92 OECD, "The Ocean Economy in 2030" (Paris: Organisation for Economic Co-operation and Development, 2016), 88.

93 Tom Bawden, "Not Only Is the Sea Level Rising – It's Doing So at an Accelerating Rate," iNews (August 11, 2016), http://inews.co.uk/essentials/news/. The first satellite measurements were taken by the TOPEX/Poseiden measurement satellite.

94 Laffoley and Baxter, eds., "Explaining Ocean Warming," 10.

95 WWF International, "Living Blue Planet Report," 46.

96 Ibid., 33.

97 See www.indianriverlagoon.org and Audubon, "Crisis in the Indian River Lagoon: Solutions for an Imperiled Ecosystem," http://fl.audubon.org/crisis-indian-river-lagoon-solutions-imperiled-ecosystem.

98 IGBP, "Ocean Acidification: Summary for Policymakers. Third Symposium on the Ocean in a High-CO_2 World" (Stockholm: International Geosphere-Biosphere Programme, 2013).

99 Alister Doyle, "Oceans Suffer Silent Storm of Acidification: International Study," Reuters (November 14, 2013).

100 Laffoley and Baxter, eds., "Explaining Ocean Warming," 10.

101 Ibid., 13.

102 Editorial, "The Marine New World: Deep Trouble," *Economist* (May 27, 2017).

103 WWF International, "Living Blue Planet Report," 6.

104 Alister Doyle, "Toxins Found in Creatures Even in Deepest Part of Oceans: Study," Reuters (February 13, 2017), citing a study by scientists mainly from the University of Aberdeen in Scotland.

105 WWF International, "Living Blue Planet Report," 45.

106 Ibid.

107 United Nations, "Life Below Water: Why It Matters," www.un.org/sustainabledevelopment/wp-content/uploads/2016/08/14_Why-it-Matters_Goal-14_Life-Below-Water_3p.pdf.

108 Editorial, "The Marine World: Deep Trouble," *Economist* (May 27, 2017); Preamble, Paris Agreement.

109 "Analysis: 'This Gets Us in the Game,'" Scripps Oceanography at COP21 (December 18, 2015).

110 Goal 14, "Transforming Our World."

111 Target 14.2, "Transforming Our World."

112 Here I am quoting Lisa Levin, a biological oceanographer at the Scripps Institute of Oceanography at the University of California San Diego, from "Analysis: 'This Gets Us in the Game.'"

113 Declaration, "Our Ocean, Our Future: Call for Action," United Nations Ocean Conference, A/CONF.230/11, (June 9, 2017); see also "193 Nations Urge Action to Protect Oceans Despite US Withdrawal from Paris Agreement," Australian Broadcasting Company (June 10, 2017), www.abc.net.au/news/2017-06-10/193-nations-urge-action-to-protect-oceans/8607390.

114 Declaration, "Our Ocean, Our Future: Call for Action."

115 OECD, "The Ocean Economy in 2030," 227.

116 Ibid.

117 Editorial, "Net Positive: How to Stop Overfishing on the High Seas," *Economist* (July 16, 2016).

118 Target 14.5, "Transforming Our World."

119 Michelle Innis, "Coast of Antarctica Will Host World's Largest Marine Reserve," *New York Times* (October 27, 2016).

120 Brian Clark Howard, "World's Largest Marine Reserve Created Off Antarctica," *National Geographic* (October 27, 2016).

121 "UN Committee Begins Work on High Seas Biodiversity Pact," *BioRes* (April 13, 2016).

122 Global Ocean Commission, "The Future of Our Ocean: Next Steps and Priorities. Report 2016" (Oxford, UK, February 2016), 22.

123 Target 14.1, "Transforming Our World."

124 Urmi Goswami, "The Plastic Menace: How Mankind Is Treating Oceans as a Global Trash Can," *Economic Times* (May 27, 2017); see also Dani Cooper, "Remote South Pacific Island Has Highest Levels of Plastic Rubbish in the World," ABC Science (May 16, 2017).

125 WWF International, "Living Blue Planet Report," 38, citing M. Erickson et al., "Plastic Pollution in the World's Oceans: More than 5 Trillion Plastic Pieces Weighing over 250,000 Tons Afloat at Sea," *PLoS ONE*, Vol. 9, No. 12 (2014).

126 Eleanor Goldberg, "Margaret Atwood Has Some Fixes for a Crisis That's Slowly 'Killing Us,'" *Huffington Post* (June 6, 2017).

127 WEF, "The New Plastics Economy: Rethinking the Future of Plastics" (Geneva: World Economic Forum, January 2016), 7.

128 Ibid., 8.

129 Target 14.a, "Transforming Our World."

130 Jim Leape, "Technology Can Help Us to Save Our Oceans: Here Are Three Reasons Why" (Geneva: World Economic Forum, April 20, 2017), https://weforum.org/agenda/2017/04.

131 Ibid.

132 Rothwell and Stephens, *The International Law of the Sea*, 342.

133 Target 14.c, "Transforming Our World." See the discussion of UNCLOS in Chapter 7.

134 Paragraph 158, "The Future We Want."
135 Paragraph 159, "The Future We Want."
136 "Our Ocean, Our Future: Call to Action."
137 Global Ocean Commission, "The Future of Our Ocean: Next Steps and Priorities. Report 2016," 5; Global Ocean Commission, "From Decline to Recovery: A Rescue Package for the Ocean" (Oxford, UK, June 2014).
138 OECD, "The Ocean Economy in 2030," 223–24.
139 Ibid.
140 "US Backs Plan to Save Oceans But Notes Plan to Quit Climate Deal," Reuters (June 10, 2017).
141 "Branson Petitions UN for Protection of Oceans," *Straits Times* (June 10, 2017).
142 Ocean Studies Board and National Resource Council, *Marine Protection Areas: Tools for Sustaining Ocean Ecosystems* (Washington, D.C.: National Academies Press, 2001), 2. See also Chelsea Harvey, "Human Impact on the Oceans Is Growing – and Climate Change Is the Biggest Culprit," *Washington Post* (July 14, 2015). See as well Chapter 2, "How Climate Change Alters Ocean Chemistry," and Chapter 5, "Climate Change Impacts on Marine Ecosystems," in "World Ocean Review: Living with the Oceans" (Kiel, Germany: Maribus, 2010), 28–55 and 102–119.
143 See James Bacchus, "Groping Toward Grotius: The WTO and International Law," in Bacchus, *Trade and Freedom*, 451.
144 U. Rashid Sumaila, "Trade Policy Options for Sustainable Oceans and Fisheries," E15 Initiative, E15 Expert Group on Oceans, Fisheries and the Trade System, Policy Options Paper (Geneva: International Centre for Trade and Sustainable Development and World Economic Forum, 2016), 6. See generally World Bank, "Fish to 2030: Prospects for Fisheries and Aquaculture," Report 83177-GLB (Washington, D.C.: World Bank, 2013).
145 Sumaila, "Trade Policy Options for Sustainable Oceans and Fisheries."
146 "Ocean Fishing: All the Fish in the Sea," *Economist* (May 27, 2017).
147 Editorial, "The Marine World: Deep Trouble," *Economist* (May 27, 2017).
148 Sumaila, "Trade Policy Options for Sustainable Oceans and Fisheries," 10.
149 E15 Initiative, "Strengthening the Global Trade and Investment System in the 21st Century," 96, citing the FAO.
150 Christopher Costello et al., "Global Fishery Prospects Under Contrasting Management Regimes," *Proceedings of the National Academy of Sciences* (March 29, 2016); see also Editorial, "How to Save the World's Fisheries," *Washington Post* (March 29, 2016).
151 Sumaila, "Trade Policy Options for Sustainable Oceans and Fisheries," 6; Tim Flannery, *Here on Earth: A Natural History of the Planet* (New York: Atlantic Monthly Press, 2010), 47. See also Wilson, *Half-Earth*, 67–78.
152 "Ocean Fishing: All the Fish in the Sea."
153 Target 14.6, "Transforming Our World."
154 Target 14.4, "Transforming Our World."
155 Sumaila, "Trade Policy Options for Sustainable Oceans and Fisheries," 6.
156 Ibid., 8, citing the FAO.
157 Dupuy and Vinuales, *International Environmental Law*, 163.
158 Editorial, "Net Positive: How to Stop Overfishing on the High Seas."
159 Ibid.

160 Agreement for the Implementation of the Provisions of the United Nations Convention on the Law of the Sea of 10 December 1982 relating to the Conservation and Management of Straddling Fish Stocks and Highly Migratory Fish Stocks, 4 August 1995, 2167 UNTS 88 (the "Straddling Fish Stocks Agreement").

161 Sumaila, "Trade Policy Options for Sustainable Oceans and Fisheries," 6.

162 Global Ocean Commission, "The Future of Our Ocean: Next Steps and Priorities. Report 2016," 7, 23.

163 Ministerial Declaration, Ministerial Conference, Fourth Session, Doha, Qatar, November 9–14, 2001, WT/MIN(01)DEC/1.

164 Sumaila, "Trade Policy Options for Sustainable Oceans and Fisheries," 13.

165 Ricardo Melendez-Ortiz, "Additionality, Innovation and Systemic Implications of Environment, Fisheries and Labour in TPP: A Preliminary Review" (March 2016) (unpublished paper in possession of the author), 3.

166 Article 20.16.5, Trans-Pacific Partnership, as updated in Da Nang, Vietnam (November 9–10, 2017), https://bilaterals.org/tpp-trans-pacific-partnership.

167 "WTO Ministerial: In Landmark Move, Country Coalitions Set Plans to Advance on New Issues."

168 Gilles Hosch, "Trade Measures to Combat IUU Fishing: Comparative Analysis of Unilateral and Multilateral Approaches" (Geneva: International Centre for Trade and Sustainable Development, 2016), 3. See also David J. Agnew et al., "Estimating the Worldwide Extent of Illegal Fishing," *PLoS ONE*, Vol. 4, No. 2 (February 25, 2009).

169 The United Nations Straddling Fish Stocks Agreement.

170 This was done pursuant to The Illegal, Unreported, and Unregulated (IUU) Fishing Enforcement Act enacted by the Congress in November 2015, and signed thereafter into law by the President of the United States.

171 Paragraph 66, FAO International Plan of Action to Prevent, Deter and Eliminate Illegal, Unreported and Unregulated Fishing (Rome: FAO, 2001).

172 This new US seafood traceability program has been applied under the authority of the Magnuson–Stevens Fishery Conservation and Management Reauthorization Act of 2006, 16 USC 1801 et seq. See Federal Register, Vol. 18, No. 24, 6210–6222 (February 5, 2016), amending 50 CFR Parts 300 and 600.

173 "WTO Members Weigh In on Measures to Tackle Illegal Fishing" (Geneva: WTO, October 6, 2015), www.wto.org/english/news_e/news15_e/envir_06oct15_e.htm.

174 Milton Haughton, "Unilateral Trade Measures and the Fight Against IUU Fishing," E15 Initiative (Geneva: International Centre for Trade and Sustainable Development and World Economic Forum, June 11, 2015), http://e15initiative.org/blogs/unilateral-trade-measures-and-the-fight-against-iuu-fishing.

175 Elinor Ostrom, *Governing the Commons: The Evolution of Institutions for Collective Action* (Cambridge: Cambridge University Press, 1990). See the discussion on Ostrom in Chapter 3.

176 Global Ocean Commission, "The Future of the Ocean: Next Steps and Priorities. Report 2016," 4.

177 Rafaella Lobo and Peter J. Jacques, "SOFIA'S Choice: Discourses, Values, and Norms of the World Ocean Regime," *Marine Policy*, Vol. 78 (2017), 26–33.

178 Dominic Waughray, "Tuna 2020 Traceability Declaration: Stopping Illegal Tuna from Coming to Market" (Geneva: World Economic Forum, June 5, 2017), https://weforum .org/2017/06.

179 Sumaila, "Trade Policy Options for Sustainable Oceans and Fisheries," 11; "Ocean Fishing: All the Fish in the Sea," *Economist* (May 27, 2017); WWF International, "Living Blue Planet Report," 29.

180 See Frank Asche and Fahmida Khatun, "Aquaculture: Issues and Opportunities for Sustainable Production and Trade," ICTSD Issue Paper No. 5 (Geneva: International Centre for Trade and Sustainable Development, 2006).

181 See the long string of proceedings in United States – Measures Concerning the Importation, Marketing and Sale of Tuna and Tuna Products, WT/DS381, starting in 2012. I served as a counsel to the complainant, Mexico, in this long-running dispute, commonly known as the "tuna–dolphin" dispute.

182 Annex 1.1, WTO Agreement on Technical Barriers to Trade.

CHAPTER 16

1 Renee Martin-Nagle, "Preserving Groundwater in a Changing Climate," *International Law News*, Vol. 45, No. 1 (Summer 2016), 14.

2 Ibid.

3 Ibid.

4 Charles Fishman, *The Big Thirst: The Secret Life and Turbulent Future of Water* (New York: Free Press, 2011), 17. See also Sandra Postel, *Replenish: The Virtuous Cycle of Water and Prosperity* (Washington, D.C.: Island Press, 2017).

5 Fred Pearce, "Good Until the Last Drop," *Washington Post* (July 10, 2011).

6 United Nations, "The Millennium Development Goals Report 2015" (New York: United Nations, 2015), 7.

7 Goal 6, "Transforming Our World."

8 Pearce, "Good Until the Last Drop."

9 Fishman, *The Big Thirst*, 18, 19.

10 OECD, "OECD Environmental Outlook to 2030" (Paris: Organisation for Economic Co-operation and Development, 2008).

11 World Bank, "High and Dry: Climate Change, Water, and the Economy" (Washington, D.C.: World Bank, 2016).

12 FAO, "Coping with Water Scarcity: An Action Framework for Agriculture and Food Security," FAO Water Reports No. 38 (Rome: UN Food and Agriculture Organization, 2012), 5–6.

13 Peter H. Gleick, "We Have Seen the Future of Water, and It Is Cape Town," *Huffington Post* (February 9, 2018).

14 Laura Poppick, "What's Behind Cape Town's Water Woes?," *Smithsonian* (February 13, 2018), www.smithsonianmagazine.com/science-nature/day-zero-looms-capte-town-water-crisis-may-signify-new-normal-180968128; Kimon de Greef, "What Happens When a Major World City Runs Dry?," *Foreign Policy* (February 14, 2018), http://foreignpolicy .com/2018/02/14/what-does-it-mean-when-a-major-world-city-runs-dry-capte-town-south-africa-day-zero/.

15 FAO, "Water Withdrawal by Sector, Around 2007" (Rome: UN Food and Agriculture Organization, 2014).

16 World Bank, "Inclusive Green Growth: The Pathway to Sustainable Development" (Washington, D.C.: World Bank, 2012), 111.

17 WEF Water Initiative, "The Bubble Is Bursting" (Davos: World Economic Forum, 2009).

18 "Water Security and the Global Water Agenda: A UN-Water Analytical Brief" (Tokyo: United Nations University, 2013), 11–12.

19 UN General Assembly Resolution 64/292 A/RES/64/292 (July 28, 2010).

20 Paragraph 7, Declaration, "Transforming Our World."

21 Target 6.1, "Transforming Our World"; "Water Security and the Global Water Agenda: A UN-Water Analytical Brief," 11–12.

22 WEF, "Global Redesign Initiative" (Geneva: World Economic Forum, 2016), 533.

23 Arjen J. Hoekstra, "The Relation Between International Trade and Freshwater Scarcity," Staff Working Paper ERSD-2010-05 (Geneva: World Trade Organization, January 2010), 7.

24 Ibid., 13.

25 Mike Muller and Christophe Bellmann, "Trade and Water: How Might Trade Policy Contribute to Sustainable Water Management?" (Geneva: International Centre for Trade and Sustainable Development, October 2016), 1.

26 Ibid.

27 Pearce, "Good Until the Last Drop."

28 Carey L. Biron, "WTO Urged Not to Treat Water Like Widgets," Inter Press Service News (December 2013).

29 United States – Final Countervailing Duty Determination with respect to Certain Softwood Lumber from Canada (Softwood Lumber IV), WT/DS257/AB/R (2004). The potential – and potentially esoteric and nuanced – differences between the concepts of "goods" and "products" are likewise relevant to this issue; the ruling of the Appellate Body in this appeal touched on this question but did not answer it because it was not necessary to do so to resolve the dispute. See the thoughtful discussion on this WTO case by two leading authorities on WTO law in Valerie Hughes and Gabrielle Marceau, "WTO and Trade in Natural Resources," in Lawrence Boisson de Chauzommes, Christina Leb, and Maria Tignino, eds., *International Law and Freshwater: The Multiple Challenges* (Cheltenham, UK: Edward Elgar, 2013), 274–77.

30 US – Softwood Lumber, para. 59.

31 Ibid.

32 Ibid., para. 65.

33 Paolo Turrini, "Virtual Water and International Law," SIS Working Paper No. 2014–8 (Trento, Italy, University of Trento School of International Studies, November 2014), 19, 20.

34 1993 Statement by the Governments of Canada, Mexico, and the United States. For a sense of this continuing controversy under the NAFTA, see UNCITRAL, Sunbelt Water Inc. v. Her Majesty the Queen, Notice of Intent to Submit a Claim to Arbitration Under Chapter 11 of the NAFTA, 27 November 1998.

35 Muller and Bellmann, "Trade and Water," 14.

36 Lane Kisonak, "Bottleneck: Reforming Water as a Consumer Good to Regulate Climate Change," *International Law News* (Summer 2016), 23–24.

37 Turrini, "Virtual Water and International Law," 7.

38 Hoekstra, "The Relation Between Water Trade and Freshwater Scarcity," 7.

39 Jenny Kehl, "The Hidden Global Trade in Water," Yale Global (February 13, 2013), citing a UNESCO study done in 2003, www.UNESCO-IHE.

40 Ibid.

41 Ibid.

42 Ibid.

43 Ashok K. Chapagain and Arjen Y. Hoekstra, "The Global Component of Freshwater Demand and Supply: An Assessment of Virtual Water Flows Between Nations as a Result of Trade in Agricultural and Industrial Products," *Water International*, Vol. 33, No. 1 (January 2006), 31.

44 Alexandre Le Vernoy and Patrick Messerlin, "Water and the WTO: Don't Kill the Messenger" (January 10, 2011), prepared for a workshop on "Accounting for Water Scarcity and Pollution in the Rules of International Trade," Amsterdam, November 25–26, 2010, 5.

45 Ibid.

46 This is done through utilities, public companies, or direct government provision: "FAQ: World Bank Group Support for Water and Sanitation Solutions," www.worldbank.org/en/topic/water/brief/working-with-public-private-sectors-to-increase-water-sanitation-access. See, for example, Ruth Caplan, "Don't Let the WTO Get Hold of Our Water!," Alliance for Democracy (2003). See also "GATS, Water and the Environment: Implications of the General Agreement on Trade in Services for Water Resources," CIEL and WWF International Discussion Paper (Geneva: Center for International Law and World Wildlife Fund, October 2003), 28.

47 "Misunderstandings and Scare Stories: The WTO Is Not After Your Water," www.wto.org/English/tratop_e/serv_e/gats_factfiction8_e.htm.

48 Le Vernoy and Messerlin, "Water and the WTO," 5.

49 "For Want of a Drink: A Special Report on Water," *Economist* (May 22, 2010), 3–5.

50 "Managing the Water-Food-Energy Nexus" (September 24, 2010), www.weforum.org/en/knowledge/ThemesEnvironment/KN_SESS_SUMM_30946?u.

51 Quoted in James E. Nickum, "Hydraulic Pressures: Into the Age of Water Scarcity?," *Foreign Affairs* (September/October 2010), 134. See Steven Solomon, *Water: The Epic Struggle for Wealth, Power and Civilization* (New York: HarperCollins, 2010), 490.

52 Smith, *The Wealth of Nations*, Book I, Chapter IV.

53 Solomon, *Water*, 379.

54 Article XX(b), General Agreement on Tariffs and Trade.

55 Article XX(g), General Agreement on Tariffs and Trade.

56 Chapeau, Article XX, General Agreement on Tariffs and Trade.

57 Le Vernoy and Messerlin, "Water and the WTO," 10.

58 Hoekstra, "The Relation Between International Trade and Freshwater Scarcity," 15.

59 WTO Agreement on the Application of Sanitary and Phytosanitary Measures.

60 WTO Agreement on Technical Barriers to Trade.

61 Hoekstra, "The Relation Between International Trade and Freshwater Scarcity," 18.

62 Ibid.

63 Edward O. Wilson, "The Global Solution to Extinction," *New York Times* (March 12, 2016).

64 "Scientists Discover 163 New Species in Greater Mekong Region: WWF," Reuters (December 18, 2016).

65 Center for Biological Diversity, "The Extinction Crisis," www.biologicaldiversity.org/programs/biodiversity/elements_of_biodiversity/extinction_crisis/. See Elizabeth Kolbert, *The Sixth Extinction* (New York: Henry Holt, 2014). See also F. S. Chapin et al., "Consequences of Changing Biodiversity," *Nature*, Vol. 405 (2000), 234–42.

66 S. L. Pimm et al., "The Future of Biodiversity," *Science*, Vol. 269 (1995), 347–50.

67 Center for Biological Diversity, "The Extinction Crisis."

68 WWF, "Living Planet Report 2016: Risk and Resilience in a New Era," 15, http://wwf.panda.org/about_our_earth/all_publications/lpr_2016/.

69 Damian Carrington, "One in Five of World's Plant Species at Risk of Extinction," *Guardian* (May 9, 2016).

70 Paraphrased here is the Center for Biological Diversity, "The Extinction Crisis."

71 Target 15.5, "Transforming Our World."

72 Sean Maxwell et al., "The Ravages of Guns, Nets and Bulldozers," *Nature*, Vol. 536 (August 11, 2016), 143.

73 Ibid.

74 Joe Cochrane, "Borneo Lost More than 100,000 Orangutans from 1999 to 2015," *New York Times* (February 15, 2018).

75 Wilson, "The Global Solution to Extinction." See Wilson, *Half-Earth*.

76 Manfred Lenzen et al., "International Trade Drives Biodiversity Threats in Developing Nations," *Nature*, Vol. 486 (June 7, 2012), 109.

77 Article 45(1)(a)(x), Havana Charter (1948).

78 Convention on International Trade in Endangered Species of Wild Fauna and Flora, 3 March 1973, United Nation, 993 UNTS 243 ("CITES").

79 CITES, "Regulating the World's Wildlife Trade" (Geneva: Convention on Internatoinal Trade in Endangered Species of Wild Fauna and Flora, 2012–13), 3.

80 Appendix I, CITES.

81 Appendix II, CITES.

82 "CITES Hosts Largest-Ever Meet, Takes Key Wildlife Decisions," *Bridges Weekly*, Vol. 20, No. 34 (October 13, 2016), 10–12; Darryl Fears, "The World Just Agreed to the Strongest Protections Ever for Endangered Animals," *Washington Post* (October 5, 2016); Jade Saunders, "CITES Conference Marks Major Breakthrough in Battle Against Endangered Rosewood Trade" (October 20, 2016), www.chathamhouse.org/expert/comment/cites-conference-marks-major-breakthrough-battle-against-endangered-rosewood-trade.

83 "National Efforts Continue to Curb Ivory Trade, Protect Elephant Populations," *Bridges Weekly*, Vol. 22, No. 4 (February 8, 2018), 14–16.

84 "President Trump's Controversial Reversal of the Elephant Trophy Ban," *Time* (November 17, 2017), http://time.com/5028798/elephant-hunting-trophy-zimbabwe.

85 Target 15.7, "Transforming Our World."

86 United States – Import Prohibition of Certain Shrimp and Shrimp Products, WT/DS58/AB/R (1998), para. 132.

87 European Communities – Measures Prohibiting the Importation and Marketing of Seal Products, WT/DS400/AB/R (2014) (Canada) and WT/DS401/AB/R (2014) (Norway).

88 Ibid., para. 5.290.

89 Convention on Biological Diversity, 5 June 1992, 1760 UNTS 79.

90 Article 2, Convention on Biological Diversity.

91 "Summary of the UN Biodiversity Conference in Cancun, Mexico, December 2–17, 2016," *Earth Negotiations Bulletin*, Vol. 9, No. 678 (December 20, 2016), 1; see Cancun Declaration on Mainstreaming the Conservation and Sustainable Use of Biodiversity for Well-Being (December 3, 2016), www.cbd.int/cop/cop-13/hls/cancun%20Declaration-en .pdf.

92 Cartagena Protocol on Biosafety to the Convention on Biological Diversity, 29 January 2000, 2226 UNTS 208; Nagoya Protocol on Access to Genetic Resources and the Fair and Equitable Sharing of Benefits Arising from their Utilization to the Convention on Biological Diversity, 29 October 2012, www.ecolex.org (TRE – 155959).

93 Articles 7–10 and, on "lack of scientific certainty," Article 10(6), Cartagena Biosafety Protocol.

94 Article 1, Cartagena Biosafety Protocol.

95 Principle 15, Rio Declaration on Environment and Development.

96 Richard P. Feynman, *The Meaning of It All: Thoughts of a Citizen-Scientist* (Reading, Mass.: Perseus Books, 1998), 26, 27. See also Carlo Rovelli, "Science Is Not About Certainty," *New Republic* (July 11, 2014), https://newrepublic.com/article/118655/theoret ical-physicist-explains-why-science-not-about-certainty.

97 See especially two of Popper's essays, "Two Kinds of Definitions" [1945], 87–100, and "The Problem of Induction" [1954], 101–17, in David Miller, ed., *Popper Selections*, Part I (Princeton: Princeton University Press, (1985); and see also Frederic Raphael, *Popper* (London: Phoenix, 1998), 5, 7.

98 Article 5.7, WTO Agreement on the Application of Sanitary and Phytosanitary Measures; and see Appellate Body Report, European Communities – Measures Concerning Meat and Meat Products, WT/DS26/AB/R (1998).

99 Article 2.2 and Article 5.1, WTO Agreement on the Application of Sanitary and Phytosanitary Measures.

100 Article 5.5, WTO Agreement on the Application of Sanitary and Phytosanitary Measures (emphasis added).

101 Article 6(1), 6(2), and 7, Nagoya Protocol: Article 15(5), Convention on Biological Diversity.

102 Article 5, Nagoya Protocol; Article 15(7), 16, and 19, Convention on Biological Diversity.

103 Target 15.6, "Transforming Our World."

104 Article 27.1, TRIPS Agreement. See generally Nuno Pires de Carvalho, *The TRIPS Regime of Patent Rights* (Alphen aan den Rijn, Netherlands: Wolters Kluwer, 2010); Molly Jamison, "Patent Harmonization in Biotechnology: Towards International Reconciliation of the Gene Patent Debate," *Chicago Journal of International Law*, Vol. 15, No. 2, Article 9 (2015), 688, https://chicagounbound.uchicago.edu/cgi/viewcontent.cgi?referer=https://www.google.co.uk/&httpsredir=1&article=1086&context=cjil; and C. Niranjan Rao, "Patents for Biotechnology Inventions in TRIPS," *Economic and Political Weekly*, Vol. 37, No. 22 (June 1–7, 2002), 2126–29.

105 Article 8.1, TRIPS Agreement.

106 Article 27.2, TRIPS Agreement.

107 Article 27.3, TRIPS Agreement. This exclusion does not apply to microorganisms or to non-biological and microbiological processes.

108 For a detailed discussion of this issue, see Oran R. Young et al., *Institutional Interplay: Biosafety and Trade* (Tokyo: United Nations University Press, 2008).

109 Geoffrey A. Fowler, "How Was Your Smartphone Made? No One Really Knows," *Wall Street Journal* (July 9, 2016).

110 Todd C. Frankel and Peter Whoriskey, "The Price of 'White Gold'," *Washington Post* (December 20, 2016).

111 Ibid.

112 Vince Beiser, "The World's Disappearing Sand," *New York Times* (June 23, 2016).

113 Ibid.

114 Ibid.

115 Bernice Lee, "This Time the Politics Must Not Be Ignored," *World Today* (June/July 2012), 10.

116 Bernice Lee et al., Executive Summary and Recommendations, "Resources Future: A Chatham House Report" (London: Royal Institute of International Affairs, December 2012), 2. In her acknowledgments for this report, Lee was kind enough to acknowledge the (very limited) role I played along with many others in assisting her and her co-authors in reaching their conclusions.

117 WTO, "World Trade Report 2010," 48–49.

118 John Gray, "The New Wars of Scarcity," in John Gray, *Heresies: Against Progress and Other Illusions* (London: Granta Books, 2004), 115.

119 Ibid. See also John Gray, "The Global Delusion," *New York Review of Books* (April 26, 2006), where he makes the same points.

120 See, for example, Sharon Burke, "Natural Security," Working Paper, Center for a New American Security (June 2009), 9, https://s3.amazonaws.com/files.cnas.org/documents/CNAS_Working-Paper_Natural-Security_SBurke_June2009_OnlineNEW_0.pdf.

121 Ibid.

122 WTO, "World Trade Report 2010," 63.

123 Lee et al., "Resources Future: A Chatham House Report," 20–23.

124 R. Sharma, "Food Export Restrictions: Review of the 2007–2010 Experience and Considerations for Disciplining Restrictive Measures," FAO Commodity and Trade Policy Research Working Paper No. 32 (Rome: UN Food and Agriculture Organization, 2011), 8.

125 Gabrielle Marceau, "The World Trade Organization and Export Restrictions," in Mitsuo Matsushita and Thomas J. Schoenbaum, eds., *Emerging Issues in Sustainable Development: International Trade Law and Policy Relating to Natural Resources, Energy, and the Environment* (Tokyo: Springer, 2016), 119. Gabrielle Marceau is a prolific and always insightful writer on the frontiers of international trade law, and this article is one of her best, an overview of the complex relationship between WTO rules and the natural resources dimension of sustainable development.

126 Ibid. See Robert Howse and Tim Josling, "Agricultural Export Restrictions and International Trade Law: A Way Forward," International Food and Agriculture Trade Policy Council (2012), www.agritrade.org/Publications.

127 Smith, *The Wealth of Nations*, Book V, Chapter I.

128 For more on ancient Athens and trade, see Chapter 5.

129 These same points were made in much the same words in James Bacchus, "Russian Export Ban Mirrors Old Error," *International Business Times* (August 31, 2010).

130 See James Bacchus, "Hoarding Resources Threatens Free Trade," *Wall Street Journal Asia* (May 9, 2010).

131 Roberta Piermartini, "The Role of Export Taxes in the Field of Primary Commodities" (Geneva: World Trade Organization, 2004).

132 Claude Barfield, "Trade and Raw Materials – Looking Ahead," Presentation at the Conference on the EU's Trade Policy and Raw Materials, Brussels, Belgium (September 29, 2008).

133 Ibid.

134 Ilaria Espa, "Energy Export Restrictions in the WTO Between Resource Nationalism and Sustainable Development," in Francesca Romanin Jacur, Angelica Bonfanti, and Francesco Seatzu, eds., *Natural Resource Grabbing: An International Law Perspective* (Leiden and Boston: Brill Nijhoff, 2016), 365.

135 Article XI, General Agreement on Tariffs and Trade.

136 For an illustrative list of quantitative restrictions, see Council on Trade in Goods, Decision on Notification Procedures for Quantitative Restrictions, adopted on 22 June 2012, G/L/59/Rev.1, dated 22 June 2012, Annex 2.

137 Article XI(2)(a), General Agreement on Tariffs and Trade.

138 Daniel Crosby, "WTO Legal Status and Evolving Practice of Export Taxes," *Bridges Weekly*, Vol. 12, No. 5 (November 6, 2008), 3–4.

139 Article II, General Agreement on Tariffs and Trade.

140 See GATT Panel Report, Canada – Measures Affecting Exports of Unprocessed Herring and Salmon, 35S/98 (1988); GATT Panel Report, Japan – Trade in Semi-conductors, 35S/116 (1988); WTO Panel Report, Argentina – Measures Affecting the Export of Bovine Hides and the Import of Finished Leather, WT/DS155/R (2001).

141 Appellate Body Report, China – Measures Related to the Exportation of Various Raw Materials, WT/DS394/AB/R (2012).

142 Appellate Body Report, China – Measures Related to the Exportation of Rare Earths, Tungsten and Molybdenum, WT/DS431/AB/R (2014).

143 See Paragraph 11.3 and Annex 6, Protocol on the Accession of the People's Republic of China, WT/L/423 (November 23, 2001).

144 See Marceau, "The World Trade Organization and Export Restrictions," 113–19.

145 Article I, Section 9, Clause 5, United States Constitution.

146 See Julia Ya Chin, "The Predicament of China's 'WTO-Plus' Obligation to Eliminate Export Duties: A Commentary on the China-Raw Materials Case," *Chinese Journal of International Law*, Vol. 11, No. 2 (2012), 237–46.

147 Article XX(b), General Agreement on Tariffs and Trade.

148 Article XX(g), General Agreement on Tariffs and Trade.

149 Article XX(j), General Agreement on Tariffs and Trade.

150 Chapeau, Article XX, General Agreement on Tariffs and Trade.

151 Principle 2, Rio Declaration on Environment and Development.

152 See Koivurova, *Introduction to International Environmental Law*, 105–06.

153 See Chapter 7.

154 Edward Wong, "China Output for Exports Is Linked to US Smog," *International New York Times* (January 21, 2014); Editorial, "Globalization of Pollution," *International New York Times* (January 25–26, 2014).

155 US – Shrimp, para. 133.

156 Panel Report, European Communities – Measures Prohibiting the Importation and Marketing of Seal Products, WT/DS400/R, WT/DS401/R (2013), para. 7.640.

157 Target 12.2, "Transforming Our World."

158 Hughes and Marceau, "WTO and Trade in Natural Resources," 269–70.

159 Christophe Bellmann and Marie Wilke, "Trade Policies for Rethinking Export Restrictions," in Ricardo Melendez-Ortiz et al., eds., *The Future and the WTO: Confronting the Challenges. A Collection of Short Essays* (Geneva: International Centre for Trade and Sustainable Development, 2012), 203.

160 Preamble, WTO Agreement.

161 WTO General Council Decision of 15 December 2006, WT/L/676, dated 19 December 2006, and extended by the WTO General Council on 11 December 2012.

162 Article II:1(b), General Agreement on Tariffs and Trade, refers only to the "importation" of products. It does not mention their exportation.

163 Christophe Bellmann, "Trade and Investment Frameworks in Extractive Industries: Challenges and Options," E15 Initiative, E15 Expert Group on Trade and Investment in Extractive Industries (Geneva: International Centre for Trade and Sustainable Development and World Economic Forum, January 2016), 6–7.

164 Annex 3 to the WTO Agreement, entitled "Trade Policy Review Mechanism."

165 Alice Tipping and Robert Wolfe, "Trade and Sustainable Development: Options for Follow-up and Review of the Trade-Related Elements of the Post-2015 Agenda and Financing for Sustainable Development" (Geneva: International Centre for Trade and Sustainable Development and International Institute for Sustainable Development, 2015), 14–17.

CHAPTER 17

1 Robert Axelrod, *The Evolution of Cooperation*, rev. edn. (Cambridge, Mass.: Perseus, 2006) [1984]. See the earlier discussion in Chapter 5 on the WTO and the evolution of cooperation.

2 Stephen C. Neff, *Justice Among Nations: A History of International Law* (Cambridge, Mass.: Harvard University Press, 2014), 241 (emphasis in original). See Emmanuelle Jouannet, *The Liberal Welfarist Law of Nations: A History of International Law* (Cambridge: Cambridge University Press, 2012), 34–48.

3 Immanuel Kant, "To Perpetual Peace: A Philosophical Sketch," in *Immanuel Kant, Perpetual Peace and Other Essays*, Ted Humphrey, trans. (Indianapolis and Cambridge: Hackett, 1983), 117 [1795].

4 Neff, *Justice Among Nations*, 241 (emphasis in original).

5 Ibid. (emphasis in original).

6 Maria Ivanova, "Global Governance in the 21st Century: Rethinking the Environmental Pillar," University of Massachusetts Boston, Conflict Resolution, Human Security, and

Global Governance Faculty Publications Series, Paper 1 (2011), http://works.bepress.com/maria_ivanova/1/, 9.

7 Leal-Arcas, "Sustainability, Common Concern and Public Goods," 9 (emphasis added). At footnote 32, he cites as authority for the proposition that the duty to cooperate may be legally enforceable an order issued by the International Tribunal for the Law of the Sea in 2001 in Mox Case (Ireland v. UK) which, in footnote 82, held that UNCLOS and general international law "make the duty to cooperate a fundamental principle for the prevention of marine pollution (in our view, a matter of common concern) and that certain rights arise from it, which the tribunal can enforce by ordering provisional measures."

8 Neff, *Justice Among Nations*, 454–55; Daniel Bodansky and Elliot Diringer, "The Evolution of Multilateral Regimes: Implications for Climate Change" (Washington, D.C.: Pew Center on Global Climate Change, December 2010), 3.

9 Bodansky and Diringer, "The Evolution of Multilateral Regimes: Implications for Climate Change," 3.

10 Ibid., 5.

11 Ibid., 5–9.

12 Ibid., 9–10.

13 Ibid., 10.

14 See David J. Bederman, *International Law in Antiquity* (Cambridge: Cambridge University Press, 2001).

15 Neff, *Justice Among Nations*, 15.

16 Bodansky and Diringer, "The Evolution of Multilateral Regimes," 5–12.

17 Alfred, Lord Tennyson, "Locksley Hall," in *Poetical Works of Alfred Lord Tennyson* (London: Macmillan and Co., 1935), 101.

18 Neff, *Justice Among Nations*, 456.

19 Ibid., 456–57.

20 See Postrel, *The Future and Its Enemies*, 142–46.

21 Targets, 16.6, 16.7, and 16.8, "Transforming Our World."

22 Postrel, *The Future and Its Enemies*, 146.

23 "Don't Expect Too Much from Leaders at Climate Summit: Report," Reuters (September 19, 2014).

24 Onora O'Neill, *Justice Across Boundaries: Whose Obligations?* (Cambridge: Cambridge University Press, 2016), 164 (emphasis added).

25 Ibid., 178.

26 "Lifting the Ambition of the Paris 2015 Agreement: Agreement on An Agenda for Lima," An Agenda for Lima, Yale Climate Dialogue, Yale Center for International Law (November 2014) (unpublished paper circulated at COP-20 in Lima, Peru). On the Yale Climate Dialogue, see https://envirocenter.yale.edu/projects/yale-climate-change-dialogue.

27 Smith, *The Theory of Moral Sentiments*, 27.

28 Neff, *Justice Among Nations*, 10.

29 Ibid.

30 W. E. H. Lecky, *History of European Morals from Augustus to Charlemagne* (New York: George Braziller, 1955), Vol. I, 100–01, 285 [1869]. See James Bacchus, "Lecky's Circle: Thoughts from the Frontier of International Law," in Bacchus, *Trade and Freedom*, 475–511.

31 "Chained to Health Ministry, Peruvians Protest Mining Pollution," Reuters (June 23, 2017).

32 Xi Jinping, President, People's Republic of China, G20 Summit 2016, China (December 1, 2015).

33 Ibid.

34 Sauvant, "The Evolving International Investment Law and Policy Regime," 8.

35 Gary Hufbauer and Sherry Stephenson, "The Case for a Framework Agreement on Investment," Columbia FDI Perspectives, No. 116 (March 3, 2014).

36 Ibid.

37 See Yang Guohua, "On the Constitution of the World Trade and Investment Organization," in "World Investment and Trade Organization: Is It Possible for Global Governance? G20, TPP and WTO," Chinese Initiative on International Law, WTO Public Forum, Geneva (September 27, 2017), 24–44 (conference booklet in the possession of the author).

38 These numbers are as of 2012. See Gary Hufbauer, Eujin Jung, Sean Miner, Tyler Moran and Jeffrey Schott, "From Drift to Deals: Advancing the WTO Agenda," commissioned by the ICC World Trade Agenda (Paris: International Chamber of Commerce, 2012), 41. In their view, "the WTO's future agenda would not be complete without its own investment agreement": ibid., 44.

39 Richard Baldwin, Simon Evenett, and Patrick Low, "Beyond Tariffs: Multilateralizing Non-Tariff RTA Commitments," in Richard Baldwin and Patrick Low, eds., *Multilateralizing Regionalism* (Cambridge: Cambridge University Press, 2009), 137.

40 Principle 3, G20 Guiding Principles for Global Investment Policy-Making.

41 Collins, *An Introduction to International Investment Law*, 222.

42 Ibid., 224–25.

43 This is why a WTO member can go straight to the WTO for the settlement of its trade dispute with another WTO member without having first to exhaust its legal remedies in the national courts of that other WTO member.

44 See Math Noortman, August Reinisch, and Cedric Ryngaert, eds., *Non-State Actors in International Law* (London: Bloomsbury Press, 2015).

45 UNCTAD, "Investment Policy Framework for Sustainable Development," 81.

46 Ibid.

47 UNCTAD, "Investment Dispute Settlement Navigator" (Geneva: UN Conference on Trade and Development, January 1, 2017), http://investmentpolicyhub.unctad.org/ISDS; UNCTAD, "World Investment Report 2017," xii.

48 Through the spring of 2017, the United States had won eighteen of eighteen ISDS disputes.

49 Scott Miller and Gregory N. Hicks, "Investor–State Dispute Settlement: A Reality Check," Center for Strategic and International Studies (Lanham, Md.: Rowman & Littlefield, January 2016), v.

50 Ibid., 10–11.

51 United Nations Convention on Transparency in Treaty-based Investor–State Arbitration (adopted 10 December 2014, opened for signature 17 March 2015, not yet in force) (the "Mauritius Convention"). See Gabrielle Kaufmann-Kohler and Michele Potesta, "Can the Mauritius Convention Serve as a Model for the Reform of Investor–State Arbitration in

Connection with the Introduction of a Permanent Investment Tribunal or an Appeal
Mechanism?" (Geneva: Geneva Center for International Dispute Settlement, June 3,
2016). The authors say yes. In contrast, Professor Robert Howse of NYU says no. See
Robert Howse, "Gabrielle Kaufman-Kohler: A Booby-Trapped Approach to Reforming
Investor–State Dispute Settlement," Parts I and II, International Economic Law and
Policy Blog (March 2, 2017).

52 UNCITRAL Rules on Transparency in Treaty-based Investor–State Arbitration (January
2014), www.uncitral.org/pdf/english/texts/arbitration/rules-on-transparency/Rules-on-Trans
parency-E.pdf.

53 Collins, *An Introduction to International Investment Law*, 227–28.

54 Principle 3, G20 Guiding Principles for Global Investment Policy-Making.

55 Ibid.

56 Sergio Puig, "Social Capital in the Arbitration Market," *European Journal of International
Law*, Vol. 25, No. 2 (2014), 387–424.

57 Giorgio Sacerdoti, "Is the Party-Appointed Arbitrator a 'Pernicious Institution'?: A Reply to
Professor Hans Smit," Columbia FDI Perspectives, No. 35 (April 15, 2011). I served with
the deservedly distinguished Professor Sacerdoti on the WTO Appellate Body.

58 See Comprehensive Economic and Trade Agreement between Canada, of the one part,
and the European Union and its Member States, of the other part (signed 30 October
2016, approved by European Parliament February 15, 2017) (the "CETA"). The dispute
settlement innovations in the CETA follow and elaborate on the earlier suggestions by the
EU for including a similar standing investment court as part of the proposed Trans-
Atlantic Trade and Investment Partnership between the EU and the United States. See
Chapter II, Investment, set out in the EU's proposal for Investment Protection and
Resolution of Investment Disputes in the TTIP, made public on November 12, 2015.
See also Jack Newsham, "Global Investment Court Will Be Good for Everyone, EU
Says," Law360 (August 4, 2016). These EU proposals are also implemented, to some
extent, in the FTA between the EU and Vietnam. See European Union – Viet Nam
Free Trade Agreement (text released 1 February 2016), Articles 12–15.

59 With 159 member countries, the ICSID is already the favored forum for the settlement of
all kinds of investment disputes. Other popular global forums include the UNCITRAL,
the London Chamber of Arbitration, the International Chamber of Commerce in Paris,
the Arbitration Institute of the Stockholm Chamber of Commerce, the international
arbitration centers in Singapore and in Hong Kong, and the Permanent Court of Arbitration in The Hague. Holdouts from the ICSID include India and Russia.

60 Article 8.30, CETA.

61 Article 8.27, CETA.

62 Article 8.29, CETA.

63 Ibid.

64 Luke Eric Peterson, "Analysis: EU and Canada Convene Dozens of Countries This Week
to Discuss Informally a Multilateral Investment Court, While 'Institutional' Ownership of
Formal Negotiations Remain Unclear," *Investment Arbitration Reporter* (December
13, 2016).

65 For a contrasting view, see David Schneiderman, "Why CETA Is Unlikely to Restore
Legitimacy to ISDS," Investor–State Arbitration Commentary Series No. 7 (Waterloo,

Canada: Centre for International Governance Innovation, May 27, 2016), www.cigionline
.org/publications/why-ceta-unlikely-restore-legitimacy-isds.

66 As one of the six original co-sponsors of the implementing legislation for the Uruguay
Round trade agreements in the United States House of Representatives, I was among those
who envisaged the WTO in this way at the outset.

67 Manfred Elsig, "The Functioning of the WTO: Options for Reform and Enhanced
Governance," E15 Initiative, E15 Expert Group on the Functioning of the WTO, Policy
Options Paper (Geneva: International Centre for Trade and Sustainable Development
and World Economic Forum, 2016), 6, 8.

68 Ibid., 11.

69 Ibid.

70 Bhagwati, *Termites in the Trading System.*

71 Ibid., xi.

72 Article XXIV, General Agreement on Tariffs and Trade.

73 Bhagwati, *Termites in the Trading System,* 49, 61, 63.

74 Carolyn Deere Birkbeck, "The Future of the WTO: Governing Trade for a Fairer, More
Sustainable Future" (Geneva: International Centre for Trade and Sustainable Development, December 2011), 2.

75 See ICC, "Mega-Regional Trade Agreements and the Multilateral Trading System"
(Paris: International Chamber of Commerce, 8 March 2016); Global Agenda Council
on Trade & FDI, "Mega-regional Trade Agreements: Game-Changers or Costly Distrac-
tions for the World Trading System?" (Geneva: World Economic Forum, July 2014); and
Kati Suominen, "Enhancing Coherence and Inclusiveness in the Global Trading System
in the Era of Regionalism," E15 Initiative (Geneva: International Centre for Trade and
Sustainable Development and World Economic Forum, January 2016).

76 See the Trade and Environment Database (TREND), www.chaire-epi.ulaval.ca/trend.

77 Jean-Frederic Morin and Rosalie Gauthier Nadeau, "Environmental Gems in Trade
Agreements: Little-Known Clauses for Progressive Trade Agreements," CIGI Papers
No. 148 (Waterloo, Canada: Centre for International Governance Innovation, October
2017), 2.

78 Ibid., 3.

79 Ibid., 4.

80 Ibid.

81 See Peter Draper and Memory Dube, "Plurilaterals and the Multilateral Trading System,
E15 Initiative, E15 Expert Group on Regional Trade Agreements and Plurilateral
Approaches" (Geneva: International Centre for Trade and Sustainable Development
and World Economic Forum, December 2013), 4.

82 Bhagwati, *Termites in the Trading System,* 90.

83 WTO, "Report on G20 Trade Measures" (Geneva: World Trade Organization, November
2016), 26.

84 See James Bacchus, "Open Up the WTO," *Washington Post* (February 20, 2004). While a
Member and Chairman of the WTO Appellate Body, I was sworn, along with my
colleagues, to uphold all WTO rules, including the rule requiring the "confidentiality"
of all WTO dispute settlement proceedings. In my first public appearance soon after
completing my service to the WTO at yearend 2003, before the Washington International

Trade Association, I called for opening the doors of the WTO to the public. My remarks then are summarized in this article, which was published soon afterwards.

85 See Annex 3, WTO Agreement.

86 Steve Charnovitz, "Addressing Government Failure Through International Financial Law," *Journal of International Economic Law*, Vol. 13, No. 3 (2010), 743. In this article, Professor Charnovitz suggested the adaptation of the WTO trade review process to support financial regulation.

87 Birkbeck, "The Future of the WTO," 6.

88 Ibid. See also Julien Chasse and Mitsuo Matsushita, "Maintaining the WTO's Supremacy in the International Trade Order: A Proposal to Refine and Revise the Role of the Trade Policy Review Mechanism," *Journal of International Economic Law*, Vol. 16, No. 1 (2013), 9–36. Professor Matsushita, widely proficient in international law, is, like me, a founding Member of the WTO Appellate Body.

CHAPTER 18

1 Article 14 and Article 17.10, WTO Dispute Settlement Understanding.

2 Target 16.6, "Transforming Our World."

3 See Appellate Body Report, European Communities – Measures Affecting Asbestos and Asbestos Containing Products, WT/DS135/AB/R (2001).

4 Article 17.9, WTO Dispute Settlement Understanding.

5 My former colleague on the WTO Appellate Body, Professor Giorgio Sacerdoti of Bocconi University in Italy, has describing this same setting and has proposed some of the same reforms that are suggested here. See Giorgio Sacerdoti, "The Future of the WTO Dispute Settlement System: Consolidating a Success Story," in Manfred Elsig, Bernard Hoekman, and Joost Pauwelyn, eds., *Assessing the World Trade Organization: Fit for Purpose? World Trade Forum* (Cambridge: Cambridge University Press, 2017), 45–68.

6 WTO Appellate Body, "Annual Report for 2014" (Geneva: World Trade Organization, July, 2015), 3.

7 Articles 3.2 and 3.7, WTO Dispute Settlement Understanding; see Sacerdoti, "The Future of the WTO Dispute Settlement System," 47.

8 Articles 3.2 and 19.2, WTO Dispute Settlement Understanding.

9 Suominen, "Enhancing Coherence and Inclusiveness in the Global Trading System in the Era of Regionalism," 7.

10 Henry Gao and Chin Leng Lim, "Saving the WTO from the Risk of Irrelevance: The WTO Dispute Settlement System as a 'Common Good' for RTA Disputes," in Debra P. Steger, ed., *Redesigning the World Trade Organization for the Twenty-First Century*, Centre for International Governance Innovation and International Development Research Centre (Ottawa: CIGI and Wilfrid Laurier University Press, 2010), 391.

11 Sacerdoti, "The Future of the WTO Dispute Settlement System," 47. This compliance percentage is a calculation by the WTO Secretariat. See Valerie Hughes, "Working in WTO Dispute Settlement: Pride without Prejudice," in Gabrielle Marceau, ed., *A History of Law and Lawyers in the GATT/WTO: The Development of the Rule of Law in the Multilateral Trading System* (Cambridge: Cambridge University Press, 2015), 414.

12 See Scott Andersen, "Administration of Evidence in WTO Dispute Settlement Proceedings," in Rufus Yerxa and Bruce Wilson, eds., *Key Issues in WTO Dispute Settlement: The First Ten Years* (Cambridge: Cambridge University Press, 2005), 177–99.

13 Article 5, WTO Dispute Settlement Understanding.

14 Birkbeck, "The Future of the WTO," 5. See, for example, the fully digital Small Claims Tribunal of the Dubai International Financial Courts, at http://difcourts.ae.

15 Article 4, WTO Dispute Settlement Understanding.

16 Article 12.8, WTO Dispute Settlement Understanding.

17 Article 8.7, WTO Dispute Settlement Understanding.

18 Article 21.3, WTO Dispute Settlement Understanding.

19 Article 21.3(c), WTO Dispute Settlement Understanding.

20 Article 22, WTO Dispute Settlement Understanding.

21 Goldsmith and Posner, *The Limits of International Law*, 162.

22 This has been done by the United States in its dispute with Brazil over illegal US cotton subsidies in implementation of Appellate Body Report, United States – Upland Cotton, WT/DS267/AB/R (2005).

23 This was agreed following the Appellate Body Report in US – Upland Cotton, WT/DS267/AB/R (2005).

24 James Flett, "How Can the Extent and Speed of Compliance of WTO Members with DSU Rulings Be Improved?," in Simon J. Evenett and Alejandro Jara, eds., *Building on Bali: A Work Programme for the WTO* (London: Center for Economic Policy Research, 2013), 95.

25 Ibid.

26 Ibid.

27 Article 19.1, WTO Dispute Settlement Understanding.

28 See Gregory Shaffer, Manfred Elsig, and Sergio Puig, "The Extensive (But Fragile) Authority of the WTO Appellate Body," *Law and Contemporary Problems*, Vol. 79 (1916), 237.

29 Article IX:1, WTO Agreement.

30 See Gregory Shaffer, "Will the US Undermine the World Trade Organization?," *Huffington Post* (May 23, 2016).

31 See Steve Charnovitz, "The Obama Administration's Attack on Appellate Body Independence Shows the Need for Reforms," International Economic Law and Policy Blog (September 22, 2016), http://worldtradelaw.typepad.com/ielpblog/2016/09/the-obama-administrations-attack-on-appellate-body-independence-shows-the-need-for-reforms-.html.

32 Gregory Shaffer, Manfred Elsig, and Mark Pollack, "Trump Is Fighting an Open War on Trade: His Stealth War on Trade May Be Even More Important," *Washington Post* (September 27, 2017).

33 "US Slammed at DSB for Blocking Korean Appellate Body Reappointment," World Trade Online (May 23, 2016).

34 See the statement by the United States to the WTO Dispute Settlement Body, "The Issue of Possible Reappointment of One Appellate Body Member" (May 23, 2016), www.wto.org/english/news_e/news16_e/dsb_agenda_23may16_e.pdf.

35 Article 17.12, WTO Dispute Settlement Understanding.

36 Article 3.2, WTO Dispute Settlement Understanding.

37 Article 3.2 and Article 17.12, WTO Dispute Settlement Understanding.

38 Letter to the Chairman of the WTO Dispute Settlement Body dated May 18, 2016. See Alex Lawson, "WTO Members Clash Over Appellate Body Reappointment," Law360 (May 23, 2016).

39 Letter to the Chairman of the WTO Dispute Settlement Body dated May 31, 2016. I was one of the thirteen former Members of the Appellate Body who wrote and signed this letter.

40 Article 17.1, WTO Dispute Settlement Understanding.

41 Letter to the Chairman of the WTO Dispute Settlement Body dated May 31, 2016.

42 Here I am taking the liberty of quoting myself. See my remarks during the opening session of the WTO@20 conference held at Harvard Law School in celebration of the twentieth anniversary of the WTO, on April 28, 2016. See https://wto20.law.harvard.edu.

43 "America's New Trade Representative: The Negotiator," *Economist* (May 20, 2017).

44 Current Members of the Appellate Body could be transitioned into this structure and rotation through a novation that could extend the terms of some of the current Members.

45 "Towards a Charter Moment: Hakone Vision on Governance for Sustainability in the 21st Century" (September 29, 2011), www.ieg.earthsystemgovernance.org/ieg/publications/towards-charter-moment-hakone-vision-governance-sustainability-21st-century; Rio+20 Policy Brief No. 3, "Transforming Governance and Institutions for a Planet Under Pressure" (2012), 7; Frank Biermann et al., "Navigating the Anthropocene: Improving Earth System Governance," *Science*, Vol. 335 (March 16, 2012), 1306–07; Norichika Kanie et al., "A Charter Moment: Restructuring Governance for Sustainability," *Public Administration and Development*, Vol. 32, Issue 3 (August 2012), 292–304.

46 "Towards a Charter Moment: Hakone Vision on Governance for Sustainability in the 21st Century."

47 Ibid.

48 "Climate Governance After the Paris Agreement," Workshop Report, University College of London Global Governance Institute (November 25, 2016), 4 (emphasis added). On the five-year cycles for committing updated national climate pledges, see Article 4.9, Paris Agreement. The Paris Agreement also provides for a "global stocktake" on the implementation of national pledges and on "the collective progress towards achieving the purpose of this Agreement and its long-term goals." A "global stocktake" is scheduled for 2023, with others following every five years thereafter: Article 14, Paris Agreement. See the discussion in Chapter 7.

49 Article 15, Paris Agreement. See the earlier discussion in Chapter 7.

50 Article 15, Paris Agreement; UNFCCC, Decision 1/CP.21, Adoption of the Paris Agreement (UN Doc. FCCC/CP/2015/10, Add. 1, 29 January 2016). See the earlier discussion in Chapter 7.

51 Article 15.2, Paris Agreement.

52 Christina Voigt, "The Compliance and Implementation Mechanism of the Paris Agreement," *Review of European Community and International Environmental Law*, Vol. 25, No. 2 (2016), 165.

53 Susan Biniez, "Elaborating Article 15 of the Paris Agreement: Facilitating Implementation and Promoting Compliance," IDDRI Policy Brief No. 10 (Paris: Institut du développement durable et des relations internationales, October 2017), 2.

54 Ibid., 3.
55 Voigt, "The Compliance and Implementation Mechanism of the Paris Agreement," 166.
56 Ibid., 161–62.
57 See Ronald B. Mitchell, "Compliance Theory: Compliance, Effectiveness, and Behaviour Change in International Environmental Law," in Bodansky et al., eds., *The Oxford Handbook of International Environmental Law*, 893–921.
58 See Nicolas Chan, "The 'New' Impacts of the Implementation of Climate Change Response Measures," *Review of European Comparative and International Environmental Law (RECIEL)*, Vol. 25, Issue 2 (July 2016), 228–37.
59 Article 3.5, UNFCCC.
60 Ibid.
61 Andrei Marcu and Wijnand Stoefs, "The Role of Response Measures in Ensuring the Sustainable Transition to a Low-GHG Economy," Policy Brief (Geneva: International Centre for Trade and Sustainable Development, January 2017), 6, 12.
62 Louis J. Kotzé, *Global Environmental Constitutionalism in the Anthropocene* (Oxford and Portland, Ore.: Hart Publishing, 2016), 215.
63 See Brownlie, *Principles of Public International Law*, 573–78; Shaw, *International Law*, 281–86.
64 Dominique Vidalon, "France's Macron to Back Push for Global Environment Rights Pact," Reuters (June 25, 2017).
65 Preamble, Universal Declaration of Human Rights, GA Res. 217A(III), UN Doc. A/810 (1948), 7.
66 Daniel Magraw, "Rule of Law and the Environment," *Environmental Policy and Law*, Vol. 44 (2014), 202.
67 For pros and cons of this proposal, see Sebastian Oberthur, "Clustering of Multilateral Environmental Agreements: Potentials and Limitations," *International Environmental Agreements*, Vol. 2, No. 4 (2002), 317–40.
68 John E. Scanlon, "Enhancing Environmental Governance for Sustainable Development: Function-Oriented Options," Governance and Sustainability Issue Brief Series: Brief 5, Center for Governance and Sustainability (Boston: University of Massachusetts Boston, 2012), 1, https://issuu.com/governance_and_sustainability/docs/cgs_brief5.
69 "The Belgrade Process Toward International Environmental Governance" emerged from the first meeting of the Consultative Group of Ministers or High-Level Representatives of the United Nations Environment Programme in Belgrade, Serbia, June 27–28, 2009.
70 See Maria Ivanova, "An Engaged Scholarship Narrative," in Simon Nicholson and Sikina Jinnah, eds., *New Earth Politics: Essays from the Anthropocene* (Cambridge, Mass.: MIT Press, 2016), 183–218; see also Maria Ivanova, "A New Global Architecture for Sustainability Governance," in Linda Starke, ed., *State of the World 2012: Jumpstarting Sustainable Economies* (Washington, D.C.: Worldwatch Institute, 2012), 104–17.
71 See the discussion of these differences in Scanlon, "Enhancing Environmental Governance for Sustainable Development," 2–3.
72 Ivanova, "Global Governance in the 21st Century: Rethinking the Environmental Pillar," 8.
73 Article 13.1, WTO Dispute Settlement Understanding.

74 Article 15.2, Paris Agreement.

75 Ernst Ulrich Petersmann, *Multilevel Constitutionalism for Multilevel Governance of Public Goods: Methodology Problems in International Law* (Oxford and Portland, Ore.: Hart Publishing, 2017), 4.

76 Joel P. Trachtman, "The World Trading System, the International Legal System, and Multilevel Choice," *European Law Journal*, Vol. 12 (2006), 469–85.

77 See Andrew J. Jordan, Dave Huitema, Mikael Hilden, Harro van Asselt, Tim J. Rayner, Jonas J. Schoenefeld, Jale Tosun, Johanna Forster, and Elin L. Boasson, "Emergence of Polycentric Climate Governance and Its Future Prospects," *Nature Climate Change*, Vol. 2725 (August 10, 2015); Hari Osofsky, "The Geography of Solving Environmental Problems: Reflections on Polycentric Efforts to Address Climate Change," *New York Law School Law Review*, Vol. 58 (2013–14), 777–827; and Daniel H. Cole, "From Global to Polycentric Climate Governance," *Climate Law*, Vol. 2 (2011), 395–413.

78 Michelle Betsill et al., "Building Productive Links Between the UNFCCC and the Broader Climate Governance Landscape," *Global Environmental Politics*, Vol. 15, No. 2 (May 2015), 1–10.

79 Elinor Ostrom, "A Polycentric Approach for Coping with Climate Change," Policy Research Working Paper No. 5095 (Washington, D.C.: World Bank, 2009), 35.

80 Betsill et al., "Building Productive Links Between the UNFCCC and the Broader Climate Landscape."

81 See Article 30, Vienna Convention on the Law of Treaties.

82 ITLOS, Conservation and Sustainable Exploitation of Swordfish Stocks in the South-east Pacific Ocean (Chile/European Community) (removed from docket 17 December 2009), www.itlos.org. See the discussion in Chapter 9.

83 Rothwell and Stephens, *The International Law of the Sea*, 448.

84 Ibid., 447.

85 Article 31, Vienna Convention on the Law of Treaties.

CONCLUSION

1 Launch Complex 39A has been leased for twenty years to a private company, Space X, which is using it as a launch facility for its heavy-lift Falcon rocket. Launch Complex 39B is expected to be used within the next decade for NASA's new deep-space launch programs, currently in development.

2 NASA Report, "Sea Level Rise Hits Home at NASA: Watching Waters Rise Right Outside the Front Door," https://earthobservatory.nana.gov/Features?NASASeaLevel/?src=eoa-fea tures, 2, 5.

3 John Schwartz, "NASA Is Facing a Climate Change Countdown," *New York Times* (April 16, 2017); Barbara Liston, "Sea Level Rise Threatening Kennedy Space Center in Florida," Reuters (December 5, 2014).

4 NASA Report, "Sea Level Rise Hits Home at NASA," 3.

5 Ibid., 1. Thanks are due to my longtime friend Dale Ketcham for his confirmation of the accuracy of these observations on the Kennedy Space Center.

6 Matthias Mengel, Alexander Nauels, Joeri Rogelj, and Carl-Friedrich Schleussner, "Committed Sea-Level Rise Under the Paris Agreement and the Legacy of Delayed

Mitigation Action," *Nature Communications*, Vol. 9, Article No. 601 (February 20, 2018), www.nature.com/articles/s41467-018-02985-8; Alister Doyle, "Seas to Rise About a Meter Even If Climate Goals Are Met," Reuters (February 20, 2018).

7 Chris Mooney, "Climate Change Turning White Antarctica Green," *Washington Post* (May 19, 2017).

8 Ben Guarino, "More 'Quiet Springs' Feared as Climate Change Upends Routines of Songbirds," *Washington Post* (May 17, 2017).

9 Chris Mooney, "As Coral Reefs Die, Huge Swaths of the Seafloor Are Deteriorating Along with Them," *Washington Post* (April 20, 2017); Chris Mooney, "As Coral Withers, So Will Florida Keys Economy," *Washington Post* (June 26, 2017); Jenny Staletovich, "Reef Rescuers Race Against Climate Change," *Miami Herald* (June 18, 2017).

10 The phrase is that of Laurence Lafore in *The Long Fuse: An Interpretation of the Origins of World War I*, 2nd edn. (Long Grove, Ill.: Waveland, 1997) [1965]. This book was – a few years ago – on my reading list as a student at Vanderbilt University.

11 See Donald Kagan, *On the Origins of War and the Preservation of Peace* (New York: Doubleday, 1995).

12 See Diamond, *Collapse: How Societies Choose to Fail or Succeed*, 113.

13 Ibid.

14 Here of course I paraphrase Edmund Burke. See Edmund Burke, "Speech to the Electors of Bristol" (November 3, 1774), in *Select Works of Edmund Burke* ,Vol. IV, *Miscellaneous Writings* (Indianapolis: Liberty Fund, 2018), 4. In this speech, Burke said, "Your representative owes you, not his industry only, but his judgement; and he betrays, instead of serving you, if he sacrifices it to your opinion."

15 Pinker, "The Enlightenment Is Working."

16 On this point, see William James, *The Moral Equivalent of War* (London: Read Books, 2011) [1910].

17 Christopher Potter, *The Earth Gazers: On Seeing Ourselves* (New York and London: Pegasus Books, 2018), 430.

18 Paragraphs 51 and 53, "Transforming Our World."